Baptist History in England and America

Baptist History *in* England *and* America

Personalities, Positions, and Practices

BY
David Beale
Xulon Press

Xulon Press
2301 Lucien Way #415
Maitland, FL 32751
407.339.4217
www.xulonpress.com

© 2018 by David Beale

All rights reserved solely by the author. The author guarantees all contents are original and do not infringe upon the legal rights of any other person or work. No part of this book may be reproduced in any form without the permission of the author. The views expressed in this book are not necessarily those of the publisher.

Scripture quotations taken from the King James Version (KJV) – *public domain*.

The front cover image is the Jordan River in Israel.

Printed in the United States of America.

ISBN-13: 9781545622193

Dedicated

———✳———

To the memory of the Baptist pastor who mentored me
during my early training and prayed for me until he
went home to be with the Lord:
Rev. Samuel E. Hyde Sr. (1932–2015)

Contents

Preface...ix

Part I: Preliminary Essentials 1
   1. Introductory Essays on Our Baptist Heritage 3

Part II: English General Baptists to the New Connection..........23
   2. The English Separatist Roots of General Baptists...........25
   3. General Baptist Beginnings: Thomas Helwys
      to Thomas Grantham 54
   4. General Baptist Doctrinal Decline and the Rise
      of the New Connection............................75

Part III: English Particular Baptists to the Down
   Grade Controversy......................................89
   5. The Politico-Religious Landscape of the
      Earliest Particular Baptist Churches.....................91
   6. Three Key Baptist Leaders: Hanserd Knollys,
      William Kiffin, and Benjamin Keach...................144
   7. Particular Baptist Confessions of Faith 200
   8. John Gill and the Modern Question:
      The Emergence of Antinomianism....................231
   9. The Rise of Evangelical Calvinism: Life of
      Andrew Fuller to the Prayer Call of 1784...............250
   10. William Carey: His Life and Ministry 288
   11. Charles Spurgeon: His Life and Ministry 322

Part IV: Baptists in America 345

    12. Roger Williams and John Clarke: Founders of
the First Two Baptist Churches in America
and Co-Founders of Rhode Island................... 347

    13. Seventeenth-Century Baptists in Massachusetts....... 391

    14. William Screven, Elias Keach, and Morgan
Edwards: Church Planting, Expansion, and
Higher Education................................. 422

    15. The Separate Baptists: Struggle for Religious
Freedom in North Carolina, Georgia,
and Virginia 441

    16. Isaac Backus, John Leland, and Their Associates:
Final Steps toward Religious Liberty 475

    17. Pioneer Missionaries: Adoniram Judson,
Luther Rice, and John Mason Peck 507

    18. Northern Baptist Seminaries and the Rise of
Theological Liberalism 520

    19. The Rise and Development of Baptist
Fundamentalism 532

    20. The Southern Baptist Convention: Its Strong
Foundation, Rise of Liberalism, and
Conservative Resurgence 551

Part V: Sources for Baptist Ecclesiology 585

    21. Additional Tools and Resources...................... 587

Appendix A: Reconciling Old Style–New Style
Calendar Dates 593

Appendix B: Overview of Free Will Baptists in America 595

Appendix C: Travel Guide to Historical Baptist Sites in
England, Wales, and America........................... 598

Index.. 621

Preface

David Beale has given us not merely a credible history, but a remarkable one. He is a conservative, independent Baptist minister and theologian. His credentials as a historian are indisputable, having authored major works including *Historical Theology In-depth: Themes and Contexts of Doctrinal Development since the First Century* (2 vols.); *The Mayflower Pilgrims: Roots of Puritan, Presbyterian, Congregationalist, and Baptist Heritage*; *A Pictorial History of Our English Bible*; and *In Pursuit of Purity: American Fundamentalism since 1850*. Beale is a Baptist not by convenience but by conviction. With careful and painstaking research, he has selected the most notable players in British and American Baptist history and provided thorough descriptions of their character and contributions. In doing so, he has offered a unique study that endears the reader to his subject.

Beale introduces his study in an unusual and captivating way, by setting Baptist beginnings in the crucible of persecution, and showing throughout the book how Baptists paid dearly for their outspoken defense of religious liberty. Like the early church of the first century, Baptists were tormented, incarcerated, and martyred for their faith. Their courageous testimony continues to stand as a beacon for perseverance in righteousness. The numerous, valuable contributions in this book, to name a few, include: (1) incontrovertible proofs that Landmarkism is based on spurious evidence; (2) how Thomas Helwys, founder of the first General Baptist church in England, made it financially possible for the future *Mayflower* Pilgrims to escape from England to the Netherlands; (3) how Thomas

Grantham, the most articulate General Baptist theologian, provided the earliest doctrinal direction to his denomination; (4) how the triumvirate of Hanserd Knollys, William Kiffin, and Benjamin Keach united Particular Baptists around confessional theology; (5) how Baptists of John Bunyan's day regarded him; (6) how evangelical Calvinism pioneered the missionary efforts of Andrew Fuller and William Carey in England, then spearheaded the missionary efforts of Adoniram Judson, Luther Rice, and John Mason Peck in America; (7) how the Down Grade Controversy unfolded between Charles Spurgeon and leaders of the British Baptist Union; and (8) how an inside look at Baptist Fundamentalism enlightens one's understanding of the Fundamentalist/Modernist conflict in America.

One of the most significant contributions of this history is its attention to detail. To support his claims, Beale cites a massive collection of primary (in numerous cases rare) source materials, indicated by the extensive bibliographical entries at the end of each chapter. These are buttressed with empirical evidence from his own travels. In his biographies of famous Baptists, for example, he not only provides fascinating insights into their personal lives gleaned from original documents, but vividly describes the locations related to them. He can do this because he has personally visited nearly every place he mentions. This gives confidence to the reader that the author knows exactly what he is talking about. Complementing these references is a final chapter with additional resources for further study in Baptist distinctives and ecclesiology, along with an appendix providing a "Travel Guide to Historical Baptist Sites in England, Wales, and America." Besides being a superb textbook for seminaries, colleges, and Baptist Heritage classes in local churches, this book is second to none as a handy reference work for Baptist historiography.

Gerald Priest, PhD
Professor of Historical Theology, Retired, Detroit Baptist Theological Seminary

---❋---

"In the hourglass of merciful opportunity, one grain of time's inestimable sand is worth a golden mountain. Let's not lose it."

– *Roger Williams,* The Bloody Tenent of Persecution
(chapter 138)

Part I
Preliminary Essentials

Chapter 1

Introductory Essays on Our Baptist Heritage

❋

Baptist Distinctives

The earliest denominational usage of the name *Baptist* appears in 1644 from the pen of an opponent who refers to "those Baptists, or Dippers, that will not be called Anabaptists."[1] Because of the Baptist practice of believer's baptism by immersion, their opponents also called them *Dippers* who rejected the name *Anabaptist*. The term *Anabaptist* means "re-baptizer." Emerging in sixteenth-century Europe, evangelical Anabaptist groups were rejecting their infant baptism and practicing re-baptism, usually by pouring. Regarding infant baptism as no baptism at all, Baptists refused the name "re-baptizers." Despite opponents calling them "Anabaptists," the Baptists described themselves as "Baptized Believers," "Baptized Churches," and other similar names. No official group ever chose a name for the denomination. Their

---

[1] I. E. [John Etherington, a.k.a. Hetherington], *The Anabaptists Ground-Work for Reformation: Or, New Planting of Churches,* "that no man, woman, nor child, may be baptized, but such as have justifying faith and doe make profession thereof, before, to the baptizer" (London: M. Simmons, 1644), 23. The work is in the form of a debate between Etherington (a Familist) and Thomas Lamb, the General Baptist. The document is in the British Library, London.

distinctive name *Baptist* became standard simply from the practice of dropping the prefix from *Anabaptist*. By the 1700s, their permanent label was appearing in denominational literature in England and America.

There are two strands of English Baptist beginnings: The General Baptists, who established their first church during 1611–12, and the Particular Baptists, who formed their first church during 1633–38. The name *General* reflects the view that Christ died for all humanity. The name *Particular* reflects the view that Christ died only for the elect. Emerging in seventeenth-century London, both groups descended from various Independent, Separatist churches that had broken from the Church of England and embraced a congregational form of polity.

By 1643, Baptists, especially Particular Baptists, had defined their ordinances: Baptism and the Lord's Supper. The word *ordinance* is that which is ordered or ordained of the Lord. Baptists believe that Jesus ordered that local churches administer baptism by immersion to converts, as a public witness of their identification with His death, burial, and resurrection. Likewise, Baptists believe that Jesus ordained that local churches observe the Lord's Supper in remembrance of Him and His redemptive work. Prior to partaking of the Lord's Supper, each believer is to examine himself in spiritual preparation for this special memorial and worship of Christ.

This book includes frequent discussion on various "Baptist Distinctives," including those listed in the BAPTIST acrostic that L. Duane Brown (b. 1933) developed for a series of Sunday-School lessons during the 1960s. Brown published the acrostic in his *Biblical Basis for Baptists* (1969):[2]

---

[2] He was then shepherding a church in New York State. Brown, *Biblical Basis for Baptists: A Bible Study of Baptist Distinctives*, revised and expanded (North Fort Myers, FL: Faithful Life Publishers, 2009). Brown was a long-time leader in the General Association of Regular Baptist Churches and the Independent Baptist Fellowship of North America. Idem, *What Is THE Apostasy? The Coming Dark Ages and Collapse of Civilization* (North Fort Myers, FL: Faithful Life Publishers, 2014), www.FaithfulLifePublishers.com; and idem, *Confronting Today's World: A Fundamentalist Looks at Social Issues* (Schaumburg, IL: Regular Baptist Press, 1986).

Biblical Authority
Autonomy of the Local Church
Priesthood of All Believers
Two Ordinances
Individual Soul Liberty
Saved Church Membership
Two Officers
Separation of Church and State

The Earliest Records of Infant Baptism, Pouring, and Sprinkling

The large corpus of primitive Christian literature provides clear and frequent evidence that the immersion of professing believers was a continuation of the biblical practice. Even triple immersion often appears. For ancient support of baptism by pouring, non-Baptists often point to *The Teaching of the Twelve Apostles*, usually called the *Didache* (Gk. the *Teaching*). This anonymous work instructs that, if there is no river, lake, or pond for administering triple immersion in cool, natural water, the baptizer may use an immersion baptistery. If there is insufficient water to use the baptistery, he may pour water three times upon the believer's head.[3] Originating from the Syrian mountains, well after the era of the twelve apostles, the *Didache* carried no authoritative weight beyond its own rural environment. Scholars have attributed its preservation to its quaint style and strange blend of apocryphal and liturgical content. No church father or any other ancient writer ever mentions the *Didache*.

Baptismal pouring and sprinkling would emerge from belief in circumcisional regeneration in the Old Testament and its supposed replacement—baptismal regeneration in the New Testament.[4] Works by Origen of Alexandria (ca. 185–254) and

---
[3] *The Teaching of the Twelve Apostles* (7), ed. Alexander Roberts and James Donaldson, in *The Ante-Nicene Fathers, Translations of the Fathers Down to A. D. 325* (Edinburgh: T. & T. Clark, 1866), 7:379.

[4] In Colossians 2:11–13, Paul is merely contrasting God's putting off spiritual, inward "flesh" in regeneration with man's putting off outward flesh in circumcision. Water baptism is in no way a replacement of Old Testament circumcision. Water baptism merely symbolizes spiritual

Cyprian of Carthage (ca. 200–58) are the earliest extant sources for such practices. Fearing that infants might die in their sins without baptism and suffer in hell, Origen insists, "Little children are baptized 'for the remission of sins.' … Through the mystery of Baptism, the stains of birth are put aside. For this reason, even small children are baptized. For, 'unless a man be born again of water and spirit, he will not be able to enter into the kingdom of heaven'" [John 3:5].[5] When Carthaginian "priests" requested Bishop Cyprian's permission to administer infant baptism on the eighth day, like the Old Testament priests administered circumcision, Cyprian promptly mandated that they administer baptism within the second or third day after birth, since (as he thought) water baptism is the circumcision that regenerates. Cyprian commands that since "no one is to be hindered from obtaining grace … spiritual circumcision ought not to be hindered."[6] Contrary to Replacement theology, Baptists find in Scripture no such baptism and no such church office as *priest*, since each believer is a priest.

Major Views on Baptist Origins, with a Reappraisal of Landmarkism

Among historians there are four basic views regarding Baptist origins. First, the *English Separatist Derivation* view, which this book teaches, is that Baptists derived in the early seventeenth century from the English Separatist-Congregationalist movement, which had separated from the national Church of

---

baptism (regeneration). Neither circumcision nor water baptism can ever regenerate or cleanse spiritually.

[5] Origen, *Homilies on Luke* (14.5), trans. Joseph T. Lienhard, in vol. 94 of *The Fathers of the Church* (Washington, DC: Catholic University of America Press, 1996), 58–59; and Origen, *Commentary on the Epistle to the Romans* (Books 1–5), trans. Thomas P. Scheck, in vol. 103 of *The Fathers of the Church* (Washington, DC: Catholic University of America Press, 2001), 366–67.

[6] Cyprian, *Epistle* 58.2 and 58.5; cf. *Epistle* 75.12, in Roberts and Donaldson, *The Ante-Nicene Fathers*, 5:353–54, 5:400–1. See also David Beale, "A Listing of Ante-Nicene Seeds of Roman Catholicism," in *Historical Theology In-Depth* (Greenville, SC: Bob Jones University Press, 2013), 1:200–6.

England.[7] Second, the *Anabaptist Influence* view, supported in this book, agrees with the first view and stresses that evangelical Anabaptists in the Netherlands influenced the earliest General Baptists in their practice of believer's baptism and in their principle of separation of church and state.[8] Third, the *Spiritual Kinship* view contends that the Baptists began with Jesus and continued to modern times through a spiritual parentage of individuals and groups such as the Donatists. Those who teach this view do not attempt to establish any historical connections among the various, ancient groups.[9] Fourth, the *Landmark* view asserts that Jesus, during His earthly ministry, established the first Baptist church—the one true church— from which a perpetual succession of connected churches with various names comprise true Baptist history.

The Origins of Baptist Landmarkism

In 1851, six years after the formation of the Southern Baptist Convention (SBC), Landmarkism originated as a movement at a mass meeting in Cotton Grove Baptist Church (SBC), near Jackson, Tennessee, as the skillful orator James R. Graves (1820-93) expounded his convictions on Baptist beginnings. The movement derived its name from a publication titled *An Old Landmark Re-set* (1856), written by James M. Pendleton (1811-91),[10] who credited Graves for the title. As

---

[7] Other representative historians of the English Separatist Derivation view include William T. Whitley (1861-1947), Champlin Burrage (1874-1951), Robert G. Torbet (1912-95), Winthrop S. Hudson (1911-2001), William G. McLoughlin (1922-92), Robert A. Baker (1910-1992), H. Leon McBeth (1931-2013), and Barrington R. White (b. 1934).

[8] Other representative historians of the Anabaptist Influence view include Alfred C. Underwood (1885-1948), Ernest A. Payne (1902-80), and William R. Estep (1920-2000).

[9] Representative historians of the Spiritual Kinship view include Thomas Crosby (1683-1751), Joseph Ivimey (1773-1834), David Benedict (1779-1874), Thomas Armitage (1818-96), Albert H. Newman (1852-1933), and Henry C. Vedder (1853-1935). Unlike the rest, Ivimey envisioned a Baptistic kinship exclusively indigenous to England; thus, he restricted its spiritual ancestry to the various forms of English medieval dissent.

[10] See J. M. Pendleton, *Reminiscences of a Long Life* (Louisville: Press Baptist

the father of the Landmark movement Graves later wrote *Old Landmarkism: What Is It?* (1880).[11] Another early, influential promoter of Landmarkism was former Presbyterian Amos C. Dayton (1813–65),[12] best known for his 1856 novel, *Theodosia*

Book Concern, 1891), 103–4. Born in Spotsylvania County, Virginia, and raised in Kentucky, Pendleton died in Bowling Green, Kentucky. During his lifetime, he served pastorates in Kentucky, Tennessee, Ohio, and Pennsylvania. In 1852, during his twenty-year Bowling Green pastorate, he embraced Landmarkism under Graves's influence, and, the following year, Pendleton published his *Three Reasons Why I Am a Baptist*. While serving as a faculty member at Union University in Murfreesborough, Tennessee, Pendleton joined Amos C. Dayton as coeditor of James R. Graves's *Tennessee Baptist*, the voice of Landmarkism. Pendleton's support for the Union during the Civil War prompted him to accept a short pastorate at Hamilton, Ohio, before moving to Upland, Pennsylvania, where he helped establish Crozer Theological Seminary and served a long pastorate (1865–83). He spent the final years of his life in the South.

[11] Born in Chester, Vermont in 1820, Graves experienced conversion and received baptism into the fellowship of the Baptist church at North Springfield, Vermont, at the age of fifteen. Following several years of teaching school in Ohio and Kentucky, he moved to Nashville, Tennessee, in 1845, at the age of twenty-five. After a one-year pastorate in Nashville, Graves, in 1848, became editor of the paper known over a thirty-year span as *The Baptist*, the *Tennessee Baptist*, and the *Baptist and Reflector*—its circulation reaching up to twelve thousand. As the most widely read paper among Southern Baptists, it was their official organ in Tennessee, Arkansas, Louisiana, and Mississippi. See O. L. Hailey, *J. R. Graves: Life, Times and Teachings* (Nashville, TN: by the author, 1929); and James E. Tull, *A Study of Southern Baptist Landmarkism in the Light of Historical Baptist Ecclesiology* (New York: Columbia University Press, 1960).

[12] Born in New Jersey and reared a Presbyterian, Dayton practiced dentistry in Mississippi for nearly fifteen years before becoming a Baptist in 1852. He would serve as author for several Southern Baptist newspapers and as pastor of several SBC churches. His tombstone in Perry, GA, acknowledges him as being the first Southern Baptist novelist. Dayton later condensed his *Theodosia Ernest* into a popular one-volume book. See Jarrett Burch, "A Tennessee Baptist Returns to Georgia: The Latter Life of A. C. Dayton," *Tennessee Baptist History* (Fall 2005): 19–28; and Dayton's *Pedobaptist and Campbellite Immersion*, "with an introductory essay by J. R. Graves" (Nashville: Southwestern Publishing House, 1858), considered by many as the classic Landmark statement against "alien immersion." Dayton aimed to stem the tide of Baptists' receiving as valid "the immersions and ordinations of Pedobaptists and Campbellites" (iii–iv).

Ernest, or Heroine of Faith, a fictional pilgrimage of Theodosia's ten-night study in search of true baptism. The second volume is *Theodosia Ernest, or Ten Days Travel in Search of the Church*. Predictably, the young Presbyterian found true baptism and the true church among the Baptists. Within the SBC, the Landmark movement's greatest strength resided in Texas, Oklahoma, Louisiana, Arkansas, southern Illinois, western Kentucky, western Mississippi, western Tennessee, northern Alabama, and portions of Missouri.

Eventually, the strength of the Baptist Landmark movement passed into the hands of Baptist churches outside the SBC. Independent Landmark Baptists formed their first state organization in Texas when, in 1899, they broke from the Southern Baptist General Convention of Texas (BGCT) and established their own Baptist Missionary Association of Texas. Other Landmark Baptists left the SBC in 1905 and organized the General Association of Baptist Churches. Finally, in March 1924, in Texarkana, Texas, the two associations merged to form the American Baptist Association (ABA), a loosely knit fellowship of missionary Baptist churches. They operate a publishing company and a few local-church seminaries such as the Missionary Baptist Seminary and Institute in Little Rock, Arkansas. Scattered throughout the Association are numerous local-church institutes. The ABA churches teach that a succession of Baptist churches began with Jesus and has continued to the present day. They reject any idea of a "universal" church and believe that the only kind of church in the Bible is the local church.[13] In addition to those churches associated with organized groups such as the ABA, many unaffiliated Baptist churches embrace various tenets of Landmarkism. It would be difficult if not impossible to measure the numerical strength of the movement. Most Landmark Baptist churches do not include the word *Landmark* in their titles displayed on letterheads and

---

[13] Robert Ashcraft, ed., *History of the American Baptist Association*, "commemorating the seventy-fifth meeting, June 20–22, 2000" (Texarkana, TX: American Baptist Association, 2000); Conrad N. Glover and Austin T. Powers, *The American Baptist Association 1924–1974* (Texarkana, TX: Bogard Press, 1979); and the 2014 *Yearbook Directory*, http://www.abaptist.org/Yearbook/Yearbook.htm.

signboards. In addition, the appearance of the word *Landmark* in a church title does not necessarily mean that the church identifies with the teachings of Landmarkism. It might simply reflect the truth of Proverbs 22:28: "Remove not the ancient landmark, which thy fathers have set."

Key Tenets of Landmarkism

While many Landmark individuals no longer embrace every detail of the system, James R. Graves essentially defined the movement with these standard components:

- The terms *kingdom* and *churches* are synonymous. Graves assumes that Daniel's words, God shall "set up a *kingdom*, which shall never be destroyed" (Dan. 2:44), find their fulfillment in Jesus' words, "I will build my *church*; and the gates of hell shall not prevail against it" (Matt. 16:18). Graves concludes that the term *kingdom* refers collectively to all true Baptist churches.[14] He concedes that true Christians exist among other denominations and that individual Baptists may have personal fellowship with them. Ecclesiastical fellowship, however, can include only Baptist assemblies.[15]
- Early in His earthly ministry, even prior to the death of John the Baptist, Jesus established the first Baptist church. Every true "gospel" church since that time has been a Baptist church.
- In Matthew 16:18, when Jesus says, "Thou art Peter, and upon this rock I will build my church; and the gates of hell shall not prevail against it," He is promising an unbroken historical succession of true gospel churches on earth until He returns for His "Baptist bride."[16]

---

[14] James R. Graves, *Intercommunion Inconsistent, Unscriptural, and Productive of Evil* (Memphis: Baptist Book House, 1881), 160. Graves emphasizes that some churches that call themselves "Baptists" are not true Baptist churches.

[15] Idem, *Old Landmarkism: What Is It?* (Memphis: Baptist Book House, 1880), 154ff.

[16] In *Old Landmarkism: What Is It?* Graves equates the one true "church" with the Baptist churches and with the one "bride" (32, 44, and 123);

According to this teaching, the succession began with Jesus and continued through various "baptistic" groups such as the Montanists, Novatians, Donatists, Paulicians, Albigenses, Petrobrusians, Waldenses, and Anabaptists. This succession, with the Manicheans added, appears in G. H. Orchard, *A Concise History of Baptists from the Time of Christ Their Founder to the 18th Century* (London, 1838). In 1855, J. R. Graves added his own "Introductory Essay" of endorsement and republished Orchard's book in America.

- Only Baptist churches are biblically qualified to function as churches and to carry out the Great Commission.[17]
- The only Christian baptism is water baptism, even in passages such as Ephesians 4:5, "One Lord, one faith, one baptism," and 1 Corinthians 12:13, "For by one Spirit are we all baptized into one body, whether we be Jews or Gentiles, whether we be bond or free; and have been all made to drink into one Spirit." According to Graves, there is no such thing as a baptism of the Holy Spirit.[18]
- The only biblical church is a local church, even in passages such as Ephesians 5:25, "… Christ also loved the church, and gave himself for it; That he might sanctify and cleanse it with the washing of water by the word, That he might present it to himself a glorious church, not having spot, or wrinkle, or any such thing; but that it should be holy and without blemish." Pendleton

---

Christ "has left his betrothed Bride till he comes again to marry her" (98); Christ "has but one Bride and will have but one wife" (20). Later, in *The Work of Christ in the Covenant of Redemption: Developed in Seven Dispensations* (Memphis: Baptist Book House, 1883), 461, Graves describes Christ's Bride as the redeemed, "from the days of Abel until the day of the rapture." This appears to be the only (though perhaps unguarded) instance in which Graves contradicts his notion of a "Baptist" Bride.

[17] James R. Graves, ed., *The Tennessee Baptist*, vol. 2, Thursday, February 1, 1849, page 2, column 2. For the most complete study, see Myron James Houghton, "The Place of Baptism in the Theology of James Robinson Graves" (ThD diss., Dallas Theological Seminary, 1971).

[18] See Houghton, "The Place of Baptism," 97ff.

disagreed with Graves on this point.[19]

Many non-Landmark Baptists do concur with the following Landmark tenets:

- Baptism administered by a non-Baptist is invalid.
- Just as each local church must restrict its administration of discipline to its own membership, so must each church restrict the ordinance of the Lord's Supper to its own membership.
- Baptist churches should not invite non-Baptist ministers to their pulpits.
- Baptist churches should not endorse mission work not sponsored by Baptist churches.

Significantly, not only has Graves' ecclesiology drawn controversy, his Christology has drawn charges ranging from Apollinarianism and Nestorianism to Arianism.[20] While maintaining the eternality of the person of Christ, Graves departed from historical orthodoxy in his adamant rejection of the eternal Sonship of Christ. Graves penned the following only ten years prior to his death and he never retracted it:

> Before the birth of creation there could have been no relationships existing as that of the Father and Son, for these are terms of *relationship*, and imply *order* of being, and consequently demand *time*. If this be so, then evidently the phrases "Eternal Father," and "Eternal Son," are inadmissible, since they involve a manifest contradiction. As certainly as the Creator must exist before the thing created, the begetter must

---

[19] Unlike Graves, J. M. Pendleton conceded that, in passages such as Eph. 5:25, there is one "aggregate" church of all the redeemed. See his *Church Manual: Designed for the Use of Baptist Churches* (Philadelphia: American Baptist Publication Society, n.d.), 5–6; idem, *Christian Doctrines: A Compendium of Theology* (Philadelphia: American Baptist Publication Society, 1878), 329; idem, *Notes of Sermons* (Philadelphia: American Baptist Publication Society, 1886), 78.

[20] E.g., James Leo Garrett Jr., *Baptist Theology: A Four-Century Study* (Macon, GA: Mercer University Press, 2009), 222–23.

exist before the begotten—Father before Son.... The phrases "Eternal Son of God," "the Eternal Father," are manifestly of human coinage.... The relationship, expressed by the terms Father and Son, originated with the conception of the Covenant of Redemption and Work of Christ, and when that work is consummated, the relationship and its inferiority will cease.[21]

Investigating the Claims of Landmarkism

In his well-known booklet, *The Trail of Blood* (1931), Southern Baptist author James Milton (J. M.) Carroll (1852-1931)[22] presents five lectures, with a pull-out chart, to argue from Mark 3:16-18 that Jesus organized the first Baptist church, and that in Matthew 16:18 Jesus promises an unbroken succession of Baptist churches from that first one down to His Second Coming. Like G. H. Orchard and J. R. Graves,[23] Carroll anachronistically, equates Anabaptists with Baptists. Like Orchard and Graves, he has the Roman Catholic Cardinal Stanislaus Hosius (1504-79) claiming, "Were it not that the Baptists have been grievously tormented and cut off with the knife during the past twelve hundred years, they would swarm in number greater than all the Reformers."[24] Many Landmark publications add the following and attribute it to Hosius:

> If the truth of religion were to be judged by the readiness and cheerfulness which a man of any sect shows in suffering, the opinions and persuasions of no sect can be truer or surer than those of the Anabaptists, whence there have been none for these twelve hundred years past that have been more grievously

---

[21] Graves, *The Work of Christ in the Covenant of Redemption*, 61-62.
[22] J. M. Carroll was the brother of B. H. Carroll, founder of Southwestern Baptist Theological Seminary, Fort Worth, Texas.
[23] Graves, "Introductory Essay," in Orchard, *A Concise History of Baptists from the Time of Christ Their Founder to the 18th Century*, 13th ed. (Nashville: Graves & Marks, 1855), xvii; cf. 304.
[24] J. M. Carroll, *The Trail of Blood* (Lexington, KY: Ashland Avenue Baptist Church, 1931), 3; cf. idem, *A History of the Texas Baptists* (1923). John Gill had also used the alleged citation.

> punished, or that have more cheerfully and steadfastly undergone and even offered themselves to the most cruel sorts of punishment than these people.[25]

Those who have circulated the alleged quotations (above) claim that both derive from "Hosius, *Letters, Apud Opera*, 112-13." They offer no volume number and no specific "Letter." Hosius wrote no work titled "*Apud Opera.*" The complete works (*opera*) of Cardinal Hosius appeared in two volumes (1564 and 1584), and all his 277 epistles are in volume two (pages 145-453). Pages "112-13" do not contain the alleged citations in either volume. It is only in *Epistle* 150 that the word *Anabaptists* appears in the same context with the words *twelve hundred years*. Even here, *Epistle* 150 does not contain the word *knife* or any other such instrument. Nor does it contain the word *Reformers*. Displaying Anabaptists as heretics, Hosius, in the same *Epistle*, presents a downward spiral from "Lutheranism to Calvinism, from Calvinism to Anabaptism, from Anabaptism to Trideism, [and] from Trideism to Atheism" (*de Lutheranismo ad Calvinismum: de Calvinismo ad Anabaptismum: de Anabaptismo ad Trideismum: de Trideismo ad Atheismum*).[26] In the next sentence, he speaks of "Anabaptists (*Anabaptistarum*) who, so we read, were pronounced heretics twelve hundred years ago and deserving of capital punishment" (*dolens, quos ante mille ducentos annes haeretisos, capitalique supplicio dignos esse pronunciatos legimus*).[27] Hosius never uses the word *Baptists*. When he speaks of *Anabaptistarum*, he likens them to individuals such as Caspar Schwenckfeld von Ossig (1489-1561) and Thomas Müntzer (d. 1525), and to groups such as Waldenses and Donatists. Normally, when Hosius uses the term *Anabaptists*, he identifies them as Donatists,[28] but there is

---

[25] E.g., Curtis Pugh, *Three Witnesses for the Baptists* (Bloomfield, NM: The Historic Baptist, 1994), 66.

[26] Hosius reaffirms the same in *Epistle* 157, 2:316.

[27] Stanislai Hosii, *Epistle* 150, in *Operum* (Coloniae: Apud Maternum Cholinum, 1584), 2:309, my translation. Hosius addresses *Epistle* 150 to Alberto Bavariae Duci. For the entire *Epistle* see 2:306-10.

[28] E.g., see Stanislaus Hosius, *A Most Excellent Treatise of the Begynnyng of Heresyes in Oure Tyme*, trans. Richard Shacklock, who describes the

no viable evidence that Baptists emerged from the Donatists or from any other ancient group.

Landmark authors appeal also to the works of two Dutch historians to argue their case for Baptist perpetuity. Annaeus Ypeij (Ypey) and Izaak Johannes Dermout, under commission from King William I of the Netherlands, authored a four-volume *History of the Dutch Reformed Church* (*Geschiedenis der Nederlandsche Hervormde Kerk*, 1819–27). For many years, Landmark Baptists, including the Southern Baptist, John T. Christian (1854–1925), have followed the lead of Orchard and Graves in circulating the following as a direct quotation from this work by Ypeij and Dermout:

> We have now seen that the Baptists who were formerly called Anabaptist, and in later times Mennonites, were the original Waldenses, and who have long in the history of the church received the honor of that origin. On this account the Baptists may be considered as the only Christian society which has stood since the days of the apostles, and as a Christian society which has preserved pure the doctrines of the Gospel through all ages. The perfectly correct external and internal economy of the Baptist denomination tends to confirm the truth, disputed by the Romish Church, that the Reformation brought about in the sixteenth century was in the highest degree necessary, and at the same time goes to refute the erroneous notion of the Catholics, that their denomination is the most ancient (Ypeij en Dermout, *Geschiedenis der Nederlandsche Hervornude Kerk*. Breda, 1819).[29]

---

work "the Hatchet of Heresies" (Antwerp: Imprinted by AEg. Diest, 1565), 27b–48; idem, *De Haeresibus Nostri Temporis*, in *Operum* (Lugduni: Apud Guliel Rovillium, 1564), 1:25–26. The Donatists, like the Catholics, were pedobaptists who held to baptismal regeneration. The state church persecuted Donatists for their separatism. See David Beale, "A Reappraisal of the Donatist Controversy and Its Significance," in *Historical Theology In-Depth* (Greenville, SC: Bob Jones University Press, 2013), 1:358–85.

[29] John T. Christian, *A History of the Baptists*, 2 vols. (Nashville: Broadman, 1925), 1:95–96.

Those who have attempted to use the alleged citation (above) have provided no volume numbers or page numbers. Parts of the citation appear scattered throughout pages 148–51 of volume one. The alleged citation contains no ellipsis points to indicate its omission of words, phrases, and even paragraphs. Landmark additions to the text include the word *Baptists*. The Dutch term for "Baptist Church" is *Baptisten Kirche*. Ypeij and Dermout never use the term. Yet, Landmark Baptists point to this work as their best historical evidence for the apostolic origin of the Baptists. The Dutch word that Ypeij and Dermout use for "Anabaptists" is *Wederdopers* (*weder* means "again" and *doper* means "baptize"). The authors describe these *Wederdopers* as having "a very harmful impact on the outer life of the Protestant community." Landmark Baptists ignore that fact. Besides the word *Mennonieten* (followers of Menno Simons), the synonymous and commonly used term for "Mennonites" was *Doopsgezinden*,[30] or "those inclined to baptism," that is, believer's baptism in this case. *Doops* is genitive of *doop* ("baptism") and *gezind* means "to favor," or "to be inclined." Unlike their negative description of the "Anabaptists" (*Wederdopers*), Ypeij and Dermout report favorably of the *Doopsgezinden* (Mennonites), as having "a beneficial influence on the inner life of the whole community of Protestant Christians in Holland." They live "beyond reproach, as diligent and hard-working citizens, good, religious Christians, avoiding worldly attractions, and steadfastly following the best moral principles." Ypeij and Dermout lament that the Mennonites were at times being "confused with" the Anabaptists (*Wederdopers*).[31] The Mennonites

---

[30] Latourette has a valuable discussion on the *Doopsgezinden*, a term that he uses exclusively for "Mennonites." Kenneth Scott Latourette, "Nineteenth-Century Protestantism in Holland (The Kingdom of the Netherlands)," in *The Nineteenth Century in Europe: The Protestant and Eastern Churches*, vol. 2 of *Christianity in a Revolutionary Age: A History of Christianity in the Nineteenth and Twentieth Centuries* (Grand Rapids: Zondervan, 1959), 237–51.

[31] A. Ypeij en I. J. Dermout, *Geschiedenis der Nederlandsche Hervormde Kerk*, 4 vols. (Breda: W. Van Bergen, 1819), 1:149–50. They spell it *Wederdoopers*. For Ypeij and Dermout, I acquired the professional translation services of Marco Schuffelen, scholar of Dutch. His website is www.heardutchhere.net.

have used the name *Doopsgezind* since the seventeenth century, and it has been the official registered name of the Mennonites in the Netherlands since 1796,[32] long before Ypeij and Dermout wrote their history.

Concerning local church successionism, Henry Vedder well concludes:

> The church that [Jesus] said he would build on the rock, to which he guaranteed victory against the gates of Hades itself, is not a visible body—that is the great falsehood of Rome—but the assembly of those in all the ages who truly love God and keep the commandments of Christ. Of these, there has been an unbroken line and here is the true apostolic succession—there is no other.... Our theory of the church as deduced from the Scriptures requires no outward and visible succession from the apostles. If every church of Christ were today to become apostate, it would be possible and right for any true believers to organize tomorrow another church on the apostolic model of faith and practice, and that church would have the only apostolic succession worth having—a succession of faith in the Lord Christ and obedience to him.[33]

Newgate Prison: The Dark Hole of Persecution

Any serious study of religious freedom and liberty of conscience must consider the noble company who suffered and paid the ultimate price for freedoms often taken for granted. Meeting in members' homes, gravel pits, and other secret places, the earliest Baptists left behind no buildings or other physical monuments. Among its multiple jails, however, London's notorious Newgate Prison became the most ominous testimonial to Baptist persecution. Its gloomy, overshadowing buildings

---

[32] See "Doopsgezind," in Harold S. Bender, et al., eds., *Mennonite Encyclopedia: Comprehensive Reference Work on the Anabaptist-Mennonite Movement*, 4 vols. (Hillsboro, KS: Mennonite Brethren Publishing House, 1955–59), 2:86.

[33] Henry C. Vedder, *Short History of the Baptists*, rev. 2nd ed. (Valley Forge: The American Baptist Publication Society, 1907), 7.

existed until the turn of the twentieth century, and, even now, there remain remnants of one of its walls. Untold numbers of Independent-Separatists and Baptists suffered incarceration here—multiple times for many of them. As in many other prisons, hundreds died within the walls of Newgate, where even a short list of dissenter inmates includes Baptist leaders Thomas Helwys, John Murton, Thomas Lamb, Edward Barber, Thomas Delaune, Richard Overton, Samuel Eaton, Hanserd Knollys, John Griffith, Hercules Collins, and William Kiffin's grandsons, Benjamin and William Hewling.

Initially, *Newgate* was the name of a gatehouse in the old London City wall. The year 1188 marks the earliest reference to the "Gaol at Newgate." In the wake of London's Great Fire of 1666, Newgate Prison was rebuilt during 1672–73. Over the years, it would be rebuilt several more times. At the junction of Old Bailey, Giltspur Street, and Newgate Street, a slightly misleading plaque reads, "Site of Newgate Demolished 1777." The year 1777 did witness the tearing down of the old gatehouse, along with a cluster of the prison's oldest buildings, but this partial demolition was only to make way for the construction of its new facilities. The final Newgate Prison opened in 1785. In 1902, the city demolished the prison once for all, making room for a larger building for Old Bailey Courthouse. Here, in the back of Amen Court, in the shadow of St. Paul's Cathedral, one can view the only surviving wall of Newgate Prison, whose public executions took place eight times each year. Execution days were public holidays, attracting immense crowds of spectators watching from windows, carts, and surrounding fields.

Inside the nearby "Church of St. Sepulchre without Newgate,"[34] a hand bell, called the "Great Bell," or "Execution Bell," still resides in a glass case situated near the entrance

---

[34] Like the Church of the Holy Sepulchre in Jerusalem, the London church once stood just outside the northwest gate of its city. When the London church took the name *Church of the Holy Sepulchre*, knights of the Crusades chose it as the most suitable place from which they would set out for the Holy Land. Later, when the London church abbreviated *Holy* to *St.*, its name became the "Church of St. Sepulchre without Newgate." The expression *without Newgate* means that the church stood just "outside Newgate" Prison.

of a blocked-up tunnel that once connected the church with Newgate Prison. Beginning in 1612, at midnight on the eve of every execution day, the church's hired bellman would walk through the tunnel and into the prison. Standing outside the cells of condemned prisoners, he would ring twelve double tolls of the Execution Bell and chant his memorized lines through the keyholes:

> All you that in the condemned hole do lie,
> Prepare you, for tomorrow you shall die;
> Watch all and pray: the hour is drawing near
> That you before the Almighty must appear;
> Examine well yourselves; in time repent,
> That you may not to eternal flames be sent.
> And when St. Sepulchre's Bell in the morning tolls,
> The Lord above have mercy on your souls.[35]

The next morning, bystanders eagerly watch, as the condemned prisoners, on their way to execution, pass by St. Sepulcher's, where the bellman tolls a funeral knell for four hours (from six to ten) and then "rings it out, till the Execution is over."[36] Those who are sentenced to death by hanging are taken three miles by ox-cart up Holborn Hill to Tyburn (a village on London's west side)[37] and led to the scaffold of the triangular "Tyburn Tree," erected at the junction where two Roman roads meet. Each victim is stripped naked—his clothes becoming the hangman's property. In those days, the "Tree"

---

[35] Stephen Halliday, *Newgate: London's Prototype of Hell* (Gloucestershire, England: Sutton Publishing, 2006), 63. See also Kelly Grovier, *The Gaol: The Story of Newgate—London's Most Notorious Prison* (London: John Murray, 2008), 76ff.

[36] B. L. [Batty Langley] of Twickenham, *An Accurate Description of Newgate* (London: Printed at the Black Boy in Paternoster Row for T. Warner, 1724), 48n. See also Anthony Babington, *The English Bastille: A History of Newgate Gaol and Prison Conditions in Britain 1188–1902* (London: Macdonald, 1971).

[37] The village obtained its name from the Tyburn stream, a tributary of the Thames. Now subterranean, the stream continues its surreptitious course underneath the streets of London.

was the dreaded scaffold, with its three legs and three crossbeams capable of dispatching twenty-four victims at a time — eight on each beam. The year 1759 marked the final demolition of the infamous gallows — after some fifty thousand executions over six centuries. Embedded in the pavement, on the traffic island at the junction of Marble Arch underground station and Edgware Road, a medallion stone displays the engraved words, "The Site of Tyburn Tree."

The area abounds with legend, most notably the location of Oliver Cromwell's body.[38] Following his death in September 1658, Cromwell received a public burial inside Westminster Abbey. The following chronicle of what happened to his corpse, a little over two years later, is probably the most accurate and certainly the most popular account of this mysterious turn of events. During the predawn hours of January 30, 1661 (twelfth anniversary of the execution of Charles I), pro-Restoration marauders removed the corpses of Cromwell and two other men from Westminster Abbey. They conveyed the corpses to the Tyburn Tree, hanged them, and decapitated them. The marauders then disposed of the three headless corpses. At daylight, news rapidly spread that the corpses were missing from the Abbey and that the three heads were on twenty-foot spikes hovering above Westminster Hall — high against London's skyline. The heads remained displayed there for several years, and no one has ever found the bodies.[39] Further details remain a mystery.

Albeit, the atrocities that occurred that same year against

---

[38] Alfred Marks, *Tyburn Tree: Its History and Annals* (London: Brown, Langham and Co., n.d.), 71; Alan Brooke and David Brandon, *Tyburn: London's Fatal Tree* (London: Sutton Publishing, 1980); and Donald Rumbelow, *The Triple Tree: Newgate, Tyburn and Old Bailey* (London: Harrap, 1982), 87, see illustration. Victims sometimes included Roman Catholics.

[39] See also Oliver Cromwell's *Letters and Speeches*, 5 vols., ed. Thomas Carlyle (London: Chapman and Hall, 1850–1903); Michael A. G. Haykin, ed., *"To Honor God": The Spirituality of Oliver Cromwell* (Dundas, Ontario, 1999); John Morley, *Oliver Cromwell* (New York: Century, 1900); Frederic Harrison, *Oliver Cromwell* (New York: Macmillan, 1889); Antonia Fraser, *Cromwell: The Lord Protector* (New York: Dell, 1975); and J. H. Merle d'Aubigné, *The Protector: A Vindication* (New York: Robert Carter, 1847).

Baptists and other separatists are known and sobering facts. "Towards the end of 1661, 289 out of 355 prisoners in Newgate were Baptists."[40] In his letter titled *A Voice from Prison*, the Baptist Hercules Collins (1646/7–1702) wrote from his Newgate cell the following meditations on Revelation 3:11: "The weathercock turns with every wind of temptation, but the established soul stands fast when the rains fall, the winds blow, [and] the waves beat.... He stands ... founded upon the Rock of Ages." Collins then proclaims, "O! Blessed state to be delivered from the fear of men, the fear of evil, the fear of prison, the fear of poverty, the fear of flames, as many have experienced through grace. And if they may be believed, [they] can speak experimentally, which is more than to read it, that Christ's yoke is easy, and ... notwithstanding all [that] befalls the saints, his burden is a light burden, and his ways are pleasant, and his paths are peace."[41]

Conclusion

From Baptists' beginnings in the early 1600s to American's Constitution and Bill of Rights in the late 1700s, the Baptist heritage is the story of courageous men and women, who faithfully spread the gospel, often suffered persecution and martyrdom, and kept the faith. This book conveys the story of our Baptist ancestors who lived and died "for the faith ... once delivered unto the saints" (Jude 3*b*).[42] The following chapter includes the life of Thomas Helwys, who befriended the *Mayflower* Pilgrims and subsidized their escape into Holland, prior to their 1620 voyage to America. Helwys, meanwhile, would

---

[40] Claire Cross, *Church and People 1450–1660: The Triumph of the Laity in the English Church*, 2nd ed. (Oxford: Blackwell, 1999), 208.

[41] Hercules Collins, *A Voice from the Prison, or, Meditations on Revelations III.X1*, "tending to the establishment of God's little flock, in an hour of temptation" (London: Printed by George Larkin, 1684), 4, 31. I slightly modernized grammar. A copy of this thirty-four-page letter is in the British Library, London.

[42] See for example, Keith E. Durso, *No Armor for the Back: Baptist Prison Writings, 1600s–1700s* (Macon: Mercer University Press, 2007); and H. Leon McBeth, *English Baptist Literature on Religious Liberty to 1689* (New York: Arno Press, 1980). Initially, McBeth's work was a ThD thesis, Southwestern Baptist Theological Seminary, 1961.

plant England's first Baptist church and die in Newgate Prison.

Select Bibliography for Further Reading

Calamy, Edmund, and Samuel Palmer. *The Nonconformist's Memorial: Being an Account of the Lives, Sufferings, and Printed Works of the Two Thousand Ministers Ejected from the Church of England, Chiefly by the Act of Uniformity, Aug. 24, 1662*. 3 vols. 2nd ed. London: J. Cundee or Button and Son, and T. Hurst, 1802–3.

Collins, Hercules, *A Voice from the Prison, or, Meditations on Revelations III. X1*. London: Printed by George Larkin, 1684.

Cook, Brenton Hunter. "Recovering the Historic View of Baptist Origins: The Seventeenth-Century Baptists' Theological Identity Interpreted through a Progressive Illumination Paradigm." PhD diss., Bob Jones University, 2005.

Durso, Keith E. *No Armor for the Back: Baptist Prison Writings, 1600s–1700s*. Macon: Mercer University Press, 2007.

Halliday, Stephen. *Newgate: London's Prototype of Hell*. Gloucestershire, England: Sutton Publishing, 2006.

Hanbury, Benjamin, ed. *Historical Memorials Relating to the Independents or Congregationalists: From Their Rise to the Restoration of the Monarchy, A. D. MDCLX*, 3 vols. London: Congregational Union of England and Wales, 1839–44.

Houghton, Myron James. "The Place of Baptism in the Theology of James Robinson Graves." ThD diss., Dallas Theological Seminary, 1971.

Langley, Batty ["B. L."]. *An Accurate Description of Newgate*. London: Printed at the Black Boy in Paternoster Row for T. Warner, 1724.

McBeth, H. Leon. *English Baptist Literature on Religious Liberty to 1689*. New York: Arno Press, 1980. Initially, this was a ThD thesis, Southwestern Baptist Theological Seminary, 1961.

McGoldrick, James Edward. *Baptist Successionism: A Crucial Question in Baptist History*. Metuchen, NJ: Scarecrow Press, 1994.

Moritz, Fred. "The Landmark Controversy: A Study in Baptist History and Polity." *Maranatha Baptist Theological Journal* 2, no. 1 (Spring 2012): 3–28.

Patterson, W. Morgan. *Baptist Successionism: A Critical View*. Valley Forge: Judson Press, 1969.

Rumbelow, Donald. *The Triple Tree: Newgate, Tyburn and Old Bailey*. London: Harrap, 1982.

Taulman, James E. "Amos Cooper Dayton: A Critical Biography." ThM thesis, Southern Baptist Theological Seminary, 1965.

Wilson, Walter. *The History and Antiquities of Dissenting Churches and Meeting Houses, in London, Westminster, and Southwark: Including the Lives of Their Ministers, from the Rise of Nonconformity to the Present Time*, 4 vols. London: Printed for the author, 1808–14.

Part II

English General Baptists to the New Connection

Chapter 2

The English Separatist Roots of General Baptists

The Rise of Puritanism

Queen Mary I (r. 1553–58), who was a daughter of Henry VIII and the wife of the Roman Catholic Philip II of Spain, had forced a restoration of Roman Catholicism upon England. It was the endeavor of her successor Elizabeth I (r. 1558–1603) to mark out a *via media* between Protestantism and "popery."[43] Elizabeth's first task was to restore the Anglican Church. For the bishops of the Church of England to continue claiming a succession from the apostles, Anglican ecclesiastics were careful to recognize the Church of Rome as a true church—though essentially corrupt in doctrine and practice. Elizabeth herself had revealed such successionism when she began her reign by appointing Matthew Parker as Archbishop of Canterbury. Parker had received his ordination in the Roman Catholic Church in 1527, prior to England's break with the papacy. To the bishops, therefore, Parker represented a continuity of "apostolic episcopacy." Elizabeth proceeded to nullify all the religious restorations of her sister Mary and persuaded

---

[43] A good discussion of the rise of Separatism during Elizabeth's reign is Barrington R. White, *The English Separatist Tradition: From the Marian Martyrs to the Pilgrim Fathers* (London: Oxford University Press, 1971), 20–43.

Parliament to restore her father's Act of Supremacy (1558), vesting all ecclesiastical jurisdictions in the Crown.

For all office holding, in both church and state, it was now necessary to take a solemn oath recognizing England's monarch as "the only Supreme Governor of this realm ... in all spiritual and ecclesiastical things." Civil penalties were in place for those refusing to take the oath. The state would tolerate Puritans only if they took the oath and obeyed the Queen. Elizabeth's transfer of ecclesiastical punishments to the state was a demonstration of *Erastianism*, a term derived from the Swiss theologian and medical doctor, Thomas Erastus (1524-83).[44] Although Erastus himself would not likely have agreed with every application of the concept, *Erastianism* quickly became the view that, under a single state-church religion, the state (in behalf of the church) must exercise coercive jurisdiction over all punitive matters. Indeed, as Robert Walton notes, "Religion as established by law under the Elizabethan settlement was ... Erastian in church order and government, and largely mediaeval in liturgy."[45] Essentially, the Elizabethan Settlement consists of two parts: The Act of Supremacy and the Act of Uniformity.

Under Elizabeth's Act of Uniformity (1559), ministers failing to subscribe to the liturgical *Book of Common Prayer* (revised 1560) and to the confessional Thirty-Nine Articles (revised 1563) would lose their pulpits and suffer imprisonment. The Act of Uniformity carried severe penalties against anyone who would not conform to the authority of the Church of England. Both Puritans and Roman Catholics would suffer persecution before the Elizabethan age ended. Many suffered fines and imprisonment for refusing to attend the services of the parish churches. Anyone in London who tried to promote

---

[44] The original name of Thomas Erastus was Thomas Lüber (Lieber, or Liebler), which became Latinized into Erastus.

[45] Robert C. Walton, *The Gathered Community* (London: Carey Press, 1946), 59. For a sympathetic discussion of Erastianism, see J. W. Allen, "The Erastian Point of View," in *English Political Thought 1603–1660* (London: Methuen and Co., 1938), 1:339–45. Richard Hooker (1593-1662), in his *Of the Lawes of Ecclesiasticall Politie*, would become perhaps the most able defender of the Erastian doctrine of secular supremacy over the church.

the notion of independent, congregational churches ran the danger of imprisonment and public execution. It was from the establishment of Elizabeth's Act of Uniformity that many Puritans acquired the label *non-conformists*.

To ensure uniformity, the Queen issued proclamations declaring null and void all preaching licenses granted prior to 1564; that year marks the beginning of *Puritanism* as a movement. Written by Archbishop Matthew Parker, the proclamations silenced all preachers and issued fresh licenses only to "conformable" ministers. Suddenly, thousands of parishes were destitute of ministers to preach to them. One third of London's clergy suffered suspension for their refusal to submit to Parker's requirements, which included the enforced use of clerical vestments such as the surplice (robe). Puritan ministers cried aloud that clerical vestments belonged not to the ministry of the church of Christ, but to the priesthood of the house of Aaron, as depicted in the "Romish rags of the pope's church!" For eighty years—1564 to 1644—a distinct body of Puritans, always in and of the Church of England, dared to speak out against corruption in the Church. The controversy lay deeper than mere outward forms. The Puritans preached from the Scriptures that the very nature and discipline of Christ's church were under attack.

When Elizabeth died on the last day of 1602[46] the kingdom that she left—so poor and defenseless at the beginning of her reign—had in forty-five years become a rich and mighty realm, the beginning of a vast empire. Elizabeth left no heir, and the throne of England passed from the Tudors to the Stuarts. James VI of Scotland succeeded her as James I of England (r. 1603-25). The Puritans hoped that from him they would receive milder treatment. Archbishop Whitgift, however, had already sent agents to Scotland to assure the King of the loyalty of the Church of England and of its bishops. In return, the new King gave them his complete support. On April 4, 1603, as James was on his way to London to assume his throne, the Puritans

---

[46] Elizabeth died on March 24, 1602 (O. S.), the last day of the year according to the Julian calendar. She died on April 3, 1602 (N. S.).

presented to him their "Millenary Petition,"[47] unsigned, but expressing in moderate language the wishes of hundreds of concerned ministers who desired a Reformation in the Church of England. A conference was set to assemble at Hampton Court Palace,[48] January 14, 16, and 18, 1604, professedly to give due consideration to the concerns listed on the Petition. James, however, was in no mood for compromise. Indeed, the only positive thing that the Puritans received from the Hampton Court Conference was the authorization to translate and publish the King James Bible.

The Rise of Separatism

Ministerial corruption was rampant in the National Church throughout the entire reign of James I. Like Roman Catholics, increasing numbers of Anglican clergymen were embracing heretical views on the doctrine of sin. Preaching man's innate abilities, the state church only encouraged the moral corruption that was already sweeping the kingdom. When Puritans cried out against such doctrines and practices, Bishop Richard Bancroft became obsessed with his intent of breaking their backs. In the spring of 1604, the *Ecclesiastical Constitutions and Canons*, edited by Bancroft, were issued in Convocation (presided over by Bancroft) on the strength of Royal Supremacy alone, without Parliamentary consent. Among other things, the canons required the wearing of ministerial surplices, the observance of prescribed religious days, and strict conformity to *The Book of Common Prayer* in worship. The formation of secret conventicles (religious gatherings) was forbidden as high crime.

The Court of High Commission, authorized by the Act of

---

[47] The Puritans had hoped for a thousand signatures on the Petition, but, realizing that they would probably get no more than 750, they decided to omit signatures altogether. The name *Millenary Petition* became permanent.

[48] Located near Kingston upon Thames and little more than ten miles SW of the city of London, Hampton Court Palace was the favorite country residence of Henry VIII (who played tennis here). Five of his wives lived here. A walk through the palace's rooms and gardens offers a unique taste of nearly five hundred years of history.

Supremacy, became the Erastian instrument used to enforce conformity. Archbishop Whitgift was now dead and Bancroft would soon become his successor, surpassing even Whitgift in his severities. Three hundred non-conformist Puritan ministers, in 1604, suffered imprisonment and exile. While the Puritans preached eloquently and faithfully, increasing numbers of sincere religious dissenters were coming to the conviction that they must go beyond Puritanism and worship the Lord outside of England's parish churches. They must become Separatists. While Puritans were not Separatists in practice, Separatists were Puritan in doctrine.

The following year (1605), officials summoned seventeen Nottinghamshire men and women to appear in court for listening to the separatist preaching of John Robinson at Sturton-le-Steeple. In the face of the continuing failure of Puritan efforts to reform the National Church, concerned Separatist clergymen in the Diocese of Lincoln wrote an *Apology* (1605),[49] setting forth bold and clear reasons for their inability, in good conscience, to obey the 1604 *Ecclesiastical Constitutions and Canons*, or to conduct their worship in conformity with *The Book of Common Prayer*. The *Apology* constitutes the Separatists' essential grievances against the Church of England:

- Widespread lack of biblical qualifications, knowledge of Scripture, and spiritual leadership among ministers
- Absence of the preaching of cardinal doctrines in most pulpits
- Absence of many books of Scripture in *The Book of Common Prayer*
- Apocrypha used alongside Scripture in *The Book of Common Prayer*
- Lack of biblical prerequisites for partaking of the Eucharist
- The office of the priesthood entrusted to forgive sins

---

[49] *An Abridgement of That Booke Which the Ministers off the Lincolne Diocese Delivered to His Maiestie upon the First of December 1605: Being the First Part of an Apologie for Themselves and Their Brethren That Refuse the Subscription and Conformitie Which is Required*, cited in Harold Kirk-Smith, *William Brewster 'The Father of New England' — His Life and Times — 1567-1644* (Boston, England: Richard Kay, 1992), 61–63.

- Confessions made to priests
- Total lack of church discipline
- Local churches forbidden from choosing their own ministers

From that landscape, the earliest General Baptists would emerge from two Separatist churches, known in those days as the Ancient Church and the Gainsborough-Scrooby Church.

The Ancient Church

Its Early Years

The Ancient Church began as a secret church. On October 8, 1587, officers arrested John Greenwood and twenty-two other Separatists for meeting secretly for worship. Local officials threw them into the infamous Clink Prison in London's Southwark area on the south bank of the Thames. On November 19, while visiting Greenwood in the Clink, Henry Barrow suffered arrest. Officials incarcerated him with Greenwood. Here, Barrow authored A True Description (1589), the secret church's first statement of faith.[50] While the brief confession includes essentials of early congregationalism, its oligarchy of elders leans more toward semi-Presbyterianism. For more than five years, Barrow and Greenwood would remain in the Clink and in nearby Fleet Prison. From their cells, Barrow and Greenwood wrote numerous treatises, pamphlets, letters, and petitions that Separatists smuggled out, a few pages at a time, and sent to Holland for printing. English Puritan, Francis Johnson (1562–1618), a Cambridge graduate and chaplain to the Church of Merchant Adventurers in Middleburg (Zeeland), learned that a book by Barrow and Greenwood was being secretly printed in the Dutch city of Dort. Authorized by the English ambassador to seize and burn all copies, Johnson spared two copies

---

[50] Henry Barrow, "A True Description out of the Worde of God, of the Visible Church," in *The Writings of Henry Barrow 1587–1590*, ed. Leland H. Carlson (London: George Allen and Unwin, 1962), 208–23; and Williston Walker, *The Creeds and Platforms of Congregationalism* (New York: Charles Scribner's Sons, 1893), 28–40.

for perusal—one for a friend and the other for himself. Upon studying this *Plaine Refutation*, whose opening dedication carries the signatures of "Henrie Barrowe & John Greenwood for the testimonie of the gospel in close prison,"[51] Francis Johnson became a Separatist. He returned to London, visited the prison cells of Barrow and Greenwood, and soon succeeded Greenwood as pastor of the secret church.

In 1593, Anglican authorities hanged Greenwood and Barrow, along with the Welshman John Penry, for their separatist worship. Francis Johnson and several others were then imprisoned, as the remnant of their secret church escaped to Holland—first to Kampen, then to Naarden, and finally to Amsterdam by 1596, when Henry Ainsworth (ca. 1570–1622)[52]— Cambridge-educated Hebrew scholar—joined them and succeeded Barrow as doctor/teacher. Other English Separatist groups escaping to Amsterdam would refer to the re-gathered secret church as the "Ancient Church," since it was the first English-speaking assembly of refugees to arrive. In addition to his celebrated Psalter (1612),[53] Ainsworth wrote the Ancient Church's True Confession of the Faith (1596).[54] All Baptists would reject Ainsworth's infant baptism (Article 35) and his designating to princes and magistrates the authority and duty "to suppress and root out" all false ministries, voluntary religions, and counterfeit worship. In agreement with traditional Puritanism and Presbyterianism, the Confession urges that governments should "establish & mayntein by their lawes

---

[51] Henry Barrow and John Greenwood, *A Plaine Refutation of M. G. Giffardes Reprochful Booke, Intituled a Short Treatise against the Donatists of England*, "wherein is discovered the forgery of the whole ministrie, the confusion, false worship, and antichristian disorder of these parish assemblies, called the Church of England" (n.p.: n.p., 1591). This copy is in the Henry E. Huntington Library and Art Gallery, San Marino, CA.

[52] See Benjamin Hanbury, ed., *Historical Memorials Relating to the Independents or Congregationalists: From Their Rise to the Restoration of the Monarchy, A. D. MDCLX*, 3 vols. (London: Congregational Union of England and Wales, 1839–44), 1:91ff.

[53] Henry Ainsworth, *The Book of Psalmes: Englished Both in Prose and Metre* (Amsterdam: Giles Thorp, 1612).

[54] William L. Lumpkin, *Baptist Confessions of Faith*, 2nd rev. edition, ed. Bill J. Leonard (Valley Forge: Judson Press, 2011), 75–91.

every part of God's word his pure Relligion and true ministerie" (Article 39).

The Ainsworth Confession's blend of Calvinism and Congregationalism would become a paradigm for Particular Baptists, as depicted in their London Confession (1644). Likewise, in London, Johnson and the remnant of the secret church signed the Ainsworth Confession; in Amsterdam, Ainsworth's Ancient Church endorsed it. Thus, Ainsworth's Confession became the centerpiece for the reorganization of the Ancient Church from semi-Presbyterian polity to congregational polity. Meanwhile, Ainsworth authored a major treatise, *The Communion of Saints* (1607),[55] with entire chapters devoted extensively to the defense of Separatist congregationalism. Most significantly, for Baptist history, during the last half of 1608 and the first half of 1609, two Separatist congregations of English refugees would be attending the Ancient Church and observing its congregationalism firsthand: (1) the *Mayflower* Pilgrim Separatists, under the leadership of John Robinson and Thomas Helwys, and (2) John Smyth's Separatist followers. Back in England, the two groups had been one congregation; thus, Smyth and Helwys would bring congregational polity into the earliest Baptist churches.

Final Years of the Ancient Church

Following their release from the London prison, in 1597, Francis Johnson and the last remnant of the secret church united with the Ancient Church in Amsterdam, where the group had purchased their meetinghouse with a monetary donation from London contributors. The congregation now consisted of some forty members. Johnson resumed his office as pastor; Ainsworth continued as teacher. Championing Presbyterian polity, Johnson insisted on a church government vested solely in the eldership. Ainsworth, on the other hand,

---

[55] Henry Ainsworth, *The Communion of Saints: A Treatise of the Fellowship That the Faithful Have with God and His Angels, and with One Another in This Present Life; Gathered out of the Holy Scriptures* (1607; repr., Edinburgh: D. Paterson, 1789).

insisted on a church government vested in the whole congregation including the elders. In 1610, the church divided over the issue. The congregation numbered some three hundred, and about half of these seceded with Ainsworth and began meeting in a former synagogue, two doors down the street. Johnson's group kept possession of the properties and excommunicated the Ainsworth group. In 1613, some of the London donors, in behalf of the Ainsworth congregation, filed a lawsuit in the Dutch courts for possession of the church properties occupied by the Johnson group. The Ainsworth supporters made the legal case that determination of property ownership must rest upon fidelity to the church's confession of faith.[56] The court accepted the argument. Since Ainsworth's True Confession of the Faith (1596) enacts congregational polity, the court ordered Johnson's elders to transfer the deed to the Ainsworth congregation for the settlement of 5,530 guilders.[57] Ainsworth seems to have been ministering in Ireland during the legal proceedings, but he soon returned.[58]

Francis Johnson and his group soon moved to Emden, East Friesland (Germany). Sadly, their earthly pilgrimage soon came to a tragic end. After Johnson's death in 1618, most of his congregation set out on a disastrous voyage bound for Virginia. "Packed together like herrings," as William Bradford reports, 130 of the 180 persons on board died.[59] As for those of the church congregation who reached shore, the Powhatan Indians by 1622 had destroyed their settlement near Jamestown.

---

[56] It is noteworthy that, in America, the attorneys for the Trinitarian secessionists would fail to reference this precedent during the notorious Dedham Case of 1820, which resulted in the Massachusetts Supreme Court relegating all church properties to the Unitarians.

[57] Keith L. Sprunger, *Dutch Puritanism: A History of English and Scottish Churches of the Netherlands in the Sixteenth and Seventeenth Centuries* (Leiden: E. J. Brill, 1982), 51; and Henry M. Dexter, *English Exiles in Amsterdam 1597–1625* (Cambridge: John Wilson and Son, 1890), a 25-page paper presented to the Massachusetts Historical Society.

[58] See the "Biographical Sketch of Henry Ainsworth," in Ainsworth's *Annotations on the Pentateuch or the Five Books of Moses; the Psalms of David; and the Song of Solomon*, 2 vols. (Glasgow: Blackie & Son, 1843), 1: i–viii.

[59] William Bradford, *Of Plymouth Plantation 1620–1647*, ed. Samuel Eliot Morison (1952; repr., New York: Alfred A. Knopf, 1998), 356–57.

Meanwhile, back in Amsterdam, Ainsworth served the Ancient Church pastorate until his death in 1622. His successor, John Canne (ca. 1590–1667), would not arrive from England until 1630, and he would become a leading Fifth-Monarchist revolutionist during the 1650s. The Ancient Church maintained a feeble existence until 1701, when the last five members closed the church and joined the English Reformed Church of Amsterdam (Presbyterian), organized in 1607 as a church for English merchants. Here at this beautiful brick church, there are plaques commemorating the *Mayflower* Pilgrims and their associations with the Ancient Church, which had deeply impacted Francis Johnson's former Cambridge student, John Smyth, whose remarkable story begins in the English town of Gainsborough, situated on the east side of the River Trent.

John Smyth and England's Gainsborough-Scrooby Church

John Smyth (ca. 1570–1612) had studied at Christ's College, Cambridge,[60] where Francis Johnson was one of his most memorable tutors.[61] Smyth earned his BA and MA, received ordination into the priesthood, and remained at Christ's College as a fellow for four more years. From 1600 to 1602, Smyth held the office of Lecturer in the City of Lincoln. The word *lecturer* in the sixteenth and seventeenth centuries referred to teachers appointed by Parliament, at the request of parishioners, to give instruction in the Christian faith where there was a scarcity of regular ministers. Many able Puritan non-conformists availed themselves of this opportunity, since their lecturing would essentially be preaching. John Smyth was one such Puritan. It was during his time in Lincoln that Smyth preached four public messages on the twenty-second Psalm, and Cambridge

---

[60] See the Smyth pedigree charts in Walter H. Burgess, "Did John Smyth the Se-Baptist Spring from Sturton?" in *The Pastor of the Pilgrims: A Biography of John Robinson* (London: Williams and Norgate, 1920), 409–17.

[61] Nathaniel Morton, nephew of William Bradford, says that Smyth suffered in "a wretched dungeon in the Marshalsea" Prison in London while Francis Johnson and John Penry were also imprisoned. See Nathaniel Morton, *New England's Memorial* (1669; repr., Boston: Congregational Board of Publications, 1855), 446.

University published the series under the title *The Bright Morning Starre* (1603).[62] Church of England authorities, however, were hearing rumors that Smyth was frequently criticizing their custom of reading public prayers from the official *Book of Common Prayer*. Smyth suddenly faced charges of "forward preaching" and "strange doctrines." Deposed from his Lincoln lectureship, in 1602, Smyth promptly began preaching in Gainsborough, where increasing numbers of people became so attracted to his ministry that they persuaded him to become their pastor.

By 1604, when James I outlawed all dissenters, Gainsborough's manorial lord, Sir William Hickman, had already befriended the Smyth group. In 1606, Hickman wrote in Smyth's defense against charges of unbridled non-conformity.[63] In his own published defense, *A Paterne of True Prayer: A Learned and Comfortable Exposition or Commentary upon the Lord's Prayer* (1605), Smyth affirms, "A set form of prayer is not unlawful." Indeed, "I am far from the opinion of them which separate from our Church, concerning the set form of prayer." He clearly expresses his intention to remain a loyal member of the Church of England.[64] Smyth served his community as a physician, and his congregation assembled for their worship in the Great Hall inside Gainsborough Old Hall Manor. Brought up as a devout Protestant, Hickman harbored a natural love for religious freedom. His parents, Anthony and Rose Hickman, had provided shelter to hunted men, including Presbyterian John Knox, during the reign of the Catholic Queen Mary I. The Hickman family had then fled into religious exile in Antwerp, where William was born. After the crown passed to Elizabeth, the family returned to England, and, in 1596, William had purchased Gainsborough's Old Hall Manor.

---

[62] Smyth, *The Bright Morning Starre* (1603), in *The Works of John Smyth, Fellow of Christ's College, 1594-8*, ed. W. T. Whitley, 2 Vols. (Cambridge: Cambridge University Press, 1915), 1:1ff.

[63] In March 1606, William Hickman, with five other citizens of Gainsborough, wrote in Smyth's defense. See Stephen Wright, *The Early English Baptists, 1603–1649* (Woodbridge, Suffolk, England: Boydell Press, 2006), 17.

[64] Smyth, *A Paterne of True Prayer* (1605), in *The Works of John Smyth*, 1:71, first page of preface, "To the Christian Reader."

Since Gainsborough was not an incorporated town, the lord of Old Hall Manor, as justice of the peace, held considerable power of his own. The regular parish priest had been absent for some time, and John Smyth's services were attracting many folks, even from other villages.[65] By now, large numbers of non-conformist ministers had suffered deprivation of their churches for disobeying orders intended to silence all dissent. In 1606, a group of these non-conformists gathered for a meeting in the Coventry home of Sir William Bowes to discuss what course of action they should take. They all considered themselves loyal Puritans. Bowes's wife, Isabel (affectionately called Lady Bowes) offered protection and financial support.[66] John Smyth was in attendance; after the meeting, he struggled over whether he should break ties with the Church of England.[67] Some of his closest friends were resisting any thought of separation. At last, Smyth determined that he had no other choice but to sever every tie with the National Church.

Harassed by ecclesiastical authorities, in 1607, John Smyth re-organized his non-conformist congregation into a Separatist church. In his *Principles and Inferences Concerning the Visible Church*,[68] written near this time, Smyth bases the local church

---

[65] Members also flocked in from surrounding communities such as Scrooby, Skegby, Sutton, Sturton-le-Steeple, North Wheatley, Retford, Broxtowe Hall, Mattersey, Worksop, and the Isle of Axholme.

[66] Timothy George, *John Robinson and the English Separatist Tradition* (Macon, GA: Mercer University Press, 1982), 82–83. With few and conflicting records, it is now impossible to know exactly how many ministers had been ousted by this time, or precisely how many attended the Coventry meeting.

[67] The Gainsborough Parish Registers reveal that John Smyth baptized one of his daughters here on March 11, 1604 (N. S.), and that he baptized another daughter here in March 1606 (N. S.), the year of the Coventry meeting. Soon after this, Smyth broke his final ties with the Church of England. For the baptismal records, see Jennifer Vernon, *Gainsborough Old Hall and the Mayflower Pilgrim Story* (Gainsborough, England: Friends of the Old Hall Association, 1991), 12–15.

[68] See also Smyth, *The Differences of the Churches of the Separation: Containing a Description of the Liturgy and Ministry of the Visible Church*, "annexed as a correction and supplement to a little treatise lately published, bearing title, *Principles and Inferences Concerning the Visible Church*" (1608), in *The Works of John Smyth*, 1:269ff.

upon the foundation of a congregational covenant. Like earlier Separatists, his congregation would have read the account of King Josiah's assembling "all the people, great and small." He "read in their ears all the words of the book of the covenant." He then "made a covenant before the Lord, to walk after the Lord, and to keep his commandments, and his testimonies, and his statutes, with all his heart, and with all his soul, to perform the words of the covenant which are written in this book." Moreover, he "caused all that were present in Jerusalem and Benjamin to stand to it" (2 Chron. 34:30–32). Likewise, "As the Lord's free people," Smyth's group "joined themselves (by a covenant of the Lord) into a church estate, in the fellowship of the gospel, to walk in all his ways, made known, or to be made known unto them, according to their best endeavors, whatsoever it should cost them, the Lord assisting them."[69] It is noteworthy that, later in Amsterdam, Smyth's foundational basis for the local church would change from the congregational covenant to believer's baptism. At present, though, he still perceived of baptism and Communion as "seals of the covenant."[70] Smyth now stood as an avowed Separatist pastor of a covenanted church, numbering at least sixty to seventy members.[71] At every meeting, the congregation stood in constant danger of arrest.

There were always local informers eager to report unusual gatherings. On every Lord's Day, a sizable number of Smyth's congregation were traveling from the Scrooby area and crossing the River Trent by ferry to reach Gainsborough. For their safety, therefore, in 1606, the Gainsborough church divided

---

[69] W. T. Whitley, "Biography," in *The Works of John Smyth*, 1:lxii. See also E. Catherine Anwyl, *John Smyth: The Se-Baptist at Gainsborough* (Gainsborough, England: G. W. Belton, 1991), no pagination; cf. Bradford, *Of Plymouth Plantation*, 9.

[70] *The Works of John Smyth*, 2:419–20.

[71] There might have been eighty or more Separatists meeting here in Gainsborough; see Harold Kirk-Smith, *William Brewster 'The Father of New England' — His Life and Times — 1567–1644* (Boston, England: Richard Kay, 1992), 84. Contrary to Kirk-Smith, however, the number of those who left England with Smyth was most likely about forty. Kirk-Smith thinks that seventy to eighty left with Smyth, but as many as half of Smyth's group most likely left with the Scrooby group, as the number of signatures on the Smyth and Helwys confessions of faith in Holland suggests.

into two congregations. The members from the Scrooby area began worshiping in the Scrooby Manor, home of postmaster William Brewster. Richard Clyfton served as their pastor, and John Robinson served as teacher. Many if not most of their congregation traveled from neighboring villages and communities. From Austerfield, eighteen-year-old William Bradford, future governor of Plymouth Plantation, New England, was a member of the Scrooby flock. Government spies traveling the North Road soon learned from local informers of the Separatist gatherings in the Scrooby and Gainsborough Manors. It was now impossible for the Separatists to remain in England and to function as normal families. Bradford describes their desperate situation:

> After these things they could not long continue in any peaceable condition, but were hunted and persecuted on every side, so as their former afflictions were but as flea-bitings in comparison of these which now came upon them. For some were taken and clapped up in prison, others had their houses beset and watched night and day, and hardly escaped their hands; and the most were fain to flee and leave their houses and habitations, and the means of their livelihood.[72]

In the fall of 1607, the Scrooby Separatists negotiated with an English sea captain who agreed to transport them across the North Sea from Boston to the Netherlands. Boston lies some sixty miles southeast from Scrooby. Once the Separatists paid their fees and boarded the ship, the king's officers suddenly appeared and arrested them all. The ship's captain had betrayed them and swindled them without mercy. The Separatists watched as officers ransacked their luggage and plundered their books in search of cash. Officers immodestly searched men and women to their inner garments for valuables. They then hauled the group into Boston as "a spectacle and wonder to the multitude which came flocking on all sides to behold them."[73]

---

[72] Bradford, *Of Plymouth Plantation*, 10.
[73] Idem, 12.

After incarcerating the Separatists for a month, magistrates ordered them to leave the area. No one knows the precise number of the group.[74] Key leaders remained in prison cells until they could be "bound over to the assizes [courts]." While no trial records have ever emerged, a legal document recently noticed in the record office at Lincoln lists fifteen of the Separatists who suffered imprisonment at Boston. Among them is Thomas Helwys who in the following year would re-gather these same Separatist families from both sides of the River Trent and subsidize their escape to the sea and beyond.[75] Prior to mid-1608—no one knows precisely when or how— John Smyth and about forty of his Gainsborough congregation made a surreptitious escape over the North Sea to Amsterdam. Helwys remained with William Bradford, William Brewster, and other future *Mayflower* Pilgrims, to assist their escape from England's tyranny to freedom in Amsterdam, where both groups—the Pilgrims and the Smyth party—would attend the Ancient Church for several months before going their separate ways. Although Governor William Bradford, in his *Of Plymouth Plantation*, recalled their escape from England as "an adventure almost desperate," he excluded any mention of Helwys or of his sacrificial contributions.[76] Bradford would begin writing his *Plymouth Plantation* in 1630—sixteen years after Helwys (by then a Baptist) died in Newgate Prison for defending freedom of conscience for all dissenters. Bradford's silence regarding Helwys could have stemmed from any of the following reasons: (1) Helwys's temporary association with Mennonites; (2) Helwys's resultant opposition to infant baptism; (3) the

---

[74] In John Robinson's petition to the Leiden magistrates for permission to settle there, he says that the group numbered "one hundred persons, or thereabouts, men and women." This is on the first phototypic plate in *Leyden Documents Relating to the Pilgrim Fathers*, trans. and annot. D. Plooij and J. Rendel Harris (Leyden: E. J. Brill, 1920), i. Robinson obviously did not include the children in that figure. Samuel Eliot Morison places the number at "about 125 members of the Scrooby congregation," who went over to Amsterdam; see his footnote in Bradford, *Plymouth Plantation*, 15.
[75] Nick Bunker, *Making Haste from Babylon* (New York: Alfred A. Knopf, 2010), 186–98, 447n36.
[76] See *Plymouth Plantation*, 11, 9, 16.

Smyth-Helwys exit from the English Separatist movement, including the Pilgrims; and (4) a mistaken identification of Helwys with Smyth's doctrinal aberrations. Below are Helwys's untold contributions to the Pilgrims' survival and to the Baptist heritage.

Thomas Helwys and the *Mayflower* Pilgrims

Thomas Helwys (ca. 1575–1615), of Nottingham, had both the desire and the means to organize and finance his fellow Separatists' escape to freedom. Having studied law as a Puritan at Gray's Inn of London,[77] Thomas had inherited the estate of his father, Sir Edmund Helwys of Broxtowe Hall, at Bilborough, only about thirty-five miles from Scrooby. At the time of the Separatists' escape from Scrooby and Gainsborough, Thomas and his wife Joan had seven children, all under the age of twelve. Court records reveal that Thomas and Joan knew the pain of persecution for having become Separatists. Accused of being "Brownists," John Drew, Thomas Jessop, and Joan Helwys ("Elwish"), on April 1, 1608 (N. S.), had suffered a three-month incarceration in York Castle.[78] At their hearing, they had "refused to take an oath" (*Quo die comparuerunt*) of allegiance to the National Church. Shortly, the courts summoned "Mr. Thomas Helwys and his wife Joan" to answer to the same charges, but the defendants had already found hiding among friends. With the Scrooby group and the Gainsborough remnant bonded as one, Brewster and Helwys agreed that the time had come to set their new escape plan into motion.

That spring (1608), they contracted a Dutch sea captain to bring his vessel to Stallingborough Haven (near Immingham Dock) at the mouth of the Humber on the North Sea. Stallingborough village is near a remote coastline about five

---

[77] Joseph Foster, *Register of Admissions to Gray's Inn, 1521–1889 Together with the Register of Marriages in Gray's Inn Chapel, 1695–1754* (London: The Hansard Publishing Union, 1889), 92. According to the record, "Thomas Elwes" matriculated at Gray's Inn on November 23, 1597.

[78] Ronald A. Marchant, *The Puritans and the Church Courts in the Diocese of York 1560–1642* (London: Longmans, Green, and Co., 1960), 156, 163n5, 162–66.

miles north of Grimsby. To help maintain a low profile during the risky trek to the sea, some sixteen of the Separatist men set out walking to Stallingborough. Meanwhile, the owner of a fifty-ton sailing barge, called the *Francis*, began at Gainsborough to gather the families, along with their possessions, and transport them up the River Trent to Stallingborough. When the vessel reached Stallingborough Haven, it had seventy-five to a hundred Separatists.

With the skies darkening and a storm rising over the North Sea, the shallow mudflats were stalling the *Francis*. The sixteen men had just boarded the Dutch vessel when the sight of armed, English soldiers, approaching on horseback and on foot, brought panic to the ship's captain. Already nervous about assisting refugees out of England, the captain swore the Dutch oath, "*Sacramente*," weighed anchor, hoisted sails, and departed. Husbands and fathers were helplessly leaving their women and children in the face of danger. The tempest raged for days upon the tiny, single-mast ship, as sailors cried, "We sink, we sink." Prayers ascended, according to Bradford, and the Lord spared them. The storm had swept their ship far to the northeast, off the coast of Norway. After fourteen days, they finally reached Holland.

Meanwhile, back on England's stormy shores, officers had arrested Thomas Helwys (Elvish) and his Separatist servant, Edward Armfield. Dated May 1608, the original depositions, now in the National Archives at Kew,[79] reveal that Thomas Helwys had arranged the details and financed the cost of the *Francis*, with its owner and crew, and the Dutch ship, with its captain and crew. John Robinson records the magnitude of the Separatists' debt to Helwys. "The truth is," says Robinson, "it was Mr. Helwisse, who above all … furthered this passage into strange countries: and if any brought oars, he brought sails, as I could show in *many particulars*, … as all that were acquainted with the manner of our coming over can witness with me."[80]

---

[79] See Bunker, *Making Haste from Babylon*, 192ff. with photo of the depositions; and Marchant, *The Puritans and the Church Courts in the Diocese of York*, 163n5, 162–66.

[80] John Robinson, "Of Religious Communion, Private and Public," in *The Works of John Robinson, Pastor of the Pilgrim Fathers*, with memoir and

The witnesses failed to record the "many particulars," but Helwys had indeed "brought sails."

Records reveal that the barge's cargo included items belonging to Thomas's cousin, Sir Gervase Helwys,[81] a sheriff of Lincolnshire whom James I had knighted in 1603. Though Gervase was not a Separatist, his familial relationship with Thomas explains why there is no trace of an official verdict and no record of how the Separatists left England. Bradford reports simply that the English "were glad to be rid of them … upon any terms, for all were wearied and tired with them…. And in the end, notwithstanding all these storms of opposition, they all got over at length, some at one time and some at another, and some in one place and some in another, and met together again according to their desires, with no small rejoicing."[82] By the end of August, the Separatists were united in Amsterdam and worshipping with the Ancient Church. In 1611–12, Thomas Helwys would return to England, where, with his family and a few supporters, he would establish the nation's first Baptist church.

John Smyth in Amsterdam

Neither the Smyth-Helwys group nor the Pilgrim group remained in Amsterdam's Ancient Church of Johnson and Ainsworth. By the spring of 1609, the Pilgrims, under John Robinson's pastoral guidance, moved to Leiden. Eleven years later, many of his congregation would sail to the New World on the *Mayflower*. Meanwhile, by late 1608 or early 1609, the Smyth-Helwys group moved into an Amsterdam bakery that produced biscuits for ships. The Mennonite Jan Munter, a wealthy ship-owner and merchant, had recently purchased the bakery from the Dutch East India Company. Situated along the Amstel River and known as the "Bakehouse," or the "Great

---

annotations by Robert Ashton, 3 vols. (London: John Snow, 1851), 3:159. Italics mine. Robinson then takes issue with Helwys on church practices; twice, he resorts to depicting Helwys as ignorant (3:175; 3:277).

[81] Bunker, *Making Haste from Babylon*, 195.
[82] *Plymouth Plantation*, 14–15.

Cake House,"[83] the facility, including its attached buildings, provided living quarters, jobs, and even a meeting hall for the congregation. It also served to bring Smyth and his flock into daily contact with Mennonite influence.

Becoming seriously attracted to the Mennonite practice of believer's baptism, Smyth and Helwys began at once to drift away from the English Separatists, whose Reformed theology mandated infant baptism as a continuation of Old Testament circumcision. Smyth and Helwys concluded that for a local church to be a true church, its covenant must reside within the framework of believer's baptism.[84] The essential nature of the local church seemed at stake, since God calls the church to be a vital part of the one body of Christ. A serious question arose. Where could they turn for a proper model for such a church? Questions also emerged over peculiar beliefs and practices among the Mennonites.

Immediately upon moving into the bakery facilities, Smyth led his group to reorganize themselves into an unaffiliated proto-Baptist church, reconstituted upon the basis of believer's baptism. After salvation there are two immediate obligations: (1) obedience to the command of public baptism, and (2) commitment by covenant into a local congregation of believers. Obedience to those obligations qualifies one to partake of Communion. Such a belief reveals a major change in Smyth's ecclesiology. He had previously taught the Reformed doctrine that baptism replaces circumcision as the seal of the Abrahamic covenant. According to Reformed doctrine, as male circumcision engrafted the Jewish infant into the family of God, infant baptism now engrafts the newborn child into the body

---

[83] Edward Arber, ed., *The Story of the Pilgrim Fathers, 1606–1623 A.D.: As Told by Themselves, Their Friends, and Their Enemies* (London: Ward and Downey, 1897), 131–40.

[84] Smyth, *The Character of the Beast*, "or the false constitution of the church discovered in certain passages betwixt Richard Clyfton and John Smyth, concerning true Christian baptism of new creatures, or new babes in Christ, and false baptism of infants born after the flesh" (1609), *in The Works of John Smyth*, 2:645. Since Smyth's former friend, Richard Clyfton, identified with the Separatist Pilgrims, the two had been close friends.

of Christ.[85] Smyth had come to the conviction that baptism is a symbol rather than a seal.

Embracing Anabaptist practice, Smyth now repositioned the covenant into the framework of *believer's* baptism—a baptism that his new local assembly was about to restore *de novo*.[86] Smyth baptized himself (*se-baptism*), but not upon his own authority. He baptized upon the authority of the local church: "It is Lawful for a man to baptize himself together with others in communion, & this warrant is a plerophory [full assurance] for the practice."[87] With his congregation fully assembled, Smyth administered baptism "out of a basin"[88] and by affusion (pouring).[89] Dexter describes their gathering around "a three-legged stool, which held a basin of water." Smyth "dipped up the water in his hand and poured it over his own forehead in the name of the Father, Son, and Holy Ghost. Then he repeated the ceremony in the case of each of the others."[90] Smyth's former friend John Robinson reported: "Mr. Smyth baptized first himself, and next Mr. Helwisse, and so the rest, making their particular confessions."[91] After this, "worship was held, ending with the Lord's Supper; and at last they felt themselves a genuine church of Christ."[92] Smyth and his church perceived baptism to be the outward symbol of the remission of sin, and the Lord's Supper to be the blessed remembrance of Jesus' New-Covenant sacrifice. Their church consisted of

---

[85] Such is the teaching of John Calvin, *Institutes of the Christian Religion* (4.15.1), trans. Henry Beveridge (Edinburgh: Edinburgh Printing Company for the Calvin Translation Society, 1845).

[86] For more on this transition, see William R. Estep, *The Anabaptist Story*, 3rd ed. (Grand Rapids: Eerdmans, 1996), 287–90.

[87] Smyth, *Character of the Beast* (1609), in *Works*, 2:660.

[88] Barrington R. White, *The English Separatist Tradition: From the Marian Martyrs to the Pilgrim Fathers*, 133.

[89] W. T. Whitley, "Biography," in *The Works of John Smyth*, 1: xciii–xcv; and Wright, *The Early English Baptists, 1603–1649*, 33n93.

[90] Henry Martyn Dexter and Morton Dexter, *The England and Holland of the Pilgrims* (Boston: Houghton, Mifflin, and Co., 1905), 456–57. This includes a picture of a three-legged stool such as the Anabaptists often used in those days.

[91] Robinson, "Of Religious Communion, Private and Public," in *Works*, 3:168.

[92] Dexter and Dexter, *The England and Holland of the Pilgrims*, 456–57.

professing, baptized believers, covenanting together to nurture their children with fervent prayers that they might come to accept Christ by faith and repentance. Described simply as "brethren," this church constituted the official break from the English Separatists.

Strangely, Smyth devised a novel doctrine that he called the "kingship of the saints" within the local church. While the saints' priesthood pertains to prayer and worship, the saints' kingship pertains to discipline and excommunication. Basing his teaching upon serious misapplications of Jesus' parables and Bible expressions such as a "royal" priesthood (1 Pet. 2:9), Smyth concluded that under the present "government of Christ," the "saints as kings rule the visible church.... The visible church is Christ's kingdom." Thus, "the members of the visible church are called the children of the kingdom." In familiar, Arminian Mennonite fashion, Smyth adds that, except they remain faithful, "the children of the kingdom shall be cast out into outer darkness: there shall be weeping and gnashing of teeth" (Matt. 8:12).[93]

Able to read Hebrew and Greek, Smyth began each of his church services with a time of "preparation for spiritual worship." Such preparation consisted of an opening prayer, followed by Bible readings (using English translations). Reacting to the heavy use of the *Book of Common Prayer* in the Church of England, Smyth restricted all prayer to impromptu prayer, and he required each Bible reader to punctuate his reading with interpretation or application of the text. Disgustingly abhorrent to Smyth were the "read and dead services" of the Church of England. Thus, as soon as the church service completed its transition from "preparation" into "spiritual worship," Smyth forbad the use of books or notes by those who prayed, preached (prophesied), or sang. All spiritual worship must be spontaneous: "We hold that the worship of the New Testament ... is spiritual, proceeding originally from the heart:

---

[93] Besides Matthew 8:12, Smyth offers additional references. See, *The Differences of the Churches of the Separation* (1608), in *Works of John Smyth*, 1:274; cf. Smyth, *Parallels, Censures, Observations* (1609), in *Works*, 2:474. The latter work includes Smyth's side of a debate with his former Puritan friend Richard Bernard. Point by point, Smyth refutes Bernard's indictment of the Separatists.

and that reading out of a book (though a lawful ecclesiastical action) is no part of the spiritual worship." Thus, "in time of prophesying it is unlawful to have the book as a help before the eye." Moreover, "singing a Psalm is a part of spiritual worship; therefore, it is unlawful to have the book before the eye in time of singing a Psalm."[94] Smyth would allow only one person at a time to sing, and he forbad the use of meter or rhythm, since these might quench the activity of the Holy Spirit. On a typical Sunday, Smyth held two four-hour services. Two of his original members, Hugh and Anne Bromhead, wrote a letter around 1609 describing a regular service in their church:

> The order of the worship and government of our church is: We begin with prayer, after[wards] read some one or two chapters of the Bible; give the sense thereof and confer upon the same; that done, we lay aside our books, and after a solemn prayer made by the first speaker, he propoundeth some text out of the Scripture, and prophesieth out of the same by the space of one hour, or three quarters of an hour. After him standeth up the second speaker and prophesieth out of the [same, or said] text the like time and [illegible], sometime[s] more, sometime[s] less. After him the third, the fourth, the fifth, so many as the time will give leave. Then the first speaker concludeth with prayer as he began with prayer; with an exhortation to contribute to the poor, which collection being made is also concluded with prayer. This Morning exercise begins at eight of the clock and continueth unto twelve of the clock; the like course of exercise is observed in the afternoon from two of the clock unto five or six of the clock. Last of all the execution of the government of the Church is handled.[95]

---

[94] Smyth, *The Differences of the Churches of the Separation* (1608), in *Works*, 1: 273; cf. 1:269–320. I modernized some of the spelling and punctuation. Another enlightening source, often overlooked, is Thomas Helwys, "An Unnoticed Letter of Thomas Helwys's (1608)," in Champlin Burrage, *The Early English Dissenters in the Light of Recent Research (1550–1641)* (Cambridge: Cambridge University Press, 1912), 2:167–68, copied from MS. 709, fol. 117, recto and verso, in Lambeth Palace Library.

[95] *Letter of the Bromheads to Sir William Hammerton* (n.d.). The original

Smyth had three primary reasons for the proactive organization of his church. (1) Since the Church of England was corrupt, its baptism was invalid and worthless. (2) Since believer's baptism is the only true, water baptism, their *pedobaptism* within the National Church had been meaningless. *Pedo* means "child." (3) Hopeful that there existed among the Waterlander Mennonites a chain of local churches traceable to New Testament times, Smyth was creating time to study Mennonite history and tradition. Earlier in his life, Smyth had expressed opposition to the idea of successionism, and there is no evidence that Waterlander Mennonites had ever held to such a notion. Thus, the issue of a visible perpetuity of churches may have been a factor in the Mennonites' hesitation in accepting the Smyth proposal for union. With few exceptions, the Mennonites could not speak English and the English could not speak Dutch. Each side did have a few who could read Latin, which became the major vehicle for serious communication.

Meanwhile, Smyth sought to convince the nearby Waterlander "Church by the Tower" (*Kerk Bij den Toren*)[96] of his increasing acceptance of Mennonite tenets. The name *Waterlander* refers to the region of their origin in the province of North Holland. In agreement with the Mennonites, most of Smyth's congregation now stood willing to abstain from taking oaths and from participating in civil government. With the Mennonites, the Smyth group was willing also to refuse the admission of government officials into church membership.[97]

---

manuscript is in the British Museum (Harleian MS 360, folio 71). I have slightly modernized some of the punctuation and spelling to preserve the meaning of the damaged text, quoted verbatim in Horton Davies, *Worship and Theology in England*, vol. 1, *From Cranmer to Hooker, 1534–1603*, vol. 2, *From Andrewes to Baxter and Fox, 1603–1690* (1970, 1975; repr., Grand Rapids: Eerdmans, 1996), 1:338–39, combined ed. It is cited with various modernizations in Champlin Burrage, *The Early English Dissenters in the Light of Recent Research*, 2:176–77; Barrington R. White, 126–27; and Dexter and Dexter, *The England and Holland of the Pilgrims*, 384–85.

[96] The tower stood by the Torensluis (Tower Lock) Bridge, the oldest and widest in this city of bridges. The bridge was completed in 1648 and still stands. The tower was taken down in 1829.

[97] See arts. 37 and 38 of the Waterlanders' 40-article Brief Confession of the

One other obstacle remained. While the Mennonites would have accepted Smyth's baptism of his followers, they may not have accepted Smyth's se-baptism. They would need to baptize him.[98] Suddenly doubting the validity of his se-baptism and hoping to hasten Mennonite acceptance, Smyth, in 1610, abruptly persuaded most of his group to dissolve their church and to apply for official recognition as an extension of the Church by the Tower.

Embracing unorthodox views, however, the Waterlander Church by the Tower was an integral part of a large group that had remained aloof from mainline Mennonites since about 1555. Smyth, nevertheless, stood prepared to declare the Waterlanders a true church and to confess his acceptance of two heretical teachings embedded within Waterlander doctrine: (1) the Christological heresy of Menno Simons and Melchior Hoffman that Jesus brought His own celestial body into Mary's womb; and (2) the hamartiological heresy of Pelagianism, that no one is born a sinner.[99] Writing in Latin, Smyth prepared a twenty-article Short Confession of Faith (1609) and delivered it to the Mennonite congregation for their inspection. In accordance with Waterlander doctrine, Smyth's confession includes Pelagianism: "There is no original sin (lit., *no sin of origin or descent*), but all sin is actual and voluntary, viz., a word, a deed, or a design against the law of God; and therefore, infants are without sin" (Art. 5). Justification consists only "partly" of the imputation Christ's righteousness (Art. 10).[100] In turn, the

---

Principal Articles of the Christian Faith (1580), trans. from a Latin text into English by W. J. McGlothlin, *Baptist Confessions of Faith* (Philadelphia: American Baptist Publication Society, 1911), 26–48. McGlothlin's translation is also in Lumpkin, *Baptist Confessions of Faith*, 45–61.

[98] Sprunger, *Dutch Puritanism*, 85.

[99] See especially arts. 4 and 8 of the Waterlanders' Brief Confession of the Principal Articles of the Christian Faith (1580), in W. J. McGlothlin, *Baptist Confessions of Faith*, 26–48. McGlothlin's translation is also in Lumpkin, *Baptist Confessions of Faith*, 45–61. See also Irvin E. Burkhart, "Menno Simons on the Incarnation," *Mennonite Quarterly Review* 4 (1930): 113–39, 178–207; and Klaus Deppermann, *Melchior Hoffman: Social Unrest and Apocalyptic Visions in the Age of Reformation*, trans. Malcolm Wren and ed. Benjamin Drewery (Göttingen, 1979; repr., Edinburgh: T. & T. Clark, 1987), 223–29.

[100] The original manuscript of Smyth's confession is in the Mennonite

Waterlanders sent to Smyth their Short Confession of Faith (1610), authored by Hans de Ries (1553–1638),[101] and it teaches Pelagianism: "None of his [Adam's] posterity are guilty, sinful, or born in original sin" (Art. 4).[102]

Ending his days without membership in any organized church, John Smyth died of tuberculosis in 1612. Handwritten in Dutch, the name *Jan Smidt* appears among the burial records in Amsterdam's City Archives (*Stadsarchief*). The entry reveals that Smyth was buried on September 1 at the New Church (*Nieuwe Kerk*). His burial fee was paid on September 8. Normally, only wealthy people received burial inside the church; thus, Smyth's remains likely received interment in one of the two cemeteries in the churchyard. Both cemeteries were eventually removed to create more space for the modern city square—Dam Square. Over the years, the *Nieuwe Kerk* would suffer through several fires. Its present structure, built in the nineteenth century, became the prestigious coronation site for the House of Orange. Situated next to the Royal Palace, the *Nieuwe Kerk* now serves only as a museum and civic center.

In *The Last Booke of John Smyth Called the Retraction of His Errours and the Confirmation of the Truth*, Smyth resolves, "I deny all succession except in the truth." On the other hand, he suggests that Jesus' flesh could have been natural and spiritual—but essentially spiritual. While conservative theology insists that Jesus must be fully God and fully human to reconcile God and man, and that spiritual flesh cannot redeem, Smyth would "not refuse brotherhood" to those who embraced celestial-flesh theology. To Smyth, "Contention about Christ's natural flesh is in comparison … to the soldiers' contention for his coat" [John

---

Archives in Amsterdam. The English translation is in B. Evans, *The Early English Baptists*, 2 vols. (London: J. Heaton & Son, 1862), 1:253–54. Lumpkin copied the Evans translation into his book on pages 93–95. For a copy of the Latin, see J. De Hoop Scheffer, *History of the Free Churchmen Called the Brownists, Pilgrim Fathers and Baptists, in the Dutch Republic 1581–1701*, ed. William Elliot Griffis (Ithaca, NY: Andrus & Church, 1922), 211–13.

[101] Hans de Ries worked with Lubbert Gerritz (1534–1612) of Amsterdam in the negotiations with the Smyth group.

[102] The Waterlanders' 38-article Short Confession of Faith (1610) is in McGlothlin, 54–65; and Lumpkin, 96–105.

19:23-24]. In agreement with the Waterlander heresy, Smyth rests his case with a fanciful appeal to Jesus' unrelated words in John 6:63*a*, "It is the spirit that quickeneth, the flesh profiteth nothing."[103]

Three years after Smyth's death, the Mennonite Church by the Tower (*Kerk Bij den Toren*) accepted his group as one of their own. The Smyth group accomplished the union by presenting to the Mennonites a reinforced one-hundred-article confession called Propositions and Conclusions Concerning True Christian Religion (1612-14). Most Baptists would have agreed with the Confession's conclusion "that there is no succession in the outward church" (Art. 81). Baptists would also have agreed that "the magistrate is not ... to meddle with religion, or matters of conscience, to force or compel men to this or that form of religion or doctrine: but to leave Christian religion free to every man's conscience, and to handle only civil transgressions (Rom. 13)." Indeed, "Christ only is the ... lawgiver of the church and conscience (James 4:12)" (Art. 84). Baptists would reject the Confession's advocacy of Pelagianism, that is, "original sin is an idle term ... because God threatened death only to Adam." The Confession claims, even "if original sin might have passed from Adam to his posterity, Christ's death ... stopped the issue and passage thereof (Rev. 13: 8)." Thus, "infants are conceived and born in innocency without sin."[104]

In a special assembly, in January 1615, each member of the Smyth congregation, with few exceptions,[105] signed the Mennonite confession and, without any further baptism, received official acceptance of the Mennonite Church by the

---

[103] *Works of John Smyth*, 2:758-60.

[104] See Articles 18-20 in the Propositions and Conclusions Concerning True Christian Religion (1612-14). This confession is in McGlothlin, 66-84 and Lumpkin, 115-29. I have modernized some punctuation and the formatting of Scripture references.

[105] There were exceptions, since the Smyth congregation had increased in numbers since their arrival: (1) the Dutch congregation required four un-baptized English individuals to receive baptism prior to membership; and (2) the Dutch congregation refused membership to four English applicants who scrupled over the Mennonite articles that refused membership to civil magistrates and that forbad taking oaths.

Tower. The English congregation would continue their meetings at the Bakehouse until 1639, when they finally moved their worship completely into the Church by the Tower. By then, the language barrier would have largely dissipated. Gradually, their descendants would become thoroughly Dutch. The Bakehouse complex, situated just outside the former city walls, would suffer demolition, but there remain the following key landmarks.

The Bakehouse properties once stretched along the Amstel River near the *Blauwe Brug* and the *Rembrantsplein*. A tiny lane, called *Engelse-Pelgrimsteeg* (English Pilgrim Lane), once led into the Bakehouse perimeters, where the street is still *Bakkersstraat* (Bakerstreet). A short walk east of the former Bakehouse area is a church called the Singelkerk, a key landmark in the history of John Smyth. Situated by the Singel Canal, the Singelkerk, in 1608, would have been putting final touches on its first building just as the English Separatists were arriving in their city. In 1639–40, the congregation replaced the original meetinghouse with a new building that has continued in use to the present day. In 2008, in celebration of its four-hundredth anniversary, the congregation launched a major restoration of the building. The following overview of its history will highlight this church's major significance as a vital part of the Baptist landscape.

The Singelkerk was a Flemish Waterlander congregation, known as the "Church at the Lamb" (*Kerk Bij 't Lam*). They were situated next to the brewery known by its sign depicting "the Lamb" (*'t Lam*). Therefore, those of the Singelkerk were the *Lamists*, a term that soon extended to the broader liberal movement among Dutch Mennonites. In 1664, some five hundred conservatives separated from the Singelkerk and organized themselves into the "Church at the Sun" (*Kerk Bij de Zon*). Their newly purchased meetinghouse was a former brewery known by its sign depicting the Sun (*Zon*). These Mennonites were the *Zonists*, a term that soon extended to the mainline, traditional conservative churches. In 1668, the Church by the Tower, which had absorbed Smyth's congregation, merged into the Church at the Lamb. Gradually, the minority Lamists dropped some of their theological aberrations such as Jesus' having celestial flesh. Thus, in 1801, the Lamists and the Zonists reconciled their differences and resumed meeting as one in the Singelkerk. This merger marked the historic beginning of a united Amsterdam Mennonite Church whose theological foundations would remain compromised in varying degrees as internal battles continued.[106]

Select Bibliography for Further Reading

Beale, David. *The Mayflower Pilgrims: Roots of Puritan, Presbyterian, Congregationalist, and Baptist Heritage*. Belfast, Northern Ireland: Ambassador-Emerald International, 2000.

Burgess, Walter H. *John Smyth the Se-Baptist, Thomas Helwys, and the First Baptist Church in England, with Fresh Light upon the Pilgrim Fathers' Church*. London: James Clarke, 1911.

Coggins, James Robert. *John Smyth's Congregation: English Separatism, Mennonite Influence, and the Elect Nation*. Scottdale, PA: Herald Press, 1991.

——— . "The Theological Positions of John Smith." *Baptist Quarterly* 30, no. 6 (April 1984): 247–64.

Culpepper, Scott. *Francis Johnson and the English Separatist Influence: The Bishop of Brownism's Life, Writings, and Controversies*. Macon, GA: Mercer University Press, 2011.

Dale, R. W. *History of English Congregationalism*. London: Hodder and Stoughton, 1907.

Deweese, Charles W. *Baptist Church Covenants*. Nashville: Broadman, 1990.

Dexter, Henry Martyn. *The Congregationalism of the Last Three Hundred Years, as Seen in Its Literature*. New York: Harper and Brothers, 1880.

——— . *The True Story of John Smyth, the Se-Baptist, as Told by Himself and His Contemporaries; with an Inquiry Whether Dipping were a New Mode of Baptism in England, in or about 1641; and Some Consideration of the Historical Value of Certain Extracts from the Alleged "Ancient Records" of the Baptist Church of Epworth, Crowle, and Butterwick*. Boston: Lee and Shepard, 1881.

Kliever, Lonnie D. "General Baptist Origins: The Question of Anabaptist Influence." *The Mennonite Quarterly Review* 36, no. 4 (October 1962): 291–321.

Lee, Jason K. *The Theology of John Smyth: Puritan, Separatist, Baptist, Mennonite*. Macon, GA: Mercer University Press, 2003.

---

[106] For more discussion, see Harold S. Bender, et al., eds., *Mennonite Encyclopedia: Comprehensive Reference Work on the Anabaptist-Mennonite Movement*, 4 vols. (Hillsboro, KS: Mennonite Brethren Publishing House, 1955–59), 3:270, 4:531, 4:738, 4:1038.

Taylor, Adam. *The History of the English General Baptists, Part First: The English General Baptists of the Seventeenth Century*. London: T. Bore, 1818.

Timmer, Kirsten T. "John Smyth's Request for Mennonite Recognition and Admission: Four Newly Translated Letters, 1610–1612." *Baptist History and Heritage* 44, no. 1 (Winter 2009): 8–19.

Chapter 3

General Baptist Beginnings:
Thomas Helwys to Thomas Grantham

―――――※―――――

The First English Baptist Church and the Development of the General Baptist Movement

Thomas Helwys and His Legacy

In 1610, when John Smyth dissolved his church, to merge with the Waterlander Mennonite Church, a remnant of eight to ten of his flock broke away. Led by Thomas Helwys (ca. 1575–1615),[107] the small remnant excommunicated Smyth. In early March 1610 (N. S.), Helwys wrote in Latin, a *Synopsis of the Faith of the True English Christian Church at Amsterdam*,[108] and delivered it to the Waterlanders. The purpose of this nineteen-point synopsis was to explain their break from Smyth. For now, the Helwys group still embraced the Pelagian heresy, as their Article 4 declares, "There is no sin from our parents through generation." In his concluding note, Helwys expresses his appreciation for much of the teaching that his group had received from the Waterlanders.[109] The following year, Helwys wrote, in behalf

---

[107] Those who remained with Helwys included John Murton, William Pygott, and Thomas Seamer.

[108] *Synopsis fidei, verae Christianae Ecclesiae Anglicanae, Amsterodamiae*.

[109] The Latin manuscript is in Champlin Burrage, *The Early English Dissenters in the Light of Recent Research (1550–1641)* (Cambridge: Cambridge

of his group, a Declaration of Faith (1611), the earliest Baptist confession in existence, embracing classical Arminianism and repudiating Pelagianism. The Confession's preface expresses the group's former devotion and loyalty to Smyth, their leaving England with him, their grieving over his apostasy and fall from grace, and the necessity of breaking from him:

> What would we not have borne or done, how willingly had we given up all we have, nay more, dug out our eyes, sacrificed our lives, if we might have continued with a good conscience to profit by his [Smyth's] teachings! God knows it! Do not men know it too? Does he himself not know it? Have we not disregarded ourselves, our wives and children, and all what is ours, in order to honor him? We own to have had all reasons for doing so, because of the excellent gifts God of his grace has so overflowingly given him. All our love was still too poor and unworthy of him. Let, therefore, every one and himself not think otherwise than that the loss of such a man we most sadly have taken and still do take to heart. But *he has denied the Lord's truth, he is fallen from grace, and, though the fowler laid the snares, the knot was broken, and we are liberated.* God be praised and thanked![110]

One of Helwys's primary purposes in the Declaration is to distinguish his church from extreme Anabaptism. From their beginnings, Baptists rejected Anabaptist tenets such as pacifism,

---

University Press, 1912), 2:182–84, copied from MS. B. 1350 in the Mennonite Archives, Amsterdam. There is an English translation in the work by Goki Saito, "An Investigation into the Relationship between the Early English General Baptists and the Dutch Anabaptists" (ThD diss., Southern Baptist Theological Seminary, 1974), 198–200 (Appendix B). Saito excludes the personal note at the end of the document.

[110] Quoted by J. De Hoop Scheffer, *History of the Free Churchmen Called the Brownists, Pilgrim Fathers and Baptists in the Dutch Republic 1581–1701*, ed. William Elliot Griffis (Ithaca, NY: Andrus & Church, 1922), 149. The italics in the citation above are mine. The original document is from the Mennonite archives in Amsterdam, and a good copy is in *Verslagen en Mededeelingen der Koninklijke Akademie van Wetenschappen, Afdeeling Letterkunde* (Amsterdam: Johannes Müller, 1881), 396, Bijlage 3.

forbidding members from taking oaths, and the exclusion of government officials from church membership. Key doctrinal points in Helwys's Declaration include the following:

- The Trinity created all things *ex nihilo*. (Arts. 1–2).
- In Adam death passed upon all men (Art. 2).
- Christ was the promised seed who died for all humanity (Art. 3).
- All are born in complete depravity; therefore, God must take the initiative in salvation (Art. 4). This is a repudiation of Pelagianism.
- Election is conditioned upon foreseen faith (Art. 5).
- Justification is by faith alone unto good works (Art. 6).
- True Christians may fall from grace and become eternally lost (Art. 7). This is Arminianism.
- The eternal Christ is the Virgin-born Son of God in one person and two natures (Art. 8).
- Jesus Christ is the Mediator of the New Testament, which for the church is the absolute and perfect rule of direction to which no power on earth may add or diminish (Art. 9).
- The local church is a company of faithful believers, separated from the world by the Word and by the Spirit, knit together by baptism, upon their own confession of faith (Art. 10).
- The church is one universal body (Eph. 4:4), yet on earth it consists of local congregations. A congregation can be a true church even with as few as two or three, and even when its officers are in prison or too ill to minister (Art. 11). No early Baptist confession denies the universal church.
- Each local church is founded upon the Word of God and is dependent upon God and His Word. As typical among early Baptist confessions, there is a strong emphasis on the independence and autonomy of the local church. Moreover, there is no visible succession of local churches (Art. 12).
- Baptism is a "washing with water," intended only for believers (Art. 14).
- Government officials who are earnest believers are

encouraged to receive baptism and to unite with a local church. "They are ministers of God to take vengeance on them that do evil, Rom. 13.... We are to pray for them, for God would have them saved and come to the knowledge of His truth (1 Tim. 2.1, 4). And therefore, they may be members of the Church of Christ, retaining their Magistracy" (Art. 24).

During 1611–12, Helwys and his followers returned to England in the face of persecution. There was no surprise among the Helwys family when they learned that the king had confiscated their estate in Nottinghamshire, including beautiful Broxtowe Hall.[111] Taking up residence in London's sparsely populated Spitalfields region, that is, the grazing fields on the east side of London's medieval hospital of St. Mary Spital,[112] the group established a Baptist church, the mother of all General Baptist churches. In 1611, Helwys wrote a *Short and Plain Proof*, dedicated to Lady Bowes, with an appeal for her support. In the treatise, Helwys candidly sets forth his Arminianism[113] as he refutes Smyth's heresies. Grounded in Puritan theology, Lady Bowes chose not to support him. Although Helwys's doctrine was Arminian, he strongly opposed as unbiblical these four teachings of John Smyth: (1) extreme emphasis on man's free will; (2) Pelagianism; (3) "heavenly-flesh" Christology; and (4) successionism.[114] Except for successionism, those teachings

---

[111] The best sources include Walter Burgess, "The Helwys Family," *Transactions of the Baptist Historical Society* 3, no. 1 (1912): 18–30; W. T. Whitley, "Thomas Helwys of Gray's Inn and Broxtowe Hall, Nottingham," *Baptist Quarterly* 7, no. 6 (April 1935): 241–55; and D. P. Dymond, D. P., ed., *The Charters of Stanton, Suffolk c. 1215–1678* (Rochester, NY: Boydell Press, 2009).

[112] The Spitalfields population would eventually grow into a stronghold of many other types of non-conformity.

[113] Thomas Helwys, *A Short and Plaine Proofe*, "by the word and works of God that God's decree is not the cause of any man's sin or condemnation, and that all men are redeemed by Christ, as also that no infants are condemned" (n.p.: n.p., 1611), signed by Thomas Helwys, "June 2, 1611." I have modernized a little of the spelling. This is in the Bodleian Library, Oxford.

[114] See also Thomas Helwys, *An Advertisement or Admonition, unto the Congregations, Which Men Call the New Fryelers, in the Lowe Countries*, "written in Dutch and published in English" (n.p.: n.p., 1611). The term

circulated widely among Anabaptists. The earliest Baptists rejected all four of them. English Baptists were convinced that any church founded on the Bible has no need for any successionism outside the Bible. To them, visible successionism was one of the false claims of the Church of Rome.

Helwys's final book, *A Short Declaration of the Mistery of Iniquity* (1612),[115] is one of the earliest appeals for full religious freedom ever published in the English language. The author pledges throughout the book that true Separatists will always obey the king when such obedience does not contradict Scripture. Kings have no divine right to coerce men in matters of faith. True churches cannot exist as departments of state. The spiritual realm belongs to God whose Word is above every human ruler. In the first of its four sections,[116] Helwys identifies the first beast of Revelation 13 as the Roman Catholic Church, known for using temporal powers to persecute believers. Helwys identifies the second beast as the bishops of the Church of England, known for imitating Rome's example. The second section[117] is a direct charge to King James I that he is leading a false church. In the third section,[118] Helwys contends that the Puritans are supporting apostasy by remaining inside the false church. In his fourth section,[119] the author offers evidence that the Brownists are an extremist movement of pseudo-Separatists. He further argues that the Separatist Congregationalist, John Robinson, is making a grave mistake in urging believers that their infant baptism from the false Church of England is a perpetually true baptism.

Fryelers probably means *Freewillers*. This copy is in the Bodleian Library, Oxford. Countering four false teachings among Waterlander Mennonites, Helwys sets forth four sound teachings: (1) since Jesus received his flesh from Mary, His body was physical; (2) Christians should observe a day of rest every first day of the week; (3) there is no ecclesiastical succession; and (4) since the civil magistracy is a holy ordinance of God, local churches should not bar civil officers from their membership.

[115] Thomas Helwys, *Short Declaration of the Mistery of Iniquity* (n.p.: n.p., 1612). This copy, in the Bodleian Library, Oxford, is the one copy with Helwys's handwritten note.

[116] Ibid., 1–36.

[117] Ibid., 37–83.

[118] Ibid., 84–123.

[119] Ibid., 123–204.

In a postscript,[120] Helwys disparages the leadership of John Smyth and others who chose to remain in the haven of Holland. Helwys describes himself and his congregation as having been "misled by deceitful-hearted leaders who ... seek to save their lives ... by perverting and misapplying the words of our Savior Christ," who "says, 'When they persecute you, or drive, or thrust you out of one city, flee into another.'" (Matt. 10:23). To Helwys, "Our Savior Christ's meaning was that when they were driven or expelled out of one city, they should go to another city in Israel to preach the gospel.... But these men," such as Smyth and his followers, "flee to cities" in "which they cannot preach the gospel, being of a strange tongue. Neither have they any intent ... to preach the gospel."[121] Using an abundance of Scripture, Helwys completes his postscript with a carefully considered defense and plea for Christians to stand strong even amid persecution. When the printer released his *Short Declaration*, Helwys wrote a personal note inside the cover of one copy. Appealing directly to King James, the handwritten note pleads for religious freedom for everyone:

> Heare O King, and dispise not the counsell of the poore, and let their complaints come before thee.
>
> The King is a mortall man, & not God, therefore hath no power over the Immortall Soules of his Subjects, to make Lawes & Ordinances for them, and to Set Spirituall Lords over them.
>
> If the King have authority to make Spirituall Lords & Lawes, then he is an Immortal God and not a mortall man.
>
> O King, be not seduced by Deceivers to Sin so against God whome thou oughtest to obey, nor against thy poore Subjects who ought and will obey thee in all thinges with body life and goods, or else let their lives be taken from the earth.
>
> God save the King.
>
> Spittalfield
> neare London   Tho. Helwys

---

[120] Ibid., 202–12.
[121] Ibid., 205. I slightly modernized some of the spelling and punctuation.

The brave soul sealed his fate. While no one knows if the king read the book, authorities promptly arrested Helwys and incarcerated him in Newgate Prison.

The following year (1613), Thomas's cousin Sir Gervase Helwys received an appointment as Lieutenant of the Tower of London. Two years later, he suffered execution on Tower Hill for allegedly withholding evidence relating to the poisoning murder of Sir Thomas Overbury. Many legal scholars have assessed Gervase's trial as a travesty based upon dubious evidence.[122] Five days prior to his execution, Gervase requested permission to stand publicly and repent of all his sins. In the thirty-page message, signed, "Geruase Ellowis," he explains, "My purpose is to rip up my very heart and to leave nothing there which may prove any clog to my conscience."[123] When interrupted by accusing shouts of his being an "Anabaptist," he succinctly denied the charge and returned to his impassioned lamentation.

Gervase Helwys was from Saundby village, two miles across the River Trent from Gainsborough. Inheriting Saundby Manor in 1599, Gervase had erected for his parents a beautiful altar tomb on the north side of the chancel in the village church of St. Martin of Tours. The stone altar is now in two pieces, embedded in a Jacobean table in the chancel. Affixed to the wall above the table, the tomb inscription reads:

---

[122] There is a good overview of the case in Alfred Marks, *Tyburn Tree: Its History and Annals* (London: Brown, Langham, and Co., 1908), 178–81; and Edward Abbott Parry, "The Martyrdom of Gervase Helwys," in *The Overbury Mystery: A Chronicle of Fact and Drama of the Law* (London: T. F. Unwin, 1925), 243–50. Written by an accomplished British barrister, judge, historian, and dramatist, this work is both engaging and profitable. The known facts in this real-life mystery could hardly be narrated without drama, and Parry was an expert narrator.

[123] Sir Gervase Helwys, *The Lieutenant of the Tower, His Speech and Repentance, at the Time of His Death, Who Was Executed upon Tower Hill, on the 20 Day of November 1615: Together with A Meditation and Vow of His That He Made Not Long before He Dyed* (London: G. Eld for Na. Butter, to be sold in his shop neere Saint Austines gate, 1615). The author humbly testifies of man's depravity and God's grace. There is no pagination, but it is completely legible. This is in the Harvard University Library.

> Here lieth buried the bodye of John Helwys Esqr sometyme lorde of this manor, and Mary his wife, the daughter of Robert Blagden of Thames Ditton in the county of Surrey Esq.: who left behind them two children, Gervase and Margaret, 7mo Decembris Anno dni: 1599.

Underneath those words, Gervase explains in Latin why he erected the monument to his parents. In translation, it reads, "This is a work of piety, not of pride, and the work of deep affection, for in their own lifetime they taught me how I ought to honor them indeed. Thus, it behooves me to live, and them to die. G. H."[124] Authorities executed Gervase Helwys in November 1615.

Thomas Helwys died in Newgate Prison prior to April 8, 1616, the day Thomas's uncle, Sir Geoffrey Helwys (sheriff of London), bequeathed ten pounds to "widow" Joan Helwys, "late wife" of Thomas Helwys.[125] We conclude by returning to his roots in Bilborough. Here, in the parish church of St. Martin of Tours, Thomas had taken Joan Ashmore to be his wife, on December 3, 1595. Nearby stood the stately Broxtowe Hall, home of Thomas's father, Sir Edmund Helwys.[126] Broxtowe Hall suffered demolition in 1937. Penned on September 24, 1590, the *Preface to the Last Will and Testament of Edmund Helwys* is his eternal memorial, testifying of his salvation by grace through faith alone:

---

[124] The Saundby church permanently closed in 1973. It is still consecrated and under the care of the Churches Conservation Trust, which suggests calling 07799 424079 to schedule a visit. The church is on Gainsborough Road and there is a local key-holder.

[125] "I give to Johane [Joan] Elwes [Helwys] widdowe lat[e] wife of Thomas Elwes deceased tenne poundes," from the "Will of Jeffrey [Geoffrey] Elwes, Citizen and Alderman of London," April 8, 1616, in *Miscellanea Genealogica et Heraldica*, ed. Joseph Jackson Howard (London: Hamilton, Adams, and Co., 1868), 1:73. See the Helwys pedigree charts on 70ff.

[126] He used the names *Edmund* and *Edward* interchangeably. Many would remember his Calvinistic tract on Revelation 12, in Edward Hellwis, *A Marvell, Deciphered* (London: Robert Robinson for Iohn Winnington, 1589). This is in the British Library.

> I, Edmund Helwis, alias Elwis, of Broxtoe in the county of Nottingham gentleman, whole and sound in body and of good and perfect remembrance, the Lord be praised, and yet considering the uncertainties of this world which is justly termed a dirty sty, a grove of thorns, wherein is nothing but fear, shame, vexation, tears, labor, sickness, sin and death, do make this my last will and testament in manner and form following under my own handwriting the xxiiii September, in the year of Christ's incarnation, 1590. First, I bequeath my soul to Almighty God my Creator which is the soul of so wicked and sinful a creation that I might despair of any acceptance of the same at his hands were it not that the Holy Scriptures comfort me, teaching in many places that Christ Jesus, the immaculate Lamb of God, being free from sin gave himself up to suffer death upon the cross for us wretched sinners to deliver us from the wicked world Gal. 2, and he is the fulfilling of the Law to justify all that believe Ro. 10. On this Christ do I believe and therefore shall not be condemned, but shall have life everlasting. Jo. 3. Through this belief I shall not abide in darkness Jo. 13. This belief is my justification Acts, 20, and St. Paul saith Ro. 13 that God is the justifier of him that believeth in Jesus. To conclude, I do believe that Christ hath delivered us from the curse of the Law in as much as he was made accursed for us. Gal. 3. This Jesus I confess with my mouth to be the Lord and believe in my heart that God raised him from death Ro. 10. And through this belief I hope with St. Paul to be purged from all my sins which I confess are many and most wicked, yea infinite and abominable and therefore say with St. Augustine, "What shall I give unto God that putteth me in remembrance of my sin and yet am afraid thereof." Wherefore the worldly goods that God hath made me steward of my will is to dispose them as, &o., &c., this testament directs.[127]

One month after the signing of the will, fifteen-year-old

---

[127] Quoted in Burgess, *John Smyth the Se-Baptist, Thomas Helwys, and the First Baptist Church in England*, 111-12.

Thomas Helwys inherited his father's estate. Sir Edmund and his daughter Anne died on the same day and were buried in the same tomb, on October 24, 1590, in the Church of St. Martin of Tours.[128]

John Murton and His Legacy

Succeeding Thomas Helwys to the London pastorate, John Murton (Morton) (ca. 1583–1626), from Gainsborough, had sided with Helwys in the separation from John Smyth in Amsterdam. By 1613, Murton was in Newgate Prison,[129] where he wrote two influential works on religious liberty. One is titled *Objections Answered by Way of Dialogue, Wherein Is Proved … That No Man Ought to Be Persecuted for His Religion* (1615), a well-written dialogue among three individuals named "Christian," "Antichristian," and "Indifferent." With that format, Murton makes his case: "How heinous it is in the sight of the Lord to force men and women by cruel persecutions, to bring their bodies to a worship whereunto

---

[128] In his will, Sir Edmund Helwys had made this request: "My body I would have buried in the church of Bilborough, either in the chancel or before the pew door, with a gravestone laid thereupon, with my first coat of arms set thereupon in brass." The family placed Sir Edmund's tomb near his pew. In the 1800s, interior alterations made it necessary to shift his tomb from its original position. During the process, the tomb was broken up, but not before the marble tablet was mercifully removed from the tomb and affixed to the chancel's north wall. In 1972, renovations made it necessary to remove the north wall to make way for expansion, and to attach the tablet to the south wall where it remains. Sir Edmund's shield of arms surmounts the tablet, whose cracked inscription in Latin verse laments the simultaneous decease of the beloved father and daughter. See also John Standish, ed., *Transactions of the Thoroton Society, 1906* (Nottingham: Thoroton Press, 1907), 10:10–13. Photos are included. For the text, see Walter H. Burgess, "The Helwys Family," *Transactions of the Baptist Historical Society* 3, no. 1 (May 1912): 18–31. The Helwys pedigree chart is on page 31. I modernized spelling and punctuation in the will of Sir Edmund Helwys.

[129] John Wilkinson, *The Sealed Fountaine Opened to the Faithful and Their Seed* (London: n.p., 1646). Wilkinson had written the book in 1613, "against John Morton, [in] prison at London" (title page). Wilkinson describes himself as "a prisoner in Colchester … 1613" (1). Wilkinson's book, now in London's British Library, was intended to refute Murton's Arminianism.

they cannot bring their spirits.... No man ought to be persecuted for his religion, be it true or false," to prove his "faithful allegiance to the king." One can sense the personal element in Murton's depiction of loyal Englishmen who did "lie many years in filthy prisons, in hunger, cold, idleness, divided from wife, family, calling, left in continual miseries and temptations, so as death would be, to many, less persecution."[130] Murton signs his preface with this description of himself and his congregation: "By Christ's unworthy witnesses, his Majesty's faithful subjects, commonly (but most falsely) called Ana-Baptists."

Murton's second work on religious liberty is a treatise titled *A Most Humble Supplication*,[131] a ten-chapter appeal for freedom of conscience. He closes his treatise with the hope that the king and all in authority "may see there is no comparison, between the Kings of Israel under the Law, and the Kings of Nations in the time of the Gospel in matters of religion." Murton signs his book, "The King's ... loyal subjects in all lawful obedience,

---

[130] *Objections Answered by Way of Dialogue* (n.p.: n.p., 1615), first and third pages of un-paginated preface. This is in the Bodleian Library, Oxford. Except for Stephen Wright, *The Early English Baptists, 1603–1649* (Woodbridge, Suffolk, England: Boydell Press, 2006), 45, who speculates that Helwys might have been the author, most have agreed that it was Murton, e.g., W. T. Whitley, *A Baptist Bibliography* (1526–1837) (London: Kingsgate Press, 1916), 1:7. A fourth edition of Murton's work appeared in 1662 under the title *Persecution for Religion Judg'd and Condemn'd: In a Discourse between an Antichristian and a Christian*, in *Tracts on Liberty of Conscience and Persecution, 1614–1661*, ed. Edward Bean Underhill (London: J. Haddon, 1846), 83–180.

[131] *A Most Humble Supplication*, "of many [of] the King's Majesty's loyal subjects, ready to testify all civil obedience, by the oath, as the law of this realm requires, and that of conscience, who are persecuted only for differing in religion, contrary to divine and human testimonies as follows" (n.p.: n.p., 1621), title page. The author addresses his supplication "to The High and Mighty Prince James by the grace of God King of Great Britain, France and Ireland, our Sovereign Lord on earth; to the excellent and noble Prince Charles, Prince of Wales; to all the right honorable nobility, grave and honorable judges; and to all other the right worshipful gentry of all estates and degrees, assembled in this present Parliament" (1). I have modernized some spelling. Scholars have unanimously attributed the work to John Murton. The document is also in Underhill, *Tracts on Liberty of Conscience and Persecution, 1614–1661*, 181–231.

unjustly called, Ana-Baptists." Roger Williams, founder of the New England Colony of Rhode Island, reported the imprisoned author's difficulty in writing his *Most Humble Supplication*. When Murton was deprived of ink, he used milk, carefully inscribing the words on the paper stoppers of the daily bottles of prison milk and smuggling the stoppers to a Christian friend who carefully browned or slightly scorched each one with a candle to make its words visible. In Williams's treatise, *The Bloody Tenent of Persecution* (1644), he describes Murton as a prisoner in Newgate, "for the truths of Jesus":

> Having not the use of pen and ink, [he] wrote these arguments in milk, on sheets of paper, brought to him by the woman his keeper, from a friend in London, as stopples of his milk bottle. In such paper written with milk nothing will appear, but the way of reading it by fire being known to this friend who received the papers, he transcribed and kept together the papers, although the author himself could not correct, nor view what himself had written.
> It was in milk, tending to soul nourishment, even for babes and sucklings in Christ. It was in milk, spiritually white, pure and innocent, like those white horses of the Word of truth and meekness, and the white linen or armor of righteousness, in the army of Jesus (Rev. 6 and 19). It was in milk, soft, meek, peaceable and gentle, tending both to the peace of souls, and the peace of states and kingdoms.

Williams laments that Murton's gentle cry for peace, written in milk, was answered "in blood," referring to John Cotton's bloody persecution against other men's conscience.[132]

Unlike Williams in doctrine, Murton authored a defense of Arminianism, titled *A Description of What God Hath Predestinated Concerning Man, in His Creation, Transgression, & Regeneration:*

---

[132] Roger Williams, *The Bloody Tenent of Persecution, for Cause of Conscience, Discussed in a Conference between Truth and Peace*, in *Publications of the Narragansett Club* (Providence, RI: Narragansett Club, 1867), 3:61–62. I have modernized some of the spelling.

As Also an Answer to John Robinson, Touching Baptisme (1620).[133] There is no record that Murton ever left Newgate alive. He died sometime during 1624–26. His wife Jane then returned to Amsterdam, where, in 1630, she and her brother Alexander Hodgkin joined the Mennonite church that had absorbed the Smyth congregation.[134] At the Smyth-Helwys division, Alexander had sided with Smyth and remained in Amsterdam. It was only natural for Jane to return to her relatives. Struggling to maintain an underground existence, during their early years in London, General Baptists had kept alive their periodic contacts with some of the Dutch Mennonites.

Thomas Lamb and Edward Barber

By 1626, General Baptist assemblies had emerged in London, Lincoln, Sarum, Coventry, Salisbury, and Tiverton. Much of the subsequent history of these congregations lies hidden in obscurity.[135] Following Murton's death, the major figure who led the General Baptist movement forward was a soapboiler,[136] Thomas Lamb (Lambe, fl. 1629–73), who, in 1640, suffered imprisonment in Fleet Prison for holding worship services. During Lamb's twenty-week incarceration, his wife, Dorcas, reached the state of poverty and petitioned the court for his release, for the sake of their six small children. Consequently, by the winter of 1641, Lamb was doing the work of an evangelist—planting churches and immersing converts in the River Severn, near Gloucester. By 1645, he was serving the pastorate

---

[133] N.p.: n.p., 1620. The original manuscript is in the Peterborough Cathedral Library, Cambridgeshire, UK. Scholars seem unanimous in attributing the authorship to John Murton. Its Epistle to the Reader is from one who is "falsely called an Ana-Baptist."

[134] Saito, "An Investigation," 135.

[135] For a good overview, see Barrington R. White, et al., eds., "The English General Baptists to 1660," in *The English Baptists of the Seventeenth Century*, rev. ed. (London: Baptist Historical Society, 1996), 15–58.

[136] For a photo of a trade token issued by Thomas Lamb to advertise his soap-boiling business, see Larry J. Kreitzer, *William Kiffen and His World*, a series of the Centre for Baptist History and Heritage Studies, Re-sourcing Baptist History: Seventeenth Century Series (Oxford: Regent's Park College, 2015), 4:29.

of a large church at Bell Alley, Coleman Street, London.[137] In October 1662, officials committed Lamb to Newgate for illegal worship.[138] He died just over a decade later (1673). We will discuss Lamb's theological treatises in the next chapter.

Meanwhile, the London General Baptist, Edward Barber (fl. 1620–49), a former Calvinist, had already authored the earliest Baptist defense of immersion: *A Small Treatise of Baptisme, or Dipping* (1641–42).[139] Refusing to use the English transliteration, *Baptize*, Barber translates Matthew 28:19a, "Go ye therefore and teach all nations, *dipping* them in the Name of the Father, and of the Son, and of the Holy Spirit." Barber had suffered imprisonment for eleven months for denying the sprinkling of infants. The second Baptist defense of immersion came from the pen of a Particular Baptist, Andrew Ritor, *A Treatise of the Vanity of Childish-Baptisme* (1642). Thus, the practice of immersion appears to have emerged almost concurrently, yet separately, among General and Particular Baptists, the latter quickly embedding the practice into their earliest doctrinal statement—the London Confession (1644).

Edward Barber also appears to have been the earliest General Baptist to require the laying on of hands, also called the "imposition of hands," to newly baptized believers. In his *A Declaration and Vindication of the Carriage of Edward Barber* (1648), Barber appeals to Hebrews 6:1–2 and proffers that the imposition of hands is necessary for immersed believers to receive the Holy Spirit.[140] Despite engendering controversy, the practice

---

[137] In 1645, Lamb moved his church to Spitalfields, where some of his members supported social issues, such as lower taxes, promoted also by local Levellers during 1647–49. Meanwhile, when General Baptists began practicing the "laying on of hands" for all newly baptized believers, Lamb strongly opposed the practice. See Murray Tolmie, "Thomas Lambe, Soapboiler, and Thomas Lambe, Merchant, General Baptists," *Baptist Quarterly* 27, no. 1 (January 1977): 4–13.

[138] Kreitzer, *William Kiffen and His World*, 4:24.

[139] Edward Barber, *A Small Treatise of Baptisme, or Dipping*, "Wherein is clearly shewed, that the Lord Christ ordained Dipping for those only that profess Repentance and Faith" (n.p.: n.p., 1641). In his Preface, Barber points to the *Book of Common Prayer* to show that immersion has been the ancient mode of baptism in England.

[140] Idem, *A Declaration and Vindication of the Carriage of Edward Barber*

eventually became standard in most General Baptist churches. A few Particular Baptists would also defend the practice to obtain "more of Christ and His Spirit,"[141] and "for an increase of the Graces and Gifts of the Holy Ghost."[142]

In his *A True Discovery of the Ministry of the Gospel* (1645), Edward Barber appears to have been the earliest General Baptist to use the office of "messenger," in addition to the offices of pastor (elder) and deacon. In quasi-Episcopal fashion, messengers exercised oversight among many congregations. To Barber, they constituted a continuation of the New Testament apostles. His qualifications for messengers include:

- He must be an immersed believer.
- He must be "a member of a true church."
- His local church must set him apart by the laying on of hands.
- He must have a good measure of self-denial.
- He "must have a holy contempt of all earthly things."
- He must possess the desire and the gifts to preach the gospel with power.
- He must refrain from preaching by "books and notes."
- He must immerse those who are converted under his ministry.
- He must lead converts into Baptist churches and strive to plant new churches.
- He must provide ordained evangelists to assist and strengthen all the churches.
- He must strive to keep the gospel free by finding his own means of livelihood.
- He must be ready to die for the cause of Christ.[143]

(London: E. B. Freeman, 1648), 5ff. (no pagination). This is in the British Library, London.

[141] Benjamin Keach, *Laying on of Hands upon Baptized Believers, as Such, Proved an Ordinance of Christ*, 2nd ed. (London: To be sold by Benjamin Harris, 1698), 78. This is in the British Library.

[142] Hercules Collins, *An Orthodox Catechism: Being a Sum of Christian Religion Contained in the Law and Gospel* (London: n.p., 1680), 34. This is in the British Library.

[143] Edward Barber, *A True Discovery of the Ministry of the Gospel: Or, Those Gifts Which Christ Gave at His Ascension* (London: n.p., 1645), 1–10. This

Barber's imprisonment in Newgate "for the Gospel of Christ" had once prompted him to write a single-sheet petition *To the Kings Most Excellent Majesty* (1641). To the King, Barber urged that compulsion "may make hypocrites, but not true Christians." Only "the Word and Spirit of God" can make Christians.[144]

Thomas Grantham: Key Theologian of General Baptists

Born in Lincolnshire,[145] Thomas Grantham (1633/34–1692) would humbly speak of the "Ancient Family of the Granthams," in which "I am one of the lowest of my Father's House."[146]

---

is in the Henry E. Huntington Library and Art Gallery, San Marino, CA.

[144] Idem, *To the Kings Most Excellent Majesty, and the Honorable Court of Parliament* (London: n.p., 1641). This is in the British Library.

[145] The best sources include Clint C. Bass, *Thomas Grantham (1633–1692) and General Baptist Theology* (Oxford: Regent's Park College, 2013); Spencer Franklin Plumlee, "Baptist Primitivist: Internal and External Religion in the Theology of Thomas Grantham, (1634–1692)" (PhD diss., Southwestern Baptist Theological Seminary, 2013); John D. Inscore Essick Jr., "Messenger, Apologist, and Nonconformist: An Examination of Thomas Grantham's Leadership among the Seventeenth-Century General Baptists" (PhD diss., Baylor University, 2008); idem, *Thomas Grantham: God's Messenger from Lincolnshire* (Macon, GA: Mercer University Press, 2013); J. Matthew Pinson, "Thomas Grantham's Theology of the Atonement and Justification," *Journal for Baptist Theology and Ministry* 8, no. 1 (Spring 2011): 7–21; Oscar C. Burdick, "Grantham, Thomas (1633/4–1692)," *Oxford Dictionary of National Biography* (Oxford University Press, 2004), online ed., http://www.oxforddnb.com/view/article/11298; William Richard, "A Sketch of the Life of Thomas Grantham," in four issues of *The Universal Theological Magazine* 3, no. 13 (January 1805): 1–10; 3, no. 14 (February 1805): 57–68; 3, no. 15 (March 1805): 109–17; 3, no. 16 (April 1805): 165–71; Samuel Edward Hester, "Advancing Christianity to Its Primitive Excellency: The Quest of Thomas Grantham, Early English General Baptist (1634–1692)" (ThD diss., New Orleans Baptist Theological Seminary, 1977); W. L. Johnson and R. L. Greaves, "Grantham, Thomas (1634–1692)," in *Biographical Dictionary of British Radicals in the Seventeenth Century*, ed. Richard L. Greaves and Robert Zaller (Brighton, England: Harvester Press, 1983), 2:23–24; Thomas Grantham, *The Loyal Baptist: Or an Apology for the Baptized Believers* (London: Printed for the author, 1684); idem, *St. Paul's Catechism, or, a Brief and Plain Explication of the Six Principles of the Christian Religion, as Recorded Heb. 6. 1, 2* (London: n.p., 1687). This is in the British Library, London.

[146] Thomas Grantham, "Epistle Dedicatory," in *Christianismus Primitivus*

Despite his noble ancestry, only scanty knowledge remains of his childhood and early training. During the Civil Wars, his parents "suffered much loss for the King." As hard-working farmers, they placed Thomas as a tailor's apprentice. He never attended a university, but, upon completing his apprenticeship, Thomas "gave himself to study."[147] The "Lord wrought repentance and faith" in his heart,[148] and, while still a teenager, he became a Separatist. In 1653, at about the age of nineteen, Grantham received baptism at a General Baptist church in Boston (Lincolnshire). The next year, he married Bridget Clay, who would bear him five children.

In 1656, Grantham was ordained to the pastorate of a recently organized General Baptist church in South Marsh, Lincolnshire, where he would serve for the next thirty years. Early in his

---

(London: Printed for Francis Smith, at the Sign of the Elephant and Castle in Cornhill, near the Royal-Exchange, 1678), 3 (no pagination is provided in this section). This copy of *Christianismus Primitivus* is in the Bodleian Library.

[147] Giles Firmin (1614–97), "To the Reader," in *Scripture-Warrant Sufficient Proof for Infant-Baptism: Being a Reply to Mr. Grantham's Presumption No Proof ...* (London: Printed for Thomas Parkhurst at the Bible and Three Crowns at the lower end of Cheapside, 1688), 2 (no pagination provided in this section). Although, Giles Firmin was antagonistic toward Grantham, he claims that he is quoting from a source favorable to Grantham. His source is no longer extant. This copy of *Scripture-Warrant Sufficient* is in Dr. Williams's Library, 14 Gordon Square, London.

[148] "Thomas Grantham to John Connould, 21 April 1691," in "John Connould, Letters to Thomas Grantham," James Marshall and Marie-Louise Osborn Collection, Beinecke Rare Book and Manuscript Library, Yale University Library, New Haven, CT. Copies of the collection are now available on microfilm. The collection consists of thirty letters to Grantham, accompanied by Grantham's replies, dated between April 17 and September 15, 1691. The two men were opponents when they wrote the thirty exchanges consisting of some two hundred and fifty pages. Nevertheless, John Connould, Church of England vicar of St. Stephen's in Norwich, would become a close friend of Grantham. When Grantham died on January 17, 1692, he was to be buried in the cemetery of St. Stephen's. Upon threatening rumors of abuse to the corpse, however, Connould arranged for Grantham's body to be interred "before the West doors, in the Middle Aisle" of St. Stephen's Church. Connould officiated at the funeral service and later requested that upon his death his body would rest next to Grantham's remains.

pastorate, the church met in Grantham's home. Although he and several of his members had suffered imprisonment, the church grew in number and moved into Northolme Chapel, near Wainfleet. Following the Fifth-Monarchist uprising under Thomas Venner, Grantham was one of the signatories of the General Baptists' *Second Humble Address* to Charles II in January 1661. Its purpose was to assure the King that Baptists had no part in the uprising and that they were law-abiding citizens. Even the Baptists' *Third Address*, however, was to no avail, as two additional imprisonments led to Grantham's tract, *The Prisoner against the Prelate* (1662), soon followed by *The Baptist against the Papist* (1663).

In 1666, multiple General Baptist churches chose Grantham as their messenger, or itinerant, church-planting evangelist. During this time, he established himself as a pamphleteer and debater against Anglican priests, Quakers, Sabbatarians, Presbyterians, and Particular Baptists. Faithful to the teachings of Edward Barber (fl. 1620–49), General Baptists still insisted that their messengers were continuing the work of the primitive apostles. Thomas Grantham, in practice and in treatises, would standardize the eminent function of messengers as travelling evangelists, responsible beyond their local congregations for creating and assisting churches in their ministries and ordinations. In 1686, Grantham moved to Norwich, where he founded a General Baptist church at White Friars Yard.

Written at the encouragement of Lincolnshire Baptists, Grantham's massive 1678 *Christianismus Primitivus* (*Primitive Christianity*) is by far his *magnum opus*. Divided into four books, the work constitutes the first systematic theology authored by a Baptist. Grantham calls for a return to the organization and simplicity of primitive Christianity. The work would standardize General Baptists' opposition to congregational singing. Following the earlier teachings of John Smyth, Grantham insists that only those who possess the spiritual gift of singing may use it and that all such singing must be in solo fashion. Grantham disallows all pre-composed rhymes, tunes, and meters.[149] His book offers instruction on many additional

---

[149] Thomas Grantham, "Of the Great Duty of Thanksgiving; or the

topics including marriage and divorce. During his final years, Grantham established churches in Great Yarmouth and King's Lynn. Following his death in 1692, his supporters erected a memorial plaque inside White Friars Yard chapel where his Norwich church met. The memorial's inscription summarizes Thomas Grantham's most significant accomplishments:

Dedicated to the singular merits of
A faithful confessor, and laborious servant of Christ,
Who with true Christian fortitude endured persecution
Through many perils, the loss of friends and substance,
And ten imprisonments for conscience sake;
A man endued with every Christian grace and virtue,
The Rev. Mr. THOMAS GRANTHAM,
A learned messenger of the Baptized Churches,
And pious founder of this church of believers baptized,
Who delivered to King Charles the Second
Our Declaration of Faith;
And afterwards presented to him
A Remonstrance against Persecution.
Both were kindly received, and redress of
grievances promised.
He died Jan. 17, 1692; aged 58 years:
And to prevent the indecencies threatened to his corpse,
was interred before the west doors
In the middle aisle of St. Stephen's Church in this city,
Through the interest, and much to the credit of
The Rev. Mr. John Connould;
By whom, with many sighs and tears,
The burial service was solemnly read to a crowded audience:
When at closing the book he added,
"This day has a very great man fallen in Israel."
For after their epistolary dispute, in sixty Letters, ended,
that very learned Vicar retained
the highest esteem and friendship for him whilst living,
And was by his own desire buried by him, May 1703.

Ordinance of God Touching the Singing of Psalms, Hymns and Spiritual Songs in the Christian Church, According to Scripture and Antiquity," in *Christianismus Primitivus*, book 2:99–117.

That Mr. Grantham was a very great man, appears
in those Letters, and in his numerous printed works;
Also, when engaged in public disputations,
Successfully displaying the well-accomplished Logician:
For to such exercises of skill and literature
he was often called in that disputing age.
Blessed are the dead which die in the Lord,
yea saith the Spirit,
they rest from their labors, and their works do follow them.[150]

---

[150] While the chapel and plaque have not survived, the inscription is in William Richard, "A Sketch of the Life of Thomas Grantham," *The Universal Theological Magazine* 3, no. 15 (March 1805): 116–17. St. Stephen's Church has undergone much renovation over the years. Vicar John Connould's burial stone has been moved close to the chancel. Grantham's burial site, somewhere underneath the stone floor, remains unmarked.

Select Bibliography for Further Reading

Bass, Clint C. *Thomas Grantham (1633–1692) and General Baptist Theology*. Oxford: Regent's Park College, 2013.

Early, Joe Jr., ed. *The Life and Writings of Thomas Helwys*. Macon, GA.: Mercer University Press, 2009.

Essick Jr., John D. Inscore. *Thomas Grantham: God's Messenger from Lincolnshire*. Macon, GA: Mercer University Press, 2013.

Payne, Ernest A. "Baptists and the Laying on of Hands." *Baptist Quarterly* 15, no. 5 (January 1954): 203–15.

_____. *The Free Church Tradition in the Life of England*. London: S. C. M. Press, 1944.

_____. *Thomas Helwys and the First Baptist Church in England*. 2nd ed. London: The Baptist Union of Great Britain and Ireland, 1966

Pinson, J. Matthew. "Thomas Grantham's Theology of the Atonement and Justification." *Journal for Baptist Theology and Ministry* 8, no. 1 (Spring 2011): 7–21.

Plumlee, Spencer Franklin. "Baptist Primitivist: Internal and External Religion in the Theology of Thomas Grantham, (1634–1692)." PhD diss., Southwestern Baptist Theological Seminary, 2013.

Saito, Goki. "An Investigation into the Relationship between the Early English General Baptists and the Dutch Anabaptists." ThD diss., Southern Baptist Theological Seminary, 1974.

Tolmie, Murray. "Thomas Lambe, Soapboiler, and Thomas Lambe, Merchant, General Baptists." *Baptist Quarterly* 27, no. 1 (January 1977): 4–13.

Underhill, Edward Bean, ed. *Confessions of Faith: And Other Public Documents Illustrative of the History of the Baptist Churches of England in the 17th Century*. London: addon, Brothers, and Co., 1854.

_____, ed. *Tracts on Liberty of Conscience and Persecution, 1614–1661*. London: J. Haddon, 1846.

White, Barrington R. "Early Baptist Arguments for Religious Freedom: Their Overlooked Agenda." *Baptist History and Heritage* 24, no. 4 (October 1989): 3–10.

_____. "The English General Baptists and the Great Rebellion, 1640–1660." *Baptist History and Heritage* 8, no. 1 (January 1973): 16–27.

Whitley, W. T. "Baptist Meetings in the City of London." *Transactions of the Baptist Historical Society* 5, no. 2 (July 1916): 74–82.

_____. *The Baptists of London 1612–1928: Their Fellowship, Their Expansion, with Notes on Their 850 Churches*. London: Kingsgate Press, n.d.

_____. *A History of the British Baptists*. Rev. 2nd ed. London: Kingsgate Press, 1932.

Wright, Stephen. *The Early English Baptists, 1603–1649*. Woodbridge, Suffolk, England: Boydell Press, 2006.

Chapter 4

General Baptist Doctrinal Decline and the Rise of the New Connection

---✳---

Common Features among General Baptists and Particular Baptists

*D*espite their doctrinal disparity, persecution often intertwined General and Particular Baptists in common causes regarding freedom of conscience and opposition toward governmental interference in their internal affairs. Baptist author Leonard Busher (born c. 1571), in his *Religion's Peace* (1614), was the first to describe forced worship as *spiritual rape*. Future Baptists, both Calvinists and Arminians, would cite Busher's vivid illustration: "Persecution for religion is to force the conscience; and to force and constrain men and women's consciences to a religion against their wills, is to tyrannize over the soul, as well as over the body." Indeed, "herein the bishops commit a greater sin than if they force the bodies of women and maids against their wills."[151]

---

[151] Leonard Busher, *Religions Peace: Or Reconciliation between Princes and Peoples, and Nations* (Amsterdam: n.p., 1614), 10. This is in the Henry E. Huntington Library and Art Gallery, San Marino, CA. The citation is in the paragraph that begins in the middle of the page. I slightly modernized some spelling and punctuation. A transcript is in Edward Bean Underhill, *Tracts on Liberty of Conscience and Persecution, 1614–1661*,

Lingering traditions, such as infant baptism and magisterial control over local churches,[152] had prompted Baptists to depart from the English-Separatist movement and to establish their own churches. From their beginnings, however, both General and Particular Baptists would preserve the English-Separatist commitment to be loyal citizens and to pay the necessary civil penalties for obeying God rather than man when such conflicts arose. Both groups would perpetuate the English-Separatists' congregational governance, their covenant commitment, and their manner of local-church discipline. The expositions of Scripture and the simplicity of worship that Baptists had learned and loved among the English Separatists would permanently facilitate their own worship. Many Baptists, mostly Particular, would also cling to the Separatists' manner of singing the Psalms of the Old Testament. Once they embedded immersion into their defining features, all Baptists would differ from English Separatists, as well as from most Anabaptist groups, on the proper mode of baptism.

Thomas Lamb

By 1644, there were forty-seven General Baptist churches. Most, including the Helwys-Murton church, were Arminian, believing that true believers can lose their salvation. On the other hand, not all General Baptists have held to strict Arminianism. Over the years, these maintained a remarkable balance in emphasis. A General Baptist, Thomas Lamb (Lambe, fl. 1629–73), authored an important work, *The Fountain of Free Grace Opened* (1645),[153] a careful defense of the doctrine that Christ suffered and

---

ed. (London: J. Haddon, 1846), 34 (15–81).

[152] Henry Ainsworth's True Confession of the Faith (1596) is an example. Baptists would reject Ainsworth's infant baptism (Art. 35) and his designating to princes and magistrates the authority and duty "to suppress and root out" all false ministries, voluntary religions, and counterfeit worship (Art. 39). See William L. Lumpkin, *Baptist Confessions of Faith*, 2nd rev. edition, ed. Bill J. Leonard (Valley Forge: Judson Press, 2011), 75–91.

[153] Thomas Lamb, *The Fountaine of Free Grace Opened* (London: n.p., 1645). This copy is in the British Library, London. Unfortunately, Lamb's

died for the sins of all humanity. Written from "the congregation of Christ in London ... [which is] falsely called Anabaptists," *The Fountain* also utilizes questions and answers to differentiate the congregation's soteriology from Arminianism—indeed, to "vindicate themselves from the scandalous aspersions of holding free will, and denying a free election by grace."[154] In his 1648 edition, Lamb presents "six propositions" that churches must agree upon for a proper doctrinal foundation. First, "Jesus Christ gave Himself a ransom for all men." Second, "remission of sins ought to be preached to all men." Third, "everyone ought to believe the forgiveness of his sins through Jesus Christ." Fourth, "no man has power by nature to believe in Christ." Fifth, "nothing can be done by us to cause God to choose us." Sixth, "whosoever hath precious faith is begotten by the power of God to salvation."[155]

In similar fashion, Lamb's *Treatise of Particular Predestination* (1642)[156] and *Absolute Freedom from Sin by Christ's Death for the World* (1656)[157] defend total depravity and unconditional election,

---

Fountain is frequently confused with an Antinomian work authored by John Saltmarsh, *Free-Grace or, the Flowings of Christ's Blood Freely to Sinners* (London: Printed for Giles Calvert, 1645). Unlike Saltmarsh, Thomas Lamb never uses the term *free grace* in an Antinomian sense.

[154] Lamb, *Fountain*, title page.

[155] Thomas Lamb, *The Fountain of Free Grace Opened*, 2nd ed. (London: Printed for Giles Calvert at the Black Spread Eagle at the west end of Paul's, 1648), 26. This copy is in the Cambridge University Library. I have modernized some spelling.

[156] Idem, *A Treatise of Particular Predestination* (London: n.p., 1642). This is in Trinity College (University of Cambridge) Library.

[157] Idem, *Absolute Freedom from Sin by Christ's Death for the World* (London: Printed by H. H. for the author, 1656). This work by Lamb is a negative critique of John Goodwin's *Redemption Redeemed* (1651). Goodwin was a radical Arminian. This is in the Harvard University Library. This Thomas Lamb has often been confused with a younger Thomas Lamb, a philanthropist who totally apostatized from the Baptist faith and died in 1686. For more on both Lambs, see Stephen Wright, "Lamb, Thomas (d. 1686)," *Oxford Dictionary of National Biography* (Oxford University Press, 2004), online ed., http://www.oxforddnb.com/view/article/15928; idem, "Lambe, Thomas (fl. 1629–1661)," *Oxford Dictionary of National Biography* (Oxford University Press, 2004), online ed., http://www.oxforddnb.com/view/article/72598; and Richard L. Greaves and Robert Zaller, eds., *Biographical Dictionary of British Radicals in the Seventeenth*

along with unlimited atonement. Some of his Calvinistic associates readily described Lamb as "a strict Calvinist."[158] During the Commonwealth Era, General Baptists from the Midlands published a remarkable confession, The Faith and Practice of Thirty Congregations (1651).[159] Among its seventy-five articles, there is frequent emphasis on the total depravity of man and the absolute sovereignty of God, who always takes the initiative in salvation. Article 25 insists "that there is not, neither ever was any man endued with any abilities and power to do the revealed will of God, but [that] it was given him from above (James 1:17)." In addition, the General Baptists' Orthodox Creed (1678)[160] asserts the perseverance of every true believer (Art. 36). For various reasons, including doctrinal ones, many General Baptists began moving into the Particular Baptist movement, especially after 1649, when London's Particular Baptists presented petitions from their churches to the House of Commons, denouncing the Leveller movement for its social radicalism. Moreover, Thomas Lamb's son, Isaac, would become a Particular Baptist and sign their Second London Confession.

Key Features of Early General Baptist Confessions of Faith

General Baptists held their first General Assembly in 1654,[161]

Century (Brighton, England: Harvester Press, 1983), 2:164–67.

[158] Walter Wilson, *The History and Antiquities of Dissenting Churches and Meeting Houses, in London, Westminster, and Southwark: Including the Lives of Their Ministers, from the Rise of Nonconformity to the Present Time*, 4 vols. (London: Printed for the author, 1808–14), 2:436.

[159] For the Faith and Practice of Thirty Congregations, see Lumpkin, 160–171.

[160] The 50-article Orthodox Creed (1678) is in W. J. McGlothlin, *Baptist Confessions of Faith* (Philadelphia: American Baptist Publication Society, 1911), 124–61; and Lumpkin, 298–348. The document was signed by fifty-four General Baptists on January 30, 1679 (N. S.). See Arnold H. J. Baines, "Signatories to the Orthodox Confession, 1679," *Baptist Quarterly* 17, no. 1 (January 1957): 35–42; continued in *Baptist Quarterly* 17, no. 2 (April 1957): 74–86; *Baptist Quarterly* 17, no. 3 (July 1957): 122–28; and *Baptist Quarterly* 17, no. 4 (October 1957): 170–78. Baines uses the N. S. date "1679." The usual "1678" is O. S., which began the civil year on the 25th of March.

[161] W. T. Whitley, ed., *Minutes of the General Assembly of the General Baptist*

and, in the same year, they published a confession called The True Gospel-Faith, the first Baptist confession to prescribe "the laying on of hands" for all believers. The confession appeals to Acts 8:15 and 17 to assert: It is "through the prayer of faith and [the] laying on of hands" that God gives His Spirit to "dipped" believers (Art. 12).[162]

In 1660, at the Restoration of the Stuart dynasty, General Baptists published A Brief Confession or Declaration of Faith.[163] With revisions in 1663, 1678, and 1700, and with the reiteration that Baptists are being "falsely called Anabaptists" (title page), this confession became the "Standard Confession" for General Baptists. Clearly embracing Arminianism (Art. 18), the Standard Confession would also become the major statement of faith among many Free Will Baptists. It proclaims Christ's return as "King over all the earth, Zech. 14:9, and [that] we shall reign with him on the earth, Rev. 5:10" (Art. 22). This is the earliest General Baptist confession to specify the method of baptism as "dipping" (Art. 11). It prescribes "laying on of hands" for all baptized believers, "that they may receive the promise of the Holy Spirit." For this "promise," the confession appeals to Acts 8:12, 15, and 17, Acts 19:6, 2 Timothy 1:6, and Hebrews 6:1-2 (Art. 12).

Despite a minority insisting that Scripture applies the laying on of hands exclusively to ordination, the all-inclusive practice became standard among most General Baptists. Known as "Six-Principle Baptists," they applied the six principles of Hebrews 6:1-2 (repentance, faith, baptism, the laying on of hands, resurrection, and judgment) to all believers. The passage reads, "Therefore leaving the principles of the doctrine of Christ, let us go on unto perfection; not laying again the foundation of repentance from dead works, and of faith toward God, of the doctrine of baptisms, and of laying on of hands, and of resurrection of the dead, and of eternal judgment." Although a few Particular Baptist churches also applied the laying on of hands to all their church members, most adherents of the inclusive

---

Churches in England, vol. 1, 1654-1728 (London: Kingsgate Press, 1909), 1-5.

[162] For the thirty-articles of "The True Gospel-Faith" (1654), see Lumpkin, 188-95.

[163] The 25-article Standard Confession (1660) is in McGlothlin, 111-22; and Lumpkin, 206-15.

practice were General Baptists. With a different application and in the spirit of Galatians 2:9, many Baptists now welcome new members into their churches by extending "the right hand of fellowship." The handclasp is a bond of acceptance and rests upon honor and integrity.

Matthew Caffyn and the Emergence of Theological Liberalism

Matthew Caffyn (1628–1714)[164] was born to a yeoman farmer of Horsham, Sussex. After completing two years at All Soul's College, Oxford, he was expelled in 1645 for promoting believer's baptism and attacking infant baptism. Caffyn returned to Horsham and took up farming,[165] but he also began visiting local churches and earning a reputation for his ability to preach and to debate the numerous Quakers in that region. Nearby, the General Baptist minister, Samuel Lover, persuaded his church to appoint Caffyn as his assistant. Shortly thereafter, Caffyn succeeded Lover to the pastorate, and, in 1654, Caffyn became one of the founding messengers for the first nationwide General Assembly of General Baptists. As such, he signed *The Humble Representation and Vindication* (1654),[166] the General Baptists' declaration of loyalty to the civil government. As a messenger, Caffyn began evangelizing and planting churches in a large southeastern region that included the counties of Kent, Sussex, and Surrey.

By 1660, the year of the Stuart Restoration, radical Anabaptist Christology had seriously influenced Matthew Caffyn; he was

---

[164] See B. R. White, "Caffyn, Matthew (1628–1714)," in *Biographical Dictionary of British Radicals in the Seventeenth Century*, 1:115–17; and Jim Spivey, "Caffyn, Matthew (bap. 1628, d. 1714)," *Oxford Dictionary of National Biography* (Oxford University Press, 2004), online ed., http://www.oxfor\ddnb.com/view/article/4332.

[165] On Worthing Road in Horsham, there stands a brick, two-storied church (built in 1721) that was once a General Baptist Church linked with Matthew Caffyn. It has long-since been the Horsham Unitarian Church, and they still claim Caffyn as one of their founders.

[166] For more on the Matthew Caffyn era and its aftermath, see Whitley, ed., *Minutes of the General Assembly of the General Baptist Churches in England*, 1654–1728, 1:10–150.

drawing large numbers of followers among southeast Baptists. Denying Christ's humanity, Caffyn preached that, "*Christ took nothing of his Body, Blood and Bones of the Virgin* Mary; but that the Eternal Word *Changed into Flesh* and so died."[167] Asserting that Christ was "not of the uncreated substance of the Father," Caffyn also denied Christ's deity. To Caffyn, Christ "is a God by Deputation from the Father, as Magistrates and Judges are."[168] Caffyn adamantly refused to describe Christ in the terminology of historic Trinitarian and Christological creeds, such as the Athanasian and Chalcedonian creeds.[169] Even the term *Trinity* was distasteful to Caffyn. Nevertheless, he could sign the General Baptists' Standard Confession (1660), since it contains no article on the Trinity or on the person and deity of Christ. Thomas Monk, a General Baptist messenger, led the opposition against the "Caffynite" heresies. In *A Cure for the Cankering Error of the New Eutychians* (1673), Monk warns General Baptists of Caffyn's subtle and contradictory denials of Christ's humanity and deity. Later that year, however, the General Assembly refused to condemn Caffyn's teachings.

Alarmed at their denomination's new direction, conservative pastors and messengers of central England (the Midlands area) produced the fifty-article Orthodox Creed (1678), described on its title page as a "Protestant Confession of Faith … to unite and confirm all true Protestants in the Fundamental Articles of the Christian Religion against the errors and heresies of Rome." The purpose of the confession reflects its authors' perceived need for trans-denominational cooperation in the face of the external threat of persecution and the internal threat of Caffynite heresy. Because of the conservatives' effort to refute Caffyn's aberrations, the first eight articles deal solely with the oneness of God in three distinct Persons. Indeed, the Orthodox Creed is the only Baptist confession to include the complete Apostles', Nicene, and Athanasian Creeds into the

---

[167] Christopher Cooper, *The Vail Turn'd Aside: Or, Heresy Unmask'd* (London: Printed for the author, and sold by J. Marshal, 1701), 108 (107–11). The italics are in the original.

[168] Ibid., 109.

[169] Anonymous, "A Sketch of the Life of Matthew Caffin," *The Universal Theological Magazine* 3, no. 17 (May 1805): 221–28.

body of its text (Art. 38). Fifty-four General Assembly messengers and pastors, primarily from the Midlands, signed the Orthodox Creed on January 30, 1679. When they presented the document for adoption at the London General Assembly, however, Matthew Caffyn handily convinced the Assembly's majority to reject the Creed. Caffyn piously argued that the New Testament should be the only standard for the Baptist faith. Caffyn's argument, however, was a tactic to conceal his interpretations and to avoid all accountability. He never suffered expulsion from the leadership of the General Baptist movement. Indeed, over the next several years, the Assembly would repeatedly exonerate Caffyn.[170]

Amid the theological turmoil over Caffynite teachings, in 1696, a group of conservative General Baptist churches separated from the General Assembly, taking the name *General Association* and publishing *The Reasons of Our Separation from the General Assembly*. The conservatives began holding their Association meetings in White's Alley Baptist Church (London). Meanwhile, the Particular Baptist, Benjamin Keach, was also warning that Caffyn was a "rank heretic,"[171] for his "detestable and damnable" doctrines.[172] The debilitating plague of apostasy continued to sweep through the General Baptist movement. By 1718, "not only all the Kent-Sussex churches, but all the London General Baptist churches except one, held a somewhat low view of the personality of Christ."[173] At Salters' Hall, London, on the 19th and 24th of February, 1719, Baptists met with Presbyterians and Independents (Congregationalists) to

---

[170] E.g., see Whitley, ed., *Minutes of the General Assembly of the General Baptist Churches in England*, 1:39–40, 43n11.

[171] Benjamin Keach, *The Display of Glorious Grace* (London: Printed by S. Bridge, and sold by Mary Fabian, Joseph Collier, and William Marshall, 1698), 136. This is in the Harvard University Library.

[172] Idem, *Beams of Divine Light* (London: Printed by K. Allwood, and sold by William Marshall at the Bible in Newgate Street, 1700), 23. This is in Dr. Williams's Library, 14 Gordon Square, London.

[173] "Salters' Hall 1719 and the Baptists," *Transactions of the Baptist Historical Society* 5, no. 3 (April 1917): 172. London's Guildhall Library has *White's Alley Church Book* for 1681–1841. See entries for June 7–8, 1693 and the 1704 General Association (L 18.2 Ms. 592). Cf. transcripts for 1699–1768 (Ms. 20953/1–6).

determine whether or not their ministers must subscribe to a Trinitarian statement of faith.[174] Plans for the meeting had emerged out of a Presbyterian conflict over the issue of subscription to a Trinitarian creed. When the meeting adjourned, the majority had voted 57 to 53 against subscription to any "human compositions, or interpretations of the doctrine of the Trinity." Among the General Baptists at Salters' Hall, there was one subscriber and fourteen non-subscribers. Among the Particular Baptists, there were fourteen subscribers and two non-subscribers.[175] The Salters' Hall decision promptly encouraged General Baptists to embrace the second edition of Samuel Clarke's newly published book, *The Scripture-Doctrine of the Trinity* (1719). As a Church of England Unitarian, Clarke was adept at applying René Descartes' method of compiling numerous Scripture verses into such an arrangement as to make the Bible appear to contradict itself. Michael Watts records, "Within a century, most Presbyterian meetings and many of the General Baptist churches connected with the General Assembly had become Unitarian."[176]

In 1731, the two General Baptist groups, representing the Assembly and the Association, agreed to a compromised reunification, based upon the six principles of Hebrews 6:1–2.[177] Disregarding the historic creeds of Christendom, the union resolved, "that all debates, public or private, respecting the

---

[174] Fred J. Powicke, "Arianism in the Exeter Assembly," *Congregational Historical Society Transactions* 7, no. 1 (May 1916): 34–43; idem, "The Salters' Hall Controversy," *Congregational Historical Society Transactions* 7, no. 2 (November 1916): 110–24; idem, "The Salters' Hall Assembly and the Advices for Peace," *Congregational Historical Society Transactions* 7, no. 4 (October 1917): 213–23; cf. Thomas Lewis, *The Anatomy of the Heretical Synod of Dissenters at Salters-Hall*, in *The Scourge in Vindication of the Church of England* (London: Printed for Charles Rivington, 1720), 359–84.

[175] "Salters' Hall 1719 and the Baptists," *Transactions of the Baptist Historical Society*, 189.

[176] Michael Watts, *The Dissenters: From the Reformation to the French Revolution* (1978; repr., Oxford: Oxford University Press, 1999), 376.

[177] See W. T. Whitley, ed., *Minutes of the General Assembly of the General Baptist Churches in England*, vol. 2, 1731–1811 (London: Kingsgate Press, 1910), 2:1ff.

Trinity, should be managed in scripture words and terms, and no other."[178] The compromise stipulated, regarding the Trinity, no member would be "permitted to ask any question, neither shall any question be asked of him, upon pain of being excluded" from membership.[179] The General Baptist movement had spiraled into a deadening mix of heresy.

Dan Taylor (1738–1816) and the New Connection (1770–1891)

Born to Azor and Mary Taylor of Northowram (Yorkshire), in 1738,[180] Dan Taylor began working with his father in the coalmines at the age of five. While growing up with no formal education, he loved to read and often took religious books with him into the mines. As a young man, Taylor rejected Calvinism and embraced the preaching and soteriology of John and Charles Wesley. Taylor preached his first sermon in 1761, at the age of twenty-three. Although a new convert to Methodism, Taylor joined with a small group of dissenters who had recently left the Methodist denomination over a dispute

---

[178] Adam Taylor, *The History of the English General Baptists, Part First: The English General Baptists of the Seventeenth Century* (London: T. Bore, 1818), 470 (463–80).

[179] Ibid., 477.

[180] The best sources on Dan Taylor include Frank W. Rinaldi, *The Tribe of Dan: The New Connexion of General Baptists 1770–1891: A Study in the Transition from Revival Movement to Established Denomination*, vol. 10 of the series, Studies in Baptist History and Thought (Eugene, OR: Wipf and Stock, 2009); Adam Taylor, *The History of the English General Baptists, Part Second: The New Connection of General Baptists* (London: T. Bore, 1818); Adam Taylor, *Memoirs of the Rev. Dan Taylor, Late Pastor of the General Baptist Church, Whitechapel, London: with Extracts from His Diary, Correspondence, and Unpublished Manuscripts* (London: Printed for the author, 1820); J. H. Wood, *A Condensed History of the General Baptists of the New Connection* (London: Simpkin, Marshall, and Co., 1847); W. Underwood, *The Life of the Rev. Dan Taylor: A Monograph* (London: Simpkin, Marshall, and Co., 1870); Frank Beckwith, "Dan Taylor (1738–1816) and Yorkshire Baptist Life," *Baptist Quarterly* 9, no. 5 (January 1939): 297–306; and E. F. Clipsham, "Taylor, Dan (1738–1816)," in *Oxford Dictionary of National Biography* (Oxford University Press, 2004), online ed., http://www.oxforddnb.com/view/article/27023.

over authority in their church polity. During their Bible studies, the dissenter group came to the conviction that the only true baptism is believer's baptism by immersion. In 1763, a General Baptist church in Gamston, Lincolnshire, immersed Taylor in the River Idle. That same year, in Wadsworth, near Hebden Bridge, Taylor organized a Baptist church consisting largely of former Methodists. Receiving his ordination, Taylor soon affiliated the church with the Lincoln Association of General Baptists. During 1767–69, he served as a representative at the General Baptist Assembly. By this time, however, he had become keenly aware of the Unitarian teachings and spiritual deadness among General Baptists.

In 1770, Dan Taylor led seven churches, consisting of about a thousand members, to separate from the old General Baptist denomination and to organize into "The Assembly of Free Grace Baptists," soon becoming "The New Connection of General Baptists," or "New Connection." Although Taylor wrote many sermons and tracts, his major work was the *Fundamentals of Religion in Faith and Practice* (1775).[181] In 1783, he moved from Wadsworth to Halifax and, in 1785, to London, which would remain his home until his death. Taylor would serve the pastorate of London's Church Lane Baptist, in Whitechapel. By 1786, the New Connection numbered thirty-one churches composed of 2,357 members. Over the next few decades, the more liberal General Baptist denomination, often called the "Old Connection," would fall into rapid decline. Some conservatives among them joined the New Connection. Others remained liberal and discarded Baptist distinctives such as immersion; many others moved into various Unitarian groups. Thus, the New Connection of General Baptists became England's major General Baptist voice. While the Old Connection had rejected church music, Taylor encouraged corporate singing and promptly provided hymnbooks. For training young men for ministry, the New Connection, in 1798, opened an academy in London under Dan Taylor's superintendence.[182] That same year, Taylor launched *The General Baptist Magazine*. Until

---

[181] Leeds, England: Printed for the author, 1775.
[182] The academy moved to Leicester in 1843.

his death, in 1816, Taylor was the leading voice of the New Connection. His official role as "moderator," often resembling the role of a Methodist bishop, would often draw the charge of "dictatorship."

Rather than providing his New Connection with a complete doctrinal statement, Dan Taylor, in 1770, composed six brief Articles of Religion. For the first five years, new ministers entering the Connection were required to subscribe to the Articles.[183] After 1775, however, the only membership requirement was a brief, spoken testimony of salvation. During the nineteenth century, liberals would train a new generation of New Connection leaders. In the spirit of modern ecumenism, a gradual process of merging the New Connection General Baptists with the Particular Baptists began as early as 1832, when the Particular Baptists modified the Constitution of the Baptist Union (est. 1813), to allow New Connection churches into membership. The Union would steadily decline. For instance, Thomas Goadby, principal of Midland College, promoted German higher criticism of the Bible. He concluded, "Religious doctrine ... can be verified only in the life and experience."[184] The Baptist, Samuel Cox (1826–93), in his *Salvator Mundi: Or is Christ the Savior of All Men?* (1877), denied eternal punishment and an eternal hell. Cox was the editor of the monthly magazine *The Expositor*.[185] John Clifford, editor of *The General Baptist Magazine*, carried innovative articles, such as those by Charles Ford of the Hyson Green Church (Nottingham). Ford denied the verbal inspiration of the Bible

---

[183] The original copy of the Dan Taylor's Articles of Religion is in *The Original Proceedings of the Yearly Meetings of the New Connexion from 1770 to 1796*, in the Angus Library and Archive, Regent's Park College, Oxford. There is also a copy in Adam Taylor, *The History of the English General Baptists, Part Second: The New Connection of General Baptists*, 139–42.

[184] Thomas Goadby, "Christian Theology and the Modern Spirit," in *The General Baptist Magazine for 1879*, ed. John Clifford (London: E. Marlborough and Co., 1879), 168 (161–69).

[185] Samuel Cox, *Salvator Mundi: Or is Christ the Savior of All Men?* 4th ed. (New York: E. P. Dutton, 1878); idem, *The Larger Hope: A Sequel to Salvator Mundi* (London: Kegan Paul, Trench and Co., 1883); idem, "Dives and Lazarus," in *Expositions*, 2nd ed. (London: T. Fisher Unwin, 1885), 155–69.

and rejected eternal punishment.[186] During this time, Charles Spurgeon, in the final years of his life, led his church to withdraw from the Baptist Union. He described the great battle against apostasy as the "Down Grade Controversy" (1887–92). Under John Clifford's direction, in 1891, the New Connection officially merged with the Baptist Union. No doctrinal confession was required, and the labels *Particular* and *General* forever disappeared. We have a full discussion in chapter 11, "Charles Spurgeon: His Life and Ministry."

---

[186] See F. M. W. Harrison, "The Nottinghamshire Baptists: Church Relations, Social Composition, Finance, Theology," *Baptist Quarterly* 26, no. 4 (October 1975): 186 (169–90). Meanwhile, the number of baptisms in the New Connection was still declining, as the following three years illustrate. 1882: 1542; 1883: 1344; and 1884: 1291. See also Briggs, "Evangelical Ecumenism: The Amalgamation of General and Particular Baptists in 1891: Part II," 167–68.

Select Bibliography for Further Reading

Beckwith, Frank. "Dan Taylor (1738–1816) and Yorkshire Baptist Life." *Baptist Quarterly* 9, no. 5 (January 1939): 297–306.

Clipsham, E. F. "Taylor, Dan (1738–1816)." In *Oxford Dictionary of National Biography*. Oxford: Oxford University Press, 2004, online ed., http://www.oxforddnb.com/view/article/2700230.

Crosby, Thomas. *The History of the English Baptists*. 4 vols. London: Thomas Crosby, 1738–40.

Gordon, Alexander. "Caffin, Matthew (1628–1714)." *Dictionary of National Biography*, edited by Leslie Stephen, 8:208–10. New York: Macmillan, 1886.

Ivimey, Joseph. *A History of the English Baptists: Comprising the Principal Events of the History of Protestant Dissenters, from the Revolution in 1668 Till 1760, and of the London Baptist Churches during that Period*. Vol. 3 of *A History of the English Baptists*. London: B. J. Holdsworth, 1823.

———. *A History of the English Baptists: Comprising the Principal Events of the History of the Protestant Dissenters, during the Reign of Geo. III, and of the Baptist Churches in London, with Notice of Many of the Principal Churches in the Country during the Same Period*. Vol. 4 of *A History of the English Baptists*. London: Isaac Taylor Hinton and Holdsworth & Ball, 1830.

Knight, Richard. *History of the General or Six Principle Baptists in Europe and America*. Providence: Smith and Parmenter, 1827.

Rinaldi, Frank W. *The Tribe of Dan: The New Connexion of General Baptists 1770–1891: A Study in the Transition from Revival Movement to Established Denomination*. Vol. 10 of the series, Studies in Baptist History and Thought. 2008. Reprint, Eugene, OR: Wipf and Stock, 2009.

Taylor, Adam. *The History of the English General Baptists, Part Second: The New Connection of General Baptists*. London: T. Bore, 1818.

———. *Memoirs of the Rev. Dan Taylor, Late Pastor of the General Baptist Church, Whitechapel, London: with Extracts from His Diary, Correspondence, and Unpublished Manuscripts*. London: Printed for the author, 1820.

———. *Memoirs of the Rev. John Taylor, Late Pastor of the General Baptist Church at Queenshead, near Halifax Yorkshire: Chiefly Compiled from a Manuscript Written by Himself*. London: Printed for the author, 1821.

Tolmie, Murray. "Thomas Lambe, Soapboiler, and Thomas Lambe, Merchant, General Baptists." *Baptist Quarterly* 27, no. 1 (January 1977): 4–13.

Underwood, A. C. *A History of the English Baptists*. London: Kingsgate Press, 1947.

Underwood, W. *The Life of the Rev. Dan Taylor: A Monograph*. London: Simpkin, Marshall, and Co., 1870.

Part III

English Particular Baptists to the Down Grade Controversy

Chapter 5

The Politico-Religious Landscape of the Earliest Particular Baptist Churches

❋

Why Separatists Were Falsely Called Brownists

*T*he sixteenth-century Reformation in England accomplished success only through great struggle and conflict. The final form of England's national church, *the* Church of England, established by law, was *Episcopalian*, which means government by bishops. There was no room for dissent from the *status quo*—no room for freedom of conscience in matters of religion. It was inevitable that opposition would arise.

While details of his early life are sketchy, Robert Browne (ca. 1550–1633),[187] in 1572, received his BA at Corpus Christi College,

---

[187] The best sources on Robert Browne include Albert Peel and Leland H. Carlson, eds., *The Writings of Robert Harrison and Robert Browne* (London: Allen and Unwin, 1953). Harrison was a colleague of Browne and teacher in Browne's church. Harrison assumed the leadership of the church in Middelburg when Browne left. See also Henry Martyn Dexter, *The Congregationalism of the Last Three Hundred Years as Seen in Its Literature* (New York: Harper and Brothers, 1880), 61–128; Barrington R. White, *The English Separatist Tradition: From the Marian Martyrs to the Pilgrim Fathers* (London: Oxford University Press, 1971), 44–66; Champlin Burrage, *The Early English Dissenters in the Light of Recent Research (1550–1641)* (Cambridge: Cambridge University Press, 1912), 1:94–117; Henry Martyn

Cambridge. Following his training, he received ordination in the Church of England and served as a domestic chaplain to the Duke of Norfolk. Almost immediately, Browne aroused much controversy by his open opposition to the authority of bishops. Robert Browne soon became the first to promote and publish the principles of independent congregationalism.

A confrontational visit to Cambridge about 1578 seems to mark Browne's break from the Church of England. By 1581, he was shepherding a small congregation he had gathered at Norwich. Browne and others of the group often faced imprisonment. He once boasted that he had been committed to thirty-two prisons. Lord Burghley, one of his relatives, often came to Browne's intervention. Sometime in late 1581 or early 1582, Browne and most of his group of some thirty to forty persons sought refuge in Middelburg, Zeeland (Netherlands). It was here that Browne wrote and published three treatises, advocating individualism and independency in the constitution and polity of local churches. Browne's treatises also protested any outside interference, either governmental or ecclesiastical, within the local churches. Separatists, of course, would agree with Browne's view of the independency of the local church. His most famous tract, *A Treatise of Reformation without Tarrying for Any* (1582), found its way into many parts of England, but Anglicans assessed it as reflective of Browne's typically hasty and often unwise decisions. William Pagett, a brewer's clerk in London, sold Browne's books to members of the English Company of Merchant Adventurers. This prompted an Elizabethan proclamation, in 1583, declaring Browne's ecclesiology as "seditious, scismaticall, and erroneous, ... tending to the depraving of the Ecclesiastical government established

---

Dexter and Morton Dexter, *The England and Holland of the Pilgrims* (Boston: Houghton, Mifflin, and Co., 1905), 188–212; and Williston Walker, *The Creeds and Platforms of Congregationalism* (Boston: The Pilgrim Press, 1960), 8–27; Walker includes extracts from Browne's writings and has a good bibliography. See also Michael E. Moody, "Browne, Robert (1550?–1633)," *Oxford Dictionary of National Biography* (Oxford University Press, 2004), online ed., http://www.oxforddnb.com/view/article/3695.

within this Realm."[188] In England, that same year, authorities hanged two of Browne's followers for distributing his books; at the executions, officers publicly burned forty copies of Browne's works.

Since independency stands completely opposed to the hierarchical system of bishops, leaders of the Church of England insisted that independent polity always leads to extreme individualism and factionalism. When internal dissension split the Brownist church in Middelburg, during 1583–84, "Trouble-church Browne" straightaway left most of his congregation in the Netherlands and moved to Scotland with a handful of his followers. In Edinburgh, his preaching met with disfavor among Presbyterians. Within a week, Browne stood before the Kirk-Session and landed in prison. On his return to England, he faced arrest in London and excommunication in Northampton. Utterly discouraged, Browne recanted and applied for re-admission into the Church of England. His Middelburg church soon ceased to exist. The content of Browne's writings differs from the teachings of the Church of England primarily in ecclesiastical polity, rather than doctrine, and Browne's view of baptism had always remained identical with that of the Church of England. Late in 1586, the religious Establishment received him back into their fold. From that year until about 1591, Browne served an appointment as headmaster of St. Olave's School, in London's Southwark area. Restored into the ministry of the Established Church, Browne, for the next forty years, would minister to the parish church of Achurch-cum-Thorpe, in Peterborough (Northamptonshire).

In his early ministry, Browne had been one of the first to espouse independency for local churches. His writings of that time contain the four basic congregational components, and these would extend far beyond the English Separatist tradition:
- The church is a covenanted community of believers.
- Persons join the local church by voluntary consent, never by coercion.
- Each local church is a gathered assembly, separate from

---

[188] For the complete document, see Peel and Carlson, eds., *Writings of Robert Harrison and Robert Browne*, 538–39, Appendix B.

- parish-church authority.
- Magistrates have no scriptural authority in the internal, spiritual affairs of churches.

In the end, being "poor, proud, and unloved," Robert Browne struck the parish constable who had come to collect his taxes. Being decrepit, past eighty years of age, and unable to walk, Browne rode on a feather bed on a cart to the Northampton jail, where he died circa 1633, just when Particular Baptists were organizing their first church. While no group would ever again claim the *Brownist* label, the above features of his congregationalism would find perpetuation among those who accepted the labels *Independent* and *Separatist*. Regardless of the Separatists' opposition to Browne, opponents would dub them as *Brownists*, and the negative epithet would become a popular and perilous weapon against them. Indeed, the charge of "Brownism" became as incriminating to Separatist Congregationalists as the indictment of "Anabaptism" would soon become to Separatist Baptists.

The First Two Pastors of the J-L-J Separatist Church from Which the Earliest Particular Baptists Emerged

The earliest Particular Baptist churches emerged in London, during 1633–38, by withdrawing from a Separatist, Independent-Congregational church, later called the "J-L-J" Church, so named for its first three pastors—Henry Jacob, John Lathrop, and Henry Jessey.[189] Our study of the J-L-J Church and its pastors will establish the background and origin of the Particular Baptist movement.

---

[189] Primary sources for this section include the following series of documents, published in the *Transactions of the Baptist Historical Society*, collected with notes, ed. W. T. Whitley: "Benjamin Stinton and his Baptist Friends," 1, no. 4 (January 1910): 193–96; "Stinton's Historical Researches," 1, no. 4 (January 1910): 197–202; "Records of the Jacob-Lathorp-Jessey Church, 1616–1641," 1, no. 4 (January 1910): 203–25; "Rise of Particular Baptists in London, 1633–1644," 1, no. 4 (January 1910): 226–36; "Debate on Infant Baptism, 1643," 1, no. 4 (January 1910): 237–45; and "The Jacob-Jessey Church, 1616–1678," 1, no. 4 (January 1910): 246–56.

Henry Jacob (ca. 1563-1624)

Henry Jacob—an atypical Oxford-trained Puritan—became a semi-Separatist and later a full Separatist, who, in 1616, established an Independent church in London's Southwark area.[190] Jacob had grown up at Cheriton (Kent) and had received his BA and MA degrees from St. Mary Hall, Oxford, during the 1580s. The Church of England had ordained him minister of the parish church near Cheriton. In 1591, he resigned his church, but he remained a Puritan. Influenced by Francis Johnson,[191] Jacob became a semi-Separatist. By 1606, he had made two visits to Holland, promoted the Puritans' Millenary Petition (calling for reform within the Church of England), and had suffered incarceration in London's Clink Prison for writing a treatise of *Reasons Taken Out of God's Word, and the Best Humane Testimonies Proving a Necessitie of Reforming Our Churches in England* (1603-4). The treatise, however, stopped short of advocating separation from the Church of England. Upon his release, Jacob fled to Holland, probably during 1605-6, and ministered to the English Merchant Adventurers Church in Middelburg, Zeeland, where Francis Johnson had served before becoming a Separatist. Jacob constantly kept abreast of England's political and spiritual climate.

In the wake of the Hampton Court Conference, where James I threatened dissenters with exile, Jacob "was gained to the side of truth" and moved to Leiden, Holland, in 1610, to confer with and sit under the ministry of the *Mayflower* Pilgrims' pastor, John Robinson, at Bell Alley. Nathaniel Morton, who had grown up

---

[190] See E. (Ephraim) Pagitt, *Heresiography or a Description of the Hereticks and Sectaries of These Latter Times*, 3rd ed. (London: Printed for W. L. for his shop in Fleet Street, 1647), 81–82. This is in the Bodleian Library, Oxford. See also Walter R. Goehring, "Henry Jacob (1563-1624) and the Separatists" (PhD diss., New York University, 1975). For discussions on the first three J-L-J pastors, see Dexter, *The Congregationalism of the Last Three Hundred Years*, 635ff.; Burrage, *The Early English Dissenters in the Light of Recent Research (1550–1641)*, 1:281–356; 2:146–66; and Benjamin Brook, *The Lives of the Puritans*, (Pittsburgh: Soli Deo Gloria, 1994), 2:330–34.

[191] Nathaniel Morton, *New England's Memorial* (1669; repr., Boston: Congregational Board of Publications, 1855), 446. He calls Jacob an early "convert of Francis Johnson."

in the home of his uncle, William Bradford, who knew Henry Jacob personally, would have accurately recorded these basic facts. According to Morton, Jacob became an "intimate friend and companion of Robinson." It was here in Leiden, while "in close conference with Robinson,"[192] that Jacob wrote to a friend in England *A Declaration and Plainer Opening of Certain Points* (1612). As a true and balanced Separatist, he distinguishes between ecclesiastical and personal separation. A minority of Separatists of every era has failed to make that distinction. Knowing the stigma of the *Separatist* label, and knowing that many had bandied it about as *Brownism*, Jacob carefully explains in a letter to a friend that he has not separated from every individual in the Church of England, and that, on rare occasion, one can still find a local assembly of godly people among the state churches. He cautions, though, that no assembly of the National Church can execute its local governance in a biblical manner. As for the Separatists, even though "in some matters" they "are stricter than I wish they were," explains Jacob, they are good people wrongly depicted as evil.[193] In the first century, each church was independent, that is, "one ordinary congregation." Thus, to Jacob, the Separatists' doctrine and congregational governance make them, in the most biblical sense, the "true churches of Christ." Coining the term *congregational*, Jacob argues that this is the New Testament "pattern of the apostles," and that "it is unlawful to hold any other form."[194] Jacob not only "agrees entirely with Robinson,"[195] he is the first to use the term *independent* to describe the local church. Jacob concludes, "Each congregation is an entire and independent Body politic, and endued with power immediately under, and from Christ, as every proper Church is, and ought to be."[196] Like John Robinson and the *Mayflower* Pilgrims, Henry Jacob

---

[192] Ibid., 444–46.

[193] Henry Jacob, *A Declaration and Plainer Opening of Certain Points* (n.p.: n.p., 1612), 5–6. Jacob wrote this from the Netherlands to a friend in England. This is in the library at Yale University.

[194] Ibid., 11, 33, and passim.

[195] Morton, 444.

[196] Jacob, *Declaration and Plainer Opening*, 13–14. I modernized the spelling of "entire," "politic," and "endued."

refused the Brownist mindset of labeling as "apostate" everyone identified with the National Church. As Independents, Jacob and Robinson were consistent Separatists. It was now Henry Jacob's "conviction that the time was come to take a firm and decided, though quiet, stand, and plant a church in Southwark on the model of the New Testament."[197] Thus, in 1616, after "conversing and discoursing much with John Robinson in Leyden,"[198] Jacob returned to London and gathered a Separatist church in a private home near London Bridge:

> [These] well-informed Saints having appointed a day to seek ye Face of ye Lord in fasting & Prayer, wherein that particular of their Union together as a Church was mainly commended to ye Lord: in ye ending of ye Day they were United, Thus, Those who minded this present Union & so joining together joined both hands each wth other Brother and stood in a Ringwise: their intent being declared, H. Jacob and each of the Rest made some confession or Profession of their Faith & Repentance, some were longer some were briefer, Then they Covenanted together to walk in all God's Ways as he had revealed or should make known to them.[199]

Jacob clearly established this church as Calvinist in doctrine, pedobaptist in practice, and Separatist in stance. John Lathrop would succeed Jacob to the pastorate, and, during his imprisonment, the congregation would begin to fall away from their Separatist beginnings. Maintaining both Calvinism and separatism, the original Particular Baptists would provide two key reasons for their 1633 secession from the Jacob-Lathrop Church. First, they were "convinced that baptism was not to be administered to infants." Second, during the time of John Lathrop's incarceration, his "congregation kept not to *their first principle of separation*."[200]

---

[197] Morton, 446.
[198] "Records of the Jacob-Lathorp-Jessey Church, 1616–1641," 206–11.
[199] Ibid., 209. I modernized some of the spelling.
[200] "William Kiffin Manuscript," preserved in Thomas Crosby, *The History of the English Baptists* (London: Thomas Crosby, 1738), 1:148 (italics mine).

Besides being Separatists, Henry Jacob's church was "the first Independent or Congregational church in England."[201] Repudiating his ordination from the Church of England, Jacob requested re-ordination from his local church. Thus, he "was chosen & Ordained Pastor" by his congregation, and "many saints were joined to them."[202] Jacob also authored their twenty-eight-article Confession and Protestation of the Faith (1616). Due to persecution, Jacob's congregation found it necessary to continue meeting in the homes of members living on both sides of the River Thames. Within the framework of independent-congregational polity, the church utilized Jacob's *Catechism* (1605), which teaches that in the New Testament there are three officers in the local church, "a pastor or bishop, with Elders, & Deacons."[203] Particular Baptists would soon reduce to two the number of church officers—pastors and deacons. Baptists, while maintaining a plurality of elders, saw that in the New Testament *elders* and *pastors* are synonymous terms.[204]

The earliest Particular Baptist churches, seceding from the J-L-J Church, had learned their basic church polity in this very place.[205] While the J-L-J Church provided for Particular Baptists their earliest *experience* in local-church autonomy, Jacob's Confession and Protestation of the Faith provided for Baptists their earliest *defense* of local-church autonomy. Notable expressions from Henry Jacob's Confession:

- The only biblical local church is a "free Congregation of Christians" with the "right and power of spiritual Administration and Government in itself and over itself by the common and free consent of the people, independently, and immediately under Christ, always in the best order they can" (Art. 4.1–2).[206]

---

[201] Morton, 444.
[202] "Records of the Jacob-Lathorp-Jessey Church, 1616–1641," 210–11.
[203] Burrage, *The Early English Dissenters in the Light of Recent Research (1550–1641)*, 2:160; cf. Jacob's Confession and Protestation of the Faith, where he also allows a plurality of elders (Art. 14).
[204] E.g., Titus 1:5–9; and compare Acts 20:17 with Acts 20:28.
[205] For more background study, see Geoffrey F. Nuttall, *Visible Saints: The Congregational Way 1640–1660* (Oxford: Basil Blackwell, 1957).
[206] Henry Jacob, *A Confession and Protestation of the Faith* (Amsterdam: G.

- A "Consociation of Congregations" may become necessary on occasion, but only on the basic condition that each local congregation will remain subject only to Christ and to the Holy Scriptures. In the spiritual realm, no church should ever find itself subjected to any higher human authority than its own flock (Art. 5).
- There is no *earthly* catholic church in the Bible (Art. 6).
- In the New Testament, there are no national, provincial, or diocesan churches. "Only a free Congregation, or ordinary Assembly, is found in the New Testament" (Art. 7).
- "The Ministry of [the Church of] England descendeth from the Pope," and any "minister" whose ordination is without the consent of the local church flock "is indeed no minister" at all. In the "Word of God," the minister is a local minister, "tied unto one congregation," or flock, and "a flock is not a realm, province, or diocese" (Arts. 10, 28).[207]

Multiple local church records reveal that in England many Independent Congregational churches embraced believer's baptism by immersion and reorganized themselves into Baptist churches.[208] Indeed, Baptists would exceed the Congregationalists in preserving congregational polity.

Besides believer's baptism, one other issue held serious ramifications for Baptists. Churches of the English Separatist tradition, including the J-L-J Church, were still clinging to a degree of state control over local churches. Like sixteenth-century magisterial Reformers, and like seventeenth-century Puritans, the English Separatists assumed an extrapolation of

---

Thorp, 1616), Article 4.1–2; I have modernized some of the spelling and punctuation. Jacob's supportive Scripture appears in this order: Matt. 18:17, 19; 1 Cor. 5:12–13; 10:15; and 7:23; 2 Cor. 2:8; 2 Thess. 3:6, 14; Acts 6:3, 5, 6; 14:23; 1:23, 26; and 15:22, 25: 1 Thess. 5:21; 1 John 4:1; Rom. 16:17; Col. 4:17; 2 John 10; 3 John 10; Gal. 1:9; 5:1; and 4:26 (Article 4.2). This is in the British Library, London.

[207] Order of supportive passages in the margin: 1 Thess. 5:21; Rom. 16:17; 1 John 4:1; Acts 14:23; 6:3, 5; and 1:23, 26; 2 Cor. 1:24; 1 Pet. 5:3; 1 Cor. 7:23; and 3:22; Matt. 18:17, 19; and 28:20 (Article 10); cf. Article 28.

[208] For examples, see H. G. Tibbutt, ed., *Some Early Nonconformist Church Books* (Bedford, England: The Bedfordshire Historical Record Society, 1972).

ecclesiastical authority to civil magistrates. Interpreting the church as "New Israel," Separatist leaders readily submitted matters of church purity and discipline to the authority of civil magistrates. Separatist Henry Ainsworth had promoted the practice in Article 39 of his True Confession (1596). Greatly alarmed, Baptists warned Separatist churches that the fear of man had steered their governance away from the New Testament pattern. Even in his Confession and Protestation of the Faith (1616), Henry Jacob's placated nuances stand opposed to the Baptist insistence that the state owns no legitimate, internal jurisdiction over the local church. Jacob states:

> We believe that we, and all true visible churches, ought to be overseen and kept in good order and peace, and ought to be governed (under Christ) both supremely and … subordinately by the civil magistrate: yea, in causes of religion when need [be]. By which rightful power of his, he ought to cherish and prefer the godly and religious, and to punish (as truth and right shall require) the untractable and unreasonable; howbeit yet always but civilly. And therefore, we, from our hearts, most humbly do desire that our gracious sovereign king would (himself so far as he seeth good, and further, by some substituted civil magistrate under him) in clemency take this special oversight and government of us, to whose ordering and protection we most humbly commit ourselves.[209] (Article 27)

On the contrary, in addition to rendering unto Caesar the

---

[209] I edited a couple of capital letters. Baptists also disagreed in part with a document that appeared later as a postscript to Jacob's Confession and Protestation of the Faith. Although some authors attribute the authorship to Jacob, we may never know who wrote this *Humble Petition to the King's Most Excellent Majestie*. To the king, the author requests, "that you would afford us, and assign to us some Civil Magistrate or Magistrates qualified with wisdom, learning, and virtue, to be (under your Highness) our Overseers for our more peaceable, orderly, and dutiful carriage of ourselves, both in our Worshipping God, and in all other our affairs, at your pleasure." Cf. *An Humble Supplication for Toleration and Libertie* (1609), addressed to James I, and often attributed to Henry Jacob. This is in the Boston Public Library.

things that are Caesar's, Baptists would call upon civil magistrates to "protect the liberty of men's consciences" in matters of worship.[210] Baptists were pioneer defenders of the autonomy of local churches and of the separation of civil government from their faith and governance.

Having fully established his Independent church, Henry Jacob resigned from its pastorate in 1622 and moved to Jamestown, Virginia,[211] where he died before his wife Sara and the children could join him. The General Court at Jamestown probated Jacob's will, and the same court testimony indicates that he died sometime during 1622-23. It is plausible that his intention was to establish churches in the Colony. He doubtlessly possessed a heavy burden to obey Christ's commission to carry the gospel to the New World. Henry Jacob's Christian life demonstrates an unselfish commitment to the Lordship of Christ. Soon after receiving the news of Henry's death, Sara sent a request for the justices of Jamestown's General Court "to sell her late husband's goods and send the proceeds to her in England."[212]

John Lathrop (1584-1653)

John Lathrop (Lothropp, Lathorp),[213] a Queens' College, Cambridge graduate, renounced his episcopal ordination and,

---

[210] 1646 edition of the Particular Baptists' London Confession (Article 48).

[211] The 1622 date coincides with the Powhatans' destruction of a small settlement established by Francis Johnson's remnant group near Jamestown.

[212] Martha W. McCartney, *Virginia Immigrants and Adventurers, 1607-1635: A Biographical Dictionary* (Baltimore: Genealogical Publishing Company, 2007), 417; cf. H. R. McIlwaine, ed., *Minutes of the Council and General Court of Colonial Virginia* (1924; repr., Richmond: Virginia State Library, 1979), 163-64.

[213] While some of his contemporaries spelled his name "Lathorp," he spelled it "Lothropp." His New England descendants later changed the spelling to "Lathrop." Occasionally, it appears as "Laythrop," representative of one of the New England pronunciations. See Richard L. Greaves, "Lothropp, John (*bap.* 1584, *d.* 1653)," *Oxford Dictionary of National Biography* (Oxford University Press, 2004), online ed., http://www.oxforddnb.com/view/article/17028.

during 1624–25, received re-ordination as the second pastor of the Independent-Congregationalist church that Henry Jacob had established in Southwark (London). Being Separatists, their sixty members met and worshipped secretly in homes and in nearby sandpits. On April 29, 1632, Lathrop and forty-two of his members were meeting for worship in the home of Humphrey Barnet in Blackfriars. Officers of King Charles discovered them, surrounded the house, seized them, and imprisoned them—some in the Clink, some in Newgate, and some in the Gatehouse. At least seven of these prisoners would become Baptists, and, upon their release, they would join John Spilsbury's Particular Baptist Church in London. Also among the prisoners was a London leather seller who owned the Lock and Key Shop in Fleet Street. His name was Praisegod Barebone (ca. 1596–1679), an Independent Separatist, who in eight years would be the pastor of a mutual wing of the J-L-J Church, and in twenty-one years a lawmaker in Cromwell's "Barebone Parliament." Meanwhile, the crime committed by Lathrop and his members was their refusal to support the Church of England. Lathrop remained in the Clink for two full years, during which time his wife died from illness. The oldest of their nine orphaned children begged the Bishop of Lambeth to intercede with the king for their father's release.[214] In 1634, authorities finally released John Lathrop on the condition that he would go into exile.

In September of that year, Lathrop and thirty-two of his members arrived in Boston, Massachusetts, on the ship *Griffin*, and settled at Scituate, in Plymouth Colony. The following year, Lathrop's daughter Jane married Samuel Fuller,[215] who had arrived on the *Mayflower* in 1620, and whose late uncle was Samuel Fuller (d. 1633), the physician of the *Mayflower* and of Plymouth Plantation. Accepting a generous offer of land from Plymouth Colony, in 1639, most of the Lathrop group moved

---

[214] A valuable source is the "Biographical Memoir of Rev. John Lothropp," by his great-grandson, John Lathrop, D. D., in *Collections of the Massachusetts Historical Society*, second series (Boston: John H. Eastburn, 1838), 1:163–78, 258–60.

[215] Eugene A. Stratton, *Plymouth Colony: Its History & People 1620–1691* (Salt Lake City, UT: Ancestry Publishing, 1986), 60–64.

to Barnstable, on Cape Cod. For the minority who remained in Scituate, Christopher Blackwood served briefly as pastor (1641), before returning to England and becoming a prominent Particular Baptist.[216] Succeeding Blackwood to the Scituate pastorate (1641–54), Charles Chauncy continued the practice of infant baptism, but insisted on baptizing only by immersion. Ironically, when Chauncy became president of Harvard College, in 1654, he was replacing Henry Dunster, whom Harvard had just ousted for practicing believer's immersion only. Dunster accepted Chauncy's Scituate pastorate (1654–59), but, with his ministry cut short by death, the church never became Baptist. Today, the church is the First Parish Unitarian Universalist Church of Scituate, Massachusetts.[217]

Meanwhile, after the fifty-mile trek along the rugged trail from Scituate, the Lathrop congregation arrived in Barnstable and promptly celebrated Communion at a place still known as Sacrament Rock. On Route 6A, a historical sign marks the location of the rock—a half mile from the site of their original meetinghouse. Some of the pewter Communion vessels that Lathrop brought over from London are still in the church's possession, including plates, a large wine tankard, and the baptismal bowl. Ten days after arriving in Barnstable, the congregation gathered in the rugged frontier home of a "poor Mr. Hull," for "a whole day" of "fasting, humiliation, and prayer." Their supplication was "for the grace of our God to settle us here in church estate and to unite us together in holy walking, and to make us faithful in keeping covenant with God and one another."[218]

---

[216] Barrington R. White, "Blackwood, Christopher (1606–1670)," in *Biographical Dictionary of British Radicals in the Seventeenth Century*, ed. Richard L. Greaves and Robert Zaller (Brighton, England: Harvester Press, 1982), 1:69–70; and Jeremy Dupertuis Bangs, *The Seventeenth-Century Town Records of Scituate, Massachusetts* (Boston: New England Historic Genealogical Society, 1997), 1:31, 1:43–44, 1:134–35.

[217] Emerging from the Scituate church during Charles Chauncey's pastorate, the nearby First Parish in Norwell, Massachusetts, is also now a Unitarian Universalist church.

[218] E. B. Huntington, "Rev. John, the Pioneer," in *A Genealogical Memoir of the Lo-Lathrop Family in the Country, Embracing the Descendants, as Far as Known, of the Rev. John Lothropp, of Scituate and Barnstable, Mass.* (Ridgefield, CT: Julia M. Huntington, 1884), 31–32.

Until the congregation completed its first meetinghouse in 1646, they met for worship in their homes, including John Lathrop's second house, built in 1644 and still standing as part of the Sturgis Library in Barnstable, Massachusetts.[219] Today's visitor can stand in the room that once served as Lathrop's study and meetinghouse. John Lathrop's personal Bible — a 1605 Bishops' Bible — is in a display case and is probably the one he had used as an Anglican priest and later as a Separatist prisoner. Late one evening during the voyage to New England, Lathrop had fallen asleep while studying. His fingers were resting between the leaves of his Bible. Unaware that a drop of tallow or a spark from his candle had fallen into his Bible, Lathrop suddenly awakened by the fire at his fingertips. The embers had burned through several pages and it was the only Bishops' Bible onboard. While still en route, however, Lathrop, with pen and ink, restored from memory all the missing text, inscribing each letter in the form of the font that had printed it. On display, his Bible is open for visitors to view the restored pages — mostly in the book of Acts.[220] Lathrop ministered in Barnstable for fourteen years until his death in 1653. His church never became Baptist, but, from its 1616 origin in London, this church was the first ever specifically designated as *Congregationalist*.

Known today as West Parish of Barnstable, Lathrop's church is the only existing remnant of London's J-L-J Church — the womb from which the first Particular Baptist churches were born. Watching high above its tower bell is a 1732, gilded weathercock, measuring over four feet from its bill to the tip of its tail. Colonial churches often chose the symbol of the rooster to warn their people of the winds of doctrinal apostasy, and of the words of Jesus to Peter, "Verily I say unto thee, That

---

[219] John Lathrop, "Scituate and Barnstable Church Records," in *The New England Historical and Genealogical Register*, "copied from Lathrop's handwritten manuscript by Yale College President Ezra Stiles in 1769" (Boston: Samuel G. Drake, 1855–56), 9:279–87, 10:37–43. These are the only extant remains of Lathrop's diary.

[220] E. B. Huntington, *Genealogical Memoir of the Lo-Lathrop Family*, 231; and Lucy Loomis, *John Lothrop in Barnstable*, 2nd ed. rev. (Barnstable, MA: Sturgis Library, 2011), 8–15.

this night, before the cock crow, thou shalt deny me thrice" (Matt. 26:34).[221] The Church Record book testifies that Lathrop was "endowed with a competent measure of gifts and earnestly endowed with a great measure of brokenness of heart and humility of spirit."[222]

Meanwhile, back in London, from the time of Lathrop's voyage to New England in 1634, the Jacob-Lathrop Church remained without a pastor until 1637, when they persuaded Henry Jessey (1601–63), a gifted man with priceless credentials, to become their third pastor. When Jessey began his pastorate, the Particular Baptists had already begun leaving the J-L-J Church. Completing the formation of their first church during 1633–38, the Baptists influenced Henry Jessey to become an immersionist. To set the stage for key developments surrounding Jessey and the Particular Baptists, we will take a birds-eye view of the conflicting forces at work in England from Charles I (1625) to the Glorious Revolution and rise of William and Mary (1689).

The Changing Political Landscape

Persecutions against Baptists and other Separatists only worsened when James I died in 1625. His successor, Charles I (r. 1625–49), married a French Roman Catholic and was soon making English ships available to Cardinal Richelieu to fight against the French Protestants. During the second quarter of the seventeenth-century, England faced widespread political, economic, and religious unrest, resulting in a great Puritan immigration to New England. The earliest non-conformist Puritans

---

[221] West Parish of Barnstable is a founding member of the United Church of Christ.

[222] Walter R. Goehring, *The West Parish Church of Barnstable: An Historical Sketch — Being an Account of the Gathering of the Church Body in London in 1616 with Henry Jacob and its Early History in the New World and Particularly of the West Parish Meetinghouse Built in 1717 in West Barnstable, Massachusetts* (West Barnstable: The West Parish Memorial Foundation, 1959), 9. Nathaniel Morton, a contemporary in Plymouth, described Lathrop as "a man of a humble and broken heart and spirit." See Nathaniel Morton, *New England's Memorial*, 168; see also 167 and 446.

arrived in Salem, Massachusetts in 1628 and in Boston in 1630. Under Charles I, the unjust and inhuman proceedings of the Council Table, the Star Chamber, and the High Commission were unparalleled. The great immigration increased when William Laud succeeded George Abbot to the archbishopric of Canterbury in 1633, and, during the next seven years, the Puritans and dissenter groups felt the full force of Laud's fiery zeal, as multitudes of them — ministers and laymen — were driven to the Netherlands and to New England.

As special executive to King Charles I, Archbishop Laud wielded unbelievable power as he drove Puritan non-conformists from one diocese to another and sought to enforce ritualism on the Presbyterians of Scotland. He instigated exceeding and unmerciful severities, harassing and persecuting both Puritans and dissenters in every corner of the land. Laud expelled the Puritan lecturers and suspended anyone who preached against his semi-Pelagianism and "popish ceremonies." In 1640, the National Church adopted new Constitutions and Canons, based directly upon Laudian practice and theology. That year, however, ongoing financial crises forced Charles I to convene the Long Parliament. This Parliament, strongly sympathetic toward Presbyterian and Puritan convictions, condemned Laud's "superstitious" and "tyrannical" Canons and Constitutions as "contrary to the Laws of this Realm, the Rights and Privileges of Parliament, the Liberty and Property of the Subject, tending also to Sedition, and of dangerous Consequence."[223] The nation was now ready to overthrow the unmitigated political and ecclesiastical tyranny. Those who were suffering from the arbitrary rule of the King joined with those who were groaning under the despotism of the bishops. In a vast effort, they would overthrow both absolute monarchy and "Anglican popery." On December 18, 1640, the House of

---

[223] "Articles of the Commons assembled in Parliament, in maintenance of their Accusation against William Laud, Archbishop of Canterbury; whereby he stands charged with High Treason, presented and carried up to the Lords by Mr. J. Pym, Feb. 26, 1640," in *Historical Collections* (1639-1640), ed. John Rushworth, "setting forth only Matter of Fact in Order of Time, without Observation or Reflection" (London: D. Browne, et al., 1721), 3:1369 (3:1365–81).

Commons impeached Archbishop Laud for high treason and placed him in confinement.[224] In March 1641, they sent Laud to the Tower. *A new era had commenced.*

During England's Civil War Era (1642–48), the Puritan immigration to New England subsided and the Age of Puritanism (1564–1644) ended. Since then, there has not existed in England a body or organized group of people properly called by the name *Puritan*. Individual English Puritans were now branching into two major parties—Independents and Presbyterians. The Civil War Era had begun with King Charles's well-trained Cavalier (Royalist) Army routing Parliament's army of Roundheads.[225] The Era soon witnessed the alliance of Parliament with the Scottish Army, the adoption of Scotland's Solemn League and Covenant, the completion of the Westminster Standards in London, and the beheading of William Laud at Tower Hill.

The Civil War Era ended with Oliver Cromwell's New Model Army defeating the Cavaliers, many of whom fled to the Virginia Colony, which had remained loyal to the Crown. With the beheading of Charles I, in January 1649, the monarchy suffered abolition and the country immediately became a Commonwealth, governed by Cromwell's Protectorate, or Interregnum (1649–60). Upon Oliver Cromwell's death in 1658, his son Richard succeeded him. After ruling only nine months, Richard's incompetent leadership forced his abdication in 1659, as England witnessed the Restoration of the Stuarts, with the

---

[224] At this time, English barrister Henry Parker desperately gathered his best arguments in favor of Erastianism and the Divine Right of Kings and published them as *The True Grounds of Ecclesiasticall Regiment: Set Forth in a Brief Dissertation Maintaining the Kings Spiritual Supremacie against the Pretended Independencie of the Prelates, etc. Together with Some Passages Touching the Ecclesiasticall Power of Parliaments, the Use of Synods, and Power of Excommunication* (London: Robert Bostock, 1641). Parker's appeal ultimately proved to be unsuccessful.

[225] Royalists went by the name *Cavaliers* because they dressed in courtly fashion, with long hair in ringlets, flamboyant hats, and bright clothes with collars and lace cuffs. While some refer to modern-day Parliamentarians as *Roundheads*, that term originated during the Civil Wars as an insult to the Puritans who wore black skullcaps and cut their hair short. The Puritans were pro-Parliamentarians.

ascension of Charles II in 1660. At the Restoration, persecution resumed, resulting in a large immigration of non-conformists and dissenters to New England. There were, between 1660 and 1688, sixty thousand non-conformists and dissenters who had suffered incarceration in England's prisons. More than five thousand had died of privation and disease.[226] The Puritans in New England would manage to keep their movement recognizable until the end of the 1680s at the latest. Following the Glorious Revolution of 1688, which deposed James II and brought William and Mary to the throne, times were changing on both sides of the Atlantic. In England, non-conformist worship enjoyed increased legalization. In New England, Plymouth Colony merged into the larger Massachusetts Bay Colony (1691). By now, Puritanism as a distinct movement was history.

The Changing Religious Landscape

Having summarized England's political changes from 1625 to 1689, we are ready to discuss a significant religious element, which will complete the landscape of the earliest English Baptist churches. The bizarre religious background of the Civil War Era (1642–48) is often depicted as a "world turned upside down."[227] These troublous times spawned numerous radical groups appealing to the common folk to join them. Any proper understanding of early Baptist history demands some grasp of the nature of these groups. We will consider how and to what degree such groups influenced Baptists. These aberrant groups have significantly influenced historians' interpretations of early Baptist doctrine and practice.

---

[226] John A. Goodwin, *The Pilgrim Republic: An Historical Review of the Colony of New Plymouth with Sketches of the Rise of Other New England Settlements, the History of Congregationalism and the Creeds of the Period* (Boston: Houghton Mifflin Co., 1920), 12.

[227] As portrayed in a title by the Marxist historian, Christopher Hill (1912–2003), *The World Turned Upside Down: Radical Ideas during the English Revolution* (1972; repr., London: Penguin, 1991).

The Seeker Movement

Emerging in England, during the mid-1630s,[228] an amorphous group called the Seekers preached that all Christendom had fallen into spiritual corruption and apostasy. In their view, the Holy Spirit had removed Himself and His gifts from all organized churches. The Seekers rejected as invalid all current forms of religious rituals, sacraments, and ordinances. The name *Seekers* derived from their search for the true church. Expecting Christ's imminent return and inauguration of the millennium, many individual Seekers began a quest for the extraordinary signs and miracles of Joel 2:28-29—hallmarks that would at last reveal the true visible church. The Particular Baptist, Thomas Kilcop, in his *Seekers Supplyed* (1646), exposed the dangers of the Seeker movement. Other Particular Baptist literature quickly followed. In his work, *Gods Ordinance, the Saints Priviledge* (1646), John Spilsbury repudiated key teachings of the Seekers. Likewise, the Particular Baptist, Hanserd Knollys (ca. 1609-91), exposed Seeker doctrine, with his powerful, biblical responses appearing in *The Shining of a Flaming-fire in Zion* (1646), and *Christ Exalted: A Lost Sinner Sought and Saved by Christ* (1646). Since Seekers rejected the use of confessions of faith, there is significant doctrinal and practical variation among those identified with the movement. Although the Seekers generally kept a low profile, many modern authors have attempted to depict well-known individuals, such as Oliver Cromwell (1599-1658), John Milton (1608-74), and Roger Williams (ca. 1603-83), as displaying Seeker traits. With growing numbers of Seekers becoming Quakers, the Seeker movement gradually went out of existence.

The Quaker Movement

The earliest devotees of the Quaker sect used the name

---

[228] See J. F. McGregor, "Seekers and Ranters," in *Radical Religion in the English Revolution*, ed. J. F. McGregor and B. Reay (Oxford: Oxford University Press, 1984), 121-39; and Robert J. Acheson, "Happy Seeker, Happy Finder: The Seekers," in *Radical Puritans in England 1550-1660* (New York: Longman, 1993), 61-64.

"Friends of the Truth." They later changed their name to the "Society of Friends." Even though many Friends were of Puritan and Presbyterian families, they apostatized under heretical influences, such as the extreme antinomianism found in translated works of the Family of Love, or Dutch Familism.[229] The Familists believed that every man possesses a divine spirit that can elevate him to a state of perfection.[230] Refusing the use of creeds or confessions, Quaker leaders expressed no essential interest in cardinal Scripture doctrines, such as the Trinity and Christology. To the present day, there has been no uniform, doctrinal belief system among Quakers. Rejecting church ordinances as dead forms, Quaker leaders internalized baptism and the Lord's Supper. They explained terms such as *resurrection* and *judgment* as a state of mind, whereby heaven is in the heart and hell is in the conscience.[231] The founder of the Friends, George Fox (1624–90), testifies that it was Justice Bennett at Derby, in 1650, "who was the first that called us Quakers, because I bade him tremble at the word of the Lord." Since "the Friends themselves were sometimes given to trembling," it was suitable that the name came into general use.[232]

Born in Leicestershire, Fox was the son of a weaver. There is no record of any formal education. As a child, he became an apprentice to a shoemaker and wool merchant. Contemplative by nature, Fox, at the age of nineteen, turned away from all organized religion and set out on a wandering pilgrimage,

---

[229] As a movement, the Familist sect, founded in Friesland by Hendrik Niclaes (ca. 1502–80), had become nearly defunct, but individual Familists had been immigrating into England since 1560.

[230] Samuel Rutherford, *A Survey of the Spiritual Antichrist: Opening the Secrets of Familism and Antinomianism* (London: J. D. & R. I. for Andrew Crooke, 1648). Rutherford exposes the Familists and Antinomians who had infiltrated England's Army during the Civil Wars.

[231] Hugh Barbour, *The Quakers in Puritan England* (New Haven: Yale University Press, 1964), 94–126; and Thomas D. Hamm, *The Quakers in America* (New York: Columbia University Press, 2003).

[232] See George Fox, *An Autobiography*, ed. Rufus M. Jones, with introduction and notes (Philadelphia: Ferris and Leach, 1909), 125–26n4. Groaning and quaking were common practices among Quakers; see T. L. Underwood, *Primitivism, Radicalism, and the Lamb's War: The Baptist-Quaker Conflict in Seventeenth-Century England* (Oxford: Oxford University Press, 1997), 94.

detailed in an autobiographical journal that constitutes the best account of early Quakerism. Believing that organized Christendom was in a state of apostasy, Fox began preaching in 1647. He was soon claiming direct mystical revelation as his inspired authority: "Now the Lord God opened to me by His invisible power that every man was enlightened by the divine Light of Christ."[233]

A personal discovery of one's "inward light," followed by obedience to that light, became at once the central teaching of Quakerism. In Quaker doctrine, no one is born with the light, but everyone receives the light. There is no imputation of Adam's sin. The mystical light is the source of immediate revelation. It is the basis of every person's possession of justification. In Quaker teachings, the universal light, also called "Jesus," "Christ," or "Spirit," provides personal oneness with deity. Experiential revelation supplements the "dead letter" of Scripture—viewed by the sect's major apologists as mere paper and ink. For the Quakers, immediate revelation is "the only sure, certain, and unmovable foundation of all Christian faith."[234] Believing that Scripture is *a* witness to the truth of inward revelation, Fox insisted that, when he preached, he possessed the same inspiration that the Scripture writers had possessed:

> I saw that Christ died for all men, and was a propitiation for all; and enlightened all men and women with his divine and saving light; and that none could be a true believer, but who believed in it. I saw that the grace of God, which brings salvation, had appeared to all men, and that the manifestation of the Spirit of God was given to every man, to profit withal. These things I did not see by the help of man, nor by the letter (though they are written in the letter), but I saw them in the light of the Lord Jesus Christ, and by his immediate Spirit and power, as did the holy men of God, by whom the Holy Scriptures were written. Yet I had no slight esteem of the Holy Scriptures, but

---

[233] *Autobiography*, 101; see also 143 and 276.
[234] Robert Barclay, *An Apology for the True Christian Divinity* (Philadelphia: Friends' Book Store, 1869), 70, 94–97, 109–10, 188ff., and passim.

> they were very precious to me, for I was in that Spirit by which they were given forth; and what the Lord opened in me, I afterwards found was agreeable to them.[235]

As a refutation to the Quaker view of Scripture, sixteen Particular Baptists, including John Spilsbury and William Kiffin, wrote *Heart-Bleedings for Professors Abominations* (1650) and included it as an appendix to the 1651 and 1652 editions of the first London Confession. Describing the Scriptures as *infallible*, the authors urge, "Dearly beloved brethren, we beg and entreat you, and every one that loves his soul, to fear and tremble at the thoughts of slighting and despising Christ and his Gospel."[236]

The Quaker movement attracted unusual attention in 1652, as Fox and his itinerants—men and women—traveled throughout every rural area of northern England preaching and converting large numbers of men, women, and children to their sect. Utilizing a designed shock factor, many of their men and women went naked in public, as a sign that they possessed the spirit of the Old Testament prophets.[237] Some Quakers burned Bibles in public to illustrate the supremacy of their inner light. The Quaker movement originated both as a mystical sect and as a societal and political force against servile occupations, high rents from heavy-handed proprietors, and state-imposed tithes for the support of the state church.

---

[235] George Fox, *A Journal or Historical Account of the Life, Travels, Sufferings, Christian Experiences, and Labor of Love*, 6th ed. in 2 vols. (Leeds: Anthony Pickard, 1836), 1:112–13. This edition of the autobiography is more complete than Rufus M. Jones's edition.

[236] John Spilsbury, William Kiffin, et al, *Heart-Bleedings for Professors Abominations* (London: Printed for Francis Tyton and to be sold at the three Daggers, Fleet Street, near the Inner-Temple-Gate, 1650), 11. This is in the British Library. In the General Baptists' Faith and Practice of Thirty Congregations (1651), Articles 45, 60, 61, and 75 militate against Quakerism. William L. Lumpkin, *Baptist Confessions of Faith*, 2nd rev. edition, ed. Bill J. Leonard (Valley Forge: Judson Press, 2011), 160–71.

[237] Underwood, *Primitivism, Radicalism, and the Lamb's War*, 89–90. Isaiah 20 was a warning to Israel that the Assyrians would soon take them as captives and force them to march completely naked.

During 1654–55, as Quakers turned southward in masse, they were feared by many as a fore-gleam of Jeremiah 1:14, "Out of the north an evil shall break forth upon all the inhabitants of the land."[238] Quakerism had become a national threat to the English people. Throughout their early history, Quaker adherents were passionate activists. Their influence in Cromwell's New Model Army forced him to expel many of them. As a counter to the serious Quaker threat, General Baptists of London reprinted Thomas Lover's confession, "The True Gospel-Faith" (1654), along with John Griffith's work, *A Voice from the Word of the Lord to Those Grand Imposters Called Quakers* (1654).[239] The Quakers' distribution of "slanderous" literature against the Baptists of South Wales prompted the Particular Baptist preacher, John Myles, to pin his erudite, fifty-one-page tract, *An Antidote against the Infection of the Times: Or a Faithful Watchword from Mt. Sion to Prevent the Ruin of Souls* (1656). When Particular Baptist churches began circulating Myles's tract as a confession of faith, George Fox responded with his usual arguments in *The Great Mystery of the Great Whore Pinfolded and Antichrist's Kingdom Revealed* (1659).

By the late 1650s, the Quakers' numerical strength in England exceeded that of the Baptists. Typically, Baptist church members were common folk, and, for the remainder of the seventeenth century, Quakerism stood as the foremost religious threat to General and Particular Baptist churches. Quaker men and women would not hesitate to barge into an established worship service, stand on pews, and disrupt worship by heaping verbal abuse upon the "university-bred priest." Records at Broadmead Baptist Church reveal that "in

---

[238] William Prynne, *The Quakers Unmasked* (London: Edward Thomas, 1655), 1ff. This is in the British Library, London.

[239] Thomas Lover, *The True Gospel-Faith Witnessed by the Prophets and Apostles, and Collected into Thirty Articles, presented to the World as the Present Faith and Practice of the Church of Christ* (London: Printed for Francis Smith in Flying-Horse Court in Fleet-Street, 1654). This is in the British Library. John Griffith, *A Voice from the Word of the Lord to Those Grand Imposters Called Quakers* (London: n.p., 1654). This is in the Angus Library and Archive, Regent's Park College, Oxford. Cf. "The True Gospel-Faith," Lumpkin, *Baptist Confessions of Faith*, 188–95.

the midst of the minister's sermon, they [Quakers] would, with a loud voice, cry out against them, calling them hirelings and deceivers, and they would say to the people, they must turn to the light within.... They would frequently trouble us—shaking, trembling, or quaking, like persons in a fit of the ague."[240]

Not until the wake of the Stuart Restoration, in 1660, did pacifism become a predominant trait among the Quakers. This, however, did not instantly stop their disruptive intrusions into Baptist assemblies, as revealed by Benjamin Keach (1640–1704), in his literary gem called *The Grand Imposter Discovered* (1675). Even in far-away Rhode Island Colony, Roger Williams faced the need of exposing the teachings of "the cunning Fox." Williams's treatise *George Fox Digg'd out of His Burrowes* (1676) met the challenge.[241] A new era did emerge in Quaker history, as the literary works of the movement's major apologists began to appear. These include the works of Robert Barclay (1648–90), author of *An Apology for the True Christian Divinity* (1678), and those of William Penn Jr. (1644–1718), author of *Primitive Christianity Revived* (1696). Both were friends of George Fox, and both were pacifists.

---

[240] Edward Bean Underhill, ed., *Records of a Church of Christ, Meeting in Broadmead, Bristol, 1640–1687* (London: J. Haddon for the Hanserd Knollys Society, 1847), 56; cf. 43–44. See similar cases in Edward Bean Underhill, ed., *Records of the Churches of Christ, Gathered at Fenstanton, Warboys, and Hexham, 1644–1720* (London: Haddon, Brothers, and Co. for the Hanserd Knollys Society, 1854), 120, 126, 141, 270, 273–74, 315; and Underwood, *Primitivism, Radicalism, and the Lamb's War*, 92.

[241] In *George Fox Digg'd out of His Burrowes* (Boston: John Foster, 1676), Williams uses the word *Burrowes* as a pun against the Quaker, Edward Burrough, author of the twenty-six-page, "Epistle to the Reader," in George Fox, *The Great Mistery of the Great Whore Unfolded: and Antichrist's Kingdom Revealed unto Destruction* (London: Printed for Thomas Simmons, 1659), no pagination. At other times, Williams uses the term in the sense of a sinister tunnel of words used for hiding the true meaning of Quaker doctrine: As Williams puts it, "G. Fox runs into his *Burrough* of the many *significations* of the word *Light* ..., willingly ignorant that Christ Jesus as Mediator ... enlightens none but those whom his Father *gives* him" (330). Later, Williams finds G. Fox "in the Burrough of the Arminians" (474). For Williams's *George Fox Digg'd*, I am using the copy in Harvard University Library, and for Fox's *Great Mistery*, I am using the copy in Duke University Library.

Due to an enormous debt owed to Penn's father, the late Navy Admiral, William Penn Sr., King Charles II granted a large proprietorship of land in the New World to Penn Jr. On that land, in 1681, William Penn Jr. established the Colony of Pennsylvania. Defending Fox's appeal to "general experience," Penn's "Holy Experiment," the Colony of Pennsylvania, ironically provided a policy of toleration that would move the center of Baptist activity from New England to Pennsylvania and to neighboring colonies.[242]

The Leveller and Ranter Movements

Especially popular among England's poor and oppressed, an ephemeral movement known as the Levellers[243] emerged about 1647 within the Army of the Long Parliament. The movement derived its name from its advocacy of "leveling" all ranks of society with a distribution of wealth, absolute equality, and a socialistic, constitutional government. The dissenters' leading propagandist was a former Puritan, John Lilburne (1615–57), whose treatise, *Foundations of Freedom; or, An Agreement of the People* (1648), became the guidebook for pamphleteering and violent agitations. In the early months of the Leveller movement, many Baptists sympathized with certain of their goals, such as freedom of the press and freedom of conscience. On the other hand, most Baptists came to reject Leveller tactics for achieving their goals. By 1649, with London's Particular Baptists denouncing Leveller activism before the House of Commons,[244] Cromwell proceeded

---

[242] William Penn's *Primitive Christianity Revived, in the Faith and Practice of the People Called Quakers* (Salem, MA: George F. Read, 1844), 10.

[243] Don M. Wolfe, ed., *Leveller Manifestoes of the Puritan Revolution* (1944; repr., New York: Humanities Press, 1967); and Brian Manning, "The Levellers and Religion," in *Radical Religion in the English Revolution*, ed. J. F. McGregor and B. Reay (Oxford: Oxford University Press, 1984), 65–90. For a sympathetic and detailed study, see Theodore Calvin Pease, *The Leveller Movement: A Study in the History and Political Theory of the English Great Civil War* (Washington, DC: American Historical Association, 1916).

[244] Anne Laurence, *Parliamentary Army Chaplains, 1642–1651*, vol. 59 of Royal Historical Society Studies in History (Woodbridge, England: Boydell Press, 1990), observes that "General Baptists continued to support the political radicals after the Particular Baptists had broken with them" (84).

to dispel the radical movement, especially since Levellers had begun to embed themselves in the New Model Army. Two years prior to his death, Lilburne became a Quaker.

At the downfall of the Leveller movement, there quickly emerged an amorphous, radical group called Ranters,[245] who harangued that the Bible cannot be trusted, that sin is a natural part of the universe, and that the devil and hell do not exist. The Ranters' antinomianism ruled out all human accountability, since a mystical, pantheistic principle (god) immunizes man against any possibility of guilt. Many Ranters became Quakers. In *Heart-Bleedings for Professors' Abominations* (1650), sixteen Particular Baptists repudiated the teachings of Ranters and Quakers.[246] Five times in his autobiographic *Grace Abounding to the Chief of Sinners*,[247] John Bunyan describes the Ranters as atheistic mystics, who promote sin that grace may abound. Urgently and pointedly, Bunyan directs his treatise, *Some Gospel Truths Opened*, against the teachings of Ranters and Quakers.[248] By 1654, the Ranter sect had faded into obscurity.

The Fifth-Monarchist Movement

The seventeenth-century English Revolution that overthrew the Stuart Dynasty also sparked the rise of a radical

---

[245] See A. L. Morton, *The World of the Ranters: Religious Radicalism in the English Revolution* (London: Lawrence and Wishart, 1970). For sample teachings from a Ranter, see Jacob Bauthumley, *The Light and Dark Sides of God* (London: William Learner, 1650), 6–7; and for a sympathetic Marxist account, see Christopher Hill, *The World Turned Upside Down: Radical Ideas during the English Revolution*, 184–258, and passim. Hill's book was turned into a play at London's Royal National Theatre.

[246] See also Underhill, ed., *Records of the Churches of Christ, Gathered at Fenstanton, Warboys, and Hexham*, 90–91n7.

[247] *Grace Abounding to the Chief of Sinners, in a Faithful Account of the Life and Death of John Bunyan* (New York: M. W. Dodd, 1844), 26–27, 76.

[248] John Bunyan, *Some Gospel Truths Opened*, in *The Whole Works of John Bunyan*, 3 vols., ed. George Offor, with prefaces, notes, and biography of Bunyan (London: Blackie and Son, 1855), 2:141–75. In the same work, see *Some Questions to Quakers*, 2:175, and *A Vindication of Gospel Truths Opened*, 2:176–214.

group called the Fifth Monarchists,[249] consisting of a peaceful wing and a violent wing. All of them believed that God was calling them to prepare the world for the immediate return of King Jesus. From Daniel 2:31–45 and Daniel 7:1–28, they saw the five monarchies prophesied: (1) the Assyrian/Babylonian Empire; (2) the Persian Empire; (3) the Grecian Empire; (4) the Roman Empire; and (5) Christ's millennial/eternal Kingdom. The monarchial power of the Roman Empire had satanically survived within the papal power of the Roman Church. Convinced that Protestant churches had themselves apostatized after breaking Roman Catholicism's power, violent Fifth Monarchists felt compelled to complete the Reformation by initiating Messiah's reign. Imagining themselves to be "the saints of the most high," to whom "the kingdom under the whole heaven … shall be given" (Daniel 7:27), the violent wing stood determined to inaugurate *its* Fifth Monarchy — by force if necessary. Extreme Fifth Monarchists found inspiration from a popular series of "Bloody Almanacs" that mixed astrology with Scripture.[250] Included among the violent and the peaceful were individuals from among Quakers, Independents, Anabaptists, and Baptists. While Baptist leaders refused to promote violence, some promoted peaceful, though at times misguided, ways to "hasten the kingdom." Typically, whenever any Baptist seemed to suggest violence, his peers would at once rebuke and shun him.

---

[249] Helpful studies include Bernard S. Capp, *The Fifth Monarchy Men: A Study in Seventeenth-century English Millenarianism* (London: Faber and Faber, 1972); and Mark R. Bell, *Apocalypse How? Baptist Movements during the English Revolution* (Macon, GA: Mercer University Press, 2000).

[250] E. g., John Booker, *The Bloody Almanack* (London: n.p., 1643); and these three by John Napier, *The Bloody Almanack Foretelling Many Certaine Predictions Which Shall Come to Passe this Present Yeare 1647: With a Calculation Concerning the Time of the Day of Judgement* (London: n.p., 1647); idem, *The Bloudy Almanack, or, Englands Looking-glass: Containing the Scots Prophesie to Their King, in Relation to the Crown, and the Present Proceedings of the English Army, with Divers Excellent Astrological Predictions for the Year, 1651* (London: n.p., 1651); idem, *The Dutch Bloudy Almanack Conteyning the Exact Astrologicall Predictions, for the Yeare of Our Lord 1653* (London: n.p., 1653).

During the decade of the Fifth-Monarchist movement — from the Commonwealth and its Rump Parliament (1649-53) to the end of Cromwell's Protectorate (1653-59) — the movement at first supported the Commonwealth, but soon turned against it for its lack of progress in setting up New Jerusalem. Far more successful than the Seekers, Levellers, and Ranters, the militant Fifth Monarchists heavily infiltrated churches and often found their strongest promoters among the various dissenter groups.[251] For instance, two notorious Seventh-day Baptists,[252] John Spittlehouse (fl. 1643-56) and John More (fl. 1650-1702), became major pamphleteers for the Fifth-Monarchist movement, calling for the abolition of the existing government. Spittlehouse wrote in defense of Fifth Monarchists in numerous works, including *A Warning Piece Discharged* (1653) and *Certaine Queries Propounded* (1654).[253] John More defended them in tracts, such as *The Trumpet Sounded: Or, the Great Mystery of the Two Little Horns Unfolded* (1654). In their *Vindication of the Continued Succession of the Primitive Church of Jesus Christ* (1652), Spittlehouse and More apply erratic Fifth-Monarchist interpretations of Scripture to historical people and events. For example, they argue that the Reformation churches had all apostatized during Martin Luther's lifetime. They regard Thomas Müntzer (d. 1525), the mystic activist in the German Peasants' War (1525), as among a hidden company of "Champions of the truth," symbolized in Revelation

---

[251] The 142 signatures on the Fifth-Monarchist *Declaration of Several of the Churches of Christ, and Godly People in and about the Citie of London* (London: Livewell Chapman, 1654) include *John Spittlehouse* and *John Clark*. This copy is in the British Library, London. No one has provided proof of this being the John Clarke who immigrated to Newport, Rhode Island. There were large numbers of Clarks in England.

[252] See William Saller and John Spittlehouse, *An Appeal to the Consciences of the Chief Magistrates of This Commonwealth, Touching the Sabbath-day* (London: Printed for the authors, 1657). On the title page, the authors explain that they are writing "in the behalf of themselves and several others, who think themselves obliged to observe the seventh day of the week." Saller died ca. 1680. This copy is in the British Library, London.

[253] Spittlehouse, *Certaine Queries Propounded to the Most Serious Consideration of Those Persons Now in Power* (London: Printed for Livewell Chapman in Popes-head Alley, 1654). This is in the British Library, London.

12:6 as the woman who fled into the "wilderness of obscurity" for 1260 days.[254] Interpreting the woman to be the true church, and counting each day as a year, Spittlehouse and More calculate that the true church began emerging from the wilderness about three years prior to Luther's death.[255] The authors expect Christ to appear at once to restore His church and its true baptism that had been lost "from about the year 406 unto this present time."[256]

In the face of societal chaos, Cromwell dissolved the Rump Parliament, in April 1653, and replaced it with the Barebone Parliament, often called the "Parliament of Saints." The Barebone Parliament quickly became so heavily dominated by Fifth Monarchists that it epitomized the radicalism of the era.[257] Praisegod Barebone served on the Committee for a New Body of Law, based largely upon Fifth-Monarchist applications of Old Testament regulations structured for Israel. The

---

[254] John Spittlehouse and John More, *Vindication of the Continued Succession of the Primitive Church of Jesus Christ (Now Scandalously Termed Anabaptists) from the Apostles unto This Present Time* (London: Gartrude Dawson for the authors, 1652). For Müntzer, see 14–15, 29–30; I am using the 1652 manuscript at the American Baptist Historical Society, Atlanta, GA. As far as I can tell, this is the only extant copy. See "Müntzer, Thomas (1488/9–1525)," in Harold S. Bender, et al., eds., *Mennonite Encyclopedia: Comprehensive Reference Work on the Anabaptist-Mennonite Movement* (Hillsboro, KS: Mennonite Brethren Publishing House, 1957), 3:785–89, 5:607–9, ed. Cornelius J. Dyck and Dennis Martin (Scottdale, PA: Herald Press, 1990); see also Thomas Müntzer, "Exposition of the Second Chapter of Daniel the Prophet Preached at the Castle of Allstedt before the Active and Amiable Dukes and Administrators of Saxony," in *Spiritual and Anabaptist Writers: Documents Illustrative of the Radical Reformation*, ed. George H. Williams (Philadelphia: The Westminster Press, 1957), 47–70.

[255] In similar manner, James R. Graves (1820–93) equates the woman of Revelation 12:6 with Baptist churches: "And the woman [church of Christ] fled into the wilderness [obscurity] where she hath a place prepared by God, that there they may nourish her a thousand two hundred and threescore days [each day representing a year]," in *Old Landmarkism: What Is It?* (Memphis: Baptist Book House, 1880), 166. Graves interprets Revelation 11:3 the same way.

[256] Spittlehouse and More, *Vindication*, 1–16. Pages 17–20 of this thirty-page treatise are missing.

[257] Tai Liu, "Saints in Power: A Study of the Barebones Parliament" (PhD diss., Indiana University, 1969).

Barebone Parliament voluntarily dissolved in December, and, within a few days, Cromwell's Protectorate emerged to restore order and stability to the realm. When Cromwell accepted the title "Lord Protector," Fifth-Monarchist extremists immediately dubbed him an anti-Christ and began plotting to kill him. There is no evidence, however, that Praisegod Barebone ever participated in any plot, and, for that reason, Fifth Monarchists attacked the Barebone home on multiple occasions.[258] With dangerous dissenters erratically realigning their allegiances within a shifting political spectrum, Baptist leaders were compelled to vindicate their people against charges of Fifth-Monarchist militancy. General Baptists, for instance, published an excellent work called *The Humble Representation and Vindication* (1655). Its twenty-five signees include the prominent Thomas Lamb.[259] In 1657, when Cromwell began receiving offers to accept the English Crown, extreme Fifth Monarchists charged that he would be accepting a crown that belonged only to King Jesus. When evidence of a plot to murder Cromwell was uncovered on April 9, 1657, many Fifth-Monarchist leaders faced imprisonment in the Tower—a measure that was lenient for the times, since English law required death.

Upon the Restoration of the Stuart Dynasty, in 1660, scores of Particular and General Baptists united in signing and publishing apologetical petitions, dissociating themselves from all radical dissenters, especially the infamous Thomas Venner (ca. 1608–61), who had already led an attempted coup against Cromwell. In the earliest such document, called *The Humble Apology of Some Commonly Called Anabaptists* (1660) and "presented to the KINGS most Excellent MAJESTY," Baptists described it as a "*Protestation* against the late wicked and most

---

[258] After the Restoration, Barebone suffered imprisonment during 1661–62.

[259] *The Humble Representation and Vindication*, "of many of the Messengers, Elders, and Brethren, belonging to several of the Baptized Churches in this Nation, of and concerning their Opinions and Resolutions touching the Civil Government of these Nations, and of their Deportment under the same: together with a Cautionary word from two of the Messengers to their Brethren, to bespeak their peaceable subjection to the present Government" (London: Printed for Francis Smith, 1655), 4, and title page. This copy is in the Union Theological Seminary Library, NYC.

horrid treasonable *Insurrection* and *Rebellion* acted in the City of LONDON."[260] Authored by William Kiffin, the Apology insists, "We who are falsely called Anabaptists" are "as ready to obey our Civil Magistrates, as to profess our subjection to them in all lawful Commands." Moreover, "whatever the Magistrate is in point of Religion, he is to be reverenced and obeyed in all those commands of his, which do not entrench upon, or rise up in opposition to the commands of God."[261] Particular Baptist signees of *The Humble Apology* included the eminent John Spilsbury. General Baptist signees included Thomas Lamb. A Particular Baptist, Henry Hills, printed the document, and a General Baptist, Francis Smith, sold it in his shop. Emphatically, these Baptists were united in affirming "that all people in every nation," as well as "members of Churches … ought for conscience sake to honor such as by the wise disposing providence of God are their Rulers, and are to submit to the Civil Commands, not only of such Rulers as are faithful, but even to infidels."[262]

As many had anticipated, Venner, the last leader of the Fifth Monarchists, led an attempted insurrection to overthrow King Charles II. Although there had been many Fifth-Monarchy sympathizers using militate language, Venner and his personal activists stood virtually alone in the use of physical violence. His extremist followers included individuals from five small Independent and Anabaptist congregations in and near London's Coleman Street. Venner led one of these churches. On

---

[260] *The Humble Apology of Some Commonly Called Anabaptists,* "in behalf of themselves and others of the same judgment with them: with their Protestation against the late wicked and most horrid treasonable Insurrection and Rebellion acted in the City of London: together with an Apology formerly presented to the Kings Most Excellent Majesty" (London: Henry Hills, to be sold by Francis Smith, at the sign of the Elephant and Castle without Temple-Bar, 1660), title page. The name "William Kiffin" heads the list of thirty signatories. Others include "John Spilsbery" and "Thomas Lamb" (14). This is in the British Library, London.

[261] Ibid., 17.

[262] Ibid., 18. I modernized the spelling of a couple of words. See also Edward Bean Underhill, ed., *Confessions of Faith,* 343–52. Underhill includes two similar apologies on pages 353–60.

the evening of Sunday January 6, 1661, Venner and his armed band (around fifty men) marched in the name of "King Jesus" from the meetinghouse toward St. Paul's Cathedral, to inaugurate the millennium. They were soundly defeated. Twenty of them, including Venner, went on trial for high treason. On January 19, Thomas Venner was hanged, drawn, and quartered outside his Swan Alley meetinghouse.[263]

Such then is the politico-religious landscape of the life and ministry of the Independent, Henry Jessey, who, in 1637, had become pastor of the J-L-J Church, the womb of the earliest Particular Baptist churches. Jessey would become an immersionist.

Henry Jessey (1601–63) — Third J-L-J Pastor

Henry Jessey was born at West Rounton, Yorkshire. His Oxford-trained father was the local rector, faithfully preaching the gospel here until his death in 1623. Following his home schooling, Henry enrolled at St. John's College, Cambridge, at the age of seventeen. By the end of his first four years at Cambridge, it had pleased the Lord to renew Henry's heart, "through the effectual working of His Holy Spirit in the Ministry of the Word."[264] Thus, Jessey "was fitted for the employment for which God designed him."[265] With strong Puritan convictions and a decisive call to the ministry, he received his BA in 1623. In 1626–27, he received his MA and his Anglican ordination.

---

[263] See Charles E. Banks, "Thomas Venner, the Boston Wine-Cooper and Fifth Monarchy Man," *New England Historical and Genealogical Register* 47 (October 1893): 437–44; Champlin Burrage, "The Fifth Monarchy Insurrections," *The English Historical Review* 25, no. 100 (October 1910): 722–47; and A. J. D. Farrar, "The Fifth Monarchy Movement," *Transactions of the Baptist Historical Society* 2, no. 3 (May 1911): 166–81.

[264] Edward Whiston, *The Life and Death of Mr. Henry Jessey, Late Preacher of the Gospel of Christ in London* (London: n.p., 1671), 3. This is in the Union Theological Seminary Library, NYC.

[265] Edmund Calamy and Samuel Palmer, *The Nonconformist's Memorial: Being an Account of the Lives, Sufferings, and Printed Works of the Two Thousand Ministers Ejected from the Church of England, Chiefly by the Act of Uniformity, Aug. 24, 1662*, 2nd ed., 3 vols. (London: J. Cundee for Button and Son and for T. Hurst, 1802–3), 1:129 (1:129–35).

Already proficient in Greek and Latin, Jessey remained at Cambridge until he became proficient in Hebrew and able to read Syriac and Chaldee. While pursuing his education, Jessey developed a passion for distributing gospel literature and practical books to the poor. For refusing to use the prescribed ceremonies in the *Book of Common Prayer* and for removing a crucifix from his church in Aughton (Yorkshire), Jessey quickly stood ejected from the Anglican ministry, in 1633, for non-conformity. Forced into separatism by state-church intolerance, he moved to London in 1635 and joined the Jacob-Lathrop Church, meeting in London's Swan Alley off Coleman Street.[266] Within two years, Jessey was making plans to sail to New England as a church planter. The J-L-J congregation, without a pastor since Lathrop's voyage to New England, finally persuaded Jessey, in 1637, to cancel his plans and become their pastor. Although he never married, Jessey loved children, and, over the span of a twenty-five-year pastorate, he would set aside time to write children's literature, such as his *Catechisme for Babes, or, Little Ones* (1652),[267] in addition to his numerous doctrinal works.

As the J-L-J congregation increased considerably in size, during the 1630s, a significant number of their members began holding church in private homes. Even as loosely-knit, Independent churches, they maintained an essential bond of fellowship. Some were becoming Baptists. During the years 1633–38, the Particular Baptists, under the leadership of John Spilsbury, had organized their earliest church, and it was committed to credo (believer's) baptism as the only true baptism by water. Meanwhile, for their safety and convenience, the growing J-L-J Church, in May 1640, divided "by mutual consent" into two separate congregations—one led by Praisegod Barebone and the other by Henry Jessey. Barebone chided

---

[266] Underhill, ed., *Records of the Churches of Christ, Gathered at Fenstanton, Warboys, and Hexham*, 345–51, 345n6. This correspondence with the Hexham church confirms that Jessey's church was on Swan Alley, Coleman Street. Hanserd Knollys's Particular Baptist church was also located on Coleman Street for a time (313, 334).

[267] Henry Jessey, *A Catechisme for Babes, or, Little Ones* (London: Printed by Henry Hills, 1652). This is in the Union Theological Seminary Library, NYC.

Baptists for what he regarded as an unauthorized return to credo immersion without a "warrant from heaven," such as that of John the Baptist.[268] Jessey, on the other hand, chose to receive immersion, in June 1645, from the Particular Baptist, Hanserd Knollys.

In New England, in 1644, the Massachusetts General Court had recently issued an order to exile any person found preaching against infant baptism. Upon learning of this law, Henry Jessey, in 1645, seven days prior to his own baptism by immersion, penned a letter to the magisterial, Puritan churches of New England, pleading with them to cease from their "smiting of fellow servants," which is "persecution for conscience sake." Jessey's letter testifies that he and sixteen others had come to embrace immersion after studying and praying for long hours and many days until they received God's perfect peace with the baptistic position.[269] Jessey then wrote to his friend, Governor John Winthrop Sr. in behalf of persecuted Baptists in New England.[270]

Although he used immersion, Jessey continued practicing pedobaptism. Particular Baptists stood in hearty agreement with Jessey's theology and soteriology, but they could not embrace his ecclesiology. Like his close friend, John Bunyan (1628–88), Jessey offered open membership and open Communion without the prerequisite of baptism. Like Bunyan, for the remainder of his life Jessey would allow non-immersed individuals to remain in full standing on the church rolls. The earliest Particular Baptists allowed only professing believers who had received immersion to partake of the Lord's Supper. Their first London Confession (1646 ed.) requires it (Art. 39). While Henry Jessey maintained fellowship with Particular Baptists, his name does not appear among the signees of any

---

[268] Praisegod Barebone, *A Discourse Tending to Prove the Baptisme* (London: R. Oulton and G. Dexter and to be sold by Benjamin Allen, 1642), 6–7. This is in the Yale University Library.

[269] Jessey's letters are transcribed in P. J. Anderson, "Letters of Henry Jessey and John Tombes to the Churches of New England, 1645," *Baptist Quarterly* 28, no. 1 (January 1979): 30–40.

[270] "Henry Jacie to John Winthrop," in *Winthrop Papers 1645–1649* (Boston: Massachusetts Historical Society, 1947), 5:204–5.

edition of the first London Confession. Perhaps the most famous refutation of open Communion came from the pen of Particular Baptist, William Kiffin, in his book, *A Sober Discourse of Right to Church-Communion* (1681).[271] Not until the late nineteenth century, would large numbers of English Baptists discontinue the prerequisite of believer's baptism by immersion for membership and the Lord's Supper. Surrendering the defining prerequisite for which Baptist pioneers had suffered, many would forfeit any honest use of the name *Baptist*.

It is only within the following span of events in Jessey's life that we can best understand the crucial issues that always encompassed his ministry and influence. Jessey had remained a faithful friend of Parliament, during the Civil Wars of 1642–48. Throughout the 1650s, he traveled widely and preached in dozens of Independent and Baptist churches. Striving for Jesus' coming as King of Kings, Jessey joined a group of Independent ministers and Particular Baptists, including John Spilsbury and Hanserd Knollys, in signing a 1657 letter, respectfully urging Oliver Cromwell to refuse the English Crown.[272] Jessey sympathized with a few individuals of the moderate wing of the Fifth-Monarchy movement, but he never advocated violence. He kept in close fellowship with many of Cromwell's Baptist supporters, such as the well-known William Kiffin. Collecting money for the relief of distressed Jews in Jerusalem, Jessey longed to hasten Israel's conversion, an event that many considered necessary for Christ's Second Advent. In addition to promoting John Eliot's missionary work among the Indians of

---

[271] William Kiffin, *A Sober Discourse of Right to Church-Communion* (London: Printed by George Larkin for Enoch Prosser, 1681), title page, "wherein is proved by scripture, the example of primitive times, and the practice of all that have professed the Christian religion that no unbaptized person may be regularly admitted to the Lord's Supper." The work endeavors to refute the open Communion and open membership practices of John Bunyan. I slightly modernized some capitalization and punctuation. This is in the Union Theological Seminary Library, NYC.

[272] Barrington White, "Knollys, Hanserd (c. 1599–1691)," in *Biographical Dictionary of British Radicals in the Seventeenth Century*, 2:160–62; idem, "Henry Jessey in the Great Rebellion," in *Reformation, Conformity and Dissent*, ed. R. Buick Knox (London: Epworth Press, 1977), 132–53.

New England,[273] Jessey challenged every disciple of Jesus to obey "the Grand Commission and Institution"[274] of Matthew 28:19. Since 1290, an Edict of Expulsion (issued by Edward I), forcing all Jews from England, had remained in force. Jessey's penchant was to see the edict annulled and to begin preparing the way for Jews to return to England. He advanced public proposals for readmitting Jews and granting them rights of citizenship and free trade. At last, in 1656, Oliver Cromwell annulled the anti-Semitic edict and officially allowed Jewish immigration.[275] In his later years, Jessey, with four or five likeminded friends, privately observed the Jewish Sabbath, but he conducted all his church services on Sunday, and he never

---

[273] Richard W. Cogley, *John Eliot's Mission to the Indians before King Philip's War* (Cambridge, MA: Harvard University Press, 1999), 207.

[274] Henry Jessey, *A Storehouse of Provision, to Further Resolution in Severall Cases of Conscience, and Questions Now in Dispute* (London: Charles Sumptner for T. Brewster and G. Moule, 1650), 59. Jessey explains that the Commission's baptism is "a dipping" of new disciples "in water, in or unto the name of the Father, the Son, and the Holy Ghost" (57–65); see also 51–103. This is in the Union Theological Seminary Library, NYC. Jessey's descriptive term *Grand* Commission was already becoming a common term among Baptists. In 1641, for example, Edward Barber had utilized the term *Great Commission*, in his *Small Treatise of Baptism* (page 4), the first Baptist defense of baptism by immersion. This is in the British Library. Baptist pastor John Norcott, immediate successor to John Spilsbury in London, uses the term *Great Commission*, in his *Baptism Discovered Plainly and Faithfully, according to the Word of God*, 2nd ed. (London: Printed for the author and sold by Benjamin Harris, 1675), table of contents. This is in the Boston Public Library.

[275] A quiet man called "Jacob the Jew" was already in England. His story is noteworthy. The famous Oxford antiquarian, Anthony Wood, recalls in his diary the constant bickering that he had witnessed between Presbyterians and Independents. The two groups seemed never to have sat down for discussion. Wood reveals the reason: "We had no coffee houses." The remedy arrived in Oxford (1651) when Jacob the Jew opened Angel Inn—the first coffee house in England. Pro-Catholic Charles II briefly silenced this free flow of ideas when he issued "A Proclamation for the Suppression of Coffee-Houses" (1675). See Andrew Clark, *The Life and Times of Anthony Wood, Antiquary, of Oxford, 1632–1695*, collected from his diaries and papers (Oxford: Clarendon Press for the Oxford Historical Society, 1891), 1:299.

attempted to impose Sabbatarianism upon anyone.[276]

For years, Jessey worked feverishly on a translation project, attempting to replace the King James Version with a more accurate one. Although the translation was never published, Jessey served as a key member of a team of scholars that produced *An English-Greek Lexicon, Containing the Derivations, and Various Significations of All the Words in the New Testament* (1661).[277] In the wake of Oliver Cromwell's death in 1658 and Richard Cromwell's abdication the following year, the inauguration of Charles II (1660–85) marked the Restoration of the Stuarts and their unmerciful retaliation toward dissenters. Jessey promptly addressed the nation's predicament with *The Lord's Loud Call to England* (1660),[278] a summons to national repentance. After some eighteen months of imprisonment (1661–63), Jessey went to his grave believing that the Restoration would be only a temporary bump in the road toward the millennium. Henry Jessey was buried in London's Bunhill Fields—graveyard of dissenters. His portrait, engraved by James Caldwall, is in *The Nonconformist's Memorial*. Although the exact location of his tombstone is unknown, a translated copy of its Latin epitaph reads:

> From storms of dangers, and from seas of grief
> Safe landed, *Jessey* finds a blest relief.
> The grave's soft bed his sacred dust contains,

---

[276] Whiston, *The Life and Death of Mr. Henry Jessey*, 67–69, 87–88. Jessey's attitude toward "Seventh-day men" was like that of Hanserd Knollys. While insisting that the first day of the week is the only proper day of Christian worship, Knollys maintained personal fellowship with some of the Seventh-day Particular Baptists. Knollys also presided over the ordination of the Seventh-day Particular Baptist Joseph Stennett. See R. L. Greaves, "Stennett, Joseph (1663–1713)," in *Biographical Dictionary of British Radicals in the Seventeenth Century*, 3:204–6; and Bryan W. Ball, *The Seventh-day Men: Sabbatarians and Sabbatarianism in England and Wales, 1600–1800* (Oxford: Clarendon Press, 1994), 111–12, 120.

[277] Printed for Lodowick Lloyd, next to the Castle in Cornhill, 1661. There is a good copy at Union Theological Seminary Library (NYC).

[278] Henry Jessey, *The Lord's Loud Call to England: Being a True Relation of Some Late, Various and Wonderful Judgments, or Handy-works of God, by Earthquake, Lightening, etc.* (London: L. Chapman and Francis Smith, 1660). This is in the British Library, London.

And with its God the soul in bliss remains.

Faith was his bark, incessant prayer his oars,
And hope his gale, that from these mortal shores
Through death's rough wave to heaven his spirit bore,
To enjoy his triumph, and, to sigh no more.[279]

The Emergence of the Earliest Particular Baptist Churches

While the broad portrait of English Particular Baptist history unfolds in a perspicuous manner, the precise details of the earliest period (1630–44) are sometimes difficult to reconstruct. The key reasons for this phenomenon include (1) the limited number of original documents; (2) the incompleteness of key sources; and (3) the sporadic appearance of tenable contradictions among the Jessey Church Records,[280] the William Kiffin Manuscript,[281] and various sources from Hanserd Knollys.

---

[279] John Andrew Jones, ed., *Bunhill Memorials: Sacred Reminiscences of Three Hundred Ministers and Other Persons of Note, Who Are Buried in Bunhill Fields, of Every Denomination, with the Inscriptions on Their Tombs and Gravestones, and Other Historical Information Respecting Them, from Authentic Sources* (London: James Paul, 1849), 116ff. Cf. Calamy and Palmer, *Nonconformist's Memorial*, 1:134; and "Henry Jessey, M.A., 1601–1663: A Puritan Versed in Scripture," *The Gospel Magazine* (November 1963): 488–92.

[280] The "So-called Jessey Records or Memoranda," Record No. 1 of documents compiled and edited by Benjamin Stinton (1676–1719), in *A Repository of Diverse Historical Matters Relating to the English Antipedobaptists, Collected from Original Papers or Faithful Extracts* (1712), in *The Early English Dissenters in the Light of Recent Research (1550–1641)*, ed. Champlin Burrage, 2:292–302. The original manuscript is in the Angus Library and Archive, Regent's Park College, Oxford.

[281] While the original manuscript apparently no longer exists, a copy from the early 1700s resides in the Angus Library and Archive, Regent's Park College, Oxford. For a transcript, see the "So-called Kiffin Manuscript," Record No. 2 of documents compiled and edited by Benjamin Stinton, in *A Repository of Diverse Historical Matters Relating to the English Antipedobaptists, Collected from Original Papers or Faithful Extracts* (1712), in *Early English Dissenters*, ed. Burrage, 2:302–5. Concluding that Kiffin may have authored the original manuscript, Barrington R. White includes a transcript in his article, "Baptist Beginnings and the Kiffin Manuscript,"

Those documents are known as the "Jessey," "Kiffin," and "Knollys" memoranda,[282] not necessarily because these men were the primary authors, but because they were the probable owners of the originals. Such records, beginning in the early 1600s, provide the earliest accounts leading to a unified Baptist standardization of the practice of baptism by immersion. While historians generally agree to disagree on minor details, the following consideration of the data offers a chronological arrangement and a historical framework for ongoing studies in this fascinating era of our Baptist heritage.

From the beginning of John Lathrop's 1632 imprisonment to the beginning of Henry Jessey's pastorate in 1637, the J-L-J Church had been without pastoral leadership. During that time, individuals and small groups had been leaving the J-L-J Church for three primary reasons. First, the congregation had increased in such numbers that their gatherings were too conspicuous for their safety. Second, many in the church had abandoned the separatist stance of its founder, Henry Jacob. Without a pastor, some non-separatist members now had no qualm about taking their infants into the parish churches for baptism.[283] Third, many Separatist members embraced Baptist

---

Baptist History and Heritage 2, no. 1 (January 1967): 27–37. See also White's two valuable articles: "Who Really Wrote the Kiffin Manuscript?" *Baptist History and Heritage* 1, no. 3 (October 1966): 3–10; and "William Kiffin — Baptist Pioneer and Citizen of London," *Baptist History and Heritage* 2, no. 2 (July 1967): 91–103 + 126.

[282] These documents are also in the *Transactions of the Baptist Historical Society*, collected with notes by W. T. Whitley: "Benjamin Stinton and his Baptist Friends," 1, no. 4 (January 1910): 193–96; "Stinton's Historical Researches," 1, no. 4 (January 1910): 197–202; "Records of the Jacob-Lathorp-Jessey Church, 1616–1641," 1, no. 4 (January 1910): 203–25; "Rise of Particular Baptists in London, 1633–1644," 1, no. 4 (January 1910): 226–36; "Debate on Infant Baptism, 1643," 1, no. 4 (January 1910): 237–45; and "The Jacob-Jessey Church, 1616–1678," 1, no. 4 (January 1910): 246–56.

[283] Separatists feared also that these same individuals might soon consider it befitting to go to the Anglican churches for their weddings and funerals. Henry Jacob had clearly relegated weddings and funerals to civil authorities, since the Roman Church had corrupted them into sacraments. As to ecclesiastics officiating at weddings and funerals, Jacob had insisted that there is not "so much as one example of any such practice in the whole Book of God" (A Confession and Protestation

tenets and abhorred the church's embrace of infant baptism. One such group, led by "its minister," John Spilsbury (ca. 1593–1668), left the J-L-J Church on friendly terms, and, on September 12, 1633, constituted a distinct church—the first recorded, organized Particular Baptist church. Disavowing their infant baptism, "most or all of them received a new baptism":

> There was *a congregation of Protestant Dissenters of the independent Persuasion* in London, gathered in the year 1616, whereof Mr. Henry Jacob was the first pastor; and after him succeeded Mr. John Lathorp, who was their minister at this time. In this society several persons, *finding that the congregation kept not to their first principle of separation*, and being also convinced that baptism was not to be administered to infants, but such only as professed faith in Christ, desired that they might be dismissed from that communion, and allowed to form a distinct congregation, in such order as was most agreeable to their own sentiments.
>
> The church, considering that they were now grown very numerous, and so more than could in these times of persecution conveniently meet together, and believing also that those persons acted from a principle of conscience and not obstinacy, agreed to allow them the liberty they desired, and that they should be constituted a distinct church; which was performed the 12th of Sept. 1633. And as they believed that baptism was not rightly administered to infants, so they looked upon the baptism they had received in that age as invalid: whereupon most or all of them received a new baptism. Their minister was Mr. John Spilsbury. What number they were [remains] uncertain, because in the mentioning of the names of about twenty men and women, it is added, "with divers others."[284]

---

of the Faith, Article 23).

[284] "William Kiffin Manuscript," in Thomas Crosby, *The History of the English Baptists* (London: Thomas Crosby, 1738), 1:148–49. I modernized some spelling. In favor of the 1638 date, Lofton argues that Crosby wrongly conjoined a 1633 Jessey Record to a 1638 portion of the Kiffin Manuscript. See George A. Lofton, *Defense of the Jessey Records and Kiffin Manuscript*

Early in Henry Jessey's pastorate, in 1638, increasing numbers, "being convinced that baptism was not for infants, but professed believers,"[285] were tansferring from the J-L-J Church to Spilsbury's Baptist church. Samuel Eaton, a London button-maker, had been among those incarcerated with John Lathrop. Upon Eaton's release and upon his profession of faith, he received from John Spilsbury "a further baptism,"[286] that is, his new baptism as a believer. The contemporary Anglican poet, John Taylor, author of *A Swarme of Sectaries, and Schismatiques* (1641), quips that Spilsbury had baptized Eaton "in Anabaptist fashion," which at the time was immersion.

> Also one *Spilsbery* rose up of late,
> (Who doth, or did dwell over Aldersgate) ....
> He rebaptiz'd in Anabaptist fashion
> One *Eaton* (of the new found separation)
> A zealous Button maker, grave and wise,
> And gave him orders, others to baptize.[287]

Eaton also received ordination into the eldership of Spilsbury's church. For his Baptist convictions, in 1639, Eaton died in Newgate Prison, leaving two small children and his faithful wife, Elizabeth, who was pregnant with twins. Assaulted by an official, Elizabeth lost the twins in a miscarriage.[288]

(Nashville: Marshall and Bruce, 1899), 19, passim. On the other hand, Crosby, as a son-in-law of Benjamin Keach (1640–1704), could have had access to manuscripts or manuscript fragments that have since been lost. If that is the case, Crosby has accurately used the 1633 date. We may never know. Crosby did make some minor mistakes.

[285] "Rise of Particular Baptists in London, 1633–1644," *Transactions of the Baptist Historical Society* 1, no. 4 (January 1910): 231.

[286] "Records of the Jacob-Lathorp-Jessey Church, 1616–1641," *Transactions of the Baptist Historical Society* 1, no. 4 (January 1910): 220.

[287] Taylor, John, *A Swarme of Sectaries, and Schismatiques* (London: n.p., 1641), 6–7. This copy is in the British Library, London.

[288] B. R. White, "Samuel Eaton (d. 1639) Particular Baptist Pioneer," *Baptist Quarterly* 24, no. 1 (January 1971): 19 (10–21); cf. "Records of the Jacob-Lathorp-Jessey Church, 1616–1641," *Transactions of the Baptist Historical*

Contrary to William H. Whitsitt in his work, *A Question in Baptist History* (1896),[289] various dissenters, including English Anabaptists, had been practicing believer's baptism by immersion prior to the 1640s. Dutch and English publications had been reporting the practice for several decades. Even as early as 1614, Dutch dissenter Leonard Busher authored a treatise teaching that the only true baptism is the immersion of believers. Busher titled the book *Religions Peace: Or Reconciliation between Princes and Peoples, and Nations* (1614) and dedicated it to King James:

> And it is well worthy [for] consideration, that as in the time of the Old Testament, the Lord would not have his offerings by constraint, but of every man whose heart gave it freely; so now in the time of the gospel, he will not have the people constrained, but as many as receive the word gladly, they are to be added to the church by baptism. And therefore, Christ commanded his disciples to *teach all nations, and baptize them*; that is, to preach the word of salvation to every creature of all sorts of nations, that are worthy and willing to receive it. And *such as shall willingly and gladly receive it, he hath commanded to be baptized in the water; that is, dipped for dead in the water.*[290]

Society 1, no. 4 (January 1910): 220-21.

[289] William H. Whitsitt, *A Question in Baptist History: Whether the Anabaptists in England Practiced Immersion Before the Year 1641?* (Louisville, KY: Charles T. Dearing, 1896), 90ff. For an abstract, see Whitsitt, "Baptists," in *Johnson's Universal Cyclopaedia*, ed. Charles Kendall Adams, et al. (New York: D. Appleton, 1898), 1:489-93; for more on Whitsitt, see James H. Slatton, *W. H. Whitsitt: The Man and the Controversy* (Macon, GA: Mercer University Press, 2009).

[290] Leonard Busher, *Religions Peace: Or Reconciliation between Princes and Peoples, and Nations* (Amsterdam: n.p., 1614), 23-24 (beginning with the last paragraph on page 23). This thirty-one-page document is in the Henry E. Huntington Library and Art Gallery, San Marino, CA. A reprint appears under the new title *Religions Peace: A Plea for Liberty of Conscience* (1614; repr., London: John Sweeting, 1646), in *Tracts on Liberty of Conscience and Persecution, 1614–1661*, compiled by Edward Bean Underhill (London: J. Haddon, 1846), 59 (1-81). While Busher befriended Anabaptists, his precise identity among the various Baptist groups remains unknown. Cf. W. T. Whitley, "Leonard Busher, Dutchman," *Transactions of the Baptist Historical Society* 1, no. 2 (April 1909): 107-13.

In 1640, while studying Colossians 2:12 and Romans 6:4, Richard Blunt, with others of Jessey's church, became "convinced of Baptism y^t also it ought to be by diping ye Body into ye Water, resembling Burial & riseing again."[291] Inevitably, there emerged the question of precisely how the earliest churches had administered immersion, "none having then so practiced in England to professed Believers, & hearing that some in ye Nether Lands had so practiced they agreed & sent over Mr Rich. Blunt (who understood Dutch) wth Letters of Commendation, who was kindly accepted there, & returned wth Letters from them Jo: Batte a Teacher there, & from that Church."[292]

The two quotations above indicate that, while Blunt and others from Jessey's church were familiar with the immersion of infants, they were seeking, apart from heretical groups, to know just how to immerse believers. The practice of immersion had not ceased in the Church of England. The official *Book of Common Prayer* (1549), largely composed by Thomas Cranmer, prescribes triple-immersion. The document allows pouring, but only as an exception for weak or sickly infants. The 1552 edition drops triple-immersion but maintains single-immersion.[293] Among the parish churches, the practice of infant immersion would only gradually disappear. There was never a mandate to cease the practice. Blunt and his group, in their search for the primitive manner of administering believer's baptism, would have known of the radical immersionist groups throughout England, but they kept their distance, fearing any appearance of identification with Anabaptists or other heretical groups.

It was no secret, though, that the quiet, country village of Rijnsburg, near Leiden, in South Holland, had become the center of a fast-growing, albeit ephemeral group known as the Collegiants, who administered believer's baptism by

---

[291] "Rise of Particular Baptists in London, 1633–1644," *Transactions of the Baptist Historical Society* 1, no. 4 (January 1910): 232.

[292] Ibid., 233.

[293] "On Baptisme, bothe publique and private," in *The Book of Common Prayer: The Texts of 1549, 1559, and 1662*, ed. Brian Cummings (Oxford: Oxford University Press, 2011), 51; and *The Book of Common Prayer* (London: Edward Whitchurch, 1552), no pagination.

immersion, that is, "dipping" or "plunging." Since Richard Blunt could speak Dutch, his brethren sent him to Rijnsburg. On foreign soil, Blunt could familiarize himself with the Collegiants' procedure of administering immersion to adults. With hardly a risk of any seeming identification or association with this remote group, he could even exchange letters of courtesy with "Jo. Batte a Teacher there,[294] & from that Church to such as sent him." The Rijnsburgers had emerged in the municipality of Warmond (near Leiden) in the aftermath of the Synod of Dort (1619). Although the Collegiants had maintained no permanent connection with the Arminian Remonstrants, they did embrace Arminianism. They met together only one Sunday a month. When they moved their monthly meeting to Rijnsburg, many began referring to them as *Rijnsburgers*. Believing that there were no true churches remaining anywhere on earth, they refrained from organizing themselves into churches. Besides their collective monthly meeting, their families met locally in their own villages, towns, and cities on the other Sundays. These local gatherings were the *collegia*. Thus, they became the *Collegiants*. They did not have pastors. Indeed, most of their leaders were lay "prophets" whose preaching without notes was an act of *prophesying*. Except for a short while in Groningen, the local *collegia* did not administer ordinances. This explains why Richard Blunt remained in Holland for several months. It was only twice a year—Pentecost and late August—that all the *collegia* came to Rijnsburg for collective, outdoor immersions and public Communion services. These activities were widely promoted and they were open to everyone. Each baptizee chose the one who would baptize him. Each baptizer informed his audience that he possessed no ecclesiastical authority and that the baptism he administered would not signify membership into any local church. The movement's single purpose was to inspire revival among evangelical Christians. The Collegiants would hold their final meeting in 1791.[295]

---

[294] Sufficient evidence is lacking for any absolute identification of "Jo. Batte."

[295] Gerard Brandt (1626–85), "An Account of the Rise and Progress of the Sect of Rynsburgers, Collegiants, or Prophets," in *The History of the Reformation and Other Ecclesiastical Transactions in and about the Low-Countries* (London: T. Wood, 1720–23), 4:49–59, translated from Brandt's original four-volume

Over the years since 1619, Collegiants had gradually established fellowship among various Mennonite groups, especially the Waterlanders, some of whom eventually accepted baptism by immersion. The Collegiants agreed with the Mennonite practices of pacifism and forbidding members from holding political offices. In view of the Collegiants' overall beliefs and practices, Richard Blunt, desiring to become a Particular Baptist, would not have been seeking a baptismal succession from such an unstable and aberrant group.[296] Blunt's single mission was to determine the precise, ancient manner of administering adult immersion. From their own origins, Particular Baptists consistently argued against successionism. In fact, Henry Jessey and his J-L-J Confession had provided biblical arguments for local church autonomy as ample authority for ordinations and ordinances. Moreover, the Particular Baptist, Thomas Kilcop, would embrace that same proposition as early as 1642, in *A Short Treatise of Baptisme*, which also insists on believer's baptism by immersion.[297]

On January 19, 1642 (N. S.),[298] soon after his return to London, Blunt immersed Samuel Blacklock, a "Teacher amongst" the group of Separatists desirous of organizing themselves into Particular Baptist congregations. Blacklock,

---

Historie der Reformatie ... (Rotterdam: Barent Bos, 1671–1704); and "Collegiants," in Harold S. Bender, et al., eds., *Mennonite Encyclopedia: Comprehensive Reference Work on the Anabaptist-Mennonite Movement*, 4 vols. (Hillsboro, KS: Mennonite Brethren Publishing House, 1955–59), 1:639–40.

[296] Some have suggested that certain of the Rijnsburgers could have been influenced by the immersionist teachings of the Polish Socinians' Racovian Catechism (1605); e.g., A. H. Newman, *A History of Anti-Pedobaptism: From the Rise of Pedobaptism to A.D. 1609* (Philadelphia: American Baptist Publication Society, 1897), 387.

[297] Thomas Kilcop, *A Short Treatise of Baptisme*, "wherein is declared that only Christs disciples or beleevers are to be baptised; and that the baptising of infants hath no footing in the word of God, but is a meere tradition, received from our forefathers" (n.p.: n.p., 1642), title, 1ff. A copy of this careful and reasonable thirteen-page work is in the British Library, London.

[298] "Rise of Particular Baptists in London, 1633–1644," 234–35. The manuscript refers to it as the "ninth day." January 9, 1641 (O. S.) is January 19, 1642 (N. S.).

in turn, baptized Blunt, and the two men then proceeded to immerse all others who were like-minded: "Mʳ Blunt Baptized Mʳ Blacklock … & Mʳ Blunt being Baptized, he & Mʳ Blacklock Baptized yᵉ rest of their friends that ware so minded, & many being added to them they increased much."[299] Including Blunt and Blacklock, the group consisted of forty-one immersed believers. A few days later, they baptized an additional twelve. These fifty-three Baptists then "met in two companies,"[300] for the purpose of organizing themselves into two Particular Baptist churches—one under the pastorate of Richard Blunt and the other perhaps under the pastorate of Thomas Kilcop,

---

[299] Ibid. Some historians, including Thomas Crosby, Joseph Ivimey, W. H. Whitsitt, and Ernest A. Payne believed the expression "Mʳ Blunt being Baptized" infers that Blunt had already baptized himself in Holland. Quite the contrary, I prefer the conclusion reached by many historians, including Robert Torbet, Barrington R. White, and Stephen Wright that those words "Mʳ Blunt being Baptized" mean that Blunt baptized Blacklock, who in turn baptized Blunt. Firsthand sources that support such a scenario include the following three. First, Henry Jessey, in his reply to a question on the restoration of immersion, appears to defend Blunt's being un-immersed at the time that he "dipped" Blacklock: "If none but *Baptized* ones, are *own'd* to be *Disciples*; then, the *first* Restorers, of Baptisme [immersion] were *not own'd* to be *Disciples*." See Jessey, *A Storehouse of Provision*, 188. With John the Baptist as an illustration, Jessey is showing that Blunt was un-immersed when he "dipped" Blacklock. As Spilsbury would explain, "Where there is a beginning, some must be first." The second source, Praisegod Barebone, describes the group's first baptizer (Blunt) as being "un-baptized," in *A Reply to the Frivolous and Impertinent Answer of R. B. to the Discourse of P. B.* (London: n.p., 1643), 30–31. This copy is in the British Library, London. Whenever Barebone does mention self-baptism, he makes no reference of it to Blunt. E.g., see Barebone's *Discourse Tending to Prove the Baptisme in, or under the Defection of Antichrist to be the Ordinance of Jesus Christ* (London: Benjamin Allen, 1643), 8. This is in the William Andrews Clark Memorial Library, University of California, Los Angeles. The third source, John Spilsbury, explains that the local church possesses "the power & authoritie of Christ within her selfe," to use her own administrators to restore true baptism. Such individuals have the authority to "administer baptisme upon the whole body, and so upon themselves in the first place as a part of the same…. Where a thing is wanting, there must be of necessitie a beginning to reduce that thing againe into being." See John Spilsbury, *A Treatise Concerning the Lawfull Subject of Baptisme* (London: n.p., 1643), 38.

[300] "Rise of Particular Baptists in London, 1633–1644," 233.

or "Killcop," whose signature appears on the 1646 edition of the Particular Baptists' first London Confession. During that same year, Kilcop wrote *Seekers Supplyed* (1646) as part of an urgent effort among Particular Baptists to expose the dangers of the Seeker movement.[301] As for Samuel Blacklock, he likely joined Blunt's church. Promptly, however, Blacklock defected into the Seeker movement. Re-emerging in 1648 with a group of Seekers and General Baptists, Blacklock accompanied two Levellers—John Lilburne and Richard Overton—as they presented a protest to General Thomas Fairfax of the New Model Army for his refusal to legitimize Lilburne's *Agreement of the People* (1648).[302] Blacklock would never return to the Particular Baptist fold. As for Richard Blunt's congregation, they disappear from history. Blunt's name does not appear among the signees of the London Baptist Confession (1644). Presbyterian antagonist, Thomas Edwards, in 1646, said of Blunt's congregation, "They broke into pieces, and some went one way, some another, divers fell off to no church at all."[303] In a 1670 record, we find a glimpse of Blunt suffering arrest and imprisonment with thirteen others, including the Baptists, Hercules Collins and Tobias Wells, for holding an unlawful assembly and for other "misdemeanors."[304] Nevertheless, in the face of persecu-

---

[301] Thomas Kilcop, *Seekers Supplyed* (London: Printed by Thomas Paine for George Whittington, 1646). This is in the British Library, London. John Spilsbury, in *Gods Ordinance, the Saints Priviledge* (1646), repudiates key teachings of the Seekers. Another Particular Baptist, Hanserd Knollys (ca. 1599–1691), in *The Shining of a Flaming Fire in Zion* (1646), and in *Christ Exalted: A Lost Sinner Sought, and Saved by Christ* (1646), provides additional refutation of Seeker doctrines.

[302] In 1649, Particular Baptists presented to the House of Commons a reproof of Leveller activism, as Cromwell expelled Leveller activists from the Army. See Richard Greaves, "Blacklock (or Blaiklocks), Samuel (fl. 1642–1648)," in *Biographical Dictionary of British Radicals in the Seventeenth Century*, 1:68.

[303] Thomas Edwards, *Gangraena: Or a Catalogue and Discovery of Many of the Errors, Heresies, Blasphemies and Pernicious Practices of the Sectaries of This Time, Vented and Acted in England in These Four Last Years* (London: Ralph Smith, 1646), Part 3, pages 112–13. Each Part begins new pagination: Part 1 has 192 pages; Part 2 has 212 pages; and Part 3 has 292 pages. This is in the Union Theological Seminary Library, NYC.

[304] G. Stephen Weaver Jr., "'Patiently to Suffer for Christ's Sake': Hercules

tion, there had emerged from the J-L-J Church a sound remnant of brave Particular Baptists whose number, by 1644, had "become Seven Churches in London."[305] These would establish the movement upon a solid doctrinal and practical foundation.

The fifty-three Blunt-Blacklock baptizees in 1642 included Thomas Shepard and his wife. The couple had participated in John Spilsbury's 1633 secession from the Jacob-Lathrop Church. Shepard would sign the Baptists' London Confession (1644) as Thomas "Skippard."[306] The fifty-three baptizees also included Mark Lucar (d. 1676) and his wife Mabel,[307] who aligned themselves with Spilsbury's group. By the mid-1640s, Lucar arrived in Newport, Rhode Island, where he assisted John Clarke (1609–76), founding pastor of the second Baptist church in America. Having received instruction from John Spilsbury, Lucar would play a key role in Clarke's ministry.

Meanwhile in London, Spilsbury had emerged as the progenitor of the Particular Baptist movement. Their study of the Scriptures brought Spilsbury and other Particular Baptists to the conviction that the only true baptism is believer's baptism by immersion. They stood certain that they had restored immersion on the authority of the Bible alone, with no requirement of any kind of visible succession. Despite a wall of opposition, Spilsbury had organized the first Particular Baptist church (1633–38), and this led to his indictment, in 1641, for holding unlawful assemblies.[308] The immersion of believers, however, was now the Baptist way.

In Southwark (London), 1642, Particular Baptists,

Collins as an Exemplar of Baptists during the Great Persecution (1660–1688)," *The Southern Baptist Journal of Theology* 18, no. 1 (Spring 2014): 83–84.

[305] "Rise of Particular Baptists in London, 1633–1644," 235.

[306] Thomas Munden, another of the Blunt-Blacklock baptizees, would sign the 1644 London Confession as Thomas "Munday."

[307] Since there is no further mention of her name, we can only assume that Mabel came to Rhode Island with Mark.

[308] See Larry J. Kreitzer, "The Indictment of John Spilsbery for Attending a Conventicle (12 September 1641)," in *William Kiffen and His World*, vols. 1–4 of a series of the Centre for Baptist History and Heritage Studies, Re-sourcing Baptist History: Seventeenth Century Series (Oxford: Regent's Park College, 2010–15), 3:191–211.

represented by William Kiffin ("*Cufin*"), engaged in a heated debate over baptism with antagonist Daniel Featley. Following the debate, Featley, a Church of England clergyman, retaliated in his work, *The Dippers Dipt: Or, the Anabaptists Duck'd and Plung'd over Head and Ears*. This was during the Civil Wars (1642–48), and Featley dedicated the work to Parliament. In his dedication, Featley complains that, "*for the past twenty years,*" Anabaptists have been doing the work of the devil in the rivers near his residence. In his Preface to the Reader, Featley bewails that such "enthusiasts" have "re-baptized hundreds of men and women … dipping them over head and ears." Equating Baptists with Anabaptist fanatics, Featley concludes his lengthy harangue with a prayer for their total destruction: "So let all the factious and seditious enemies of the Church and State perish: but upon the Head of King Charles [I] let the Crowne flourish. Amen."[309]

Spilsbury and Kiffin seem to have merged their churches at times, during 1650–53.[310] From their earliest years, the Spilsbury

---

[309] Daniel Featley, *The Dippers Dipt: Or, the Anabaptists Duck'd and Plung'd over Head and Ears*, 5th ed. (London: Printed for N. B. and Richard Royston at the Angel in Ivy-lane, 1647), last page of the Epistle Dedicatory (no pagination in this section); Preface to the Reader, page 3; and page 258 (the final page of the book). This copy is in the Bodleian Library, Oxford. Featley's section on "Anabaptists" (235–58) attempts to identify Baptists with Anabaptists. Cf. E. (Ephraim) Pagitt, *Heresiography or a Description of the Hereticks and Sectaries of These Latter Times*, 3rd ed. (London: Printed for W. L. for his shop in Fleet Street, 1647), 32–33, also in the Bodleian Library.

[310] Kreitzer, "The Merger of the Churches of John Spilsbery and William Kiffen," in *William Kiffen and His World*, 3:201–5. In June 1653, the churches of the Abingdon Association addressed a letter "to the church of Christ of which our brethren John Spilsberie and William Kiffin are members, and to the rest of the churches in and neere London," in "Association Records of the Abingdon Association to 1660," Part 3 of the *Association Records of the Particular Baptists of England, Wales, and Ireland to 1660*, ed. Barrington R. White (London: Baptist Historical Society, 1974), 131; cf. Obadiah Holmes's 1651 letter "unto the well beloved Brethren John Spilsbury, William Kiffin, and the rest that in London stand fast in that Faith, and continue to walk stedfastly in that Order of the Gospel which was once delivered unto the Saints by Jesus Christ," in John Clarke, *Ill Newes from New-England* (London: Printed by Henry Hills living in Fleet-Yard next door to the Rose and Crown, 1652), 17. This copy is in the

church had met in various places (including homes) in Old Gravel Lane, Wapping. Their earliest known meetinghouse was on James Street, Wapping, where their attendance reached almost four hundred. During 1730–1855, the congregation maintained a chapel on Prescot Street. In 1855, they relocated to a building on Commercial Street, where they remained until 1914, when they moved to the Walthamstow section, where the church remains to this day in Kevan Court, on the corner of Cairo Road and Church Hill. As London's oldest Baptist church, its current name is *Church Hill Baptist Church*.[311] At Spilsbury's death, John Norcott became his successor, and Hercules Collins would become the third pastor.[312] A long list of noble pastors would succeed them, including Abraham Booth (1734–1806).

The Emergence of the Baptist Name and Ordinances

The earliest reference to the designation *Baptists* appears in 1644 from the pen of an opponent, John Etherington, who describes "those Baptists, or Dippers, that will not be called Anabaptists."[313] The Greek term *Anabaptist* (*ana*, "again," + *baptizo*) literally means "re-baptizer." With opponents negatively designating Baptists as *Anabaptists*, the name *Baptist* as a denominational label emerged from the simple practice of dropping the prefix from *Anabaptist*. By the turn of the

---

Henry E. Huntington Library and Art Gallery, San Marino, CA.

[311] See Ernest F. Kevan, *London's Oldest Baptist Church: Wapping 1633 – Walthamstow 1933* (London: Kingsgate Press, 1933); and Robert W. Oliver, *From John Spilsbury to Ernest Kevan: The Literary Contribution of London's Oldest Baptist Church* (London: Grace Publications Trust, 1985).

[312] For more on Hercules Collins, see Michael A. G. Haykin and Steve Weaver, *"Devoted to the Service of the Temple": Piety, Persecution, and Ministry in the Writings of Hercules Collins* (Grand Rapids: Reformation Heritage Books, 2007).

[313] I. E. [John Etherington, a.k.a. Hetherington], *The Anabaptists Ground-Work for Reformation: Or, New Planting of Churches*, "that no man, woman, nor child, may be baptized, but such as have justifying faith and doe make profession thereof, before, to the baptizer" (London: M. Simmons, 1644), 23. The work is in the form of a debate between Etherington (a Familist) and Thomas Lamb, the General Baptist. The document is in the British Library, London.

eighteenth century, the *Baptist* label was rapidly becoming permanent and widespread on both sides of the Atlantic.[314]

In 1642, the Particular Baptist Andrew Ritor produced two major volumes in defense of believer's baptism by immersion, including *A Treatise of the Vanity of Childish-Baptisme*.[315] In addition, by 1644, the two Baptist ordinances of Baptism and the Lord's Supper had emerged well defined. Seeing no wisdom in seeking connections with Anabaptists or with General Baptists, John Spilsbury stood convinced that, on the sole authority of the Bible, Particular Baptist churches were true churches and that, by virtue of their union with Christ their supreme Head, their ordinances were true and valid. Particular Baptist leaders had set the tone for their first London Confession (1644).[316]

For the instruction of his people and for future generations, John Spilsbury wrote *A Treatise Concerning the Lawfull Subject of Baptisme* (1643), a major Baptist defense of independent, congregational polity and believer's baptism by immersion, under the immediate authority of the local church. Spilsbury was also confident that to embrace visible successionism is "to shut up the ordinance of God in such a strait, that none can come by it, but through the authority of the Popedome of Rome."[317] When Spilsbury reached the end of his *Treatise*, he earnestly desired for his readers to understand the broader, biblical foundation of Particular Baptist churches, and specifically of his own

---

[314] See also the brief article by Robert B. Hannen, "Historical Notes on the Name 'Baptist,'" *Foundations* 8, no. 1 (January 1965): 62–71.

[315] Andrew Ritor, *A Treatise of the Vanity of Childish-Baptisme: Wherein the Deficiency of the Baptisme of the Church of England Is Considered in Five Particulars Thereof: and Wherein Also Is Proved, That Baptizing Is Dipping, and Dipping Baptizing* (London: n.p., 1642); idem, *The Second Part of the Vanity & Childishnes of Infants Baptisme Wherein the Grounds from Severall Scriptures Usually Brought for to Justifie the Same, Are Urged and Answered: As also the Nature of the Divers Covenants Made with Abraham and His Seed, Briefly Opened and Applied* (London: n.p., 1642). Both treatises are in the British Library.

[316] Cf. Article 39 of the 1646 edition.

[317] Spilsbury, *A Treatise Concerning the Lawfull Subject of Baptisme* (London: n.p., 1643), 39. This is in the Union Theological Seminary Library, NYC. The forty-four-page treatise includes a two-page "Epistle to the Reader," signed "John Spilsbery."

personal position and practice. Following a valuable introductory paragraph, the author set forth a ten-point doctrinal statement that would provide the essential framework of the London Confession of 1644.[318]

Select Bibliography for Further Reading

Bell, Mark R. *Apocalypse How? Baptist Movements during the English Revolution*. Macon, GA: Mercer University Press, 2000.

Brown, Louise Fargo. *The Political Activities of the Baptists and Fifth Monarchy Men in England during the Interregnum*. Oxford: Oxford University Press, 1912.

Burrage, Champlin. "The Restoration of Immersion by the English Anabaptists and Baptists (1640-1700)." *The American Journal of Theology* 16, no. 1 (January 1912): 70-89.

Capp, Bernard S. "The Fifth Monarchists and the Popular Millenarianism." In *Radical Religion in the English Revolution*, edited by J. F. McGregor and B. Reay, 165-89. Oxford: Oxford University Press, 1984.

Farnell, James E. "The Usurpation of Honest London Householders: Barebone's Parliament." *The English Historical Review* 82, no. 322 (January 1967): 24-46.

Farrar, A. J. D. "The Fifth Monarchy Movement." *Transactions of the Baptist Historical Society* 2, no. 3 (May 1911): 166-81.

"The Fifth-Monarchy Manifesto of 1654." *Transactions of the Baptist Historical Society* 3, no. 3 (May 1913): 129-53.

Jacob, Henry. "Papers of Henry Jacob's Written during 1603-1605." *The Early English Dissenters in the Light of Recent Research (1550-1641)*, by Champlin Burrage, 2:146-66. Cambridge: Cambridge University Press, 1912.

Light, Alfred. *Bunhill Fields*. London: C. J. Farncombe & Sons, 1913.

Loomis, Lucy. *John Lothrop in Barnstable*. 2nd ed. Barnstable, MA: Sturgis Library, 2011.

Moore, Walter Levon. "Baptist Teachings and Practices on Baptism in England 1600-1689." ThD diss., The Southern Baptist Theological Seminary, 1950.

Oliver, Robert W. *From John Spilsbury to Ernest Kevan: The Literary Contribution of London's Oldest Baptist Church*. London: Grace Publications Trust, 1985.

Reay, B. "Quakerism and Society." In *Radical Religion in the English Revolution*, edited by J. F. McGregor and B. Reay, 141-64. Oxford: Oxford University Press, 1984.

Spilsbury, John, William Kiffin, et al. *Heart-Bleedings for Professors Abominations*. London: Printed for Francis Tyton and to be sold at the

---

[318] Idem, 43-44.

three Daggers, Fleet Street, near the Inner-Temple-Gate, 1650.

Stassen, Glen H. "Anabaptist Influence in the Origin of the Particular Baptists." *The Mennonite Quarterly Review* 36, no. 4 (October 1962): 322–48.

Taber, Helen Lathrop. *A New Home in Mattakeese: A Guide to Reverend John Lathropp's Barnstable*. Yarmouth Port, MA: n.p., 1995.

Tolmie, Murray. *The Triumph of the Saints: The Separate Churches of London 1616–1649*. Cambridge: Cambridge University Press, 1977.

Turner, George Lyon, ed. *Original Records of Early Nonconformity under Persecution and Indulgence*. 3 vols. London: T. F. Unwin, 1911–14.

Underhill, Edward Bean, ed. *Tracts on Liberty of Conscience and Persecution, 1614–1661*. London: J. Haddon, 1846.

Underwood, T. L. *Primitivism, Radicalism, and the Lamb's War: The Baptist-Quaker Conflict in Seventeenth-Century England*. Oxford: Oxford University Press, 1997.

Watts, Michael R. *The Dissenters: From the Reformation to the French Revolution*. Oxford: Clarendon Press, 1978.

White, Barrington R. "Early Baptist Arguments for Religious Freedom: Their Overlooked Agenda." *Baptist History and Heritage* 24, no. 4 (October 1989): 3–10.

_____. "Henry Jessey: A Pastor in Politics." *The Baptist Quarterly* 25, no. 3 (July 1973): 98–110.

_____. "How Did Kiffin Join the Baptists?" *Baptist Quarterly* 23, no. 5 (January 1970): 201–7.

_____. "The Organization of the Particular Baptists, 1644–1660." *The Journal of Ecclesiastical History* 17, no. 2 (October 1966): 209–26.

_____, ed. *The English Puritan Tradition*. Nashville: Broadman, 1980.

_____, and Roger Haydon, eds. *English Baptists of the Seventeenth Century*. Rev. London: Baptist Historical Society, 1996.

Whitley, W. T. "Baptist Meetings in the City of London." *Transactions of the Baptist Historical Society* 5, no. 2 (July 1916): 74–82.

_____. *The Baptists of London 1612–1928: Their Fellowship, Their Expansion, with Notes on Their 850 Churches*. London: Kingsgate Press, n.d.

_____. *A History of the British Baptists*. Rev. 2nd ed. London: Kingsgate Press, 1932.

_____. "The Seven Churches of London." *Review and Expositor* 7, no. 3 (July 1910): 384–413.

Wright, Stephen. "Baptist Alignments and the Restoration of Immersion, 1638–44, Part I." *Baptist Quarterly* 40, no. 5 (January 2004): 261–82. Part II." *Baptist Quarterly* 40, no. 6 (April 2004): 346–68.

_____. *The Early English Baptists, 1603–1649*. Woodbridge, Suffolk, England: Boydell Press, 2006.

_____. "Jessey, Henry (1601–1663)." In *Oxford Dictionary of National Biography*. Oxford: Oxford University Press, 2004, online ed., http://www.oxforddnb.com/view/article/14804.

Chapter 6

Three Key Baptist Leaders: Hanserd Knollys, William Kiffin, and Benjamin Keach

---

Hanserd Knollys (ca. 1609–91)

The Early Years

*B*orn and raised in the home of a Cambridge graduate and Church of England vicar, in northeastern Lincolnshire, Hanserd Knollys (pronounced nōlz) would have already acquired a keen understanding of Puritan doctrine prior to his 1627 matriculation at St. Catherine's Hall, in Cambridge.[319] Following his ordination into the priesthood of

---

[319] For the date of Knollys's birth, I favor the year 1609, as argued by Dennis C. Bustin, "Hanserd Knollys' Date of Birth," in *Paradox and Perseverance: Hanserd Knollys, Particular Baptist Pioneer in Seventeenth-Century England*, vol. 23 of the series, Studies in Baptist History and Thought (Milton Keynes, England: Paternoster, 2006), 324–28. Earlier works dated the birth 1598/1599. Other valuable sources on Knollys include Hanserd Knollys and William Kiffin, *The Life and Death of That Old Disciple of Jesus Christ, and Eminent Minister of the Gospel, Mr. Hanserd Knollys, Who Dyed in the Ninety-Third Year of His Age*, written by Knollys to the year 1672 and completed by William Kiffin in 1692 (London: Printed for John Harris, 1692). See also Barry H. Howson, *Erroneous and Schismatical Opinions: The Question of Orthodoxy regarding the Theology of Hanserd Knollys (c. 1599–1691)*, vol. 99 of the series, Studies in the History of Christian Thought

the National Church, in 1629, Knollys served a little over a year as schoolmaster in the Free School of Gainsborough, an area saturated in Separatist history.[320] By 1631, Hanserd was Vicar of Humberstone (Humberston).[321] The following year, he married Anne Cheney, whom he described as "a holy, discreet woman, and a help meet for me in the ways of her household, and also in the way of holiness; who was my companion in all my sufferings, travels, and hardships, that we endured for the gospel."[322] Their marriage of nearly forty years would produce seven sons and three daughters. Anne died in 1671, two decades prior to Hanserd's death.

Becoming a Christian and a Separatist

Near the time of his marriage, Hanserd was beginning to question some of the Church of England's practices, such as

---

(Leiden: E. J. Brill, 2001); Michael A. G. Haykin, *Kiffin, Knollys and Keach: Rediscovering Our English Baptist Heritage* (Leeds, England: Reformation Today Trust, 1996), 54–61; James Culross, *Hanserd Knollys: "A Minister and Witness of Jesus Christ" 1598–1601* (London: Alexander and Shepheard, 1895); Pope A. Duncan, *Hanserd Knollys: Seventeenth-Century Baptist* (Nashville: Broadman, 1965); James Muriel, *Religious Liberty on Trial: Hanserd Knollys – Early Baptist Hero* (Franklin, TN: Providence House Publishers, 1997); Barrington R. White, *Hanserd Knollys and Radical Dissent in the 17th Century* (London: Dr. Williams's Trust, 1977); idem, "Knollys, Hanserd (c. 1599–1691)," in *Biographical Dictionary of British Radicals in the Seventeenth Century*, ed. Richard L. Greaves and Robert Zaller (Brighton, England: Harvester Press, 1983), 2:160–62; and Walter Wilson, "Hanserd Knollys," in *The History and Antiquities of Dissenting Churches and Meeting Houses, in London, Westminster, and Southwark: Including the Lives of Their Ministers, from the Rise of Nonconformity to the Present Time*, 4 vols. (London: Printed for the author, 1808–14), 2:562–71.

[320] In 1602, John Smyth had begun serving the pastorate of a congregation of persecuted Separatists in Gainsborough. By about the end of 1607, he had led some forty of them in a successful escape across the North Sea to Amsterdam.

[321] The town of Humberston lies just a few miles from Immingham Dock, from which the *Mayflower* Pilgrims had escaped to Amsterdam in 1608.

[322] Knollys and Kiffin, *Life and Death*, 8–9. I have modernized some capitalization and punctuation. This is in the Henry E. Huntington Library and Art Gallery, San Marino, CA.

allowing the parish churches to admit the unconverted to the Communion Table. Alarmed that there had been no conversions under his own ministry, Knollys renounced his ordination and seriously began to question his own spiritual state. Hearing of John Wheelwright, a former Church of England minister who had become "instrumental to convert many souls," Knollys sought him out and spent several days under his counsel. When Wheelwright revealed to him "the nature of the covenant of free grace," Knollys confessed his being a stranger to grace and being under bondage to legalism. He could soon testify of God's inward preparation, followed by conversion and full assurance:

> [I] went home exceeding sorrowful about my soul's condition, but I gave myself to prayer, and begged of God to teach me the covenant of grace, and to that end I searched the scriptures, and I heard one Mr. How preach upon Gal. 2: 20, *I live by the faith of the Son of God*; whereby I saw that I had lived a life of works, and not of faith. Then I began to see a necessity of believing in Christ for pardon and salvation; and hearing the minister say that Christ was the Author, Root, and only foundation of saving faith, and that God did give the faith of *evidence*, Heb. 11:1, in some New Covenant promise, Gal. 3:14, and that those promises were given of God, 2 Pet. 1:4. I prayed that night, and next morning, and in the night season, that God would give me such a promise. The next day I locked myself in the church, and in the chancel, or quire so called, I prayed very earnestly, mourning and bemoaning myself and my soul's condition, fearing, and with great brokenness of spirit, and many tears expressed my fears that God would leave me and forsake me, and that I should utterly perish forever. And then that promise, Heb. 13:5, *I will never leave thee, nor forsake thee*, was given me, which promise stopped me a little in prayer, and I brake forth into this kind of expostulation with God, saying, "Lord who am I! I am a vile sinful sinner, the chief of sinners, most unworthy of pardon and salvation! How, Lord! Never leave me, nor forsake thee?

O infinite mercy! Oh, free grace! Who am I? I have been a graceless soul, a formal professor, a legal performer of holy duties, and have gone about to establish mine own righteousness, which I now see is but filthy rags, &c. Then God gave me those two promises, Isa. 43:22–25 and Isa. 54:9–10 and filled my soul with joy and peace in believing, so that I brake forth into praises and thanksgiving."[323]

Of his itinerate ministry over the next three or four years, Knollys testifies, "Very many sinners were converted, and many believers were established in the faith."[324] Highly offended at Knollys's non-conformity, the Church of England silenced him, and the High Commission Court had him arrested in Boston (Lincolnshire). The officer responsible for Knollys became so conscience smitten that he allowed him to escape. Knollys went to London to await the next ship to Massachusetts Bay Colony. Because of prolonged delays, by the time Hanserd, Anne, and their baby embarked, Hanserd had only "six brass farthings" left in his pocket.[325] Later, when a serious need arose, Anne would give Hanserd the £5 that she had secretly saved for such a time. He would have also taken courage in knowing that his friend Wheelwright would be in Boston to greet them and to assist them in establishing themselves in the New World.

John Wheelwright, Anne Hutchinson, and the Antinomian Charges against Hanserd Knollys in New England

Although John Wheelwright (1592-1679)[326] had studied at Cambridge and had served for a decade as vicar of Bilsby (Bilsbury), his commitment to Scripture over ecclesiastical conformity had prompted Archbishop William Laud to

---

[323] Ibid., 12–14. I slightly modernized some of the grammar. Knollys died in 1691.
[324] Ibid., 16. Grammar slightly modernized.
[325] Ibid., 16–17.
[326] See Charles H. Bell, "Memoir," in *John Wheelwright: His Writings, Including His Fast-Day Sermon, 1637, and His Mercurius Americanus, 1645, with a Paper upon the Genuineness of the Indian Deed of 1629*, ed. Charles H. Bell (Boston: The Prince Society, 1876), 1–78.

silence him from preaching. Due to the Laudian persecutions, Wheelwright had embarked for New England, in 1636, in hopes of finding religious freedom. He was completely unaware that, in January, Boston's authorities had forced Separatist Roger Williams out of their colony and into the wilderness. Moreover, the Massachusetts Bay founders were intent on modeling their "New Canaan" after the civil laws of Israel.

One Thursday morning, in January 1637, John Cotton (1584–1652), the teaching elder at First Church, preached Boston's Fast-Day sermon. He invited his friend John Wheelwright to preach the evening message. In his sermon,[327] Wheelwright expressed concern that many ministers in both Old and New England were preaching a "covenant of works," that is, a legal system that many understood to be the pillar of their salvation. While mentioning no specific names, Wheelwright contended that many ministers were ignoring the "covenant of free grace" that God had made with His elect. For the sake of propriety, Wheelwright cautioned his audience, "Let us have a care that we give not occasion to others to say we are libertines or Antinomians, but Christians."[328] Nevertheless, his sermon prompted the General Court of Massachusetts to accuse Wheelwright of insubordination and of spreading hyper-Calvinist Antinomianism, a doctrine that the Court equated with the teachings of Wheelwright's sister-in-law, Anne Hutchinson (1591–1643), who had arrived in Boston in 1634. Having lived since birth at Alford (Lincolnshire), Anne's favorite pastor, John Cotton (1584–1652), had mentored her in nearby St. Botolph's Church, in Boston, until he immigrated to New Boston, Massachusetts, in 1633, to serve as teacher with Pastor John Wilson, at First Church. Her devotion to Cotton's teachings had been Anne's fundamental reason for immigrating to New England, where she served as a community midwife. Esteeming Cotton as one of the few ministers who still preached free grace (rather than works), Anne opened her

---

[327] Wheelwright, "A Sermon Preached at Boston in New England upon a Fast Day … January 1636," in *Writings*, 153–79. For more on fast days see W. DeLoss Love, *The Fast and Thanksgiving Days of New England* (Boston: Houghton, Mifflin, and Co., 1895).

[328] Wheelwright, "A Sermon Preached at Boston," 175.

Boston home on various week-days to any of the women who wished to attend her Bible studies. Male informers were often present. Anne and her listeners never ceased attending First Church on Sundays. Along with Governor Henry Vane (the Younger), John Cotton silently agreed with Hutchinson's doctrinal teachings and openly appealed for tolerance toward her. Nevertheless, the pressures of politico-religious correctness began to restrain Cotton's congeniality toward Anne. As for Wheelwright, neither Cotton nor Vane viewed his teachings as in any sense heretical. Cotton never criticized Wheelwright's fast-day sermon, and he never commended the General Court's action.

The tides turned, in 1637, when votes from outside Boston decided an election that replaced Henry Vane with John Winthrop as the new governor.[329] Winthrop had already charged Hutchinson with teaching "two dangerous errors": First, "that the person of the Holy Ghost dwells in a justified person"; and second, "that no [works of] sanctification can help to evidence to us our justification."[330] The charges against Hutchinson were rooted in the Puritan notion of "progressive conversion" attained through repeated means of grace. Under this teaching, parishioners struggled to obtain assurance of

---

[329] Returning to England in 1637, Henry Vane became Joint Treasurer of the Navy in 1639. He was knighted in the following year. He supported the parliamentary cause during England's Civil Wars. He took no part in the execution of King Charles I. For his opposition to the Restoration, however, he was tried for high treason and executed in 1662. Vane should be remembered as a true champion of religious freedom. Like John Cotton and most key New England Puritans, Vane also taught historic premillennialism. See George Sikes, *The Life and Death of Sir Henry Vane, Knight: Or, A Short Narrative of the Main Passages of His Earthly Pilgrimage; Together with a True Account of His Purely Christian, Peaceable, Spiritual, Gospel-Principles, Doctrine, Life, and Way of Worshipping God, for Which He Suffered Contradiction and Reproach from All Sorts of Sinners, and at Last, a Violent Death, June 14, Anno, 1662* (London: n.p., 1662). This is in the Henry E. Huntington Library and Art Gallery, San Marino, CA.

[330] John Winthrop, "History of New England 1630–1649," in *Winthrop's Journal*, ed. James Kendall Hosmer, 2 vols. (New York: Charles Scribner's Sons, 1908), 1:195.

their salvation. The Puritans were charging Hutchinson with heresy for teaching the women that every true believer has the witness of the indwelling Holy Spirit, and that one must regard good works as the fruit rather than the proof of a believing heart. Hypocrites can do works that appear to be holy. While her opponents charged Hutchinson (rightly or wrongly) with claiming direct revelation from God, John Cotton himself, in his sermon on Revelation 4:1-2, had "declared his belief in the possibility of direct revelation in his day, giving an almost ecstatic evocation of the heights of inspiration to which the Holy Spirit might lift a believer."[331] The General Court branded both Hutchinson and Wheelwright as "seditious heretics,"[332] confiscated their properties, and banished them "forever" from the Bay Colony.

The General Court's action occurred in November 1638 — just as Hanserd and Anne Knollys were on a ship to Boston in search of freedom from religious persecution. After their three-month voyage, on which the Knollys's firstborn died, Hanserd and Anne at once faced oppression of conscience in vital matters regarding their faith. Reports of Hanserd's acquaintance with Wheelwright had reached Boston. Depending solely upon hearsay, Puritan officials at once regarded Knollys as a dangerous adherent of hyper-Calvinist Antinomianism.

---

[331] Sydney V. James, *John Clarke and His Legacies: Religion and Law in Colonial Rhode Island 1638–1750*, ed. Theodore D. Bozeman (University Park, PA: Pennsylvania State University Press, 1999), 29; and George Selement, "John Cotton's Hidden Antinomianism: His Sermon on Revelation 4:1-2," *The New England Historical and Genealogical Register* 129 (July 1975): 278-94.

[332] The best studies on this era include David D. Hall, ed., *The Antinomian Controversy, 1636–1638: A Documentary History* (Middletown, CT: Wesleyan University Press, 1968); Michael P. Winship, *Making Heretics: Militant Protestantism and Free Grace in Massachusetts, 1636–1641* (Princeton: Princeton University Press, 2002); Mark Jones, *Antinomianism: Reformed Theology's Unwelcome Guest?* (Phillipsburg, NJ: P&R Publishing, 2002); Charles Francis Adams, ed., *Antinomianism in the Colony of Massachusetts Bay 1636–1638* (Boston: The Prince Society, 1894); and David R. Como, *Blown by the Spirit: Puritanism and the Emergence of an Antinomian Underground in pre-Civil-War England* (Stanford, CA: Stanford University Press, 2004).

Knollys promptly received orders to leave the colony, because "the Magistrates were told by the Ministers that I was an *Antinomian*," thus, "they would not suffer me to abide in their Patent."[333] Upon his departure from the Bay Colony, Knollys assisted a Congregational church in Dover, New Hampshire, where he soon suffered slander from evil men.[334] With his pregnant wife and their three-year-old child, he returned to London in 1641, at the bidding of his aged father.[335] As for the banished Anne Hutchinson, she and most of the family had moved to Portsmouth, founded by John Clarke on Aquidneck Island, which soon became *Rhode Island*. Following her husband's death, Anne and about six of the children moved to New Netherland—renamed *New York* in 1665. The family settled into a remote farming area on Long Island Sound, between the modern Bronx and New Rochelle. In 1643, a disgruntled band of Native Americans massacred Anne Hutchinson and all but one of the children; the assassins took nine-year-old Susanna captive.

---

[333] Knollys and Kiffin, *Life and Death*, 17.

[334] On the slander, see Terry Wolever, "The Knollys-Larkham Controversy of 1640-1641," in *A Noble Company: Biographical Essays on Notable Particular-Regular Baptists in America*, ed. Terry Wolever (Springfield, MO: Particular Baptist Press, 2006), 1:395–404, Appendix A. Defending Knollys, Cotton Mather explains, "There were some … whose names deserve to live in our *book* for their *piety*, although their particular *opinions* were such, as to be disserviceable unto the declared and supposed *interests* of our churches. Of these there were some godly *Anabaptists*; as namely, Mr. *Hanserd Knollys*, (whom one of his adversaries called, *Absurd Knowles*) of *Dover*, who afterwards removing back to *London*, lately died there, *a good man, in a good old age*. And Mr. *Miles*, of *Swansey*, who afterwards came to *Boston*, and is now gone to his *rest*. Both of these have a respectful character in the churches of this wilderness." This is in Mather, *Magnalia Christi Americana* (Hartford: Silas Andrus, 1820), 1.3.221. See also Isaac Backus, *A History of New England: with Particular Reference to the Denomination of Christians Called Baptists*, 2 vols., 2nd ed., with notes by David Weston (Newton, MA: The Backus Historical Society, 1871), 1:81–83n2; and J. Newton Brown, "Memoir of Hanserd Knollys, M. A.," *New-Hampshire Historical Society Collections* 5 (1837): 175–79; idem, "Hanserd Knollys," in *Annals of the American Baptist Pulpit*, by William Sprague (New York: Robert Carter & Brothers, 1860), 6:1–7.

[335] Knollys and Kiffin, *Life and Death*, 17–18.

Meanwhile, with a few loyal friends, John Wheelwright, traveling during the winter over land and water, reached Exeter, New Hampshire, where he erected a meetinghouse and soon became the town's leading founder. When Exeter came under the jurisdiction of Massachusetts, Wheelwright took refuge in Wells, Maine, where he erected a meetinghouse for worship and a sawmill for their livelihood. For the next fifteen years, he ministered to the locals. Meanwhile, in Boston, the Puritans had never produced credible evidence that Wheelwright had ever been an Antinomian. Finally invited to return to Massachusetts, Wheelwright received pardon from the Bay Colony. As an official Commissioner to England for the Colonies, Wheelwright returned to England during the Commonwealth. His old friend and Cambridge classmate, Lord Protector Oliver Cromwell, joyfully entertained him. Wheelwright preached in numerous churches, but, at the Stuart Restoration, he returned to New England where, for the remainder of his life, he served as a faithful, Congregational pastor in Salisbury, Massachusetts. Due to their bold, courageous, and persistent stand in behalf of freedom of conscience, through the hardest of times, John Wheelwright, Henry Vane, Roger Williams, Hanserd Knollys, and John Clarke, with their families, had suffered the persecution of "heretics." Today, we often take for granted the precious freedoms that cost an inestimable price to untold numbers of noble men and women. For the Knollys family, moreover, the suffering would continue.

Knollys's Early Years as a Baptist

Back in London, Hanserd Knollys's success as a schoolmaster was helping to provide for his family and to care for his sick wife and father. Eventually, this work would help to support his preaching tours, as he encouraged a growing network of Particular Baptist churches. Regrettably, Knollys provides but few specifics on how he became a Baptist. During 1643, he was serving as a chaplain in the Parliamentary Army.[336]

---

[336] Ibid., 18–24. We find Knollys in Cromwell's New Model Army chaplaincy during 1649; see Anne Laurence, *Parliamentary Army Chaplains, 1642–1651*,

Following his return to civilian life, authorities arrested him several times for preaching without a license. Knollys soon began attending Henry Jessey's services at London's J-L-J Church where, in March 1644, Knollys and William Kiffin initiated a discussion on baptism.[337] In 1645, Knollys embraced believer's baptism by immersion and even enjoyed the opportunity of baptizing Jessey by immersion. In that same year, in London, Knollys established a Baptist church, whose pastorate he would serve for the remainder of his life. Over the years, due to persecution, his church would move to several locations within the city,[338] including Coleman Street and Great St. Helen's, where his congregation frequently numbered as many as a thousand. At the time of his death, Knollys's church was located at Broken Wharf, on Thames Street, near the north bank. His congregation would continue experiencing the seasons of persecution. Early in his ministry, in 1646, Knollys had signed the second edition of the London Baptist Confession, which calls upon civil magistrates to "protect the liberty of men's consciences" in matters of worship (Art. 48).

The Four Charges of Heresy

In his autobiography, Knollys speaks of having to "prove and vindicate" himself, over many years, from charges of being an

---

vol. 59 of Royal Historical Society Studies in History (Woodbridge, England: Boydell Press, 1990), 58. Leveller presence in the Army, however, may have prompted Knollys's decision to return to civilian life. Indeed, it was in 1649 that Particular Baptists, including Knollys, publicly and completely renounced the Leveller movement.

[337] W. T. Whitley, "Debate on Infant Baptism, 1643," *Transactions of the Baptist Historical Society* 1, no. 4 (January 1910): 237–45; and Whitley, "The Jacob-Jessey Church, 1616–1678," *Transactions of the Baptist Historical Society* 1, no. 4 (January 1910): 254 and passim.

[338] The names of the streets on which Knollys's church met up to its extinction are listed in W. T. Whitley, "Baptist Meetings in the City of London," *Transactions of the Baptist Historical Society* 5, no. 2 (July 1916): 81–82; idem, *The Baptists of London 1612–1928: Their Fellowship, Their Expansion, with Notes on Their 850 Churches* (London: Kingsgate Press, n.d.), 13–15, 107; and Walter Wilson, "Hanserd Knollys," in *The History and Antiquities of Dissenting Churches and Meeting Houses*, 2:559–61.

Anabaptist and of teaching hyper-Calvinist Antinomianism.[339] During the Westminster Assembly (1643–53), Presbyterian officials expressed disgust over the large crowds that gathered to hear Knollys's sermons.[340] The 1645 minutes of the Westminster Assembly refer to Knollys's "venting his Antinomian opinions."[341] Meanwhile, the pro-Presbyterian Thomas Edwards, in his *Gangraena*, accused Knollys of Anabaptist and Antinomian heresies.[342] Over the years, opponents brought four basic charges of heresy against Hanserd Knollys:[343] (1) Antinomianism,[344] (2) hyper-Calvinism,[345] (3) Anabaptism,[346] and (4) Fifth Monarchism.[347]

---

[339] Knollys and Kiffin, *Life and Death*, 22ff.

[340] Especially repugnant to many Presbyterians was Knollys's Baptist defense known as *A Moderate Answer unto Dr. Bastwicks Book Called "Independency not God's Ordinance"* (London: Jane Coe, 1645). Bastwick was a Presbyterian. Knollys argues not for a loose democracy but for a representative polity that could protect what Baptists saw as biblical independency for the local church. Knollys was convinced that Presbyterian churches had failed to protect the autonomy of the local churches. Knollys's *Moderate Answer* is in the British Library, London.

[341] *Minutes of the Sessions of the Westminster Assembly of Divines*, ed. Alexander F. Mitchell and John Struthers (London: William Blackwood and Sons, 1874), 96.

[342] Thomas Edwards, *First and Second Part of Gangraena: Or a Catalogue and Discovery of Many of the Errors, Heresies, Blasphemies and Pernicious Practices of the Sectaries of This Time, Vented and Acted in England in These Four Last Years*, 3rd. ed. (London: Ralph Smith, 1646), Part 1, section 2, pages 39–40. Part 1 ends on page 116, and Part 2 commences with new pagination. This is in Trinity College (Dublin, Ireland) Library.

[343] For valuable discussions and rebuttals of each of the four charges against Knollys, see Howson, *Erroneous and Schismatical Opinions: The Question of Orthodoxy regarding the Theology of Hanserd Knollys (c. 1599–1691)*.

[344] Ibid., 79–132. In 1690, Samuel Crisp, son of Tobias Crisp (d. 1643), republished his father's popular Antinomian work under the title *Christ Alone Exalted: Being the Complete Works of Tobias Crisp, D. D., Containing XLII Sermons*. Of the fifty-two sermons, eight had never appeared in print. To assure readers that the eight sermons were authentic, a certificate signed by twelve London pastors was placed inside each book. Hanserd Knollys was a signatory, but, rather than being an endorsement, it was merely a confirmation of the authenticity of the eight additions.

[345] Howson, *Erroneous and Schismatical Opinions*, 133–93.

[346] Ibid., 194–242.

[347] Ibid., 243–306.

Essentially, however, his beliefs and practices are clearly within the boundaries of orthodoxy.

Concerning the first charge, "Antinomianism," Knollys agreed with the Antinomians that Christ saves sinners from four aspects of the law. First, He saves us "from all the Ceremonies or Elements of the Law." Secondly, He saves us "from under the penalties, and curse of the Law." Thirdly, He saves us "from the school-mastership of the Law," for "we have a new schoolmaster, to wit, Jesus Christ." Fourthly, Christ saves us "from the old Covenant of the Law." Yet, contrary to strict Antinomianism, Knollys insists, "We do not hereby make void the Law, but establish it." For, "in newness of spirit," we "fulfill the Royal law according to the Scriptures." We are not "without Law to God, but under the Law to Christ."[348] Knollys clearly disagreed with the extreme Antinomian assertions that true repentance can never lead to salvation, that Christ abrogated the moral law,[349] and that works of sanctification are peripheral.

Concerning the charge of "hyper-Calvinism," while he embraced the soteriology of John Calvin, Knollys's passion for evangelism, conversions, and church planting guarded him against any form of hyper-Calvinism.[350] For example, in his *World That Is to Come*, Knollys compassionately calls sinners to

---

[348] Knollys, *Christ Exalted: A Lost Sinner Sought, and Saved by Christ* (London: Printed by Jane Coe, according to Order, 1646), 23–25. A copy is in the British Library, London.

[349] Knollys makes it clear that God's elect are saved "from the *Law*, not from *Evangelical* obedience unto the *moral part* of the Law … but from the *Ceremonial* part of the Law … and from the curse of the Law," in *An Exposition of the Whole Book of the Revelation* (London: Printed for the author and for bookseller William Barthall, 1689), 93. Knollys adds, "By the *Keys* of the Kingdom, we are to understand that … our Lord Jesus Christ gave unto his Apostles and Elders *to Rule well*, and to *govern* in his Churches of Saints according to his *own* Institutions, Laws, and Ordinances" (106). All italics are in the original. The copy of Knollys's *Exposition* that I am using is in the Union Theological Seminary Library, NYC.

[350] Ibid., 241–42, where Knollys closes his commentary on Revelation with an invitation: "The Church of God, and the Spirit of God, and all converted persons, do invite all sorts of sinners, *especially*, thirsty sinners, without exception against any Persons, that are willing, and without any price, to take Christ freely."

faith and repentance:

> Consider, God offers Jesus Christ to poor, lost, miserable sinners (Rev. 3:17–18), yea to the chief of sinners (1 Tim. 1:12–15), upon Gospel-terms of Free Grace (Isa. 55:1–7), without exception of person, and without respect of price, Revelation 22:17: "And the Spirit and the bride say, Come. And let him that heareth say, Come. And let him that is athirst come. And whosoever will, let him take the water of life freely." In other words, any one, every one that is *willing*, may come to Christ, and receive Christ, and have Christ *freely*; for HE is the free Gift of God to sinners, who are without Christ in the World (John 3:16). Be but *willing* to take Christ, and the work is done. Christ complained of them that would not come to him, that they might have life (John 5:39–40).
>
> …. I *counsel* you poor, lost, perishing Sinners, *first*, suffer the Lord Jesus Christ to *come* by his Spirit and Word into your hearts, and set up the *Kingdom* of his Grace in your souls; that where *Sin* hath abounded, *Grace* may much more abound; and where *Sin* hath Reigned unto Death, there *Grace* might Reign through Righteousness unto *eternal* Life by Jesus Christ our LORD (Rom. 5:20–21). Do not resist the Holy Spirit, as they did (Zech. 7:7–9, 11–13) and their Children after them (Acts 7:51).
>
> *Secondly*, open your hearts to Christ, when he knocks at the Door of your Souls, and calls you to come to him, to receive him, and let him come into your hearts, and dwell in your hearts by his Holy Spirit, and sanctifying Grace, Revelation 3:20: "Behold, I stand at the door, and knock: if any man hear my voice, and open the door, I will come in to him, and will sup with him, and he with me." If the Sinner be *willing* to open the door of his heart, Christ will come in by his Holy Spirit, and he will communicate of his Grace to his Soul.
>
> *Thirdly*, let the Lord Jesus Christ have the *Throne*, and be exalted above ALL in your Souls, Isaiah 2:17: "And

the Lord alone shall be exalted in that day." Let your *own imaginations* be cast down, and every high thing that exalteth it *Self* against the knowledge of God, that every Thought may be brought into Captivity to the Obedience of Christ [2 Cor. 10:5]. Be *willing* to resign your whole Man — *Spirit, Soul,* and *Body* — unto the Government of Christ, as Lord and King, to Reign and Rule, Guide and Govern you by his Holy Spirit, and Written Word.

Not that you can do those things of yourselves; I have told you, without Christ you can do nothing (John 15:5). But it is your duty to do them, and it is the Free Grace of God, to work in you to will and to do, according to his good pleasure (Phil. 2:12–13), that he so working in you, you may work out your own salvation with fear and trembling.[351]

Concerning the charge of "Anabaptism," while agreeing with Anabaptists on believer's baptism, congregational polity, and opposition to state intrusion into local churches, Knollys stood repulsed over the manifold heresies and anarchies among the various Anabaptist groups.

Finally, regarding the charge of "Fifth Monarchism," Knollys shared the Fifth Monarchists' longing for the millennial reign of Christ, but he rejected any use of force to establish it.[352] He also shared the Fifth Monarchists' concerns over high taxes for the poor, and Royal trade monopolies' running small independent businesses out of existence, but he never joined any Fifth-Monarchist organization.

---

[351] Knollys, "The World That Is to Come," in *The World That Now Is; and the World That Is to Come: Or the First and Second Coming of Jesus Christ, Wherein Several Prophecies Not Yet Fulfilled Are Expounded* (London: Thomas Snowden, 1681), 34–36. Knollys begins new pagination in this section. I have modernized some grammar and punctuation. This copy is in the Bodleian Library, Oxford.

[352] Knollys insists that "ecclesiastical Power ordained by Christ and given to his Ministers, is not Magisterial, but Ministerial; not the Power of the Sword but of the Word," in *An Exposition of the Whole Book of the Revelation*, 129.

Knollys and the Restoration of the Stuarts

From the mid-1640s to 1660, Knollys traveled regularly in behalf of evangelistic outreach and church planting. While preaching in Suffolk, he "was stoned out of the pulpit (as he was preaching) by a company of rude fellows … set on by a malignant High-Constable who lives in the same Town." Knollys promptly published his sermon, *Christ Exalted* (1645), and dedicated it to the Committee of Examination who had condemned it.[353] During a shocking turn of events, the 1660 Restoration of the monarchy—albeit a limited monarchy—brought the Stuart King Charles II to England's throne. Intense persecution would soon commence against anyone suspected of dissent.

In April 1660, in Breda, Holland, Charles II had signed "The Declaration of Breda," promising "liberty for tender consciences," ensuring "that no man shall be disquieted or called in question for differences of opinion in matter of religion, which do not disturb the peace of the kingdom."[354] The following month, London's House of Lords and House of Commons heard a reading of the Declaration. Amid great jubilance, Charles soon landed in Dover on his way to London to secure his throne. Cheering crowds greeted him all the way to the capital city. Twelve months later, his supporters again took to the streets in celebration of his Coronation. Many were eagerly anticipating their promised "liberty for tender consciences." If Charles ever desired religious toleration, however, it was only in behalf of the Roman Church, which would receive him into her bosom on his deathbed. Meanwhile, to maintain his Crown, Charles, a crypto Catholic, first needed the support of a Restoration Parliament that would stand determined to reestablish total conformity to the National Church. All religious dissent must be rooted out. To accomplish that goal, Charles persuaded Parliament to annul every religious law established during the previous twenty years.

---

[353] Knollys, *Christ Exalted* (London: n.p., 1645), title page. This copy is in the British Library, London.

[354] "The Declaration of Breda," in *Documents Illustrative of English Church History*, ed. Henry Gee and William John Hardy (London: Macmillan, 1914), 587.

Knollys and the Clarendon Code

During 1661–65, Parliament passed a series of four acts, collectively called the Clarendon Code, whose primary purpose was the reestablishment, in England and Wales, of the absolute supremacy of the Church of England.[355] Until 1688, these and other acts regarding social issues, such as marriage and burial, would relegate Baptists to second-class citizenship. The four acts of the Clarendon Code are:

- The Corporation Act (1661) required all officers of municipal corporations to receive Communion "according to the rites of the Church of England." The act excluded all non-conformists, including Baptists, from public offices.
- The Act of Uniformity (1662) compelled every minister in the realm to declare in public his "unfeigned assent and consent to all and everything contained and prescribed in and by the *Book of Common Prayer*" for all corporate worship.[356] The Particular Baptist, John Norcott (d. 1676), successor to John Spilsbury at Wapping, was among the first of nearly two thousand non-conformists and dissenters ejected from their pulpits. Norcott found refuge in Holland during this time.[357]
- The Conventicle Act (1664) specified that, for persons sixteen years of age or older, the first offence of attending a non-conformist Conventicle (assembly) would result in a fine of five shillings, or a three-month prison sentence. A second offence would bring a fine of ten pounds, or a six-month imprisonment. A third offence would incur a fine of one hundred pounds, or a seven-year exile.[358]

---

[355] The Code was named in honor of the Lord Chancellor of Charles II, Edward Hyde, the first Earl of Clarendon.

[356] Andrew Browning, ed., "Early Modern 1660–1714," in *English Historical Documents, 1660–1714*, ed. David C. Douglas (1966; repr., London: Routledge, 1996), 375–82.

[357] Geoffrey F. Nuttall, "Another Baptist Ejection (1662): The Case of John Norcott," in *Pilgrim Pathways: Essays in Baptist History in Honor of B. R. White*, ed. William H. Brackney and Paul S. Fiddes, with John H. Y. Briggs (Macon, GA: Mercer University Press, 1999), 185–88.

[358] John Raithby, ed., *Statutes of the Realm: 1628–80* (London: History of Parliament Trust, 1819), 5:516–20.

A 1670 revision of the Conventicle Act would forbid all religious gatherings of more than five persons who were not of the same household. In addition, any person guilty of permitting an illegal assembly on his property would receive a fine of twenty-pounds.[359]

- The Five-Mile Act (1665) forbade all expelled non-conformist clergy from coming within five miles of their former places of worship and from coming within five miles of "any city, town corporate, or borough that sends burgesses to the Parliament." Moreover, the act forbade such ministers from teaching at any "public or private school." Violation of any part of the Five-Mile Act carried a fine of forty pounds.[360] In a word, those who refused to comply with unjust laws usually ended up paying heavy fines. Those unable to pay such fines faced imprisonment or exile.

Following the Venner uprising in 1661, authorities dragged Hanserd Knollys from his home and committed him to Newgate Prison for eighteen weeks on suspicion of supporting Fifth Monarchists. While he had sympathized with certain of the non-violent goals of the Fifth Monarchists, Knollys had never joined any such group. Nor had he signed the Fifth-Monarchist Manifesto. In fact, Knollys had joined with other Baptists in publishing declarations of loyalty toward the Crown. Now he found it unsafe to remain in any one place in England for more than a few days. We find the Knollys family, during this time, visiting Wales, Lincolnshire, Holland, and even Germany, where they remained for two or three years, as Hanserd resumed writing his Hebrew, Greek, and Latin grammars and lexicons.[361] Returning to London by way of Rotterdam, the

---

[359] Browning, 384–86.
[360] Ibid., 382–84.
[361] E.g., Hanserd Knollys, *Rhetoricae Adumbratio* (London: n.p., 1663); *Grammaticae Graecae Compendium* (London: n.p., 1664); *Grammaticae Latinae Compendium* (London: n.p., 1664); *Grammaticae Latinae, Graecae & Hebraicae Compendium* (London: Tho. Roycroft, 1665); *Linguae Hebraicae Delineatio* (London: n.p., 1664); *Radices Hebraicae Omnes, Quae in S. Scriptura, Veteris Testamenti Occurrunt* (London: n.p., 1664); and *Radices*

family discovered that, in their absence, the English government had confiscated all their property. Incredibly, the story of the Knollys family seems never to have been without grief; Hanserd seems never to have complained. In the wake of the Great Plague, in 1665, that killed at least 68,596 of London's population,[362] a ten-month drought turned the city into a tinderbox. The Great Fire of 1666 raged for four days and three nights, destroying two thirds of central London and leaving sixty-five thousand persons homeless. Almost ninety churches suffered utter destruction.[363] There is little wonder that, in the following year, Hanserd Knollys authored *Apocalyptical Mysteries* (1667), the first of his six treatises on prophecy,[364] emphasizing the imminence of Christ's return and the urgency for all to repent and turn to Christ as Lord and Savior.

In 1670, officers suddenly arrested Hanserd as he was ministering to his church assembled at Broken Wharf. He suffered

---

Simplicium Vocum, Flexilium Maxime, Novi Testamenti (London: n.p., 1664). Copies of these are at the University of Illinois (Urbana-Champaign Campus). Harvard University Library has a copy of Knollys, *The Rudiments of the Hebrew Grammar in English* (London: Moses Bell, 1648).

[362] "According to the Report made to the King's Most Excellent Majesty by the Company of the Parish Clerks of London," in *A Collection of the Yearly Bills of Mortality, from 1657 to 1758 Inclusive, Together with Several Other Bills of an Earlier Date* (London: Printed for A. Millar, 1759), n.p.

[363] See Neil Hanson, *The Great Fire of London: In That Apocalyptic Year, 1666* (Hoboken, NJ: John Wiley and Sons, 2002).

[364] Hanserd Knollys, *Apocalyptical Mysteries* (London: n.p., 1667), in the University of Chicago Library. Cf. Knollys, *The Parable of the Kingdom of Heaven Expounded: Or, an Exposition of the First Thirteen Verses of the Twenty Fifth Chapter of Matthew* (London: Benjamin Harris, 1674), in the Harvard University Library; Knollys, *Mystical Babylon Unvailed ... Also, a Call to the People of God to Come Out of Babylon* (London: n.p., 1679), in the Henry E. Huntington Library and Art Gallery, San Marino, CA. The book teaches that Rome is mystical Babylon, that the pope is the beast, that the Church of Rome is the great whore, and that the Roman priests mirror the false prophet. See Knollys, *An Exposition of the Eleventh Chapter of the Revelation* (London: n.p., 1679), in the Henry E. Huntington Library and Art Gallery, San Marino, CA; Knollys, *The World That Now Is; and the World That Is to Come* (1681); and Knollys, *An Exposition of the Whole Book of the Revelation* (1689).

imprisonment for violating acts of the Clarendon Code.[365] Even during times of sickness, Knollys rejoiced that he could preach to the inmates. Soon after his release, as he was under a near-terminal illness, death snatched away many his closest family members—including two grandchildren, three sons, and his faithful wife, Anne. Through it all, Hanserd continued his pastoral duties—encouraging his congregation and fellow Baptist pastors in the work of the Lord. Persecution lingered, though, and, in the spring of 1684, seventy-five-year-old Hanserd Knollys spent six more months in Newgate Prison. Again, he rejoiced in the opportunities to minister to the other prisoners.[366]

Knollys's Final Years amid Political Change

Charles II died in 1685 and the Crown passed to his brother James II (r. 1685-89). James, however, was a Roman Catholic, and large numbers of non-conformists and dissenters openly opposed his kingship. Many of them rallied to the support of the Duke of Monmouth, James Scott, an illegitimate son of Charles II. Claiming to be the rightful heir to the throne, Scott gathered an army and attempted a *coup d'état* known as Monmouth's Rebellion (1685). Howbeit, the Royal Army defeated James Scott and beheaded him for treason. Hundreds among Scott's vastly outnumbered military were captured, tried, and, in the "Bloody Assizes," were condemned to death by hanging—followed by drawing and quartering. Their gruesome remains were set up for public display in towns and villages. As we will see below, among the condemned "rebels" who suffered death were two grandsons of the Particular Baptist William Kiffin, a dear friend of Hanserd Knollys.

When the Queen of James II gave birth to a son in 1688, English Protestants once again awakened to the imminent threat of a Roman Catholic dynasty. Their deliverer was the Protestant, Prince William of Orange, son-in-law of James II. Unopposed by the Royal Navy, Prince William landed on England's Devon coast in November 1688, with 463 Dutch ships and a Dutch army

---

[365] Knollys and Kiffin, *Life and Death*, 24–32.
[366] Bustin, *Paradox and Perseverance*, 188–89.

of fourteen thousand troops. Receiving a grand welcome, Prince William drew over twenty thousand English supporters along the way, as he marched his army toward London. In the ensuing Glorious Revolution, Prince William issued his now-famous declaration that he would maintain "the liberties of England and the Protestant Religion." With James II fleeing to France and prominent Roman Catholics vacating London in disarray, Prince William of Orange became William III, King of Great Britain and Ireland. At their ascendency to the throne, William III (r. 1689-1702) and his wife Mary II (r. 1689-94) accepted Parliament's Declaration (Bill) of Rights, which initiated measures to assure the nation that Mary's Protestant sister, Anne, would be the next queen of England. On the heels of the Bill of Rights came the Toleration Act of 1689, which Baptist historian Joseph Ivimey would hail as "the Magna Charta of the Protestant Dissenters, by which they were relieved from all pains and penalties for separating from the Church of England."[367]

Indeed, the Toleration Act was a great victory and a marvelous beginning, but it was not a complete victory. Some features of the Clarendon Code remained in place, and all dissenters would still be required to pay tithes and parochial taxes for the maintenance of the Church of England.[368] On the other hand, though, in 1701, the nation incorporated into law the Act of Settlement, designed to secure a permanent Protestant succession to England's throne. It proclaimed that no Roman Catholic or anyone married to a Roman Catholic could ever hold the English Crown. Every Sovereign would swear to uphold the Church of England.[369] Mary died in 1694. Upon William's death, in 1702, Mary's sister, Anne, succeeded to the

---

[367] Joseph Ivimey, *A History of the English Baptists* (London: Printed for the author, 1811), 1:477–78.

[368] Bustin, *Paradox and Perseverance*, 236.

[369] *An Act for the Further Security of His Majesties Person, and the Succession of the Crown in the Protestant Line, and for Extinguishing the Hopes of the Pretended Prince of Wales and All Other Pretenders, and Their Open and Secret Abettors* (London: Printers to the Kings most excellent Majesty, 1701); see also Edmund Gibson, ed., *Codex Juris Ecclesiastici Anglicani*, 2nd ed. (Oxford: Clarendon Press, 1756), 614–18; and John Raithby, ed., *Statutes of the Realm: 1695–1701* (London: History of Parliament Trust, 1820), 7:747–50.

throne. Meanwhile, in the broader scope, France's Louis XIV, in 1685, had revoked the Edict of Nantes, which had protected the Protestant French Huguenots who were now fleeing to England, Germany, Holland, and the New World—South Carolina, New York, and New Jersey. These highly skilled tradesmen would enhance the spiritual welfare of Protestant lands by spreading the pure gospel of Christ. A new era had begun for Baptists and for many others on both sides of the Atlantic.

In July 1689, Hanserd Knollys, William Kiffin, Benjamin Keach, and four other pastors sent a letter to Baptist leaders throughout England and Wales, inviting them to London for the first General Assembly of Particular Baptists. Hosted by Knollys's church in George Yard, leading down to Broken Warf, the Assembly convened during September 3–12, 1689. Representing 107 Particular Baptist churches, the Assembly adopted the Second London Confession (1677, 2nd ed. 1688). The theological content of this confession, often called the "Assembly Confession," should dispel any question of Knollys's orthodoxy.

Even in the heated, internal controversy over congregational singing, Hanserd Knollys, during the final months of his life, wrote in behalf of the great majority who were longing for corporate singing of hymns as well as Psalms.[370] At that time, English Presbyterians and Independents generally frowned upon the corporate singing of any type of music other than Psalms. Some feared that if believers and unbelievers mingled their voices in song it would desecrate their worship. Others insisted that if congregations sing they should sing silently, in the heart, since (as they thought) women must refrain from uttering even a song. Nevertheless, London's Particular Baptists would become the first to popularize the corporate singing of hymns. Soon after Knollys's death, his congregation moved to Bagnio Court, then to Newgate Street, where the church remained for several years.

---

[370] Hanserd Knollys, *An Answer to a Brief Discourse concerning Singing in the Publick Worship of God in the Gospel-Church* (London: Printed for the author, 1691). This copy is in the Folger Shakespeare Library. Knollys is briefly but brilliantly answering Isaac Marlow's *A Brief Discourse concerning Singing in the Publick Worship of God in the Gospel-Church* (London: Printed for the author, 1690). This copy is in the Bodleian Library, Oxford. Marlow was a Baptist merchant who vehemently opposed corporate singing in church.

In about 1705, the congregation leased Curriers' Hall, situated in the ward of Cripplegate,[371] and remained there until 1799, when they moved to Red Cross Street. Soon thereafter, they moved to Aldersgate Street, where the church permanently closed about 1859. The spiritual fruit of Hanserd Knollys's ministry, however, will never cease.

Shortly before his death, Hanserd Knollys wrote his "Last Legacy to the Church"[372] he had founded and served for near half a century. Having endured many severe trials for his biblical convictions, Knollys died on September 19, 1691, in his 93rd year. The family buried him near his wife in Bunhill Fields. While the precise location of their graves is unknown, Anne's tomb inscription appears in a 1720 London survey:

Here lyeth the Body of Mrs. Anne Knollys, Daughter of John Cheney, Esq; Wife of Hanserd Knollys (Minister of the Gospel) by whom he had Issue 7 Sons and 3 Daughters; who dyed April 30th, 1671, and in the 63d Year of her Age.

Underneath that is an inscription of Hanserd's love poem to:

My only Wife, that in her Life,
Liv'd Forty Years with me,
Lyes now at Rest, forever blest
With Immortality.
My Dear is gone, left me alone,
For Christ to do, and dye;
Who did for me, and dy'd to be
My Savior God most High.[373]

---

[371] During its location in Cripplegate, the church was often designated the Cripplegate Baptist Church. The area of Cripplegate is now the well-known site of Barbican Centre and Barbican Estate. In the 1700s, hyper-Calvinists John Skepp and John Brine would serve as the Cripplegate Baptist pastors, opposing any offer of the gospel to the lost. Their opponents included Andrew Fuller and John Sutcliff.

[372] This is in Knollys and Kiffin, *Life and Death*, 44–50.

[373] *The Inscriptions upon the Tombs, Grave-Stones, etc. in the Dissenters Burial Place Near Bunhill-Fields* (London: Printed for E. Curll, 1717), 32; cf. John Stow, *A Survey of the Cities of London and Westminster*, ed. John Strype, 2

William Kiffin (1616-1701)
The Early Years

Born in or near London, William Kiffin (Kiffen)[374] was orphaned by the London plague of 1625 when he was only nine years old. The official record of the number of burials within the city of London attributes 35,417 deaths to the plague—about a third of the city's population.[375] Although expecting to die

---

vols. (London: Printed for A. Churchill, et al., 1720), vol. 2, bk. 4, chap. 2, p. 55. Volume one contains books 1-3 and volume two contains books 4-6, plus appendices; John Andrew Jones, ed., *Bunhill Memorials: Sacred Reminiscences of Three Hundred Ministers and Other Persons of Note, Who Are Buried in Bunhill Fields, of Every Denomination, with the Inscriptions on Their Tombs and Gravestones, and Other Historical Information Respecting Them, from Authentic Sources* (London: James Paul, 1849), 140-44; and *History of the Bunhill Fields Burial Ground: With Some of the Principal Inscriptions*, "printed by order of the City Lands Committee of the Corporation of London," with content contributions by Charles Reed, Chairman of the Preservations Committee (London: Charles Skipper and East, Printers, 1893), 32, 49-50.

[374] William's signature appears in two spellings: *Kiffin* and *Kiffen*. Larry J. Kreitzer prefers the latter in his excellent work, *William Kiffen and His World*, vols. 1-4 of a series of the Centre for Baptist History and Heritage Studies, Re-sourcing Baptist History: Seventeenth Century Series (Oxford: Regent's Park College, 2010-15), see 1:8-9. I have chosen to retain the spelling *Kiffin*. Other helpful works include William Kiffin, *Remarkable Passages in the Life of William Kiffin*, edited from the original manuscript with additional notes by William Orme (London: Burton and Smith, 1823); B. A. Ramsbottom, *Stranger than Fiction: The Life of William Kiffin* (1989; repr., Harpenden [Hertfordshire], England: Gospel Standard Trust Publications, 2008); Paul R. Wilson, "William Kiffin (1616-1701)," in *The British Particular Baptists 1638-1910*, ed. Michael A. G. Haykin, 1:64-77; Barrington R. White, "Kiffin, William (1616-1701)," in *Biographical Dictionary of British Radicals in the Seventeenth Century*, 2:155-57; idem, "William Kiffin—Baptist Pioneer and Citizen of London," *Baptist History and Heritage* 2, no. 2 (July 1967): 91-103 + 126; Michael A. G. Haykin, *Kiffin, Knollys and Keach*, 41-52; idem, "Kiffin, William (1616-1701)," in *Oxford Dictionary of National Biography* (Oxford: Oxford University Press, 2004), online ed., http://www.oxforddnb.com/view/article/15521.

[375] "According to the Report made to the King's Most Excellent Majesty by the Company of the Parish Clerks of London," in *A Collection of the Yearly Bills of Mortality, from 1657 to 1758* (London: Printed for A. Millar, 1759), n.p. This report is for December 16, 1624 to December 15, 1625. See Kiffin, *Remarkable Passages*, 2.

from "plague-boils," young William recovered. Friends of the family took the boy under their care. To some degree, we are dependent upon the *Remarkable Passages* (memoirs) that Kiffin wrote after arriving at an "old age," thinking it "my duty to leave behind me some account of those many footsteps of his grace and goodness towards me."[376] Kiffin was the first Baptist to write an autobiography. In his teen years, he began serving an apprenticeship with a local glove maker.

Early one Sunday morning, Kiffin decided, without just cause, to run away from his master. "Wandering up and down the streets, and passing by St. Antholin's church, I saw people going in, which made me return and go in also." The Puritan, Thomas Foxley, was preaching on Moses' commandment concerning "the duty of servants to masters." The message "made me greatly wonder," says Kiffin, "as thinking he had known me, and only preached to me." In fact, it had the "effect of making me immediately return to my master." Moreover, the "sermon dwelt very much upon my thoughts, and provoked in me a desire to hear some of them they called Puritan Ministers."[377] As Kiffin continued hearing and reading Puritan preaching, he came to know Christ as his Savior. After struggling for many months for assurance of salvation, he received full confidence. In 1638, twenty-two-year-old Kiffin became a freeman of the Leathersellers' Company of London, and, over the years, he would acquire wealth as a successful merchant and stockholder.[378] Kiffin and philosopher John Locke (1632–1704), decades later, would become two of the eleven partners in the Bahama Adventurers Company and invest in trade from the Caribbean Islands.[379]

Baptist Defender of the Faith during

---

[376] Kiffin, *Remarkable Passages*, 1ff.
[377] Ibid., 3.
[378] See Kreitzer, "William Kiffen's Apprentices within the Leathersellers' Company of London," in *William Kiffen and His World*, 2:258–61.
[379] Kreitzer has documented this information from correspondence in the Bodleian Library between William Kiffen and John Locke. See Kreitzer, "William Kiffen, John Locke, and the Bahama Adventurers of 1672," in *William Kiffen and His World*, 1:363–410; cf. 2:150–54 and 3:35–151.

DAVID BEALE

Seasons of Persecution

During 1638, Kiffin accepted an invitation to preach in London for an "Independent congregation,"[380] identified in the Kiffin manuscript as ""Spilsbury's congregation."[381] Kiffin soon joined this church and married Hanna, who was already a member.[382] In 1642, the congregation birthed another church, later known as "Devonshire Square Baptist Church."[383] Following Spilsbury's tutelage, William Kiffin accepted the Devonshire Square pastorate, where he served for the remainder of his life. The consensus among scholars is that Kiffin coauthored with John Spilsbury the first London Confession (1644). Kiffin describes why he became a Baptist:

> [I had] concluded that the safest way was to follow the Footsteps of the Flock (namely) that Order laid

---

[380] Kiffin, *Remarkable Passages*, 14. With Henry Jessey just recently accepting the J-L-J pastorate in 1637, Kiffin would be in close fellowship with the J-L-J Church, along with some of its offspring groups. For further discussion on the "Independent congregation" that Kiffin joined in 1638, see the "Rise of the Particular Baptists in London, 1633–1644," *Transactions of the Baptist Historical Society* 1, no. 4 (January 1910): 230–31; see also Barrington R. White, "How Did Kiffin Join the Baptists?" *Baptist Quarterly* 23, no. 5 (January 1970): 201–7; idem, "William Kiffin—Baptist Pioneer and Citizen of London," *Baptist History and Heritage* 2, no. 2 (July 1967): 91–103 + 126; and Walter Wilson, "William Kiffin," *The History and Antiquities of Dissenting Churches and Meeting Houses, in London, Westminster, and Southwark: Including the Lives of Their Ministers, from the Rise of Nonconformity to the Present Time*, 4 vols. (London: Printed for the author, 1808–14), 1:408.

[381] This is available in Ernest F. Kevan, *London's Oldest Baptist Church: Wapping 1633 – Walthamstow 1933* (London: Kingsgate Press, 1933), 16.

[382] At least three sons and three daughters would be born to this couple, and they would have at least a dozen grandchildren. See Kreitzer, *William Kiffen and His World*, 3:379.

[383] Due to persecution and the London fire of 1666, Kiffin's congregation would change locations many times before settling in Devonshire Square, near Bishopsgate Street on the north side of the Thames. See "Names of the Churches and Messengers," in *The Narrative of the Proceedings of the General Assembly* (London: n.p., 1689), 22. This copy is in the British Library. See Kreitzer, "Devonshire Square Baptist Church Membership Lists, c. 1664–90," in *William Kiffen and His World*, 1:177–307.

down by Christ and his Apostles, and Practiced by the Primitive Christians in their times, which I found to be, that after Conversion they were Baptized, added to the Church, and Continued in the Apostles' Doctrine, Fellowship, Breaking of Bread, and Prayer; according to which I thought myself bound to be Conformable.[384]

On October 17, 1642, in Southwark (London), Kiffin debated the Church of England clergyman, Daniel Featley, on believer's baptism by immersion; Featley published his retaliation, called *The Dippers Dipt*.[385] During the same year, as Kiffin was visiting the home of a friend who had broken his leg, authorities suddenly apprehended him for holding an unlawful religious service. Kiffin had shared a message from Hosea 2:7-8. Upon release from White-Lyon Prison, he published the Hosea sermon, dedicating it "to the right worshipful ... Justices of [the] Peace for his Majesties County of Surrey." His message was a plea for liberty of conscience.[386]

During the late 1630s and early 40s, Kiffin took business trips to Holland. During the late 40s and early 50s, he was able to spend more time with his family and church. He also served as a member of Oliver Cromwell's final Parliament (1656-58). At a meeting at Dorchester in 1658, Kiffin openly opposed the Fifth-Monarchist movement. He earnestly promoted due respect and obedience toward civil powers. The name *William Kiffin* heads the list of thirty signatories on *The*

---

[384] William Kiffin, "To the Christian Reader," in *A Sober Discourse of Right to Church-Communion* (London: Printed by George Larkin for Enoch Prosser, 1681), i-ii. This is in the Union Theological Seminary Library, NYC. I have modernized the spelling of a few words.

[385] Daniel Featley, *The Dippers Dipt: Or, the Anabaptists Duck'd and Plung'd over Head and Ears*, 4th ed. (London: Printed for Nicholas Bourn and Richard Royston in Ivy-lane, 1646), 1-16. Kiffin's name, spelled *Cufin* (suggesting a Welsh origin), appears in the margins (3-13). This is in Henry E. Huntington Library and Art Gallery, San Marino, CA.

[386] Kiffin, *Certaine Observations upon Hosea the Second [Chapter], the 7th and 8th Verses* (London: Printed for William Larner, at the Bible in Little-Eastcheap, 1642). This is in the Bodleian Library, Oxford.

Humble Apology of Some Commonly Called Anabaptists (1660),[387] insisting, "We who are falsely called Anabaptists" … obey our Civil Magistrates." Moreover, "whatever the Magistrate is in point of Religion, he is to be reverenced and obeyed in all those commands of his, which do not entrench upon, or rise up in opposition to the commands of God."[388] *The Humble Apology* affirms as well that Christians "are to submit to the Civil Commands, not only of such Rulers as are faithful, but even to infidels."[389] In spite of Kiffin's obedience, he suffered imprisonment as a suspect in the wake of the Venner uprising (1661).[390] In 1663, he intervened to secure the release of twelve General Baptists of Aylesbury who had been condemned to death for observing the Lord's Day in their homes.[391]

In 1670, Kiffin was elected sheriff of London and Middlesex.[392] Amid increasing state-church resistance, he quietly stepped down from office. The following year, he was elected Master of the propitious Leathersellers' Company of London.[393] Even as an entrepreneur, Kiffin kept his focus on local church order and doctrine, as well as on the personal care of his fellow-believers. On one occasion, his friend, Hanserd

---

[387] *The Humble Apology of Some Commonly Called Anabaptists* (London: Henry Hills, to be sold by Francis Smith, at the sign of the Elephant and Castle without Temple-Bar, 1660), title page; and 14. This is in the British Library, London. See also Kreitzer, "William Kiffen's Indictments at the Surrey Assizes in March 1642," in *William Kiffen and His World*, 1:6–41.

[388] *Humble Apology*, 17.

[389] Ibid., 18. I have modernized the spelling of a couple of words.

[390] See Kreitzer, "'Unlawfully assembled and mett together': William Kiffen's Arrest on 24 February 1661 at the House of Robert Malbon," in *William Kiffen and His World*, 1:148–76. Kiffin makes a brief reference to the incident in *Remarkable Passages*, 32.

[391] Thomas Crosby, *The History of the English Baptists*, 4 vols. (London: Thomas Crosby, 1738–40), 2:180–85; and Kreitzer, "William Kiffen and the Release of the Aylesbury Twelve," in *William Kiffen and His World*, 4:225–63.

[392] Edward Duane Burton, "The World of English Artisans and Traders: 1600–1750" (PhD diss., Purdue University, 2007), 152–53.

[393] William Henry Black, *History and Antiquities of the Worshipful Company of Leathersellers, of the City of London* (London: Printed by Edward J. Francis, 1871), 67.

Knollys, was suffering from illness. Knollys recalls that "Mr. Kiffin & Mr. Vavasor Powel … prayed over me, and anointed me with Oil in the Name of the Lord: and the Lord did hear Prayer and heal me."[394] Powel (1617–71) suffered martyrdom as a Baptist; he lies buried in Bunhill Fields graveyard. Although his tombstone deteriorated with time, its inscription was mercifully preserved:

Vavasor Powell, a successful Teacher of the past,
A sincere Witness of the present, and an useful Example to the future Age, lies here interr'd, who in the Defection of so many, obtained Mercy to be found Faithful; for which being called to several Prisons, he was there tried, and would not accept Deliverance, expecting a better Resurrection. In hope of which, he finished this Life, & Testimony, in the 11th year of his Imprisonment,
And in the 53d Year of his Age, Octob. 27. An. 1671.
In vain Oppressors do themselves perplex,
To find out Arts how they the Saints may vex:
Death spoils their Plots, and sets the oppressed free;
Thus Vavasor obtained true Liberty.
Christ him released, and now he's joyned among
The martyred Souls, with whom he cries, *How long*.
Rev. 6.10.[395]

Following a Declaration of Indulgence, issued by Charles II in 1672, some Baptists began securing preaching licenses and registration certificates for their meetinghouses. To obtain the certificates, the churches had to provide the names of their pastors and of their members, along with the addresses of their meeting places. On March 8, 1673, Parliament, however, pressured Charles into retracting the Indulgence and recalling the licenses and certificates. As persecution resumed, many Baptist pastors suffered incarceration in Newgate. Keenly astute with

---

[394] Knollys and Kiffin, *Life and Death*, 35–36.
[395] *The Inscriptions upon the Tombs, Grave-Stones, etc. in the Dissenters Burial Place Near Bunhill-Fields*, 39; cf. Edward Bagshaw, *The Life and Death of Mr. Vavasor Powell* (London: n.p, 1671), 208.

politics inside the capital, William Kiffin would have anticipated the ephemeral benefits of governmental gifts. Hence, he appears to have refrained from applying for licenses and certificates for his London congregation.[396] Indeed, many Baptists had firmly expressed their conviction that only the local church has authority to license its preachers. According to the 1674 section in the Record Book of Bristol's Broadmead Baptist Church, renewed persecution was now making it necessary for churches to guard their doors during services:

> We ... ordered one of the doors of our meeting place to be made fast, and all to come in at one, ... and to appoint some youth, or two of them, to be out at the door, every meeting, to watch when ... informers or officers, were coming: and so to come in, one of them, and give us notice thereof. Also, some of the hearers, women and sisters, would sit and crowd in the stairs, when we did begin the meeting with any exercise, that so the informers might not too suddenly come in upon us; by reason of which they were prevented divers times.[397]

Some of Broadmead Church's pastors were in Newgate Prison. With informers continually gaining access into their services, the church began seating unknown attendees inside a curtained-off section, where they could hear the ministers but could not identify them. Such methods frequently failed. The Broadmead Record Book reveals heart-wrenching examples of pastors beaten and imprisoned, despite their desperate attempts at using curtains, trap doors, and even escape routes through underground tunnels. On one occasion, in 1674, a pastor had almost escaped, when "the bishop's men got hold of his legs, others of his arms, and so, with much violence,

---

[396] See W. T. Whitley, "The Baptist Licenses of 1672," *Transactions of the Baptist Historical Society* 1, no. 3 (October 1909): 166; and Frank Bate, *The Declaration of Indulgence 1672: A Study in the Rise of Organized Dissent* (University Press of Liverpool, 1908), 130–43.

[397] Edward Bean Underhill, ed., *Records of a Church of Christ, Meeting in Broadmead, Bristol, 1640–1687* (London: J. Haddon for the Hanserd Knollys Society, 1847), 223.

dragged him out, and carried him away to Bridewell, where he remained some time, and then was committed to Newgate."[398]

During these persecutions, Edward Terrill (1635–86), ruling elder of the Broadmead Baptist Church, felt compelled to execute a trust fund for the support of a minister for Broadmead, specifically "a holy man, well skilled in Greek and Hebrew," and "whose chief task would be that of preparing young men for ministry among the Baptist churches of the land."[399] Dated June 3, 1679, Terrill's endowment would become the seed money toward the establishment of the earliest Baptist institution of higher learning—Bristol Baptist Academy (later College). After feeble beginnings, the Academy established a firm local-church foundation, under the thirty-eight-year tutorship of Bernard Foskett (1685–1758). Characteristically, the tutor was also the Broadmead Baptist pastor. During the earliest decades, the students lived and received their training in the pastor's home. With Baptist churches standing in dire need of well-trained ministries, Bristol Baptist Academy began to meet that need. There were important issues at stake—in both doctrine and practice.

Already, in two published works, John Bunyan had defended open membership and open Communion—practices deemed by serious Baptists as contrary to the New Testament. Disregarding the New Testament order of believer's baptism by immersion, Bunyan regarded one's baptism as simply an individual choice, rather than a local church ordinance. Among the membership at the Bunyan Church, some had received immersion as believers, but many of the older members had received nothing more than a mere sprinkling as infants in the National Church. Typically, these members had no desire for a scriptural baptism. This would rarely be an issue today. Among mainstream British Baptists of the twenty-first-century, the practice of open Communion and the theology of ecumenical Sacramentalism hold sway.[400]

---

[398] Ibid., 232.
[399] Norman S. Moon, *Education for Ministry: Bristol Baptist College 1679–1979* (Bristol, England: Bristol Baptist College, 1979), 1.
[400] The best studies on this topic include Peter Naylor, *Calvinism, Communion and the Baptists: A Study of the English Calvinistic Baptists from the Late*

Prior to the 1770s, most Baptist churches restricted membership and Communion to immersed believers. A century later, larger numbers of Baptists would be dropping the restriction. Alarmed at the confusion resulting from Bunyan's practices and lack of discernment, William Kiffin wrote *A Sober Discourse of Right to Church-Communion* (1681), "wherein is proved by scripture, the example of primitive times, and the practice of all that have professed the Christian religion that no un-baptized person may be regularly admitted to the Lord's Supper."[401] Kiffin recognized that these were critical years for Baptists. This was no time for turning back. While appealing to church fathers, Kiffin most often appeals to New Testament churches and their prescribed order of conversion and baptism preceding the breaking of bread: Acts 2:41–42: "Then they that gladly received his word were baptized: and the same day there were added unto them about three thousand souls. And they continued stedfastly in the apostles' doctrine and fellowship, and in breaking of bread, and in prayers."

In 1682, the deepest sorrow filled William Kiffin's life.[402] In grief, he recalls the death of Hanna, "my dear and faithful wife, with whom I had lived nearly forty-four years. Her tenderness to me and faithfulness to God, were such as cannot by me be expressed…. Her death was to me the greatest sorrow I ever met with in this world."[403] Kiffin later married Sarah Reeves, who, with multiple lapses of character, would bring grief to William and to the church.

1600s to the Early 1800s, vol. 7 of the series, Studies in Baptist History and Thought (2003; repr., Eugene, OR: Wipf and Stock, 2006); Stanley K. Fowler, *More than a Symbol: The British Baptist Recovery of Baptismal Sacramentalism* (Milton Keynes, England: Paternoster, 2002); Anthony R. Cross and Philip E. Thompson, eds., *Baptist Sacramentalism* (Milton Keynes, England: Paternoster, 2003); idem, *Baptist Sacramentalism 2* (Milton Keynes, England: Paternoster, 2008); and Ian M. Randall, *The English Baptists of the Twentieth Century* (Didcot, England: The Baptist Historical Society, 2005).

[401] Kiffin, *A Sober Discourse of Right to Church-Communion*, title page; 16ff. and passim.

[402] Idem, *Remarkable Passages*, 22ff.

[403] Ibid., 50.

The Final Years

Among those captured in Monmouth's Rebellion,[404] in 1685, were two of William Kiffin's grandsons: Captain Benjamin Hewling of the Cavalry (ca. twenty-two years of age) and Lieutenant William Hewling (age nineteen) of the Red Regiment.[405] They were the sons of Kiffin's widowed daughter, Hannah. Upon the recent death of their father, in 1684, Benjamin and William had gone to the Netherlands. They had returned to England the following year with the Duke of Monmouth. Since Benjamin and William were among the most important prisoners, their captors transported them to London for interrogation. Offering praise to the Lord that they had acted only in behalf of "English Liberties and the Protestant Religion," the young men suffered immediate incarceration in Newgate Prison. Officers weighted them down with irons and placed them in solitary confinement. Benjamin testifies that God's presence had never been as powerful to them as during those days in Newgate.[406] During their childhood, the

---

[404] Among the best sources, see Robert Dunning, *The Monmouth Rebellion: A Guide to the Rebellion and Bloody Assizes* (Dovecote Press: Stanbridge, Wimborne, Dorset, United Kingdom, 1985); and Peter Earle, *Monmouth's Rebels: The Road to Sedgemoor 1685* (New York: St. Martin's Press, 1977).

[405] *A List of the Names of the Rebells That Were Executed at Lyme, Bridport, Weymouth, Melcombe Regis, Sherbourn, Pool, Wareham, Exeter, Taunton, and Several Other Places* (London: Printed by E. Mallet, next door to Mr. Shiptons Coffee-House near Fleet-Bridge, 1686). Issued as a broadsheet, this is a list of executions after the final battle at Sedgemoor. This is in the British Library, London.

[406] "The Hewlings," in *A New Martyrology: Or, the Bloody Assizes, Now Exactly Methodized in One Volume, comprehending a Complete History of the Lives, Actions, Trials, Sufferings, Dying Speeches, Letters, and Prayers of All Those Eminent Martyrs Who Fell in the West of England, and Elsewhere, from the Year 1678 to 1689*, 3rd ed. (London: Printed according to the original copies for John Dunton at the Black Raven in the Poultry, 1689), 154–56. This is in the Union Theological Seminary Library, NYC. The author's name is not provided. Although it has been long assumed that the authors of *A New Martyrology* included John Tutchin and Titus Oates, the 1693 fourth edition provides a single author's name, "Thomas Pitts," who, in his title, changes "Martyrs" to "Protestants," and changes "from the Year 1678 *to 1689*" to "from the Year 1678 to This Present Time."

boys had lived for some time in the home of Grandfather Kiffin, who now offered £3000 for their acquittal,[407] *but to no avail.* William Hewling was hanged in Lyme and buried in the Lyme churchyard. Benjamin was hanged in Taunton and buried at Taunton's St. Mary Magdalene's Church. Surprisingly, their corpses were spared from drawing and quartering. Their sister, Hannah, paid the unjust fee of a thousand pounds for permission to have a Christian burial for Benjamin. Chief Justice George Jeffreys, during the trial hearings, had attempted to torment William Hewling with a warning that "his grandfather did as well deserve that death, which he was likely to suffer."[408]

In an unexpected turn of affairs, only two years after the Hewling executions, King James II nominated the elderly William Kiffin for the office of Alderman for the City of London. When the King entreated him to commence his post, Kiffin expressed reluctance.[409] "'Sire,' replied Kiffin, 'I am a very old man, and have withdrawn myself from all kind[s] of business for some years past, and am incapable of doing any service in such an affair to your majesty in the city. Besides, Sire' — the old man went on, fixing his eyes steadfastly on the king, while the tears ran down his cheeks — 'the death of my grandsons gave

---

See Thomas Pitts, "The Hewlings," in *A New Martyrology: or, the Bloody Assizes, Now Exactly Methodized in One Volume, comprehending a Complete History of the Lives, Actions, Trials, Sufferings, Dying Speeches, Letters, and Prayers of All Those Eminent Protestants Who Fell in the West of England, and Elsewhere, from the Year 1678 to This Present Time*, 4th ed. (London: Printed according to the original copies for John Dunton at the Black Raven in the Poultry, 1693), 184ff. This is in the British Library, London. There are some mistakes in the pagination of this edition.

[407] Joseph Ivimey, *The Life of Mr. William Kiffin, upwards of Sixty Years Pastor of the Baptist Church, Devonshire Square, London, from 1639 to 1701* (London: Printed for the author, 1833), 63.

[408] Kiffin, *Remarkable Passages*, 82. As James II was fleeing the country in 1688, Judge Jeffreys was already in the Tower of London, where he died the next year at the age of forty-four. Ironically, his supporters had placed him in the Tower for his safety.

[409] As part of a concerted effort to weaken the influence of the National Church, James II, a Roman Catholic at heart, was bypassing traditional Church of England clergy for government roles. Thus, James was seeking to use dissenters such as Kiffin for his own purposes.

a wound to my heart which is still bleeding, and never will close but in the grave.'"[410] The King sat in total silence. "In a minute or two, however, he recovered himself enough to say, 'Mr. Kiffin, I shall find a balsam for that sore.'"[411] Suddenly, the King turned toward a Lord in Waiting and left the room. Much against his will, Mr. Kiffin did serve as Alderman, but he declined from acting as Justice of the Peace, since that would have required his taking the sacrament of the Church of England. After nine months, Kiffin was discharged from office. He never again heard from the King, on the matter of the grandsons. The King's "balsam" turned out to be more persecution.

In the following year (1686), authorities were again harassing Kiffin's Devonshire Square Church, for holding "illegal" assemblies. The church was holding two services every Sunday.[412] Remarkably, Knollys and Kiffin were the major Baptist figures who experienced these long years of persecution and still lived to see the turning point toward freedom — the Toleration Act of 1689. Among those who had signed the Baptists' London Confession, in 1644, only William Kiffin lived to witness the approval of the Second London Confession, formally adopted by the first General Assembly of Particular Baptists from England and Wales, in 1689.

As requested in his will, when Kiffin died in 1701, the family interred his body in the grave of his first wife Hanna, in Bunhill Fields. Although the tombstone no longer exists, its copied inscriptions are as follows:

---

[410] Joseph Ivimey, *History of the English Baptists* (London: Printed for the author, 1811), 1:473–74. The heart-wrenching account is preserved in these sources: Kiffin, *Remarkable Passages*, 55–82; Mark Noble, *Memoirs of the Protectoral-House of Cromwell*, 3rd ed. (London: Printed for G. G. J. and J. Robinson, 1787), 2:454–64; and "The Hewlings," in *A New Martyrology: Or, the Bloody Assizes*, 3rd ed., 143–65.

[411] Wilson, "William Kiffin," in *History and Antiquities of Dissenting Churches and Meeting Houses*, 1:427.

[412] See Kreitzer, "'Riotously assembled': Conventiclers arrested at the Devonshire Square Baptist Church (11 February 1686)," in *William Kiffen and His World*, 1:308–14. Kiffin's name, however, is not included with the eight who were arrested.

> Hanna, late wife of William Kiffin, fell asleep in the Lord the 6th of October [1682] in the 67th year of her age.
> William Kiffin, the elder, of London, merchant, ... [died] Dec. 29th, 1701, in the 86th year of his age.

At least four additional family members lie buried in William Kiffin's tomb. From extant copies, we have the tombstone inscriptions for his eldest son William (d. August 31, 1669, at age 20); for his daughter Priscilla Liddel (d. March 15, 1679, at age 24); for his son Henry (Harry) (d. December 8, 1698, at age 44); and for his granddaughter Henrietta (d. 1698) — all resting in one grave.[413]

Benjamin Keach (1640–1704)

The Early Years

Born on February 29, 1640, at Stoke Hammond (Buckinghamshire), to John and Fedora (Joyce) Keach,[414] Benjamin received infant baptism in the local parish church.[415] England was, at the time, on the brink of the Civil War Era (1642–48. Since his parents were unable to provide him with a college education, Benjamin earned his living as a tailor. He had a brilliant mind, and, even from his youth, he was an avid reader of Scripture and of theological books by Puritan and Independent authors. Upon profession of faith in Christ,[416]

---

[413] Stow, *A Survey of the Cities of London and Westminster*, vol. 2, bk. 4, chap. 2. p. 57; *History of the Bunhill Fields Burial Ground: With Some of the Principal Inscriptions*, 49; John Andrew Jones, ed., *Bunhill Memorials*, 124–34; cf. Haykin, *Kiffin, Knollys and Keach*, 52; idem, "Kiffin, William (1616–1701)," *Oxford Dictionary of National Biography* (Oxford University Press, 2004), online ed., http://www.oxforddnb.com/view/article/15521.

[414] On the name of Keach's mother, see Austin Walker, *The Excellent Benjamin Keach* (Dundas, Ontario: Joshua Press, 2004), 39n6.

[415] The local parish church in Stoke Hammond still exists. It underwent major restoration in 1852. Its twelfth-century stone font could be the one used for Benjamin Keach's infant baptism.

[416] Helpful sources on Keach include Walker, *The Excellent Benjamin Keach*;

Benjamin, at age fifteen, received baptism by immersion at a nearby General Baptist church. By the age of eighteen, he was preaching among General Baptist congregations in the area. At the beginning of the Stuart Restoration (1660), twenty-year-old Benjamin married Jane (née Grove), of nearby Winslow. They would have four girls and an only son, Elias. Two of the girls died at a young age.

King Charles's Declaration of Breda, with its promise of freedom of worship, had encouraged Baptist congregations to reopen their meetinghouse doors for public worship. Immediately, they faced the broken promises and sharp restrictions of the Clarendon Code. With the abolition of the Declaration of Breda, Baptists faced the piercing reality that King Charles's promise "to allow freedom of conscience in religious matters" applied only to the National Church.[417] Baptist historian, Thomas Crosby, future son-in-law of Keach, reported

---

Jonathan W. Arnold, *The Reformed Theology of Benjamin Keach (1640–1704)*, vol. 11 of a series for the Centre for Baptist History and Heritage Studies (Oxford: Regent's Park College, 2013); Thomas Crosby, *The History of the English Baptists*, 4:268–314; Wilson, "Benjamin Keach," in *The History and Antiquities of Dissenting Churches and Meeting Houses, in London, Westminster, and Southwark*, 4:243–50; Tom J. Nettles, "Benjamin Keach (1640–1704)," in *The British Particular Baptists 1638–1910*, ed. Michael A. G. Haykin (Springfield, MO: Particular Baptist Press), 1:94–131; Michael A. G. Haykin, *Kiffin, Knollys and Keach*, 82–97; R. L. Greaves, "Keach (or Keeche), Benjamin (1640–1704)," in *Biographical Dictionary of British Radicals in the Seventeenth Century*, 2:155–57; William Eugene Spears, "The Baptist Movement in England in the Late Seventeenth Century as Reflected in the Work and Thought of Benjamin Keach, 1640–1704" (PhD diss., University of Edinburgh, 1953); and D. B. Riker, *A Catholic Reformed Theologian: Federalism and Baptism in the Thought of Benjamin Keach, 1640–1704*, vol. 35 of the series, Studies in Baptist History and Thought (2009; repr., Eugene, OR: Wipf and Stock, 2010).

[417] Arthur Clear, *The King's Village in Demesne: Or a Thousand Years of Winslow Life* (Winslow, England: Edwin J. French, 1894), 91–92; see also 88–98. Erected ca. 1696 — eight years prior to Keach's death — the quaint, little brick church in Winslow claims to be "Benjamin Keach's Meeting House," http://www.westgallerychurches.com/index.html. According to local history, while Keach never served as pastor of the Winslow church, the congregation did set him apart for the gospel ministry and sent him out to preach. See also Kenneth Dix, *Benjamin Keach and a Monument to Liberty* (Dunstable, England: Faucomberg Press, 1985), 16, 22.

that Benjamin "was often seized, while preaching, and committed to prison ... and sometimes his life was threatened."[418]

Keach's Trial

Keach's newly published primer, *The Child's Instructor* (1664),[419] quickly incited the rector of Stoke Hammond to complain to the civil authorities that the book contained "damnable doctrines" against infant baptism and in support of lay preaching and of a millennial reign of Christ on earth. On October 9, 1664, Keach appeared before Lord Chief Justice Hyde. During Keach's trial at the Aylesbury Assizes (Courts), Judge Hyde falsely accused him of being a radical Fifth Monarchist. Hyde was seeking grounds to impose the death sentence upon his victim. When the jury found Benjamin Keach guilty only of misquoting a verse of Scripture, Hyde bullied the jurors into finding the defendant guilty of other charges. Crosby preserves the text of the final verdict and the sentence that Judge Hyde read aloud to the court:

> *Benjamin Keach,* you are here convicted, for writing, printing and publishing, a seditious and schismatical book, for which the court's judgment is ... that you shall go to *gaol* for a fortnight without bail ... and the next *Saturday,* to stand upon the *pillory* at *Aylesbury,* in the open market, for the space of two hours, with a paper upon your head with this inscription, "For writing, printing, and publishing a schismatical book entitled *The Child's Instructor, or a New and Easy Primer."* And the next *Thursday,* to stand in the same manner, and for the same time, in the market of *Winslow;* and there your book shall be openly burnt, before your face, by the common hangman, in disgrace of you and your doctrine: and you shall forfeit to the King's Majesty the sum of *twenty pounds*; and shall remain in *gaol,* until you find *sureties* for your good behavior, and appearance at the next *Assizes,* there to *renounce your doctrines,*

---

[418] Thomas Crosby, *The History of the English Baptists,* 2:185–86.
[419] *The Child's Instructor: or, a New and Easie Primmer* (London: n.p., 1664). There are no extant copies of this edition.

and make such public submission as shall be enjoined upon you: Take him away, keeper.[420]

Benjamin Keach would never renounce his doctrine. Even as he watched the common hangman publicly burning all copies of *The Child's Instructor*, Keach, with his head in a pillory, preached the gospel to spectators. Crosby recorded the opening words of Keach's message: "Good people, I am not ashamed to stand here this day, with this paper on my head; my Lord *Jesus* was not ashamed to suffer on the cross for me; and it is for his cause that I am made a gazing-stock. Take notice, it is not for any wickedness that I stand here; but for writing and publishing his truths, which the Spirit of the Lord hath revealed in the Holy Scriptures."[421] Keach's preaching was so convincing that the sheriff threatened to gag him. Normally, the throngs would jeer at a person whose head and hands were locked into a public pillory. They would pelt him with stones. In this case, the crowds stood in sympathy with the man of God. When a Church of England clergyman raised his voice against the humble preacher, the crowd reproached the clergyman for his being recently "pulled drunk out of a ditch" and being "found drunk under a hayrick." The disgraced minister hurried out of sight. Keach would count the experience as "the greatest honor that ever the Lord was pleas'd to confer upon me."[422] His wife Jane remained by his side through the entire

---

[420] Crosby, *History of the English Baptists*, 2:202–03; see also 2:185–209 and 2:207; cf. Arthur Clear, *The King's Village in Demesne*, 92–93. Crosby's account is from "The Tryall of Mr Benja: Keach who was prosecuted for Wrighting against Infant Baptism &c, with an Account of ye Punishment inflicted on him for ye same. Anno 1664," in *A Repository of Divers Historical Matters relating to the English Antipedobaptists, Collected from Original Papers or Faithful Extracts*, no. 21, 93–104, comp. and ed. Benjamin Stinton (Angus Library and Archive, Regent's Park College, Oxford, 1712). Stinton, who was Keach's son-in-law and successor, explains that the account is "taken from Manuscript found among Mr Keachs Papers after his Death, which, as he informed me when alive, was sent [to] him from one in yt Country who was present both at his tryall & Punishment, & took what passed in Wrighting."

[421] Crosby, *History of the English Baptists*, 2:204.

[422] Ibid., 2:204–5; 2:207; cf. Francis Hargrave, "The Trial of Mr. Benjamin Keach, at the Assizes at Ailsbury in Buckinghamshire, for a Libel, October

ordeal. It is tenable, as many believe, that Keach rewrote much of the *Child's Instructor* from memory and included it in two later primers, *The Child's Delight*[423] and *Instructions for Children*[424] — precursors of the *New England Primer*.[425]

Establishment and Outreach of Keach's Horsleydown Church

In 1668, Benjamin, Jane, and the children, moved to London, whose citizens were still recovering from the Plague and the Great Fire. Deeply burdened for suffering Christians and lost souls on every hand, Benjamin received ordination as pastor of a General Baptist church, meeting in a home on Tooley Street, Southwark. The previous pastor, William Rider, had deceased, and the church had been without a pastor for some time. Two years after arriving in London, Jane, the wife of Benjamin's youth passed into eternity. The couple had been married only ten years. To the memory of his "first dear and beloved wife," Keach published his poem, *A Pillar Set Up* (1670), inspired by the biblical account of Rachel's death in Genesis 35:20, "Jacob set a pillar upon her grave: that is the pillar of Rachel's grave unto this day." Keach rejoiced when numerous individuals testified of their conversion through Jane's witness.[426] After nearly two years as a widower with three youths, he married Susannah Partridge (née Skidmore) with Hanserd Knollys officiating the

---

8 and 9, 1664," in *A Complete Collection of State Trials, and Proceedings for High Treasons, and Other Crimes and Misdemeanours in Great Britain, Commencing with the Eleventh Year of the Reign of King Richard III and Ending with the Sixteenth Year of the Reign of King George III* (Dublin: printed by Graisberry and Campbell for P. Byrne, 1795), 2:601–5.

[423] *The Child's Delight: Or Instructions for Children and Youth*, 3rd ed. (London: printed for William and Joseph Marshall, n.d.). This copy is in the British Library.

[424] *Instructions for Children: Or, the Child's and Youth's Delight; Teaching an Easy Way to Spell and Read True English*, 30th ed. (London: printed for J. How, n.d.). Thus, we know that this primer went through at least thirty editions.

[425] See Gillian Avery, "Origins and English Predecessors of the New England Primer," *Proceedings of the American Antiquarian Society* 108, part 1 (1998): 33–61.

[426] Crosby, *History of the English Baptists*, 4:274.

wedding. "A woman of extraordinary piety," Susannah "had a good report of all."[427] She would bear Benjamin five daughters and survive him by some twenty years.

In Southwark, Keach quickly acquired faithful friends and doctrinal influence from among the leading Particular Baptists, including Knollys, William Kiffin, and John Norcott.[428] Keach's identification with these brethren resulted in the reorganization of his little flock into a Particular Baptist Church. While this General Baptist congregation could well have divided over such a transformation, there is no evidence of any splinter group.[429] Under the brief Declaration of Indulgence issued by Charles II, Keach's newly organized congregation, in 1672, erected a chapel on Goat Street, Horsleydown, in Southwark. Experiencing steady growth, this evangelistic congregation enlarged their chapel several times, until it could hold "near a thousand hearers." Like many Separatist chapels of those days, the wooden building probably had no seating. Keach would serve the Horsleydown pastorate for the remainder of his life. The church's future buildings would include Charles Spurgeon's New Park Street chapel and the Metropolitan Tabernacle.[430] Spurgeon once noted that Keach "was by no

---

[427] Ibid., 4:275.

[428] John Norcott and Hercules Collins were the first two successors to John Spilsbury at the Wapping church. Keach read an evangelistic, poetic eulogy at Norcott's funeral in 1676. A copy of the two-columned sheet is in the British Library, London.

[429] W. T. Whitley, ed., *Minutes of the General Assembly of the General Baptist Churches in England*, vol. 1, 1654–1728 (London: Kingsgate Press, 1909), 34n10; cf. Riker, *A Catholic Reformed Theologian*, 40n131.

[430] Charles H. Spurgeon, *The Autobiography of C. H. Spurgeon 1854–1860*, compiled from his diary, letters, and records by his wife and his private secretary (London: Passmore and Alabaster, 1898), 2:329. Keach served the Horsleydown congregation from 1668 to 1704. In 1757, the congregation would build a new chapel at Carter Lane, off Tooley Street, Southwark, for John Gill, who served the pastorate from 1720 to 1771. During 1773–1836, John Rippon (1751–1836) would serve the pastorate. In 1830, six years prior to Rippon's death, Carter Lane chapel would suffer demolition to make room for wider access to the nearby London Bridge. Three years later, the congregation would move into their new chapel on New Park Street. Nineteen-year-old Charles Spurgeon (1834–92) would assume the New Park Street pulpit in 1854.

means [as] highly Calvinistic as his great successor, Dr. Gill; but evidently held much the same views as are now advocated from the pulpit of the Tabernacle."[431]

Keach contributed immensely to the cause of Christ in Baptist ministries and outreach. By the end of his life, he had published at least fifty works on a wide range of topics, some in multiple editions. He was the leading Baptist theologian of his era. Typical among his strong defenses of believer's baptism by immersion are *Gold Refin'd* (1689) and *The Ax Laid to the Root* (1693). Unlike most Particular Baptists, Keach defended and practiced the *Laying on of Hands upon Baptized Believers, as Such, Proved an Ordinance of Christ* (1698).[432] His key theological works include *Tropologia, or, a Key to Open Scripture Metaphors* (1681),[433]

---

[431] *The Autobiography of C. H. Spurgeon 1834–1854* (London: Passmore and Alabaster, 1897), 1:306.

[432] This is Keach's revision of his earlier work, *Darkness Vanquished: Or, Truth in Its Primitive Purity* (1675).

[433] The Particular Baptist scholar, Thomas Delaune, assisted Keach with the *Tropologia* and co-signed its epistle "to the reader." Widely recognized as being well versed in the classics and in the church fathers, Delaune also had a firm grasp of Hebrew, Greek, and Latin. He joined with William Kiffin, Hanserd Knollys, and three others in writing a defense of believer's baptism, *The Baptists Answer to Mr. Obed. Wills, His Appeal against Mr. H. Danvers* (London: Printed for Francis Smith, 1675). This is in the Union Theological Seminary Library, NYC. Most importantly, Delaune authored *Compulsion of Conscience Condemned* (London: Printed for John How and Thomas Knowles, 1683). This copy is in the British Library, London. The next year he wrote *A Plea for the Nonconformists* (London: Printed for the author, 1684). This copy is in Dr. Williams's Library, 14 Gordon Square, London. Daniel Defoe would write the preface of the 1706 edition. There is bitter irony in Delaune's fate. For his urgent warnings that persecution was already stripping dissenters of "their Liberties, Estates, yea Lives," Delaune was tried in Old Bailey on the false charge of sedition. The common hangman publicly burned his books in front of the Royal Exchange. Unable to pay his fine of a hundred marks (ca. £67), Delaune was incarcerated among felons, in Newgate Prison, where his wife and two children would soon join him. Under miserable conditions, the entire family died in the prison within fifteen months. Being the last to die (1685), Thomas had witnessed the horrific death of each member of his family. See his *Narrative of the Sufferings of Thomas DeLaune, for Writing, Printing and Publishing a Late Book Called, 'A Plea for the Nonconformists'* (London: Printed for the author, 1684). This

A Golden Mine Opened (1694), *The Glory of a True Church and its Doctrine Display'd* (1697), and *The Jewish Sabbath Abrogated* (1700). His important premillennial,[434] eschatological works include *Antichrist Stormed: Or, Mystery Babylon the Great Whore, and Great City, Proved to Be the Present Church of Rome* (1689), and *Gospel Mysteries Unveil'd* (1701). His allegory, *War with the Devil* (1673), predates the first volume of John Bunyan's *Pilgrim's Progress* by five years. Two additional allegories by Keach—*The Progress of Sin* (1684) and *The Travels of True Godliness* (1684)—appeared concurrently with the second volume of Bunyan's *Pilgrim's Progress*. A more polemical work by Keach is his rhymed dialogue, *The Grand Imposter Discovered* (1675), a critique and exposé of the key beliefs of George Fox and his Quakers.

Keach as the Father of Baptist Hymnody

While the singing of vernacular hymns was already commonplace among German churches of the seventeenth-century, English Independents and Presbyterians still favored only the singing of Psalms in corporate worship. While most Particular Baptists favored the practice of congregational hymn singing, a loud minority, led by Isaac Marlow, protested in a heated, internal debate on the topic. In his *Brief Discourse*

---

is in the Union Theological Seminary Library, NYC. See also Keith E. Durso, "Thomas Delaune: A Martyred Champion for Religious Liberty," in *No Armor for the Back: Baptist Prison Writings, 1600s–1700s* (Macon: Mercer University Press, 2007), 106–11; for an excellent overview, see Michael A. G. Haykin, "Delaune, Thomas (d. 1685)," *Oxford Dictionary of National Biography* (Oxford University Press, 2004), online ed., http://www.oxforddnb.com/view/article/7451).

[434] Keach says, "His [Christ's] second personal coming I judge will be at the beginning of the thousand years reign, when 'God will tabernacle with men,' Rev. 21:3," in *Gospel Mysteries Unveil'd: Or an Exposition of All the Parables and Many Express Similitudes Contained in the Four Evangelists* (London: Printed by R. Tookey to be sold by William Marshall,1701), 3:95. Keach adds, "The peaceable and universal reign will not be until the king comes" (3:175); cf. 2:158, 3:142, and Supplement 111–12. Keach partitions this work into a three-book division. This copy is in the British Library, London. See also the valuable discussion by Jonathan W. Arnold, *The Reformed Theology of Benjamin Keach (1640-1704)*, 217ff.

concerning Singing in the Public Worship of God in the Gospel-Church (1690), Marlow presented five reasons for rejecting corporate singing: (1) In Ephesians 5:19, the essence of singing is not vocal, rather, it is singing "in your heart to the Lord."[435] (2) Although the early churches sang David's Psalms, the New Testament never prescribes the practice.[436] (3) Prescribed and pre-composed songs and hymns are tantamount to the pre-composed forms of prayer found in the Anglican *Book of Common Prayer*.[437] (4) Congregational singing violates the principle that "women ought neither to teach nor pray vocally in the Church of Christ."[438] (5) Vocal singing would introduce "legal worship" and disorder in the church.[439] Marlow concludes, "Vocal singing together, either of David's Psalms or any human pre-composed forms, is a corrupting of the pure worship of Jesus Christ.... It will lead us to apostasy."[440] In his *Answer*, Keach exhibits Marlow's case as exegetically flawed.[441]

Under Keach's tutelage, congregational singing at Horsleydown Baptist emerged with the simple singing of a Psalm after the Lord's Supper. Keach pointed to the scene of Jesus and His disciples as they were finishing the initial Lord's Supper: "When they had sung an hymn, they went out into the mount of Olives" (Matt. 26:30). Keach published some of his own hymns as early as 1664 in *The Child's Instructor*. He would now begin incorporating some of these hymns into special services, such as Thanksgiving days. In about 1690, the majority of the Horsleydown congregation voted in favor of singing a hymn every Lord's Day. They agreed to sing after the sermon, so that those who were unwilling to sing

---

[435] Isaac Marlow, *A Brief Discourse concerning Singing in the Public Worship of God in the Gospel-Church* (London: Printed for the author, 1690), 5–9. This is in the Bodleian Library, Oxford.

[436] Ibid., 9–15.

[437] Ibid., 15–21.

[438] Ibid., 21–22.

[439] Ibid., 22–23.

[440] Ibid., 44–50.

[441] Benjamin Keach, *An Answer to Mr. Marlow's Appendix* (London: Printed for the author, and sold by John Hancock in Castle-Alley on the west side of the Royal-Exchange, and by the author at his house near Horsleydown in Southwark, 1691). This is in the British Library, London.

could "go freely forth." Although the church used no musical instruments, which would have deeply offended many, their corporate singing still led to a breach in the church.[442] The following year, however, Keach published *The Breach Repaired in God's Worship, or Singing of Psalms, Hymns, and Spiritual Songs, Proved to Be a Holy Ordinance of Jesus Christ with an Answer to All Objections* (1691).[443] Benjamin Keach had now established himself as a Baptist pioneer, by normalizing the practice of congregational hymn singing, as "an ordinance of the Lord," in all regular church services.[444] In his *Spiritual Melody* (1691),[445] Keach published some three hundred of his hymns. An additional one hundred of his hymns would appear five years later, in his *Feast of Fat Things Full of Marrow* (1696).[446] Keach was the

---

[442] Those who split from Keach's church established a church on Tooley Street in Southwark. It was later called the Maze Pond Church, and eventually it embraced congregational singing.

[443] Benjamin Keach, *The Breach Repaired in God's Worship, or, Singing of Psalms, Hymns, and Spiritual Songs, Proved to Be an Holy Ordinance of Jesus Christ with an Answer to All Objections* (London: Printed for the author, and sold by John Hancock in Castle-Alley on the West side of the Royal-Exchange, and by the author at his House near Horsleydown in Southwark, 1691). This first-edition copy is in the British Library.

[444] The most helpful studies on Keach and the issue of music include Robert H. Young, "The History of Baptist Hymnody in England from 1612 to 1800" (DMA diss., University of Southern California, 1959); W. T. Whitley, *Congregational Hymn-Singing* (London: J. M. Dent and Sons, 1933), 94–101, 121–23; Henry S. Burrage, *Baptist Hymn Writers and Their Hymns* (Portland, ME: Brown Thurston and Co., 1888), 30–32, 627–28; James C. Brooks, "Benjamin Keach and the Baptist Singing Controversy: Mediating Scripture, Confessional Heritage, and Christian Unity" (PhD diss., Florida State University, 2006); and Hugh Martin, *Benjamin Keach (1640-1704): Pioneer of Congregational Hymn Singing* (London: Independent Press, 1961).

[445] Benjamin Keach, *Spiritual Melody: Containing near Three Hundred Sacred Hymns* (London: Printed for John Hancock, in Castle-Alley, near the Royal-Exchange in Cornhill, 1691). This is in the Bodleian Library, Oxford. See also W. T. Whitley, "The First Hymnbook in Use," *Baptist Quarterly* 10, no. 7 (July 1941): 369–75.

[446] Benjamin Keach, *A Feast of Fat Things Full of Marrow Containing Several Scripture Songs Taken out of the Old and New Testaments*, "together with one hundred divine hymns" (London: Printed by B. H., 1696). This is in the British Library, London.

father of Particular Baptist hymnody. As W. T. Whitley notes, these Baptists "were pioneers. They were the first to popularize the singing of English hymns by the congregation."[447]

The Final Years

Keach had participated in the first Particular Baptist General Assembly of 1689. In 1697, he published for his congregation thirty-nine Articles of Faith—a condensed version of the Second London Confession (1677, 2nd ed. 1688). Departing from the latter confession, Keach broadened the application of the term *ordinance*. Most Particular Baptists recognized two standard ordinances—Baptism and the Lord's Supper. When he was a General Baptist, Keach had advocated the laying on of hands upon each new member, and he practiced it for the rest of his life. Believing that, through baptism, accompanied by the imposition of hands, the believer will "meet with more of Christ and His Spirit,"[448] Keach regarded both acts as important prerequisites for partaking of the Lord's Supper. In his Articles of Faith, Keach recognizes five "holy ordinances" in this order: Baptism (Art. 21), the Laying on of Hands (Art. 23), the Lord's Supper (Art. 24), Prayer (Art. 26), and the Singing of Psalms (Art. 27).[449]

Leaving a notable legacy, Keach was succeeded in the Horsleydown pastorate by his son-in-law Benjamin Stinton. A second son-in-law was Thomas Stinton, and a third was Thomas Crosby, the Baptist historian.[450] In about 1688, Benjamin's son,

---

[447] W. T. Whitley, *A History of the British Baptists*, rev. 2nd ed. (London: Kingsgate Press, 1932), 184.

[448] Benjamin Keach, *Laying on of Hands upon Baptized Believers, as Such, Proved an Ordinance of Christ*, 2nd ed. (London: To be sold by Benjamin Harris, 1698), 78. This copy is in the British Library, London.

[449] Idem, *The Articles of the Faith of the Church of Christ, or Congregation Meeting at Horsley-down, Benjamin Keach, Pastor, as Asserted This 10th of the 6th Month, 1697* (London: n.p., 1697). This copy is in the library of Union Theological Seminary, NYC.

[450] The Stinton men were brothers. Benjamin Stinton married Keach's daughter Susanna; Thomas Stinton married Elizabeth; and Thomas Crosby married the youngest daughter, Rebecca. The nearest first-hand account of the life and ministry of Benjamin Keach is in Crosby's

Elias (1666-99), immigrated to the Colony of Pennsylvania and established, near Philadelphia, the Pennepack Baptist Church—now the oldest Baptist church in the state. Upon his return to London, in 1692, Elias began presenting a morning lectureship in Pinners' Hall,[451] where as many as 1500 persons frequently attended. The following year, he gathered a Baptist church at Wapping, Middlesex, in London's east end, where Hercules Collins, pastor of the nearby Spilsbury church, ordained him before "a great congregation." Within some nine months, Elias had baptized 130 believers.[452] He died at the age of thirty-three—his father Benjamin surviving him by five years. The Baptists had purchased enough real estate for a little burial ground. This land had once been part of the nearby "Park" connected with the palace of the Winchester bishops in Southwark. From the official records of the *Trade Tokens*, we read that, "In the Park was the first Baptist burial-ground, where was buried Mr. Benjamin Keach, who died July 16, 1704 (*vide* Jacob Street and Goat Yard [passage])."[453] A member of his congregation lamented:

Is he no more? Has Heaven withdrawn his light,
And left us to lament, in sable shades of night,

---

four-volume *The History of the English Baptists*, 4:268-314. See B. R. White, "Thomas Crosby, Baptist Historian," Part I, *Baptist Quarterly* 21, no. 4 (October 1965): 154-68; and Part II, *Baptist Quarterly* 21, no. 5 (January 1965): 219-34.

[451] Earlier known as the "Glass House," in Old Broad Street, the building became "Pinners' Hall" when the Pinners' Company (a manufacturer of pins and needles) bought it. Supported by the merchants, the weekly Tuesday-morning lectureship had begun in 1673. There were six regular lecturers—four Presbyterians and two Independents. See "The Ancient Merchants' Lecture," *Congregational Historical Society Transactions* 7, no. 6 (April 1918): 300-09.

[452] Morgan Edwards, *Materials towards a History of the Baptists in Pennsylvania both British and German*, vol. 1 of his *Materials* (Philadelphia: Joseph Crukshank and Isaac Collins, 1770), 1:109-15 (Appendix 5). Elias dated his letter "the 12th month, 20th day, 1693-94."

[453] George C. Williamson, ed., *Trade Tokens Issued in the Seventeenth Century in England, Wales, and Ireland, by Corporations, Merchants, Tradesmen, Etc.* (London: Elliot Stock, 1891), 2:1033.

Our loss?
Death boasts his triumph; for the rumor is spread
Through Salem's plains, that Keach, dear Keach, is dead.[454]

The Life and Ministry of John Bunyan: With Consideration of His Place in Baptist History

John Bunyan (1628-88) was born in Elstow, near Bedford. Baptized as an infant in the Elstow Parish Church,[455] John was the eldest of three sons born to Thomas and Margaret Bunyan. Although Thomas earned his living as a local brazier, he managed to own a cottage at the far eastern end of Elstow Parish, bordering the hamlet of Harrowden. The cottage no longer stands, but a stone marks the site. Forced to learn his father's trade, John ended his formal education after a few years of grammar school. In 1644, when John was sixteen, his mother and sister died within the same month. His father soon remarried, and, by year's end, John enlisted in the Army of Parliament, when England's Civil War Era was in its second year.

Bunyan would often testify of God's sovereign and merciful providence, in an event from this period of his life. He was stationed to garrison duty in the company of Newport Pagnell, twelve miles from Elstow. Bunyan's company assigned him to a group commissioned to besiege a certain location. "When I was just ready to go," recalls Bunyan, "one of the company desired to go in my room [stead] .... When I consented, he took my place; and coming to the siege, as he stood sentinel, he was shot into the head with a musket bullet, and died."[456] When

---

[454] Edward Walford, *Old and New London* (London: Cassell and Co., 1873), 6:110.
[455] The Elstow Abbey Church of St. Helena and St. Mary possesses the Communion table used at that time, along with the font used to christen the infant John Bunyan.
[456] John Bunyan, *Grace Abounding to the Chief of Sinners* (1666), in *The Whole Works of John Bunyan*, 3 vols. ed. George Offor, with prefaces, notes, and biography of Bunyan (London: Blackie and Son, 1855), 1:7, hereafter called *Works of John Bunyan*.

the Army disbanded the Newport Pagnell company, in 1647, Bunyan returned to Elstow and resumed his work as a "tinker," or repair man, soldering metal household wares.[457] It is noteworthy that the most crucial years of John Bunyan's spiritual pilgrimage to conversion would coincide precisely with the years of Oliver Cromwell's Commonwealth (1649-1653).

In 1649, Bunyan married his first wife, and, in the following year, their blind daughter, Mary, was born. Three other children would be born of this marriage. While her first name is unknown, Mrs. Bunyan's meager dowry brought two books of spiritual influence into their home: Arthur Dent's *The Plaine Man's Pathway to Heaven* (1601), "wherein every man may clearly see whether he shall be saved or damned," and Lewis Bayly's *The Practice of Piety* (1612), "directing a Christian how to walk that he may please God." Especially helpful to John Bunyan during this time was his discovery of an old copy of Martin Luther's *Commentary on Galatians*. During 1652-53, after passing through severe spiritual conflict and conviction of sin, John Bunyan attained God's inward peace. In his autobiography, *Grace Abounding to the Chief of Sinners* (1666), he provides a clear testimony of his conversion.

Bunyan immediately joined the Bedford Church, known as "Bedford Meeting," an Independent congregation, recently gathered by John Gifford, who had counseled Bunyan and immersed him in the River Great Ouse.[458] Having no building of its own, Bedford Meeting received permission to hold its services in the facilities of St. John's Church, situated on the south side of the river. Like many Independent congregations during this time, Bedford Meeting regarded itself as both congregationalist and baptistic.[459] Greater clarity would gradually lead

---

[457] In Bedford's Bunyan Museum, there is a tinker's anvil with this inscription on three sides: "J Bunyan/Helstowe/1647." The museum also has a tinker's iron fiddle (or violin) with the inscription, "John Bunyan Helstowe."

[458] The site of Bunyan's baptism is on the river's south bank, between Bedford Town Bridge and the Duck Mill Lane car park.

[459] Joseph D. Ban, "Was John Bunyan a Baptist? A Case Study in Historiography," *Baptist Quarterly* 30, no. 8 (October 1984): 367-76; and W. T. Whitley, "The Bunyan Christening, 1672," *Transactions* of *the Baptist*

many Independents to define themselves as *Congregationalists*, while others would designate themselves as *Baptists*. Calvinistic in doctrine and congregational in practice, Gifford's church resembled many Baptist churches—with one major exception. His church did not require immersion as a prerequisite to membership and Communion. With John Gifford's death in 1655, the Bunyan family moved into Bedford,[460] and the congregation often called upon John to preach. Beginning in the late 1650s, he traveled extensively throughout Bedfordshire, Hertfordshire, Cambridgeshire, Surry, and London, powerfully preaching the gospel in churches and fields. Bunyan's wife died in 1658.[461] The following year, he married his second wife, Elizabeth, and published his most ambitious theological treatise, *The Doctrine of Law and Grace Unfolded*.

In 1660, at the Restoration of the Stuart dynasty, authorities issued a warrant for Bunyan's arrest for breaking the Conventicle Act. Bunyan was opening his Bible to preach in a farmhouse, in the hamlet of Lower Samsell (Bedfordshire), when officers captured him, conveyed him to Bedford, and incarcerated him in the County Gaol. Had Bunyan promised to stop preaching, the authorities would have released him immediately; John Bunyan could never yield to such demands. Except for a few brief periods of parole, he remained in Bedford County Gaol until 1672.[462] During the twelve-year imprisonment, Bunyan wrote *Christian Behavior* (1663), *The Holy City* (1665), and *Grace Abounding* (1666—the year of London's great fire). In 1672, a Declaration of Indulgence, issued by Charles II, made Bunyan a free man. Still without a permanent pastor or place to worship, Bedford Church began praying for God's will in both matters. The *Church Book* records the divine answer:

> After much seeking God by prayer, and sober

Historical Society 2, no. 4 (1910–11): 255–63.

[460] A blue plaque on the building at No. 17 St. Cuthbert's Street reads, "On this site stood the cottage where John Bunyan lived from 1655."

[461] This was also the year of Oliver Cromwell's death.

[462] At the corner of Silver Street and High Street, a plaque in the pavement marks the site of the County Gaol, demolished in 1801. Two of its doors are in Bedford's Bunyan Museum.

conference formerly had, the Congregation did at this meeting in joynt consent (signifyed by solemne lifting up of their hands) call forth and appoint our bro. John Bunyan to the pastoral office, or eldership: And he accepting thereof, gave up himself to serve Christ, and his church in that charge; and received of the elders the right hand of fellowship.[463]

Soon after becoming pastor of Bedford Church, Bunyan (for the sum of £50) purchased land containing a barn and a little orchard on Mill Street. The church converted the barn into a meetinghouse, whose burial ground, "the Garden of Remembrance," would supplant the orchard. (In 1707, a three-gabled building would replace the barn.)[464] The size of Bunyan's congregation was rapidly increasing, and his preaching tours were drawing large crowds.

In the summer of 1672, the Declaration of Indulgence emboldened some Congregationalists and Baptists to apply for church licenses; Bunyan's church was among those seeking a license. Illustrative of his neutral position on baptism, when Bunyan filled out the applications for his church and for several others, he described them all as "Congregational" rather than Baptist.[465] At the beginning of his pastorate, Bunyan had written *A Confession of My Faith, and a Reason of My Practice* (1672), in which he insisted that the church must not make immersion a prerequisite for full standing. Like the Baptists,

---

[463] *A Booke Containing a Record of the Acts of a Congregation of Christ in and about Bedford and a Brief Account of Their First Gathering*, later published under the title *The Church Book of Bunyan Meeting, 1650–1821: Being a Reproduction in Facsimile of the Original Folio in the Possession of the Trustees of Bunyan Meeting* (London: J. M. Dent and Sons, 1928), 50 (January 21, 1672). This is a handwritten, folio-size manuscript, limited edition, number 39 of 675 copies. The first occurrence of Bunyan's name appears on page 5, on line twenty-six of a list of members.

[464] The present church building on the site was erected during 1849–50. Known as "Bunyan Meeting" and self-described as "independent," the church presently holds full membership in the Baptist Union of Great Britain and in the Congregational Federation. The Bunyan Museum preserves priceless memorabilia of his life and times.

[465] W. T. Whitley, "The Baptist Licenses of 1672," *Transactions of the Baptist Historical Society* 1, no. 3 (October 1909): 165.

Bunyan recognized two ordinances for the local church. Like the Baptists, he believed that baptism is symbolic of the believer's death, burial, and resurrection in Christ, and that Communion is a memorial, established by Jesus as a remembrance of His sacrificial atonement. Of these ordinances, though, Bunyan added, "I count them not the fundamentals of our Christianity." [466]

Many Baptists leaders expressed alarm at Bunyan's quasi-Baptist refusal to make believer's baptism by immersion a requirement for church membership. This was a Baptist distinctive. Indeed, Baptists had earned their label by their firm conviction in this matter. They feared that Bunyan's loose practices would increasingly lead others to inclinations even more precarious. As a Baptist, William Kiffin responded to Bunyan's *Confession* with *Serious Reflections* (1673). Bunyan countered with *Differences in Judgment about Water Baptism, No Bar to Communion* (1673), and *Peaceable Principles and True* (1674).[467] Kiffin answered with *A Sober Discourse of Right to Church Communion* (1681). Bunyan relegated baptism to personal preference, rather than a New Testament church ordinance. Under the pastorate of Ebenezer Chandler (1691–1720), Bunyan's immediate successor, the Bedford Church would make infant baptism its normal practice, thus solidifying its traditional and exclusive identification with the Congregationalist denomination.[468]

In 1673, Charles II withdrew the Declaration of Indulgence. During 1676–77, Bunyan was imprisoned, this time on a technicality—and this time in the Town Gaol, located on the Town Bridge. He spent his six-month term writing two thirds of the first volume of his immortal allegory, *The Pilgrim's Progress*. The first edition of the first volume appeared in 1678, and the first authorized edition of the second volume appeared six years later (1684 O. S.).[469] *Pilgrim's Progress* would undergo

---

[466] Bunyan, *A Confession of My Faith, and a Reason of My Practice*, in Works of John Bunyan, 2:604.

[467] See *Works of John Bunyan*, 2:591–655; cf. Thomas Armitage, *A History of the Baptists* (New York: Bryan, Taylor, and Co., 1887), 528–39.

[468] Ban, "Was John Bunyan a Baptist?" 371.

[469] John Bunyan, *The Pilgrim's Progress from This World to That which is to*

widespread publication and translation into many languages.[470] Meanwhile, Bunyan had published his books, *The Life and Death of Mr. Badman* (1680) and *The Holy War* (1682).[471] Amid uncertainty surrounding the inauguration of the Roman Catholic James II, in 1685, Bunyan deeded his property to his wife, Elizabeth, to avoid confiscation. Happily, the threat was short-lived. In a rapid turn of events, England, by 1688, was now standing at the brink of a Glorious Revolution that would bring William and Mary to the throne and religious tolerance for her people. Bunyan would not live to see the Revolution.

In August of 1688, he set out on a forty-mile journey, on horseback, in a driving rain, from Reading to London. Upon arrival, Bunyan preached the gospel, but it was to be his final sermon. He had contracted a severe fever, a "sweating sickness," that quickly developed into pneumonia. Twelve days later, August 31 — three months short of his sixtieth birthday — John Bunyan completed his earthly pilgrimage and entered the eternal presence of His Lord and Savior. His body lies buried in a vault in Bunhill Fields, in London. Towering nine feet tall, at the north end of Bedford's High Street, there stands a three-ton bronze statue of John Bunyan. This statue symbolizes the greatness of this man's never-ending spiritual influence upon untold millions.

Select Bibliography of Works by and About John Bunyan

Ban, Joseph D. "Was John Bunyan a Baptist? A Case Study in Historiography." *Baptist Quarterly* 30, no. 8 (October 1984): 367–76.
Brown, John. *John Bunyan (1628–1688): His Life, Times, and Work*. Tercentenary edition revised by Frank Mott Harrison. London: The Hulbert Publishing Co., 1928. This is the most complete of all Bunyan

---

Come, 2 vols. (London: Nath. Ponder, 1678–84). The original is in Henry E. Huntington Library & Art Gallery, San Marino, CA.
[470] John Brown, *John Bunyan (1628–1688): His Life, Times, and Work*, revised by Frank Mott Harrison (London: Hulbert Publishing Co., 1928), 239–91, 472. At the present Town Bridge, built in 1813, the inscription on a historical plaque states that Bunyan served his six-month sentence in the earlier bridge that was here.
[471] Other pertinent titles among John Bunyan's sixty books include *The Jerusalem Sinner Saved* (1688) and *The Heavenly Footman* (1698).

biographies. John Brown was minister of the Bunyan Church from 1864 to 1903.

Bunyan, John. *The Whole Works of John Bunyan*. 3 vols. Edited by George Offor with prefaces, notes, and biography. London: Blackie and Son, 1855.

The Church Book of Bunyan Meeting 1650-1821. London: J. M. Dent and Sons, 1928 facsimile reprint.

Poe, Harry L. "John Bunyan." In *Baptist Theologians*, edited by Timothy George and David S. Dockery, 26-48. Nashville: Broadman, 1990.

Smith, Allen, "John Bunyan (1628-1688)." In *The British Particular Baptists 1638-1910*, ed. Michael A. G. Haykin. 1:78-93. Springfield, MO: Particular Baptist Press, 1998.

Whitley, W. T. "The Bunyan Christening, 1672." *Transactions* of *the Baptist Historical Society* 2, no. 4 (1910-11): 255-63.

Winslow, Ola Elizabeth. *John Bunyan*. New York: Macmillan, 1961.

Select Bibliography of Works by and About Hanserd Knollys

Brown, J. Newton. "Memoir of Hanserd Knollys, M. A." *New-Hampshire Historical Society Collections* 5 (1837): 175-79.

Bustin, Dennis C. *Paradox and Perseverance: Hanserd Knollys, Particular Baptist Pioneer in Seventeenth-Century England*. Vol. 23 of the series, Studies in Baptist History and Thought. Milton Keynes, England: Paternoster, 2006.

Culross, James. *Hanserd Knollys: "A Minister and Witness of Jesus Christ" 1598-1601*. London: Alexander and Shepheard, 1895.

Duncan, Pope A. *Hanserd Knollys: Seventeenth-Century Baptist*. Nashville: Broadman, 1965.

Howson, Barry H. *Erroneous and Schismatical Opinions: The Question of Orthodoxy regarding the Theology of Hanserd Knollys (c. 1599-1691)*. Vol. 99 of the series, Studies in the History of Christian Thought. Leiden: E. J. Brill, 2001.

James, Muriel. *Religious Liberty on Trial: Hanserd Knollys – Early Baptist Hero*. Franklin, TN: Providence House Publishers, 1997.

Knollys, Hanserd. *An Answer to a Brief Discourse concerning Singing in the Publick Worship of God in the Gospel-church*. London: Printed for the author, 1691.

_____. *Apocalyptical Mysteries*. London: n.p., 1667.

_____. *Christ Exalted: A Lost Sinner Sought, and Saved by Christ*. London: Printed by Jane Coe, according to Order, 1646.

_____. *An Exposition of the Eleventh Chapter of the Revelation*. London: n.p., 1679.

_____. *An Exposition of the Whole Book of the Revelation*. London: Printed for the author and for bookseller William Barthall, 1689.

_____. *Mystical Babylon Unvailed ... Also a Call to the People of God to Come Out of Babylon*. London: n.p., 1679.

_____. *The Shining of a Flaming-fire in Zion*. London: Printed by Jane Coe, according to Order, 1646.

_____. *The World That Now Is; and the World That Is to Come: Or the First and Second Coming of Jesus Christ, Wherein Several Prophecies Not yet Fulfilled Are Expounded*. London: Thomas Snowden, 1681.

_____, and William Kiffin. *The Life and Death of That Old Disciple of Jesus Christ, and Eminent Minister of the Gospel, Mr. Hanserd Knollys, Who Dyed in the Ninety-Third Year of His Age*, "written with His Own Hand to the Year 1672 and Continued in General in an Epistle by Mr. William Kiffin." London: Printed for John Harris, 1692.

Muriel, James. *Religious Liberty on Trial: Hanserd Knollys – Early Baptist Hero*. Franklin, TN: Providence House Publishers, 1997.

White, Barrington R. *Hanserd Knollys and Radical Dissent in the 17th Century*. London: Dr. Williams's Trust, 1977.

Select Bibliography of Works by and About William Kiffin

Ivimey, Joseph. *The Life of Mr. William Kiffin, upwards of Sixty Years Pastor of the Baptist Church, Devonshire Square, London, from 1639 to 1701*. London: Printed for the author, 1833.

Kiffin, William. *Remarkable Passages in the Life of William Kiffin*. Edited from the original manuscript with notes by William Orme. London: Burton and Smith, 1823.

_____. *A Sober Discourse of Right to Church-Communion*. London: Printed by George Larkin for Enoch Prosser, 1681.

Kreitzer, Larry J. *William Kiffen and His World*. Vols. 1–4 of a series for the Centre for Baptist History and Heritage Studies, Re-sourcing Baptist History: Seventeenth Century Series. Oxford: Regent's Park College, 2010–15.

Ramsbottom, B. A. *Stranger than Fiction: The Life of William Kiffin*. 1989. Reprint, Harpenden (Hertfordshire), England: Gospel Standard Trust Publications, 2008.

White, Barrington R. "How Did Kiffin Join the Baptists?" *Baptist Quarterly* 23, no. 5 (January 1970): 201–7.

_____. "William Kiffin—Baptist Pioneer and Citizen of London." *Baptist History and Heritage* 2, no. 2 (July 1967): 91–103 + 126.

Select Bibliography of Works by and About Benjamin Keach

Arnold, Jonathan W. *The Reformed Theology of Benjamin Keach (1640–1704)*. Vol. 11 of a series for the Centre for Baptist History and Heritage Studies. Oxford: Regent's Park College, 2013.

Brooks, James C. "Benjamin Keach and the Baptist Singing Controversy: Mediating Scripture, Confessional Heritage, and Christian Unity." PhD diss., Florida State University, 2006.

Hicks, Thomas Eugene Jr. "An Analysis of the Doctrine of Justification in the Theologies of Richard Baxter and Benjamin Keach." PhD diss., The Southern Baptist Theological Seminary, 2009.

Keach, Benjamin. *The Ax Laid to the Root.* London: Printed for the author, and are to be old by John Harris, 1693.

———. *The Child's Delight: Or Instructions for Children and Youth.* 3rd ed. London: Printed for William and Joseph Marshall, n.d.

———. *An Exposition of the Parables and Express Similitudes of Our Lord and Savior Jesus Christ.* London: Aylott and Co., 1858.

———. *Instructions for Children: Or, the Child's and Youth's Delight; Teaching an Easy Way to Spell and Read True English.* 30th ed. London: Printed for J. How, n.d.

———. *Tropologia: A Key to Open Scripture Metaphors, in Four Books, to which are Prefixed, Arguments to Prove the Divine Authority of the Holy Bible, Together with Types of the Old Testament.* London: William Hill Collingridge, 1856.

Riker, D. B. *A Catholic Reformed Theologian: Federalism and Baptism in the Thought of Benjamin Keach, 1640–1704.* Vol. 35 of the series, Studies in Baptist History and Thought. 2009. Reprint, Eugene, OR: Wipf and Stock, 2010.

Spears, William Eugene. "The Baptist Movement in England in the Late Seventeenth Century as Reflected in the Work and Thought of Benjamin Keach, 1640–1704." PhD diss., University of Edinburgh, 1953.

"The Tryal of Mr. Benjamin Keach, at the Assizes held at Ailsbury in Buckinghamshire, October 8 and 9, 1664." In *The History of the English Baptists*, by Thomas Crosby, 2:185–209. London: Thomas Crosby, 1739.

Walker, Austin. *The Excellent Benjamin Keach.* Dundas, Ontario: Joshua Press, 2004.

Young, Robert H. "The History of Baptist Hymnody in England from 1612 to 1800." DMA diss., University of Southern California, 1959.

Select Bibliography of Relevant Works Pertaining to the Whole Chapter

Crosby, Thomas. *The History of the English Baptists.* 4 vols. London: Thomas Crosby, 1738–40.

Greaves, Richard L., and Robert Zaller, eds. *Biographical Dictionary of British Radicals in the Seventeenth Century.* 3 vols. Brighton, England: Harvester Press, 1982–84.

Haykin, Michael A. G., ed. *The British Particular Baptists: 1638–1910.* 3 vols. Springfield, MO: Particular Baptist Press, 1998–2003.

Terrill, Edward. *The Records of a Church of Christ Meeting in Broadmead, Bristol A.D. 1640 to A.D. 1688.* Edited by Nathaniel Haycroft. London: J. Heaton and Son, 1865. Edward Terrill, an elder in the church, recorded this account from firsthand knowledge. He and Broadmead Baptist Church founded Bristol Baptist College.

Underhill, Edward Bean, ed. *Records of the Churches of Christ, Gathered at Fenstanton, Warboys, and Hexham, 1644–1720.* London: Haddon, Brothers, and Co. for the Hanserd Knollys Society, 1854.

White, Barrington R. "The English Particular Baptists and the Great Rebellion, 1640–1660." *Baptist History and Heritage* 9, no. 1 (January 1974): 16–29.

_____. "The Organization of the Particular Baptists, 1644–1660." *The Journal of Ecclesiastical History* 17, no. 2 (October 1966): 209–26.

_____. "Who Really Wrote the Kiffin Manuscript?" *Baptist History and Heritage* 1, no. 3 (October 1966): 3–10.

_____, ed. *Association Records of the Particular Baptists of England, Wales, and Ireland to 1660.* London: Baptist Historical Society, 1971–77.

_____, and Roger Haydon, eds. *The English Baptists of the Seventeenth Century.* Rev. London: Baptist Historical Society, 1996.

Chapter 7

Particular Baptist Confessions of Faith

London Confession (1644)

The Background

In 1642, at the brink of England's Civil War Era (1642-48), London booksellers were disseminating two anonymous tracts, slandering and endangering the lives of all Baptists. The authors designed the tracts to engender fear and hatred throughout a city whose estimated population at the time was above three hundred thousand.[472] The first pamphlet was *A Short History of the Anabaptists of High and Low Germany*. The second was *A Warning for England Especially for London in the Famous History of the Frantick Anabaptists* [with] *Their Wild Preachings and Practices in Germany*. Capriciously equating Baptists with the heretical and violent Anabaptists who had revolted against the German government in Muenster in 1534-35, the *Short History* closes with the urgent summons of "suppressing the growth of *Anabaptism*, which is the canker of Religion and the gangrene of the State, and that speedily, before it eats us up to the heart."[473] Likewise, the *Warning for*

---

[472] Roger Finlay, *Population and Metropolis: The Demography of London, 1580-1650* (Cambridge: Cambridge University Press, 1981), 6ff.
[473] *A Short History of the Anabaptists of High and Low Germany* (London:

England concludes with an appeal for unbridled action: "So, let all the factious and seditious enemies of the church and state perish; but, upon the head of King Charles, let the Crown flourish! Amen."[474] In the summer of 1644, a third provocation proceeded from the pen of Thomas Blakewell, *A Confutation of the Anabaptists and All Others Who Affect Not Civil Government*.[475]

The 1644 Edition

Small wonder, therefore, that on the title page of their London Confession, published in the fall of 1644, Baptists declare that they are being "falsely called Anabaptists." The Confession's preface refers to critics who, "in pulpit and print," charge Baptists "with holding free-will, falling away from grace, denying original sin," advocating lawlessness, and administering baptism in "unseemly" ways, "not to be named amongst Christians." Particular Baptists disclaimed all such charges as "notoriously untrue."[476] Indeed, the manifold dis-

---

Printed by T. Badger for Samuel Brown, 1642), 56. I modernized some of the spelling. This is in the British Library, London.

[474] *A Warning for England Especially for London in the Famous History of the Frantick Anabaptists* [with] *Their Wild Preachings and Practices in Germany* (London: n.p.), 25. This document is in the British Library, London. Its author was revealed to be Daniel Featley, when the work appeared verbatim in his, *The Dippers Dipt: Or, the Anabaptists Duck'd and Plung'd over Head and Ears*, 5th ed. (London: Printed for N. B. and Richard Royston, 1647), 217–34, 258. This is in Oxford's Bodleian Library.

[475] Thomas Blakewell, *A Confutation of the Anabaptists and All Others Who Affect Not Civil Government* (London: Printed by M. O. for T. Bankes, 1644). This is in the British Library, London.

[476] The first edition was published as *The Confession of Faith, of Those Churches Which Are Commonly (Though Falsely) Called Anabaptists* (London: n.p., 1644). The copy that I am using is in the Thomason Collection/ E. 12[24] in the British Library, London (Wing/C5789). See G. K. Fortescue, ed., *Catalogue of the Pamphlets, Books, Newspapers, and Manuscripts Relating to the Civil War, the Commonwealth, and Restoration, Collected George Thomason, 1640–1661* (London: Trustees of the Thomason Collection, 1908), 1:344 (October 16, 1644). Transcriptions are available in W. J. McGlothlin, *Baptist Confessions of Faith* (Philadelphia: American Baptist Publication Society, 1911), 171ff. McGlothlin's transcript is in William L. Lumpkin, *Baptist Confessions of Faith*, 2nd rev. edition, ed. Bill J. Leonard (Valley Forge:

tinctions between Baptists and Anabaptists have convinced most Baptist historians that any theory of Baptist churches emerging prior to the early seventeenth century would "be in the highest degree unscientific."[477] In fact, the twofold purpose of the Baptists' London Confession was (1) to combat general accusations that all Baptists were either Arminians or Pelagians, and (2) to distinguish Particular Baptists from both General Baptists and Anabaptists. There were a few General Baptists, however, who rejected Arminianism. His reading of the London Confession prompted the four-point Calvinist, Thomas Lamb, a General Baptist, to write *The Fountaine of Free Grace Opened* (1645), a defense of unlimited atonement. In this book, Lamb seeks to distance his church from the *Arminian* label and to "vindicate" them from "scandalous aspersions of holding free will, and denying a free election by grace." Lamb held to the perseverance of all the elect.

Later called "the First London Confession," the Confession of Faith (1644), made its debut prior to the Presbyterians' Westminster Confession (1647), and its primary authors likely included John Spilsbury and William Kiffin. Their names are among the confession's fifteen signatures, representing seven local churches. An obvious influence upon the confession's Calvinism was William Ames's *The Marrow of Theology* (*Medulla Theologiae*, 1623). Independent-Congregational influences included Henry Ainsworth's True Confession of the Faith (1596), Ainsworth's *Communion of Saints* (1607), and Henry Jacob's Confession and Protestation of the Faith (1616). Baptists have generally agreed that the New Testament prescribes only two ordained offices for the local church—pastor and deacon. The word "priest," corresponding to the Latin *sacerdos*, is one who offers sacrifices. Christ abolished the old sacrificial system,

---

Judson Press, 2011), 141–60. For a brief background on the confession, see Michael A. G. Haykin, *Kiffin, Knollys and Keach: Rediscovering Our English Baptist Heritage* (Leeds, England: Reformation Today Trust, 1996), 33–40; see also Barrington R. White and Roger Haydon, eds., *The English Baptists of the Seventeenth Century*, rev. (London: Baptist Historical Society, 1996).

[477] E.g., Henry C. Vedder, *Short History of the Baptists*, rev. 2nd ed. (Valley Forge: The American Baptist Publication Society, 1907), 5.

every Christian is a priest, and Christ alone is our great High Priest. Perhaps inadvertently, Baptists copied into the first edition of their 1644 Confession the four church offices that they had observed in Independent-Separatist churches—pastors, teachers, elders, and deacons (Arts. 36–38). All later editions would include only two offices—elders (pastors) and deacons. The gifts of the pastor include teaching.

Baptists have generally agreed that the New Testament prescribes only two ordained offices for the local church: pastor (overseer) and deacon (servant). In 1 Timothy 3:1–13, the apostle Paul reveals the qualifications of pastors and deacons. The New Testament packages the terms *pastor*, *elder*, *bishop*, *shepherd*, and *presbyter* all into a single office, as Luke does in Acts 20. In Acts 20:17, Paul, in Miletus, sends for the Ephesian "elders" (Gk. *presbyters*). Then, in 20:28, he describes them as "bishops" (Gk. overseers), who shepherd the flock: "Take heed therefore unto yourselves, and to all the flock, over [Gk. in] which the Holy Ghost hath made you overseers [Gk. *bishops*], to feed [Gk. *shepherd* or *pastor*] the church of God, which he hath purchased with his own blood." Likewise, when Paul left Titus in Crete to "ordain elders in every city" (Titus 1:5), his qualifications for these "elders" (Gk. *presbyters*) begin with the words, "A bishop [Gk. *overseer*] must be blameless" (vv. 6–9).[478] Baptists recognize ordination as the "laying on of the hands of the presbytery" (1 Tim. 4:14), and many believe that, in Ephesians 4:11, Paul is describing pastors as "shepherd-teachers," a singular term, rather than "pastors and teachers."[479]

The Confession distinctively differs from the English Separatist tradition concerning two ways: The first is separation of church and state. The London Confession clearly and respectfully articulates well-nuanced distinctions between the two entities (Article 49). The second difference is Baptism.

---

[478] Cf. 1 Pet. 5:1–2. For more discussion see Stewart Custer, *Witness to Christ: A Commentary on Acts* (Greenville: Bob Jones University Press, 2000), 294–95; and Thomas M. Lindsay, *The Church and the Ministry in the Early Centuries* (London: Hodder and Stoughton, 1902), 162–64 and passim. Lindsay was principal of the Glasgow College of the United Free Church of Scotland.

[479] E.g., see *ESV Study Bible*, 2268n3.

As the earliest Baptist confession to specify immersion as the only proper mode of baptism, the London Confession designates baptism as an "ordinance of the New Testament, given by Christ only upon persons professing faith" (Art. 39). It adds that, according to Scripture, the "manner of dispensing" this ordinance is "to be dipping or plunging the whole body under water." Furthermore, baptism is not a seal; the Holy Spirit is our seal. Baptism serves as an outward symbol of three truths. First, it symbolizes the "washing of the whole soul in the blood of Christ." Secondly, it symbolizes "the death, burial, and resurrection" of Christ. Thirdly, it symbolizes the future resurrection of all believers: "As the body is buried under the water and rises again, so certainly shall the bodies of the saints be raised by the power of Christ, in the day of the resurrection, to reign with Christ" (Art. 40). Moreover, the second edition (1646) would add that only baptized believers are to partake of the Lord's Supper (Art. 39).[480]

Influence of Daniel Featley upon the Second Edition (1646)

Particular Baptists would utilize great care in preparing their Confession's second edition. This was largely due to the caricature and crude slander, contained in censures written by Church of England clergymen against the first edition. Ephraim

---

[480] The second edition is *A Confession of Faith of Seven Congregations or Churches of Christ in London, Which Are Commonly (But Unjustly) Called Anabaptists* (London: Printed by Matthew Simmons to be sold by John Hancock in Popes-head Alley, 1646). This copy is in the British Library, London and in *Confessions of Faith: And Other Public Documents Illustrative of the History of the Baptist Churches of England in the 17th Century*, ed. Edward Bean Underhill (London: Haddon, Brothers, and Co., 1854), 11–48. For a twenty-article reinforcement to the Calvinism of the second edition, see Benjamin Cox, *An Appendix to a Confession of Faith, Or, a More Full Declaration of the Faith and Judgement of Baptized Beleevers: Occasioned by the Inquiry of Some Well-affected and Godly Persons in the Country; Written by Benjamin Cox, a Preacher of the Gospel of Jesus Christ, Published for the Further Clearing of Truth, and Discovery of Their Mistake Who Have Imagined a Dissent in Fundamentals Where There Is None*, 2nd ed. (London: n.p., 1646). This copy of Cox's *Appendix* is in the British Library; cf. Underhill, ed., *Confessions of Faith*, 49ff.

Pagitt (1582–1645), in his *Heresiography* (1645), charges Baptists with teaching that

> women sin grievously that lye [lie] with their husbands that are not rebaptized, ... but ... [that it is] no sin at all for them to lye [lie] with any man that hath been re-baptized.... Thus they [the Baptists] deceive the poor people, they persuade simple women under pretense of God's commandment that they cannot be saved except they prostitute their bodies to their brethren, and play the harlots.[481]

Such literature flagrantly distorted public opinion of all Baptists during the seventeenth century. Earlier in the same year, Daniel Featley (1582–1645),[482] in his *Dippers Dipt* (1645), had claimed that Baptists "strip themselves stark naked, not only when they flock in great multitudes, men and women together, to their *Jordans* to be dipt; but also upon other occasions, when the season permits."[483]

Featley titles his final chapter "A Censure of a Book Printed Anno 1644, [titled] the Confession of Faith of Those Churches Which are Commonly (Though Falsely) Called Anabaptists."[484] Featley's critical remarks on Articles 38–40 would significantly lead the Baptists to make unnecessary concessions in

---

[481] Ephraim Pagitt, *Heresiography: Or, a Description of the Heretickes and Sectaries of These Latter Times* (London: Printed by M. Okes, 1645), 36–37. This copy is in the British Library.

[482] See Arnold Hunt, "Featley, Daniel (1582–1645)," *Oxford Dictionary of National Biography* (Oxford University Press, 2004), online ed., http://www.oxforddnb.com/view/article/9242.

[483] Found guilty for the charge of being a spy for Charles I during the Civil War, Featley spent his final years in prison, where he wrote this work. Even though he died in 1645, this popular and entertaining book went through six editions in as many years, plus a seventh edition in 1660. I am using the first edition: Daniel Featley, *The Dippers Dipt: Or, The Anabaptists Duck'd and Plung'd over Head and Eares* (London: Printed for Nicholas Bourne and Richard Royston, 1645), 203. This is in the Union Theological Seminary Library, NYC.

[484] Ibid. The table of contents labels this as chapter 8, "The Animadversions upon the Anabaptists Confession, printed at London, Anno Donn. 1644" (pages 219–27).

their second edition. In fact, the noted historian, William J. McGlothlin (1876–1933), says, "One is positively amazed at ... three concessions on matters that were then and are now regarded as essential Baptist doctrines."[485] We will briefly note these concessions.

First, Article 38, in its original edition, confronts the nation's civil law that compels all citizens to pay tithes for the support of the clergy of the Church of England:

> That the due maintenance of the officers aforesaid, should be the free and voluntary communication of the Church, that according to Christ's ordinance, they that preach the Gospel, should live on the Gospel and not by constraint to be compelled from the people by a forced Law. 1 Cor. 9:7, 14; Gal. 6:6; 1 Thess. 5:13; 1 Tim. 5:17-18; Phil. 4:15-16.

To Featley, the closing phrase, "and not by constraint to be compelled from the people by a forced Law," was "impious, sacrilegious, and directly repugnant to the Law of God."[486] His argument is that, in the Old Testament, Israel was the church, whose tithing laws now apply to the Church of England. In their revision of the article (1646), the Baptists omit the entire phrase and only affirm that "the ministers of Christ ought to have whatsoever they shall need, supplied freely by the church, that according to Christ's ordinance, they that preach the gospel should live of the gospel by the law of Christ." McGlothlin assesses the revised article this way: "The Baptist point of religious freedom and separation between church and state is so far blunted that Dr. Featley himself could have signed it without hesitation or reservation."[487]

---

[485] W. J. McGlothlin, "Dr. Featley and the First Calvinistic Baptist Confession," The *Review and Expositor* 6, no. 4 (October 1909): 588 (579–89).

[486] Featley, *Dippers Dipt*, 221–22.

[487] McGlothlin, "Dr. Featley," 587. To their credit, the framers of the Second London Confession (1677, 2nd ed. 1688) would restore the Baptist conviction of separation between church and state: "God alone is Lord of the Conscience, and hath left it free from the Doctrines and Commandments of men.... The requiring of ... blind obedience is to destroy Liberty of Conscience, and Reason also" (Art. 21.2; cf. Art. 24).

Secondly, Featley took offence with the word *only* in Article 39, since it eliminates infant baptism.[488] The Article states "that Baptism is an Ordinance of the New Testament, given by Christ, to be dispensed *only* upon persons professing faith, or that are Disciples, or taught, who upon a profession of faith, ought to be baptized. Acts 2:37-38; 8:36-38; 18:8." In their revision of the article (1646), the Baptists omit the word *only*. "Again," says McGlothlin, "the point of the Baptist contention is gone and their critic could sign the revised article without constraint of conscience. One can here scarcely defend them against the charge of unfaithfulness to their convictions."[489]

Thirdly, in the first line of Article 40, Featley took offense with the phrase, "the Scripture holds out to be."[490] It states, "The way and manner of the dispensing of this Ordinance *the Scripture holds out to be* dipping or plunging the whole body under water." In their revision of the article (1646), the Baptists omit the entire phrase. As McGlothlin notes, "They cling to their mode, but give up or at least do not any longer assert it on Scripture authority."[491] McGlothlin's point is totally valid, but he could have noted that the revision does retain the Scripture references, including Matthew 3:6, 16; Mark 1:5, 9; John 3:23; Acts 8:38; and Romans 6:3-6. The revision also appeals to Mark 1:9, where the Greek preposition depicting *into* portrays John as baptizing (dipping) Jesus *into* the Jordan, rather than merely being in the Jordan. The word *in* generally refers to being already positioned inside something, while the word *into* generally refers to movement toward the inside. Thus, in this verse, Baptists see a plunging into the Jordan.

---

[488] Featley, *Dippers Dipt*, 222-23.

[489] McGlothlin, "Dr. Featley," 587. Again, and to their credit, the framers of the Second London Confession would restore the Baptist conviction that water baptism is only for believers: "Those who do actually profess repentance towards God, faith in, and obedience, to our Lord Jesus, are the only proper subjects of this ordinance" (Art. 29.2).

[490] Featley, *Dippers Dipt*, 223-24.

[491] McGlothlin, "Dr. Featley," 588. Appropriately, the Second London Confession would introduce the Baptist position on water baptism as "an Ordinance of the New Testament, ordained by Jesus Christ" (Art. 29). An abundance of Scripture references corroborates the entire article.

Second London Confession (1677, 2nd ed. 1688)

In July 1689, Hanserd Knollys, William Kiffin, Benjamin Keach, and four other pastors sent a letter to Baptist churches throughout England and Wales,[492] inviting them to send messengers to London for the first General Assembly of Particular Baptists, convening September 3-12, 1689.[493] Representing 107 Particular Baptist churches, the Assembly adopted the Second London Confession. For helpful patterns, the framers of the Second London Confession[494] relied partly upon the Congregationalists' Savoy Declaration of Faith and Order (1658),[495] and partly upon the Presbyterians' Westminster Confession (1647).[496] As the major and most complete of all

---

[492] The other four were John Harris, George Barrett, Edward Man, and Richard Adams.

[493] Among Particular Baptists, the "messengers" were not only pastors but also evangelists and church planters representing groups of supporting churches. See W. T. Whitley, *A History of the British Baptists*, rev. 2nd ed. (London: Kingsgate Press, 1932), 87-88; and J. F. V. Nicholson, "The Office of 'Messenger' amongst British Baptists in the Seventeenth and Eighteenth Centuries," *Baptist Quarterly* 17, no. 5 (January 1958): 206-25.

[494] A 1677 first edition of the Assembly or Second London Confession, titled "A Confession of Faith, Put Forth by the Elders and Brethren of Many Congregations of Christians, (Baptized upon Profession of Their Faith) in London and the Country," is in the library of Union Theological Seminary, NYC. A transcript is in W. J. McGlothlin, *Baptist Confessions of Faith* (Philadelphia: American Baptist Publication Society, 1911), 220-89. McGlothlin's transcript is copied into Lumpkin's, *Baptist Confessions of Faith*, 216-97. A copy of the Confession's second edition (London: Printed for John Harris, 1688) is in the library of the University of Illinois (Urbana Champaign campus). (This edition includes an appendix on baptism). A transcript is in Underhill, ed., *Confessions of Faith*, 169-246. There would be numerous editions but the first two became standard. Underhill also includes the *Baptist Catechism* that many Particular Baptist pastors would utilize (247-70); see also Benjamin Beddome, *A Scriptural Exposition of the Baptist Catechism*, 2nd. (Bristol: W. Pine, 1776).

[495] *A Declaration of the Faith and Order Owned and Practiced in the Congregational Churches in England: Agreed upon and Consented unto by Their Elders and Messengers in Their Meeting at the Savoy, October 12, 1658* (London: John Field, 1658); and *The Savoy Declaration of Faith and Order*, ed. A. G. Matthews (London: Independent Press, 1959).

[496] Philip Schaff *The Creeds of Christendom, with a History and Critical Notes*

Particular Baptist confessions, the Second London was the first of them to use the word *infallible* to describe the Bible. The word appears three times (1.1; 1.5; 1.9). The centrality of the Bible is foremost throughout the work.

The Five-fold Purpose of the Confession

In the wake of the Toleration Act of May 24, 1689, the Particular Baptists' Second London Confession was necessary for five key reasons. First, it would help establish a united doctrinal front, showing areas of "hearty agreement" with Presbyterians and Congregationalists. Second, the Confession would combat the influence of Quakerism. Third, it would combat Seventh-Day Sabbatarianism. Fourth, it would help serve as an antidote to the hyper-Calvinist, antinomian doctrine of supra-temporal justification. Such hyper-Calvinism would continue far into the next century—eliminating active faith from justification, silencing the saving gift of repentance, and reducing conversion to passivity. Fifth, the Confession would help meet the pressing need to combat the Trinitarian, Christological, hamartiological, and soteriological heresies of Thomas Collier. We will begin with the latter.

The Influence of Thomas Collier (d. ca. 1691)

Details of Thomas Collier's early life in Somerset County, situated in England's West Country,[497] lie hidden in obscurity. For a time, Collier was a member of William Kiffin's London church,[498] but, by 1651, he had returned to his roots in the West.

(New York: Harper and Brothers, 1877), 3:600-73; For a comparison of the Savoy Declaration with the Westminster Confession, see 1:829-33 and 3:707-29.

[497] *West Country* is the loosely defined designation for the region of dialects and accents encompassing at least the six counties of Gloucestershire, Wiltshire, Somerset, Dorset, Devon, and Cornwall.

[498] For more detail see Richard Dale Land, "Doctrinal Controversies of English Particular Baptists (1644-1691) as Illustrated by the Career and Writings of Thomas Collier" (PhD diss., Oxford University, 1979), 25ff. See also Barrington R. White, ed., "Associational Records of the Particular

His earliest publications, *Certaine Queries* (1645)[499] and *Three Great Queries* (1645),[500] were of a practical nature and innocuous in doctrine. Often called the "Apostle of the West," Collier distanced himself from the Particular Baptists of London and began plunging into Unitarian theology. As early as 1648, he was contending that God "is not ... as some imagine, Three Persons, yet one God."[501] In his best-known book, *The Body of Divinity* (1674), Collier denies the personhood of God: "That there is any personality in God, or three Persons in the Divine Essence, is a Language I do not yet understand is made use of in the Scriptures; therefore, I avoid the terms." To Collier, "The word *Person* being not at all, as I know, given either to the Father or holy [sic] Spirit, but to the Son, as God and Man in one Person."[502] In Sabellian subtlety, Collier's *Additional Word to the Body of Divinity* (1676) adds, "There are not three Persons in the Trinity, but various titles and discoveries."[503] Moreover, Christ possessed both natures, divine and human, from eternity past.[504] Christ "is the Son of God only as considered in both

---

Baptists of the West Country to 1659," Part 2 of *Association Records of the Particular Baptists of England, Wales, and Ireland to 1660* (London: Baptist Historical Society, 1973), 53–109.

[499] Thomas Collier, *Certaine Queries: Or, Points now in Controversy Examined, and Answered by Scripture, for the Satisfaction of All those that Desire Information in the Truth* (n.p: n.p., 1645). This copy is in the British Library. Collier sets forth four queries and provides answers for Baptists: (1) What are the materials of a true church? (2) What is the form of a true church? (3) What is the discipline and government thereof? (4) What authority does the civil magistrate possess regarding church-government?

[500] A copy is in the Angus Library and Archive, Regent's Park College, Oxford. See also B. R. White, "Thomas Collier and Gangraena Edwards," *Baptist Quarterly* 24, no. 3 (July 1971): 99–110.

[501] Thomas Collier, *A General Epistle to the Universal Church of the First Born: Whose Names are Written in Heaven* (London: Printed for Giles Calvert, 1648), 4–5. This is in Cambridge University Library.

[502] Idem, *The Body of Divinity, or, a Confession of Faith* (London: Printed for Nathaniel Crouch, 1674), 43. This is in the Cambridge University Library.

[503] Idem, *An Additional Word to the Body of Divinity, or Confession of Faith* (London: Printed for the author, 1676), 11–12. This is in the Universität Göttingen Bibliothek in Göttingen, Germany.

[504] Idem, *Body of Divinity*, 30–31.

Natures."[505] In the midst of great disruption in the Western Association over Collier's *Additional Word*, western conservatives assembled at Warminster and agreed to call upon London Particular Baptists to arbitrate the matter.[506]

Having examined Collier's works, the London Baptists sent a letter to the concerned churches. The letter labeled Collier "a heretic" and warned that conservatives were prepared to expose and to refute his false teachings. Troubled over the response, Collier's congregation at Southwick, in 1676, called for a delegation of London ministers to come over to the West Country and converse with Collier concerning his views. Headed by William Kiffin and Nehemiah Coxe, the delegation of five pleaded with Collier to renounce his errors. Upon Collier's headstrong refusal, Kiffin "admonished him as a Heretic." When summoned to London for further interrogation,[507] Collier vowed never to set foot in London. Many among the Southwick congregation supported him, but the church remained divided over the issue for years.[508] London's Particular Baptists promptly rejected Collier as a heretic, and, in the following year, their scholarly conservative, Nehemiah

---

[505] Idem, *Additional Word to the Body of Divinity*, 1ff.

[506] In addition to their organization in London, the earliest Particular Baptist associations in England were the Western, the Midland, and the Abingdon Associations. There was also an association in Wales and one in Ireland. See Barrington R. White, ed., *Association Records of the Particular Baptists of England, Wales, and Ireland to 1660* (London: Baptist Historical Society, 1971-77). Abingdon Baptist Church originated in 1649, with John Pendarves as the first pastor. Since the erection of the present building in 1841, there have been several renovations. The Abingdon library, including the Record book, is housed in the Angus Library and Archive, Regent's Park College, Oxford.

[507] Kiffin thought that Collier should appear for questioning before his church in London. Apparently, Collier had never requested his name to be dropped from Kiffin's church membership.

[508] Edward Bean Underhill, ed., *Records of a Church of Christ, Meeting in Broadmead, Bristol, 1640-1687* (London: J. Haddon for the Hanserd Knollys Society, 1847), 358-59; and W. T. Whitley, "Notes and Queries: Thomas Collier," *Transactions of the Baptist Historical Society* 1, no. 2 (April 1909): 121-22.

Coxe,[509] completed his *Vindiciae Veritatis, or A Confutation of the Heresies and Gross Errours Asserted by Thomas Collier in His Additional Word to His Body of Divinity* (1677).[510] By now, Collier's Pelagianism had also emerged, in his assertion that humanity cannot be accountable for Adam's sin. Therefore, Adam's sin brought judgment to himself alone.[511]

Additionally, Collier contended that Christ's work of redemption was for the whole world, but, to assure that the work of redemption would not be in vain, God elected some to "special salvation."[512] In addition to the special salvation of the elect, who can never fall from grace, there will be "a more general and common salvation of the world." After this life, says Collier, "the majority of the world" will escape the second death, after they have borne whatever punishment God assigns to them.[513] While God enables and preserves the elect through "special salvation," those who are non-elect, yet regenerate and true believers, may fall away from God and temporarily perish.[514] Since, the dead will continue to hear the gospel, the majority of the non-elect will receive salvation and

---

[509] Nehemiah Coxe, of Petty France Baptist Church (London), was a learned physician and theologian, skilled in Latin, Greek, and Hebrew. His father Benjamin "Cockes" had signed the 1646 edition of the first London Confession of Faith with John Spilsbury. See James M. Renihan, "An Excellent and Judicious Divine: Nehemiah Coxe," *Reformed Baptist Theological Review* 4, no. 2 (July 2007): 61–78; and Walter Wilson, *The History and Antiquities of Dissenting Churches and Meeting Houses, in London, Westminster, and Southwark: Including the Lives of Their Ministers, from the Rise of Nonconformity to the Present Time*, 4 vols. (London: Printed for the author, 1808–14), 2:185–87.

[510] Nehemiah Coxe, *Vindiciae Veritatis, or A Confutation of the Heresies and Gross Errours Asserted by Thomas Collier in His Additional Word to His Body of Divinity* (London: Printed for Nathaniel Ponder, 1677). This is in the British Library, London.

[511] Collier, *Body of Divinity*, 111.

[512] Ibid., 447–49.

[513] Thomas Collier, *A Compendious Discourse about Some of the Greatest Matters of Christian Faith, Propounded and Explained between a Minister and an Enquiring Christian* (London: Printed by H. H. for Thomas Fabian, 1682), 135. This is in the Bodleian Library, Oxford.

[514] Idem, *Additional Word to the Body of Divinity*, 36.

bear a temporary punishment.[515] Escaping the second death, "none shall be Eternally Damned, but those who sin against the Holy Spirit, Matthew 12:31."[516] As for the duration of sinners in the "fiery Lake," some will spend "perhaps a 100, some a 1000 and some perhaps 10000 years, and at last must be glad with a freedom from their Torment." After that, they will be "engaging in strictness [of] holiness."[517] In the bargain, Collier thinks that sinners can believe the gospel without the aid of the Holy Spirit. Such ability levels the playing field, offering proportionate opportunity to every individual. Since justification rests largely upon man's good works, God does not require perfection.[518]

Realizing that a vital purpose of the Second London Confession (1677) was to refute his teachings, Collier published a counter Confession that included a postscript attack against seven teachings that he considered heretical in the Second London Confession.[519] Collier's influence, largely in the western counties, corrupted some of the most cardinal doctrines historically embraced by Baptists. In 1691, these western-area Baptists published their Somerset Confession, also known as A Short Confession or a Brief Narrative of Faith. It denies total depravity (Art. 8) and asserts the possibility of true believers eternally apostatizing from the faith (Art. 17).[520] Mainstream Particular Baptists would soundly reject the Somerset Confession as a flawed protest to the soteriological doctrines of their Second London Confession.

---

[515] Ibid., 48.
[516] Ibid., 47; see 47–55.
[517] Ibid., 52.
[518] Ibid., 31–32; and *Body of Divinity*, 184–85.
[519] Thomas Collier, *A Confession of Faith Published on Special Occasion* (London: Printed for Francis Smith at the Elephant and Castle, 1678), 42–64. This is in the British Library, London.
[520] The full text of the 27-article Somerset Confession of 1691 is in Thomas Crosby, *The History of the English Baptists* (London: Thomas Crosby, 1740), 4:1–42 (Appendix 1). An earlier 46-article Somerset Confession (1656) is in William L. Lumpkin, *Baptist Confessions of Faith*, 2nd rev. edition, ed. Bill J. Leonard (Valley Forge: Judson Press, 2011), 184–98. For the 1691 confession, Lumpkin provides only selected articles (pages 348–52).

The Confession Endorses the Puritans' Sabbath Lord's Day Model

Over the years, small minorities of Baptist churches, both General and Particular had embraced the Seventh-day Sabbath, broken away from the mainstream, and joined the Seventh-day Baptist movement. On a larger scale, both General and Particular Baptists readily embraced the Puritans' Sabbath Lord's Day, which Presbyterians had inscribed into their Westminster Confession (21.7–8). General Baptists placed it into their Orthodox Creed (1678, Article 40). Particular Baptists, in their Second London Confession (Chapter 22), copied it almost verbatim from the Westminster Confession. Contrary to the teachings of the church Fathers, and of first-generation, sixteenth-century Reformers, the Puritans moved the Sabbath from the seventh to the first day of the week, depicting it as perpetually binding upon all humanity, from creation to consummation.

Adherents of the Puritans' Sabbath Lord's Day believe that the inclusion of the Sabbath commandment within the Ten Commandments (Exod. 20:8–11) makes Sabbath observance a vital part of God's moral law. Arthur W. Pink, a defender of this view, writes, "It should thus be quite evident that this law for the regulation of man's time was not a temporary one, designed for any particular dispensation, but is continuous and perpetual in the purpose of God."[521] For example, in the New England Colonies, such as Massachusetts and Connecticut, a government-enforced Puritan Sabbath began at sundown on Saturday of each week.[522]

On the contrary, while traditionalists celebrate the sacredness of the Lord's Day, that is, the first day of the week, they do not call it the "Sabbath" Lord's Day. They understand from Genesis 1:31 and 2:1–3, that upon completion of His work, God took pleasure in all that He had made. He blessed and sanctified that day in anticipation of the eternal rest that His entire

---

[521] Arthur W. Pink, *The Ten Commandments* (n.p.: Jay P. Green Sr., 2003), 29.
[522] For full coverage, see David Beale, "The Sabbath Day: Christian Views from New Testament Times to the Present," in *Historical Theology In-Depth* (Greenville, SC: Bob Jones University Press, 2013), 2:102–41.

creation will ultimately enjoy. The passage is not about what man is to do, but about what God has done and what He will do. Even as they received specific instructions (Gen. 2:16–17), Adam and Eve never received so much as an implied command to observe the Sabbath.

Traditionalists agree with the consensus of patristic literature. For example, in his *Dialogue with Trypho* the Jew, Justin Martyr explains that although the pre-Mosaic patriarchs "kept no Sabbaths," they were still "righteous" and "pleasing to God." There was "no need" of "the observance of Sabbaths" (19–27). Irenaeus of Lyon echoes the same sentiment in *Against Heresies* (4.16.2). In similar manner, the first-generation, sixteenth-century Reformers, including Martin Luther,[523] Philipp Melanchthon,[524] and John Calvin,[525] plainly assert that the Sabbath observance of the fourth commandment (Exod. 20:8–11) is part of the distinct covenant document that God made exclusively with Israel at Sinai (Exod. 34:27–28). It is part of the ceremonial law. One might ask, "Why was the ceremonial Sabbath observance included with the moral commandments if it were not a part of the moral law?" John Reisinger, a Reformed Baptist, answers that, since "the Tablets of Stone were a distinct covenant," the tablets "were accompanied with a specific 'covenant sign.'" The Sabbath was the "*sign of the covenant and therefore it had to be* part of the covenant of which it *was the sign.*"[526] Harold H. P. Dressler further explains: "As a sign of the covenant, the Sabbath can only be meant for Israel, with whom the covenant was made. It has a 'perpetual'

---

[523] Martin Luther, *The Large Catechism*, in *Triglot Concordia: The Symbolical Books of the Evangelical Lutheran Church*, trans. F. Bente and W. H. T. Dau (St. Louis: Concordia, 1921), 603–9.

[524] Augsburg Confession (Part II, Article 7); and L. Fuerbringer, Th. Engelder, and P. E. Kretzmann, eds., *The Concordia Cyclopedia: A Handbook of Religious Information, with Special Reference to the History, Doctrine, Work, and Usages of the Lutheran Church* (St. Louis: Concordia, 1927), 669–72.

[525] John Calvin, *The Institutes of the Christian Religion*, trans. Henry Beveridge (Edinburgh: Calvin Translation Society, 1845), 2.8.34; idem, *The Sermons of M. John Calvin upon the Fifth Booke of Moses, Called Deuteronomie*, trans. Arthur Golding (London: Henry Middleton for Thomas Woodcocke, 1583), 204–5 (200–205).

[526] John Reisinger, *Tablets of Stone* (Southbridge, MA: Crowne, 1989), 43.

function, i.e., for the duration of the covenant, and derives its importance and significance from the covenant itself."[527]

Thus, traditionalists believe that Old Testament regulations governing Sabbath observances were ceremonial rather than moral aspects of the law. As such, those regulations passed away with the sacrificial system, the Levitical priesthood, and all other ceremonial laws prefiguring Christ. Paul, in Colossians 2:16–17, refers to the Sabbath as a "shadow" of Christ. Since the substance (Christ) has come, the shadow is no longer binding or necessary. In the Colossians passage, expressions such as "festivals" and "Sabbath days" refer to the annual, monthly, and weekly holy days of the Jewish calendar.[528] The early churches followed the pattern of designating the first day of the week as the Lord's Day, on which His people gathered for divine worship.

Traditionalists insist that, prior to Moses the lawgiver, there are no commands in the Bible to keep the Sabbath and that there is no evidence of anyone keeping the Sabbath before the time of Moses. Nowhere in the Bible are Gentile nations commanded to keep the Sabbath; nor are they condemned for not keeping it. The Sabbath was Israel's sign of the Mosaic Covenant (Exod. 31:16–17; Ezek. 20:12; Neh. 9:13–14). God does not instruct the church to observe the sign of the Mosaic Covenant. The command to observe the Sabbath was to those who were under the Mosaic Covenant that God made with the people of Israel at Mount Sinai.[529] When the apostles met at the Jerusalem council, they did not impose Sabbath keeping upon Gentile believers or upon anyone else (Acts 15). The apostle Paul clearly corrected the Galatians who thought that God expected them to observe special days, such as the Sabbath (Gal. 4:10–11). Each day for the believer is a day of resting in the assurance of salvation and cleansing, by the Spirit of God through the Word of God (Heb. 4:9–11). Even in the Genesis account, our blessed Creator and

---

[527] Harold H. P. Dressler, "The Sabbath in the Old Testament," in *From Sabbath to Lord's Day: A Biblical, Historical, and Theological Investigation*, ed. D. A. Carson (Grand Rapids: Zondervan, 1982.), 30.

[528] See, e.g., 1 Chron. 23:31; 2 Chron. 2:4; 31:3; Ezek. 45:17; and Hosea 2:11.

[529] See Myron Houghton, *Law and Grace* (Schaumburg, IL: Regular Baptist Books, 2011), 19, 119, 157, 169–75.

Redeemer, who needed no rest, provides for His redeemed a gracious reminder of His promise of eternal rest. Like the church fathers, such as Justin Martyr, and like the Reformers, such as John Calvin, every Christian with his conscience submitted to the Lordship of Christ embraces God's gracious benefit of rest and celebration. To committed believers, the Lord's Day is the most important day of the week. Every true and obedient congregation of Christ delights in gathering in celebration of Christ's glorious resurrection, and in fulfillment of the inspired instructions concerning His church—its edification, its proclamation, its offices, and its ordinances. These functions are of foremost importance in God's design for the local church. A central emphasis in the New Testament is the eternal serenity resulting from the redemptive work of Christ. The redeemed will fully realize their rest after the final battle, when the church militant becomes the church triumphant.

The Lord's Day speaks of both the pedagogical rest that followed God's *original* creation, and of the perpetual rest that will follow His *redeemed* creation. The Scriptures speak of a future time when all of God's redeemed since the creation will sit down together as one at the Marriage Supper of the Lamb (Rev. 19:6-9; Luke 13:29). There is a beautifully designed confluence, where the perfect oneness of God's people flows into eternal rest in the New Heavens and New Earth (Heb. 3:18-4:11; Rev. 21-22).

> Let us therefore fear, lest, a promise being left us of entering into his rest, any of you should seem to come short of it. For unto us was the gospel preached, as well as unto them: but the word preached did not profit them, not being mixed with faith in them that heard it. For we which have believed do enter into rest, as he said, As I have sworn in my wrath, if they shall enter into my rest: *although the works were finished from the foundation of the world. For He spake in a certain place of the seventh day on this wise, And God did rest the seventh day from all his works. And in this place again, If they shall enter into my rest.* (Heb. 4: 1-5; italics added)

Reformation Background on the Issue of Baptism

The *Book of Common Prayer* (1549), thought to be largely composed by Thomas Cranmer, prescribes triple immersion as the proper mode of baptism. This official document allows pouring but only for weak infants: "Then the priest shall take the child in his hands, and ask the name. And naming the child, shall dyppe it in the water thryse. First, dypping [immersing] the ryght side: Second, the left side: the thyrde tyme, dippyng the face towarde the fonte: So it be discretly and warely done.... And if the childe be weake, it shall suffice to power [pour] water upon it."[530] The 1552 edition drops triple immersion but maintains single immersion. It also maintains the allowance of pouring for the weak babies: he "shall dippe it in the Water, so it be discreetely and warily done . . . . And if the childe be weake, it shal suffice to power [pour] water upon it."[531]

Nevertheless, the Presbyterians who wrote the Westminster Confession (1647) fine-tuned their teachings on baptism by adhering to John Calvin (1509–64), whose distinctive views are clear. First, Calvin taught that the "sacraments" of baptism and Communion are "means of grace." Thus, in baptism, infants are passively "renewed by the Spirit of God, according to the capacity of their age, till that power which was concealed within them grows by degrees, and becomes fully manifest at the proper time."[532] Second, Calvin taught that, even though *baptism* means immersion, and that, even though immersion was the only mode used in the earliest churches, God's people now possess the liberty to use divergent modes. He expresses it this way. "Whether the person baptized is to be wholly immersed, and that whether once or thrice, or whether he is only to be sprinkled with water, is not of the least consequence:

---

[530] "On Baptisme, bothe publique and private," in *The Book of Common Prayer: The Texts of 1549, 1559, and 1662*, ed. Brian Cummings (Oxford: Oxford University Press, 2011), 51.

[531] *The Book of Common Prayer* (London: Edward Whitchurch, 1552), no pagination.

[532] Calvin, *Commentary on a Harmony of the Evangelists: Matthew, Mark, and Luke*, trans., Wm. Pringle (Edinburgh: Calvin Translation Society, 1845), 2:390, on Matt. 19:14.

churches should be at liberty to adopt either according to the diversity of climates, although it is evident that the term *baptize* means to immerse, and that this was the form used by the primitive Church."[533] Third, Calvin accepted Roman Catholic baptism as completely valid: "We condemn the papal assemblies. . . . Nevertheless, as some trace of the [true] Church is left in the papacy, and the virtue and substance of baptism remain, and as the efficacy of baptism does not depend upon the person who administers it, we confess that those baptized in it do not need a second baptism."[534]

Calvin's influence would prove to be a powerful factor in England. By the mid-seventeenth century, the practice of immersion in England would give way to pouring and sprinkling. The Presbyterians' *Book of Common Prayer as Amended by the Westminster Divines, A. D. 1661*, stipulates, "Then will the Minister (taking the Child into his hands, or leaving it in the hands of the Parent) ask of the Parents the name, and naming the Child after them, will pour water upon it."[535] In the Westminster Confession, "Dipping of the person into the water is not necessary; but baptism is rightly administered by pouring or sprinkling water upon the person" (28.3).

The Second London Confession on Baptism

Seventeenth-century Baptists were longing to restore that method of baptism employed by New Testament churches prior to the enormous ecclesiastical baggage accumulated over the centuries. While the Westminster and Savoy confessions had designated baptism and Communion as *sacraments*,[536]

---

[533] *Institutes* (4.15.19), in John Calvin, *Institutes of the Christian Religion*, 3 vols., trans. Henry Beveridge (Edinburgh: Edinburgh Printing Company for the Calvin Translation Society, 1845), 3:344. All references to the *Institutes* are from this translation.

[534] Calvin, "On the Sacrament of Baptism," Article 28 of the French (Gallican) Confession (1559), in Philip Schaff, *The Creeds of Christendom, with a History and Critical Notes* (New York: Harper and Brothers, 1877), 3:376.

[535] *Book of Common Prayer as Amended by the Westminster Divines, A. D. 1661*, ed. Charles W. Shields (Philadelphia: James S. Claxton, 1867), 258.

[536] It was Jerome, in his Latin Vulgate (380–404), who first substituted

the Baptist authors of the Second London Confession (1677) avoid that designation and replace it with the term *ordinance*,[537] meaning that which is ordained and orderly arranged. Thus, baptism is "an Ordinance of the New Testament, ordained by Jesus Christ" to be a "sign" of the believer's fellowship with Christ in His death and resurrection, and of his walking in newness of life.[538] The Confession makes it clear that only those who "profess repentance towards *God*, faith in, and obedience, to our Lord Jesus, are the only proper subjects of this ordinance.... Immersion, or dipping, of the person in water is necessary to the due administration of this ordinance" (29.1-4). It would be well into the nineteenth century before most Baptist churches in England and America had the luxury of indoor baptisteries. Prior to that time, they generally held baptismal services in rivers, lakes, ponds, or streams. There is no evidence that baby dedications ever became a common practice among Baptist churches prior to the nineteenth century.[539]

Calvin's Doctrine of the Lord's Supper and Its Influence upon Reformed Baptists

On the Lord's Supper, John Calvin held to a mediating view between what he considered the two extremes within Protestant circles. On the one hand, there was Martin Luther's

---

the word *sacrament* ("a sacred thing") for the Greek word *mystery*. "Sacramentalists" believe that the sacraments are inherently efficacious, as seals that impart grace to recipients.

[537] The rare, early Baptist sources that use the term *sacrament* include the General Baptists' Orthodox Creed of 1678 (Art. 27) and the Particular Baptist Hercules Collins, *An Orthodox Catechism* (London: n.p., 1680), 25ff. This catechism is Collins's edition of the German Reformed Heidelberg Catechism. Collins still adds the "ordinance" of "Laying on of Hands" and concludes with "An Appendix Concerning the Ordinance of Singing." Collins's work is in the British Library.

[538] For Baptist views on the proper administrator, see E. P. Winter, "Who May Administer the Lord's Supper?" *Baptist Quarterly* 16, no. 3 (July 1955): 128-33.

[539] See T. L. Underwood, "Child Dedication Services among British Baptists in the Seventeenth Century," *Baptist Quarterly* 23, no. 4 (October 1969): 165-69.

literal view of a consubstantial real presence of Christ's body and blood in, with, and under the elements of bread and wine. On the other hand, there was the symbolic position of Ulrich Zwingli and the Anabaptists,[540] who rested their memorial view upon the words of Christ at the Last Supper: "This do in remembrance of me" (Luke 22:19; 1 Cor. 11:24–25). To them, the saying, "This is my body," is as the expression, "Behold the Lamb" (John 1:29). Jesus had come *as* "the lamb," *as* "a sheep" (Isa. 53:7), *as* "the door" (John 10:9*a*), and *as* "the true vine" (John 15:1*a*).

Calvin's distinctive view begins with the Lord's Supper as "a heavenly action," whereby the faithful are elevated to heaven, where Christ dwells in glory. It is here that Christ nourishes the souls of believers.[541] Yet, Calvin declares a *spiritual-yet-real presence* of Christ's flesh and blood within the sacramental elements for the nourishment of the elect unto eternal life. He bases "spiritual presence" upon the marriage relationship in Ephesians 5, and "real presence" upon the Bread of Life in John 6:48–59—passages that many believe have nothing to do with the Lord's Supper. While opposing the Roman Catholic view of marriage as "a great *sacramentum*," Calvin contends that Ephesians 5:31*b*, "they two shall be one flesh," is the "mystery" of the Lord's Supper. To Calvin, Paul's declaration that we are members "of his flesh, and of his bones" (5:30) means that Christ "holds out his body to be enjoyed by us, and to nourish us unto eternal life." Therefore, in verse 32*a*, Paul's expression, "This is a great mystery," means that Christ mysteriously feeds us with His flesh and blood. To Protestant critics of such handling of the text, Calvin responds, "I am overwhelmed by the depth of this mystery."[542] In his *Institutes*, Calvin reiterates, "It

---

[540] Three German terms most accurately depict the views of the leading Reformers: Luther's view is *wunderhaft*, Zwingli's is *historisch*, and Calvin's is *mystisch*. E.g., see Alexander Barclay, *The Protestant Doctrine of the Lord's Supper: A Study in the Eucharistic Teaching of Luther, Zwingli, and Calvin* (Glasgow: Jackson, Wylie & Co., 1927), 270.

[541] On 1 Corinthians 11:24, see Calvin, *Commentary on the Epistles of Paul the Apostle to the Corinthians*, trans. John Pringle (Edinburgh: Calvin Translation Society, 1848), 1:380.

[542] On Ephesians 5:28–33, see Calvin, *Commentaries on the Epistles of Paul to*

is too high a mystery either for my mind to comprehend or my words to express; and to speak more plainly, I rather feel than understand it" (4.17.32). From Jesus' discourse in John 6:48–59, Calvin adds the "real" presence of Christ to the bread of Communion, especially in verse 53, "Verily, verily, I say unto you, Except ye eat the flesh of the Son of man, and drink his blood, ye have no life in you" (4.17.1, 5, 33, 34). Today, many Reformed individuals are seeking to revive Calvin's view.[543]

Conversely, William Cunningham, of the Free Church of Scotland, described Calvin's argument as "altogether unsuccessful" and "about as unintelligible as Luther's consubstantiation." Cunningham thought that it was "perhaps, the greatest blot in the history of Calvin's labors as a public instructor."[544] Southern Presbyterian theologian, Robert Lewis Dabney, described Calvin's view as "strange," "curious," and so "impossible" that the framers of the Westminster Confession "had to modify all that was untenable and unscriptural in it."[545] Reformed theologian, Robert L. Reymond, speaks of Calvin's "inappropriateness" in using the language of John chapter six. Reymond explains, "By urging that Christians feed by faith upon the *literal* flesh and blood of Christ," Calvin "comes perilously close to suggesting the Godhead's apotheosizing [deifying] of Christ's humanity and to transferring, at least

---

the *Galatians and Ephesians*, trans. William Pringle (Edinburgh: Thomas Clarke, 1841), 305–8. There are valuable discussions in Randall C. Zachman, ed., *John Calvin and Roman Catholicism: Critique and Engagement, Then and Now* (Grand Rapids: Baker, 2008), 177, passim.

[543] E.g., Keith A. Mathison, *Given for You: Reclaiming Calvin's Doctrine of the Lord's Supper* (Phillipsburg, NJ: P&R Publishing, 2002). The forward is by R. C. Sproul. The German Reformed, yet pro-Roman Catholic "Mercersburg Theology," crafted by John W. Nevin (1803–86), had likewise defended Calvin's view; see Nevin, *The Mystical Presence: A Vindication of the Reformed or Calvinistic Doctrine of the Holy Eucharist* (Philadelphia: S. R. Fisher, 1867); and D. G. Hart, *John Williamson Nevin: High-Church Calvinist* (Phillipsburg, NJ: P&R Publishing, 2005).

[544] Cunningham, *The Reformers and the Theology of the Reformation* (Edinburgh: T. & T. Clark, 1862), 240.

[545] Dabney, *Syllabus and Notes of the Course of Systematic and Polemic Theology Taught in Union Theological Seminary, Virginia*, 2nd ed. (St. Louis: Presbyterian Publishing Co. of St. Louis, 1878), 810–14.

in the Lord's Supper, the saving benefits of Christ's atoning death directly to his human nature now localized in heaven."[546] Criticism of Calvin's usage of John 6:48–59 for the Lord's Supper essentially consists in four critical points:

- Jesus spoke those words to a largely unsaved and hostile audience inside a Jewish synagogue in Capernaum.
- It is inconceivable that such an audience would have connected the Lord's Supper to this message.
- Jesus did not reveal this ordinance until just before His crucifixion.
- The view compromises the veracity of the complete, orthodox doctrine of the person of Christ as Theanthropic, that is, deity and humanity.[547]

The Second London Confession on the Lord's Supper

Unlike General Baptists, who celebrated the Lord's Supper at associational meetings, Particular Baptists maintained that the New Testament ordinances are exclusively for the local church.[548] On the other hand, unlike the 1646 edition of the first London Confession, the Second London Confession is silent regarding baptism as a prerequisite to partaking of the Lord's Supper.[549] Apparently, there was some disagreement on this issue. From their earliest days, however, most Baptists had agreed on what they perceived as the threefold, scriptural order—conversion, baptism, and the Lord's Supper (Matt.

---

[546] Reymond, *A New Systematic Theology of the Christian Faith* (Nashville: Thomas Nelson, 1998), 963.

[547] For a fuller discussion, see David Beale, *Historical Theology In-Depth* (Greenville, SC: Bob Jones University Press, 2013), 2:61–67.

[548] See the valuable discussion by E. P. Winter, "The Administration of the Lord's Supper among the Baptists of the Seventeenth Century," *Baptist Quarterly* 18, no. 5 (January 1960): 196–204; cf. Michael Walker, "The Presidency of the Lord's Table among Nineteenth Century English Baptists," *Baptist Quarterly* 32, no. 5 (January 1988): 208–23.

[549] The 1646 edition of the first London Confession clearly states that new disciples, "upon profession of faith, ought to be baptized, and after to partake of the Lord's Supper" (Art. 39). See also E. P. Winter, "The Lord's Supper: Admission and Exclusion among the Baptists of the Seventeenth Century," *Baptist Quarterly* 17, no. 6 (April 1958): 267–81.

28:18–19; Acts 2:41–42). While the majority of the 1689 General Assembly still agreed with that arrangement, they decided to "leave every Church to their own liberty."[550] Howbeit, the catechism that the same Assembly prepared and published maintains, "The proper subjects" for the Lord's Supper are those "who have been baptized upon a personal Profession of their Faith in Jesus Christ, and Repentance from dead works." Many have mistakenly called this "Keach's Catechism."[551] Although there have been a few notable exceptions, such as John Bunyan, Robert Hall Jr., and Charles Spurgeon,[552] until the late nineteenth century, most Baptists insisted on baptism by immersion as prerequisite to membership and the Lord's Supper. While Spurgeon's practice of open *Communion* contradicted the old Baptist way, he did require immersion before *membership*.

In agreement with the historic Baptist position, the Second London Confession first states that the bread and wine "*represent ... the body and blood of Christ*" (30.5). It describes the

---

[550] *A Narrative of the Proceedings of the General Assembly of Divers Pastors, Messengers and Ministering-Brethren of the Baptized Churches, Met Together in London, from September 3–12, 1689, from Divers Parts of England and Wales: Owning the Doctrine of Personal Election, and Final Perseverance* (London: n.p., 1689), 10.

[551] *A Brief Instruction in the Principles of Christian Religion: Agreeable to the Confession of Faith, Put Forth by the Elders and Brethren of Many Congregations of Christians, (Baptized upon Profession of Their Faith) in London and the Country, Owning the Doctrine of Personal Election, and Final Perseverance*, 5th ed. (London: n.p., 1695), 21 (Question 103). This is the Particular Baptists' edition of the *Shorter Catechism* of the Presbyterians' Westminster Assembly. This is the earliest extant edition, and it is in the British Library, London. The work was later published by the Philadelphia Baptist Association as *The Baptist Catechism: Or a Brief Instruction in the Principles of the Christian Religion, Agreeable to the Confession of Faith* (Philadelphia: Robert Aitken, 1786). The title page adds that this catechism was "put forth by upwards of a hundred congregations in Great Britain, July 3, 1689; adopted by the General Association of Philadelphia, September 22, 1742 and now received by churches of the same Denomination in most of the United States, to which are added the proofs from Scripture."

[552] W. Y. Fullerton, *C. H. Spurgeon: A Biography* (London: Williams and Norgate, 1920), 291; and Lewis A. Drummond, *Spurgeon: Prince of Preachers* (Grand Rapids: Kregel, 1992), 481, 580.

Lord's Supper as "a perpetual remembrance" and as "only a memorial" of Jesus offering Himself:

> The Supper of the Lord Jesus, was instituted by him, the same night wherein he was betrayed, to be observed in his Churches unto the end of the world for the perpetual remembrance, and showing forth the sacrifice in his death confirmation of the faith of believers in all the benefits thereof, their spiritual nourishment, and growth in him, their further engagement in, and to, all duties which they owe unto him; and to be a bond and pledge of their communion with him, and with each other. In this ordinance Christ is not offered up to his Father, nor any real sacrifice made at all, for remission of sin of the quick or dead; but only a memorial of that one offering up of himself, by himself, upon the cross, once for all. (30.1–2)

Contrariwise, at this point, the confession displays a paradox that historians seldom mention. Copying the Westminster Confession (29.1–8) almost verbatim, the Particular Baptists embed into their confession Calvin's *spiritual-yet-real presence* of Jesus' flesh and blood, as well as the mystical "feeding." In the Second London Confession, "Worthy receivers, outwardly partaking of the visible Elements in this Ordinance, do then also inwardly by faith, really and indeed … spiritually receive, and feed upon Christ crucified & all the benefits of his death," which are "spiritually present to the faith of Believers, in that Ordinance, as the elements themselves are to their outward senses" (30.7). When one partakes of the elements of the Supper, he is partaking of "holy mysteries" (30.8). Embracing that view, Benjamin Keach urged that, in the Lord's Supper, "there is a mystical conveyance, or communion, of all Christ's blessed merits to our souls through faith held forth hereby, and in a glorious manner received, in the right participation of it."[553] Keach's colleague Hercules Collins

---
[553] Benjamin Keach, *Tropologia: A Key to Open Scripture Metaphors, in Four Books, to which are Prefixed, Arguments to Prove the Divine Authority of the*

(1646/7–1702) clearly followed Calvin's view that, in the Bread of Life, in John chapter six, Jesus is offering His flesh in the Lord's Supper.[554] Among current British Reformed Baptists, both liberals and conservatives, many continue to adhere to the Confession's Calvinistic "mystery" of "feeding upon Jesus."[555] In America, Calvin's ecclesiology prompted Wayne Grudem to insist that baptism and the Lord's Supper should be regarded as "means of grace," and not "*merely symbolic.*"[556] Reformed Baptist, Richard Barcellos, in *The Lord's Supper as a Means of Grace* (2013),[557] also defends Calvin's spiritual-yet-real elements in the Supper.

Calvin's view has not prevailed among most conservative Baptists, especially in America.[558] Most Baptists have maintained an unencumbered memorial view, signifying "an act of remembrance." They see nothing in Scripture instructing anyone to feed in any way on Jesus' body and blood. To them, Jesus instituted the ordinance as a token, "in remembrance" of

---

Holy Bible, Together with Types of the Old Testament (London: William Hill Collingridge, 1856), 4:639.

[554] "Of the Lord's Supper," in *An Orthodox Catechism* (1680), 38ff. This copy is in the British Library, London.

[555] E.g., Anthony R. Cross and Philip E. Thompson, eds., *Baptist Sacramentalism* (Milton Keynes, England: Paternoster, 2003); idem, *Baptist Sacramentalism 2* (Milton Keynes, England: Paternoster, 2008); Michael J. Walker, *Baptists at the Table: The Theology of the Lord's Supper amongst English Baptists in the Nineteenth Century* (Didcot, England: The Baptist Historical Society, 1992); cf. Anthony R. Cross, *Baptism and the Baptists: Theology and Practice in Twentieth-Century Britain* (Carlisle, England: Paternoster, 2000).

[556] Wayne Grudem, *Systematic Theology* (Grand Rapids: Zondervan, 1994), 954–55; italics are in the original. Grudem professes to be "A Baptist Because of the Bible," in *Why I am a Baptist*, ed. Tom J. Nettles and Russell Moore (Nashville: B&H Publishing Group, 2001), 201–8.

[557] Richard Barcellos, *The Lord's Supper as a Means of Grace: More than a Memory* (Geanies House, Fearn, Ross-shire, Scotland, UK: Mentor, 2013).

[558] Michael A. G, Haykin, a Reformed Baptist, laments that, even "in Calvinistic Baptist circles," the "Zwinglian perspective on the Lord's Supper would eventually come to be the overwhelming consensus in the late eighteenth and nineteenth centuries." See Haykin, "The Second London Confession of Faith: Its Theology," in *Kiffin, Knollys and Keach: Rediscovering Our English Baptist Heritage* (Leeds, England: Reformation Today Trust, 1996), 81.

Him. Essentially, the Lord's Supper, preceded by serious, personal self-examination, becomes a worshipful, corporate oneness with one another in our risen Lord who gave Himself for us and promised, "Lo, I am with you always, even unto the end of the world [age]. Amen." (Matt. 28:20). Below are seven American statements of faith, representing a cross section of Baptists who require believer's baptism by immersion as prerequisite to membership and the Lord's Supper:[559]

- The Principles of Faith of the Sandy Creek Association (1816) insist, "The church has no right to admit any but regular baptized church members to communion at the Lord's Table" (Art. 10).
- The New Hampshire Confession (1833) states that believer's baptism by immersion "is prerequisite to the privileges of a church relation; and to the Lord's Supper, in which the members of the church, by the use of bread and wine, are to *commemorate* together the dying love of Christ; preceded always by solemn self-examination" (Art. 14.)
- The Treatise on the Faith of the Free Will Baptists (1948) instructs, "Believers in Christ are admitted to this church on giving evidence of faith in Christ ... [and] being baptized" (Chap. 15). The Lord's Supper is "a *commemoration* of the death of Christ for our sins" (Chap. 18).
- The Independent Baptist Fellowship of North America (1991) maintains, "The Lord's Table is a precious *reminder* of the broken body and shed blood of our Savior, Jesus Christ. It is also a joyous reminder that one day we will drink it new with Him in the Father's kingdom." Like baptism, "this ordinance is also fulfilled by a local church and is preceded by salvation and believer's baptism. Great care should be exercised in self-examination so that no one eats the broken bread or drinks the fruit of the vine unworthily" (Art. E).
- The Articles of Faith of the General Association of Regular Baptist Churches (2014) proclaim that Christian

---

[559] I have excluded Scripture references. Each group held that the Lord's Supper is *only* symbolic.

baptism by immersion "is to be performed under the authority of the local church; and that it is prerequisite to the privileges of church membership." The Lord's Supper "is the *commemoration* of His death until He come, and should be preceded always by solemn self-examination." In addition, "the Biblical order of the ordinances is baptism first and then the Lord's Supper, and that participants in the Lord's Supper should be immersed believers" (Art. 15).
- The Statement of Faith of the Foundations Baptist Fellowship International (2013) explains that believer's baptism by immersion "is a prerequisite to church membership. The Lord's Supper is the *commemoration* of the Lord's death until He comes, is a reminder of our continual fellowship with Him, and should be preceded by careful self-examination" (Sect. 10).
- The Baptist Faith and Message of the Southern Baptist Convention (2000) asserts that Christian baptism by immersion, "being a church ordinance ... is prerequisite to the privileges of church membership and to the Lord's Supper." Moreover, the Supper "is a *symbolic* act of obedience whereby members of the church, through partaking of the bread and the fruit of the vine, *memorialize* the death of the Redeemer and anticipate His second coming" (Art. 7).

The Demise of the General Assembly of Particular Baptists

Within local churches, vulnerability toward apathy generally emerges in the wake of great victory. Indeed, with Parliament's 1689 Toleration Act, lethargy quickly fell upon congregations that had long struggled for their biblical convictions, their separatist stance, and for their very existence. Weary from the long battle for survival, congregations were now letting down their guard and failing to seize the moment. The first generation was quickly passing off the scene. Knollys passed into eternity in 1691, followed by Kiffin in 1701, and Keach in 1704. Along with a serious shortage of pastors, there also existed a critical lack of ministerial training.

The second and third General Assemblies convened in London, in June of 1690 and 1691. Although the Second London Confession contains nothing about music, the ongoing controversy over corporate singing resulted in the fourth General Assembly's becoming the last national assembly. Convening in London, in 1692, the final national assembly agreed that future assemblies would divide, with one assembly "in the West, and one here for the East." The one in the West would meet annually at Easter in Bristol. The one in the East would meet annually in London at Whitsuntide.[560] Due to ongoing controversies and meager attendance, however, the London meetings ceased after 1694.[561] Meanwhile, the Bristol meetings developed into the "Western Association." With Bristol Baptist College providing its vitality, this Association, over the years, would experience significant growth. In the eighteenth century, though, Particular Baptists would face new challenges, not the least of which was High Calvinism, addressed in the next chapter.

---

[560] The word *Whitsuntide* refers to the week that begins with *Whitsunday* (White Sunday), which is the Day of Pentecost, the seventh Sunday and fiftieth day after Easter.

[561] In 1812, a few Particular Baptists in London attempted to revive their annual Assembly meetings. They held feeble and meagerly attended meetings during 1813–17, then ceased. See R. Philip Roberts, *Continuity and Change: London Calvinistic Baptists and Evangelical Revival 1760–1820* (Wheaton, IL: Richard Owen Roberts Publishers, 1989). This was originally prepared as a doctoral dissertation for the Free University of Amsterdam, June 22, 1989.

Select Bibliography for Further Reading

Bulley, Colin. *The Priesthood of Some Believers: Developments from the General to the Special Priesthood in the Christian Literature of the First Three Centuries*. Carlisle, England: Paternoster, 2000.

Collier, Jay Travis. "The Sources behind the First London Confession." *American Baptist Quarterly* 21, no. 2 (June 2002): 197–214.

Haykin, Michael A. G. "The Second London Confession of Faith." In *Kiffin, Knollys and Keach: Rediscovering Our English Baptist Heritage*, 62–81. Leeds, England: Reformation Today Trust, 1996.

_____, ed. *The British Particular Baptists: 1638–1910*. 3 vols. Springfield, MO: Particular Baptist Press, 1998–2003.

Land, Richard Dale. "Doctrinal Controversies of English Particular Baptists (1644–1691) as Illustrated by the Career and Writings of Thomas Collier." PhD diss., Oxford University, 1979.

Moore, Walter Levon. "Baptist Teachings and Practices on Baptism in England 1600–1689." ThD diss., Southern Baptist Theological Seminary, 1950.

Naylor, Peter. *Calvinism, Communion and the Baptists: A Study of the English Calvinistic Baptists from the Late 1600s to the Early 1800s*. Vol. 7 of the series, Studies in Baptist History and Thought. 2003. Reprint, Eugene, OR: Wipf and Stock, 2006.

Nelson, Stanley A. "Reflecting on Baptist Origins: The London Confession of Faith of 1644." *Baptist History and Heritage* 29, no. 2 (April 1994): 33–46.

Patterson, W. Morgan. "The Lord's Supper in Baptist History." *Review and Expositor* 66, no. 1 (Winter 1969): 25–34.

Payne, Ernest A. *The Fellowship of Believers: Baptist Thought and Practice Yesterday and Today*. 2nd ed. enlarged. London: The Carey Kingsgate Press, 1952.

Taylor, James B. (Barnett). *Restricted Communion: Or, Baptism an Essential Prerequisite to the Lord's Supper*. Charleston: Southern Baptist Publication Society, 1856.

Watts, Michael. *The Dissenters: from the Reformation to the French Reformation*. 1978. Reprint, Oxford: Oxford University Press, 1999.

White, Barrington R. "The Doctrine of the Church in the Particular Baptist Confession of 1644." *Journal of Theological Studies* 19, no. 2 (1968): 570–90.

_____. "The Origins and Convictions of the First Calvinistic Baptists." *Baptist History and Heritage* 25, no. 4 (October 1990): 39–47.

Whitley, W. T. "Baptist Churches till 1660." *Transactions of the Baptist Historical Society* 2, no. 4 (1910-11): 236–54.

Chapter 8

John Gill and the Modern Question: The Emergence of Antinomianism

※

Introduction

From seven churches in 1646, there were 131 Particular Baptist congregations in England by 1660.[562] During the early eighteenth century, Particular Baptists throughout England recorded 206 congregations with 40,520 "hearers," or 0.74% of the English population. In Wales, during the early eighteenth century, there existed fourteen Particular Baptist congregations with 4,050 "hearers," or 1.31% of the Welsh population.[563] The above numbers total 220 Particular Baptist congregations in England and Wales combined. "By 1750," however, the total "had shrunk to about 150."[564] Such decline was due to three major factors. First, many churches were isolated in remote regions,

---

[562] W. T. Whitley, "Baptist Churches till 1660," *Transactions of the Baptist Historical Society* 2, no. 4 (1910–1911): 236; see also 236–54.

[563] In contrast, there were only 122 General Baptist congregations in England and none reported in Wales. For details see Michael Watts, *The Dissenters: From the Reformation to the French Revolution* (1978; repr., Oxford: Oxford University Press, 1999), 509–10.

[564] Michael A. G. Haykin, ed., *The Life and Thought of John Gill (1697–1771): A Tercentennial Appreciation*, vol. 77 of the series, Studies in the History of Christian Thought (Leiden: Brill, 1997), 1; and Arthur S. Langley, "Baptist Ministers in England about 1750 A.D.," *Transactions of the Baptist Historical Society* 6, no. 2 (1918): 138–57.

with meager communication or fellowship with churches of like faith and practice. Second, prolonged controversies over such topics as corporate singing had discouraged many congregations and led to factionalism. Third, in many churches, High Calvinism and hyper-Calvinist Antinomianism were stifling the free offer of Christ to unconverted sinners.[565] John Gill would become a vital part of this factor.

John Gill (1697–1771)

His Life and Works

John Gill was born to Edward and Elizabeth Gill in Kettering, Northamptonshire, on November 23, 1697.[566] As a deacon in the local Particular Baptist church, Edward Gill developed strong convictions. For example, when the headmaster at the Kettering Grammar School suddenly required every student to attend daily services in the parish church, John's formal education ended. Nevertheless, while only eleven years old at the time, John was already excelling in Latin and Greek. Finding access to Johannes Buxtorf's Hebrew grammar and lexicon, he quickly learned to read the Old Testament in its original language. Hebrew studies became his first love.[567] The

---

[565] Michael A. G. Haykin, *One Heart and One Soul: John Sutcliff of Olney, His Friends and His Times* (Durham, England: Evangelical Press, 1994), 20–33.
[566] The best works on Gill include an anonymous "Summary of the Life, Writings, and Character of the Author," in *A Collection of Sermons and Tracts*, 3 vols., by John Gill and published posthumously (London: George Keith, 1773–78), 1:ix–xxxv; Haykin, ed., *The Life and Thought of John Gill (1697–1771)*, 1997; Robert W. Oliver, *History of the English Calvinistic Baptists 1771–1892: From John Gill to C. H. Spurgeon* (Edinburgh: Banner of Truth Trust, 2006), 3–15; John Rippon, *A Brief Memoir of the Life and Writings of the Late Rev. John Gill, D. D.* (London: John Bennett, 1838); Walter Wilson, "Carter-Lane, Tooley-Street," in *The History and Antiquities of Dissenting Churches and Meeting Houses, in London, Westminster, and Southwark: Including the Lives of Their Ministers, from the Rise of Nonconformity to the Present Time*, 4 vols. (London: Printed for the author, 1814–18), 4:212–24; and George M. Ella, *John Gill and the Cause of God and Truth* (Eggleston, Co. Durham, England: Go Publications, 1995).
[567] Some years later, when he began preaching, Gill received a gift of £17 from the Particular Baptist Fund and used it to purchase Hebrew books.

ancient languages opened the door to studies in biblical commentaries and classical literature, as well as logic and rhetoric. Kettering's bookshop became John's favorite resort, as the shopkeeper and local ministers helped guide his studies. The boy's long hours in the bookshop became proverbial, as locals frequently described their expectations as being "as sure as John Gill is in the bookseller's shop." Upon hearing Pastor William Wallis preaching on Genesis 3:9, "And the Lord God called unto Adam, and said unto him, Where art thou?" John experienced conversion at the age of twelve. He waited until he was almost nineteen to make a public confession of faith and to receive baptism. At his baptism service, the congregation sang a hymn that John himself had written. He immediately began accepting opportunities to preach in various churches. In 1718, Gill married Elizabeth Negus.

The following year, twenty-two-year-old John Gill accepted the London pastorate of the Particular Baptist church at Goat Yard, Horsleydown (Southwark), where he would serve until his death, on October 14, 1771, at the age of seventy-three.[568] The Horsleydown church had been founded by the famed pastor-evangelist Benjamin Keach (1640–1704). In 1729, Gill led the church to replace Keach's thirty-nine Articles of Faith with his own twelve-article Declaration of the Faith and Practice,[569] thus eliminating Keach's evangelistic offer of the gospel. The Keach Confession had proclaimed that, in God's "effectual calling," He "doth persuade and enable us to embrace Jesus Christ freely, as He is offered in the Gospel" (Article 2).[570]

When he became a pastor, Gill would serve for fifty years as a manager of the Particular Baptist Fund.

[568] B. R. White, "John Gill in London, 1719–1729," *Baptist Quarterly* 22, no. 2 (April 1967): 72–91. Gill became the fourth pastor of the Horsleydown Church, succeeding founder Benjamin's Keach's son-in-law, Benjamin Stinton, who died suddenly in 1719 at the age of forty-two.

[569] John Gill, "A Declaration of the Faith and Practice of the Church of Christ, in Carter Lane, Southwark, under the Pastoral Care of Dr. John Gill, Read and Assented to at the Admission of Members," in *A Collection of Sermons and Tracts*, 3:626–31.

[570] Benjamin Keach, *The Articles of the Faith of the Church of Christ, or Congregation Meeting at Horsley-down, Benjamin Keach, Pastor, as Asserted This 10th of the 6th Month, 1697* (London: n.p., 1697), 11–12.

To Gill's credit, during his pastorate, believer's baptism by immersion remained a prerequisite for membership and the Lord's Supper, and, in 1757, the congregation built a new chapel on Carter Lane (Southwark).[571] Gill's successor, John Rippon (1751–1836), an evangelical Calvinist, would minister here at Carter Lane from 1773 until his death.[572] The tombs of Gill and Rippon are in London's Bunhill Fields burial ground. In 1830, six years prior to Rippon's death, the Carter Lane chapel suffered demolition to make room for wider access to nearby London Bridge. Three years later, the congregation moved into their new chapel on New Park Street. Nineteen-year-old Charles Spurgeon (1834–92) would assume the New Park Street pulpit in 1854.[573] Keach, Gill, Rippon, and Spurgeon were indeed the most prominent pastors of this church's history. With the completion of his *Exposition of the New Testament* (1748), John Gill became the first person to produce a verse-by-verse exposition of the entire Bible in the English language.[574] The University of Aberdeen conferred upon him the Doctor of Sacred Divinity degree in recognition of his distinction "in Sacred Literature, the Oriental Languages, and Jewish Antiquities."[575] Gill's major published works include:

- *The Glory of God's Grace Displayed* (a funeral sermon, 1724);
- *An Exposition of the Book of Solomon's Song* (1728);
- *The Doctrine of Justification by the Righteousness of Christ,*

---

[571] Carter Lane (off Tooley Street) connects with St. Olave's Street, near London Bridge.

[572] For a good study of Rippon, see Ken R. Manley, '*Redeeming Love Proclaim*': *John Rippon and the Baptists*, vol. 12 of the series, Studies in Baptist History and Thought (2004; repr., Eugene, OR: Wipf and Stock, 2006).

[573] See Charles Spurgeon, "John Rippon, D. D.," in *The Metropolitan Tabernacle: Its History and Work* (London: Passmore and Alabaster, 1876), 48–54. Spurgeon and his congregation moved into their final, new building, the Metropolitan Tabernacle, in 1861.

[574] For his eschatology, see Barry Howson, "The Eschatology of the Calvinistic Baptist John Gill (1697–1771) Examined and Compared," *Eusebia* 5 (Autumn 2005): 33–66.

[575] Joseph Ivimey, *A History of the English Baptists* (London: Printed for B. J. Holdsworth, 1823), 3:437.

Stated and Maintained (1730);
- *Treatise on the Doctrine of the Trinity Stated and Vindicated* (1731; 2nd ed. 1768);
- *The Doctrines of God's Everlasting Love to His Elect, and Their Eternal Union with Christ* (1732);
- *The Cause of God and Truth* (4 vols. 1735–38);
- *The Necessity of Good Works unto Salvation Considered* (1739);
- *Exposition of the New Testament* (3 vols. 1746–48);
- *The Doctrine of the Saints' Final Perseverance, Asserted and Vindicated* (1752);
- *The Doctrine of Predestination Stated, and Set in the Scripture Light* (1752);
- *Exposition of the Books of the Prophets of the Old Testament, Both the Larger and Lesser* (2 vols. 1757–58);
- *Exposition of the Old Testament* (4 vols. 1763–66);
- *Baptism a Divine Commandment to Be Observed* (1765);
- *Infant-Baptism: A Part and Pillar of Popery* (1766);
- *A Dissertation Concerning the Antiquity of the Hebrew Language, Letters, Vowel-Points, and Accents* (1767);
- *A Dissertation Concerning the Eternal Sonship of Christ* (1768);
- *A Complete Body of Doctrinal and Practical Divinity* (1769–70);[576]
- *A Collection of Sermons and Tracts* (3 vols. 1773–78, posthumous).

The Development of Antinomianism

Seventeenth-century Church of England ministers, including many Puritans, failed to preach instantaneous conversion. In fact, testimonies of instant conversions had become passé. Parishioners struggled at great length for assurance, as they listened to "means-of-grace" sermons that conveyed the expectation of a *progressive conversion* through various duties, or means of grace, such as sacraments, works of holiness, and

---

[576] For this study, I am using John Gill, *A Complete Body of Doctrinal and Practical Divinity: Or, a System of Evangelical Truths, deduced from the Sacred Scriptures*, new ed. 3 vols. (London: Printed for W. Winterbotham, 1796).

church attendance.[577] Antinomianism emerged in protest to a means-of-grace gospel that appeared void of grace and on the brink of a works (law) righteousness. The term *Antinomian* literally means "against law or duty." The controversial Puritan, Richard Baxter (1615–91), was one of its first opponents.[578] Until the end of the eighteenth century, elements of hyper-Calvinist Antinomianism would plague the Particular Baptist movement. Key components of extreme Antinomianism include the following:

- By His *free grace*,[579] God in eternity past has already justified all the elect and united them into Christ. This eliminates saving faith as a condition of justification.
- Salvation is completely passive; so, offering Christ to a sinner is an insult to God.
- God has totally abrogated the Moral Law.
- Even when an elect individual is living in sin, God sees no sin in him.
- Works of sanctification can never provide evidence of justification.
- The only assurance of justification is the inward testimony of the Holy Spirit.
- If one doubts his salvation, he has never received salvation.[580]

---

[577] Means-of-grace ministers would accuse New England pastor Jonathan Edwards of corrupting Reformed doctrine when he reported three hundred instant and surprising conversions in his town.

[578] See "Works on Antinomianism," in William Orme, *The Life and Times of Richard Baxter*, 2 vols. (London: James Duncan, 1830), 2:311–35. Baxter was Amyraldian in doctrine. For discussions on Amyraldianism, including Baxter's views, see John McClintock and James Strong, eds., *Cyclopaedia of Biblical, Theological, and Ecclesiastical Literature*, 1:701–3; and David Beale, *Historical Theology In-Depth* (Greenville, SC: Bob Jones University Press, 2013), 2:91ff.

[579] One should note that *free grace* is not exclusively an Antinomian term. Many Baptists, both Calvinists and Arminian, have utilized the term *free grace* without any trace of Antinomian doctrine.

[580] See also E. Pagitt, *Heresiography or a Description of the Hereticks and Sectaries of These Latter Times*, 3rd ed. (London: Printed for W. L. for his shop in Fleet Street, 1647), 109–10, 105–18. This is in the Bodleian Library, Oxford.

Gill Revives Crispian Antinomianism

Tobias Crisp (1600–43), Anglican author of the two-volume work, *Christ Alone Exalted* (1643),[581] had been the foremost representative of the key elements of seventeenth-century Antinomianism. In the next century, John Gill revived Antinomianism by reproducing Crisp's volumes and adding his own editorial footnotes in defense of Crispian theology. Gill sought to convince his readers that Crisp's doctrines were free of Antinomianism. Contrary to radical Antinomians, Crisp and Gill concede that God's moral law remains in effect as a restraint against the outward evils of society. According to Crisp, "In respect of the rules of righteousness, or the matter of obedience, we are under the law still, or else we are lawless, to live every man as it seems good in his own eyes."[582] Unlike radical Antinomians, Crisp and Gill also challenge believers to pursue sanctification.[583]

Although they represent an overall, moderate Antinomianism,[584] the doctrinal writings of Crisp and Gill embed key elements of hyper-Calvinism. Gill, for instance, strongly defends supralapsarianism, a doctrine that finds no expression in John Calvin's works or even in the canons of the Synod of Dort (1619). For God's "order of salvation" (*ordo*

---

[581] Tobias Crisp, *Christ Alone Exalted*, vol. 1 (London: Printed by Richard Bishop, at the charge of M. C., 1643), consisting of fourteen sermons; idem, *Christ Alone Exalted*, vol. 2 (London: Printed for the edification of the faithful, 1643), consisting of seventeen sermons. The work was republished as *Christ Alone Exalted: Being the Complete Works of Tobias Crisp, D. D., Containing XLII Sermons* (London: William Marshal, 1690). The republishing would revive the controversy for decades. Copies of both editions are in the British Library, London.

[582] Tobias Crisp, *Christ Alone Exalted, in the Perfection and Encouragement of the Saints, Notwithstanding Sins and Trials: Being the Complete Works of Tobias Crisp, Containing Fifty-Two Sermons*, 7th ed., 2 vols., ed. John Gill, with introductory "Memoirs" of the life of Tobias Crisp (London: John Bennett, 1832), 2:401. This is the most accessible edition. All future references to this title will be from this edition.

[583] Ibid., 2:316ff.

[584] The theology of Crisp and Gill was moderately Antinomian when compared with the radical Antinomianism described in Ephraim Pagitt's *Heresiography*.

salutis), supralapsarianism places the decree of election prior to or above (*supra*) His decree to permit the fall (*lapse*) of all humanity. Such an order makes the fall necessary; that is, it appears to make God the author of sin. The fivefold order of supralapsarianism is as follows:

(1) Election of some to eternal life and reprobation of all others
(2) Creation of the world and the human race
(3) Fall of all humanity
(4) Redemption provided for the elect by Christ's atonement
(5) Application of redemptive benefits to the elect[585]

The authors of *History of Dissenters* (1812) concluded that Tobias Crisp had been "one of the first patrons of Calvinism run mad."[586] In his *Christ Alone Exalted*, Crisp repeatedly denies the charge of "extremism," while advancing at least six interrelated elements of hyper-Calvinist Antinomianism. In his editorial notes, John Gill expresses no disagreement. Rather, he adds support and frequently uses nuance to restate Crisp's hyper-Calvinism into a more broadly palatable High Calvinism. The six components of hyper-Calvinism in Crisp's work are as follows.

First, Crisp teaches that *the Old Testament law was a schoolmaster, but only for national Israel. God never gave to an elect individual a law that could only condemn.* While agreeing with Crisp, Gill, to his credit, also stresses that God's moral law, "in the hands of Christ," operates in subordination to the higher, spiritual law of Christ and His mercy.[587]

---

[585] Gill, "Truth Defended," in *A Collection of Sermons and Tracts*, 2:65–106; Gill, *The Cause of God and Truth*, new ed. (London: W. H. Collingridge, 1855), 151ff.; and David Beale, *Historical Theology In-Depth* (Greenville, SC: Bob Jones University Press, 2013), 2:89ff.

[586] David Bogue and James Bennett, *History of Dissenters: From the Revolution in 1688 to the Year 1808* (London: Printed for the authors, 1812), 4:392–94.

[587] Crisp, *Christ Alone Exalted* (1832), 1:261–62. Gill improves Crisp's statement on the law. See Gill, "Of the Abrogation of the Old Covenant and the Introduction of the New," in *A Complete Body of Doctrinal and Practical Divinity* (1796), 2:40–41 (2:24–41). See also Gill, "The Law in the Hand of Christ" (Deut. 10:5), sermon 17, in *A Collection of Sermons and Tracts*, 1:268–83; idem, "The Law Established by the Gospel" (Romans

Second, *the sinner "is first justified before he believes, then he believes that he is justified."*[588] Thus, while God saves His elect in the realm of space and time, He has already justified them in eternity past. Gill argues that, even though Jesus' "active" and "passive" obedience for His elect took place in "the fullness of time" (Gal. 4:4), He was still "the Lamb slain from the foundation of the world" (Rev. 13:8). Gill concludes, therefore, that justification "does not begin to take place in time, or at believing, but is antecedent to any act of faith." Thus, in eternity past, God imputed the elects' sins to Christ and Christ's righteousness to the elect. In other words, Crisp and Gill identify the *decree* to justify with the *act* of justifying. To Gill, active justification is God's *supra-temporal* act of forgiving all his elect of all their sin. Passive justification is the *temporal* flowing of God's grace "from his sovereign good will and pleasure" to each of His elect.[589] Passive justification results, therefore, in the believer's sensibility of God's gracious, eternal gift of forgiveness.

The Westminster Confession teaches the eternal *decree* of justification, but, unlike Crisp and Gill, it rejects any eternal *act* of justification. The Westminster article asserts that "God did, from all eternity, decree to justify all the elect, and Christ did, in the fullness of time, die for their sins, and rise again for their justification: nevertheless, they are not justified until the Holy Spirit doth, in due time, actually apply Christ unto them."[590] Like the framers of the Confession (and unlike Gill), evangelical Particular Baptists have understood the following from the corpus of Scripture: Justification is the judicial act of God whereby He declares righteous the believing sinner. The

---

3:31), sermon 13, in *A Collection of Sermons and Tracts*, 1:200–16.
[588] Crisp, *Christ Alone Exalted* (1832), 1:91. In his editorial footnote, Gill appeals to the works of several Dutch and English hyper-Calvinists in favor of eternal justification.
[589] Gill, *A Complete Body of Doctrinal and Practical Divinity*, 1:298 (1:299–306); idem, "The Doctrine of Justification by the Righteousness of Christ, Stated and Maintained," in *A Collection of Sermons and Tracts*, 3:161–80 (3:147–84).
[590] Philip Schaff, "The Westminster Confession of Faith" (11.4), in *The Creeds of Christendom, with a History and Critical Notes* (New York: Harper and Brothers, 1877), 3:627.

act of justification is temporal, but it originated in the heart of God. He is under no obligation to justify anyone. God did not *excuse* our sins; he *punished* them in the person of Christ, our substitute. The ground of our justification is the saving work and resurrection of our Lord Jesus Christ. Faith is the condition of justification. Our justification is not *for* faith, but *through* faith, which is the gift of God. Saving faith is inseparable from the gift of repentance from sin and unto God. In justification, God imputes Christ's righteousness to us. Saving faith and true repentance produce good works.

Third, *"an elect person is united in Christ before he can believe on him."*[591] While Gill is in full agreement with Crisp, he slightly qualifies the Antinomian claim that a true believer's sins can never harm him. Gill concedes that the sins of the saved elect can bring God's temporal chastisement. It is worth noting, though, that in his defense of the eternal *union* with Christ, Gill contends for the supra-temporal *adoption* of the elect.[592]

Fourth, *none of God's elect are born in a state of condemnation.* That is, an unconditional, supra-temporal "covenant of grace," made by the Holy Trinity in behalf of all the elect, resulted in God's full forgiveness in eternity past. Crisp counsels that "their sins are forgiven, and whatsoever [sins] they commit, being believers, they shall do them no hurt."[593] Historian Joseph Ivimey views Crisp's advice as "entirely opposed to the doctrine of Paul, who, speaking of himself (whom no one will doubt to have been an elect person) and of other believers, says ... ' were by nature the children of wrath, even as others'" (Eph. 2:3*b*).[594] Yet, Crisp insists, "The Lord hath not one sin to charge upon an elect person, from the first moment of conception, till the last minute of his life; there is not so much as original sin

---

[591] Crisp, *Christ Alone Exalted* (1832), 2:234–35. Crisp argues at length that faith is the fruit of our union with Christ (2:232–45). In his editorial footnote, Gill defends the doctrine of the supra-temporal union of all the elect in Christ.

[592] Gill, "The Doctrines of God's Everlasting Love to His Elect, and Their Eternal Union with Christ," in *A Collection of Sermons and Tracts*, 3:185–206; and Gill, *A Complete Body of Doctrinal and Practical Divinity*, 1:290–306.

[593] Crisp, *Christ Alone Exalted* (1832), 2:160.

[594] Ivimey, *A History of the English Baptists*, 3:55.

to be laid on him; and the ground is, the Lord hath laid it on Christ already."[595] While avoiding any express disagreement with Crisp's statement, Gill adds that, when the regenerated elect commit sin, they should forsake it and worship God in gratitude for His gift of eternal forgiveness.[596]

Fifth, *faith has no effect on the divine forgiveness of sin.*[597] Gill equivocates, "There is a special faith, which is peculiar to God's elect, and is by some called saving faith, though strictly speaking salvation is not in faith, nor in any other grace." Obviously, Gill's doctrine of eternal justification made him uncomfortable with any suggestion of "saving faith," or justification *by* faith. Gill advocates *preaching* the gospel to all, but *offering* Christ to none. He urges that if a minister "does not warn and instruct both the Righteous and the Wicked, their Blood will be required at his hand."[598] It is not until the sinner is pleading for salvation, however, that the Christian is to offer Christ. Gill instructs those who are dealing with sinners who are "under a sense of sin and guilt," and "crying out, 'What shall we do to be saved?'" In this case, says Gill, "Your work is to lead men … to the blood of Christ, shed for many for the remission of sin; and in his name, you are to preach the forgiveness of it to them."[599] In so doing, you "may be useful in the Conversion, and so in the Salvation of precious and immortal Souls, which are of more Worth than a World."[600]

Sixth, *repentance has no effect on the divine forgiveness of sin.* Crisp insists that any exercise of faith or act of repentance for

---

[595] Crisp, *Christ Alone Exalted* (1832), 1:358–59.
[596] Gill, "The Doctrines of God's Everlasting Love to His Elect, and Their Eternal Union with Christ," in *A Collection of Sermons and Tracts*, 3:214–19; and Gill, *A Complete Body of Doctrinal and Practical Divinity*, 1:361–74.
[597] Crisp, *Christ Alone Exalted* (1832), 2:94–110.
[598] John Gill and Samuel Wilson, *The Mutual Duty of Pastor and People*, "represented in two discourses preached at the ordination of the Reverend George Braithwaite, M.A., March 28, 1734" (London: Printed for Aaron Ward, 1734), 26. This is in the British Library, London.
[599] Gill, *The Doctrine of the Cherubim Opened and Explained*, "in a sermon preached at the ordination of the Reverend Mr. John Davis, at Waltham-Abbey, August 15, 1764" (London: Printed and sold by G. Keith, J. Robinson, and W. Leopard, 1766), 16. This is in the British Library.
[600] Gill, *The Mutual Duty of Pastor and People*, 27.

DAVID BEALE

forgiveness is an insult to the God of grace who forgave His elect in eternity past.[601] Gill says that repentance can be "either evangelical or legal." Evangelical repentance is a gift of God, given exclusively to each of His elect. Legal repentance is a useless work performed by the godless — whether individually or nationally. According to Gill, "Legal repentance may be performed by particular individuals, who are destitute of God's grace, and by all the inhabitants of a place, as the Ninevites, who repented externally at the preaching of Jonah." Gill is certain that the Ninevites remained without grace and that this resulted in their eventual destruction. Gill's estimation of Jesus' preaching in the four Gospels is as follows: "That there are universal offers of grace and salvation made to all men, I utterly deny."[602] Gill insists that all the Bible's commands to repent are commands to a legal repentance.

Citing Acts 3:19*a*, "Repent ye therefore, and be converted, that your sins may be blotted out," Gill explains that, whether we interpret that command as applying nationally to the Jews, or individually to others, the intended conversion "is not an internal conversion ... but an outward reformation of life." Gill finds one exception: The future conversion of Israel (Rom. 11:25–26. He explains that, except "the Jews upon their call and conversion shall return to their own land, in a literal sense, I see not how we can understand this, and many other prophecies." In his ministry, Gill avoided the use of open invitations for lost people to believe or to *do* anything.[603] "How irrational is it," Gill asked, "for ministers to stand offering Christ, and salvation by him to man, when, on the one hand, they have neither power nor right to give; and, on the other hand, the persons they offer to, have neither power nor will to receive?" He explains:

---

[601] Crisp, *Christ Alone Exalted* (1832), 1:91, 1:267, 1:335, 2:58–61, 2:214–15, 2:267; and passim.

[602] Gill, "The Doctrine of Predestination Stated," in *A Collection of Sermons and Tracts*, 3:269–70.

[603] Gill, *The Cause of God and Truth*, 35 (34–46); idem, on Jeremiah 30:3, http://www.sacred-texts.com/bib/cmt/gill/jer030.htm; and idem, "The Glory of the Church in the Latter Day" (Psalm 87:3), sermon 4, in *A Collection of Sermons and Tracts*, 1:62–63.

> The gospel is a declaration of salvation already wrought out by Christ, and not an offer of it on conditions to be performed by man. The ministers of the gospel are sent to *preach the gospel to every creature*; that is, not to offer, but to preach Christ, and salvation by him; to publish peace and pardon as things already obtained by him. The ministers are ... *criers* or *heralds*; their business is ... to *proclaim* aloud, to publish facts, to declare things that are done, and not to offer them to be done on conditions.[604]

While Gill sometimes cites Scripture that appears to teach active faith and repentance, his explanations reduce faith and repentance to a passive conversion.[605] It should not be surprising that Gill's reticence toward the term *justifying faith*, together with his insistence on totally-passive conversions, led many professing Christians to an unwholesome introspection—followed by uncertainty and doubt, regarding their calling and election. Gill's opponents believed that a straightforward reading of 1 John 1:9 could remove all doubt, "If we confess our sins, he is faithful and just to forgive us our sins, and to cleanse us from all unrighteousness." Gill persistently sought to explain away the meaning of words such as *world* and *all* when they occur in passages inviting men to believe, to repent, or to come unto Christ.[606]

Charles Spurgeon would assess Gill's soteriology this way. "The system of theology with which many identify his name has chilled many churches to their very soul, for it has led them to omit the free invitations of the gospel, and to deny that it is the duty of sinners to believe in Jesus: but for this, Dr. Gill must not be altogether held responsible."[607] Indeed, the propagation of hyper-Calvinism by Gill's followers would become seriously detrimental to the advancement of the Great Commission. On the other hand, Gill's biblical discussions on

---

[604] Gill, *A Collection of Sermons and Tracts*, 2:146–47.
[605] Gill, *A Complete Body of Doctrinal and Practical Divinity*, 3:37 (3:25–37).
[606] E.g., Gill, *The Cause of God and Truth*, 41–44, 53.
[607] Charles H. Spurgeon, *The Autobiography of C. H. Spurgeon 1834–1854*, compiled from his diary, letters, and records by his wife and his private secretary (London: Passmore and Alabaster, 1897), 1:310.

the Trinity provided positive weapons in the Baptist battles against inroads of Unitarianism and Christological heresies.[608]

Hyper-Calvinist Impact of Joseph Hussey, John Skepp, and John Brine

Joseph Hussey (1660-1726), hyper-Calvinist pastor of a Congregational church near Cambridge, published the first major treatise against inviting sinners to come to Christ. A great admirer of the works of Tobias Crisp,[609] Hussey wrote *God's Operations of Grace, but No Offers of His Grace* (1707). The book exhorts ministers to preach "gospel doctrine"—but never in the form of an offer. To Hussey, any human invitation for a sinner to accept Christ is "a piece of robbery committed upon the Holy Ghost."[610] Any "undertaking to work persuasion" toward salvation—even the act of "propounding the offer of Christ"—is mere "flattery." "The offer of salvation is enticing in the very ears of a natural man that never knows a saving change."[611] Moreover, says, Hussey, "Proffering the Gospel debases the Sovereignty of God, instead of exalting it. How abject and precarious is it in the Great and Glorious Name of Jehovah, to stand up and say, 'Here Sinners, I offer you Christ, why don't you take him?' Ah! It is a taking of God's Name in vain, and perverting of God's Message." Contrasting true preaching with offering Christ and His grace, Hussey explains, "Preaching is supreme; it breaks in upon a man by authority. Offers are servile; they make parleys, and debase Majesty, and so cannot be the same thing with preaching that exalts it."[612] In

---

[608] E.g., John Gill, "The Doctrine of the Trinity, Stated and Vindicated," in *A Collection of Sermons and Tracts*, 3:1-96; idem, "The Doctrine of the Resurrection, Stated and Defended," in *A Collection of Sermons and Tracts*, 3:97-146.

[609] Walter Wilson, "Joseph Hussey," in *The History and Antiquities of Dissenting Churches and Meeting Houses, in London, Westminster, and Southwark*, 4:411-22.

[610] Joseph Hussey, *God's Operations of Grace, but No Offers of His Grace* (London: Printed by D. Bridge, 1707), 11. This is in the British Library, London. I modernized a few spellings and punctuations.

[611] Ibid., 16.

[612] Ibid., 29. For more discussion on this issue, see R. Phillip Roberts,

a word, according to Hussey, Christians mock God when they urge the unregenerate to come to Christ. Moreover, the unregenerate have no duty to respond to the gospel.

Just as John Gill had brought Tobias Crisp's hyper-Calvinism into Particular Baptist circles, John Skepp (1675-1721) and John Brine (1703-65) embedded Joseph Hussey's most extreme views into the same circles. A former member of Hussey's Congregational church, John Skepp,[613] by 1715, had accepted the pastorate of Curriers' Hall (Cripplegate) Baptist Church in London.[614] The fervent, pastor-evangelist Hanserd Knollys had founded this church in 1645. In Skepp's *Divine Energy: Or the Efficacious Operations of the Spirit of God upon the Soul of Man* (1722),[615] he views any free offer of the gospel as tantamount to the Pelagian heresy.[616] Dedicating his book to Curriers' Hall Baptist Church, Skepp cunningly insinuates to his congregation that his teachings are compatible with those of "that eminent servant and sufferer for Christ, Mr. Hanserd Knollys."[617] Skepp had wielded an enormous influence upon John Gill—successor of evangelist Benjamin Keach. Skepp had presided at Gill's ordination and guided him in his choices of theology books. Upon Skepp's death, Gill acquired key books from his library and later published a second edition of Skepp's *Divine Energy* (1751), dividing it into chapters with introductory summaries, and adding a recommendatory preface.

In 1730, within a decade after Skepp's death, another

Continuity and Change: London Calvinistic Baptists and the Evangelical Revival, 1760-1820 (Wheaton, IL: Richards Owen Roberts, 1989), 36-43.

[613] Walter Wilson, "John Skepp," in *The History and Antiquities of Dissenting Churches and Meeting Houses, in London, Westminster, and Southwark*, 2:572-74.

[614] Cripplegate is an area near present-day Barbican Centre.

[615] John Skepp, *Divine Energy: Or the Efficacious Operations of the Spirit of God upon the Soul of Man in His Effectual Calling and Conversion, Stated, Prov'd, and Vindicated, Wherein the Real Weakness and Insufficiency of Moral Suasion ... for Conversion to God, Are Fully Evinced, Being an Antidote against the Pelagian Plague* (London: Printed for Joseph Marshall at the Bible in Newgate Street and for Aaron Ward at the King's-Arms in Little Britain, 1722). A first-edition copy is in the British Library, London.

[616] Ibid., 56-57.

[617] Ibid., Dedication.

hyper-Calvinist, John Brine, accepted the Curriers' Hall pastorate. In his *Refutation of Arminian Principles*, Brine wrongly labels as *Arminians* all who freely offer the gospel.[618] Like his friend, John Gill, Brine was born in Kettering, Northamptonshire, where they grew up attending the same Baptist church. Both entered the Particular Baptist ministry in Kettering, and both went on to serve London pastorates. Both were well-known scholars of Latin, Greek, and Hebrew, and both became prolific authors, sounding forth the depths of man's depravity. Howbeit, even when their remains rested near each other in Bunhill Fields,[619] these men left Baptists with perplexing questions on the vital issue of evangelism.

The Modern Question

In view of the Particular Baptist doctrines of limited atonement, unconditional election, and total depravity, vital questions of eternal moment emerged from the "gospel offer" controversy. Concerned pastors were now asking, "Should ministers of the gospel indiscriminately offer Christ to sinners?" "How could such an offer be well intended?" "Are all unregenerate sinners under a moral obligation to believe, repent, and accept Christ as Lord and Savior?" "Are unsaved people spiritually capable of responding to the offer of salvation?" Simply put, "Is saving faith a duty?" That last question—the common denominator of all such inquiries—emerged as "the modern

---

[618] John Brine, *A Refutation of Arminian Principles, delivered in a Pamphlet, Entitled, The Modern Question Concerning Repentance and Faith* (London: Printed for A. Ward, 1743). This copy is in the British Library. Brine further develops his hyper-Calvinism in *A Defense of the Doctrine of Eternal Justification* (London: Printed for and sold by A. Ward and H. Whitridge, 1732). Brine had served as minister of the Baptist church in Coventry prior to his call to London in about 1730. A valuable source on Brine is Walter Wilson, "John Brine," *The History and Antiquities of Dissenting Churches and Meeting Houses, in London, Westminster, and Southwark*, 2:574–79. For a complete listing of Brine's published works, see Gale Cengage Learning, Gage Inc. http://microformguides.gale.com/BrowseGuide.asp?colldocid=2019000&Item=&Page=1792.

[619] For the tomb inscriptions of Gill and Brine, see Alfred W. Light, *Bunhill Fields* (London: C. J. Farncombe and Sons, 1913), 123ff., 166ff.

question," as seen in a rapid succession of publications such as *A Modern Question Modestly Answer'd* (1737), written by an Independent Congregationalist—a Welshman named Matthias Maurice (1684-1738), who since 1723 had been serving a pastorate in Rothwell, Northamptonshire. From his consideration of thirty passages of Scripture, Maurice proposes, "Any Person surely, who ... sincerely and unfeignedly makes the Bible the Rule of his Faith, must say, that God does by his *Word* plainly and plentifully make it the Duty of unconverted Sinners, who hear the Gospel, to believe *in Christ*."[620] Maurice appeals to passages such the following three: First Timothy 2:6 says that Christ "gave himself a ransom for all." Hebrews 2:9 says that Christ tasted death "for every man." First John 2:2 says that Christ is "the propitiation for our sins: and not for ours only, but also for the sins of the whole world." Maurice concludes, "There is nobody who hears the Gospel preached, [who] can justly say, *Christ* did not die for him; it would be a great Sin in any one to say so." According to the Scriptures, says Maurice, "Wherever the Gospel is preached and heard, Faith in *Christ* is a moral Duty, and Repentance towards God is a moral Duty."[621]

Maurice further buttressed his position in another book, *The Modern Question Affirm'd and Prov'd: viz. That the Eternal God Does by His Word Make It the Duty of Poor Unconverted Sinners, Who Hear the Gospel Preach'd or Publish'd to Believe in Jesus Christ* (posthumously published, 1739). In essential agreement with Maurice, another Independent, Abraham Taylor, published a pamphlet titled *The Modern Question Concerning Repentance and Faith* (1742).[622] John Brine's *Refutation of Arminian Principles* (1743) had emerged as a direct attack against Taylor's *Modern Question*. Brine inaccurately dubs Taylor's book a compilation of "Arminian principles." To increasing numbers of Baptists, many of whom defended five-point Calvinism, such attacks against offering Christ would prove unconvincing.

---

[620] Matthias Maurice, *A Modern Question Modestly Answer'd* (London: Printed for James Buckland, 1737), 4. This is in the British Library, London.
[621] Ibid., 22, 24.
[622] Abraham Taylor, *The Modern Question Concerning Repentance and Faith, Examined with Candor in Four Dialogues* (London: Printed for James Blackstone, 1742), published anonymously.

Select Bibliography for Further Reading

Brine, John *A Defense of the Doctrine of Eternal Justification*. London: Printed for and sold by A. Ward and H. Whitridge, 1732.

Brown, Raymond. *The English Baptists of the Eighteenth Century*. London: The Baptist Historical Society, 1986.

Crisp, Tobias. *Christ Alone Exalted, in the Perfection and Encouragement of the Saints, Notwithstanding Sins and Trials: Being the Complete Works of Tobias Crisp, Containing Fifty-Two Sermons*. 7th ed., 2 vols., edited by John Gill, with introductory "Memoirs" of the life of Tobias Crisp. London: John Bennett, 1832.

Ella, George M. *John Gill and the Cause of God and Truth*. Eggleston, Co. Durham, England: Go Publications, 1995.

Gill, John. *The Cause of God and Truth*. New ed. London: W. H. Collingridge, 1855.

———. *A Collection of Sermons and Tracts*. 3 vols. London: Printed for George Keith, 1773–78.

———. *A Complete Body of Doctrinal and Practical Divinity: Or, a System of Evangelical Truths, Deduced from the Sacred Scriptures*. New ed. 3 vols. London: Printed for W. Winterbotham, 1796.

Haykin, Michael A. G., ed. *The Life and Thought of John Gill (1697–1771): A Tercentennial Appreciation*. Vol. 77 of the series, Studies in the History of Christian Thought. Leiden: Brill, 1997.

Howson, Barry. "The Eschatology of the Calvinistic Baptist John Gill (1697–1771) Examined and Compared." *Eusebia* 5 (Autumn 2005): 33–66.

Hussey, Joseph. *God's Operations of Grace, but No Offers of His Grace*. London: Printed by D. Bridge, 1707.

Maurice, Matthias. *A Modern Question Modestly Answer'd*. London: Printed for James Buckland, 1737.

Oliver, Robert W. *History of the English Calvinistic Baptists 1771–1892: From John Gill to C. H. Spurgeon*. Edinburgh: Banner of Truth Trust, 2006.

Rippon, John. *A Brief Memoir of the Life and Writings of the Late Rev. John Gill, D. D.* London: John Bennett, 1838.

Roberts, R. Phillip. *Continuity and Change: London Calvinistic Baptists and the Evangelical Revival, 1760–1820*. Wheaton, IL: Richards Owen Roberts, 1989.

Sell, Alan P. F. *The Great Debate: Calvinism, Arminianism and Salvation*. 1982. Reprint, Grand Rapids: Baker, 1983.

Skepp, John. *Divine Energy: Or the Efficacious Operations of the Spirit of God upon the Soul of Man in His Effectual Calling and Conversion, Stated, Prov'd, and Vindicated, Wherein the Real Weakness and Insufficiency of Moral Suasion … for Conversion to God, Are Fully Evinced, Being an Antidote against the Pelagian Plague*. London: Printed for Joseph Marshall at the Bible in Newgate Street and for Aaron Ward at the King's-Arms in Little Britain, 1722.

Taylor, Abraham. *The Modern Question Concerning Repentance and Faith, Examined with Candor in Four Dialogues.* London: Printed for James Blackstone, 1742.

White, B. R. "John Gill in London, 1719–1729." *Baptist Quarterly* 22, no. 2 (April 1967): 72–91.

Chapter 9

The Rise of Evangelical Calvinism: Life of Andrew Fuller to the Prayer Call of 1784

❋

Fuller's Early Years

Born on February 6, in the village of Wicken, Cambridgeshire, Andrew Fuller (1754–1815)[623] was the youngest of

---

[623] The best sources for Andrew Fuller's life and ministry include the following: John Ryland [Jr.], *The Work of Faith, the Labor of Love, and the Patience of Hope, Illustrated in the Life and Death of the Reverend Andrew Fuller*, 2nd ed. (London: Button and Son, 1818); Fuller's son, Andrew Gunton Fuller, *Andrew Fuller* (London: Hodder and Stoughton, 1882); Paul Brewster, *Andrew Fuller: Model Pastor-Theologian* (Nashville: B&H Publishing Group, 2010); Chris Chun, *The Legacy of Jonathan Edwards in the Theology of Andrew Fuller*, vol. 162 of the series, Studies in the History of Christian Traditions (Leiden: Koninklijke Brill, 2012); Keith S. Grant, *Andrew Fuller and the Evangelical Renewal of Pastoral Theology*, vol. 36 of the series, Studies in Baptist History and Thought (2013; repr., Eugene, OR: Wipf and Stock, 2013); Michael A. G. Haykin, ed., *The Armies of the Lamb: The Spirituality of Andrew Fuller* (Dundas, Ontario: Joshua Press, 2001); Michael A. G. Haykin, ed., *'At the Pure Fountain of Thy Word': Andrew Fuller as an Apologist*, vol. 6 of the series, Studies in Baptist History and Thought (2004; repr., Eugene, OR: Wipf and Stock, 2006); Gilbert Laws, *Andrew Fuller: Pastor, Theologian, Ropeholder* (London: Carey Press, 1942); A. Chadwick Mauldin, *Fullerism as Opposed to Calvinism: A Historical and Theological Comparison of the Missiology of Andrew Fuller and John Calvin* (Eugene, OR: Wipf and Stock, 2011); Peter J. Morden, *Offering Christ to the World: Andrew Fuller (1754–1815) and the Revival of*

the three sons of Robert and Philippa Fuller. Robert provided for his family by renting and operating a succession of dairy farms. From their earliest years, the Fuller boys were acquainted with hard work and discipline. They received no formal education. When Andrew was seven years old, the family moved to nearby Soham, where they regularly heard the hyper-Calvinist preaching of John Eve, at the Particular Baptist church. Eve preached to the Christian elect, but he "entirely neglected to point sinners to the Lamb of God."[624] Andrew Fuller, during his teen years, began reading evangelical works, such as John Bunyan's autobiography, *Grace Abounding to the Chief of Sinners*, and Ralph Erskine's *Gospel Sonnets*. Through these means, Andrew began to realize the depths of his sinful condition. While walking alone on a November morning, in 1769, Andrew came under great conviction and received salvation in Christ alone. He later testifies that God saved him despite "erroneous views of the gospel," preached by hyper-Calvinists who insisted that lost sinners must never receive a human offer of Christ:

> The reproaches of a guilty conscience seemed like the gnawing worm of hell. I thought surely that [it] must be an earnest of hell itself. The fire and brimstone of the bottomless pit seemed to burn within my bosom.... I saw that God would be perfectly just in sending me to hell.... I can remember I was like a man drowning, looking every way for help.... I thought of the resolution of Job, "Though he slay me, yet will I trust in him." I paused, and repeated the words over and over. Each repetition seemed to kindle a ray of hope mixed with a determination, *if I might*, to cast my perishing soul upon the Lord Jesus Christ for salvation, to be both pardoned

---

Eighteenth-Century Particular Baptist Life, vol. 8 of the series, Studies in Baptist History and Thought (Carlisle, England: Paternoster, 2003); idem, *The Life and Thought of Andrew Fuller (1754–1815)* (Milton Keynes, England: Paternoster, 2015); and *The Andrew Fuller Center Review*, for The Andrew Fuller Center for Baptist Studies, edited and directed by Michael A. G. Haykin at The Southern Baptist Theological Seminary, http://www.andrewfullercenter.org/.

[624] Andrew Gunton Fuller, *Andrew Fuller*, 24.

and purified; for I felt that I needed the one as much as the other. I was not then aware that *any* poor sinner had a warrant to believe in Christ for the salvation of his soul.... Yet it was not altogether from a dread of wrath that I fled to this refuge; for I well remember that I felt something attracting in the Savior. I must—I will—yes, I will trust my soul—my sinful lost soul in his hands. If I perish, I perish. However it was, I was determined to cast myself upon Christ, thinking peradventure he would save my soul; and, if not, I could but be lost. In this way I continued above an hour, weeping and supplicating mercy for the Savior's sake ... and, as the eye of the mind was more and more fixed upon him, my guilt and fears were gradually and insensibly removed. I now found rest for my troubled soul; and I reckon that I should have found it sooner, if I had not entertained the notion of my having no warrant to come to Christ without some previous qualification. This notion was a bar that kept me back for a time, though through divine drawings I was enabled to over-leap it.... If at that time I had known that any poor sinner *might* warrantably have trusted in him for salvation, I conceive I should have done so, and [should] have found rest to my soul sooner than I did. I mention this because it may be the case with others, who may be kept in darkness and despondency by erroneous views of the gospel much longer than I was.[625]

**Fuller's Earliest Ministry and Doctrinal Influences
His Emergence out of Hyper-Calvinism**

In April 1770, Pastor John Eve baptized sixteen-year-old Andrew Fuller into the membership of Soham Baptist. About a month earlier, in another church, Fuller had witnessed the

---

[625] Andrew Gunton Fuller, ed., *Memoirs of the Rev. Andrew Fuller*, in *The Complete Works of the Rev. Andrew Fuller*, 2 vols. (Boston: Gould, Kendall, and Lincoln, 1836), 1:20–21. For a one-volume reprint of this set, see *The Works of Andrew Fuller*, ed. Andrew Gunton Fuller (Carlisle, PA: The Banner of Truth Trust, 2007). Henceforth, however, all references to this title will shorten to *Memoirs*, and all references to the *Memoirs* will be to volume one of the 2-volume 1836 set.

"solemn immersion" of two young people, upon "profession of faith in Christ." Although he had grown up attending a Baptist church, this was the first time Fuller had ever seen the ordinance administered. He later recalled that the occasion "carried such a conviction with it that I wept like a child."[626] Within months, Fuller was exercising the gift of preaching. In late 1771, Eve and most of his members left the Soham church over a dispute concerning the extent of man's fallen volition. For the next two years, the small church relied upon lay members to do the preaching.

Early in 1774, the church called upon twenty-year-old Andrew Fuller to preach on a trial basis. "Being now devoted to the ministry," Fuller recalls, "I took a review of the doctrines I should preach." Consequently, he "durst not for some years address an invitation to the unconverted to come to Jesus."[627] Fuller was struggling over the hyper-Calvinism that had influenced him from youth. "But," says Fuller, "as I perceived this reasoning would affect the whole tenor of my preaching, I moved on with slow and trembling steps; and, having to feel my way out of a labyrinth, I was a long time ere I felt satisfied."[628] In May of the following year, the church ordained him as pastor, with Robert Hall Sr., from Leicestershire, participating. Fuller would recall that Pastor Hall "came seventy miles to my ordination, and continued my father and friend till his death."[629] In the interrogation, Hall had suggested to Fuller that he read Jonathan Edwards's *Freedom of the Will*.

One of Fuller's most unforgettable theological turning points came during a visit to London, in the fall of 1775. Here he "met with" Abraham Taylor's *Modern Question*. As he perused the book, nothing really caught his attention until he came to Taylor's discussion on "the addresses of John the Baptist, Christ, and the apostles, which he [Taylor] proved to be delivered to the ungodly and to mean spiritual repentance and faith.... This set me fast," says Fuller. "I read and examined the Scripture passages, and the more I read and thought, the

---

[626] Andrew Gunton Fuller, ed., *Memoirs*, 1:22.
[627] Ibid., 1:25.
[628] Ibid., 1:25–26.
[629] Ibid., 1:27.

more I doubted the justice of my former views."[630]

In December 1776, Fuller married Sarah Gardiner, a member of his church. Soham Baptist had recently joined the Northamptonshire Association,[631] placing Fuller into a close relationship with a small company of Particular Baptist pastors who, like himself, were in the midst of a theological transition out of hyper-Calvinism and into a missions-minded, evangelical Calvinism. Each of these men would soon be exhorting sinners to come to Christ. They included Robert Hall Sr. (1728–91),[632]

---

[630] Ibid., 1:28. Fuller testifies on the same page that another great help to him during this time was John Martin, *The Rock of Offence the Sinner's Last and Only Refuge: A Discourse on Romans x. 3 Wherein the Cause and Consequence of Not Submitting to the Righteousness of God, are Considered* (London: Printed for the author, 1771). This is a classic evangelistic message from a Calvinist.

[631] It remains unclear why the founders called it the "Northamptonshire" Association, since only two of its churches were located within that county. For more discussion, see Thornton S. H. Elwyn, "Particular Baptists of the Northamptonshire Baptist Association as Reflected in the Circular Letters 1765–1820," *Baptist Quarterly* 36, no. 8 (October 1996): 368–81.

[632] For the life of Robert Hall Sr., see John Rippon, ed., "The Rev. Mr. Robert Hall," *The Baptist Annual Register, for 1790, 1791, 1792, and Part of 1793* (London: Sold by Dilly, Button, and Thomas, in London, 1793), 226–40; Robert Hall [Jr.], "Life of the Author," in *Help to Zion's Travelers: Being an Attempt to Remove Various Stumbling-Blocks Out of the Way Relating to Doctrinal, Experimental and Practical Religion*, by Robert Hall [Sr.], ed. Joseph A. Warne, 3rd ed. (Boston: Lincoln, Edmands, and Sons, 1833), 247–68; Graham W. Hughes, "Robert Hall of Arnesby: 1728–1791," *Baptist Quarterly* 10, no. 8 (October 1941): 444–47; and Michael A. G. Haykin, "Robert Hall, Sr. (1728–1791)," in *The British Particular Baptists 1638–1910*, ed. Michael A. G. Haykin (Springfield, MO: Particular Baptist Press, 1998), 1:202–11). For the heart-wrenching story of the last four years of the life of Hall's first wife Jane, see Robert Hall [Sr.], *Mercy Manifested* (London: Sold by G. Keith, Gracechurch Street; G. Robinson, Paternoster Row; T. Vallance, Cheapside; J. Matthews, in the Strand; and Mr. Watts Bookseller, Windmill-hill, near the Foundry, Moorfields, 1777). This edition, signed on April 12, is the first of two editions published in the same year. For a valuable study on Robert Hall Jr. (1764–1831), see Cody Heath McNutt, "The Ministry of Robert Hall, Jr.: The Preacher as Theological Exemplar and Cultural Celebrity" (PhD diss., Southern Baptist Theological Seminary, 1956).

of Arnesby,[633] John Ryland Jr. (1753–1825),[634] co-pastor with his father at College Lane Baptist Church,[635] in Northampton, and John Sutcliff (1752–1814) of the Baptist church in Olney (Buckinghamshire).

Encouragement from John Fawcett and John Sutcliff

Born in Yorkshire,[636] John Sutcliff, during his teenage years, had come under the wise tutelage of John Fawcett Sr.

---

[633] Robert Hall Sr. served the pastorate of Arnesby Baptist church (est. 1701) from 1753 until his death. Situated on St. Peter's Road, its present chapel, erected 1798–99, stands on the site of the original 1719 building. The older spelling of the village's name is *Arnsby*. I am using the modern spelling. See also William Bassett, *History of the Baptist Church Assembling at Arnsby, in the County of Leicester: With A Memoir of the Rev. Robert Hall, Sen., and Biographical Notices of His Successors* (London: B. L. Green, 1856).

[634] For more on John Ryland Jr., see James Culross, *The Three Rylands: A Hundred Years of Various Christian Service* (London: Elliot Stock, 1897), 67–91; L. G. Champion, "The Theology of John Ryland: Its Sources and Influences," *Baptist Quarterly* 28, no. 1 (January 1979): 17–29; idem, "The Letters of John Newton to John Ryland," *Baptist Quarterly* 27, no. 4 (October 1977): 157–63; H. W. Robinson, "The Experience of John Ryland," *Baptist Quarterly* 4, no. 1 (January 1928): 17–26; and E. F. Clipsham, "Ryland, John (1753–1825)," *Oxford Dictionary of National Biography* (Oxford University Press, 2004), online ed., http://www.oxforddnb.com/view/article/24412.

[635] See John Taylor, *History of College Street Church, Northampton with Biographies of Pastors, Missionaries, and Preachers*, bi-centenary volume (Northampton: Taylor and Son, the Dryden Press, 1897); and Ernest A. Payne, *College Street Church, Northampton, 1697–1947* (London: Kingsgate Press, 1947).

[636] The best source on Sutcliff is Michael A. G. Haykin, *One Heart and One Soul: John Sutcliff of Olney, His Friends and His Times* (Durham, England: Evangelical Press, 1994); see also R. M. Thomson, "John Newton and His Baptist Friends," *Baptist Quarterly* 9, no. 6 (April 1939): 368–71; Kenneth W. H. Howard, "John Sutcliff of Olney," *Baptist Quarterly* 14, no. 7 (July 1952): 304–9; and Andrew Fuller, *The Principles and Prospects of a Servant of Christ*, "delivered at the funeral of the Rev. J. Sutcliff, of Olney, June 28, 1814," Sermon 25, in *The Complete Works of the Rev. Andrew Fuller*, ed. Andrew Gunton Fuller, 2 vols. (Boston: Gould, Kendall, and Lincoln, 1836), 2:328–37; and Andrew Fuller, "Memoir of the Rev. John Sutcliff," *The Baptist Magazine* 7 (February 1815): 45–53. See also John Newton, *Olney Hymns* (Philadelphia: Printed by William Young, 1792).

(1740–1817),[637] who had become a Christian in 1755, after hearing George Whitefield preach from John 3:14, "And as Moses lifted up the serpent in the wilderness, even so must the Son of man be lifted up." Following a brief time as a Methodist preacher, Fawcett became an evangelical Particular Baptist. In 1763, he began preaching for Wainsgate Baptist Church, overlooking the township, Hebden Bridge, in West Yorkshire.[638] In July 1765, the Wainsgate church ordained Fawcett as their pastor. In 1769, when seventeen-year-old John Sutcliff became a Christian, he joined Wainsgate Baptist, where Fawcett mentored him at Ewood Hall Theological Academy, in Fawcett's home, and persuaded him to enroll at Bristol Baptist College. In 1772, London's Carter Lane Baptist Church invited Fawcett to replace their recently deceased pastor, the celebrated John Gill (1697–1771). After preaching at Carter Lane fifty-eight times, during a nine-week visit, and establishing favor with the church, Fawcett accepted their offer.

When he returned to Wainsgate with the news, the congregation displayed enormous grief over the impending loss of their beloved pastor and his family. When Fawcett's farewell sermon ended, and the family boarded the wagons loaded with all their household possessions, "the love and tears of his attached people prevailed." Unable to leave his congregation, Fawcett remained in Wainsgate, and Carter Lane brought in John Rippon (1751–1836) as Gill's successor. Like Rippon, John Fawcett was a hymn writer. The love and loyalty that bonded the Wainsgate congregation to the Fawcett family inspired John Fawcett to write his venerable hymn, "Blest Be the Tie

---

[637] The best sources on John Fawcett Sr. include John Fawcett Jr., *An Account of the Life, Ministry, and Writings of the Late Rev. John Fawcett, D. D.* (London: Baldwin, Cradock, and Joy, 1818); and Michael A. G. Haykin, "'Dissent Warmed Its Hands at Grimshaw's Fire.' William Grimshaw of Haworth and the Baptists of Yorkshire," *Perichoresis* 7, no. 1 (2009): 23–37.

[638] In 1815, the Wainsgate church replaced its 1750 building with a new one. The present building was erected in the late 1850s. In 2001, the church permanently closed, and their building came under the care of the Historic Chapels Trust. In its graveyard is John Fawcett's tombstone. See Charles W. Thomson, *Wainsgate Baptist Chapel, West Yorkshire: A History and Guide* (London: N.p., 2012); and *A Brief Guide to Wainsgate Baptist Church* (London: Historic Chapels Trust, n.d).

that Binds."[639] Fawcett included the song in his book of *Hymns* (1782), and John Rippon popularized it in his own hymn collections. Originally, its title was "Brotherly Love." Of its six stanzas this is the first:

> Blest be the tie that binds
> Our hearts in Christian love;
> The fellowship of kindred minds
> Is like to that above.

Stanza 3 especially reflects the "woes" and "tears" at Wainsgate:

> We share our mutual woes;
> Our mutual burdens bear;
> And often for each other flows
> The sympathizing tear.[640]

In 1777, the congregation assisted Fawcett in planting a sister church, two miles away, in the valley community of Hebden Bridge, where they gathered a flock, erected a building, and named it Ebenezer Baptist Church.[641] Again, preferring to stay with his people, Fawcett, in 1792, declined the office of president of Bristol Baptist College.

Meanwhile, as John Sutcliff commenced his Olney pastorate,

---

[639] John Julian, ed., *A Dictionary of Hymnology* (2nd rev. ed., 1907; repr., New York: Dover Publications, 1957), 1:373; cf. Fawcett Jr., *An Account of the Life, Ministry, and Writings of the Late Rev. John Fawcett*, 171–75; and Charles Seymour Robinson, *Annotations upon Popular Hymns* (New York: Hunt and Eaton, 1893), 407.

[640] John Fawcett, *Hymns: Adapted to the Circumstances of Public Worship, and Private Devotion* (Leeds: Printed by G. Wright and Son, 1782), 188–89 (Hymn 104).

[641] Ebenezer Baptist Church used this building until 1858, when the need for more space compelled them to erect a new one a few hundred yards away. With their new building, the congregation changed its name to Hope Baptist Church. Since then, the older building has been the home of the Hebden Bridge Times, an arts center, and an antique shop. On the right side of its front door is the grave of John Fawcett's daughter. See also *A Brief History of the Baptist Church, Hebden Bridge, Yorkshire*, with addresses at the centenary services on November 20th, 1877 (London: Yates and Alexandria, 1878).

in 1775, his neighbors included the Church of England minister, John Newton (1725-1807), author of the hymn, "Amazing Grace." Sutcliff's first four years in Olney were Newton's last four before his transferring to London's St. Mary Woolnoth Church. The hymn writer and poet, William Cowper (1731-1800), was a member of Newton's Olney parish, and, at the time of Sutcliff's arrival, Newton and Cowper were composing their popular *Olney Hymns*. After attending John Sutcliff's ordination, in August 1776, John Newton recorded in his diary that the Baptist pastor's answers were "pertinent and modest."[642] It was in such a setting that Sutcliff (1752-1814), John Ryland Jr. (1753-1825), and Robert Hall Sr. (1728-91) commenced to bond with Andrew Fuller in their struggle for a biblical theology of evangelism and missions. They would soon discover powerful influences in the writings of Colonial Americans, Jonathan Edwards and his students.

Influence of New Divinity Theology

Jonathan Edwards, Joseph Bellamy, and Samuel Hopkins. In 1777, two years after Robert Hall Sr. had advised Fuller to read Edwards's *Freedom of the Will*,[643] Fuller began to absorb this book. It would help transform his soteriology. In multiple treatises, Edwards had made the metaphysical and paradoxical distinction between man's "moral" (spiritual) inability and his "natural" (rational) ability, with only the former being lost in Adam's fall. Edwards based his speculations upon the theory of a twofold image of God in man:

> As there are two kinds of attributes in God, according to our way of conceiving Him, His moral attributes, which are summed up in His holiness, and His

---

[642] Haykin, *One Heart and One Soul: John Sutcliff of Olney*, 119.
[643] I am using the third edition of Edwards, *A Careful and Strict Enquiry into the Modern Prevailing Notions of that Freedom of the Will, which is supposed to be Essential to Moral Agency, Virtue and Vice, Reward and Punishment, Praise and Blame*, 3rd ed. (London: J. Johnson, 1768). Future references to this title will shorten to *Freedom of the Will* (3rd ed.). Fuller was likely using the third rather than the first (1754) edition.

natural attributes of strength, knowledge, etc., that constitute the greatness of God; so there is a twofold image of God in man: His moral or spiritual image, which is His holiness, that is the image of God's moral Excellency (which image was lost by the fall) and God's natural image, consisting in man's reason and understanding, his natural ability, and dominion over the creatures, which is the image of God's natural attributes.[644]

Edwards's discussion of an inherent "natural ability" in the unregenerate would open the door, ever so slightly, for a softening of the Old Calvinist doctrine of total depravity. In Edwards's view, "Sin destroys spiritual principles, but not the natural faculties.... There seems to be nothing in the nature of sin or moral corruption that has any tendency to destroy the natural capacity, or even to diminish it, properly speaking."[645] To Edwards, natural ability at least provides the possibility for an unregenerate person to reason correctly concerning God's natural revelation, and even to understand the special revelation of the gospel message.

Regarding the seeming paradox between an unsaved individual's natural ability to believe the gospel, and his moral (spiritual) inability to be willing to believe, Andrew Fuller would concur with Edwards and Edwards's two students, Joseph Bellamy (1719-90) and Samuel Hopkins (1721-1803), that only those whom God has unconditionally elected will receive the grace to believe and to repent. Edwards, Bellamy, Hopkins, and Fuller also agreed that regeneration is the Holy Spirit's miraculous infusion of life into a dead sinner, and that "natural ability" is not the same as the "common grace" of Arminianism. Indeed, they feared any apparent agreement or possible association with Arminianism. These men also

---

[644] Jonathan Edwards, *Treatise Concerning the Religious Affections*, 2nd ed. (Boston: J. Parker, 1768), 207 (Part 3 sect. 3). Cf. Edwards, "Of the Distinction of Natural and Moral Necessity, and Inability," in *Freedom of the Will* (3rd ed.), 28–38 (Part 1 sect. 4).

[645] Jonathan Edwards, *True Grace Distinguished from the Experience of Devils* (New York: James Parker, 1753), "Improvement" 2.

insisted that regeneration is never the fruit of any outward "means of grace," such as sacraments.

On the other hand, the total silence of Edwards toward the Governmental (Moral) Atonement theory would leave an open door for leaders of the next generation to accept such a view. Dutch theologian Hugo Grotius (1583–1645) had designed the Governmental theory to justify the Moral Governor of the universe in His eternal punishment of unbelievers. The theory rests upon the premise of a genuine, universal ability of sinners to desire Christ as Lord and Savior. While Edwards never teaches the Governmental *system*, he fails to criticize it. In his *Freedom of the Will*, he frequently employs the term *moral government* of God.[646] Edwards also contributed a laudatory preface to Joseph Bellamy's *True Religion Delineated* (1750),[647] which contains numerous metaphorical implications of the Governmental system. A subsequent London edition of Bellamy's book would include Andrew Fuller's endorsement.[648]

Samuel Hopkins, upon graduating from Yale College, studied theology in the home of Jonathan Edwards Sr. and eventually accepted the pastorate of the Congregationalist, First Church of Newport, Rhode Island. Due to his denial of the imputation of Adam's sin and guilt to all humanity, the name *Hopkinsian* became synonymous with *New Divinity* theology. In subtle nuance, Hopkins explains that, while there is a "certain connection" between Adam's first sin and humanity's sin and guilt, each person, in the earliest stage of life, willfully rebels and becomes a guilty sinner. Thus, there is no real or direct imputation of sin and guilt from Adam:

---

[646] E.g., see Edwards, *Freedom of the Will*, 3rd ed., 17, 152, 225–26, 385, 406, and 412.

[647] Joseph Bellamy, *True Religion Delineated: As Distinguished from Formality on the One Hand, and Enthusiasm on the Other; Set in a Scriptural and Rational Light*, in 2 discourses (1750; repr., Boston: Henry P. Russell, 1804), preface by Edwards. In this work, Bellamy advances an unlimited atonement.

[648] See Fuller, "Address to the Editor," in Bellamy's *True Religion Delineated*, 3rd ed. (London: W. Heney, 1812), vii. Fuller adds that he does not agree with every detail in the book.

> It is not to be supposed that the offence of Adam is *imputed* to them [his posterity] to their condemnation, while they are considered as in themselves, in their own persons innocent: or that they are guilty of the sin of their first father, *antecedent to their own sinfulness.* But all that is asserted, as what the scripture teaches on this head is, that by a divine constitution, there is a certain connection between the first sin of Adam, and the sinfulness of his posterity; so that as he sinned and fell under condemnation, they in consequence of this became sinful and condemned. Therefore, when Adam had sinned, by this the character and state of all his posterity were fixed, and they were by virtue of the covenant made with Adam, constituted or made sinners like him; and therefore, were considered as such, before they had actual existence. It was made certain, and known and declared to be so, that all mankind should sin as Adam had done, and fully consent to his transgression, and join in the rebellion which he began; and, *by this,* bring upon themselves the guilt of their father's sin, by consenting to it, joining with him in it, and making it their own sin.[649]

Stephen West, Nathaniel Emmons, and Jonathan Edwards Jr. Yale graduate and pastor of the Congregational church in Stockbridge, Massachusetts, Stephen West (1735-1819), in his *Scripture Doctrine of Atonement* (1785), popularized the incipient New Divinity doctrine. Combining warmth with scholarship, West displays an array of Scripture passages to demonstrate Christ's atonement as substitutionary[650] and unlimited.[651] Much of his teaching is well within the bounds of orthodoxy. West is careful to add that God never designed unlimited atonement with the intent "that mankind would be universally saved."

---

[649] Samuel Hopkins, *The System of Doctrines, Contained in Divine Revelation, Explained and Defended, showing their Consistence and Connection with Each Other, to which is added, a Treatise on the Millennium*, 2nd ed. in 2 vols. (Boston: Lincoln and Edmands, 1811), 1:268.

[650] Stephen West, *The Scripture Doctrine of Atonement, Proposed to Careful Examination* (New Haven: Meigs, Bowen, and Dana 1785), 53-65.

[651] Ibid., 141-64.

Rather, unlimited atonement is the divine "foundation ... for the general invitations of the gospel ... that whoever will, may come and take of the waters of life freely." Thus, the "free and general invitations of the gospel" are expressions of "the very character of God."[652]

Nevertheless, West frequently emphasizes a Governmental Atonement. To him, the primary design of Christ's death was to display God's wrath as an even-handed distribution of forgiveness for all repentant sinners.[653] Most significantly, the Governmental system depicts Christ's atonement in terms of law, rather than of love, which is an essential apparel of the gospel. The yearning of a loving father for his lost, prodigal son is in the background, or missing altogether, from Governmental expositions. Andrew Fuller and his circle of friends in England would treasure the works of Edwards, Bellamy, Hopkins, and West.[654] Fuller at times uses terms such as *moral government of the universe*,[655] *moral governor of the world*,[656] and *moral government of God*,[657] but he always stops far short of teaching the whole *system*. In fact, Fuller's works, including his intriguing discussions on paradoxes, would provide the theological basis for evangelical Calvinism.

---

[652] Ibid., 146–48.

[653] Ibid. 30.

[654] Cf. Haykin, *One Heart and One Soul: John Sutcliff of Olney, His Friends and His Times*, 300–301.

[655] Except as otherwise indicated, titles by Fuller will be from *The Works of the Rev. Andrew Fuller*, vol. 1 (Philadelphia: Anderson and Meehan, 1820); and *The Works of the Rev. Andrew Fuller*, vols. 2–8 (New Haven: S. Converse, 1824–25). Henceforth, all references to these eight volumes will shorten to *Works*.

[656] Andrew Fuller, *The Gospel Its Own Witness: Or the Holy Nature and Divine Harmony of the Christian Religion Contrasted with the Immorality and Absurdity of Deism* (1799), in *Works*, 3:145, 3:157n. This outstanding work made a wide appeal. It militates against the Deism and rationalism set forth in Tom Paine's *Age of Reason* and in the writings of other infidels such as David Hume and Jean-Jacques Rousseau.

[657] Andrew Fuller, *Antinomianism Contrasted with the Religion Taught and Exemplified in the Holy Scriptures* (n.d.), in *Works*, 4:159; idem, *The Calvinistic and Socinian Systems Compared* (1793), in *Works*, 2:57 (Letter 5). This work is a series of fifteen letters addressed to "Friends of Vital and Practical Religion."

In New England, though, after the passing of Edwards Sr., typical New Divinity theologians would move the Governmental Atonement to heretical levels. Nathaniel Emmons (1745–1840), for instance, urged upon all men the obligation to practice self-regeneration through moral exercises. One of his most popular sermons was *The Duty of Sinners to Make Themselves a New Heart* (1812). A Yale graduate and pastor at Second Church, Wrentham (later Franklin), Massachusetts, Emmons trained in his home as many as a hundred Christian leaders in an extreme New Divinity theology.[658]

Jonathan Edwards Jr. (1745–1801), a prolific author,[659] became president of Union College in Schenectady, New York. His deadliest contributions are his attacks against the doctrines of man's total depravity and against the substitutionary nature of Christ's death. Edwards Jr. advanced the notion that, under an impartial (moral) government, there can be no imputation or transfer of Adam's sin and guilt to anyone. To Edwards Jr., humanity, in child-conception, receives only the consequences of Adam's sin, that is, the "habitual disposition to sin." Thus, it is only when each person sins that he becomes a sinner and acquires guilt. Moreover, under a just government, there can be no imputation or transfer of Christ's righteousness. Believers receive only "beneficial consequences" of Christ's death.[660] Edwards's

---

[658] Nathaniel Emmons, *The Works of Nathaniel Emmons*, 6 vols., ed. Jacob Ide (Boston: Crocker and Brewster, 1842), 2:263, 2:441, 2:683; 4:357, 4:373ff; 5:122–31, 5:277–90. Biographical material is in 1:ix–clxxv. The best reviews are Henry B. Smith, "The Theological System of Emmons," in *Faith and Philosophy: Discussions and Essays*, ed. George L. Prentiss (New York: Scribner, Armstrong & Co., 1877); and Edwards A. Park, *Memoir of Nathaniel Emmons: with Sketches of his Friends and Pupils* (Boston: Congregational Board of Publication, 1861).

[659] *The Works of Jonathan Edwards* Jr., 2 vols. including a memoir of his life and character by Tryon Edwards (Andover: Allen, Morrill, Wardwell, 1842).

[660] Jonathan Edwards Jr., "Clearer Statements of Theological Truth," in *Memoirs of Jonathan Edwards* [Sr.], by Sereno E. Dwight, in *The Works of Jonathan Edwards* [Sr.], rev. Edward Hickman, 2 vols. (London: F. Westley and A. H. Davis, 1834), 1:ccxxxvi–vii. See also Jonathan Edwards Jr., *The Necessity of the Atonement, and the Consistency between that and Free Grace, in Forgiveness*, in *Theological Tracts*, ed. John Brown, 3 vols. (1785; repr.,

Governmental model of the atonement has no Good Shepherd laying down His life in behalf of His sheep. Christ's death was not an expiatory payment to an offended party. Instead, God designed Christ's death to be merely a satisfaction to the requirements of the divine law. Thus, the death of Christ was simply the Father's public demonstration of moral government. A truly moral Governor, according to Edwards Jr., could have devised no other plan.[661] The Fuller circle would reject such teachings.

Fuller's Agonizing Transition from Soham to Kettering

Meanwhile, back at Cambridgeshire, Andrew Fuller—now locked in conflict with hyper-Calvinism—was pouring over *Freedom of the Will* by Edwards Sr. Key members of Soham Baptist Church were refusing to share the gospel, or even to welcome the lost into their services. With most of his members financially poor, Fuller's entire yearly income from the church had never exceeded thirteen pounds. He had tried part-time work, but to no practical benefit. Discouragement set in, and his health began to fail. Meanwhile, the Baptist church at Kettering, Northamptonshire, extended an invitation for Fuller to consider becoming their pastor. Reminiscent of John Fawcett's dilemma, the normal expectation in those days was that pastors remain with their church until death. Fearing the very thought of leaving the place where God in His providence had assigned him, Fuller, on January 10, 1780, made "a solemn vow or renewal of covenant with God." The key section of that vow is as follows:

> Lord, thou hast given me a determination to take up no principle at second-hand; but to search for everything at the pure fountain of *thy word*. Yet, Lord, I am afraid, seeing I am as liable to err as other men, lest I should be led aside from truth by mine own imagination. Hast thou not promised, "The meek thou wilt

---

London: A. Fullarton and Co., 1853), 1:380 (1:333–84).

[661] For fuller discussion, see David Beale, "The New Divinity Theology," and "The New Haven Theology," in *Historical Theology In-Depth* (Greenville, SC: Bob Jones University Press, 2013), 2:274–307.

guide in judgment, and the meek thou wilt teach thy way" [Psalm 25:9]? Lord, thou knowest, at this time, my heart is not haughty, nor are mine eyes lofty. O "guide me by thy counsel, and afterwards receive me to glory" [Psalm 73:24].[662]

Suffering from depression, Fuller agonized in prayer for months, seeking three things: (1) victory over sin—especially pride; (2) the will of God concerning his place of service; and (3) the knowledge, understanding, and wisdom of God regarding the ever-present doctrinal and practical issues facing him. In Fuller's case, every doctrinal issue had become a practical issue. God's perfect peace flooded his soul, as Fuller realized that victory over sin requires daily cross bearing and death to self. In addition to his prayers, Fuller's study of God's Word had begun to solidify and to stabilize his soteriology and his practical ministry. Never wavering in his belief that Arminianism was laden with doctrinal aberrations, Fuller stood convinced that his steadfast embrace of unconditional election could never bridle the free offer of the gospel. By 1781, he had written a treatise that would eventually appear in print—*The Gospel Worthy of All Acceptation*. Fuller's original composition of the work was not for publication, but for sorting out perplexing theological issues he encountered every day.

In October 1782, Fuller resigned from the Soham church and accepted the pastorate of the Baptist church in Kettering, whose population numbered about three thousand. On the solemn occasion of Fuller's formal installation, Robert Hall Sr. and John Ryland Jr. preached the charge. Fuller presented to the church his Confession of Faith.[663] For the rest of his life, he would remain with Kettering Baptist, at 51 Gold Street, and known since 1860–61 as "Fuller Baptist Church."[664] Although he worked at his desk ten hours a day, Andrew Fuller remained

---

[662] Andrew Gunton Fuller, *Memoirs*, 1:31 (1:30–41).
[663] For a copy of Fuller's 20-article Confession of Faith, see John Ryland [Jr.], *The Work of Faith, the Labor of Love, and the Patience of Hope*, 2nd ed. (1818), 64–70.
[664] In 1860–61, the Kettering congregation erected its present chapel, named in honor of Andrew Fuller, and built to accommodate about a thousand people.

constantly committed to his pastoral duties. He loved and visited his flock, cared for the poor, and kept in touch with influential business and political figures of the day—such as the eminent William Wilberforce (1759-1833). During the Fuller pastorate, believer's baptism by immersion remained a prerequisite for membership and the Lord's Supper.[665] With a powerful voice, he preached practical and evangelistic sermons—mostly textural or topical. By 1786, the Kettering congregation was compelled to enlarge their chapel. With increasing growth, by 1804-5, the congregation again enlarged their chapel—this time to seat nine hundred persons.[666]

Development of the Theology of Fullerism
The Struggle for Balance

The first published edition of Fuller's *The Gospel Worthy of All Acceptation* appeared in 1785, followed by the revised, second edition of 1801, which is the standard edition.[667] Published under the persuasion of friends, *Gospel Worthy* became Fuller's best-known book. Not only is it a microcosm of Fuller's entire corpus of theology, it marks the beginning of a new era for missions—both at home and abroad. While Fuller was foremost a theologian, his special-occasion sermons, ordination messages, and advice to the churches were highly sought after in his day. Few were aware that he suffered almost daily with severe headaches. As Ernest Clipsham said of Fuller, "It was because he was a pastor that he was compelled also

---

[665] Andrew Fuller, *The Admission of Unbaptized Persons to the Lord's Supper, Inconsistent with the New Testament: A Letter to a Friend (in 1814)* (London: Printed by H. Teape, on Tower Hill, and sold by Gardiner, on Princes Street, and Button and Son, and Gale and Co. on Paternoster Row, 1815). I am using a copy of Princeton University's twenty-nine-page original, but a transcript of the text appears in *The Complete Works of the Rev. Andrew Fuller*, ed. Andrew Gunton Fuller, 2 vols. (Boston: Gould, Kendall, and Lincoln, 1836), 2:670-75.

[666] In 1804-5, the Kettering church enlarged its chapel by lengthening it by eighteen feet and raising its walls by four feet.

[667] Andrew Fuller, *The Gospel Worthy of All Acceptation: Or, The Duty of Sinners to Believe in Jesus Christ* (2nd ed. 1801), in *Works*, 1:1-162. Henceforth, references to this title will shorten to *Gospel Worthy* (2nd ed. 1801), in *Works*.

to be a theologian."[668] In a letter to a friend, C. H. Spurgeon would later hail Andrew Fuller as "the greatest theologian of the century."[669] Awarded an honorary Doctor of Divinity degree from Princeton and another from Yale, Fuller modestly declined using the title *Doctor*. During his entire ministerial life, he was engaged non-stop in theological controversy. Clipsham correctly notes that Fuller would hammer out his doctrine "on the anvil of his own experience. Whether sinners should be exhorted to repentance and faith was not merely an academic question to him, but a living issue of fundamental importance."[670] With hyper-Calvinists equating Fullerism with *Duty-faith* and *Duty-repentance*, and with Arminians accusing Fullerism of caricaturing God's character with unconditional election, Fuller's defense of evangelical Calvinism refuted hyper-Calvinism on the one hand and Arminianism on the other. His close circle of fellow pastors, especially John Ryland Jr. and John Sutcliff, would stand with him in full accord.

Opposition to Sandemanianism

Meanwhile, Fuller found it necessary to expose an unusual form of hyper-Calvinism that had originated in Scotland. Its name *Sandemanianism* derived from Robert Sandeman (1718-71), son-in-law and disciple of John Glas (1695-1773). Deposed for heresy by the established Presbyterian churches, Glas established a sect-chapel near Dundee, Scotland. His followers were called *Glasites*. In England and America, they were *Sandemanians*. The prominent doctrinal aberration of Sandemanianism was that saving faith is a mere intellectual assent to the basic facts of the gospel. Justifying faith, in other words, is "no more than a simple assent to the Divine testimony, passively received by the understanding."[671] Replying to such a dismissal of faith

---

[668] Ernest F. Clipsham, "Andrew Fuller and Fullerism I," *Baptist Quarterly* 20, no. 3 (July 1963): 100.

[669] See Gilbert Laws, *Andrew Fuller: Pastor, Theologian, Ropeholder*, 27.

[670] Ernest F. Clipsham, "Andrew Fuller and Fullerism IV," *Baptist Quarterly* 20, no. 6 (April 1964): 269.

[671] J. Harris Gibson, "The Religious Sect of the Sandemanians in Liverpool," in *Transactions of the Historic Society of Lancaster and Cheshire for the Years*

and repentance, Fuller emphasized that saving faith "produces repentance."[672] To Fuller, "The faith of the gospel, or a believing in Jesus for the salvation of our souls, is represented in the New Testament as implying repentance for sin."[673]

Brotherly Criticism from Abraham Booth (1734–1806)

Fuller's major opponents would emerge from both Calvinists and Arminians. During the interval between the first and second editions of *Gospel Worthy* (1785–1801), Fuller altered his emphases on the doctrines of imputation and atonement. His adjustments would prompt some Calvinists, such as Abraham Booth, to dub "Fullerism" as "a half-way house" to the New Connection of General Baptists.[674] While disagreement on theological emphases would remain between Fuller and Booth, they came to regard one another with genuine respect. A noble laborer in the work of evangelism, at home

---

1891–92 (Liverpool: Printed for the Society, 1893), 43:322 (43:321–23).

[672] Andrew Fuller, *Strictures on Sandemanianism: In Twelve Letters to a Friend*, in *Works* (1810), 3:339–501; see especially Letter 3, "Containing a More Particular Inquiry into the Consequences of Mr. Sandeman's Notion of Justifying Faith" (3:373ff.); and Letter 5, "On the Connection between Repentance toward God, and Faith toward Our Lord Jesus Christ" (3:397–409). Fuller wrote the twelve letters to a friend, regarding the criticism emerging from the pen of Archibald McLean (1733–1812), who was once a member of the Sandemanian church in Glasgow, Scotland. McLean later left the Sandemanian church, served the pastorate of a Baptist Church at Edinburgh, and even supported the Baptist Missionary Society (est. 1792). Nevertheless, as Fuller kindly cautioned, McLean retained nuances of Sandemanian soteriology throughout his ministry. Compare with Michael A. G. Haykin, "Andrew Fuller and the Sandemanian Controversy," in *'At the Pure Fountain of Thy Word'*, 223–36.

[673] Fuller, *Gospel Worthy* (2nd ed. 1801), in *Works*, 1:131–32 (Appendix).

[674] Mainly, Fuller and Booth would disagree on the imputation of sin and the sufficiency of the atonement. See Fuller, "On Imputation," in *Six Letters to Dr. Ryland, Respecting the Controversy with the Rev. A. Booth* (1803), Letter 2, in *The Complete Works of the Rev. Andrew Fuller*, ed. Andrew Gunton Fuller, 1:669–72; see also Robert W. Oliver, "Andrew Fuller and Abraham Booth," in *History of the English Calvinistic Baptists 1771–1892: From John Gill to C. H. Spurgeon* (Edinburgh: Banner of Truth Trust, 2006), 149–72.

and abroad, Abraham Booth,[675] pastor of Little Prescot Street Baptist Church, in Goodman's Fields, London, would take the lead in the 1796 establishment of the Baptist Society in London for the Encouragement and Support of Itinerant and Village Preaching. According to its rules, the Society existed for "Calvinistic Ministers of the Baptist Persuasion," and, in 1821, it would become the Particular Baptist Home Missionary Society. At Little Prescott Street,[676] Abraham Booth, an evangelical Calvinist, was a strong link in the long chain of noble successors from John Spilsbury, who had gathered this church in 1633.[677] Booth defined *Particular Baptists* as "those who have

---

[675] The best sources for his life and works include Abraham Booth, *The Works of Abraham Booth*, 3 vols. (London: Printed by J. Haddon and sold by Button and Son, 1813); Anonymous, "Memoir of the Author," in *The Works of Abraham Booth*, 1:xvii–lxxx; Abraham Booth, *Pedobaptism Examined*, 3 vols. (London: Printed for Ebenezer Palmer, 1829); idem, *Defense of Pedobaptism Examined* (London: Printed for the author and sold by C. Dilly, 1792); John Rippon, *A Short Memoir of the Rev. Abraham Booth*, "incorporated with the address delivered at his interment, in Maze Pond, February 5, 1806," in *A Sermon Occasioned by the Death of the Rev. Abraham Booth*, preached in Little Prescot Street, Goodman's Fields, by James Dore (London: Printed by C. Whittingham, 1806), 41–98; Raymond Arthur Coppenger, *A Messenger of Grace: A Study of the Life and Thought of Abraham Booth* (Ontario, Canada: Joshua Press, 2009); William Jones, *An Essay on the Life and Writings of Mr. Abraham Booth* (Liverpool: Printed for the author by James Smith, 1808); Michael A. G. Haykin and Victoria J. Haykin, eds., *"The First Counsellor of Our Denomination": Studies on the Life and Ministry of Abraham Booth (1734–1806)* (Springfield, MO: Particular Baptist Press, 2011); Ernest A. Payne, "Abraham Booth 1734–1806," *Baptist Quarterly* 26, no. 1 (January 1975): 28–42; and Oliver, *History of the English Calvinistic Baptists 1771–1892*, 149–72.

[676] Many years ago, one end of the street was Great Prescot Street while the other end was Little Prescot Street. Today, the entire street is simply "Prescot Street."

[677] During times of persecution, Spilsbury's congregation met in secret places. On occasions, the congregation worshipped with the Particular Baptist church where William Kiffin served as pastor. These two churches appear to have merged for a brief time during 1650–53. Later, the Spilsbury church met in various places (including homes) in Old Gravel Lane, Wapping. Their earliest known meetinghouse was on James Street, Wapping, where their attendance reached almost four hundred. During 1730–1855, the church was located on Little Prescot Street, then

been solemnly immersed in water, upon a personal confession of faith, and who profess the doctrines of Three Divine Persons in the Godhead, Eternal and personal Election, Original Sin, Particular Redemption, Efficacious Grace in Regeneration and Sanctification, Free Justification by the imputed Righteousness of Christ, and the Final Perseverance of the Saints."[678]

Among Booth's written works, *Reign of Grace* (1768) remains the most popular — appearing in nine English editions, besides one Scottish and three American editions.[679] Along with other strong leaders, such as historian Joseph Ivimey,[680] and Pastor Joseph Kinghorn, of the Baptist Church at St. Mary's (Norwich),[681] Abraham Booth taught that the Scriptures

---

on Commercial Street from 1855 to 1914, when they relocated to the Walthamstow section, where the church remains to this day in Kevan Court, on the corner of Cairo Road and Church Hill. As London's oldest Baptist church, its current name is *Church Hill Baptist Church*. See Ernest F. Kevan, *London's Oldest Baptist Church: Wapping 1633 – Walthamstow 1933* (London: Kingsgate Press, 1933); and Robert W. Oliver, *From John Spilsbury to Ernest Kevan: The Literary Contribution of London's Oldest Baptist Church* (London: Grace Publications Trust, 1985).

[678] Godfrey and Ward, *History of Friar Lane Baptist Church, Nottingham*, 268.

[679] Abraham Booth, *The Reign of Grace: From Its Rise to Its Consummation* (9th ed.), *Works*, 1:1–327.

[680] The best sources for Joseph Ivimey (1773–1834), pastor of the Baptist Church on Eagle Street, London, and buried in Bunhill Fields, include George Pritchard, *Memoir of the Life and Writings of the Rev. Joseph Ivimey, Late Pastor of the Church in Eagle Street, London* (London: George Wightman, 1835); J. C. Doggett, "Joseph Ivimey (1773–1834)," in *The British Particular Baptists 1638–1910*, ed. Michael A. G. Haykin, 3:112–31; and John Andrew Jones, ed., *Bunhill Memorials: Sacred Reminiscences of Three Hundred Ministers and Other Persons of Note, Who Are Buried in Bunhill Fields, of Every Denomination, with the Inscriptions on Their Tombs and Gravestones, and Other Historical Information Respecting Them, from Authentic Sources* (London: James Paul, 1849), 100–107.

[681] The best sources for Joseph Kinghorn (1766–1832) include Martin Hood Wilkin, *Joseph Kinghorn of Norwich: a Memoir* (Norwich: Fletcher and Alexander, 1855); Joseph Kinghorn, *Baptism, a Term of Communion at the Lord's Supper* (Norwich: Bacon, Kinnebrook, and Co., 1816); Robert Hall, *A Reply to the Rev. Joseph Kinghorn: Being a Further Vindication of the Practice of Free Communion* (Leicester: Thomas Combe, 1818); Joseph Kinghorn, *A Defense of "Baptism a Term of Communion," in Answer to the Rev. Robert Hall's Reply* (Norwich: Wilkin and Youngman, 1820); Dean

restrict church membership and Communion to immersed believers. Booth's habit of reading a chapter from the Greek New Testament every morning enabled him, by the end of his life, to have read the New Testament numerous times in its original language.[682] When Adoniram Judson, a pedobaptist, left New England for India, in 1812, he brought with him the most scholarly books available, on baptism, to prepare himself for the inevitable discussions with William Carey. During Judson's voyage, he studied Abraham Booth's multi-volume *Paedobaptism Examined*–a powerful influence. Not long after reaching India, Judson and his wife became Baptists by conviction. Booth's impact was far-reaching.

Even during his final years, Booth worked with the London Baptist Education Society (est. 1752) to set the stage for the 1810 founding of Stepney Academy, located in East London. Moving to the center of Regent's Park, London, in 1855, Stepney Academy became Regent's Park College, a constituent College of the University of London. In 1927, Regent's Park College moved to Oxford, and, since 1957, it has been a Permanent Private Hall of the University of Oxford. The Angus Library and Archive at Regent's Park College holds a large, priceless treasure of Baptist history. The valuable manuscript collection includes documents and letters of William Carey and his colleagues, Joshua and Hannah Marshman, and William Ward.

Fullerism Explained

Fuller's doctrinal adjustments positioned his evangelical Calvinism as antithetical to High Calvinism, but sympathetic with elements of moderate New Divinity theology. Contrary to the oft-repeated illustration of a dead, human corpse as a description of total depravity, Fuller reasons that, since a dead corpse can do nothing good *or evil*, it is incomparable

---

Olive, "Joseph Kinghorn (1766–1832)," in *The British Particular Baptists 1638–1910*, ed. Michael A. G. Haykin, 3:84–111; and Terry Wolever, ed., *The Life and Works of Joseph Kinghorn*, 3 vols. (Springfield, MO: Particular Baptist Press, 1995–2010).

[682] Payne, "Abraham Booth 1734–1806," 33.

to spiritual death. A spiritually dead person is still willing to sin.[683] Thus, a dead corpse fails to illustrate man's condition. Fuller further reflects as follows: As Christ's atonement and justification are applied individually and willfully, by active faith, even so, Adam's sin and guilt are applied individually and willfully by acting on a propensity toward sin.[684] In his 1803 letter "On imputation," Fuller carefully "endeavors to define" his ideas on the matter. He explains the meaning of *impute* as merely "to regard," or "to consider." Ignoring the historic, Protestant interpretation of the term, Fuller insists that the word *impute* does not include any kind of "transfer." To Fuller, God does not transfer Christ's righteousness to anyone, but all true believers receive its beneficial effects. Likewise, God did not transfer Adam's sin and guilt to anyone, but all receive its penal effects:

> *Imputation* ought not to be confounded with *transfer*. In its proper sense, we have seen there is no transfer pertaining to it. In its figurative sense, as applied to justification, it is righteousness itself that is imputed; but its effects only are transferred. So also in respect of sin: sin itself is the object of imputation; but neither this nor guilt is strictly speaking transferred, for neither of them is a transferable object. As all that is transferred in the imputation of righteousness is its beneficial effects, so all that is transferred in the imputation of sin is its penal effects.[685]

Fuller explains that these "penal effects" of Adam's sin result in each person entering the world "at once free and enslaved." Fuller's paradox unfolds this way. At conception, each person receives a "proclivity," or "propensity," toward sin, rather than toward holiness. From each individual's "very birth," says

---

[683] Fuller, *Gospel Worthy* (2nd ed. 1801), in *Works*, 1:56, 60.

[684] See for example, Fuller, *Three Conversations* (n.d.), in *Works*, 4:79–90 (Conversation 1, "on imputation"); cf. Letter 2, "On the Importance of a True System," in *Works*, 4:269.

[685] Fuller, *Six Letters to Dr. Ryland, Respecting the Controversy with the Rev. A. Booth* (1803), Letter 2 in *The Complete Works of the Rev. Andrew Fuller*, ed. Andrew Gunton Fuller (1836), 1:671.

Fuller, this inclination is "so interwoven through all his powers, so ingrained, as it were, in his very soul, as to grow up with him and become natural to him."[686] The "equity" embedded in Governmental doctrine becomes Fuller's premise for depicting each individual as "a free moral agent," who, as Fuller explains, "is an intelligent being who is at liberty to act according to his choice, without compulsion or restraint."[687] Although a sinner will never come to Christ on his own, "it is not a want of *ability* but of *inclination* that proves his ruin," says Fuller.[688] "Our mind hath such an inclination to vanity that it can never cleave fast to the truth of God."[689] Even from the womb, each person willfully sins in "private self-love," which is the "root of depravity." It is *willful* depravity, therefore, that makes each person "at once free and enslaved,"[690] and such depravity constitutes the basis of each person's "original" guilt.[691]

Like Jonathan Edwards Sr., Fuller declares that God must always take the initiative in salvation, and that "God doth only open the eyes of the elect, that they may seek him by faith."[692] To the objections of an Arminian critic, Fuller writes:

> The scriptures not only represent salvation as being *through faith*, but they ascribe *faith itself* to the operation of the Spirit of God. Those who come to Christ are described as having first *heard* and *learned* of the Father, and as being *drawn* by him; nor can any man come to Him, except it be *given* him of the Father.... *Faith*, as well as love, joy, peace, long-suffering, gentleness, and goodness, is a *fruit* of the Spirit. We

---

[686] *Gospel Worthy* (2nd ed. 1801), in *Works*, 1:97.
[687] Fuller, *The Reality and Efficacy of Divine Grace* (1790), in *Works*, 1:353 (Letter 3).
[688] Ibid., 1:401 (Letter 10); cf. Fuller, *Gospel Worthy* (2nd ed. 1801), in *Works*, 1:93–99.
[689] *Gospel Worthy* (2nd ed. 1801), in *Works*, 1:101.
[690] See also Clipsham, "Andrew Fuller and Fullerism IV," 275.
[691] Fuller, *Dialogues and Letters between Crispus and Gaius* (1793–95), in *Works*, 4:41 (Dialogue 8, on human depravity).
[692] Fuller, *Six Letters to Dr. Ryland, Respecting the Controversy with the Rev. A. Booth* (1803), Letter 5 in *The Complete Works of the Rev. Andrew Fuller*, ed. Andrew Gunton Fuller (1836), 1:676.

> *believe, according to the working of his mighty power*; a power equal to that which raised our Lord from the dead. *Faith* is expressly said to be *of the operation of God*. We are not only saved *by grace through faith*; but even that is *not of ourselves*: it the gift of God. If regeneration be brought about by any exertion of ours, it is not only contrary to all ideas of generation (to which, undoubtedly, it alludes), but also to the express testimony of scripture, which declares that we *are born not of the will of the flesh, nor of the will of man, but of God* (John 6:44–45, 65, Galatians 5:22, Ephesians 1:19, Colossians 2:12, John 1:13).[693]

Like Edwards Sr., Fuller never loses sight of the substitutionary nature of Christ's atonement—limited to the elect in its application.[694] Indeed, in Fuller's new emphasis, the atonement is sufficient for all,[695] but efficient only for the elect. He illustrates it this way: "The obedience and death of Christ, *in themselves considered*, were like the sun in the heavens, necessary for an individual, but sufficient for a world." Similarly, Christ's atonement is "sufficient for all, but effectual only to the elect."[696] Fuller

---

[693] Fuller, *A Defense of a Treatise, Entitled, "The Gospel of Christ Worthy of All Acceptation"* (Preface dated 1787), in *Works*, 1:248. For the entire work, see 1:163–333. In this *Defense*, published in 1787, Fuller buttresses his views against critiques coming from the High Calvinist (hyper-Calvinist), William Button, and from the Arminian "Philanthropos," Fuller's pseudonym for Dan Taylor of the New Connection of General Baptists.

[694] E.g., Fuller, *The Reality and Efficacy of Divine Grace* (1790), in *Works*, 1:391-95 (Letter 9) and 1:401-7 (Letter 11). For the entire work, see (1:335–424). This was the only work that Fuller wrote under the pseudonym "Agnostos." It consists of Fuller's thirteen letters of rebuttal against recent letters from "Philanthropos," Fuller's pseudonym for Dan Taylor, the Arminian General Baptist, whose views Fuller had refuted three years earlier in his *Defense* of *Gospel Worthy*.

[695] Andrew Fuller and Abraham Booth would disagree on the sufficiency of the atonement. Robert W. Oliver, "Andrew Fuller and Abraham Booth," in *History of the English Calvinistic Baptists 1771-1892*, 149–72.

[696] Andrew Fuller, *The Abuse of Reviews* (n.d.), in *The Complete Works of the Rev. Andrew Fuller*, ed. Andrew Gunton Fuller (1836), 2:846. See also the discussion by Michael A. G. Haykin, "Particular Redemption in the Writings of Andrew Fuller (1754-1815)," in *The Gospel in the World*, ed. David Bebbington, vol. 1 of the series, Studies in Baptist History and

joined the practical outworking of this teaching with a twofold axiom: (1) the "infinite sufficiency of Christ's sacrificial work" and (2) the "indiscriminate preaching of the gospel."[697] Fuller continued, at times, to explain Christ's atonement in governmental vocabulary. For instance, the atonement was significantly a "reparation of the injury done by sin to the divine government, and for the consistent exercise of free mercy to the unworthy."[698] Howbeit, Fuller never hesitates to offer a battery of Scripture,[699] along with logical argument, to demonstrate that a designed and limited application of the atonement is consistent with a genuine and universal invitation to sinners:

> As the application of redemption is solely directed by sovereign wisdom; so, like every other event, it is the result of *previous design*. That which is actually done was *intended* to be done. Hence, the salvation of those that are saved is described as the *end* which the Savior had in view... There is no contradiction between this peculiarity of *design* in the death of Christ, and a universal obligation on those who hear the gospel to believe in him, or a universal invitation being addressed to them.[700]

In view of the inevitable tension within human systems of theology, Fuller warns that, since certain of God's mysteries are unfathomable and inexplicable, it is vital that Christians hold fast to the perspicuity of Scripture, that they may know with certainty that God does all things well:

> Paul invariably takes it for granted that *whatsoever God doth is right*: nor will he dispute with any man on a contrary principle, but cuts him short in this manner: *Is there unrighteousness with God? God forbid!*

Thought (Carlisle, England: Paternoster Press, 2002), 107–28.
[697] See Box, "The Atonement in the Thought of Andrew Fuller," 216.
[698] Fuller, *Antinomianism Contrasted with the Religion Taught and Exemplified in the Holy Scriptures* (n.d.), in *Works*, 4:177.
[699] Fuller, *A Defense of a Treatise, Entitled, "The Gospel of Christ Worthy of All Acceptation"* (Preface dated 1787), in *Works*, 1:292–333.
[700] *Gospel Worthy* (2nd ed. 1801), in *Works*, 1:90.

> It was enough for him that God hath said to Moses, *I will have mercy on whom I will have mercy*. This, as if he should say, is the *fact: He hath mercy on whom he will have mercy, and whom he will he hardeneth*. He knew what would be the heart-risings of the infidel—*Thou wilt say then unto me, Why doth he yet find fault? For who hath resisted his will?* But does he attempt to answer this objection? No, he repels it as Job did: *He that reproveth God, let him answer it—Nay but, O man, who art thou that repliest against God? Shall the thing formed say to him that formed it, Why hast thou made me thus?*[701]

On any given issue in which the Bible appears, in the eyes of frail humanity, to be portraying two contradictory propositions, Fuller forthrightly advises:

> The truth is, there are but two ways for us to take: one is, to reject them *both* and the Bible with them, on account of its inconsistencies; the other is, to embrace them both, concluding that, as they are both revealed in the Scriptures, they are both true, and both consistent, and that it is owing to the darkness of our understandings that they do not appear so to us.[702]

Pathway to the Prayer Call of 1784

Fuller received immense encouragement, in 1781,[703] when Robert Hall Sr. published his landmark treatise, *Help to Zion's Travelers*.[704] Its purpose was to remove every doctrinal and prac-

---

[701] Andrew Fuller, *Three Conversations: on Imputation, Substitution, and Particular Redemption* (n.d.), in *Works*, 4:114–15.
[702] *Gospel Worthy* (2nd ed. 1801), in *Works*, 1:78.
[703] Ten years later, Fuller would preach an "Oration Delivered at the Grave of the Rev. Robert Hall [Sr.], of Arnsby, March 1791," in *Works*, 8:475–78.
[704] Robert Hall [Sr.], *Help to Zion's Travelers: Being an Attempt to Remove Various Stumbling Blocks Out of the Way, Relating to Doctrinal, Experimental, and Practical Religion* (Bristol: Printed by William Pine and sold by Buckland and Keith in London and by T. Evans and T. Mills in Bristol, 1781). This first edition copy is in the British Library. I have changed the

tical obstacle that, for five decades, had hindered Particular Baptists from obeying the Great Commission (Matthew 28:18-20). Hall's text was Isaiah 57:14, "Cast ye up, cast ye up, prepare the way, take up the stumblingblock out of the way of my people." The treatise emerged from a sermon that Hall had preached two years earlier to the Northamptonshire Association. Numerous, urgent requests were demanding its publication. Not only does the book offer an able vindication of Bible truth against Sabellianism and Socinianism (Unitarianism),[705] it delineates the author's strong differences with Arminianism. Citing Scripture, such as Isaiah 45:22, "Look unto me, and be ye saved, all the ends of the earth: for I am God, and there is none else,"[706] and defending unconditional election, limited atonement, and eternal security,[707] Hall demonstrates that the free offer of the gospel can in no way constitute Arminianism. Recalling his first reading of Hall's *Help to Zion's Travelers*, William Carey reminisces, "I do not remember ever to have read any book with such raptures as I did that. If it was poison, as some then said, it was so sweet to me that I drank it greedily to the bottom of the cup; and I rejoice to say, that those doctrines are the choice of my heart to this day."[708] Young Carey, who would soon become the father of Baptist foreign missions, would often walk twenty miles to hear the preaching of Robert Hall Sr.

In April 1784, John Ryland Jr., at College Lane Baptist Church, in Northampton, received a box of books from the distinguished, Scottish theologian, John Erskine (1721-1803) of Edinburgh. One of these books, authored by Jonathan Edwards Sr., is *An Humble Attempt to Promote Explicit Agreement and Visible Union of God's People in Extraordinary Prayer for the Revival of Religion and the Advancement of Christ's Kingdom on*

---

spelling, *travellers*, to *travelers*. See also *The Works of Robert Hall*, 6 vols. (London, 1832-46).

[705] *Help to Zion's Travelers*, 5-25.

[706] Ibid., 118.

[707] E.g., Ibid., 42-52 (unconditional election); and 161-65 (particular redemption and final perseverance).

[708] Eustace Carey, *Memoir of William Carey, D. D.* (Boston: Gould, Kendall, and Lincoln, 1836), 11.

Earth, Pursuant to Scripture-Promises and Prophecies Concerning the Last Time (1747), henceforth referred to as *Humble Attempt*. The book is a revision of a 1747 sermon Edwards had preached from Zechariah 8:20–22, "Thus saith the Lord of hosts; It shall yet come to pass, that there shall come people, and the inhabitants of many cities: And the inhabitants of one city shall go to another, saying, Let us go speedily to pray before the Lord, and to seek the Lord of hosts: I will go also. Yea, many people and strong nations shall come to seek the Lord of hosts in Jerusalem, and to pray before the Lord." Unlike premillennial scholars, who maintain that Christ will establish His kingdom at His Second Coming, Edwards, a postmillennialist, appeals to vast portions of Scripture to predict that the revivals of his day were the latter-day outpouring of God's Spirit. Edwards's longing is that the recent revivals in New England (during the 1730s and 40s) and the concert of prayer and revival in Scotland (beginning in 1744) will spread over the earth until Christ returns. "The people of God, in the latter days, will … become the instruments of pulling down the kingdom of Satan, by prayer."[709] Edwards is confident that the Reformation, now revitalized by Pietistic influences, such as Moravian missions[710]

---

[709] Jonathan Edwards, *An Humble Attempt to Promote Explicit Agreement and Visible Union of God's People in Extraordinary Prayer for the Revival of Religion and the Advancement of Christ's Kingdom on Earth, Pursuant to Scripture-Promises and Prophecies Concerning the Last Time*, in *The Works of President Edwards* (Worcester: Isaiah Thomas, 1808), 3:404. Henceforth, this reference will shorten to *Humble Attempt*, in *Works*.

[710] Founded in 1722, the Moravian movement sent out their first missionaries in 1732. Only fifteen years later, at the publishing of Edwards's *Humble Attempt* (1747), the Moravians had commissioned scores of missionaries. By this time, they held mission stations in St. Thomas, in the West Indies (1732), Greenland (1733), Georgia, North America (1734), Lapland (1735), Surinam, or Dutch Guiana, on the north coast of South America (1735), Cape Town, South Africa (1737), Elmina, Dutch headquarters in the Gold Coast (1737), Guyana, South America (1738), and among the Pennsylvania Indians (1741). Admittedly, their type of missionary work was predominantly cultural and sometimes mystical in nature. See J. E. Hutton, *A History of Moravian Missions* (London: Moravian Publication Office, 1922), 24–120; cf. J. M. Van der Linde, "The Moravian Church in the World, 1457–1957," *International Review of Mission* 46, no. 184 (October 1957): 417–23.

and Oxford's Holy Club,[711] had already initiated the end of the spiritual kingdom. Edwards extrapolates from multiple passages, such as Zechariah 12:10a, that current revivals are glimpses of the end-time "effusion of the Spirit of God" upon His church.[712] Edwards's *Humble Attempt* was a call for Christians everywhere to unite in prayer for "the promised restoration of the church of God, after the Babylonish captivity."[713] Andrew Fuller[714] and John Sutcliff[715] would echo the same message. Edwards assured them that, even if his extrapolations prove to be "premature," the revivals will have edified the churches.[716] Edwards's catena of Scripture passages on prayer and revival stirred many to seek God's face. The *Humble Attempt* left a profound impression upon John Ryland Jr., Andrew Fuller, and John Sutcliff. Making evangelical Calvinism understandable to children, Sutcliff published *The First Principles of the Oracles of God, Represented in a Plain and Familiar Catechism, for the Use of Children*. For parents, Sutcliff even included a discussion on natural ability and moral inability.[717]

In the summer of 1784, Particular Baptist ministers of the Northamptonshire Association, whose churches spread from Hertfordshire to Lincolnshire, assembled for their meeting in Nottingham. Sixteen of the twenty Association churches sent

---

[711] Oxford University students, John and Charles Wesley, had established the Holy Club in 1729, in Christ Church College. Often joined by George Whitefield, the group regularly met for prayer, studied the New Testament, fed the poor, and visited the sick and imprisoned. Not long after that, in 1735, George Whitefield experienced conversion to Christ. The Wesley brothers experienced conversion in the spring of 1738.

[712] Edwards, *Humble Attempt*, in *Works*, 3:373–418.

[713] Ibid., 3:360.

[714] E.g., Andrew Fuller, *The Promise of the Spirit the Grand Encouragement in Promoting the Gospel*, in *Works*, 8:462–69.

[715] E.g., John Sutcliff, *The Divinity of the Christian Religion Considered and Proved, in a Circular Letter, from the Baptist Association, at Leicester, Northampton* (London: Printed by T. Dicey and Co., 1797).

[716] Edwards, *Humble Attempt*, in *Works*, 3:487–88.

[717] John Sutcliff, *The First Principles of the Oracles of God, represented in a Plain and Familiar Catechism, for the Use of Children*, 3rd ed. (Halifax, Yorkshire: Printed and sold at Ewood Hall, near Halifax; sold also by the author, at Olney, and by W. Button, in London, n.d.), 7–8. This copy is in the British Library.

representatives, but none could have realized the historical significance of this occasion. On Tuesday evening and Wednesday morning (June 1-2), the brethren met "for prayer, and reading the letters from the churches." At the 10:30 AM session on Wednesday, John Sutcliff preached from 1 Corinthians 6:19-20, "What? know ye not that your body is the temple of the Holy Ghost which is in you, which ye have of God, and ye are not your own? For ye are bought with a price: therefore, glorify God in your body, and in your spirit, which are God's." According to the official Minutes, "Divine worship was also attended with singing at proper intervals." For the 2:30 session, John Gill (1730-1809) (nephew of his legendary namesake), pastor of the Baptist congregation in St. Albans (Hertfordshire), preached from Luke 11:28, "But he said, Yea rather, blessed are they that hear the word of God, and keep it." At the 7:00 PM service, Andrew Fuller preached from 2 Corinthians 5:7, "For we walk by faith, not by sight." Soon published under the title, *The Nature and Importance of Walking by Faith* (1784),[718] this message would become Fuller's earliest publication,[719] and it clearly echoes Edwards's *Humble Attempt*, urging the importance of prayer for missions. In the published format of his sermon, Fuller appends seven points of *Persuasives to a General Union in Extraordinary Prayer, for the Revival and Extent of Real Religion*. He addresses his points to those "Christian Brethren" who stand willing to get serious about humbling themselves, praying, and seeking God's face.[720]

The Association Minutes state that, on "the same evening," a "Circular Letter, which had been drawn up by Brother Ryland Jr., was read and approved, and ordered to be signed by the

---

[718] Andrew Fuller, *The Nature and Importance of Walking by Faith: A Sermon Delivered at the Annual Association of the Baptist Ministers and Churches Met at Nottingham, June 2, 1784* (Northampton: Printed by T. Dicey and Co., 1784).

[719] Fuller's *Gospel Worthy* would appear in print the following year (1785).

[720] Fuller, *Persuasives to a General Union in Extraordinary Prayer, for the Revival and Extent of Real Religion* (1784), an appendix to *The Nature and Importance of Walking by Faith*, 41-47. I am indebted to Michael A. G. Haykin for providing a copy of this document. The sermon is in *Works*, 7:3-38, but without the valuable appendix.

Moderator." This Circular Letter, titled *The Nature, Evidences, and Advantages of Humility* (1784), is Ryland's fervent call for a season of humiliation before the Lord. The "Postscript" to the Minutes reports that on Thursday (June 3) the representatives heard a motion that they lead their congregations in focused prayer, "to bewail the low estate of religion, [to] … earnestly implore a revival of our churches, and … to wrestle with God for the effusion of his Holy Spirit." In response to that motion, the pastors, led by Sutcliff, Fuller, and Ryland, "unanimously RESOLVED to recommend to all our churches" that we unite for "one hour in prayer, on the first Monday in every calendar month." Following some practical suggestions, the Resolution concludes with the "Prayer Call of 1784," as described by later authors:

> The grand object in prayer is to be, that the Holy Spirit may be poured down on our ministers and churches, that sinners may be converted, the saints edified, the interest of religion revived, and the name of God gloried. At the same time remember, we trust you will not confine your requests to your own societies [churches]; or to our own immediate connection [denomination]; let the whole interest of the Redeemer be affectionately remembered, and the spread of the gospel to the most distant parts of the habitable globe be the object of your most fervent requests. We shall rejoice if *any other Christian societies* of our own or other denominations will unite with us, and do now invite them most cordially to join heart and hand in the attempt.
>
> Who can tell what the consequences of such a united effort in prayer may be! Let us plead with God the many gracious promises of His Word, which relate to the future success of His gospel. He has said, "I will yet for this be enquired of by the House of Israel to do it for them, I will increase them with men like a flock." Ezekiel xxxvi.37. Surely, we have love enough for Zion to set apart *one hour* at a time, twelve times in a year, to seek her welfare.[721]

---

[721] "Minutes," an addendum at the end of John Ryland Jr., *The Nature,*

Thornton S. H. Elwyn concluded, "This Northamptonshire Association prayer call was one of the most decisive events in the life of [that] period, and probably for all Christendom."[722] The response of the churches was so overwhelming that prayer meetings were soon spreading among the churches of Yorkshire, Warwickshire, and the Western Association (centered in Bristol). William Staughton reported that the resolution "was attended to for about seven years with some degree of zeal and importunity."[723] In 1786, Kettering Baptist, under Fuller's leadership, enlarged its chapel to accommodate its increasing attendance. As a further encouragement to the concert of prayer, Sutcliff, in 1789, published a pocket-sized edition of Jonathan Edwards's *Humble Attempt*.

An Eternal Bond Established between Fuller and William Carey

One day, during the 1780s, an unforgettable incident occurred at a Baptist ministers' meeting in Northampton's College Lane Baptist. After the final service, John Collett Ryland Sr. (1723–92) called upon two young ministers—each to propose a question for general discussion. The first was John Webster Morris (1763–1836), who was serving the Baptist pastorate in Clipston,

---

Evidences, and Advantages of Humility, "a Circular Letter from the ministers of the Baptist Association assembled at Nottingham, June 2, 3, 1784" (n.p.: n.p., 1784), 11–12. On its last page, "Richard Hopper, Moderator, signed in behalf of the brethren." I am using a facsimile of the copy in London's British Library. Perhaps unaware that the Resolution *is* the "Prayer Call of 1784," Ernest A. Payne states that the Prayer Call is in Ryland's Circular Letter. See Payne, *The Prayer Call of 1784* (London: Baptist Laymen's Missionary Movement, 1941), 2. Payne's suggestion, however, that John Sutcliff wrote the Prayer Call is probably correct, since the Prayer Call is the Resolution. Michael A. G. Haykin concurs that Sutcliff "most likely" wrote it. See Haykin, *One Heart and One Soul: John Sutcliff of Olney, His Friends and His Times*, 164 (153–71); cf. Haykin, "John Sutcliff and the Concert of Prayer," in *Reformation and Revival: A Quarterly Journal for Church Leadership* 1, no. 3 (1992): 74 (65–88).

[722] Thornton S. H. Elwyn, "Particular Baptists of the Northamptonshire Baptist Association as Reflected in the Circular Letters 1765–1820," *Baptist Quarterly* 36, no. 8 (October 1996): 380 (368–81).

[723] William Staughton, *The Baptist Mission in India* (Philadelphia: Hellings and Aitken, 1811), 13.

Northamptonshire. With a bit of hesitation, he proposed a discussion on the last part of 2 Peter 2:1, describing false teachers as "denying the Lord that bought them." Dismissing Morris "and his Arminian questions," Ryland Sr., an outspoken and moderately High Calvinist, instructed Morris "to go home and read Gill and Brine, and various other commentators."[724] The other young man was William Carey (1761–1834), who was serving the Baptist pulpit in Moulton, not far from Clipston. Since he was un-ordained and a stranger to most of the audience, Carey begged to decline, but Ryland Sr. was adamant. Speaking in slightly nervous tones, Carey proposed the question, "Whether the command given to the apostles to 'teach all nations,' was not obligatory on all succeeding ministers to the end of the world, seeing that the accompanying promise was of equal extent." Carey urged upon his hearers the duty of compassionating the heathen by sending the saving gospel of Christ to regions beyond. Carey's message stunned most of his audience. Everyone knew that Ryland Sr. stood firmly with the teachings of the Protestant Reformers, that is, that Jesus addressed the Great Commission of Matthew 28 exclusively to the first-century apostles. No one would have been surprised when Ryland Sr. turned to Carey and called him "a most miserable enthusiast for asking such a question. Certainly nothing can be done before another Pentecost, when an effusion of miraculous gifts, including the gifts of tongues, will give

---

[724] J. W. Morris, *Memoirs of the Life and Writings of the Rev. Andrew Fuller*, ed. Rufus Babcock Jr. (Boston: Lincoln and Edmands, 1830), 84–85. A printer by trade, the author, John Webster Morris (1763–1836), joined the Baptist Missionary Society (BMS) staff in 1793 and later edited and printed the BMS *Periodical Accounts* from 1798 to 1809. In 1803, Morris accepted the pastorate of the Baptist church in Dunstable, Bedfordshire, but, after his wife's death, he accumulated a large debt that led to personal difficulties. Leaving the ministry in 1810, Morris would continue his writing and printing. Over time, he would preach when invited for special occasions. This material on Morris is from the *Baptist Autographs in the John Rylands University Library of Manchester, 1741–1845*, transcribed and ed. Timothy Whelan (Macon, GA: Mercer University Press, 2009), 423. See also J. W. Morris, *Biographical Recollections of the Rev. Robert Hall [Jr.], A.M.* (London: George Wightman, 1833).

effect to the commission of Christ as at first."[725] Ryland's pastorates had included the Baptist church in Warwick. An 1815 history of this town includes a general assessment of Ryland: He "was possessed of considerable abilities," says the author, William Field, "but a strong and ardent imagination was not controlled by equal soundness, or strength of Judgment: and a great degree of what is usually called *eccentricity*, marked not only the manner of his public services, but even his conduct in private life."[726] It might come as no surprise, therefore, that in Joseph Belcher's account of the Northampton meeting, Ryland Sr. thunders out to William Carey, "Young man, sit down; when God pleases to convert the heathen world, he will do it without your help or mine either."[727] Culross reports that,

---

[725] This is in the first edition of J. W. Morris, *Memoirs of the Life and Writings of the Rev. Andrew Fuller* (London: Printed for the author and sold by T. Hamilton, 1816), 96–97. John Ryland Jr. denied that the incident ever occurred; see John Ryland [Jr.], *The Work of Faith, the Labor of Love, and the Patience of Hope, Illustrated in the Life and Death of the Reverend Andrew Fuller*, 112n. On the other hand, William Carey's nephew, Eustace Carey, defends Morris's account; see Eustace Carey, *Memoir of William Carey* (Boston, 1836), 35–36. Other defenders of Morris's account include the following: S. Pearce Carey, *William Carey, D. D., Fellow of Linnaean Society* (Philadelphia: Judson Press, 1923), 50; George Smith, *The Life of William Carey, D. D., Shoemaker and Missionary* (London: John Murray, 1885), 31–32; and Peter Naylor, "John Collett Ryland (1723–1792)," in *The British Particular Baptists 1638–1910*, ed. Michael A. G. Haykin, 1:193–94 (1:184–201).

[726] William Field, *An Historical and Descriptive Account of the Town and Castle of Warwick* (Warwick: Printed by and for H. Sharpe, 1815), 140. Even so, Ryland Sr. was loved and highly respected. On July 29, 1792, John Rippon, from 2 Timothy 4:6, preached Ryland's funeral sermon in the College Lane church, where family and friends entombed Ryland's remains at the end of the baptistery inside the auditorium. John Taylor, *History of College Street Church, Northampton*, 33–34.

[727] Joseph Belcher, *William Carey: A Biography* (Philadelphia: American Baptist Publication Society, 1853), 18–19. The fact that this is the earliest appearance of this specific utterance from Ryland Sr. might provide reason to question Belcher's accuracy. Most sources seem to agree, though, that Ryland did say something similar. Belcher's work as secretary of the Baptist Union enhances his credentials for many researchers. For an overall portrayal of Ryland Sr., see William Newman, *Rylandiana: Reminiscences Relating to the Rev. John Ryland, A.M. of Northampton*

as Carey was descending the pulpit steps, there came "through the throng of village pastors a round-headed, rustic-looking country minister, broad-shouldered, tall, and powerfully built, with a joyful light gleaming from under the dark shaggy eyebrows and brightening the homely countenance, who seized the preacher's hand and exclaimed, 'Brother, we must know each other better.'" This was Andrew Fuller; he was in his early thirties.[728] On August 1, 1787, Fuller would preach Carey's ordination sermon to the church in Moulton.[729] This church would promptly join the Particular Baptist Association, and the bond of friendship between Andrew Fuller and William Carey would never cease.

Select Bibliography for Further Reading

Anonymous. "Memoir of the Author." In *The Works of Abraham Booth*, 1: xvii–lxxx. London: Printed by J. Haddon and sold by Button and Son, 1813.

Ascol, Thomas Kennedy. "The Doctrine of Grace: A Critical Analysis of Federalism in the Theologies of John Gill and Andrew Fuller." PhD diss., Southwestern Baptist Theological Seminary, 1989.

Barrett, Gladys M. *A Brief History of Fuller Church, Kettering 1696–1946*. St. Albans: Printed by Parker Brothers, n.d.

Booth, Abraham. *The Works of Abraham Booth*. 3 vols. London: Printed by J. Haddon and sold by Button and Son, 1813.

Box, Bart D. "The Atonement in the Thought of Andrew Fuller." PhD diss., New Orleans Baptist Theological Seminary, 2009.

Brewster, Paul. *Andrew Fuller: Model Pastor-Theologian*. Nashville: B&H Publishing Group, 2010.

Chun, Chris. *The Legacy of Jonathan Edwards in the Theology of Andrew Fuller*. Vol. 162 of the series, Studies in the History of Christian Traditions. Leiden: Koninklijke Brill, 2012.

Clipsham, Ernest F. "Andrew Fuller and Fullerism I." *Baptist Quarterly* 20, no. 3 (July 1963): 99–114. Part II. *Baptist Quarterly* 20, no. 4 (October 1963): 146–54. Part III. *Baptist Quarterly* 20, no. 5 (January 1964): 214–25. Part IV. *Baptist Quarterly* 20, no. 6 (April 1964): 268–76.

Coppenger, Raymond Arthur. *A Messenger of Grace: A Study of the Life and Thought of Abraham Booth*. Ontario, Canada: Joshua Press, 2009.

(London: G. Wightman, 1835).

[728] James Culross, "Andrew Fuller," in *Founders and Pioneers of Modern Missions* (Northampton: Taylor and Son, 1899), 5.

[729] A sketch of this sermon is in *The Complete Works of the Rev. Andrew Fuller*, ed. Andrew Gunton Fuller, 2 vols. (1836), 2:423–24.

Ella, George M. *The Law and the Gospel in the Theology of Andrew Fuller.* Eggleston, Co. Durham, England: Go Publications, 1996.

Elwyn, Thornton S. H. *The Northamptonshire Baptist Association.* London: The Carey Kingsgate Press, 1964.

Fuller, Andrew. *The Complete Works of Andrew Fuller.* 3 vols. Edited by Joseph Belcher. 1845. Reprint, Harrisonburg, VA: Sprinkle Publications, 1988.

_____. *The Works of the Rev. Andrew Fuller.* Volumes 2–8. New Haven: S. Converse, 1824–25.

_____. *The Gospel Worthy of All Acceptation: Or, The Duty of Sinners to Believe in Jesus Christ.* Vol. 1 of *The Works of the Rev. Andrew Fuller.* Philadelphia: Anderson and Meehan, 1820.

Fuller, Andrew Gunton. *Andrew Fuller.* London: Hodder and Stoughton, 1882. The author was a son of Andrew Fuller by his second wife.

_____, ed. *Memoirs of the Rev. Andrew Fuller.* In *The Complete Works of the Rev. Andrew Fuller.* 2 vols. Boston: Gould, Kendall, and Lincoln, 1836. For a one-volume reprint of this set, see *The Works of Andrew Fuller,* ed. Andrew Gunton Fuller. Carlisle, PA: The Banner of Truth Trust, 2007.

Godfrey, John T., and James Ward. *The History of Friar Lane Baptist Church, Nottingham.* Nottingham: Henry B. Saxton, 1903.

Grant, Keith S. *Andrew Fuller and the Evangelical Renewal of Pastoral Theology.* Vol. 36 of the series, Studies in Baptist History and Thought. 2013. Reprint, Eugene, OR: Wipf and Stock, 2013.

Haykin, Michael A. G., ed. *The British Particular Baptists: 1638–1910.* 3 vols. Springfield, MO: Particular Baptist Press, 1998–2003.

_____, ed. *'At the Pure Fountain of Thy Word': Andrew Fuller as an Apologist.* Vol. 6 of the series, Studies in Baptist History and Thought. 2004. Reprint, Eugene, OR: Wipf and Stock, 2006.

Kirkby, Arthur H. "Andrew Fuller—Evangelical Calvinist." *Baptist Quarterly* 15, no. 5 (January 1954): 196–202.

_____. "The Theology of Andrew Fuller and Its Relation to Calvinism." PhD diss., University of Edinburgh, 1956.

Laws, Gilbert. "Andrew Fuller, 1754–1815." *Baptist Quarterly* 2, no. 2 (April 1924): 76–84.

Mauldin, A. Chadwick. *Fullerism as Opposed to Calvinism: A Historical and Theological Comparison of the Missiology of Andrew Fuller and John Calvin.* Eugene, OR: Wipf and Stock, 2011.

Morden, Peter, J. *The Life and Thought of Andrew Fuller (1754–1815).* Milton Keynes, England: Paternoster, 2015.

_____. *Offering Christ to the World: Andrew Fuller (1754–1815) and the Revival of Eighteenth-Century Particular Baptist Life.* Vol. 8 of the series, Studies in Baptist History and Thought. Carlisle, England: Paternoster, 2003.

Morris, J. W. *Memoirs of the Life and Writings of the Rev. Andrew Fuller, Late Pastor of the Baptist Church at Kettering, and First Secretary to the Baptist Missionary Society.* Edited by Rufus Babcock. Boston: Lincoln and Edmands, 1830).

_____. *Miscellaneous Pieces on Various Religious Subjects: Being the Last Remains of the Rev. Andrew Fuller.* "Collected and arranged with occasional notes, intended as a supplement to his memoirs of the author." London: Wightman and Cramp, 1826.

Naylor, Peter. *Calvinism, Communion and the Baptists: A Study of the English Calvinistic Baptists from the Late 1600s to the Early 1800s.* Vol. 7 of the series, Studies in Baptist History and Thought. 2003. Reprint, Eugene, OR: Wipf and Stock, 2006.

_____. *Picking up a Pin for the Lord: English Particular Baptists from 1688 to the Early Nineteenth Century.* London: Grace Publications Trust, 1992.

Nuttall, Geoffrey F. "Northamptonshire and the Modern Question: A Turning-point in Eighteenth-Century Dissent." *Journal of Theological Studies* 16, no. 1 (1965): 101–23.

Pike, Godfrey Holden. *Ancient Meeting-Houses: Or, Memorial Pictures of Nonconformity in Old London.* London: S. W. Partridge and Co., 1870.

Roberts, R. Philip. *Continuity and Change: London Calvinistic Baptists and Evangelical Revival 1760–1820.* Wheaton, IL: Richard Owen Roberts Publishers, 1989. This was originally prepared as a doctoral dissertation for the Free University of Amsterdam, June 22, 1989.

Sell, Alan P. F. *The Great Debate: Calvinism, Arminianism and Salvation.* 1982. Reprint, Grand Rapids: Baker, 1983.

Toon, Peter. *The Emergence of Hyper Calvinism in English Nonconformity 1689–1765.* 1967. Reprint, Weston Rhyn, Oswestry, Shropshire, England: Quinta Press, 2003.

Whitley, W. T. "Baptist Meetings in the City of London." *Transactions of the Baptist Historical Society* 5, no. 2 (July 1916): 74–82.

_____. *The Baptists of London 1612–1928: Their Fellowship, Their Expansion, with Notes on Their 850 Churches.* London: Kingsgate Press, n.d.

Chapter 10

William Carey: His Life and Ministry

---※---

The Early Years in Paulerspury, Piddington, and Hackleton

William Carey (1761–1834)[730] was born the eldest of five children to Edmund and Elizabeth Carey, on August 17, in Paulerspury, an obscure village in South Northamptonshire.[731]

---

[730] The best sources on William Carey include the following: Eustace Carey, *Memoir of William Carey, D. D.*, with "Introductory Essay" by Francis Wayland, president of Brown University (Boston: Gould, Kendall, and Lincoln, 1836). Eustace Carey was William Carey's nephew. John Clark Marshman, *The Life and Times of Carey, Marshman, and Ward: Embracing the History of the Serampore Mission* (London: Longman, Brown, Green, Longmans, and Roberts, 2 vols. 1859). John Clark Marshman was the son of Joshua and Hannah Marshman, co-workers with William Carey in the establishment of the Serampore Mission. George Smith, *The Life of William Carey, D. D. Shoemaker and Missionary* (1885). Having visited Serampore, George Smith was familiar with William Carey's descendants, as well as many of Carey's Indian converts. S. Pearce Carey, *William Carey, D. D., Fellow of Linnaean Society* (1923). S. Pearce Carey was William Carey's great-grandson. His work remains the classic biography of Carey. Joseph Belcher, *William Carey: A Biography* (1853). After serving as secretary of the Baptist Union, Belcher settled in America. See also Timothy George, *Faithful Witness: The Life and Mission of William Carey* (Birmingham, AL: New Hope, 1991); and Ernest A. Payne, "Carey and His Biographers," *Baptist Quarterly* 19, no. 1 (January 1961): 4–12.

[731] The Carey cottage, William's birthplace, stood on what is now Carey Road, at Pury End, a hamlet on the edge of Paulerspury. The cottage suffered

When William was six years old, his father, a weaver by trade, received an appointment to the office of village schoolmaster at the local charity school, and to the clerkship of St. James Parish Church, where his family faithfully attended.[732] Inside the church, one can still see the font used for William's christening when he was six days old. At an early age, Carey acquired a love for learning. When he was fourteen, he moved to the nearby village of Piddington and took up residence with Clarke Nichols, a shoemaker, who apprenticed him as a cobbler. Multiple influences, including the fellow apprentice and roommate, John Warr, helped to create a desire in Carey to seek a genuine relationship with the Lord. While still holding an inbred contempt for any religious services outside the National Church, Carey reluctantly accompanied Warr to a thatched cottage in the nearby village of Hackleton, where a few non-conformists were holding regular prayer meetings.

One day, Mr. Nichols caught young William in deception. The boy had attempted to use a counterfeit shilling and told a lie to cover his sin. Terrified with the thought of the whole neighborhood hearing about it, Carey feared to go out in public. Conscience stricken, he began looking to Warr for spiritual advice. A national crisis would come to Cary's assistance. Prompted by ongoing loses in the American War of Independence, King George III proclaimed Wednesday, February 10, 1779, a day of prayer and fasting.[733] Seventeen-year-old William Carey would never forget that day when he accompanied his friend Warr to the cottage prayer meeting at Hackleton. The speaker, Thomas Chater of Olney, preached on the cost of true discipleship. He pointed his audience to Hebrews 13:13, "Let us go forth therefore unto him without the camp, bearing his reproach." Those words, says Carey, "broke me off from the Church of England." He was now willing to "bear the reproach of Christ among the Dissenters; and accordingly," says Carey, "I always afterwards

---

demolition in 1965 to make room for modern homes. A memorial cairn, built from the original stones, preserves a tangible memorial of the cottage.
[732] In the porch of St. James Church, a plaque commemorates William Carey. A few feet away, just to the right of the porch, Edmund Carey's grave carries this inscription: "Reader, time is short, prepare to meet thy God."
[733] France had already recognized America's independence by this time.

attended divine worship among them." William Carey was now an Independent Separatist. While Carey never pinpointed the precise day and hour of his conversion and assurance, Chater challenged and encouraged him with Scripture until, as Carey testifies, "I was by these means ... brought to depend on a crucified Savior for pardon and salvation."[734] In Clarke Nichols' workshop, Carey found a New Testament commentary with text printed in Greek. With such a tool at his fingertips, he borrowed a concordance and Greek grammar and taught himself Greek.

Upon Nichols' death, in September 1779, Carey completed his shoemaker training under his brother-in-law, Thomas Old, in Hackleton. It was here that Carey met the Anglican clergyman Thomas Scott (1747–1821) of Olney whose urgent, spiritual autobiography, *The Force of Truth* (1779), was now fresh off the press. After struggling for years as an unregenerate minister of the Church of England, Scott had come under the embrace of John Newton's friendship and letters of counsel, and had experienced salvation by grace through faith. As a Bible-believing preacher and pastor, Scott would author many works, including his venerated *Commentary on the Whole Bible*. He would join another famous Anglican, William Wilberforce, in founding the Church Missionary Society (1799). During his preaching visits to Hackleton, Scott would drop by and advise Carey's studies in Greek and Latin. He jovially dubbed the cobbler's workshop as "Carey's College." Forty years later, as Scott lay dying, he was consoled to learn of Carey's muse, "If there be anything of the work of God in my soul, I owe much of it to Mr. Scott's preaching when I first set out in the ways of the Lord."[735]

Carey assisted in reorganizing Hackleton's little non-conformist house of prayer into an Independent Congregationalist church, which would gradually become a Baptist church—now called Carey Baptist Church.[736] He preached his first sermon

---

[734] Eustace Carey, *Memoir of William Carey*, 9.

[735] S. Pearce Carey, *William Carey*, 33.

[736] In one of the rooms of Carey Baptist Church, one can see the pulpit from which John Warr and William Carey once preached in the thatched cottage. In 1809, when the thatched cottage could no longer accommodate the growing congregation, the church moved to a nearby site and erected a "24 feet by 36 feet" room. In 1813, they had seventy-six members. There

here. Another of this church's founders of special interest is Daniel Plackett—father of Dorothy ("Dolly," 1756–1807), who married William Carey in June 1781. The newly-weds set up housekeeping in Piddington—just a short walk from Hackleton. Sadly, their first child, Ann, would die of a severe fever before reaching two years of age. Finding encouragement and doctrinal stability from Robert Hall Sr.'s *Help to Zion's Travelers*, Carey, in 1782, began a three-year-period of preaching every other Sunday at Earls Barton, six miles from Hackleton.[737] Meanwhile, he had been searching the Scriptures for the truth about baptism. Finally, on October 5, 1783, William Carey walked five miles from Piddington to Northampton in time for John Ryland Jr. to immerse him in the River Nene at 6:00 AM.[738] Carey was now a Baptist. During the same year, he began reading accounts of Captain James Cook's *Voyages* of discovery in the Pacific Ocean. From the leather, world-map that Carey constructed and placed on the cobbler-shop wall, he painfully began to realize what a small portion of humanity possessed any knowledge of the gospel. He later recalled, "Reading Cook's voyages was the first thing that engaged my mind to think of missions."[739] Meanwhile, Carey had been sharpening his language skills in Latin, Greek, and Hebrew.

Carey's Earliest Pastorate: Moulton Baptist Church

In March 1785, he and Dorothy moved into a cottage in Moulton, where William opened a village school. His pay was

---

were 129 members in 1862, at which time the church added a Sunday-School room and a vestry. The thatched cottage eventually suffered demolition. The present edifice of Carey Baptist Church dates to 1888–89. See Dorothy Tippleston, *William Carey and Hackleton Baptist Church* (Northampton: Printed by Billingham and Son, 1955).

[737] The present building of Earls Barton Baptist Church dates to the nineteenth century.

[738] Carey was baptized on the spot where the modern railway station is now located. The building of the station necessitated the rerouting of the River Nene. Carey's baptism took place where the station's "platform one" ends. In 2011, for the 250th anniversary of Carey's birth, a "William Carey" plaque was unveiled here at the railway station.

[739] Eustace Carey, *Memoir of William Carey*, 12.

pitiful. Providentially, in bygone years, the builder of the cottage home had designed it to facilitate a shoemaker. A trough for soaking shoe leather was already set in the wall. Driven by necessity, Carey set up shop and made shoes and boots for Thomas Gotch, a Christian merchant whose business was in Kettering. Every two weeks, William walked to Kettering to deliver Gotch's order and to pick up leather for the next batch. When Gotch, a deacon under Andrew Fuller, learned of Carey's family responsibilities, pastoral work, and language studies, he made it possible for the young man to stop making shoes and to devote his time to his calling. Gotch continued giving Carey ten shillings a week—the weekly profit that Carey had been making as a cobbler. By July of 1785, Carey had placed himself under the tutelage of Pastor John Sutcliff of Olney and under the watch-care of the Olney church, where he held membership. After Carey preached his first sermon to the Olney congregation, the unanimous conclusion was that the young man needed more time for preparation before they could ordain him. They promised to hear him again. Operating a little theological academy, like John Fawcett's, Sutcliff was establishing a good reputation for preparing young men for ministry.

Since it was unusual in those days for ministers to move from one pastorate to another, churches often ordained their ministers anew, at the beginning of each pastorate. They commonly used the word *induction*, as well as *ordination*, to describe a re-ordination. Generally, pastors practiced the laying on of hands at the ordinations. On August 10, 1786, Sutcliff led in Cary's initial ordination, and Olney Baptist commissioned Carey to minister wherever the Lord might lead. In those days, pastors felt especially accountable to their "sending" churches. Carey had been preaching at the Baptist church at Moulton, where, in May 1787, he moved his membership. On August 1, 1787, he received his ordination into the Moulton pastorate and, indeed, "to preach wherever God in his providence might call him."[740] On this solemn occasion, John Ryland Jr. asked the ques-

---

[740] John Taylor, comp., *Biographical and Literary Notices of William Carey, D. D., the English Patriarch of Indian Missions and the First Professor of the Sanskrit and Other Oriental Languages in Indian Missions: Comprising Extracts from*

tions, John Sutcliff preached the charge from 2 Timothy 4:5, and Andrew Fuller preached a challenge directed to the members.[741] Always encouraging on such occasions, Fuller typically advised each young minister to begin with a small church, since, as he added, "It will be like cultivating a garden before you undertake a field."[742] Carey followed that advice. When he began his ministry at Moulton, the small, elderly, and discouraged congregation was meeting sporadically for Sunday services. Carey at once initiated weekly services and a renovation program for the deteriorated, twenty-five-year-old chapel. In October 1787, he baptized Dorothy. He served the Moulton congregation until the summer of 1789, when he accepted a probationary pastorate at Harvey Lane Baptist Church, in Leicester.

Settling into the Harvey Lane Pastorate in Leicester

When William and Dorothy moved into the cottage across the street from the Harvey Lane church, they had three

---

Church Books, Autograph MSS., and Other Records; also A List of Interesting Mementoes Connected with Carey, with Bibliographical Lists of Works Relating to, or Written by Carey; and Pertaining to Baptist Missions in the East, etc. and Addenda (Northampton: The Dryden Press, Taylor and Son, 1886), 1–9.

[741] Carey raised the money and led the Moulton Baptist congregation in the reconstruction of their building (made of brick) and the enlargement of its dimensions to thirty feet square. In 1870, the church enlarged the structure to its present size. In 1958, they added the William Carey Memorial Hall whose renovation in the 1990s included a multi-panel mural depicting the story of Carey's life and work. Church rooms underwent renovation in 2002. The year 2009 witnessed major refurbishment of the auditorium. Next to the church is Carey's cottage home, where the trough he had used to soak his shoe leather is still set in the wall. Part of the cottage is a museum that includes Carey's pulpit. On the exterior wall, a tablet records that Carey lived here from 1785 to 1789. It pays tribute to Carey's achievements: "shoemaker, schoolmaster, preacher, scholar, and missionary pioneer. While beneath this roof, he conceived and developed the great missionary idea that has changed India and awakened worldwide movements." The tablet also quotes Carey's dictum: "Expect great things from God; attempt great things for God." Adjoining Carey's cottage is a pub called The Telegraph.

[742] Andrew Fuller, "To a Young Minister in Prospect of Ordination" (dated August 30, 1810), *The Baptist Magazine* 7 (October 1815): 420.

sons—Felix, William Jr., and Peter. Lucy was born about 1791, but, like Ann, she died before her second birthday. At Carey's May 1791 ordination into the Harvey Lane pastorate,[743] Bristol Baptist Academy graduate, Samuel Pearce (1766-99),[744] preached from Galatians 6:4 for the evening message.[745] A close bond had already forged between Carey and Pearce,[746] who, since 1789-90, had been serving the pastorate at Cannon Street Baptist Church (est. 1737), in Birmingham. Pearce would become one of the founders of the Baptist Missionary Society and an ardent supporter of foreign missions. He would die of pulmonary tuberculosis when only thirty-three years of age.[747] John Ryland Jr. would speak for many when he described Pearce as "that seraphic young man."[748] Samuel and his devout

---

[743] Deposited in the Leicestershire Record Office, at 57 New Walk, are the minute books of the Harvey Lane Baptist Church.

[744] See the valuable biography of Samuel Pearce by his great-grandson, S. Pearce Carey, *Samuel Pearce, M. A., The Baptist Brainerd*, 3rd ed. (London: The Carey Press, n.d.). S. Pearce Carey was also William Carey's great-grandson through the marriage of Anna Pearce (daughter of Samuel Pearce) to Jonathan Carey (son of William Carey). As noted above, S. Pearce Carey also wrote a fine biography of William Carey. Other valuable sources include Jason Edwin Dees, "The Way to True Excellence': the Spirituality of Samuel Pearce" (PhD diss., Southern Baptist Theological Seminary, 2015); Andrew Fuller, *Memoirs of the Late Rev. Samuel Pearce A. M. Minister of the Gospel in Birmingham, with Extracts from Some of His Most Interesting Letters* (Clipstone: Printed by J. W. Morris, 1800); and Tom Wells, "Samuel Pearce (1766-1799)," in *The British Particular Baptists 1638-1910*, ed. Michael A. G. Haykin (Springfield, MO: Particular Baptist Press, 2000), 2:182-99. Many of Pearce's letters are in Michael A. G. Haykin, ed., *Joy Unspeakable and Full of Glory: The Piety of Samuel and Sarah Pearce* (Kitchener, Ontario, Canada: Joshua Press, 2012).

[745] For the morning service, Ryland Jr., Sutcliff, and Fuller were key participants. For Carey's own account of the day, see John Rippon, ed., "Ordinations in 1791," in *The Baptist Annual Register, for 1790, 1791, 1792, and Part of 1793* (London: Sold by Dilly, Button, and Thomas, in London, 1793), 519.

[746] Cf. Andrew Fuller, *The Works of the Rev. Andrew Fuller* (New Haven: S. Converse, 1824-25), 6:273-468. Except as otherwise indicated, titles by Fuller will be from this set, shortened to *Works*.

[747] Angus Library and Archive, Regent's Park College, Oxford, houses much of Pearce's correspondence.

[748] In John Ryland [Jr.], *The Work of Faith, the Labor of Love, and the Patience*

wife, Sarah, had five children at the time of his death.

The Making of Carey's *Enquiry*

William Carey would find special encouragement at the 1791 Easter-week assembly of the Northamptonshire Baptist ministers at Clipston. John Sutcliff and Andrew Fuller brought stirring messages. Preaching from 1 Kings 19:10, *On Being Very Jealous for the Lord God of Hosts*, Sutcliff exhorted the churches to be as Elijah. Answering the question, "Who is my neighbor?" (Luke 10:29), Sutcliff gave the clarion challenge that one's neighbor is any person on earth: "Let him be an ignorant Negro, dwelling in the unexplored regions of Africa; or an untutored Savage, wandering in the inhospitable forests of America; he is your fellow creature; he is your neighbor; he is your brother. He has a Soul—a Soul that will exist for ever."[749] Fuller followed Sutcliff with a dynamic warning against *The Pernicious Influence of Delay in Religious Concerns*. His text was Haggai 1:2, "Thus speaketh the Lord of hosts, saying, This people say, The time is not come, the time that the Lord's house should be built." Beginning with that passage, Fuller warned against five areas of procrastination: (1) attending to the small things of life that prevent or destroy a spiritual life; (2) obeying the Great Commission; (3) making a public confession of faith; (4) self-examination and self-denial; and (5) preparation for death.[750] William Carey's passion for missions would soon intensify, as he read Jonathan Edwards's *Account of the Life of the*

---

of Hope, Illustrated in the Life and Death of the Reverend Andrew Fuller, 2nd ed. (London: Button and Son, 1818), 143–44.

[749] John Sutcliff, *Jealousy for the Lord of Hosts*, and Andrew Fuller, *The Pernicious Influence of Delay in Religious Concerns*, "two discourses delivered at a meeting of ministers at Clipston, in Northamptonshire, April 27, 1791" (London: Sold by Vernor, Ash, Matthews, Button, and Gardiner, all in London, and Smith, in Sheffield, 1791), 7 (1–16). A copy of this book is in the British Library. Sutcliff's message also appears in Haykin, *One Heart and One Soul*, 355–65. Fuller's message later appears under a revised title, *The Instances, the Evil Nature, and the Dangerous Tendency of Delay, in the Concerns of Religion*, in *Works*, 7:57–68.

[750] Fuller, *The Pernicious Influence of Delay in Religious Concerns*, 17–30.

Rev. David Brainerd.[751] Finally, in 1792, in Leicester, Carey published his most enduring work, *An Enquiry into the Obligations of Christians to Use Means for the Conversion of the Heathens*.[752] In this book, Carey sets forth answers to objections against missions. Establishing a biblical foundation, Carey first outlines the Christian obligation to obey the Great Commission. He then provides a brief overview of the history of missions, along with statistical data that challenges the reader to recognize the world's need for the gospel. He offers a proposal for the formation of a society (board) that could support such an enterprise, and he culminates his *Enquiry* with a strong challenge for believers to give generously toward financing the endeavor.

The Deathless Sermon: "Expect Great Things — Attempt Great Things"

Carey's most unforgettable opportunity to open his heart's concern to his fellow Baptists came on Wednesday morning, May 30, 1792, at the meeting of the Northampton Association.[753] Friar Lane Baptist, in Nottingham, hosted the meeting,[754] and copies of Carey's eighty-seven-page *Inquiry* were available. The day began with prayer at 6:00 AM; Carey preached at 10:00 AM. His sermon would earn the epitaph "The Deathless Sermon." His text was Isaiah 54:2–3, "Enlarge the place of thy tent, and let them stretch forth the curtains of thine habitations: spare not, lengthen thy cords, and strengthen thy stakes.

---

[751] Jonathan Edwards, *An Account of the Life of the Late Rev. David Brainerd* (Boston: D. Henchman, 1749).

[752] William Carey, *An Enquiry into the Obligations of Christians to Use Means for the Conversion of the Heathens* (Leicester: Ann Ireland, 1792).

[753] John Rippon, ed., "Minutes of the Northamptonshire Association Assembled at Nottingham, May 29, 30, and 31, 1792," in *The Baptist Annual Register, for 1790, 1791, 1792, and Part of 1793*, 418.

[754] The Friar Lane congregation would place a commemorative plaque on their wall to celebrate Carey's sermon. Richard Hopper was their pastor at the time of Carey's visit. In 1815, the Friar Lane (later renamed Park Street) congregation moved to George Street. It closed permanently about 1946–48. Presently, an arts theater occupies the George Street building. John T. Godfrey and James Ward, *The History of Friar Lane Baptist Church, Nottingham* (Nottingham: Henry B. Saxton, 1903), 13–14, 186–91.

For thou shalt break forth on the right hand and on the left; and thy seed shall inherit the Gentiles, and make the desolate cities to be inhabited." Carey addressed the words of the text to the typical, sleepy church—abiding alone in its little cottage. He reminded the church that, since her God is the God of the whole earth, she must enlarge the place of her tent, stretch her habitations, lengthen her cords, and strengthen her stakes. She must send forth missionaries to faraway regions. No one transcribed the sermon, but, according to William Staughton, who was in the audience, the spirit of Carey's message was two-pronged. "Expect great things—Attempt great things."[755] Frequent repetition would expand the expression to "Expect great things from God; attempt great things for God." The message called for action; but the men hesitated. The next morning, their discussion turned to other matters, and Ryland Jr. was about to close the meeting. Suddenly, Carey tugged at Andrew Fuller's sleeve and asked, "Is there again nothing going to be done, sir?" Fuller instantly proposed to the brethren an October meeting of any individuals willing to assist in making plans for the establishment of a Baptist society for propagating the gospel among the heathen.

Formation of the Particular Baptist Missionary Society (BMS)

Finally, at Kettering, on October 2, 1792, at least fourteen men,[756] mostly pastors, assembled in the home of Mrs. Beeby Wallis, affectionately called "Widow Wallis,"[757] for the founding

---

[755] William Staughton, *The Baptist Mission in India* (Philadelphia: Hellings and Aitken, 1811), 15.

[756] Brian Stanley, *The History of the Baptist Missionary Society 1792–1992* (Edinburgh: T&T Clark, 1992), 14–15.

[757] As faithful members of Andrew Fuller's church, Beeby and Martha Wallis had used their home as an inn for traveling evangelists. Many still call it the "Gospel Inn." Situated on Lower Street, in the heart of Kettering, the historic, well-preserved Wallis house is now called the "Carey Mission House," the featured attraction of "Martha Wallis Court," a residential facility for the elderly. The room where the BMS was born contains the table and chairs that the men used on October 2, 1792. (Fuller Baptist Church has the snuffbox.). There is a bronze memorial plaque near the

of "The Particular Baptist Society for Propagating the Gospel among the Heathen," later shortened to The Baptist Missionary Society (BMS). With the men seated at a table in the back parlor, Fuller collected faith-based, financial pledges by passing around his silver snuffbox—its lid embossed with a picture of the Apostle Paul's conversion. The pledges amounted to thirteen pounds, two shillings, six pence, plus all proceeds from Carey's *Enquiry*. This seemingly meager but sacrificial collection was the seed money of all future faith-promise offerings in behalf of overseas Baptist missions. The pastors who made these initial pledges were from poor and obscure, separatist churches. Their founding of the BMS enjoyed no newspaper coverage and no special attention. Nonetheless, the five key leaders among them were relatively young men with a fresh vision: Samuel Pearce (26), William Carey (31), Andrew Fuller (38), John Ryland Jr. (39), and John Sutcliff (40). On the day of its inception, the BMS appointed its first committee—John Ryland Jr., Reynold Hogg,[758] William Carey, John Sutcliff, and Andrew Fuller. Hogg was the treasurer and Fuller was secretary.

Also present at the 1792 founding of the BMS was William Staughton (1770–1829). Baptized by Samuel Pearce and recently graduated from Bristol Baptist Academy, Staughton

---

street. Across the street is the "Chesham House," home of Thomas Gotch, the merchant for whom Carey had made shoes while at Moulton.

[758] Reynold Hogg (1752–1843), longtime supporter of the BMS, was the first pastor of the Baptist church at Thrapston, Northamptonshire. In 1797, the congregation officially organized into a Baptist church, and the following year they ordained Rev. Hogg as pastor. He would serve here for seventeen years. The congregation entombed the earthly remains of Reynold and his wife Ann underneath the church, and a tablet inside the church commemorates them. The Thrapston Church Record Book still exists, and the congregation still uses the original 1787 two-storied, brick building. I am grateful to Neil Mathieson at Thrapston Baptist Church for his kind assistance. See also John Rippon, ed., *The Baptist Annual Register for 1794 –1797* (London: Sold by Dilly, Button, and Thomas, 1797), 10; James Culross, "Reynold Hogg," in *Founders and Pioneers of Modern Missions*, 21–24; *The Roots and Shoots of Thrapston Baptist Church*, a booklet produced in 1997 for the church's 200th anniversary. See also http://www.britishlistedbuildings.co.uk/en-424473-thrapston-baptist-church-thrapston-north.

had placed a pledge of ten shillings into the silver snuffbox. Due to his youth, he had humbly entered the abbreviation for *anonymous*, "Anon," rather than writing his name. In 1793, Staughton immigrated to America, where he became a pastor and educator. His most notable pastorates were First Baptist Church and Sansom Street Baptist in Philadelphia. Having originated in First Baptist, Philadelphia, in 1814, the Triennial Convention, at its second meeting (1818), approved the establishment of a "classical and theological seminary" for training young preachers. Staughton established the seminary in his Philadelphia home the following year. In 1821, upon Luther Rice's founding of Columbian College (later George Washington University) in Washington D. C., the Convention appointed Staughton as the college's first president. Staughton moved his Philadelphia seminary to Washington and it became the theology department of Columbian College, where he served twice as Chaplain of the United States Senate.[759]

Andrew Fuller's Unending Loyalty

As secretary of the BMS, Andrew Fuller would work himself to the grave, promoting and raising funds for the Society. Fuller's wife, Sarah, had died in August 1792, just prior to the formation of the BMS. For almost three months prior to her death, Sarah had suffered from a deranged mind, resulting in unspeakable misery to the entire family.[760] Andrew and Sarah had eleven children, but only two would live to survive their father. Andrew lamented many years in fervent prayer for their unsaved son, Robert, who died while he was in the Royal Marines. In his *Memoirs*, Fuller

---

[759] Thomas J. Nettles, "William Staughton 1770–1829," in *A Noble Company: Biographical Essays on Notable Particular-Regular Baptists in America*, ed. Terry Wolever (Springfield, MO: Particular Baptist Press, 2016), 7:84–140; and S. W. Lynd, *Memoir of the Rev. William Staughton, D. D.* (Boston: Lincoln, Edmands, and Co., 1834).

[760] Andrew Gunton Fuller, ed., *Memoirs of the Rev. Andrew Fuller*, in *The Complete Works of the Rev. Andrew Fuller*, 2 vols. (Boston: Gould, Kendall, and Lincoln, 1836) 1:58–60. Henceforth, references to this title will shorten to *Memoirs*. All references to the *Memoirs* are to volume one of this 1836 set.

reveals a heart-wrenching letter that he had sent to Robert.[761] After Robert died aboard ship off the coast of Lisbon, in 1809, his captain, along with a messmate, testified that Robert's exemplary character and conduct commanded respect from those who knew him. Robert's final letters to the family also brought some hope that he might have become a Christian. Thirty years after Andrew Fuller's death, Andrew Gunton Fuller (1799-1884), one of Fuller's sons by his second wife, was in Scotland when he met up with a Mr. Waldy, a deacon in the Baptist church in Falkirk. During their conversation, Waldy related that he had been with young Robert Fuller during his final voyage, and that he and Robert had "opened our minds much to each other." Best of all, Waldy reported that Robert "was a very pleasing, nice youth, and became a true Christian man."[762]

Continuing for the remainder of his life as the first secretary of the BMS, Andrew Fuller traveled over England, Ireland, Wales, and Scotland, raising funds for the cause of missions. In 1794, he suffered a stroke that left a temporary facial paralysis. That same year, he married Ann Coles, of Ampthill, Bedfordshire. Of the six children born of this marriage, only three would survive their father. Fuller served the pastorate of Kettering Baptist until his death at age sixty-one. At that time, the church recorded a membership of 174 and about a thousand attendees.[763] Fuller

---

[761] *Memoirs*, 1:66-69.

[762] Andrew Gunton Fuller, *Andrew Fuller* (London: Hodder and Stoughton, 1882), 73.

[763] The Kettering church's 1792 membership of eighty-eight was up to 174 in 1815. During 1804-5, an increased attendance had compelled the church to enlarge its chapel. They replaced that building with the present Lombardian style edifice during 1860-61, when the church's name changed from Kettering Baptist Church to "Fuller Baptist Church." Inside the church, a Heritage Room displays memorabilia including Andrew Fuller's pulpit, communion table, desk, and sermon notes, along with Widow Wallis's teapot. Tombs in the small graveyard at the rear of the premises include, in addition to that of Fuller, those of Beeby and Martha Wallis (Widow Wallis). Gladys M. Barrett, *A Brief History of Fuller Church, Kettering 1696-1946* (St. Albans: Printed by Parker Brothers, n.d.), 7, 10, 16; and the *Church Book*, 145. Located at Fuller Baptist Church, at 51 Gold Street, the *Church Book* is an unpublished, bound, autograph manuscript covering circa 1768-1815.

died on Sunday May 7, 1815, leaving an aged mother, a widow, three sons, and two daughters to mourn the loss of this beloved man. An estimated two thousand persons attended the funeral. His tomb is in the small burial ground behind Fuller Baptist Church. Although he died young, he had outlived twelve of his seventeen children. His service to foreign missions was immeasurable. His wise mentor, John Sutcliff, had passed into glory the previous year. Fuller's missionary friend, William Carey, would live another nineteen years.

Acceptance of John Thomas and William Carey as Missionaries to India

During the second meeting of the Baptist Missionary Society, on October 31, 1792, at Northampton, Samuel Pearce presented a contribution of seventy pounds from Cannon Street Baptist, in Birmingham. The BMS elected him a member of the committee. At the third BMS meeting, on November 13, 1792, in Northampton, the brethren read a letter from William Carey, informing them of John Thomas (1757–1801), an evangelical, Calvinistic Baptist who had been in India for several years preaching and translating portions of Scripture into the Bengali language. Thomas was now in England raising support and seeking a missionary who would return with him to India. Learning of Thomas, the committee requested its secretary, Andrew Fuller, to make inquiry concerning the man's character and qualifications.

When the committee met in Kettering on Wednesday, January 9, 1793, to hear Fuller's report, they were pleased to learn more of John Thomas. Born to devout Christian parents in Fairford, Gloucestershire, Thomas, as a young adult, in 1785, had professed his conversion to Christ and received baptism under the ministry of Samuel Stennett (1727–95) of the Baptist Church in Little Wild Street, London. This church's history describes Thomas as "the first Baptist Missionary in India."[764]

---

[764] Anonymous, *A Brief History of the Baptist Church in Little Wild Street* (London: Sold by G. Wightman, 1835), 11. Little Wild Street, in the Holborn section of London, is now Keeley Street, and the Baptist church

Thomas was a trained medical doctor and had served as a ship's surgeon. While in India, he had written frequent letters to three English Baptist pastors—Samuel Stennett, John Collett Ryland Sr., and Abraham Booth. Besides acquiring documents from several other sources, Fuller had obtained access to Thomas's correspondence with Booth. Upon careful examination of all the documents, the committee, "being fully of opinion that a door was now open in the East Indies, for preaching the gospel to the heathen, agreed to invite Mr. Thomas to go out under the patronage of the Society." In addition, if Thomas accepted the offer, the Society would endeavor to procure another missionary for him. Asked if he would be that missionary, Cary "readily answered in the affirmative."[765] That afternoon, Carey preached to the brethren from Revelation 22:12, "And, behold, I come quickly; and my reward is with me, to give every man according as his work shall be." Due to a foot injury, Thomas had declined an invitation to join the Committee for this occasion. Late in the evening, however, everyone was surprised at the announcement that Thomas had arrived. When Thomas limped into the room, he and Carey "fell on each other's neck and wept."[766] Andrew Fuller reflects that, upon hearing Thomas's account, "We saw," that "there was a gold mine in India, but it seemed almost as deep as the centre of the earth. Who will venture to explore it? 'I will venture to go down,' said Carey to his brethren, 'but remember that you must hold the ropes.' We solemnly engaged to do so, nor while we live shall we desert him."[767] In those words, Fuller unveils an eternal moment, an unforgettable glimpse into the depth of his

---

no longer exists.

[765] The question to Carey was simply for the record. In the recent October and November sessions of the BMS, Carey had already "offered himself as a missionary, and was accepted." See J. W. Morris, *Memoirs of the Life and Writings of the Rev. Andrew Fuller,* ed. Rufus Babcock Jr. (Boston: Lincoln and Edmands, 1830), 87; cf. Cox, *History of the Baptist Missionary Society from 1792 to 1842,* 1:20.

[766] Cox, *History of the Baptist Missionary Society from 1792 to 1842,* 1:20; Morris, *Memoirs of the Life and Writings of the Rev. Andrew Fuller,* 87; cf. Marshman, *The Life and Times of Carey, Marshman, and Ward,* 1:52.

[767] Cox, *History of the Baptist Missionary Society, from 1792 to 1842,* 1:20.

personal commitment to his friend. We knew, says Fuller, "that while *we* lived, we should *never* let go the rope. You understand me. There was great responsibility attached to us who began the business."[768] With Thomas and Carey bonded as colleagues, the long session ended past midnight, with much rejoicing.[769] While, in sermons and conversations, Carey's passion for the mission field had been obvious to everyone, it still must have been difficult for him to speak of it to Dorothy for the first time, as actually being "official." He and Thomas would now begin traveling and raising funds.[770] Progress would be slow—every step of the way. The world would relentlessly oppose these pioneer missionaries, who possessed no manual and no earthly instructor. Both believed that, in Christ, they could reach India with the gospel.

The Five-Month Preparation for the Voyage

William and Dorothy Carey readily agreed that he would take eight-year-old Felix with him to India, set up housekeeping, initiate a ministry, and return in two to three years for the rest of the family. During the interval, Dorothy, William Jr., and Peter would live in Piddington with her younger sister Catherine (Kitty). The BMS would help support Dorothy with £50 a year, during the interval. The Carey family's final Sunday at Harvey Lane Baptist came on March 17, 1793,[771]

---

[768] Andrew Gunton Fuller, *Memoirs*, 1:64–65.
[769] C. B. Lewis, *The Life of John Thomas: Surgeon of the Earl of Oxford East Indiaman, and First Baptist Missionary to Bengal* (London: Macmillan and Co., 1873), 218–20. Lewis cites key letters from Andrew Fuller.
[770] Staughton, *The Baptist Mission in India*, 18–20.
[771] The Harvey Lane building no longer exists. When the church outgrew its building, in 1845, the congregation moved to Belvoir Street and changed its name to Belvoir Street Baptist. In 1940, Belvoir Street Baptist and Charles Street Baptist (planted by Harvey Lane in 1831) merged to form the United Baptist Church, situated in the Charles Street facilities. In 1983, United Baptist Church and the Victoria Road Church merged to form the present Central Baptist Church, still in Charles Street. Meanwhile, in 1915–16, the William Carey Cottage had become the Carey Museum, called "House of Memories." Due to street additions in the 1960s, the Carey Museum suffered demolition, and a Holiday Inn now occupies the

and Dorothy was now about five and a half months pregnant. Harvey Lane held its final farewell for the Carey family on Wednesday March 20, with morning prayers and an afternoon session with John Thomas sharing his experiences in India. The evening service included a message by Reynold Hogg, from Acts 21:12-14, followed by a stirring farewell charge from Andrew Fuller to Carey and Thomas. Fuller's text came from the words of Jesus, in John 20:21, "Peace be unto you: as my Father hath sent me, even so send I you." Carey spent the next six days getting Dorothy and the children settled in Piddington. On Tuesday March 26, he kissed his wife and children goodbye. That night, Carey, with Felix, traveled to Olney to deliver a final sermon at the church that had first commissioned him. Preaching from Romans 12:1, Carey closed with the words of a hymn written by the Baptist hymn writer, Benjamin Beddome (1717-95), who, for fifty-two years, served the pastorate of the Baptist church at Bourton-on-the-Water,[772] in Gloucestershire. Beddome titled this hymn "Self-Denial":

---

site. Besides a memorial tablet to Carey, Central Baptist Church has its own Carey Museum, displaying the artifacts once housed in the Carey Museum at Harvey Lane. See also Sheila Mitchell, *Not Disobedient: A History of United Baptist Church, Leicester Including Harvey Lane 1760–1845, Belvoir Street 1845–1940 and Charles Street 1831–1940* (Leicester: Sheila Mitchell, 1984); and Graham Lee, "A Brief History of United Baptist Church 1940–1983," in *Not Disobedient*, by Sheila Mitchell, 179–89.

[772] For more on his life and works, see "Rev. Benjamin Beddome, A. M.," *The Baptist Annual Register for 1794-1797*, ed. John Rippon, 314–26; "Memoir of the Rev. Benjamin Beddome, A.M.," *The Baptist Magazine* 35 (October 1843): 509–12; Thomas Brooks, *Pictures of the Past: The History of the Baptist Church, Bourton-on-the-Water* (London: Judd and Glass, 1861); Michael A. G. Haykin, "Benjamin Beddome (1717–1795)," in *The British Particular Baptists 1638–1910*, ed. Michael A. G. Haykin, 1:166–83; Henry S. Burrage, *Baptist Hymn Writers and Their Hymns* (Portland, ME: Brown Thurston and Co., 1888), 49–52; Benjamin Beddome, *Sermons*, "with a brief memoir of the author" (London: William Ball, 1835); idem, *Hymns Adapted to Public Worship, or Family Devotion* (London: Sold by Burton and Briggs, 1818); idem, *A Scriptural Exposition of the Baptist Catechism*, 2nd ed. (Bristol: W. Pine, 1776).

> 1. And must I part with all I have,
> Jesus, my Lord, for Thee?
> This is my joy, since thou hast done
> Much more than this for me.
> 2. *Yes let it go!* One look from thee
> Will more than make amends
> for all the losses I sustain,
> Of credit, riches, friends.
> 3. Savior of souls! Could I from Thee
> A single smile obtain,
> Tho' destitute of all things else,
> I'd glory in my gain.[773]

The next morning, the missionaries proceeded to London and visited the office of the British East India Company for their licenses to enter India. Humanly speaking, the timing of their request could not have been worse. The East India Company's charter had recently come up for renewal and a controversy had emerged. Two evangelical members of Parliament, Charles Grant (1746-1823)[774] (on the East India Company's board of trade) and William Wilberforce (1759-1833),[775] had made a resolution before the House of Commons for the addition of a "pious clause" (as some called it) into the Company's charter. Designed to increase spiritual, cultural, and educational opportunities for Christian missionaries, the clause resolved:

> That it is the peculiar and bounden duty of the Legislature to promote by all just and prudent means, the interests and happiness of the inhabitants of the British Dominions in India; and that, for these ends, such measures ought to be adopted as may gradually

---

[773] S. Pearce Carey, *William Carey, D. D., Fellow of Linnaean Society*, 117. The italics are in Carey's book. A later edition of the hymn is in Beddome, *Hymns Adapted to Public Worship, or Family Devotion*, 225.

[774] See Henry Morris, *The Life of Charles Grant: Sometimes Member of Parliament for Inverness-Shire and Director of the East India Company* (London: John Murray, 1904), 207. Grant was quite familiar with Thomas's work in India.

[775] Among the many sources on Wilberforce, see especially the work by his sons, Robert Isaac Wilberforce and Samuel Wilberforce, *The Life of William Wilberforce*, 5 vols. (London: John Murray, 1838).

> tend to their advancement in useful knowledge, and to their religious and moral improvement.[776]

While the House agreed to hear the proposal, worldly-minded politicians and bishops argued that Christian conversions in India would kindle political uprisings. Deplorably, such trepidation of cultural change won the day. Fearing that evangelistic work would hinder the Company's lucrative trade, both Houses of Parliament defeated the clause and renewed "the Court of Directors' standing order requiring the expulsion of all unlicensed persons arriving in India."[777] In the wake of the defeat, Wilberforce wrote in his private journal, "How mysterious, how humbling, are the dispensations of God's providence!"[778] By 1813, Wilberforce would be successful in the matter, but, for now, Carey and Thomas had walked into a political hornets' nest. Even so, they agreed with Wilberforce that Providence not Parliament is foremost in bringing God's decrees to pass with precision and perfection. Without licenses to leave the country, the Carey team must now travel secretly and enter India as illegal immigrants. As a ship's surgeon, John Thomas had previously traveled with a "Captain White," who now agreed to take the missionaries to India without licenses.

On Easter Sunday, March 31, Carey preached for John Rippon at London's Carter Lane Baptist, at Walnut Tree Alley. In the audience was twenty-three-year-old William Ward, a printer from Derby who was visiting with friends. After the service, Ward and Carey walked along the street by the Thames conversing over the work of the Lord. Before they realized it, their conversation had taken them many blocks to Pudding Lane—near Sir Christopher Wren's Monument to the Great Fire of London. As they were finally departing, Carey placed his hand on William Ward's shoulder and told him that he hoped to have the Bible translated into Bengali and ready for a printer in four to five years. Carey then added, "You must

---
[776] See Penelope Carson, *The East India Company and Religion 1698–1858* (Woodbridge, Suffolk, UK: The Boydell Press, 2012), 37 (37–44).
[777] Ibid., 52ff.
[778] Wilberforce, *The Life of William Wilberforce*, 2:27.

come and print it for us."[779] The two would never forget this conversation.

On Thursday April 4, 1793, William and Felix Carey, John Thomas, his wife, daughter, two cousins (Samuel and Sarah Powell), and Thomas's "black boy Andrew"[780] boarded the *Earl of Oxford* for their voyage to Calcutta. It was too dangerous, however, for passenger ships to depart alone. The French Revolutionary and Napoleonic Wars (1792–1815) had already set England and France at war against one another. While waiting for a naval escort to the high seas, the captain anchored his ship in the narrow strait separating the Isle of Wight from England's mainland. Meanwhile, Carey had sent a letter to Dorothy to keep her posted on his location. During the six-week delay, all passengers were required to wait on shore. Thus, the missionaries spent their time at Ryde, on the Isle of Wight, where Carey received a letter from Dorothy telling him their son had been born. William returned a tender letter to his wife.

Meanwhile, on Sunday May 19, Captain White received an anonymous letter from the East India House, warning him that "a person" on his ship was trying to leave the country without a license. The Court of Directors' standing order for such a person was expulsion. The letter cautioned that Captain White could forfeit his command if he allowed this individual to remain on the ship. White promptly ordered both John Thomas and William Carey off his ship and refunded Carey £150 in cash. Thomas, Carey, and Felix retrieved their baggage and returned to Ryde. Carey had evidence to believe that one of Thomas's creditors, discovering that he was leaving the country without a license, had reported him to keep him in England. To play it safe, Captain White had ejected Carey as well, but permitted Thomas's family to remain aboard the ship if they so desired. They chose to stay aboard; Thomas would join them in Calcutta. As for Carey, he had no license, but he had no debts either, and, in the ensuing years, he would become increasingly distraught over Thomas's instability and perpetual lack

---

[779] S. Pearce Carey, *William Carey, D. D., Fellow of Linnaean Society*, 119.
[780] Lewis, *Life of John Thomas*, 237.

of wisdom concerning finances. Once in India, Thomas would often display an argumentative and even hot-tempered disposition when conversing controversial issues. Despite Thomas's flaws, however, Carey would regard him as a gifted, compassionate, generous, and well-meaning man sent from God to assist the team.[781]

Meanwhile, attending to the dire situation at hand, Thomas, Carey, and Felix hastily caught a boat from Ryde to Portsmouth, where they stored their baggage and took a stagecoach to London in search of another sympathetic sea captain. As Carey was writing to Dorothy that she could expect him home in the morning, the sea-savvy Thomas was entering a seafarers' coffeehouse on London's east side. He knew that this was the perfect place to discover the table talk of the quays. Aware that the eastbound shipping season was almost over, Thomas enquired of a waiter "whether any Swedish or Danish ship expected to sail from Europe to Bengal, or any part of the East Indies, that season." Then, "to the great joy of a bruised heart," reports Thomas, "the waiter put a card into my hand, whereon were written these life-giving words: 'A Danish East Indiaman, No. 10, Cannon Street.'"[782] A quick visit to the address revealed that a Danish ship would be sailing from Copenhagen to Calcutta. The captain was planning his embarkation from Dover, England, within five days.

After booking the voyage, Thomas, Carey, and Felix caught an overnight stagecoach to Northampton and arrived in Piddington early the next morning. Overjoyed at seeing his wife and family, especially three-week-old Jabez, Carey was saddened that Dorothy still refused to travel. Of course, he understood her fears. She was illiterate. In the parish church, she had signed the marriage register with an X. She had never traveled beyond her surrounding neighborhood. Besides that, she was nursing a baby, and the boys were all under nine years old. William knew that Dorothy had named their latest baby

---

[781] Cf. Ronald B. Dietrick, "The Man the Church Forgot: John Thomas," in *The Man the Church Forgot: and Other Early Missionaries Who Made a Difference* (Maitland, FL: Xulon Press, 2012), 21–48, http://www.xulonpress.com/bookstore/.

[782] Lewis, *Life of John Thomas*, 238.

Jabez because she "bare him with sorrow" (1 Chron. 4:9). Carey believed that, at some point, God would bestow upon Dorothy the strength to follow him, as he pursued a divine call that to him was so clear and so urgent.

Suddenly, in an unexpected turn of events, as Carey, Felix, and Thomas were making their way back into Northampton for a stagecoach to Portsmouth, Thomas suddenly insisted on returning alone to Piddington to plead once more with Dorothy. William tried to dissuade him, but Thomas went back. Dorothy agreed to go if her sister Catherine would accompany them. After a time of solitary prayer in her room, Catherine announced that she was willing. Thomas rushed the good news back to William, who promptly returned for his family. The Carey team now consisted of eight: William, Dorothy, Catherine, the four Carey boys (Felix, William Jr., Peter, and Jabez), and John Thomas. Meanwhile, there was much to do and little time left to reach the ship. As the Careys were packing their belongings, John Ryland Jr. was desperately raising the minimum £700 cash needed for the additional passengers. John Thomas, a sort of treasurer for the team, oversaw the cash supply, and he grossly underestimated the amount of monetary support the team would need during their first year in India.

When the group reached London, Thomas purchased the additional tickets for the overseas voyage and then caught a boat to Portsmouth to retrieve their baggage. Within a couple of days, they all met in Dover in time to board the six-hundred-ton sailing ship, the *Kron Princessa Maria*—only to learn that the Danish vessel was in a delay and would not arrive in Dover until two-weeks later. Finally, on June 13, 1793, as they watched the white cliffs of Dover slowly fading behind them, the missionaries were underway for India. One hundred and fifty-days had passed since Carey declared, "I will venture to go down, but you must hold the ropes." Writing in his diary that night, Carey spiritually "raised" his "Ebenezer" stone in joyful thanksgiving to God for all His providences. The word *Ebenezer*, from 1 Samuel 7:12, means "Stone of help," and it described the memorial that Samuel set up after the Hebrews returned to the Lord and routed the Philistines by His mighty hand. Even from his childhood, Carey would have sung the familiar usage of *Ebenezer*, in the hymn "Come, Thou Fount of Every Blessing" (1758), by Robert Robinson (1735–90),[783] pastor of Stone-Yard Baptist Chapel in Cambridge. Though Carey would never again see his English homeland, his eye of faith looked for a heavenly city "whose builder and maker is God" (Heb. 11:10). He would have especially pondered the lyrics of Robinson's second stanza: "Here I raise my Ebenezer; Here by Thy great help I've come; And I hope, by Thy good pleasure, Safely to arrive at home."

Highlights of the Carey Mission Team to 1800

The voyage of Carey's missionary team would be a fifteen-thousand-mile journey through many treacherous storms. Five months later, on November 9, 1793, their ship entered India's Hooghly (Hugli) River, a tributary of the Ganges River, which flows into the Bay of Bengal. As illegal immigrants, the missionaries were compelled to enter Calcutta surreptitiously. At the mouth of the Hooghly, therefore, the ship stopped for them to board a native boat for the remaining few miles to Calcutta. Traveling upriver, they stopped at a "bazaar or market," where, as Carey reports, Mr. Thomas "preached [in Bengali] to the people. They left their merchandise, and listened for three hours with great attention. One of them prepared us a dinner, which we had on a plantain-leaf for dish and plates; and instead of knives and forks, we used our fingers." Carey adds, "When we left them, they desired us to come again."[784]

On November 11, the missionaries arrived at Calcutta (now spelled *Kolkata*). In search of a piece of land to cultivate, they soon moved thirty miles north to the Portuguese settlement of Bandel, then returned to Calcutta, where Thomas attempted to use his medical skills for money to square up his debts. During this time, Carey learned to his dismay that Thomas in ten weeks had used

---

[783] While conservatives would disagree with his opposition to creeds and confessions, this Robert Robinson must not be confused with the English Unitarian, Robert Robinson (1726–91).

[784] William Carey, "Letter to the Society for the Propagation of the Gospel amongst the Heathen," written from the Bay of Bengal (1793), in Eustace Carey, *Memoir of William Carey, D. D.*, 80. For more of Carey's letter, see Rippon, ed., *The Baptist Annual Register for 1794 –1797*, 154.

up nearly a year's allowance from the missionary budget. No longer would Thomas handle the team's finances. Still in search of land, the Carey family moved to Maniktala, which is today a northern suburb of Calcutta. During this time, Dorothy and Felix were suffering with severe dysentery. Receiving an offer of a few acres of land, the Carey family, early in 1794, moved near Debhata, which was forty miles east of Calcutta and today is just over the border into Bangladesh. Charles Short, a moral but non-Christian business executive, allowed the Carey family to live in his home for as long as they needed it. Meanwhile, Carey, with the help of a Hindu scholar, was learning to translate the Bible into the Bengali language.

Within four months, John Thomas had befriended and encouraged a Christian entrepreneur in Malda named George Udny, who, out of gratitude, offered Thomas the management of an indigo factory in Moypaldiggy. Determined to pay his endless line of creditors, Thomas accepted the offer, but on one condition—that Udny extend to Carey the management of his factory in Mudnabati, situated north of Malda up the Tangan River. Carey accepted and his family began packing for the move. While Dorothy's sister, Catherine, remained in Debhata to marry Charles Short,[785] the rest of the team journeyed the 250 miles to Mudnabati, where a spacious home awaited them. With some ninety hired workers (*munshi*), Carey operated the indigo plantation and processed its leaves into blue dye for textile manufacturers. The seasonal nature of the work provided abundant time for Carey's translation work and for evangelism. Able to preach in Bengali for up to thirty minutes, Carey was now preaching to some five hundred persons—both Hindu and Muslim. John Thomas, meanwhile, was suffering from depression. It was his habit, when depressed, to find relief by changing his environment. Thus, in 1797, he abandoned the indigo plant and traveled alone for weeks on end. Penniless and in debt, Thomas preached in remote vil-

---

[785] During a visit to England with his wife and for his health, Charles, in 1801, made a return trip to India, where he suddenly died in 1802. Catherine never returned to India. She spent her final years in Clipston, where she died in 1827.

lages and ministered to the sick. His family had no way of contacting him. Carey, nevertheless, with capital from his indigo production, was reaching two hundred villages and running two schools to teach the locals how to read the Bible.

Suddenly, a flood, followed by severe drought, destroyed the indigo harvest. On top of that, a severe fever spread through Carey's workforce and reached his own family. On October 11, 1794, five-year-old Peter Carey died of the fever. His parents were devastated. At Christmas, the family took a little holiday trip to Malda. By April 1795, Dorothy was pregnant with their seventh child, Jonathan (b. January 1796), and, sadly, she was sinking into an abyss of mental illness. During the fits of delusion and paranoia, Dorothy's language became obscene, abusive, and even violent. She imagined William having affairs with all the women. As she began threatening to cut William's throat with the kitchen knife, the missionaries were compelled to confine her to her room. The situation heaped incredible discouragement upon William. For the next twelve years, until her death in 1807, at age fifty-one,[786] Dorothy's condition would only deteriorate. Locked into a cause that was greater than she was able mentally and emotionally to grasp, Dorothy had proven herself a worthy instrument in the hands of her Creator. Only eternity will reveal Mrs. Carey's true excellence and full reward from the One who is just in all His ways. Besides bearing and nursing his children, Dorothy had made it possible for William never to put his ministry on hold for return trips to England. He would entreat the Baptist Missionary Society for more missionaries and eventually for a transfer of his own monetary support to the other missionaries.

The First Two Decades of Missionary Work in Serampore

Compelled to abandon the ruined indigo factory in Mudnabati and to build a new one about twelve miles away, in Kidderpore, Carey made a special appeal to the BMS for missionaries. In late 1798, he received an encouraging letter

---

[786] The best source for Dorothy Carey is James R. Beck, *Dorothy Carey: The Tragic and Untold Story of Mrs. William Carey* (Grand Rapids: Baker, 1992).

from the young printer, William Ward (1769-1823),[787] who had conversed with Carey five years earlier at Carter Lane. Since that conversation, Ward had received baptism by immersion, studied under John Fawcett at Ewood Hall Theological Academy, and assisted the ailing Samuel Pearce (1766-99) in his Birmingham pastorate. Ward's letter was to inform Carey that he was coming to India. On October 13, 1799, Ward, along with a group that included Joshua (1768-1837) and Hannah (1767-1847) Marshman,[788] docked at Serampore, a small trading colony of Danish India. Learning that these new arrivals were English missionaries, British authorities demanded their immediate return to England. Impounded and awaiting their return, the missionaries suddenly learned that a compassionate Danish Lutheran Christian, Colonel Ole Bie, Crown regent of Serampore, had come forth to offer them political asylum. William Carey quickly heard the news with great delight. On the morning of January 1, 1800, the Carey group, with all their cargo, set sail on the ten-day, three-hundred-mile downriver trip to Serampore to join the new missionaries. By now, the three oldest Carey boys, Felix, William Jr., and Jabez were speaking fluent Bengali. Even three-year-old Jonathan was speaking it quite naturally. Meanwhile, George Udny, the Christian entrepreneur, had already purchased a printing press for the Carey team. In India, printing presses were rare and expensive. Taking great interest in Carey's ministry, Governor Bie offered the team complete freedom to purchase houses, to preach the gospel, establish schools, print the Scriptures, and even to obtain passports into British territories.

William Carey would spend the remainder of his life here in Serampore, an international port, situated on the west bank of

---

[787] See A. Christopher Smith, "William Ward (1769-1832)," in *The British Particular Baptists 1638-1910*, ed. Michael A. G. Haykin, 2:254-71; and Samuel Stennett, *Memoirs of the Life of the Rev. William Ward* (London: Printed by J. Haddon, 1825).

[788] See Sunil Kumar Chatterjee, *Hannah Marshman: The First Woman Missionary in India* (Sheoraphuli, Hoogly District, West Bengal: Sri Sunil Chatterjee, 1987); and A. Christopher Smith, "Joshua (1768-1837) and Hannah Marshman (1767-1847)," in *The British Particular Baptists 1638-1910*, ed. Michael A. G. Haykin, 2:236-53.

the Hooghly and only sixteen miles from Calcutta, the center of British trade in India. These would be the most productive years for the Carey team. The missionaries purchased a building by the river to serve as their Mission House. By March, they had established the Serampore Mission Press. On April 24, 1800, the team observed a day of thanksgiving for the Mission House, the Press, and for the completion of additional buildings. Their thanksgiving began at sunrise with a session of prayer, followed by a special service for recognizing Carey as their pastor and for a congregational sharing of conversion testimonies. Following Carey's evening sermon, called "Rejoicing in Hope," the congregation listened to the reading of encouraging letters of support from back home. By August, the team had published the first book ever printed in Bengali type. It was the Gospel of Matthew.

In late November 1800, some young girls appeared at the Mission House requesting urgent medical help for their father, a Hindu carpenter named Krishna Pal (1764–1822). He was a half mile away. Having fallen and dislocated his shoulder, Krishna had learned that John Thomas was staying at the Mission House. Thomas, Carey, and Joshua Marshman rushed to Krishna's side. Positioning him against a tree, Thomas set Krishna's shoulder in place and shared the gospel with him. The next morning, Carey took Krishna to the Mission House for relief from his pain and for sharing more Scripture. Having heard of Jesus while doing some carpentry work for Moravian missionaries, Krishna had been seeking truth outside of strict Hinduism. More recently, he had been listening to an Islamic sect, but he had found no peace. For several weeks, the Carey team ministered the gospel to him. Finally, on December 22, John Thomas asked Krishna pointedly whether he understood the Christian message of salvation. To his enquirer's utter delight, Krishna replied that the "Lord Jesus Christ had given His very life for the salvation of sinners, and that he and his friend Gokul did unfeignedly believe this."[789] Thirty-six-year-old Krishna Pal had become the team's first Bengali

---

[789] S. Pearce Carey, *William Carey, D. D., Fellow of Linnaean Society*, 195. See also *The First Hindoo Convert: A Memoir of Krishna Pal, a Preacher of the Gospel to His Countrymen More than Twenty Years* (Philadelphia: American Baptist Publication Society, 1852).

convert. This was seven years and forty-three days since Carey's arrival in India. Krishna and Gokul (Go Kul) immediately abandoned the caste system by joining with the missionary families for a meal.

The next day, John Thomas lapsed into emotional incoherence to the point of insanity, described as non-violent, but uncontrollable ecstatic wildness, punctuated with raptures of joy. Mournfully, the team found it necessary to quarantine Thomas inside the mission schoolhouse.[790] On Sunday December 28, 1800, at a solemn baptismal service at the river in front of the Mission, Carey immersed his son Felix and then Krishna. Those in attendance included Governor Bie, along with a great host of Europeans, Hindus, and Muslims. The Governor wept openly with incredible joy. Krishna's wife, sister, and four daughters soon confessed Christ as Lord and Savior. With Gokul receiving his immersion in the spring of 1801, his wife and a widowed neighbor also accepted Christ. Indeed, Krishna and Gokul would become instrumental in bringing many more to the Lord. Meanwhile, on the first day of 1801, Carey and Marshman were compelled to admit Thomas into Calcutta's hospital for the insane. Later released, Thomas never recovered. He would die on October 13, 1801, of a serious heart condition. Mightily used in the service of his Lord for some fifteen years, John Thomas had earnestly loved God and borne his cross for the sake of lost souls.

Meanwhile, by March 1801, William Carey had completed his translation of the entire New Testament into Bengali. In April, he accepted the governor's offer of a professorship in Bengali studies at Fort William College in Calcutta. From Serampore, Carey would row the sixteen-mile round trip. His schedule allowed him to stay in Calcutta Tuesday–Thursday and to

---

[790] William Staughton speaks wisely when he says of Thomas, "We feel disposed to pity rather than censure him; as little or no doubt remains with us that his unevenness of mind and temper, with other irregularities, proceeded from a *tendency* in his constitution to that which at length came upon him." Staughton, *The Baptist Mission in India*, 283; cf. Dietrick, *The Man the Church Forgot*, 42–45; and Michael Haykin, "John Thomas and the Mission to India," in *A Cloud of Witnesses: Calvinistic Baptists in the 18th Century* (Faverdale North, Darlington, England: Evangelical Times, 2006), 53–58.

DAVID BEALE

remain in Serampore during the four-day weekend. Ecclesiastes 4:12 says, "A threefold cord is not quickly broken." During these years, a threefold cord — Carey, Ward, and Marshman — became the "triumvirate of Serampore," as historians have described them. William Ward had taken a special interest in Carey's two oldest boys, Felix and William, and led them both to Christ. The Serampore Mission Press, under Ward's direction, soon became one of the largest in the world, employing fifty artisans, purchasing a steam engine, and manufacturing their own paper and ink. Felix Carey worked as Ward's assistant and, with a few local pundits, proofread Carey's translations.

In 1807, the year of Dorothy's death, William Carey published his Sanskrit New Testament, and Brown University, in Providence, Rhode Island, conferred upon him the Doctor of Divinity degree. The following year, Dr. Carey married Charlotte Emilia Rumohr (1761–1821), who faithfully upheld him, his family, and every aspect of his ministry — for better, for worse; for richer, for poorer; and indeed, in sickness, and in health, until her death. When a devastating fire, on March 11, 1812, destroyed the Carey team's five printing presses in Serampore, many precious manuscripts perished. When news of the fire reached England, such generous monetary gifts began pouring into the Mission House that, by the end of the year, new presses were up and running — with unprecedented production.[791] Meanwhile, as John Ryland Jr. was preaching to a great host at a BMS annual meeting in London, he referred to Dr. Carey's joy in having his two sons, Felix and William, dedicated to missions. "But," he added, "there is a third who gives him pain, he is not yet turned to the Lord." After a long pause, with tears flowing down his face, Ryland exclaimed, "Brethren, let us send up a united, universal, and fervent prayer to God, in solemn silence, for the conversion of Jabez Carey!" The congregation of "perhaps two thousand" prayed for the soul of nineteen-year-old Jabez Carey. The next mail from India brought the news of Jabez's conversion, which had occurred "quite synchronous with the season of fervent supplication."[792]

---

[791] See S. Pearce Carey, "The Fire," in *William Carey, D. D., Fellow of Linnaean Society*, 283–92.
[792] F. A. Cox, *History of the Baptist Missionary Society, from 1792 to 1842*, 1:241.

In 1818, Carey led in the founding of Serampore College, a divinity school for nationals.[793] Hailed in India as the Father of Modern Bengal, Carey translated the whole Bible into India's six major languages: Bengali, Oriya, Marathi, Hindi, Assamese, and Sanskrit. He translated portions of the Bible into more than thirty-six Asian languages and into numerous dialects. Often assisted by students, he published grammatical and lexicographical works. Besides biblical studies, he published Bengali textbooks on chemistry, medical science, and geography. To assist in finances and to spread the gospel, Joshua and Hannah Marshman opened boarding schools for the children of wealthy Europeans. These schools quickly became the best in Bengal. The couple established additional schools for Bengali boys and girls in and around Serampore. For every work they established, the Carey team's threefold purpose was evangelism, edification, and the improvement of Indian culture. Carey's study of Indian flora led him, in 1820, to establish the Agri Horticultural Society in Calcutta, which continues to this day as one of India's most prestigious societies. By 1821, the Carey team had baptized more than 1,400 converts.

Carey's Final Years

On May 30, 1821, Charlotte Carey died, soon after her sixtieth birthday. During her final years, she had become a complete invalid. Of their "thirteen years and three weeks" of marriage, Carey wrote, "We had as great a share of conjugal happiness as ever was enjoyed by mortals."[794] Two years later, William Ward died of cholera. In 1823, Carey married Grace Hughes (1777–1835), who cared for him through his remaining eleven years on earth. Grace would survive William by only one year. Carey

---

[793] Conservatives must caution that the divinity school is no longer doctrinally sound.

[794] Carey's tribute to Charlotte is in *The Missionary Register for MDCCCXXIII* (London: L. B. Seeley and Son, 1823), 40. Carey adds, "She was eminently pious, and lived very near to God. The Bible was her daily delight.... She was full of compassion for the poor and needy; and entered most heartily into all the concerns of the Mission, and into the support of Schools, particularly those for Female Native Children."

had joyfully baptized all three of his wives. His indefatigable work and persistent pressure resulted in governmental legislation that, in 1829, permanently ended the Hindu practice of sati, that is, the requirement of widows to sacrifice their lives to the flames of their husbands' funeral pyres. Carey's influence also led to the abolition of assisted suicide of the aged, and the abolition of infanticide, including the Hindu sacrifices of millions of infants to the alligators of the "sacred" waters of the Ganges.

Without question, Carey was the Father of Baptist Foreign Missions. He had spent the final forty-one years of his life in India. Two years prior to his death, he completed the eighth and final edition of his Bengali New Testament (1832). At the time of his death, fifty missionaries were serving eighteen mission stations. At sunrise, on June 9, 1834, as seventy-two-year-old William Carey lay dying, his surviving sons—Jabez, William, and Jonathan—joined with those who had gathered around his bed. Suddenly, Carey beckoned the celebrated Scottish missionary, Alexander Duff, to his bedside and whispered these words, "Mr. Duff! You have been speaking about Dr. Carey, Dr. Carey; when I am gone, say nothing about Dr. Carey. Speak about Dr. Carey's Savior."[795] In his will, Carey had expressed his desire to be "buried by the side of my second wife, Charlotte Emilia Carey." He also requested two lines, and nothing more, from an Isaac Watts hymn, as the inscription on the stone slab of his grave:

A wretched, poor, and helpless worm,
On Thy kind arms I fall.[796]

---

[795] The couch on which Carey died is at Regent's Park College, Oxford, together with his Bible, many letters, and various other artifacts.

[796] On his own deathbed, in 1878, Charles Hodge recited the two lines, "A guilty, weak, and helpless worm, On thy kind arms I fall." As his fleeting breath suddenly expired, Dr. Hodge's grieving wife quickly voiced the final lines, "Be thou my Strength and Righteousness, My Savior and my All." See Charles Seymour Robinson, *Annotations upon Popular Hymns* (New York: Hunt and Eaton, 1893), 247. This edition of Watts's first line differs slightly from the one that Carey had used.

Not only did William Carey inspire thousands of missionaries, including Adoniram Judson (1788–1850) to Burma, Hudson Taylor (1832–1905) to China, and David Livingstone (1813–73) to Africa, the Baptist Missionary Society touched off the formation of a host of mission agencies on both sides of the Atlantic.[797] Even within England's Particular Baptist churches, evangelistic fervor had, after 1702, increased rapidly. John Rippon, editor of *The Baptist Annual Register*, reported remarkable growth in membership and in the establishment of new churches among Particular Baptists in England and Wales.[798] In 1798, Rippon further reported, "More of our meeting houses have been enlarged, within the last five years, and more built within the last fifteen, than had been built and enlarged for thirty years before."[799] In 1949, the Baptist Missionary Society (BMS) donated to London's Westminster Abbey a beautiful, hand carved lectern, commemorating the sesquicentennial of the BMS that Carey had helped to establish. Situated near the Abbey's High Altar, the lectern displays the words, "Attempt great things for God." In 1993, India honored the memory of William Carey by printing a six-rupee postage stamp with a picture portraying the missionary sitting at his desk translating Scripture.

---

[797] Even prior to Carey's death, there had emerged numerous missionary outlets, including the London Missionary Society (1795); Scottish and Glasgow Missionary Societies (1796); Church Missionary Society (1799); Religious Tract Society (1799); British and Foreign Bible Society (1804); American Board of Commissioners for Foreign Missions (1810); Baptist Board for Foreign Missions (1814); New England Tract Society (1814); American Bible Society (1816); Baptist General Tract Society (1824); and the American Baptist Home Mission Society (1832).

[798] John Rippon, ed., *The Baptist Annual Register for 1794 –1797* (London: Sold by Dilly, Button, and Thomas, 1797), 1–24.

[799] Idem, ed., *The Baptist Annual Register for 1798 –1800 and Part of 1801* (London: Sold by Button, and Conder, 1801), 41 (1–44). There are some errors in the book's pagination in this section.

Select Bibliography for Further Reading

Beck, James R. *Dorothy Carey: The Tragic and Untold Story of Mrs. William Carey.* Grand Rapids: Baker, 1992.
Belcher, Joseph. *William Carey: A Biography.* Philadelphia: American Baptist Publication Society, 1853.
Carey, Eustace. *Memoir of William Carey, D. D.* Boston: Gould, Kendall, and Lincoln, 1836. This includes an "Introductory Essay" by Francis Wayland, president of Brown University. Eustace Carey was William Carey's nephew.
Carey, S. Pearce. *William Carey, D. D., Fellow of Linnaean Society.* Philadelphia: Judson Press, 1923. The author was William Carey's great-grandson and Samuel Pearce's great-grandson. He wrote biographies of both of his great-grandfathers.
_____. *Samuel Pearce, M. A., The Baptist Brainerd.* 2nd ed. London: The Carey Press, 1913.
_____. *Serampore Letters: Being the Unpublished Correspondence of William Carey and Others with John Williams 1800–1816.* Edited by Leighton and Mornay Williams. London: G. P. Putnam's Sons, 1892.
The Centenary Celebration of the Baptist Missionary Society, 1892–3. Edited by John Brown Myers. London: Printed by Alexander and Shepheard for the Baptist Missionary Society, 1893.
Chatterjee, Sunil Kumar. *Hannah Marshman: The First Woman Missionary in India.* Sheoraphuli, Hoogly District, West Bengal: Sri Sunil Chatterjee, 1987.
Cox, F. A. *History of the Baptist Missionary Society from 1792 to 1842.* London: T. Ward, 1842.
Culross, James. *Founders and Pioneers of Modern Missions.* Northampton: Taylor and Son, 1899.
Dietrick, Ronald B. "The Man the Church Forgot: John Thomas." In *The Man the Church Forgot: And Other Early Missionaries Who Made a Difference*, 21–48. Maitland, FL: Xulon Press, 2012. http://www.xulonpress.com/bookstore/.
George, Timothy. *Faithful Witness: The Life and Mission of William Carey.* Birmingham, AL: New Hope, 1991.
Lewis, C. B. *The Life of John Thomas: Surgeon of the Earl of Oxford East Indiaman, and First Baptist Missionary to Bengal.* London: Macmillan and Co., 1873.
Marshman, John Clark. *The Life and Times of Carey, Marshman, and Ward.* London: Longman, Brown, Green, Longmans, and Roberts, 2 vols. 1859.
Payne, Ernest A. *The First Generation: Early Leaders of the Baptist Missionary Society in England and India.* London: Carey Press, 1936.
Pease, Paul. *Travel with William Carey.* Leominster: Day One, 2005.
Smith, A. Christopher. "William Ward (1769–1832)." In *The British Particular Baptists 1638–1910*, edited by Michael A. G. Haykin, 2:254–71. Springfield, MO: Particular Baptist Press, 2000.

———. "Joshua (1768–1837) and Hannah Marshman (1767–1847)." In *The British Particular Baptists 1638–1910*, edited by Michael A. G. Haykin, 2:236–53. Springfield, MO: Particular Baptist Press, 2000.

Smith, George. *The Life of William Carey, D. D. Shoemaker and Missionary*. London: John Murray, 1885.

Stennett, Samuel. *Memoirs of the Life of the Rev. William Ward*. London: Printed by J. Haddon, 1825.

Taylor, John. *Historical Sketches of the Congregations of Protestant Dissenters in Northamptonshire, 1700–1800*. Northampton: The Dryden Press, Taylor and Son, 1885.

Tippleston, Dorothy. *William Carey and Hackleton Baptist Church*. Northampton: Printed by Billingham and Son, 1955.

Chapter 11

Charles Spurgeon: His Life and Ministry

---※---

Early Years, Conversion, and Initial Ministries

Charles Spurgeon (1834–92)[800] was born in Kelvedon (Essex), England, on June 19, ten days after the Baptist missionary, William Carey (1761–1834), died in India. Charles was the eldest son of John Spurgeon (1810–1902), pastor of an Independent, Congregational church in Tollesbury, near Colchester (Essex), and later the pastor of a similar church in Cranbrook (Kent).[801]

---

[800] Valuable sources include Arnold Dallimore, *Spurgeon* (Chicago: Moody Press, 1984); Eric Hayden, *The Unforgettable Spurgeon* (Greenville, SC: Emerald House Group, 1997); Heinz Dschankilic, "Charles Haddon Spurgeon (1834–1892)," in *The British Particular Baptists 1638–1910*, ed. Michael A. G. Haykin (Springfield, MO: Particular Baptist Press, 2003), 3:260–77; Iain H. Murray, *The Forgotten Spurgeon* (London: Banner of Truth Trust, 1966); idem, *Spurgeon v. Hyper-Calvinism: The Battle for Gospel Preaching* (Edinburgh: Banner of Truth Trust, 2000); Craig Skinner, *Spurgeon & Son: The Forgotten Story of Thomas Spurgeon and His Famous Father, Charles Haddon Spurgeon* (1984; repr., Grand Rapids: Kregel, 1999); Elizabeth Ruth Skoglund, *Bright Days, Dark Nights: With Charles Spurgeon in Triumph over Emotional Pain* (Grand Rapids: Baker, 2000); Don Theobald, "Susannah Spurgeon (1832–1902)," in *The British Particular Baptists 1638–1910*, ed. Michael A. G. Haykin, 3:278–94; and http://www.spurgeon.org/mainpage.htm.

[801] Occasionally, during his childhood years, Charles lived with his grandfather, James Spurgeon (1776–1864), pastor of an Independent-Congregational church in Stambourne, Essex.

Charles received his basic education at Colchester, Maidstone (Kent), and Newmarket (Cambridgeshire), where he worked as tutor while continuing his study of philosophy and mastering Latin, Greek, and French.

Spurgeon became a Christian during his Newmarket days, when his father was still serving the Tollesbury pastorate. Charles's conversion occurred on Sunday, January 6, 1850, while he was back at home in Colchester for Christmas holidays. Already under conviction for the sins of his youth, fifteen-year-old Spurgeon rose early that morning to read his Bible and pray. Later in the morning, in a heavy snowfall, he set out looking for a church that his mother had recommended. The blinding snow compelled him to turn down a side street, where he noticed a Primitive Methodist Church, in Artillery Street. Charles took refuge inside this little chapel. Although the storm had prevented the minister from being there, twelve to fifteen persons arrived. Soon, a lay-member entered the pulpit and announced his text. Spurgeon recalls the scene:

> Blessed be God for that poor local preacher. He read his Text. It was as much as he could do. The text was [Isaiah 45:22], "Look unto me and be ye saved all the ends of the earth [for I am God, and there is none else]." He was an ignorant man, he could not say much; he was obliged to keep to his text. Thank God for that. He began, "*Look*, that is not hard work. You need not lift your hand; you do not want to lift your finger. *Look*, a fool can do that. It does not need a wise man to look. A child can do that. It don't need to be full-grown to use your eyes. *Look*, a poor man may do that, no need of riches to look. *Look*, how simple; how simple." Then he went on, "Look unto Me. Do not look to yourselves, but look to me, that is, Christ.... I am sweating great drops of blood for you; look unto *me*, I am scourged and spit upon; I am nailed to the cross, I die, I am buried, I rise and ascend, I am pleading before the Father's throne, and all this for you." Now that simple way of putting the gospel had enlisted my attention, and a ray of light had poured into my heart. Stooping down, he looked under the

gallery and said, "Young man, you are very miserable." So, I was, but I had not been accustomed to be addressed in that way. "Ah," he said, "and you will always be miserable if you don't do as my text tells you; that is, look unto Christ." And then he called out, with all his might, "Young man, look; in God's name look, and look now!" I did look, blessed be God! I know I looked, then and there; and he who but that minute ago had been near despair, had the fullness of joy and hope; and in that instant, he who was ready to destroy himself could have stood up there and then to "Sing of him, whose pardoning blood had washed sins away."[802]

On May 3, 1850, Spurgeon walked eight miles to Isleham, for a Baptist pastor to immerse him in the River Lark. Back in Newmarket, he would make time in his schedule to distribute tracts, by visiting an average of seventy homes every Saturday afternoon. In August 1850, he moved to a Cambridge school, operated by E. S. Leeding, and worked without salary as a tutor and as assistant to the headmaster. Leeding was fine-tuning Spurgeon's gifts for things to come. Here in Cambridge, Spurgeon joined St. Andrew's Street Baptist Church and quickly became active in their Sunday school outreach. He joined the Lay Preachers' Association and began preaching on Sundays in surrounding villages. In the tiny village of Teversham, he preached his first sermon, at the age of sixteen. In January 1852, he accepted the pulpit of the Baptist chapel in the small village of Waterbeach. Every weekend, he walked six miles from

---

[802] Spurgeon, "Temple Glories" (Sermon 375, delivered on Sunday evening, March 31, 1861), in *Metropolitan Tabernacle Pulpit* (1862; repr., Pasadena, TX: Pilgrim Publications, 1969), 7:224. The best firsthand sources on Spurgeon's life include C. H. *Spurgeon's Autobiography 1834–1854*, vol. 1 (London: Passmore and Alabaster, 1897); idem, C. H. *Spurgeon's Autobiography 1854–1860*, vol. 2 (London: Passmore and Alabaster, 1898); idem, *C. H. Spurgeon's Autobiography 1856–1878*, vol. 3 (London: Passmore and Alabaster, 1899); idem, *C. H. Spurgeon's Autobiography 1878–1892*, vol. 4 (Chicago: Curts and Jennings, 1900). After Spurgeon's death, his private secretary, J. W. Harrald, and Mrs. Spurgeon compiled all four volumes of the *Autobiography* from her husband's diary, letters, and records.

Cambridge to Waterbeach; the people joyfully accepted him. With villagers crowding in to hear "the boy preacher," attendance rapidly soared from forty to a hundred.

New Park Street Baptist Church
Spurgeon's Predecessors, with Special Notice of John Rippon

The history of the New Park Street Baptist Church began in a home on Tooley Street, Southwark, where William Rider, in ca. 1653, organized a General Baptist church and served its pastorate until ca. 1665, the time of his decease. The tiny congregation was without a pastor, until 1668, when they ordained Benjamin Keach (1640–1704). Keach and his flock soon reorganized themselves into a Particular Baptist Church, and, in 1672, they erected a chapel on Goat Street, Horsleydown, in Southwark. Keach's son-in-law, Benjamin Stinton, succeeded him, and, when he died at the age of forty-two, John Gill became the fourth pastor. During Gill's pastorate, the congregation, in 1757, built a new chapel on Carter Lane, off Tooley Street.[803] John Rippon became Gill's successor. In 1830, six years prior to Rippon's death, Carter Lane chapel suffered demolition, to make room for wider access to nearby London Bridge. Three years later, the congregation moved into their new chapel on New Park Street. As the church's fifth pastor, Rippon would make significant contributions toward setting the stage for the church's ninth pastor, Charles Spurgeon, and for the future of English Baptists. We will take a panoramic view of Rippon's influence.

Born of Baptist parents, at Tiverton (Devonshire), John Rippon (1751–1836)[804] grew up in a devout Christian home and

---

[803] Carter Lane connects with St. Olave's Street, near London Bridge, Southwark.

[804] The best sources for John Rippon include Ken R. Manley, *'Redeeming Love Proclaim': John Rippon and the Baptists*, vol. 12 of the series, Studies in Baptist History and Thought (2004; repr., Eugene, OR: Wipf and Stock, 2006); John Andrew Jones, ed., *Bunhill Memorials: Sacred Reminiscences of Three Hundred Ministers and Other Persons of Note, Who Are Buried in Bunhill Fields, of Every Denomination, with the Inscriptions on Their Tombs and Gravestones, and Other Historical Information Respecting Them, from*

received three years of training at Bristol Baptist Academy.[805] As an evangelical Calvinist, he served the Carter Lane pastorate from 1773 to the end of his life. He wrote a laudatory memoir of his predecessor John Gill.[806] From 1790 to 1802, Rippon edited the *Baptist Annual Register*, the first periodical to chronicle Particular Baptist involvement in missions and revivals in England and America, along with the BMS outreach in India and Sierra Leone. Like many British Baptists, Rippon supported the Americans in their War of Independence. In 1773, John Collett Ryland Sr. (1723-92), in a letter to President James Manning, at the Baptist College of Rhode Island (later Brown University), includes John Rippon in a list of the twenty-one Baptist ministers in England who could read the Greek New Testament.[807] In 1792, the College of Rhode Island conferred upon Rippon an honorary Doctor of Divinity degree. In 1813, Rippon became the first chairman of the Baptist Union of Great Britain. With help from his son, John Jr., Rippon copied from the official Register all the "nearly forty thousand names" of those interred in Bunhill Fields graveyard, from 1713 (where the records began) to the year 1790. When John Jr. brought the list up to the year 1826, there were six handwritten volumes. Tediously copying the tombstone inscriptions, Rippon and his son filled six additional manuscript volumes. For genealogical research, the College of Herald's Library, in London, still utilizes the twelve volumes.[808] One day, two visitors in

---

Authentic Sources (London: James Paul, 1849), 232-36; Charles Spurgeon, "John Rippon, D. D.," in *The Metropolitan Tabernacle: Its History and Work* (London: Passmore and Alabaster, 1876), 48-54; and Sharon James, "John Rippon (1751-1836)," in *The British Particular Baptists 1638-1910*, ed. Michael A. G. Haykin, 2:56-75.

[805] See also John Rippon, *A Brief Essay towards an History of the Baptist Academy at Bristol*, "read before the Bristol Education Society at their anniversary meeting in Broadmead, August 26, 1795" (London: Sold by Dilly and Button, 1796).

[806] John Rippon, *A Brief Memoir of the Life and Writings of the Late Rev. John Gill, D. D.* (London: John Bennett, 1838).

[807] Reuben Aldridge Guild, *Early History of Brown University: Including the Life, Times, and Correspondence of President Manning, 1756-1791* (Providence, RI: Snow and Farnham, 1897), 245.

[808] Manley, *'Redeeming Love Proclaim': John Rippon and the Baptists*, 211-14;

Bunhill Fields came upon Mr. Rippon at his work. One of them recorded the scene in her diary:

> Mr. Rippon ... was laid down upon his side between two graves, and writing out the epitaphs word for word. He had an ink-horn in his button-hole, and a pen and book. He tells us that he has taken most of the old inscriptions, and that he will, if God be pleased to spare his days, do all, notwithstanding it is a grievous labor, and the writing is hard to make out by reason of the oldness of the cutting in some, and defacings of other stones. It is a labor of love to him, and when he is gathered to his fathers, I hope someone will go on with the work.[809]

Rippon was also a well-known hymn writer, with his *Selection of Hymns* (1787) appearing in twenty-seven editions during his lifetime.[810] Until the publication of Charles Spurgeon's *Our Own Hymnbook* (1866), the Metropolitan Tabernacle used Rippon's *Selection*. After sixty-three years as a pastor, John Rippon died on December 17, 1836, well into the eighty-sixth year of his life. His remains rest in Bunhill Fields.

T. G. Crippen, ed., "The Tombs in Bunhill Fields," in *Transactions of Congregational Historical Society* 4, no. 6 (September 1910): 347–63; *The Official Guide to Bunhill Fields* (London: Corporation of London, 1991), 11, 25–26. In 1892, George Gatfield reported "Collections Relating to the Dissenters' Burial-ground at Bunhill Fields, London, by John Rippon, in 11 volumes, Brit. Mus. Add. MSS. 28513–28523," in *Guide to Printed Books and Manuscripts Relating to English and Foreign Heraldry and Genealogy* (London: Mitchell and Hughes, 1892), 158.

[809] *History of the Bunhill Fields Burial Ground: With Some of the Principal Inscriptions*, "printed by order of the City Lands Committee of the Corporation of London," with content contributions by Charles Reed, Chairman of the Preservations Committee (London: Charles Skipper and East, Printers, 1893), 22, 58–59.

[810] Rippon was the foremost authority in his day on the hymns of Isaac Watts. See Rippon, *A Selection of Hymns*, "from the best authors, intended to be an Appendix to Dr. Watts's Psalms and Hymns" (Burlington, England: Printed by S. C. Ustick, 1801).

Spurgeon's Ministry at New Park Street

In April 1854, nineteen-year-old Charles Spurgeon accepted the pastorate of the New Park Street Church. His ministry here in the capital city would last thirty-eight years, to the time of his death. In 1855, the church commenced the weekly publication of his sermons—eventually appearing in twenty-nine languages across the globe. On January 8, 1856, he married Susannah Thompson, the brightest human encouragement of his life. Spurgeon's ministry would never be without challenge and opposition. As the largest building of London's 113 Baptist churches, New Park Street was capable of seating twelve hundred persons. When Spurgeon arrived, this area on the south bank of the Thames had become one of the worst places in the city, and the congregation had dwindled to two hundred persons. Despite new extensions to the building, the structure remained utterly inadequate for the crowds arriving to hear the future "Prince of Preachers." Having no formal college training, Spurgeon read an average of six books a week, expanding his knowledge in a broad range of categories, including not only theology and biblical commentaries, but also science, history, biographies, and Shakespearean plays. He read Foxe's *Book of Martyrs* multiple times and Bunyan's *Pilgrim Progress* more than a hundred times. Above all else, Spurgeon was a theologian, with the ability to discern between biblical truth and subtle nuances of false doctrine.

The Surrey Gardens Music Hall Incident (1856)

In 1855, the church rented Exeter Hall (Strand), with its 4,500 seats, for their Sunday services, but even this could not accommodate the crowds. The following year, they rented the newly-built Surrey Gardens Music Hall (Walworth), with its ten thousand seats.[811] On opening night, on October 19, 1856,

---

[811] The Surrey Gardens Music Hall was built in 1856 in the Surrey Zoological Gardens. It would suffer greatly from a fire in 1861 and was rebuilt the same year. In 1872, it was demolished and replaced with small, terraced houses. See Ben Weinreb and Christopher Hibbert, eds., *The London Encyclopedia* (1983; repr., Bethesda, MD: Adler and Adler Publishers, 1986), 847.

an estimated crowd of twelve thousand filled every seat and packed every aisle and stairway, as ten thousand others stood outside, hoping to hear the preacher's voice. Following an opening prayer, hymn, and Scripture reading, Spurgeon, almost overwhelmed at the sight of the vast audience, was beginning to pray, just prior to his message, when a voice from the galleries shouted, "FIRE!" There was no fire, but another adversary on the ground floor cried out, "The galleries are falling!" A third voice quickly yelled, "The whole place is collapsing!" Panic swept over the terrified assembly, as many stumbled and fell on top of one another on the staircase, breaking down the railings. Seven persons died, twenty-eight hospitalized, and many more suffered injuries. Charles Spurgeon was only twenty-two years old. He later recalls, "Perhaps never soul went so near the burning furnace of insanity, and yet came away unharmed."[812] Though Spurgeon would carry this grief to the grave, the Lord provided strength and encouragement. Just one month earlier, Susannah had given birth to twin sons, Thomas and Charles. During the boys' teenage years, Spurgeon would have the joy of baptizing them upon their professions of faith. Both would attend their father's Pastors' College, established in 1856–57 and founded upon the model of Bristol Baptist College. Both sons would become pastors, and both would support their father in every battle. Using admission tickets for extra security, Spurgeon would hold Sunday morning services at the Music Hall until the Metropolitan Tabernacle was built. Meanwhile, an unexpected crisis gripped the nation.

The National Humiliation in London's Crystal Palace (1857)

To gain their independence from England, in 1857, India carried out a massacre, killing 2,163 British military officers. The mutiny resulted in the proclamation of a National Fast Day on Wednesday, October 7, "to obtain pardon of our sins."[813]

---

[812] In Darrell W. Amundsen, "The Anguish and Agonies of Charles Spurgeon," *Christian History and Biography* (January 1, 1991): 23.
[813] Spurgeon, "Fast-Day Service," held at the Crystal Palace, Sydenham, on

The day would conclude with an evening service of National Humiliation, in London's Crystal Palace (Sydenham).[814] The appointed speaker was Charles Spurgeon, who, in behalf of his country, would express grief over England's mistreatment of India and over the massacre. A day or two prior to the event, Spurgeon entered the Crystal Palace to test its acoustics and to determine the best location for the platform. He repeatedly cried, "Behold the Lamb of God, which taketh away the sin of the world" (John 1:29*b*). Later, he would learn that a lone worker, high up in one of the galleries, had heard those words as "a message from heaven." Smitten with conviction, the worker had abandoned his tools and gone to his home where, after "a season of spiritual struggle," he repented of his sins and trusted Christ as his Lord and Savior. Meanwhile, as the crowds poured into Crystal Palace, the turnstiles counted 23,654 persons—reported to be the largest indoor congregation ever addressed by a preacher.

The Years at Metropolitan Tabernacle

When the Prayer Meeting Awakening crested in the city of London, in 1859, Spurgeon's congregation had already begun construction on the Metropolitan Tabernacle, at the junction of Elephant and Castle Streets (Southwark). At the groundbreaking ceremony, Spurgeon sealed three items under the cornerstone: A copy of the Scriptures, Rippon's *Hymns*, and the Second London Confession.[815] A Grecian-style building, with six massive Corinthian columns forming an imposing façade and porch, the Tabernacle was the largest separatist church in the world. From its opening service, on Monday afternoon March 25, 1861, to the time of Spurgeon's death—thirty-one years later—its attendance averaged five thousand persons every Sunday, both morning and evening. Emerging from

---

Wednesday, October 7, 1857 (New York: Sheldon, Blakeman, and Co., 1857), title page.

[814] A fire leveled the Crystal Palace in 1936. Its concrete foundation is the only thing that remains of the original building. Nearby, there is a sports stadium called "Crystal Palace."

[815] *The Autobiography of C. H. Spurgeon 1854–1860*, 2:160.

all manner of life, the crowds poured in—from the common people to nobility—from factory workers to the Prime Minister. The Tabernacle's multiple ministries continued non-stop, establishing mission stations across London and planting Baptist churches throughout the country. Spurgeon's multifaceted ministry seems endless. It included the weekly *Sword and Trowel* magazine (est. 1865),[816] the Colportage Association for the spread of wholesome literature (1866), the Stockwell Boys' orphanage (1867), the almshouses (1868), the first building for the Pastors' College (1873), the inauguration of Mrs. Spurgeon's Book Fund for young ministers (1875), and the girls' orphanage (1879). To provide help for their pastor, the congregation, in 1868, appointed Spurgeon's brother, James, as "co-pastor." The congregation made it clear from the beginning, however, that James would not inherit succession to the Tabernacle's pastorate. James would undertake much of the administrative work and some outreach ministries.

The New Connection

In his final years, C. H. Spurgeon would witness, within England's Baptist churches, a doctrinal departure, or "Down Grade," from the cardinal doctrines of the Christian faith. Baptist apostasy had originated among the General Baptists. Dan Taylor (1738-1816), serving as a representative at the

---

[816] Of approximately 140 titles, Spurgeon's most important writings include, *The New Park Street Pulpit,* 6 vols. (London: Passmore and Alabaster, 1855-60); idem, *Metropolitan Tabernacle Pulpit,* 57 vols. (London: Passmore and Alabaster, 1861-1917); idem, *The Metropolitan Tabernacle: Its History and Work* (1876); idem, *The "Down Grade" Controversy: Collected Materials Which Reveal the Viewpoint of the Late Charles Haddon Spurgeon,* compiled by the publisher (Pasadena, TX: Pilgrim Publications, n.d.). Spurgeon's *Lectures to My Students,* providing wisdom on the work of the ministry, originated as a three-volume set. There have been many editions. His *Treasury of David* is a commentary on the Psalms. It originated in weekly installments over a twenty-year span and later appeared as a seven-volume set. There have been multiple editions. From 1865 to 1892, Spurgeon produced his monthly magazine *The Sword and the Trowel: A Record of Combat with Sin and of Labor for the Lord.* See also http://pilgrimpublications.auctivacommerce.com/Default.aspx.

General Baptist Assembly, during 1767-69, had become aware of the Unitarianism and spiritual deadness among these Baptists. In 1770, Taylor had led seven churches, consisting of about a thousand members, to separate from the old General Baptist denomination, and to organize into "The New Connection of General Baptists." Taylor was the leading voice of the New Connection until his death in 1816. After 1775, however, no member was required to subscribe to Taylor's doctrinal Articles of Religion. The only requirement for new members was an oral testimony of salvation. The General Baptist denomination, or "Old Connection," had long fallen into disarray, and, even prior to Spurgeon's day, the compromised New Connection had infiltrated the Particular Baptist movement with voices of apostasy.

The Emergence and Doctrinal Decline of the Baptist Union

The Baptist Union of Great Britain (est. 1813), under the leadership of Joseph Ivimey (1773-1834) and John Rippon (1751-1836), had emerged as a sound, voluntary association of Particular Baptist churches. With Rippon as its first chairman the Baptist Union's theological foundations included the immediate imputation of sin, unconditional election, limited atonement, the imputed righteousness of Christ, justification by faith, efficacious grace in regeneration, final perseverance of all true believers, the resurrection of the dead, future judgment, the eternal bliss of the righteous, and the eternal misery of the impenitent. In 1832, however, the Particular Baptists changed the Constitution of the Baptist Union to allow New Connection churches into its membership. Ivimey, now at sixty years of age, and Rippon, the eighty-one-year-old moderator, would both be with the Lord within the next four years. Rippon's advancing senility prevented him from discerning the theological dangers at hand.[817] Reducing its doctrinal statement to a formula palatable to liberals, the Union's requirement for membership was a verbal agreement with "the sentiments usually denominated

---

[817] Manley, *'Redeeming Love Proclaim': John Rippon and the Baptists*, 78, 271.

evangelical."[818] From that time forward, the Baptist Union had no doctrinal foundation. In 1842, J. G. Pike, a General Baptist, was the president of the Baptist Union. Another General Baptist, Jabez Burns, occupied the presidential chair in 1850. In 1873, with increasing centralization of Union control over its agencies, Union leaders repealed its membership requirement of agreeing with "evangelical sentiments." Such action left only one requirement: Baptism by immersion.[819] Long gone were the great seasons of revival, as increasing numbers of non-evangelical, New Connection churches began flooding the Union's membership.[820]

Liberalism within the New Connection had already destroyed the missionary emphasis of its founder, especially after the publication of Charles Darwin's *Origin of Species* (1859),[821] which challenged the biblical account of man's origin. Four months later, there appeared seven popular *Essays and Reviews* (1860),[822] authored by six Church of England clergymen and a parishioner. Collectively, these works favored higher criticism and assaulted the integrity of Scripture. Equally significant was the appearance of Darwin's *The Descent of Man* (1871),[823] which challenged the biblical account of the origin and nature of sin. Even popular literature, such as the *Christian*

---

[818] Ernest A. Payne, *The Baptist Union: A Short History* (London: The Carey Kingsgate Press, 1959), 61. In 1830, "the New Connection was calculated to embrace about 11,000 members in 109 churches with 82 full-time ministers." See J. H. Y. Briggs, "Evangelical Ecumenism: The Amalgamation of General and Particular Baptists in 1891: Part I," *Baptist Quarterly* 34, no. 3 (July 1991): 103.

[819] Payne, *The Baptist Union,* 109.

[820] By 1864, the New Connection had 21,000 members in about 150 churches served by about a hundred clergy. In 1862, however, baptisms and membership began a rapid decline. J. H. Y. Briggs, "Evangelical Ecumenism: The Amalgamation of General and Particular Baptists in 1891: Part II," *Baptist Quarterly* 34, no. 4 (October 1991): 161–62.

[821] Charles Darwin's *On the Origin of Species by Means of Natural Selection, or the Preservation of Favored Races in the Struggle for Life* (London: John Murray, 1859).

[822] *Essays and Reviews,* 2nd ed. (London: John W. Parker and Son, 1860).

[823] Charles Darwin, *The Descent of Man, and Selection in Relation to Sex* (London: John Murray, 1871).

World Magazine, helped to spread the message of modernism and the social gospel. Such an avalanche of literature would have its effects on the New Connection. Throughout the second half of the nineteenth century, the New Connection included Universalists, such as Samuel Cox (1826-93), who sought to assure his readers that all humanity would ultimately receive salvation. In his *Salvator Mundi: Or is Christ the Savior of All Men?* (1877), Cox argues adamantly against the reality of hell and eternal punishment.[824] Cox was pastor of the Mansfield Road Baptist Church, Nottingham (1863-88). As editor of the monthly magazine *The Expositor*, Cox radically influenced a new generation of New Connection Baptists.[825]

Meanwhile, thinly veiled elements of biblical criticism had begun making inroads into New Connection colleges. This divided the academic community between traditional conservatives on one side and "progressives," such as William Underwood and Thomas Goadby on the other side. Underwood was principal of the General Baptist College at Chilwell (1857-73), and Goadby was principal of the Midland College (1873-89). While studying in German universities Underwood and Goadby had acquired an addictive sympathy toward higher criticism of the Bible. While Underwood took a "moderate liberal" stance, Goadby took a carefully nuanced, but far more radical, stance. Goadby urged his students and his denomination that the modern spirit of higher criticism could pose no threat, if Christians would base their core beliefs on life and experience rather than on Scripture and creeds. Goadby asserted, "The doctrines and truths of Christianity belong to the sphere of the religious life and to the experience of the spirit within us .... Religious doctrine ... can be verified only in the life and experience."[826] Also contributing to the theological

---

[824] Samuel Cox, *Salvator Mundi: Or is Christ the Savior of All Men?* 4th ed. (New York: E. P. Dutton, 1878); idem, *The Larger Hope: A Sequel to Salvator Mundi* (London: Kegan Paul, Trench and Co., 1883).

[825] E.g., Samuel Cox, "Dives and Lazarus," in *Expositions*, 2nd ed. (London: T. Fisher Unwin, 1885), 155-69.

[826] Thomas Goadby, "Christian Theology and the Modern Spirit," in *The General Baptist Magazine for 1879*, ed. John Clifford (London: E. Marlborough and Co., 1879), 168 (161-69).

demise, *The General Baptist Magazine*, edited by John Clifford, carried innovative articles such as those by Charles Ford of the Hyson Green Church, Nottingham. Describing himself as a "Liberal Orthodox," Ford denied the verbal inspiration of the Bible and rejected eternal punishment.[827]

The Down Grade Controversy and Spurgeon's Final Years

Such was the scenario that set the stage for the "Down Grade Controversy" (1887–1892), a conflict that would engage Charles Spurgeon for the remainder of his life. Keenly aware of the embedded liberalism within both the Baptist Union and the Baptist Missionary Society, Spurgeon, since 1883, had declined all speaking invitations from both groups.[828] For years, he had warned of the constant belittling and downgrading of the fundamentals of the faith. With much of his documentation residing in private, confidential correspondence, Spurgeon avoided naming names. He refused to allow the conflict to degenerate into a personality contest.[829] In March and April 1887, his *Sword and the Trowel* magazine published two anonymous,[830] pungent articles titled, "The Down Grade," which gave the controversy its name. The articles warned of apostasy within the New Connection and the Baptist Union.

---

[827] See F. M. W. Harrison, "The Nottinghamshire Baptists: Church Relations, Social Composition, Finance, Theology," *Baptist Quarterly* 26, no. 4 (October 1975): 186; 169–90. Meanwhile, the number of baptisms in the New Connection was still declining, as the following three years illustrate. 1882: 1542; 1883: 1344; and 1884: 1291. See also Briggs, "Evangelical Ecumenism: The Amalgamation of General and Particular Baptists in 1891: Part II," 167–68.

[828] Ernest A. Payne, "The Down Grade Controversy: A Postscript," *Baptist Quarterly* 28, no. 4. (October 1979): 148; 146–58.

[829] Mark Hopkins, "Spurgeon's Opponents in the Downgrade Controversy," *Baptist Quarterly* 32, no. 6 (April 1988): 274–94; idem, "The Down Grade Controversy: New Evidence," *Baptist Quarterly* 35, no. 6 (April 1994): 262–78.

[830] Robert Shindler, a Baptist pastor and close friend of Spurgeon, authored the two articles in *The Sword and the Trowel*, March and April 1887. See the Spurgeon Archive, at http://www.romans45.org/spurgeon/s_and_t/dg01.htm.

In full agreement with the two initial *Sword and Trowel* articles, Spurgeon authored the remainder of the series. It is obvious, wrote Spurgeon, "The Atonement is scouted, the inspiration of Scripture is derided, the Holy Spirit is degraded into an influence, the punishment of sin is turned into fiction, and the resurrection into a myth, and yet these enemies of our faith expect us to call them brethren and maintain a confederacy with them!"[831] It was obvious to anyone acquainted with the two organizations that an official merger of the Connection with the Union was now at hand. Already, in 1887, John Clifford (1836–1923), a liberal General Baptist, was vice-president of the Union. Spurgeon requested that the Union adopt a substantive creed and hold members accountable to its content. The Union refused. The Council would make it clear that, no matter how much documentation of liberalism they might receive, there would be no doctrinal standard for examining anyone's teachings.

On October 28, 1887, Spurgeon registered the official withdrawal of the Metropolitan Tabernacle from the Baptist Union. As Spurgeon expresses it, "Believers in Christ's atonement are now in declared religious union with those who make light of it; believers in Holy Scripture are in confederacy with those who deny plenary inspiration; those who hold evangelical doctrine are in open alliance with those who call the fall a fable." Such believers, Spurgeon adds, are in alliance with "those who deny the personality of the Holy Spirit, who call justification by faith immoral, and hold that there is another probation after death, and a future restitution for the lost." Facing us now, says Spurgeon is "the wretched spectacle of professedly orthodox Christians publicly avowing their union with those who deny the faith, and scarcely concealing their contempt for those who cannot be guilty of such gross disloyalty to Christ. To be very plain," says Spurgeon, "We are unable to call these things Christian Unions, [as] they begin to look like Confederacies in Evil…. Fellowship with known and vital error is participation in sin."[832]

---

[831] Spurgeon, "Another Word Concerning the Down-Grade," in *The Sword and the Trowel* (August 1887): 29. This also appears in *The "Down Grade" Controversy: Collected Materials Which Reveal the Viewpoint of the Late Charles Haddon Spurgeon*, 17.

[832] Spurgeon, "A Fragment upon the Down-Grade Controversy," in *The*

In a meeting on January 18, 1888, the Baptist Union Council discussed Spurgeon's withdrawal and voted to censure him, by passing a resolution of condemnation against him and his separatist position.[833] On April 23, 1888, Union president, John Clifford, chaired a full assembly that overflowed London's City Temple.[834] By a vote of 2000 to 7,[835] the cheering crowd approved a Declaratory Statement that offered no restraint upon the doctrinal teachings of its churches and institutions. The Statement listed six general topics, but provided "no doctrinal basis except the belief that 'the immersion of believers is the only Christian baptism.'"[836] The Statement's over-generalization rendered its list of topics accessory to a wide range of interpretation. For instance, its expression "justification by faith" omits the word *alone* and offers nothing definitive.[837] The Statement includes nothing on the Trinity, the inerrancy of Scripture, the Virgin Birth, or even the vicarious atonement of Christ. The vote of the Assembly constituted a public

---

Sword and the Trowel (November 1887): 558–59; and *The "Down Grade" Controversy: Collected Materials Which Reveal the Viewpoint of the Late Charles Haddon Spurgeon*, 34–35.

[833] Spurgeon, "The Baptist Union Censure," in *The Sword and the Trowel* (February 1888): 81–83; and *The "Down Grade" Controversy: Collected Materials Which Reveal the Viewpoint of the Late Charles Haddon Spurgeon*, 44–46.

[834] The City Temple was the Congregational church, led by Joseph Parker, a critic of Spurgeon.

[835] E. J. Poole-Connor, *Evangelicalism in England*, 2nd ed. (Worthing, England, 1966), 242.

[836] Spurgeon, "The Baptist Union Censure," in *The Sword and the Trowel* (February 1888): 81; and *The "Down Grade" Controversy: Collected Materials Which Reveal the Viewpoint of the Late Charles Haddon Spurgeon*, 44.

[837] The six topics are: (1) the divine inspiration and authority of the Holy Scriptures; (2) the fallen and sinful state of man; (3) the person and work of Jesus Christ; (4) justification by faith; (5) the work of the Holy Spirit; and (6) the resurrection and the judgment at the last day. Added to the list is a statement of non-endorsement: "It should be stated, as an historical fact, that there have been brethren in the Union, working cordially with it, who, while reverently bowing to the authority of Holy Scripture, and rejecting dogmas of Purgatory and Unitarianism, have not held the common interpretation of these words of our Lord." See Payne, *The Baptist Union*, 140.

condemnation upon Spurgeon. Henry Oakley, who would soon separate from the Union, was present at the Assembly. He describes the unforgettable scene when Bible critic Charles Williams made the motion (seconded by James Spurgeon) to censure Charles Spurgeon:

> I was present at the City Temple when the motion was moved, seconded, and carried. Possibly the City Temple was as full as it could be. I was there very early, but found only a "standing seat" in the aisle of the back of the gallery. I listened to the speeches. The only one of which I have any distinct remembrance was that of Mr. Charles Williams. He quoted Tennyson in favor of a liberal theology.... The moment of voting came.... When the motion of censure was put a forest of hands went up. "Against," called the chairman, Dr. John Clifford. I did not see any hands, but history records there were *seven*.... The vast assembly broke into tumultuous cheering, and cheering, and cheering yet. From some of the older men their pent-up hostility found vent; from many of the younger men wild resistance of "any obscurantist trammels," [meaning Spurgeon's preaching] broke loose. It was a strange scene. I viewed it almost with tears. I stood near a "Spurgeon's man," whom I knew very well. Mr. Spurgeon had welcomed him from a very lowly position. He went wild almost with delight at this censure of his great and generous master. I say it was a strange scene, that that vast assembly should be so outrageously delighted at the condemnation of the greatest, noblest, and grandest leader of their faith.[838]

While openly claiming the title *evangelical*, John Clifford, pastor of the Westbourne Park Baptist Church (New Connection),[839] was liberal in his view of Scripture.[840] He was

---

[838] Poole-Connor, *Evangelicalism in England*, 247–48.
[839] Clifford had earlier served the pastorate of London's Praed Street Baptist Church, Paddington. He would become the first president of the Baptist World Alliance (1905–11) and the Baptist Union would become one of its members.
[840] Willis B. Glover, *Evangelical Nonconformists and Higher Criticism in the*

clearly "of radical social and political sympathies."[841] His ecumenical mindset was encouraging the practice of open Communion and open membership as the norm in Baptist churches. In 1933, E. J. Poole-Connor would observe, "What Mr. Spurgeon saw as a stream now runs at full flood."[842] Under Clifford's direction, the New Connection merged with the Baptist Union in 1891. No doctrinal confession was required. The labels *Particular* and *General* forever disappeared. Among Clifford's supporters was the well-known, Alexander Maclaren (1826–1910), pastor of Union Chapel, Manchester. Like Clifford, Maclaren rejected the Bible's inerrancy.[843]

Spurgeon had warned, "Assuredly the New Theology can do no good towards God or man.... If it were preached for a thousand years by all the most earnest men of the school, it would never renew a soul, nor overcome pride in a single human heart."[844] The following year (the year of Spurgeon's death), Union leaders welcomed the publication of John Clifford's new book, *The Inspiration and Authority of the Bible*, a non-stop attack against the verbal inspiration and inerrancy of the Scriptures.[845] The New Connection of Dan Taylor's bold independency had morphed into a Baptist Union of John Clifford's irenic ecumenicity. Spurgeon had often stressed that

---

Nineteenth Century (London: Independent Press, 1954), 173.

[841] Payne, *The Baptist Union,* 107–08; See also David Thompson, "John Clifford's Social Gospel," *Baptist Quarterly* 31, no. 5 (January 1986): 199–217; and W. S. Stroud, "John Clifford," *Baptist Quarterly* 6, no. 7 (July 1933): 304–11.

[842] E. J. Poole-Connor, "A Watchman's Warning," in *The Apostasy of English Nonconformity* (London: Thynne and Co., 1933), 28. For a vivid depiction of the ongoing apostasy within the Baptist Union well into the twentieth century, see Poole-Connor, *Evangelicalism in England*, 249–66.

[843] Glover, *Evangelical Nonconformists and Higher Criticism*, 173ff; and A. C. Underwood, *A History of the English Baptists* (London: The Baptist Union, 1947), 230ff. Underwood was writing as a voice of the Baptist Union. The evangelical, W. Y. Fullerton, who wrote biographies of Charles and Thomas Spurgeon, was also a friend of liberals and modernists. See E. J. Poole-Connor, *The Apostasy of English Nonconformity*, 18, 20–32, 45–56.

[844] Spurgeon, "Down-Grade Controversy," *The Sword and Trowel* (annual edition 1887): 2.

[845] Clifford, *The Inspiration and Authority of the Bible*, 2nd ed. (London: James Clarke and Co., 1895).

the Baptist battle was not between Calvinists and Arminians. The battle was between conservatives and liberals. Spurgeon had poignantly warned of the unsuspecting Presbyterians, who had been the first to fall into false doctrine:

> The Presbyterians were the first to get on the down line. They paid more attention to classical attainments and other branches of learning in their ministry than the Independents, while the Baptists had no academical institution of any kind. It would be an easy step in the wrong direction to pay increased attention to academical attainments in their ministers, and less to spiritual qualifications; and to set a higher value on scholarship and oratory, than on evangelical zeal and ability to rightly divide the word of truth.[846]

The Next Generation and Beyond

On May 17, 1891, Charles Spurgeon entered his pulpit, but he was too ill to preach. He preached his final sermon on the morning of June 7. In October, family and friends took him for his final time to Menton, on the French Riviera, along the Mediterranean coastline of the southeast corner of France. Spurgeon always loved this quiet retreat. In his Menton hotel room, on January 31, 1892, the fifty-seven-year-old Prince of Preachers passed into the presence of his Lord. The family transported his body back to London and buried his remains in West Norwood Cemetery. The Tabernacle's membership was 5,307 at the time.

Determined to remain in the Union, Charles Spurgeon's brother James resigned from the co-pastorate. During the

---

[846] Spurgeon, "The Down Grade," *The Sword and the Trowel* (March 1887): 123; also in *The "Down Grade" Controversy: Collected Materials Which Reveal the Viewpoint of the Late Charles Haddon Spurgeon*, 5. For more on Presbyterian and General Baptist Unitarianism, see Jerom Murch, *A History of the Presbyterian and General Baptist Churches in the West of England: With a Memoir of Some of Their Pastors* (London: R. Hunter, 1835); and *The Manchester Socinian Controversy* (London: C. J. Westley and G. Tyrrell for Francis Westley, 1825). An appendix to this work provides a list of the Unitarian chapels in England, Wales, and Scotland.

Down Grade Controversy, both of Spurgeon's sons faithfully supported him. The younger Charles had included his name among the separatist signatories of his father's "final manifesto," a powerful, 1891 conference message, titled "The Greatest Fight in the World."[847] For the rest of his life, Charles Jr. would faithfully serve a variety of ministries. Besides taking charge of the huge orphanage that his father had founded, Charles would take many invitations to preach the gospel and even to serve the pulpits of several local churches. Meanwhile, his brother Thomas, in New Zealand at the time, had also supported his father in every battle. Since neither of the sons offered to succeed to the Tabernacle's pastorate,[848] the American Fundamentalist Arthur Tappan (A. T.) Pierson (1837–1911) accepted an offer to serve the pulpit for about a year.[849] Then, Thomas Spurgeon, in 1893, left Auckland Baptist Tabernacle, in New Zealand, to accept the Metropolitan Tabernacle pulpit. He enjoyed a fruitful, fifteen-year pastorate, until 1908, when illness forced his resignation.[850] Another American Fundamentalist, A. C. Dixon (1854–1925), succeeded Thomas and served the pastorate until 1919, after the Great War.[851]

---

[847] First published in *The Sword and the Trowel*, August 1891, the sermon also appeared the next year: Charles H. Spurgeon, *The Greatest Fight in the World* (London: Passmore and Alabaster, 1892).

[848] See Eric Hayden, *The Spurgeon Family* (Pasadena, TX: Pilgrim Publications, 1993).

[849] The twenty pastors of the church, along with the dates of their pastorates, are as follows: William Rider (ca. 1653–65), Benjamin Keach (1668–1704), Benjamin Stinton (1704–18), John Gill (1720–71), John Rippon (1773–1836), Joseph Angus (1837–39), James Smith (1841–50), William Walters (1851–53), Charles Spurgeon (1854–92), Arthur Tappan Pierson (1891–93), Thomas Spurgeon (1893–1908), Archibald G. Brown (1908–11), Amzi Clarence (A. C.) Dixon (1911–19), Harry Tydeman Chilvers (1919–35), W. Graham Scroggie (1938–43), W. G. Channon (1944–49), Gerald B. Griffiths (1951–54), Eric W. Hayden (1956–62), Dennis Pascoe (1963–69), and Peter Masters (1970–present).

[850] Hayden, *The Spurgeon Family*; W. Y. Fullerton, *Thomas Spurgeon: A Biography* (London: Hodder and Stoughton, 1919).

[851] Craig Skinner, *Spurgeon and Son: The Forgotten Story of Thomas Spurgeon and His Famous Father, Charles Haddon Spurgeon* (Grand Rapids: Kregel, 1999), 193–222. This book has strong bias against the inerrancy of the original autographs of Scripture and against those who still teach it; e.g., pages 205ff.

Since 1861, three Tabernacles have occupied the site. The original, with seating space for five to six thousand, burned to the ground, in 1898, six years after Spurgeon's death and during Thomas Spurgeon's pastorate. Only the Corinthian columns, portico, and outer walls remained. The second Tabernacle could accommodate four thousand. In 1941, during the pastorate of W. Graham Scroggie, German bombs in the Nazi blitz demolished most of the building. Once again, only the portico and basement survived. In 1957, during Eric Hayden's pastorate, the church erected its third Tabernacle, retaining its original perimeter walls, but displaying a different design. This time, it had 1,750 seats, and the addition of an interior wall further reduced the auditorium's size. One interesting addition to the auditorium was a glass-fronted baptistery. As the only elevated baptistery in Britain at the time, it provided for the congregation a clear view of baptism by immersion.

In 1950, George Beasley-Murray became principal of Spurgeon's College and, in 1955, he persuaded the Metropolitan Tabernacle to re-join the Baptist Union. In 1970, Peter Masters, a former member of Martyn Lloyd-Jones's congregation at Westminster Chapel, accepted the Tabernacle's pastorate, on the condition that the church separate from the Baptist Union.[852] In February of the following year, the church officially withdrew from the Union. The legacy of Charles Spurgeon—English counterpart to American Fundamentalism—continues to inspire separatists around the globe.

Select Bibliography for Further Reading

Albert, William Brian. "'When the Wind Blows Cold': The Spirituality of Suffering and Depression in the Life and Ministry of Charles Spurgeon." PhD diss., The Southern Baptist Theological Seminary, 2015.

Bacon, Ernest W. *Spurgeon: Heir of the Puritans*. Grand Rapids: Baker, 1967.

Curnow, Tim, et al. *A Marvelous Ministry: How the All-round Ministry of C. H. Spurgeon Speaks to Us Today*. Ligonier, PA: Soli Deo Gloria, 1993.

---

[852] Cf. Ian M. Randall, *The English Baptists of the Twentieth Century* (Didcot, England: The Baptist Historical Society, 2005), 285, 370; see also Willis B. Glover, *Evangelical Nonconformists and Higher Criticism in the Nineteenth Century*.

Dallimore, Arnold. *Spurgeon*. Chicago: Moody Press, 1984.

Drummond, Lewis A. *Spurgeon: Prince of Preachers*. Grand Rapids: Kregel, 1992.

Fountain, David G. *Contending for the Faith: E. J. Poole-Connor, a 'Prophet' amidst the Sweeping Changes in English Evangelicalism*. London: The Wakeman Trust, 2005. This is a revision of Fountain's 1966 work titled *E. J. Poole-Connor, 'Contender for the Faith.'*

Glover, Willis B. *Evangelical Nonconformists and Higher Criticism in the Nineteenth Century*. London: Independent Press, 1954.

Hayden, Eric. *The Spurgeon Family*. Pasadena, TX: Pilgrim Publications, 1993.

_____. *The Unforgettable Spurgeon*. Greenville, SC: Emerald House Group, 1997.

Manley, Ken R. *'Redeeming Love Proclaim': John Rippon and the Baptists*. Vol. 12 of the series, Studies in Baptist History and Thought. 2004. Reprint, Eugene, OR: Wipf and Stock, 2006.

Murray, Iain H. *The Forgotten Spurgeon*. London: Banner of Truth Trust, 1966.

_____. *Spurgeon v. Hyper-Calvinism: The Battle for Gospel Preaching*. Edinburgh: Banner of Truth Trust, 2000.

Pike, G. Holden. *The Life and Work of Charles Haddon Spurgeon*. 6 vols. London: Cassell and Company, Limited, n.d., circa 1895.

Poole-Connor, E. J. *The Apostasy of English Nonconformity*. London: Thynne and Co., 1933.

_____. *Evangelical Unity*. London: The Fellowship of Independent Evangelical Churches, 1941.

_____. *Evangelicalism in England*. 2nd ed. Worthing, England: Henry E. Walter, 1966.

Sheehan, R. J. *C. H. Spurgeon and the Modern Church: Lessons for Today from the 'Downgrade' Controversy*. London: Grace Publications, 1985.

Spurgeon, Charles. *C. H. Spurgeon's Autobiography 1834-1878*. Vols. 1-3. London: Passmore and Alabaster, 1897-99.

_____. *C. H. Spurgeon's Autobiography 1878-1892*. Vol. 4. Chicago: Curts and Jennings, 1900.

_____. *The "Down Grade" Controversy: Collected Materials Which Reveal the Viewpoint of the Late Charles Haddon Spurgeon*. Pasadena, TX: Pilgrim Publications, n.d.

_____. *The Metropolitan Tabernacle: Its History and Work*. London: Passmore and Alabaster, 1876.

_____. *Metropolitan Tabernacle Pulpit*. 57 vols. London: Passmore and Alabaster, 1861-1917.

_____. *The New Park Street Pulpit*. 6 vols. London: Passmore and Alabaster, 1855-60.

Part IV
Baptists in America

Chapter 12

Roger Williams and John Clarke — Founders of the First Two Baptist Churches in America and Co-Founders of Rhode Island

---❋---

Roger Williams (ca. 1603–83)

Early Years in England

Roger Williams was born in London to James and Alice Williams. James was a successful merchant tailor.[853] While growing up in the parish of St. Sepulchre without Newgate, Roger would have been keenly aware of Separatist

---

[853] The best biographies of Roger Williams include Ola Elizabeth Winslow, *Master Roger Williams: A Biography* (New York: Macmillan, 1957); Howard M. Chapin, *Report upon the Burial Place of Roger Williams* (Providence: Rhode Island Historical Society, 1918); W. Clark Gilpin, *The Millenarian Piety of Roger Williams* (Chicago: University of Chicago Press, 1979); James D. Knowles, *Memoir of Roger Williams, the Founder of the State of Rhode-Island* (Boston: Lincoln, Edmonds and Co., 1834); Perry Miller, *Roger Williams: His Contribution to the American Tradition* (1953; repr., New York: Atheneum, 1974); LeRoy Moore Jr., "Roger Williams and the Historians," *Church History* 32, no. 4 (December 1963): 432–51; and William R. Staples, *Annals of the Town of Providence, from Its First Settlement, to the Organization of the City Government, in June, 1832*, vol. 5 of *Collections of the Rhode Island Historical Society* (Providence, RI: Knowles and Vose, 1843).

prisoners in Newgate, and of martyrs, both heroes and heretics, burned in nearby Smithfield. When Roger was about eight years old, King James's men brought Bartholomew Legate, an Arian, from Newgate Prison and burned him at the stake in sight of the Williams's home. This appears to have been the approximate time of Roger's conversion, which he mentions twice. In a 1632 letter to Governor John Winthrop, Williams reminisces of the time when he was but "a child in everything, though in Christ called, and persecuted even in and out of my father's house these 20 years."[854] Late in life, in his introduction to a treatise against Quaker doctrine, he again recalls that day when "the Father of *Lights* and *Mercies* toucht my Soul with a love to himself, to his only begotten, the true *Lord Jesus*, to his *Holy Scriptures*, &c."[855] During his teens, Roger became a protégé of famed lawyer and Chief Justice of England, Sir Edward Coke (1552–1634), author of the 1628 Petition of Right and advocate of the sovereignty of common law. Williams achieved academic recognition during his pre-college training at London's Charterhouse School. Pembroke College, at Cambridge, granted him one of eight available scholarships, based upon excellence in Hebrew, Greek, and Latin. Receiving the BA degree, in 1626/27, Williams continued for nearly two years of graduate training, after which he received ordination as a Puritan minister and became chaplain to Sir William Masham of Otes, High Laver (Essex). Here, in December 1629, Williams married Mary Barnard at All Saints Church in High Laver. They would have six children—all born in the New World.

Separatism versus New England Puritanism

Abandoning a promising future in the Church of England,

---

[854] Roger Williams, "Letter to John Winthrop," in *Letters of Roger Williams, 1632–1682*, ed. John Russell Bartlett, in *Publications of the Narragansett Club* (Providence, RI: The Narragansett Club, 1874), 6:2.

[855] Roger Williams, *George Fox Digg'd out of His Burrowes* (1676), first page of an un-paginated prefatory statement, "To the People Called Quakers," a facsimile reproduction with footnotes added by J. Lewis Diman, vol. 5 of *Publications of the Narragansett Club* (Providence, RI: Narragansett Club, 1872).

BAPTIST HISTORY IN ENGLAND AND AMERICA

Williams became a Separatist and immediately came under the persecuting hand of Bishop William Laud of London. To avoid arrest, Roger and Mary boarded the ship *Lyon* and immigrated to New England, arriving at Boston in February 1631. Boston was the hub of the Massachusetts Bay Colony, where the Puritans were apparently unaware of Williams's becoming a Separatist. Upon arrival, he declined their invitation to become the teaching elder at First Church. Williams later explained, "I conscientiously refused … because I durst not officiate to an un-separated people" from the Church of England.[856] Before sailing from England, in 1630, the soon-to-be governor of Massachusetts, John Winthrop, and his Puritans had assured the National Church, their "dear mother," that they would forever cling to her as faithful sons, even

> … as those who esteem it our honor to call the Church of England, from whence we rise, our dear Mother, and cannot part from our native Country, where she specially resideth, without much sadness of heart, and many tears in our eyes, ever acknowledging that such hope and part as we have obtained in the common salvation we have received in her bosom, and sucked it from her breasts.[857]

After a brief ministry as assistant teacher at Salem, which was under the jurisdiction of Massachusetts Bay Colony, Williams moved down to Plymouth, an independent colony that, since 1620, had been home to the Separatist, *Mayflower* Pilgrims. At Plymouth Plantation, Williams served as teaching elder in the Pilgrims' First Church. Both Salem and Plymouth gladly received his preaching. In New England, both the Puritans and the Separatists established their churches upon the governance of congregationalism, as opposed to the episcopacy (rule of bishops) in the Church of England. In those days,

---

[856] Roger Williams, "Letter to John Cotton of Plymouth, 25 March 1671," in *Letters of Roger Williams: 1632–1682*, 6:356. I have added the hyphen to the word *un-separated*.
[857] *The Humble Request* (London: Printed for Iohn Bellamie, 1630), 3–4. This copy is in the Henry E. Huntington Library and Art Gallery.

many Congregational churches had two elders (pastors) — a teaching elder and a ruling elder. Normally, each would preach every other Sunday morning. As early as 1605, Separatist ministers in the Diocese of Lincoln had published an *Apology*,[858] setting forth clear and bold reasons for their inability, in good conscience, to participate in the worship of the Church of England. Their grievances included:

- Widespread lack of biblical qualifications, knowledge of Scripture, and spiritual leadership among the clergy
- Non-biblical offices such as archdeacons and archbishops
- The office of the priesthood entrusted to mere men to forgive sins
- Confessions made to priests
- Absence of preaching the cardinal doctrines of Scripture
- Absence of many books of Scripture in the official *Book of Common Prayer*
- Apocrypha used alongside Scripture in *The Book of Common Prayer*
- Lack of any biblical prerequisites for partaking of Communion
- Lack of church discipline
- Local churches forbidden from choosing their own ministers

At Plymouth, Governor William Bradford began expressing concern that Roger Williams might follow the pattern of John Smyth and Thomas Helwys, who had promoted the rebaptism of those believers who had received infant baptism in the National Church. Like their counterparts in England, the Plymouth Separatists would never tolerate rebaptism. Moreover, any such rhetoric as "separation of the church from governmental intrusion" would have sounded unorthodox to Separatists on both sides of the Atlantic. In the summer of 1633, Williams returned to Salem, built a home for his family,

---

[858] *An Abridgement of That Booke Which the Ministers off the Lincolne Diocese Delivered to His Maiestie upon the First of December 1605: Being the First Part of an Apologie for Themselves and Their Brethren That Refuse the Subscription and Conformitie Which is Required* (1605; repr., Leiden: W. Brewster, 1617). This 102-page book is in the British Library, London.

and served unofficially as Pastor Samuel Skelton's assistant. The Salem church was Puritan, but the congregation had an independent spirit and refused to fall in line with Boston on every issue. Later that summer, when Skelton died, Williams became acting pastor and quickly gained rapport with the people. Despite opposition from the Boston magistrates, the Salem church officially installed Williams as pastor, in May 1635. This infuriated the Boston clergy, whose chief spokesperson, Cotton Mather, was already describing Roger Williams as "a certain windmill of the low countries, whirling around with extraordinary violence."[859]

Williams's Core Teachings and Key Tenets

Contrary to Cotton Mather's distortion, Roger Williams was a peaceful and rational man, as testified by both friend and foe. He was thoroughly Puritan in the doctrine of soteriology. Unlike the Puritans, though, he saw in Scripture five major distinctions between Israel and the church. These contrasts formed the basis for Williams's essential differences between Puritans and Separatists:[860]

- Israel's geographical boundaries were limited, but Christ commissioned his church to spread over the whole world (e.g., Matt. 28:18–20).
- Israel was one elect nation, but the church consists of a great host of elect individuals scattered among a multitude of nations (e.g. Eph. 2:11–16).
- God commanded Israel to use a literal sword, but He has instructed His church to wield the spiritual, double-edged sword of the Word (e.g., Eph. 6:17; Heb. 4:12; Rev. 1:16).

---

[859] Cotton Mather, *Magnalia Christi Americana*, in seven "book" divisions (London: Printed for Thomas Parkhurst, at the Bible and Three Crowns in Cheapside, 1702), book 7, chapter 2, page 7. This is from the John Adams Library at the Boston Public Library.

[860] Roger Williams, *The Bloudy Tenent of Persecution, for Cause of Conscience Discussed in a Conference between Truth and Peace*, a facsimile reproduction, with footnotes added by Samuel L. Caldwell, in *Publications of the Narragansett Club* (Providence, RI: Narragansett Club, 1867), 3:316–23.

- Israel's Levitical priesthood and ceremonial worship, including festivals, Sabbaths, and holy days, passed away with the old sacrificial system, as shadows of better things (e.g., Col. 2:16–17). The church enjoys the reality of Christ's presence through His Word and by His Spirit.
- All Hebrews are Abraham's physical seed. In Christ, both Jews and Gentiles are the spiritual seed of Abraham (e.g., Gal. 3:29). Christian Jews are complete Jews, since they are Abraham's physical *and* spiritual seed. The apostle Paul distinguishes three separate groups—the Jews, the Gentiles, and the Church of God (1 Cor. 10:32). As a Christian Jew, Paul added, "My heart's desire and prayer to God for Israel is, that they might be saved" (Rom. 10:1).

The above distinctions between Israel and the church form the basis of Williams's four fundamental tenets (beliefs) that the Massachusetts Bay clergy and magistrates found repulsive. Insisting that their nascent colony was the "New Canaan," in federal covenant with God, the leading Puritans judged Williams as an enemy.[861] Roger Williams's four basic tenets are as follows:

- *Unlike Israel's Old Testament system, New England's civil magistrates possess no biblical authority over the inner, spiritual governance of local churches.*
- *The Colony should abolish its required Freeman's (Citizen's) Oath.* At that time, only freemen could legally vote and hold any government office in town or province. The prerequisite for becoming a freeman (citizen) was a compulsory oath, forcing all applicants, including non-Christians, to pledge loyalty to Christ, to support the local parish churches, and to attend worship every Sabbath Lord's Day. Williams viewed this oath as forced hypocrisy; refusal to take the oath robbed one of any right to vote.

---

[861] One of the best studies on the Puritan ideal is Harry S. Stout, *The New England Soul* (New York: Oxford University Press, 1986).

- *The Indians are the rightful owners of the lands on which they have long occupied and found food for their sustenance.* The Massachusetts Bay Colony had received these lands by Charter (1629), from King Charles I, who justified the seizure of Native American lands by appealing to his status as a "Christian King" and "Defender of the Faith," just as Moses, God's representative, had commanded Israel to take the Promised Land. Thus, the Puritans, as the New Canaan, confiscated the land by the authority of a "Christian" King who claimed to represent the only true God. To Williams, Charles I more closely resembled one of the ten horns of the apocalyptic beast of Revelation seventeen.
- *The Church of England, as a state-church, is apostate, and any participation in its worship is disobedience to God.* When the New England Puritans visited England, they worshiped in the National Church. Williams believed that by imitating Rome's religious persecutions, England's state church had spiritually aligned herself with the harlot of Revelation 17:1-6. The marginal notes in the Geneva Bible had made it clear to many Puritans that Revelation 17 is describing the Roman Catholic Church. To Williams, though, the kingdoms of the beast were not only Roman Catholic; they were all governments that practiced religious persecution. Aligned with the Church of England, therefore, the Puritans had the blood of martyrs on their hands.

Williams's Trial and Exile

Regarding Williams's teachings as "seditious doctrines," the Massachusetts General Court, in April 1635, summoned him to Boston to defend his four tenets. The hearing resulted in total confusion and indecision. In July, the Court again summoned Williams to Boston. During the hearing, Williams again made clear his belief that God appoints the divine ordinance of civil magistracy and equips it exclusively to preserve the peace and order of affairs pertaining to the state, even with the sword in just causes. Williams also made clear his belief that

God appoints spiritual leaders and equips them exclusively to superintend spiritual affairs pertaining to the local church. To the modern reader, the courtroom drama of Williams's trial is a strange scene. On one side, there is amassed the whole power of civil government, upheld by the collective voice of the state clergy. On the other side, there stands a doctrinally sound minister of the gospel, with a brilliant mind, a blameless life, and a bold defense for the purity of the local church and the freedom of every person's conscience before God. During Williams's trial, the court heard no witnesses in behalf of the defendant. In the end, the magistrates and ministers judged Roger Williams's "opinions" to be "erroneous and very dangerous." Governor John Haynes (Haines) summoned Williams to return on October 1635 for his final hearing. For weeks, the trial would be the talk of all the towns.

Finally, the eagerly-anticipated day arrived, and all the ministers gathered inside Boston General Court. The Governor presided, as Thomas Hooker (1586–1647), a prominent Puritan clergyman, engaged Williams in debate over various aspects of the four disputed tenets. Hooker's intent was to bring Williams to repentance on each point. Upon Williams's refusal to retract his tenets, the Governor issued a decree to banish him from the Bay Colony and all its jurisdictions. While all the Boston ministers consented, the town of Salem, whose church still revered Williams and his family, made an uproar over the Court's ruling. Finally, with the stipulation that Williams would cease from publicly expressing his views, the magistrates decided that the sentence would not become effective until the passing of winter. At Salem, citizens began flocking to the Williams home, on Essex Street, to hear his teachings. Hearing that Williams was voicing his doctrine in his home, and that he "had drawn above twenty persons to his opinion,"[862] the General Court decreed, in January 1636, to deport him to England immediately.

---

[862] John Winthrop, *Winthrop's Journal: "History of New England" 1630–1649*, ed. James Kendall Hosmer (New York: Charles Scribner's Sons, 1908), 1:168.

Founding of Providence and the Work among the Native Americans

Forewarned in a merciful note from former Governor, John Winthrop, that the General Court intended to force him onto a ship, Williams escaped into the wilderness "in the midst of a New England winter." He fled three days before Captain John Underhill and his soldiers arrived at the Williams home, in Salem, to apprehend him. Mary and their two daughters (both under the age of three),[863] would be safe in Salem until Roger could build a home in Rhode Island.[864] The Williams home in Salem remains the oldest house in the city. It would become the property of Jonathan Corwin, one of the judges in the 1692 Salem Witch Trials. Due to its connection with Corwin, the home later became the popular "Witch House," now included in Salem's tour guides. At the time of his departure, Williams was frail with illness. He traveled in a southwest direction, by canoe and by land. In a letter, he later recalled, "I was sorely tossed for ... fourteen weeks, in a bitter winter season, not knowing what bread or bed did mean."[865]

Finally, on land that he purchased from Narragansett sachems, Canonicus and Miantonomi, at the headwaters of Narragansett Bay, Williams established the town that, in gratitude to God, he named *Providence*, the future capital of Rhode Island.[866] From England, as well as from Massachusetts and Connecticut, settlers began pouring into this refuge from religious persecution. This resulted in the establishment of several more towns. With

---

[863] Roger and Mary would have three daughters and three sons: (1) Mary, born at Plymouth, August 1633; (2) Freeborn, a daughter, born at Salem, October 1635; (3) Providence, a son, born at Providence, September 1638; (4) Mercy, a daughter, born at Providence, July 1640; (5) Daniel, born at Providence, February 1641; and (6) Joseph, born at Providence, December 1643.

[864] For Williams's account, see Reuben Aldridge Guild, "A Biographical Introduction to the Writings of Roger Williams," in *Publications of the Narragansett Club* (Providence, RI: Narragansett Club, 1866), 1:29ff.

[865] Roger Williams, "Letter to Major Mason, June 22, 1670," in *Letters of Roger Williams: 1632–1682*, 6:333-36.

[866] The original deed for the land, the original 1648 Charter, and the original 1663 Royal Charter reside in the Archives of the City of Providence. The Archives are on the 5th floor of City Hall, at 25 Dorrance Street.

the colonies of Massachusetts, New Haven, Plymouth, and Connecticut refusing to recognize the land rights of Rhode Island and Providence Plantations, Williams sailed to London, in 1643, to negotiate a patent for his Colony. To Williams, the timing of his arrival in London was providential. England's emerging Civil War (1642-48) had forced King Charles I to flee from London, and Parliament was ruling without a king. Williams's friends, including Oliver Cromwell, Sir Henry Vane the Younger (1613-62), and the notable author, John Milton, assisted him in achieving successful negotiations with the Parliamentary Commissioners for Plantations. Roger Williams returned to New England with the 1643 Patent for "The Colony of Providence Plantations in the Narragansett Bay in New England."[867] For three years (1654-57), Williams would serve as the Colony's "president," an office equivalent to governor.

Williams devoted much of his life in the New World to reaching and teaching the Native Americans. In a letter of 1677, he reminisces to a friend, "My soul's desire was to do the natives good and to that end to learn their language." He spent much time translating portions of Scripture into their tongue. "God was pleased," testifies Williams, "to give me a painful, patient spirit to lodge with them in their filthy, smoky holes, (even while I lived at Plymouth and Salem) to gain their tongue."[868] Williams possessed a rare gift for languages. At Cambridge University, he had become proficient in Latin, Greek, Hebrew, French, and Dutch. In Salem, Massachusetts, he had remarkably mastered the Narragansett Indian tongue. As an aid to his memory, during his first voyage to England, Williams wrote his *Key into the Language of America* (1643),[869] the earliest of his

---

[867] John Russell Bartlett, ed., *Records of the Colony of Rhode Island and Providence Plantations, in New England*, vol. 1, 1636-1663, (Providence, RI: A. Crawford and Brother, 1856), iii.

[868] Knowles, *Memoir of Roger Williams*, 108-9; cf. Roger Williams, *The Bloody Tenent yet More Bloody* (1652), a facsimile reproduction, with footnotes added by Samuel L. Caldwell, in *Publications of the Narragansett Club* (Providence, RI: Narragansett Club, 1870), 4:372n2.

[869] Roger Williams, *Key into the Language of America* (1643), facsimile reproduction with footnotes added by J. Hammond Trumbull, in *Publications of the Narragansett Club* (Providence, RI: Narragansett Club,

written works. Published in London, the *Key* includes abundant first-hand knowledge of the Native Americans' religion and customs.[870]

Sadly, an increasing English encroachment of Indian lands forced the Native Americans into slavish dependence upon the colonists. That would contribute to the outbreak of New England's most devastating conflict, King Philip's War (1675-76), against all English settlements. Successor to Massasoit of the Wampanoag tribe, Philip (d. 1676), whose real name was Metacom, was irrational, haughty, and ambitious. The English called him *Philip*,[871] as his vicious onslaught annihilated most of the "Praying Indian" villages established by the Puritan John Eliot (1604–90), "Apostle to the Indians." When the Indians fell upon Providence, on March 29, 1676, most of the town's population of five hundred fled to the Island of Aquidneck. In hopes that seventy-three-year-old Roger Williams could somehow calm the madness, the town had chosen him as captain of twenty-seven men who would remain in a blockaded house. As the Indian warriors drew near, Williams, with staff in hand, ventured outside to converse with them. "Brother Williams," said their chief, "you are a good man; you have been kind to us many years; not a hair of your head shall be touched."[872] All Williams's pleading fell upon deaf ears, though, as he witnessed the burning of most of the town, including his own home. All told, some ninety towns (half of New England) suffered attack. The bitter war ended with the shooting, quartering, and beheading of Philip. Happily, Roger Williams would live to see Providence rebuilt and to thank God for His mercies.

1866), 1:62–279.

[870] Ibid. Cf. Roger Williams, *Christenings Make Not Christians, or a Brief Discourse Concerning That Name Heathen, Commonly Given to the Indians: as also Concerning That Great Point of Their Conversion* (London: Printed by Iane Coe for I. H., 1645). This is in the British Library.

[871] Perhaps evoking Philip II, the ruthless Macedonian warrior and father of Alexander the Great.

[872] William G. McLoughlin, *Rhode Island: A History* (New York: W. W. Norton, 1986), 43–44; George Washington Greene, *A Short History of Rhode Island* (Providence: J. A. and R. A. Reid, 1877), 75; and Nathaniel Philbrick, *Mayflower* (New York: Viking, 2006), 300–01.

David Beale

The Founding and Early Years of America's First Baptist Church[873]

At Providence Plantation, in 1638, Roger Williams had gathered the first Baptist church in America.[874] Most of his charter members had left the Salem church with him. Beginning with at least nineteen members, including wives,[875] the group

---

[873] The best histories of the First Baptist Church, Providence, include William Hague, *An Historical Discourse Delivered at the Celebration of the Second Centennial Anniversary of the First Baptist Church, in Providence, November 7, 1839* (Providence, RI: B. Cranston and Co., 1839); Henry Melville King, *Historical Discourse in Commemoration of the One Hundred and Twenty-Fifth Anniversary of the Dedication of the First Baptist Meeting-House, Providence, R. I., Sunday, May 27, 1900* (Providence: F. H. Townsend, 1900); idem, *The Mother Church: A Brief Account of the Origin and Early History of the First Baptist Church in Providence* (Philadelphia: American Baptist Publication Society, 1896); J. Stanley Lemons, "Churches Founded by First Baptist," in *First Baptist, Providence*, vol. 2 of the series, Baptists in Early North America, ed. William H. Brackney (Macon, GA: Mercer University Press, 2013), 455; idem, *The First Baptist Church in America* (East Greenwich, RI: Charitable Baptist Society, 1988); idem, "Historical Introduction to First Baptist, Providence," in *First Baptist, Providence*, vol. 2 of the series, Baptists in Early North America, ed. William H. Brackney (Macon, GA: Mercer University Press, 2013), xi–lxv; and *Records of the First Baptist Church*, ed. J. Stanley Lemons, in *First Baptist, Providence*, vol. 2 of the series, Baptists in Early North America, ed. William H. Brackney (Macon, GA: Mercer University Press, 2013), 1–455.

[874] *A Review of a Report, Presented to the Warren Baptist Association, at Its Meeting in 1849, of the Subject of the True Date of the First Baptist Church in Newport, R. I.*, "prepared by a committee of the First Baptist Church in Providence, and read to the Warren Baptist Association, September 12, 1850" (Providence, RI: Press of H. H. Brown, 1850); see also Henry Melville King, ed., *Historical Catalogue of the Members of the First Baptist Church in Providence, Rhode Island* (Providence: F. H. Townsend, 1908), 185–86.

[875] Omitting the wives, Henry Melville King names these thirteen charter members of First Church: Roger Williams, Ezekiel Holliman, Thomas Olney, William Arnold, William Harris, Stukely Westcott, John Greene, Richard Waterman, Thomas James, Robert Cole, William Carpenter, Francis Weston, and John Throckmorton. King, *Historical Catalogue of the Members*, 187–89. Six women charter members appear in a letter from the Salem church to the "Reverend and dearly beloved in the Lord" at the Dorchester church: "We thought it our bounden duty to acquaint you with the names of such persons as have had the great censure passed

selected Ezekiel Holliman, "a poor man,"[876] but a man of "gifts and piety,"[877] to baptize Mr. Williams, who in turn baptized Holliman and the others. As we have seen in earlier chapters, a common awareness of the practice of baptism by immersion was already widespread in England. Such awareness was equally common in New England,[878] and there is no valid reason to doubt that Holliman and Williams baptized by immersion. In his treatise, *Christenings Make Not Christians* (1645), Williams describes his baptism as immersion.[879] Williams became the church's first pastor, with Holliman as his assistant. There is no record of Holliman ever receiving ordination. Soon after the group received their new baptism, the Salem church formally excommunicated all of these who had been members there. Most of Puritan society publicly ostracized all Baptists.

Along with the Puritans, Roger Williams had fled from state-church persecution in England. Now, in New England, Baptists were fleeing from Puritan persecution. As frequently indicated in his writings, Williams never abandoned the

---

upon them in this our church, with the reasons thereof, beseeching you in the Lord, not only to read their names in public to yours, but also to give us like notice of any dealt with in like manner by you." Those named include Roger Williams and his wife, Thomas Olney and his wife, Stukely Westcott and his wife, Mary Holliman, and Widow Reeves. Thomas Hutchinson, *The History of the Colony of Massachusetts Bay*, 2nd ed. (London: M. Richardson, 1765), 1:420–21; cf. Knowles, *Memoir of Roger Williams*, 176–77n†.

[876] Knowles, *Memoir of Roger Williams*, 165n†.

[877] David Benedict, *A General History of the Baptist Denomination in America, and Other Parts of the World* (Boston: Printed by Lincoln and Edmands, 1813), 1:475.

[878] For instance, in the previous year (1637), Plymouth Plantation had rejected the eminent Cambridge scholar, Charles Chauncey (1592–1671), "a reverend, godly, and very learned man," from serving their pastorate, solely because immersion was the only mode that he would administer to infants or adults. William Bradford, *Of Plymouth Plantation 1620–1647*, ed. Samuel Eliot Morison (1952; repr., New York: Alfred A. Knopf, 1966), 313–14.

[879] Roger Williams, *Christenings Make Not Christians*, 36. He adds that, like a national church, he could have easily persuaded Indians to submit to mass baptisms, even by immersion. He could never do that, since he believed that conversion must precede baptism.

Calvinistic doctrines of soteriology. Never in his life, though, had Williams observed a church that followed the simple pattern of the New Testament. Since his arrival in New England, Williams had hoped to find such a church, but now he abandons hope. Modifying his doctrine of the church, Williams now introduces his familiar metaphor of the "wall of separation between the garden of the church and the wilderness of the world." Historians have frequently interpreted this metaphor as an appeal for separation of church and state. Earlier, he would have held that view, but Williams is now teaching that, when God's people opened a gap in the wall of separation and wedded the church to the state, then God Himself tore down the wall, in judgment upon His church. There will be no true church on earth until Christ restores it. Whenever God's people have

> opened a gap in the hedge or wall of Separation between the Garden of the Church and the Wilderness of the world, God hath ever broke down the wall itself, removed the Candlestick, and made his Garden a Wilderness, as at this day. And that therefore if he will ever please to restore his Garden and Paradise again, it must of necessity be walled in peculiarly unto himself from the world, and that all that shall be saved out of the world are to be transplanted out of the Wilderness of the world, and added unto his Church or Garden.[880]

In Williams's view, God, from the beginning, had established the wall of separation between the church and the state, to prevent encroachment of the church into Caesar's realm, and to prevent encroachment of civil government into the church. The Puritans' doctrinal statement, the Cambridge Platform, had confounded the two realms by granting to civil magistrates the responsibility of keeping their churches pure, by the power of the sword. Civil magistrates were given authority

---
[880] Roger Williams, *Mr. Cotton's Letter Examined and Answered* (1644), ed. Reuben Aldridge Guild, in *The Complete Works of Roger Williams* (New York: Russell and Russell, 1963), 1:392.

to punish those deemed guilty of heresy, pernicious opinions, Sabbath breaking, idolatry, and schism.[881] Holding fast to the notion that their "Holy Commonwealth" had replaced Israel, Puritan ministers scorned any idea of a wall of separation. Roger Williams believed that Christ had torn down the wall, removed His Spirit from organized Christendom, and promised to restore His church in the prophetic future. It seemed best to Williams that individual believers simply preach the gospel, expose heresy, be good citizens, and wait for Christ to return and restore His church, with its new ordinances.

Within four months, therefore, after forming First Baptist Church at Providence, Williams doubted the validity of both of his baptisms. Without breaking personal fellowship with their faithful friends, he and his family left the church, and, for the rest of their lives, he and Mary remained disconnected from any organized church.[882] Convinced that all Christendom had apostatized, Williams concluded that there existed no true, spiritual descendants of Jesus' original disciples to officiate the ordinances. With no churches with apostolic authority, there was no valid baptism. He explains:

> In the poor small span of my life, I desired to have been a diligent and constant observer, and have been myself many ways engaged in city, in country, in court, in schools, in universities, in churches, in Old and New England, and yet cannot in the holy presence of God bring in the result of a satisfying discovery, that either the begetting ministry of the apostles or messengers to the nations, or the feeding and nourishing ministry of pastors and teachers,

---

[881] "The Cambridge Platform, 1648" (17.8–9), in *The Creeds and Platforms of Congregationalism*, ed. Williston Walker (New York: Charles Scribner's Sons, 1893), 237.

[882] Williams also embraced John Calvin's view that Sabbath-keeping was for Israel, not the church. This view, of course, ran contrary to the Puritan's more rigid view that Sunday is a "Sabbath Lord's Day." See Williams, "Letter to Samuel Hubbard," in *Letters of Roger Williams: 1632–1682*, 6:361. For a full coverage of Calvin's view, see David Beale, "The Sabbath Day: Christian Views from New Testament Times to the Present," in *Historical Theology In-Depth* (Greenville, SC: Bob Jones University Press, 2013), 2:121–24.

> according to the first institution of the Lord Jesus, are yet restored and extant.[883]

Although critics have sought to define Williams as a "Seeker," and even to call him the "Father of the Seekers," there is no evidence that he ever identified with the Seeker movement or communicated with any of their followers. Longing for the return of Christ to restore His true church, Williams would have found all Seeker heresies, such as universalism, deplorable.[884] In truth, Williams's ideal for local Christian gatherings was more in line with the Mennonite Collegiants than with any other group. There is no evidence, though, that he ever had any contact with them.

As a *historic premillennialist*, Williams viewed the book of Revelation as a symbolic unfolding of history from the time of Jesus' First Advent down to the seventeenth century and beyond. As Williams saw it, since the fourth-century apostasy of Christendom, God has used faithful individuals as His instruments for propagating the gospel and of denouncing false doctrine. Christ's First Advent fulfilled all of God's plans for national Israel. As Williams expressed it, "The state of the Land of Israel, the kings and people thereof in peace and war, is proved figurative and ceremonial, and no pattern nor precedent for any kingdom or civil state in the world to follow."[885] Thus, in Williams's view, God will never restore the nation of Israel, nor will He ever abandon His promised remnant of individual Jews. A unique feature of Williams's eschatology and ecclesiology is his insistence that, when Christ returns to establish His millennial kingdom, He will restore true churches with true apostles who will administer true ordinances. Miraculous gifts will return, as Christ fulfills the prophecies of Joel 2:28–32.

---

[883] Roger Williams, *The Hireling Ministry None of Christ's: Or a Discourse Touching the Propagating of the Gospel of Christ Jesus* (1652), in *The Complete Writings of Roger Williams*, a facsimile reproduction with footnotes added by Perry Miller (New York: Russell & Russell, 1963), 7:160. I modernized some of the spelling and the use of italics.

[884] See the discussion by Edmund S. Morgan, *Roger Williams: The Church and the State* (1967; repr., New York: W. W. Norton, 2006), 152.

[885] Williams, *The Bloudy Tenent of Persecution* (1644), 3:3 (Preface).

Believing that most of Acts 2:16–21 will find fulfillment in the millennium, Williams adds that Christ will inaugurate His millennial kingdom by worldwide, church evangelism. Far from being anti-Semitic, Williams believed that it is God's plan to save the Jewish remnant and to gather them into the church during the worldwide campaign. Having earlier speculated over the popular view that the Indians might be the lost tribes of Israel, Williams had come to reject that view.[886] Nevertheless, his own misguided notion that Christians should not establish local churches prevented him from any attempt at organizing his Indian converts. He had observed, though, that John Eliot's attempts to organize Indian churches had largely failed, as had the Indian school that Henry Dunster established at Harvard College.

Despite Williams's faults, to the end of his life he would clearly express Baptist convictions—even in a trans-Atlantic debate over infant versus believer's baptism. The debate developed between John Norcott (d. 1676) and the Puritan missionary John Eliot (ca. 1604–90). Norcott was the immediate successor to John Spilsbury, founder of the first Particular Baptist church in London (1633). In circa 1672, Norcott published the first edition of his *Baptism Discovered Plainly and Faithfully, According to the Word of God*, a work that immediately became the most popular treatise on baptism—outliving its author by decades.[887] The book prompted a response from

---

[886] In terms of Williams's hermeneutical method of biblical exegesis, Byrd's *The Challenges of Roger Williams* corrects Perry Miller's *Roger Williams: His Contributions to the American Tradition* (1953; repr., New York: Atheneum, 1974). While Miller restricts Williams's hermeneutic to typology, Byrd organizes Williams's Scripture citations into natural categories within the passages explained most often by Williams throughout his lifetime. Byrd focuses primarily on Williams's use of Jesus' parable of the wheat and tares (Matt. 13:24–30, 36–43), of Paul's teaching on the civil magistrate (Rom. 13), and of John's Revelation 2–3 and 17. Also indispensable is W. Clark Gilpin, *The Millenarian Piety of Roger Williams*, 56–62, 116–34.

[887] See John Norcott, *Baptism Discovered Plainly and Faithfully, according to the Word of God*, 2nd ed. (London: Printed for the author and sold by Benjamin Harris, 1675). This is in the Boston Public Library. There appears to be no extant copy of the first edition. See also Norcott, *Baptism Discovered Plainly and Faithfully, according to the Word of God*, ed. William

John Eliot, in *A Brief Answer to a Small Book Written by John Norcot against Infant-Baptism* (1679).[888] Upon reading Eliot's counter arguments, Roger Williams, during the final two or three years of his life, took up his pen once more. Due to the scarcity of paper, he pulled a 230-page book from one of his shelves, and, using shorthand that he had learned as a boy, he filled virtually every margin, developing a point-by-point refutation of Eliot's defense of infant baptism and of Eliot's rejection of immersion. Housed in the John Carter Brown Library, in Providence, Rhode Island, the book containing Williams's essay is missing its title page. Thus, no one knows its title or precise date of publication. Until recently, no one had ever confirmed its authorship.[889] The library had referred to it as the "mystery book," since no one had ever deciphered Williams's shorthand. In 2012, a team of researchers at Brown University cracked the code and translated Williams's marginalia, an essay described as *A Brief Reply to a Small Book Written by John Eliot*.[890] This discovery confirms that, to the end of his life, Williams held Baptist convictions. McBeth notes that even Williams's earlier "writings on religious liberty may be viewed as Baptist productions."[891] Moreover, Williams refused to regard doctrin-

---

Kiffin and Richard Claridge, "with an appendix by another hand," 3rd ed. ("Printed at Rotterdam, and now re-printed at London, by the assigns of Widow Norcott, and sold by William Marshal at the Bible in Newgate Street," 1694). It is in Dr. Williams' Library, 14 Gordon Square, London.

[888] Boston: John Foster, 1679. This is in the New York Public Library, NYC. Eliot appears to be the only author to spell *Norcott* as "Norcot." Eliot's book never again appeared in print. See also Geoffrey F. Nuttall, "Another Baptist Ejection (1662): The Case of John Norcott," in *Pilgrim Pathways: Essays in Baptist History in Honor of B. R. White*, ed. William H. Brackney and Paul S. Fiddes, with John H. Y. Briggs (Macon, GA: Mercer University Press, 1999), 185–88.

[889] Some had used the heading on its first page, "An Essay towards the Reconciling of Differences among Christians," as the book's title.

[890] While Williams did not provide a formal title to his essay, his first line of text begins, "A Brief Reply to a Small Book Written by John Eliot." See Linford D. Fisher, J. Stanley Lemons, and Lucas Mason-Brown, *Decoding Roger Williams: The Lost Essay of Rhode Island's Founding Father* (Waco, TX: Baylor University Press, 2014). On page 83, Williams defends immersion as the only biblical mode of baptism.

[891] H. Leon McBeth, *English Baptist Literature on Religious Liberty to 1689*

ally sound Christians as "unsaved" or "apostate," for gathering and worshiping in organized churches. Indeed, Williams describes his pastoral successor, Chad Brown, as "that noble spirit," and, on another occasion, "that holy man." As Williams saw it, all of God's elect are capable of erring, especially in matters of practice:

> I dare not ... condemn thousands, and ten thousands, yea the whole generation of the righteous, who since the falling away (from the first primitive Christian state or worship) have and do err fundamentally concerning the true matter, constitution, gathering, and governing of the Church: and yet far be it from any pious breast to imagine that they are not saved, and that their souls are not bound up in the bundle of eternal life.[892]

Subsequent Highlights of First Baptist Church, Providence

Meanwhile, at First Baptist, Chad Brown (mentioned above) had succeeded Williams to the pastorate. From its founding, as a Particular Baptist church, its pastors had allowed the laying on of hands after baptism to those who requested it. When Thomas Olney, a charter member, became pastor, his opposition to the laying on of hands upon every member led to a church split. In 1652, Olney led his supporters, known as "Five Point Baptists,"[893] to organize their own church.[894] When Olney died in 1682, his son, Thomas Jr., succeeded him to the pastorate, and, by circa

---

(1961; repr., New York: Arno Press, 1980), 122–23n2. This was a ThD thesis, Southwestern Baptist Theological Seminary, 1961.

[892] Roger Williams, *The Bloudy Tenent of Persecution* (1644), 3:64. I modernized some of the spelling and use of italics.

[893] By the term *Five Point*, Olney meant *Five Principle*. This is no reference to Calvinism.

[894] Henry Melville King, *The Mother Church: A Brief Account of the Origin and Early History of the First Baptist Church in Providence*, 45–63. For more discussion, see John Callender, *An Historical Discourse on the Civil and Religious Affairs of the Colony of Rhode-Island and Providence Plantations in New-England in America: from the First Settlement, 1688, to the End of the First Century* (Boston: S. Kneeland and T. Green, 1739), 61.

1715–20, the congregation merged back into First Baptist Church. At that time, First Baptist was under the pastorate of Pardon Tillinghast, who, at his own expense, in 1700, had erected the congregation's first meetinghouse—a small structure situated on the west side of North Main Street, near its junction with Smith Street. The building was "in the shape of a hay cap, with a fireplace in the middle, the smoke escaping from a hole in the roof."[895] Up until then, the congregation had worshiped in private homes and even under the trees when weather permitted. The deed to their first meetinghouse describes the congregation as "Six-Principle."[896] Some twenty-five years later, they replaced that building with a new one—measuring forty feet square.

First Baptist of Providence would face times of trial, but John Cotton's bleak description of it is totally erroneous: "That separate church, (if it may be called a church) which separated with Mr. Williams, first broke forth … into Anabaptism, and then into Anti-baptism and Familism, and now finally into no church at all." Cotton Mather published John Cotton's distortion as "history" against the Baptists.[897] As we have seen, however, First Baptist Church did not disappear into oblivion at Roger Williams's departure. In 1771, James Manning (1738–91) became the church's twelfth pastor.[898] Having graduated second in his class of twenty-one students, at Princeton, Manning became the first college educated pastor at First Baptist since Roger Williams. Manning was the first of the church's pastors to receive a salary, to own the title *pastor* (rather than *elder*), and to enter the pulpit wearing a wig and clerical collar bands. In 1764, he became founding president of Rhode Island College. In 1774, the earliest glimmers of the Second Great Awakening appeared under his ministry. In 1775, increasing attendance compelled the First Church to erect its present, majestic building, on North Main Street, and James Manning would live to serve as a delegate to the 1786 Continental Congress.

---

[895] Knowles, *Memoir of Roger Williams*, 175n.
[896] King, *The Mother Church*, 51–52.
[897] Cotton Mather, *Magnalia Christi Americana*, book 7, chapter 2, page 9.
[898] See Reuben Aldridge Guild, *Early History of Brown University, Including the Life, Times, and Correspondence of President Manning: 1756–1791* (Providence, RI: Snow and Farnham, 1896).

Williams's Major Works on the Proper Relationship between Church and State[899]

During the bitter winter of Williams's banishment (1635–36), John Cotton of Boston had written a letter to him. Under the assumption that Williams would inform London of the mistreatment he had received at the hands of Boston Puritans, Cotton sent this letter to Williams as his best line of defense. Seven years later (1643), during his first trip back to London, Williams was surprised to find his letter from John Cotton on London's newsstands and bookstores.[900] London's political and religious climate at the time reveals Cotton's motive for publishing the letter in London. The Independents and Presbyterians of the Westminster Assembly were competing for political power. In a well-orchestrated strategy to gain advantage over their Presbyterian rivals, the Independents, for the sake of expediency,

---

[899] The best works on Williams's contributions toward separation of church and state include John M. Barry, *Roger Williams and the Creation of the American Soul: Church, State, and the Birth of Liberty* (New York: Viking Penguin, 2012); Samuel Hugh Brockunier, *The Irrepressible Democrat Roger Williams* (New York: The Ronald Press Co., 1940); James P. Byrd Jr., *The Challenges of Roger Williams* (Macon, GA: Mercer University Press, 2002); Romeo Elton, *The Life of Roger Williams: The Earliest Legislator and True Champion for a Full and Absolute Liberty of Conscience* (London: Albert Cockshaw, 1852); William Gammell, *Life of Roger Williams, the Founder of the State of Rhode Island* (Boston: Gould and Lincoln, 1854); Edwin S. Gaustad, *Liberty of Conscience: Roger Williams in America* (Valley Forge: Judson Press, 1999); Timothy L. Hall, *Separating Church and State: Roger Williams and Religious Liberty* (Champaign: University of Illinois Press, 1998); W. J. McGlothlin, *New England Dissent 1630–1833: The Baptists and the Separation of Church and State*, 2 vols. (Cambridge, MA: Harvard University Press, 1971); idem, *Soul Liberty: The Baptists' Struggle in New England, 1630–1833* (Hanover, NH: University Press of New England, 1991); Irwin H. Polishook, *Roger Williams, John Cotton and Religious Freedom: A Controversy in New and Old England* (Englewood Cliffs, NJ: Prentice-Hall, 1967); Oscar S. Straus, *Roger Williams: The Pioneer of Religious Liberty* (New York: The Century Co., 1894); and Arthur B. Strickland, *Roger Williams: Prophet and Pioneer of Soul Liberty* (Boston: Judson Press, 1919).

[900] John Cotton, *A Letter of Mr. John Cotton, Teacher of the Church in Boston, in New England, to Mr. Williams a Preacher There* (London: N.p., 1643). This is in the British Library.

were running on the popular platform of "limited toleration" toward dissenters. The Presbyterians scorned *any* degree of toleration. To bolster their numbers, the Independents were making a tacit appeal to recruit persecuted Separatists to their cause. As the foremost Independent of New England, John Cotton had published his defensive letter in London to justify the Bay Colony's verdict against Williams. On his premise that Reformed ecclesiology constituted the very conscience of any person who desired the right to vote, Cotton insisted that the colony had punished Williams, not "for his conscience," but for sinning against his conscience.[901] To Cotton's chagrin, Williams immediately published a carefully nuanced rebuttal, containing compelling evidence of Cotton's intolerance.[902]

A few days later, in his *Queries of Highest Consideration* (1644), Williams crossed theological swords even with London's Independents, by demonstrating that the *root* of persecution was London's state-church system. Dedicated to both Houses of Parliament, Williams's *Queries* were self-described as "humbly bold in the name of the Lord Jesus Christ."[903] No government, Williams argues, can "force the consciences of all [its citizens] to one Worship," or one church, without committing "spiritual rape." Williams warns the Parliamentarians how eternally dangerous it is to "commit that rape."[904] To Williams, state churches inevitably force sheep and goats into the same fold.[905]

Following his *Queries*, Williams hastily wrote *The Bloudy Tenent of Persecution* (1644). Propitiously, he had already obtained his 1643 Patent prior to this book's publication.

---

[901] See also Polishook, *Roger Williams, John Cotton and Religious Freedom*, 71–75 and passim.

[902] Roger Williams, *Mr. Cotton's Letter Lately Printed, Examined and Answered* (1644), a facsimile reproduction with footnotes added by Reuben Aldridge Guild, in *Publications of the Narragansett Club* (Providence, RI: Narragansett Club, 1866), 1:285–396.

[903] Roger Williams, *Queries of Highest Consideration* (1644), facsimile reproduction with footnotes added by Reuben Aldridge Guild, in *Publications of the Narragansett Club* (Providence, RI: Narragansett Club, 1866), 2:254. Williams published this work anonymously.

[904] Ibid., 2:260.

[905] Ibid., 2:261.

Baptist History in England and America

Without apology, Williams's *Bloudy Tenent of Persecution* is a brilliant defense of soul liberty.[906] The "conscience ought not to be violated or forced." Indeed, says Williams, "it is most true that … spiritual rape is more abominable in God's eye than to force and ravish the bodies of all the women in the world."[907] The House of Commons ordered a public burning of Williams's treatise, and John Cotton replied to it with *The Bloudy Tenent, Washed and Made White in the Bloud of the Lambe* (1647).[908] In 1651, Williams's return voyage to London (with John Clarke, of First Baptist, Newport, Rhode Island) provided him time to reply to Cotton with *The Bloody Tenent yet More Bloody* (1652). This includes Williams's defense of Obadiah Holmes, who had suffered a bloody, public beating at the hands of Boston Puritans. Williams adds that John Cotton, who had fled from religious persecution in England, was now in New England "sipping at the bloody cup of the great whore" of Revelation seventeen.[909] On the flyleaf, inside Clarke's gift copy, Roger Williams, in his own handwriting, expresses highest esteem for the Newport pastor: "For his honored and beloved Mr. John Clarke, an eminent witness of Christ Jesus, ag'st ye bloodie Doctrine of persecution, &c."[910]

In his "Letter to the Town of Providence" (January 1654–55), Williams offers his illustration of a ship at sea to depict a workable relationship between religion and state:

---

[906] In *Bloudy Tenent of Persecution, for Cause of Conscience, Discussed in a Conference between Truth and Peace* (1644), 3:61–62), Williams preserves the account of John Murton — Baptist prisoner in Newgate Prison — writing his *Humble Supplication* on milk bottle stoppers and smuggling them to believers.

[907] Ibid., 3:182.

[908] London: Printed by Matthew Symmons for Hannah Allen, 1647. This copy is from the British Library.

[909] Roger Williams, *The Bloody Tenent Yet More Bloody* (1652), 4:107.

[910] Baptist historian Isaac Backus (1724–1806) later bequeathed this signed copy to the library at Brown University. See Samuel L. Caldwell, "Editor's Preface," to *The Bloody Tenent Yet More Bloody* (1652), 4:ix. See also Roger Williams, "Letter to Major Endicott, Governor of Massachusetts, upon Occasion of the Late Persecution against Mr. Clarke and Obadiah Holmes, and Others at Boston, the Chief Towne of Massachusetts in New England," in *The Bloody Tenent Yet More Bloody* (1652), 4:502 (4:502–18).

There goes many a ship to sea, with many hundred souls on one ship, whose weal and woe is common, and is a true picture of a commonwealth, or a human combination or society. It hath fallen out sometimes, that both Papists and Protestants, Jews and Turks, may be embarked in one ship; upon which supposal I affirm, that all the liberty of conscience, that ever I pleaded for, turns upon these two hinges—that none of the Papists, Protestants, Jews, or Turks be forced to come to the ship's prayers or worship, nor compelled from their own particular prayers or worship if they practice any. I further add, that I never denied, that notwithstanding this liberty, the commander of this ship ought to command the ship's course, yea, and also, command that justice, peace, and sobriety be kept and practiced, both among the seamen and all the passengers. If any of the seamen refuse to perform their services, or passengers to pay their freight; if any refuse to help, in person or purse, toward the common charges or defense; if any refuse to obey the common laws and orders of the ship, concerning their common peace or preservation; if any shall mutiny and rise up against their commanders and officers; if any should preach or write that there ought to be no commanders or officers because all are equal in Christ, therefore, no masters or officers, no laws nor orders, nor corrections nor punishments; I say, I never denied, but in such cases, whatever is pretended, the commander or commanders may judge, resist, compel, and punish such transgressors, according to their deserts and merits. This, if seriously and honestly minded, may, if it so please the Father of lights, let in some light to such as willingly shut not their eyes.

I remain studious of your common peace and liberty.

Roger Williams.[911]

---

[911] Roger Williams, *Letters of Roger Williams: 1632–1682*, 6:278–79.

Memorials

Gradually, many Puritans came to realize the virtue of Williams's character, as he negotiated peace treaties with Native Americans in behalf of the Bay Colony. Williams recalls, "It pleased the Father of Spirits to touch many hearts, dear to him, with some relenting; amongst which, that great and pious soul, Mr. Winslow,[912] melted, and kindly visited me, at Providence, and put a piece of gold into the hands of my wife, for our supply."[913] Even Plymouth Governor William Bradford paid tribute to Williams for helping to pacify the Pequot Indians.[914] Although Williams would maintain cordial correspondence with the leading men of his day, including Governor John Winthrop,[915] his reputation still suffers from the slander that notable men published. Shamefully, many continue to propagate the slander.

When Roger Williams died, in 1683, family, friends, and admirers buried his remains on one of the slopes of Providence Hill, behind his house on Towne Street. "A considerable parade" accompanied the funeral, and "guns fired over his grave."[916] An apple orchard would eventually occupy the unmarked gravesite, and the Williams house no longer exists. In 1860, his descendants exhumed his dust and reinterred it in a more respectable family crypt, in the North Burial Ground. Adoniram Judson (A. J.) Gordon (1836–95), in his 1885 address for the celebration of Forefathers' Day in Plymouth, recalled witnessing Williams's re-interment. He recalled that the taproot of an apple tree had grown along Williams's skeleton, from the top of the vertebrae downward, remarkably preserving the skeletal shape. Gordon allegorically likened the fruit that grew above Williams's grave

---

[912] Edward Winslow (1595–1655), author of *Good Newes from New England* (1625), traveled to the New World on the *Mayflower* and served three times as governor of Plymouth Plantation.

[913] Roger Williams, "Letter to Major Mason, June 22, 1670," in *Letters of Roger Williams: 1632–1682*, 6:337–38.

[914] Bradford, *Of Plymouth Plantation 1620–1647*, 300.

[915] Also, John Winthrop Jr.; see *Letters of Roger Williams: 1632–1682*, vol. 6, passim.

[916] John M. Barry, *Roger Williams and the Creation of the American Soul*, 389.

to John Wyclif's ashes cast into the River Avon, whose waters carried them into mighty oceans that span the globe. To Gordon, "That invincible backbone of Roger Williams … was spread throughout the whole world dispersed, and reproduced in generations of his adherents."[917] It was as if to say, "The righteous are fruitful of good even in the dust of their moldering."[918] Mounted on a board in the basement of the John Brown House Museum, the symbolic "Williams root" is still part of the collection of the Rhode Island Historical Society.

Built in 1909 in Geneva, Switzerland, the International Monument of the Reformation—better known as the Reformation Wall—displays a large statue of Roger Williams. In 1936, in honor of Rhode Island's tercentenary, the Legislature of the Commonwealth of Massachusetts passed a House Bill formally revoking its order of banishment against Roger Williams. It reads, "Resolved, that in so far as it is constitutionally competent for the general court to revoke the sentence of expulsion passed against Roger Williams by the General Court of Massachusetts Bay Colony in the year sixteen hundred and thirty-five, the same is hereby revoked."[919] Three years later, the City of Providence unveiled, at Prospect Terrace, a fourteen-foot-high statue of Roger Williams: With eyes closed, Williams is standing on the bow of his canoe interceding with God for his town and colony. With his right arm extended in supplication, Williams clutches in his left hand a book inscribed with the words *Soul Liberty*. His dust found its third and final interment underneath the base of this statue.

---

[917] For a scholarly confirmation of Gordon's account, see Zachariah Allen, "Memorial of Roger Williams," a paper read before the Rhode Island Historical Society, May 18, 1860. This copy is in the Library of Congress, Washington, DC.

[918] Thomas Armitage, *A History of the Baptists* (New York: Bryan, Taylor, and Co., 1887), 648.

[919] Edwin Powers, *Crime and Punishment in Early Massachusetts, 1620–1692: A Documentary History* (Boston: Beacon Press, 1966), 119.

John Clarke (1609–1676)

Background

Born in Westhorpe (Suffolk), England, on October 3, 1609,[920] John Clarke would become cofounder of the Colony of Rhode Island and Providence Plantations. On both sides of the Atlantic, there were so many contemporaries with the common name *John Clarke* that the early life of our John Clarke lies hidden in obscurity. Soon after he married Elizabeth Harges, daughter of John Harges, Esq. of Bedfordshire, the couple boarded a ship for Massachusetts Bay Colony and arrived in November 1637. Highly regarded for his knowledge of law, medicine, and theology, Clarke would use his skills in Latin, Greek, and Hebrew to write *A Concordance of the Bible*.[921] Massachusetts Governor John Winthrop would describe Clarke as "a physician and a preacher to those of the island."[922] The Newport Medical Society, in

---

[920] Biographies of John Clarke include Louis Franklin Asher, *John Clarke (1609–1676): Pioneer in American Medicine, Democratic Ideals, and Champion of Religious Liberty* (Pittsburg, PA: Dorrance Publishing Co., 1997); Thomas W. Bicknell, *Story of Dr. John Clarke: The Founder of the First Free Commonwealth of the World on the Basis of "Full Liberty in Religious Concernments,"* 2nd ed. (Providence, RI: Published by the author, 1915); Sydney V. James, *John Clarke and His Legacies: Religion and Law in Colonial Rhode Island 1638–1750*, ed. Theodore Dwight Bozeman (University Park, PA: Pennsylvania State University Press, 1999); and Wilbur Nelson, *The Hero of Aquidneck: A Life of Dr. John Clarke* (New York: Fleming H. Revell, 1938).

[921] John Clarke, *A Concordance of the Bible* (London: Henry Hill, 1655. No copies of Clarke's *Concordance* have survived. On the same day that he died, Clarke wrote his two-page will, now at the Newport Historical Society. Clarke wrote, "Unto my loving friend, Richard Bailey, I give and bequeath my concordance and Lexicon to it belonging, written by myself, being the fruit of several years."

[922] John Winthrop, "History of New England 1630–1649," in *Winthrop's Journal*, ed. James Kendall Hosmer (New York: Charles Scribner's Sons, 1908), 1:277; see also Morgan Edwards, *Materials for a History of the Baptists in Rhode Island*, in *Collections of the Rhode Island Historical Society* (Providence, RI: Hammond Angell and Co, 1867), 6:326; and Isaac Backus, *A History of New England: with Particular Reference to the Denomination of Christians Called Baptists*, 2nd ed., with notes by David Weston (Newton, MA: The Backus Historical Society, 1871), 1:125–212, 1:277–81, and 1:348–49.

December 1885, erected a plaque inside the Newport Historical Society: "To John Clarke, Physician, 1609–1676, Founder of Newport, and of the Civil Polity of Rhode Island."

Clarke as Cofounder of Rhode Island

Arriving in Boston during the religious persecution and turmoil of Anne Hutchinson's banishment, the Clarke family, with about three hundred others, took a ship up the Sakonnet River to Pocasset, situated at the northeast end of Aquidneck Island, in Narragansett Bay. At the advice of Roger Williams, Clarke and others purchased land from the Indians and organized Pocasset into the town of Portsmouth. In 1638, the Clarkes and several other families moved to the south end of Aquidneck Island and founded the town of Newport. In 1640, Portsmouth and Newport united to form the colony of Rhode Island. They elected William Coddington as governor. As previously mentioned, in 1643, Roger Williams traveled to England and secured a patent that, by 1647, incorporated the towns of Portsmouth, Newport, Providence, and Warwick into "The Colony of Providence Plantations in the Narragansett Bay in New England." John Coggshall became the colony's first "president."

In 1649, the execution of King Charles I placed the security of Roger Williams's 1643 patent in serious jeopardy. William Coddington promptly made a secret trip to England. His objective was to acquire a Commission that would annul the Patent by separating the island towns of Portsmouth and Newport from the mainland towns of Providence and Warwick. Coddington's ultimate purpose was to make himself sovereign governor for life over the islands of Aquidneck and nearby Conanicut, named for Chief Canonicus of the Narragansett tribe. Terrified at Coddington's schemes, in 1651, the four towns sent John Clarke and Roger Williams to London to obtain a revocation of Coddington's Commission and to obtain a renewal of their 1643 Patent.[923] Upon arrival in London, Clarke and

---

[923] During this trip, Williams published his book *The Hireling Ministry None of Christ's: Or a Discourse Touching the Propagating of the Gospel of Christ Jesus* (1652).

Williams received valuable assistance from diplomat Sir Henry Vane the Younger and poet John Milton, who had tutored his friend Roger Williams in Hebrew in exchange for lessons in Dutch. Not surprisingly, the Williams-Clarke mission was successful—at least for now.[924] Within three years, family obligations prompted Williams's return to Providence,[925] but John Clarke remained in London as an agent for the colony. His wife, Elizabeth, was with him and they had no children. Besides working as a physician during his tenure in London, Clarke mortgaged his property in Newport to help meet expenses. Advantageously, Clarke was still in London at the Restoration of the Stuart monarchy, in 1660, when Charles II came to the throne. This transfer of power instantly annulled the 1643 Patent of Providence Plantations and necessitated a Royal Charter. Moreover, Charles II bitterly opposed the Plantations and their appeals for liberties.

Meanwhile, in a harrowing turn of events, the Clarkes were in London on the tense night of January 6, 1661,[926] as Thomas Venner led the final Fifth-Monarchist uprising on the city.

---

[924] Robert H. Pfeiffer, "The Teaching of Hebrew in Colonial America," *The Jewish Quarterly Review* 45, no. 4 (April 1955): 365 (363–73).

[925] During this time, Williams wrote a letter to his wife as she was recovering from a time of discouragement and sickness. The published title is *Experiments of Spiritual Life and Health, and their Preservatives in Which the Weakest Child of God May Get Assurance of His Spiritual Life and Blessedness, and the Strongest May Find Proportionable Discoveries of His Christian Growth, and Means of It* (1652), a facsimile reproduction with footnotes added by Perry Miller, in *The Complete Writings of Roger Williams* (New York: Russell & Russell, 1963), 7:42–114.

[926] Every attempt to link our John Clarke with hardcore Fifth Monarchists has failed. Cf. Richard L. Greaves, "A Colonial Fifth Monarchist? John Clarke of Rhode Island," *Rhode Island History* 40, no. 2 (May 1981): 41–47. The name *John Clarke* was common, and some who owned it were non-Baptist rioters. Like many other peaceful Christians, Clarke undoubtedly would have held sympathies with some Fifth-Monarchist issues, such as unreasonable taxes, but there is no evidence that he was ever a member of the group, or that he ever promoted violence, which would be entirely antithetical to his character. Abundant evidence of Clarke's humble, pastoral tone is in two recently-discovered letters, written in 1655 and 1658, now in the library archives at Southern Baptist Theological Seminary. See also Asher, *John Clarke*, 74–75.

Authorities quickly captured Venner and hanged him. Within hours, John Clarke issued a message to the citizens of London. Titled *The Plotters Unmasked, Murderers No Saints*, his message was "a word in season to all those that were concerned in the late rebellion against the peace of their King and country." In celebration of the defeat of the Fifth Monarchists, Clarke comforts believers with Bible promises and exhorts sinners with Christ's gospel. Appealing to Scripture—Romans 13:1-8, Titus 3:1, 1 Peter 2:13-19, and 1 Timothy 2:2—Clarke calls upon all to obey the civil authorities whom God has set over them. He signed his message, "a friend of righteousness; and a lover of all men's souls, knowing that one is of more worth than ten thousand worlds, John Clarke."[927]

Keenly astute in British diplomacy, Clarke was aware that, in Breda, Holland (April 1660), Charles II had signed "The Declaration of Breda," promising "liberty for tender consciences," ensuring "that no man shall be disquieted or called in question for differences of opinion in matter of religion, which do not disturb the peace of the kingdom."[928] English Baptists would soon learn that the King never intended such promises for them. Against all odds, in 1662, John Clarke presented two petitions to the King for a Royal Charter. He saturates his second petition with words and expressions derived directly from the King's Declaration of Breda. Clarke pleaded, for example, that his people in New England "have it much on their hearts (if they may be permitted) to hold forth a lively [living] experiment, [in order] that a flourishing civil state may stand, yea, and best be maintained … with a full liberty in religious concernments." Indeed, they humbly desire "that no person within the said colony, at any time hereafter shall be anywise molested, punished, disquieted, or called in question, for any differences in opinion in matters of religion."

---

[927] John Clarke, *The Plotters Unmasked* (London: Printed for John Clarke and to be sold at the Exchange, 1661), title page. The writing style is completely compatible with that of our John Clarke. This copy is in the British Library, London.

[928] "The Declaration of Breda," in *Documents Illustrative of English Church History*, ed. Henry Gee and William John Hardy (London: Macmillan, 1914), 587.

Continuing to paraphrase the King's own Declaration, Clarke explains that true liberty of conscience can abide only with those who are "behaving themselves peaceably and quietly, and not using this liberty to licentiousness and profaneness, nor to the civil injury or outward disturbance of others."[929]

Amazingly, in July 1663, Clarke obtained the signature and seal of King Charles II upon the Royal Charter of Rhode Island and Providence Plantations, granting absolute, religious liberty of conscience to every individual.[930] Charles's motive for legalizing such a document continues to baffle historians, but McLoughlin reminds us that the King simply "enjoyed annoying the Puritans." For years, Americans would celebrate this charter. At the election of every future governor of Colonial Rhode Island, officials would ceremoniously remove the revered Charter from its royal box and publicly read the complete document to assembled voters. "Like the Ark of the Covenant, the charter ... became the sacred symbol of the colony's special mission in the New World."[931] It would become the constitution of the "State of Rhode Island and Providence Plantations," and it would remain in force for 180 years. The constitution that Rhode Island adopted in 1843 would retain much of the language of the 1663 Charter.[932] Upon the Clarkes' arrival in Newport, in 1664, citizens took to the streets in jubilant celebration. The greatest joy for the Clarkes, after being away for thirteen years, was the little Baptist congregation who had prayed and longed for their return.

---

[929] Thomas Williams Bicknell, *The History of the State of Rhode Island and Providence Plantations* (New York: The American Historical Society, 1920), 2:435–36.

[930] The charter promises "that no person within the said colony, at any time hereafter, shall be any wise molested, punished, disquieted, or called in question, for any differences in opinion in matters of religion, and do not actually disturb the civil peace of our said Colony." See the copy of the charter in Greene, *A Short History of Rhode Island*, 292 (Appendix).

[931] McLoughlin, *Rhode Island*, 38–39.

[932] Rhode Island's most recent constitution dates to 1987.

John Clarke and Obadiah Holmes — Patriarchs of Baptists in America

There are no records of John Clarke's baptism and ordination. However, from the time of his founding of Newport, in 1638, Clarke had preached and ministered to the people around him. In 1644, he gathered the charter members for the First Baptist church in Newport—the second Baptist church in America.[933] Although some still debate the founding date of the church, its fifth pastor, John Comer, in 1725, recorded that its founders had constituted the church in 1644.[934] "It is said," reports John Callender, the church's sixth pastor, "that in 1644, Mr. *John Clark*, and some others, formed a Church, on the Scheme and Principles of *the Baptists*," and "it is certain that in 1648 there were fifteen Members in full Communion." The names *John Clark* and *Mark Lukar* are first in Callender's list of ten male members.[935] Mark Lucar (d. 1676) had arrived in Newport by the mid-1640s. Having received ministerial training from John Spilsbury, Lucar (a significant link between London and Newport) would play a key role at the Newport church. He served as John Clarke's assistant and outlived him by less than a year. Samuel Hubbard and his wife, Tacy, arrived in Newport, in October 1648, and received immersion from Clarke. Hubbard reports that he and Tacy "became identified with the little Baptist church under the pastorate of John Clarke, then four years old, and yet having but fifteen members, of

---

[933] *Historical Sketch of the First Baptist Church, Newport, R.I.*, "a discourse delivered on Thanksgiving Day, November 30, 1876, by C. E. Barrows, pastor of the church" (Newport: John P. Sanborn, 1876); cf. *A Review of a Report Presented to the Warren Baptist Association, at Its Meeting in 1849, on the Subject of the True Date of the First Baptist Church in Newport, R. I.*, "prepared by a committee of the First Baptist Church in Providence, and read to the Warren Baptist Association, September 12, 1850" (Providence, RI: H. H. Brown, 1850).

[934] The oldest Records of First Baptist Church are at the Newport Historical Society.

[935] John Callender, *An Historical Discourse on the Civil and Religious Affairs of the Colony of Rhode-Island and Providence Plantations in New-England in America: from the First Settlement, 1688, to the End of the First Century*, 63 (62–66).

whom nine were males."[936]

In 1649, Clarke and Lucar traveled to Seekonk (Rehoboth) to organize a group of Separatists into a Baptist church. Puritan officials swiftly forced a halt to their mission.[937] Before leaving Seekonk, Clarke immersed several believers, including Obadiah Holmes (1606/7-82). During the following year, Holmes and the other newly baptized moved to Newport and joined First Baptist Church, where Holmes became Clarke's assistant.[938] In a letter dated 1649 and addressed to John Winthrop Jr., Roger Williams comments on Clarke's administration of believer's baptism by immersion at Seekonk. Williams describes it as a "new baptism," not because it was immersion, but because it was *rebaptism* — a repudiation of infant baptism. While fully agreeing with Clarke, that the only true baptism by water is the immersion of believers, Williams could not endorse its administration, since he was uncertain of the precise manner by which the apostles had administered immersion. Equally important to Williams, there can be no true churches on earth until Christ establishes His premillennial kingdom and anoints new apostles to establish new churches. Williams summarizes:

---

[936] Ray Greene Huling, "Samuel Hubbard, of Newport 1610-1689," *The Narragansett Historical Register* 5, no. 1 (December 1887): 307, cf. 303 (289-327). Prior to arriving in Newport, Hubbard and his wife had been Baptists for several years and, due to persecution, they had fled from Massachusetts and Connecticut. His wife had become a Baptist first and then persuaded Samuel to embrace Baptist distinctives. They served here faithfully until 1671, when they joined the splinter group led by Stephen Mumford, who established a Seventh-Day Baptist Church in Newport. See Thomas Barber, "Samuel Hubbard," *The Narragansett Historical Register* 2, no. 2 (October 1883): 97-101.

[937] Rehoboth was situated less than fifty miles southwest of Boston and less than ten miles east of Providence. While Plymouth Colony, in 1642, had purchased from Massasoit the land that would become the township of Rehoboth, the town incorporated, in 1643, as Rehoboth, Massachusetts. In 1812, Rehoboth's western half, already known as the "Seekonk" section, would break away and incorporate as the township of Seekonk, Massachusetts.

[938] Holmes would serve the Newport pastorate during 1651-64, when Clarke was in England negotiating a charter. Clarke resumed the pastorate upon his return.

> At Seekonk a great many have lately concurred with Mr. John Clarke and our Providence men about the point of a new Baptism, and the manner by dipping: and Mr. John Clarke hath been there lately (and Mr. Lucar) and hath dipped them. I believe their practice comes nearer the first practice of our great Founder Christ Jesus than other practices of religion do, and yet I have not satisfaction, neither in the authority by which it is done, nor in the manner; nor in [their interpretation of] prophecies concerning the rising of Christ's Kingdom.[939]

On Sunday, July 20, 1651, John Clarke and Obadiah Holmes,[940] accompanied by John Crandall (a deacon), responded to a request to visit the home of an elderly member,[941] William Witter, a blind brother who resided about two miles outside Lynn, Massachusetts. As Clarke was sharing with the Witter home a message from Revelation 3:7-13 (Christ's message to the church at Philadelphia), four or five others came in unexpectedly. Suddenly, two constables entered the home and, with "clamorous tongues," interrupted Clarke's message, apprehended Clarke, Holmes, and Crandall, and escorted them into the nearby Puritan meetinghouse. Forced into such worship, the captives kept their hats on inside the room. A constable quickly pushed off the hats, and the three spent the night as prisoners in a nearby inn. The next day, after officials arraigned them, the three managed to return to the Witter home, where Holmes baptized three believers by immersion and Clarke

---

[939] *Letters of Roger Williams: 1632–1682*, 6:188.

[940] Obadiah Holmes, *The Last Will and Testimony of Obadiah Holmes*, in *Baptist Piety*, ed. Edwin S. Gaustad (1978; repr., Tuscaloosa, AL: University of Alabama Press, 2005).

[941] In London, the following year, John Clarke published his account of the episode, in his *Ill Newes from New-England: Or A Narrative of New-Englands Persecution* (London: Henry Hills, 1652). The first edition copy is in the Bodleian Library, Oxford. Its pagination differs from the printings found in vol. 2 of the fourth series of *Collections of the Massachusetts Historical Society* (Boston: Crosby, Nichols, and Co., 1854), 2:1–113. The pagination also differs from the edition published by the Baptist Standard Bearer, Paris, Arkansas, n.d. My pagination is from the Henry Hills, 1652, first printing.

served the Lord's Supper. Officials promptly transported Clarke, Holmes, and Crandall to a Boston prison and charged them for conducting illegal church services, disrupting Puritan worship, teaching that infant baptism is false, and for administering heretical rebaptism and Communion.

Holmes reported that, during the court session, the pastor of Boston's First Church, John Wilson, "struck me … saying, 'The Curse of God … go with thee.'" Publicly upbraiding Clarke for denying infant baptism, Deputy Governor Endicott informed the Baptist pastor that he "deserved death," adding that he "would not have such trash brought into their jurisdiction." Endicott then belittled Clarke that he would be incapable of defending his beliefs "before our Ministers." In a letter penned from his cell, Clarke responded to Endicott with a plea for a public debate between himself and their most capable Puritan minister—undoubtedly referring to John Cotton. Endicott at first approved the debate, but then changed his mind. Clarke wrote two additional pleas for debate, but to no avail.[942] Instead, on July 31, John Cotton delivered a sermon urging the County Court that those who deny infant baptism are "soul-murderers," guilty of "capital offense." Following the sermon, Endicott declared to the defendants, "You deserve to die."[943] He then read the verdicts: Holmes must pay a fine of thirty pounds; Clarke must pay a fine of twenty pounds; and Crandall must pay five pounds. The condemned men were to remain in prison until they paid their fines, or until someone paid for them—or else all of them would be "well whipped." Crandall received a dismissal on payment of his fine. A friend, without Clarke's knowledge, paid his fine. Clarke finally accepted, but with strong objections. Obadiah Holmes politely passed the word along that he must refuse all offers of paying his fine. He informed officials that his acceptance might appear as an acknowledgment that he had sinned against God.[944] He remained in prison until September 5, the day of his beating. Led to the whipping post, near the market by Boston's Old State House, Holmes refused a friend's offer of wine and proceeded

---

[942] Clarke, *Ill Newes*, 1–10.
[943] Ibid., 26–27.
[944] Ibid., 11–15, 19.

to address the assembled crowd: "Though my flesh should fail, and my spirit should fail, yet God [will] not fail."[945] With the victim's hands tied to the post and his clothing stripped to his waist, the whipping began. With each blow, the flogger paused to spit his hands three times. "With all his strength," the man thrashed his victim with thirty lashes from a three-corded whip—placing ninety stripes upon Holmes's naked back.[946] Holmes testified that he had never "had such a spiritual manifestation of God's presence." Following the ordeal, Holmes informed the magistrates, "You have struck me as with roses." Authorities imprisoned two bystanders, John Spur and John Hazel, for extending a brotherly hand to Holmes. The court sentenced each with a fine of forty shillings or be whipped.[947] John Hazel was above sixty years of age. He had traveled over fifty miles through a wilderness, all the way from Seekonk (Rehoboth), to stand by his Christian brother. From the aftereffects of his imprisonment, Hazel died before reaching his home. He was the first martyr for Baptist principles in America. Holmes, with his body bruised and bleeding, would endure weeks of sleepless nights, able to allow only his knees and elbows to touch the bed.[948] The ultimate crime charged to Clarke and Holmes was that *they were Anabaptists.*

The next year, while in England with his friend Roger Williams, John Clarke reported the above episode in his book, *Ill Newes from New-England*: "In our examination," writes Clarke, "the Governor upbraided us with the name of *Anabaptists*; to whom I answered, 'I disown the name, I am neither an Anabaptist, nor a Pedobaptist,'"[949] that is, one who baptizes babies. The Greek prefix *Pedo* means *child*. In his

---

[945] Ibid. 20–21. The Old State House (built 1713) still stands at the head of State Street. This would also become the site of the 1770 Boston Massacre. See Samuel G. Drake, *The History and Antiquities of Boston: From Its Settlement in 1630, to the Year 1770* (Boston: Luther Stevens, 1856), 325n†

[946] Clarke, *Ill Newes*, 32–33.

[947] Ibid., 21–22; cf. George H. Tilton, *A History of Rehoboth, Massachusetts: Its History for 275 Years 1643–1918* (Boston: Printed by Louis E. Crosscup, 1918), 41.

[948] Isaac Backus, *A History of New England: with Particular Reference to the Denomination of Christians Called Baptists*, 1:193n1.

[949] Clarke, *Ill Newes*, 5.

book's "Epistle Dedicatory to the Right Honorable the House of Parliament, and Counsel of State for the Commonwealth of England," Clarke urges that it is not the Lord's will that any man should have dominion over another man's conscience. Indeed, one's conscience "is such a sparkling beam, from the Father of lights, and spirits, that it cannot be lorded over, commanded, or forced, either by men, devils, or angels."[950] Reinforcing Clarke's message, Roger Williams, that same year, explained, "To force the Consciences of the Unwilling is a Soul-rape."[951] Baptist author Leonard Busher, in his *Religion's Peace* (1614), had been the first to describe forced worship as *spiritual rape*: "Persecution for religion is to force the conscience; and to force and constrain men and women's consciences to a religion against their wills, is to tyrannize over the soul, as well as over the body.... Herein the bishops commit a greater sin than if they force the bodies of women and maids against their wills."[952]

During Clarke's tenure in England (1651–64), First Baptist of Newport, led by Obadiah Holmes, had remained small in membership but sound in doctrine. Holmes continued to fill the pulpit frequently, during 1664–69, when Clarke was serving in the Colony's General Assemble and two terms as Deputy Governor. In 1656, when the First Baptist membership was numbering under fifty, twenty-one members withdrew to form Second Baptist Church, a "Six Principle" church, so-named for its practice of the laying on of hands to each baptizee as an additional prerequisite to membership and the Lord's Supper. The defectors embraced Arminianism, while the Clarke/Holmes congregation continued the doctrinal stance of John Spilsbury's London church, as seen in the introduction to

---

[950] Ibid., Epistle Dedicatory, 4. There is no printed pagination in this section.

[951] Roger Williams, *The Examiner – Defended in a Fair and Sober Answer* (1652), a facsimile reproduction, with footnotes added by Perry Miller, in *The Complete Writings of Roger Williams* (New York: Russell & Russell, 1963), 7:268.

[952] Leonard Busher, *Religions Peace: Or Reconciliation between Princes and Peoples, and Nations* (Amsterdam: n.p., 1614), 10. This is from the Henry E. Huntington Library and Art Gallery, San Marino, CA. I slightly modernized some spelling and punctuation.

the Clarke/Holmes, thirty-five-article Confession:

> The decree of God is that whereby God hath from eternity set down with himself whatsoever shall come to pass in time. Eph. 1:2. All things with their causes, effects, circumstances, and manner of being are decreed by God, Acts 2:23. "Him being delivered by the determinate counsel and foreknowledge of God," &c. Acts 4:28. This decree is most wise: Rom. 11:33; most just: Rom. 9:13–14; eternal: Eph. 1:4–5, 2 Thess. 2:13; necessary: Ps. 33:2, Prov. 19:21; unchangeable: Heb. 6:17; most free: Rom. 9:13; and the cause of all good: James 1:17; but not of any sin: 1 John 1:5. The special decree of God concerning angels and men is called predestination, Rom. 8:30. Of the former, viz., angels, little is spoken of in the Holy Scripture; of the latter more is revealed, not unprofitable to be known. It may be defined, the wise, free, just, eternal and unchangeable sentence or decree of God, determining to create and govern man for his special glory, viz., the praise of his glorious mercy and justice, Rom. 9:17–18, 11:36. Election is the decree of God, of his free love, grace and mercy, choosing some men to faith, holiness and eternal life, for the praise of his glorious mercy, 1 Thess. 1:4, 2 Thess. 2:13, Rom. 8:29–30. The cause which moved the Lord to elect them who are chosen, was none other but his mere good will and pleasure, Luke 12:32. The end is the manifestation of the riches of his grace and mercy, Rom. 9:23, Eph. 1:6. The sending of Christ, faith, holiness, and eternal life are the effects of his love, by which he manifests the infinite riches of his grace. In the same order, God doth execute this decree in time, he did decree it in his eternal counsel, 1 Thess. 5:9, 2 Thess. 2:13. Sin is the effect of man's free will, and condemnation is an effect of justice inflicted upon man for sin and disobedience.... A man in this life may be sure of this election, 2 Pet. 1:10, 1 Thess. 1:4; yea of his eternal happiness ... but not of his eternal reprobation; for he that is now profane, may be called hereafter.[953]

---

[953] "Confession of Faith of John Clarke and Obadiah Holmes, First Baptist

In early 1665, soon after John Clarke returned from England, Stephen Mumford, of the Bell Lane Seventh-Day Baptist Church in London, arrived in Newport. Finding no Sabbatarians in town, he attended First Baptist. Immediately, Mumford began proselytizing members toward having church on Saturday rather than Sunday. In December 1671, Mumford and his wife, along with five First Baptist members, withdrew to establish a Seventh-Day Baptist church — the first in America. The faithful at First Baptist agonized over the loss of John Crandall and of the Samuel Hubbard family to the Sabbatarians.[954] Even though several other First Baptist members would later defect to the Quakers, the little church under the leadership of Clarke and Holmes would stand firm for a time. Much later, in 1946, Second Baptist would merge back into First Baptist, to form the United Baptist Church, John Clarke Memorial, which would drop the Clarke/Holmes Confession and join the Northern Baptist Convention, now the American Baptist Churches USA. United Baptist Church's edifice at 30 Spring Street, Newport, dates to 1846. (See the Tour Guide in Appendix C.).

The Clarke/Holmes legacy still survives in innumerable ways. Upon Clarke's decease, on April 20, 1676 (during King Philip's War), Obadiah Holmes, ancestor of Abraham Lincoln,[955] succeeded as the lead pastor. Holmes died at Newport, on October 16, 1682, at the age of seventy-six. His remains lie buried in the Holmes family cemetery in Middletown, Rhode Island, where a memorial tombstone stands to his honor. Eight children survived him, and, by 1790, an estimated report had his descendants numbering five thousand.[956] One

---

Church, Newport, Rhode Island," in Isaac Backus, *A History of New England: with Particular Reference to the Denomination of Christians Called Baptists*, 2nd ed. with notes by David Weston (Newton, MA: Backus Historical Society, 1871), 1:202–9. I slightly modernized some punctuation and formatting of Scripture references.

[954] Don A. Sanford, *A Choosing People: The History of Seventh Day Baptists* (Nashville: Broadman, 1992), 94–101; and Albert N. Rogers, ed., *Seventh Day Baptists in Europe and America* (Plainfield, NJ: American Sabbath Tract Society, 1910), 1:122–24; 2:589ff.

[955] J. T. Holmes, *The American Family of Rev. Obadiah Holmes* (Columbus, OH: n.p., 1915).

[956] Tilton, *A History of Rehoboth, Massachusetts*, 41. The Holmes family

illustrative branch of Obadiah Holmes's far-reaching influence begins with his granddaughter, Susanna Holmes, who married Valentine Wightman (1681–1747),[957] who, at Groton, Connecticut, in 1705, planted the earliest Baptist church in that colony.[958] Wightman would serve this pastorate until his death forty-two years later.[959] In 1743, First Baptist of Groton organized a mission church at North Stonington, Connecticut, and Wightman ordained Wait Palmer as its first pastor. In 1751, Palmer baptized Shubal Stearns in the Willimantic River, at Tolland, Connecticut, and conducted his ordination. Stearns carried the First Great Awakening to the South and, in 1755, planted the first Baptist church in North Carolina.

Endless Memorials

Even though John Clarke married three times, his only child, a daughter by his second wife, Jane,[960] died in infancy. Clarke's third wife, Sarah,[961] survived him. In the John Clarke Family Cemetery in Newport,[962] Clarke's tombstone stands between those of Elizabeth and Jane. A small park adjoining the cemetery has two monuments to John Clarke—a plaque on a small rock and a large monument placed there in 2003 by the Baptist History Preservation Society. As St. Paul's Cathedral, in

---

cemetery is on the west side of Vaucluse Ave., just north of Green End Ave., Route 138, in Middletown, Rhode Island.

[957] Valentine Wightman readily rejected the Unitarianism of his great grandfather, Edward Wightman, who was the last religious martyr burned at the stake in England. Stephen Wright, "Wightman, Edward (bap. 1580? d. 1612)," *Oxford Dictionary of National Biography* (Oxford University Press, 2004), online edition, http://www.oxforddnb.com/view/article/29371.

[958] Frederic Denison, "The Wightmans," in *Annals of the American Baptist Pulpit*, ed. William B. Sprague (New York: Robert Carter and Brothers, 1860), 6:26–31.

[959] In 1844, First Baptist Church of Groton moved to nearby Mystic, Connecticut.

[960] Jane (née Fletcher) died in 1672.

[961] Sarah (widow of Nicholas Davis) died in 1692.

[962] The John Clarke Family Cemetery is on the west side of Dr. Marcus Wheatland Boulevard, in Newport. The key to the cemetery's padlocked gate is available at the United Baptist Church office.

London, was the masterpiece of Sir Christopher Wren, Rhode Island Colony was the masterpiece of Roger Williams and John Clarke. An inscription at Wren's Cathedral tomb describes the great architect as one who lived "not for himself but for the public good." It closes with the exhortation: "Reader, if you seek his monument look around you."[963] If we seek Williams and Clarke's monument, we need only to look at the early history of Rhode Island. Unlike the Puritans' description of Rhode Island Colony as "that sewer," in which "the Lord's debris has collected and rotted," the Rhode Island of Williams and Clarke was the world's first free republic, unstained by religious persecution. Like other colonies, it was not perfect, but its civil government was the first in the world to achieve religious freedom. Its 1663 Charter guaranteed freedom of conscience so long as the exercise of that freedom did not disturb the fundamental rights belonging to all citizens. Rhode Island was the only American colony established squarely upon the principle that government must allow the free exercise of worship. Rhode Island welcomed the Jewish people, and Touro Synagogue (est. 1763) in Newport is the oldest surviving Jewish building of worship in America. Its members still observe the annual reading of George Washington's historic letter "To the Hebrew Congregation at Newport."

Select Bibliography for Further Reading

Asher, Louis Franklin. *John Clarke (1609–1676): Pioneer in American Medicine, Democratic Ideals, and Champion of Religious Liberty*. Pittsburg, PA: Dorrance Publishing Co., 1997.

Barry, John M. *Roger Williams and the Creation of the American Soul: Church, State, and the Birth of Liberty*. New York: Viking Penguin, 2012.

Bicknell, Thomas W. *Story of Dr. John Clarke: The Founder of the First Free Commonwealth of the World on the Basis of "Full Liberty in Religious Concernments."* 2nd ed. Providence, RI: Published by the author, 1915.

Brockunier, Samuel Hugh. *The Irrepressible Democrat Roger Williams*. New York: The Ronald Press Co., 1940.

Byrd, James P. Jr. *The Challenges of Roger Williams*. Macon, GA: Mercer University Press, 2002.

Chapin, Howard M. *Report upon the Burial Place of Roger Williams*. Providence:

---

[963] *Lector, si monumentum requiris, circumspice.*

Rhode Island Historical Society, 1918.

Clarke, John. *Ill Newes from New-England: Or A Narrative of New-Englands Persecution*. London: Henry Hills, 1652.

Elton, Romeo. *The Life of Roger Williams: The Earliest Legislator and True Champion for a Full and Absolute Liberty of Conscience*. London: Albert Cockshaw, 1852.

Fisher, Linford D., J. Stanley Lemons, and Lucas Mason-Brown. *Decoding Roger Williams: The Lost Essay of Rhode Island's Founding Father*. Waco, TX: Baylor University Press, 2014.

Gaustad, Edwin S. *Liberty of Conscience: Roger Williams in America*. Valley Forge: Judson Press, 1999.

Gilpin, W. Clark. *The Millenarian Piety of Roger Williams*. Chicago: University of Chicago Press, 1979.

Guild, Reuben Aldridge. "A Biographical Introduction to the Writings of Roger Williams." In *Publications of the Narragansett Club*, 1:1–60. Providence, RI: Narragansett Club, 1866.

Hall, Timothy L. *Separating Church and State: Roger Williams and Religious Liberty*. Champaign: University of Illinois Press, 1998.

Holmes, Obadiah. *The Last Will and Testimony of Obadiah Holmes*. In *Baptist Piety*. Edited with historical introduction by Edwin S. Gaustad. 1978. Reprint, Tuscaloosa, AL: The University of Alabama Press, 2005.

James, Sydney V. *John Clarke and His Legacies: Religion and Law in Colonial Rhode Island 1638–1750*. Edited by Theodore Dwight Bozeman. University Park, PA: The Pennsylvania State University Press, 1999.

King, Henry Melville, ed. *Historical Catalogue of the Members of the First Baptist Church in Providence, Rhode Island*. Providence: F. H. Townsend, 1908.

_____. *Historical Discourse in Commemoration of the One Hundred and Twenty-Fifth Anniversary of the Dedication of the First Baptist Meeting-House, Providence, R. I., Sunday, May 27, 1900*. Providence: F. H. Townsend, 1900.

_____. *The Mother Church: A Brief Account of the Origin and Early History of the First Baptist Church in Providence*. Philadelphia: American Baptist Publication Society, 1896.

Lemons, J. Stanley. "Churches Founded by First Baptist." In *First Baptist, Providence*. Vol. 2 of the series, Baptists in Early North America, edited by William H. Brackney, 455. Macon, GA: Mercer University Press, 2013.

_____. *The First Baptist Church in America*. East Greenwich, RI: Charitable Baptist Society, 1988.

_____. "Historical Introduction to First Baptist, Providence." In *First Baptist, Providence*. Vol. 2 of the series, Baptists in Early North America, edited by William H. Brackney, xi–lxv. Macon, GA: Mercer University Press, 2013.

Mead, Sidney E. *The Lively Experiment*. New York: Harper and Row, 1963.

Morgan, Edmund S. *Roger Williams: The Church and the State*. 1967. Reprint, New York: W. W. Norton & Co., 2006.

Nelson, Wilbur. *The Hero of Aquidneck: A Life of Dr. John Clarke*. New York: Fleming H. Revell, 1938.

Records of the First Baptist Church. Edited by J. Stanley Lemons. In *First Baptist,*

Providence. Vol. 2 of the series, Baptists in Early North America, edited by William H. Brackney, 1–455. Macon, GA: Mercer University Press, 2013.

Sheffield, William P. "John Clarke, Physician, Philanthropist, Preacher, and Patriot." *Journal of the American Medical Association* 13, no. 8 (August 24, 1889): 253–57, an address presented to the American Medical Association, June 25, 1889.

Strickland, Arthur B. *Roger Williams: Prophet and Pioneer of Soul Liberty*. Boston: Judson Press, 1919.

Terry, David J. "Mark Lucar: Particular Baptist Pioneer." *Baptist History and Heritage* 25, no. 1 (January 1990): 43–49.

Williams, Roger. *The Bloudy Tenent of Persecution, for Cause of Conscience, Discussed in a Conference between Truth and Peace*. A facsimile reproduction with footnotes added by Samuel L. Caldwell. Vol. 3 of *Publications of the Narragansett Club*. Providence, RI: Narragansett Club, 1867.

———. *The Bloody Tenent yet More Bloody* (1652). A facsimile reproduction with footnotes added by Samuel L. Caldwell. Vol. 4 of *Publications of the Narragansett Club*, 1–501. Providence, RI: Narragansett Club, 1870.

———. *Experiments of Spiritual Life and Health, and their Preservatives in Which the Weakest Child of God May Get Assurance of His Spiritual Life and Blessedness, and the Strongest May Find Proportionable Discoveries of His Christian Growth, and Means of It* (1652). A facsimile reproduction with footnotes added by Perry Miller. In *The Complete Writings of Roger Williams*, 7:42–114. New York: Russell & Russell, 1963.

———. *George Fox Digg'd out of His Burrowes* (1676). A facsimile reproduction with footnotes added by J. Lewis Diman. In vol. 5 of *Publications of the Narragansett Club*. Providence, RI: Narragansett Club, 1872.

———. *The Hireling Ministry None of Christ's: Or a Discourse Touching the Propagating of the Gospel of Christ Jesus* (1652). A facsimile reproduction with footnotes added by Perry Miller. In *The Complete Writings of Roger Williams*, 7:142–91. New York: Russell & Russell, 1963.

———. *A Key into the Language of America* (1643). A facsimile reproduction with footnotes added by J. Hammond Trumbull. In *Publications of the Narragansett Club*, 1:62–279. Providence, RI: Narragansett Club, 1866.

———. *Letters of Roger Williams: 1632–1682*. A facsimile reproduction with footnotes added by John Russell Bartlett. In vol. 6 of *Publications of the Narragansett Club*. Providence, RI: Narragansett Club, 1874.

———. *Mr. Cotton's Letter Lately Printed, Examined and Answered* (1644). A facsimile reproduction with footnotes added by Reuben Aldridge Guild. In *Publications of the Narragansett Club*, 1:285–396. Providence, RI: Narragansett Club, 1866.

———. *Letter to Major Endicott, Governor of Massachusetts, upon Occasion of the Late Persecution against Mr. Clarke and Obadiah Holmes, and Others at Boston*. A facsimile reproduction with footnotes added by Samuel L. Caldwell. In *Publications of the Narragansett Club*, 4:502–18. Providence, RI: Narragansett Club, 1870.

———. *Queries of Highest Consideration* (1644). A facsimile reproduction with footnotes added by Reuben Aldridge Guild. In *Publications of the Narragansett Club*, 2:241–75. Providence, RI: Narragansett Club, 1867.

Chapter 13

Seventeenth-Century Baptists in Massachusetts

------------ ❋ ------------

Henry Dunster (ca. 1609–1658/9): First President of Harvard College

Introduction

While the earliest New England Puritans settled first in Salem, in 1628, it was Boston with her fine harbor that soon became the hub of Massachusetts Bay Colony. Deeply concerned for the education of their youth, the Puritans acquired a charter from the English Crown in 1636 to establish a college. Situated in Cambridge, just across the Charles River from Boston, Harvard College emerged as America's first institution of higher learning. Its express purpose was to train ministerial successors for Puritan churches.[964] The plaque on the brick wall, just outside the Johnston Gate at Harvard Yard, captures the

---

[964] Major histories of Harvard include Samuel F. Batchelder, *Bits of Harvard History* (Cambridge: Harvard University Press, 1924); Samuel Morison, *The Founding of Harvard College* (Cambridge: Harvard University Press, 1968); idem, *Harvard College in the Seventeenth Century*, 2 vols. (Cambridge: Harvard University Press, 1936); idem, *Three Centuries of Harvard 1636–1936* (Cambridge: Harvard University Press, 1964). See also Donald G. Tewksbury, *The Founding of American Colleges and Universities before the Civil War* (New York: Columbia University, 1932).

founders' priorities:

> After God had carried us safe to New England,
> and we had builded our houses,
> provided necessaries for our livelihood, reared
> convenient places for Gods worship,
> and settled the Civil Government:
> One of the next things we longed for, and
> looked after was to advance learning and perpetuate it to posterity,
> dreading to leave an illiterate ministry to the Churches, when our
> present ministers shall lie in the dust.[965]

The founders named the college for John Harvard (1607–38), who having no children willed half of his estate and his entire library to the school. This amounted to some four hundred books and between £700 and £850.[966] The school opened its doors in 1637 with Nathaniel Eaton as headmaster. By 1639, Eaton was unsuccessfully defending himself against bitter charges of failing to feed the students properly and of being a tyrant. The school quickly ousted him and the church excommunicated him. Eaton and his wife escaped to Virginia while the college closed temporarily to recover from its failed beginnings. Like a breath of fresh air, Henry Dunster would step in as Harvard's first president and establish the school on a firm foundation.

Dunster's Early Life

The fifth of nine children born to Henry and Isabel Kaye Dunster, in Bury (Lancashire), England, Henry Jr. received his infant baptism in the local parish and his earliest training at the Bury Grammar School.[967] He then matriculated at Magdalene

---

[965] *New Englands First Fruits* (London: Printed by R. O. and G. D. for Henry Overton, 1643), 12. This copy is in the British Library, London.

[966] A good biography of John Harvard is Henry C. Shelley, *John Harvard and His Times* (Boston: Little, Brown, and Co., 1907).

[967] Biographies of Henry Dunster include Arseny James Melnick, *America's Oldest Corporation and First CEO: Harvard & Henry Dunster* (West Conshohocken, PA: Infinity, 2008); Samuel Dunster, *Henry Dunster and His Descendants* (Central Falls, RI: E. L. Freeman, 1876); and Jeremiah

College, Cambridge, receiving the BA (1630) and MA (1634) degrees. Upon leaving the University and beginning his preparation to teach at the local free school in Bury, Henry experienced conversion to Christ by faith and repentance.[968] He soon received an appointment as headmaster of the Bury Grammar School and eventually became the curate of Saint Mary's Parish Church in Bury. In the summer of 1640, two years prior to the outbreak of England's Civil Wars, Henry and his brother Richard immigrated to Cambridge, Massachusetts. Not surprisingly, the magistrates and elders elected Henry Dunster to the presidency of Harvard College. Dunster's reputation had gone before him, as one "fitted from the Lord for the work, and … reported to be … proficient in … Hebrew, Greek, and Latin languages, an orthodox preacher of the truths of Christ, very powerful through his blessing."[969] The following year, he married Elizabeth (Harris) Glover, widow of Joseph Glover,[970] who had died in 1638 during the family's voyage to the New World. Although Elizabeth had no offspring with Mr. Glover, he had brought along five children from a previous marriage. Upon Elizabeth's death in 1643, Henry Dunster became guardian of the Glover children. Two of the Glover daughters would grow up to marry two of Governor John Winthrop's sons. In 1644, Dunster married his second wife, Elizabeth Atkinson, who would bear him three sons and two daughters. Elizabeth (d. 1690) would outlive Henry by three decades. Since settling in Cambridge in 1640, the Dunster family had belonged to First Church, where Puritan Thomas Shepard was pastor. When Shepard died, in 1649, Dunster briefly served as interim until Jonathan Mitchell assumed pastoral duties. With the church closely identified with

---

Chaplin, *Life of Henry Dunster, First President of Harvard College* (Boston: James R. Osgood, 1872).

[968] Dunster's salvation testimony is preserved in Chaplin, *Life of Henry Dunster*, 262–65.

[969] Edward Johnson, "Wonder-Working Providence of Zion's Savior," in *A History of New England: from the English Planting in the Year 1628 until the Year 1652* (London: Printed for Nath: Brooke at the Angel in Cornhill, 1654), 168. I have slightly modernized some of the spelling. This copy is in the British Library, London.

[970] Some sources call him "Jesse" Glover, but "Joseph" is correct.

the college, Mitchell often yielded his pulpit to Dunster.

Dunster as Harvard's Founder and President

As the true founder of Harvard College, Henry Dunster arguably became the greatest president ever to serve the office there. Throughout his presidency, he "often suffered from the smallness of his salary, or from the delay of payment long after it was due."[971] Nevertheless, he not only set the academic, moral, and spiritual standards that prevailed for generations, he also established a strong, permanent administrative and financial base for the institution:

> Dunster found Harvard College deserted by students, devoid of buildings, wanting income or endowment, and unprovided with government or statutes. He left it a flourishing university college of the arts, provided with several buildings and a settled though insufficient income, governed under the Charter of 1650 by a body of fellows and officers whose duties were regulated by statute. The Harvard College created under his presidency and largely through his efforts endured in all essential features until the nineteenth century, and in some respects, has persisted in the great university of today.[972]

Equally important, Dunster set respectable academic standards, not unlike the colleges of Scotland, Ireland, England, and the Continent. Entrance requirements included first, the ability to read basic classical Latin and to make practical use of it. Second, the applicant had to know the basic vocabulary and declensions of New Testament Greek. Most importantly, however, the young scholar, once enrolled, could never escape the constant reminders of the primary purpose of his Harvard training, and the only source of all wisdom. The statement is as follows:

---

[971] Alden Bradford, "Historical Sketch of Harvard University," *The American Quarterly Register* 9, no. 4 (May 1837): 334 (321–66).
[972] Morison, *Founding of Harvard College*, 246.

1. When any Scholar is able to understand Tully,[973] or such like classical Latin author extempore, and make and speak true Latin in verse and prose, *suo ut aiunt Marte*;[974] and decline perfectly the paradigms of nouns and verbs in the Greek tongue: Let him then, and not before, be capable of admission into the College.

2. Let every student be plainly instructed, and earnestly pressed to consider well, the main end of his life and studies is, *to know God and Jesus Christ which is eternal life*, John 17:3, and therefore to lay *Christ* in the bottom, as the only foundation of all sound knowledge and learning. And seeing the Lord only giveth wisdom, Let every one seriously set himself by prayer in secret to seek it of him. Prov. 2, 3.[975]

As he daily taught his students, Dunster combined scholarship with Christian compassion and godliness.[976] He believed

---

[973] In the 17th century, the word *Tully* referred to the Latin of Cicero (*Marcus Tullius Ciceronis*).

[974] Seldom translated from the Latin, the expression *suo (ut aiunt) Marte* was a Latin proverb, meaning "by one's own power," or "without any assistance."

[975] *New Englands First Fruits*, 13–14).

[976] Indicative of this was his promotion of the founding of an Indian College at Harvard. Concerned for providing the New England Indians with a good education, Dunster took seriously the statement in the Charter of 1650 that one of the purposes of the college was "the education of the English and Indian Youth of this Country." Consequently, the Commissioners and the Corporation approved the financing of a substantial brick structure in Harvard Yard. Completed about a year after Dunster himself left the school, the building could accommodate some twenty students. Only about six individuals ever attended Harvard's Indian College. Only one of those completed the four-year program (class of 1665), and he died within a year of graduation. Only one of the six lived more than a decade after attending classes. The Indian College, however, is symbolic of a sincere Christian mission to help Native Americans. Although the school's records provide no specifics, the Puritans must have offered some concessions to assist these students in overcoming deficiencies with the entrance requirements. The Indian College maintained its feeble existence into the next century. See Alden T. Vaughan, *New England Frontier: Puritans and Indians 1620–1675* (Boston:

that the only reason for education was the cultivation of spirituality for the glory of God. Spiritual and intellectual discipline was at the forefront of his curriculum, as Batchelder unsympathetically notes:

> The spiritual life of the undergraduates—the only thing that really mattered in this vale of tears—was pried into, dissected, and stimulated with relentless vigor. The scholars read the Scriptures twice a day; ... they had to repeat or epitomize the sermons preached on Sunday, and were frequently examined as to their own religious state.... (At first, the sole requirement for the degree of A.B. was the ability "to read the original of the Old and New Testament into the Latin tongue and to resolve them logically.") Morning prayers were held at an hour that would have made an anchorite blush.[977]

Dunster as an Anti-Pedobaptist

After fourteen years of faithful service, Henry Dunster became a problem to the college's General Court of Overseers. Undoubtedly influenced by the recent whipping of the Baptist, Obadiah Holmes, in nearby Boston, Dunster had embraced the Baptist ordinance of believer's baptism. The conflict surfaced in 1653, when, as Isaac Backus reports, Dunster "boldly preached against infant baptism, and for believer's baptism, in the pulpit at Cambridge."[978] The young pastor, Jonathan Mitchell, sat bewil-

---

Little, Brown, 1965), 280–85.
[977] Batchelder, 4.
[978] Isaac Backus, *A History of New England: with Particular Reference to the Denomination of Christians Called Baptists*, 2 vols., 2nd ed., with notes by David Weston (Newton, MA: The Backus Historical Society, 1871), 2:418. Cotton Mather reports, "Our Mitchell, presently upon his becoming the pastor of Cambridge, met with more than an ordinary trial, in that the good man, who was then the president of the college, and a member of the church there, was unaccountably fallen into the briars of anti-pedobaptism; and being briar'd in the scruples of that persuasion, he not only forbore to present an infant of his own unto the baptism of our Lord, but also thought himself under some obligation to bear his testimony, in some sermons against the administration of baptism to

dered throughout the entire message. After sleepless nights of finding no answers to Dunster's sermon points, Mitchell paid Dunster a visit to discuss the matter. Almost persuaded, Mitchell returned home pondering grim thoughts of what might happen to him if he accepted Dunster's position. Mitchell's internal battle between truth and error intensified to the point of nauseating depression. He describes his ordeal: "That day after I came from him, I had a strange experience: I found hurrying [driving] and pressing suggestions against pedobaptism, and injected scruples and thoughts whether the other way might not be right, and infant baptism an invention of men; and whether I might with good conscience baptize children, and the like. And these thoughts were darted in with some impression, and left a strange confusion and sickliness upon my spirit." Mitchell finally resorted to convincing himself by the traditions of men that all Dunster's arguments were "from the evil one."[979]

Meanwhile, in the fall of 1653, Dunster refused to present his newborn fourth child, Jonathan, to the church for baptism. Aware that opposition to infant baptism was at odds with Puritan law, Dunster stood confident that the Bible never authorizes the baptism of babies. In 1644, Massachusetts Bay Colony had established the first law in New England against Anabaptists and Baptists. While the law mentions only "Anabaptists,"[980] Puritans caricatured Baptists by defining them as *Anabaptists*. Dunster's opposition to infant baptism would prove sufficient to condemn him as a "heretic." Infant baptism was essential to the Reformed theology of the tax-supported, ecclesiastical Standing Order of the Puritan colony. In 1654, Harvard's Board of Overseers called for a series of debates between Dunster

---

any infant whatsoever." *Magnalia Christi Americana*, in seven "book" divisions (London: Printed for Thomas Parkhurst, at the Bible and Three Crowns in Cheapside, 1702), book 4, chapter 4, page 175. I modernized some of the capitalization. This copy is from the John Adams Library at the Boston Public Library.

[979] Mather, *Magnalia Christi Americana*, book 4, chapter 4, page 175.

[980] "Anabaptists" (1644), in *The Book of the General Laws and Liberties Concerning the Inhabitants of the Massachusetts*, "collected out of the records of the General Court" (Cambridge, MA: Printed according to order of the General Court, to be sold at the shop of Hezekiah Usher in Boston, 1648), 2–3.

and a panel of nine ministers and two elders. (Their most proficient debater, John Cotton, had died two years earlier.). The board positioned John Norton and Richard Mather as their primary debaters against Dunster, who would be in his element, since the debates would be in Latin. Dunster's thesis was *Soli visibiliter fideles sunt baptizandi* ("Only visible believers are to be baptized"). He used the word *visible* in opposition to his opponents' insistence that invisible faith resides within infants of elect parents. Puritans considered the act of cutting the infant off from baptism to be worse than cutting him out of his mother's womb. Believing that the church is under the Abrahamic Covenant, Puritans feared that infants who died outside the covenant would be eternally without Christ. In Puritan doctrine, one enters the Abrahamic covenant through the rite of water baptism, which, as they supposed, replaced the old rite of circumcision, Like John Calvin,[981] they urged that water baptism "engrafts" the infant "into Christ." Thus, the Puritans regarded denial of infant baptism as *soul-murder*.

Dunster would not budge on his stand that infant baptism was not only absent from the earliest churches, it was also absent from Scripture. Morison observes that Dunster "not only believed infant baptism to be unscriptural; he meant to testify against it upon every proper opportunity. Incidentally," adds Morison, "Dunster was right. Infant baptism was unknown in the Christian Church until more than two centuries after the death of Christ." Refusing to silence his convictions, in June 1654, Dunster submitted a letter of resignation to the college overseers.[982] In reply, the board urged him to retain his presidency by recanting. In July, just prior to a Sunday morning infant baptism, in First Church of Cambridge, Dunster calmly rose from his seat and once more explained from Scripture the spiritual dangers of baptizing the unconverted.[983] On October 24, he submitted his second letter of resignation to the college.[984] The board accepted, and, on

---

[981] John Calvin, *Institutes of the Christian Religion* (4.15.1), trans. Henry Beveridge (Edinburgh: Edinburgh Printing Company for the Calvin Translation Society, 1845).
[982] Chaplin, *Life of Henry Dunster*, 125–26.
[983] Ibid., 130–31; cf. Morison, *Harvard College in the Seventeenth Century*, 1:308.
[984] Chaplin, *Life of Henry Dunster*, 135.

November 10, they inaugurated Charles Chauncy (1592–1672) into the presidency. Although a Cambridge University graduate, Chauncy firmly believed that baptism should be by immersion—for adults and infants. He had practiced immersion for years in Plymouth Colony, but now he agreed to keep quiet about it. The contrast between the two men is obvious: While Dunster forfeited the presidency to maintain his convictions, Chauncy forfeited his convictions to gain the presidency.

Dunster requested permission to remain temporarily in the president's home. He was willing to assist the campus family in multiple ways during the transition of leadership. Dunster had contributed to the college a hundred acres of land,[985] on which he had built the home with his own hands. Moreover, Dunster's first wife had inherited America's first printing press from her deceased husband, Joseph Glover, and she had bequeathed it to Henry. In their home, Dunster had turned out the first printed works in America, including the venerable *Bay Psalm Book* (1640). Following a second printing, in 1647, Dunster and his assistant, Richard Lyon, had revised the *Bay Psalm Book* and reprinted it under the title *The Psalmes Hymns and Spiritual Songs of the Old and New Testament* (1651). Described by Cotton Mather as "a very good Hebrician," Dunster "bore a very great part in the metrical version of the Psalms, now used in our churches."[986] The Psalter had already become so popular that the churches would use it for more than a century after Dunster's death.[987] Dunster had passed the ownership of the press to the college, and, upon arrangement with the school, he had continued to operate the press in his home. Now, with his wife and youngest child ill, and with a bitter winter approaching, he received an order to vacate immediately. With four small children, ranging from one to nine years of age, Dunster once again pleaded in behalf of his

---

[985] Backus, *A History of New England: with Particular Reference to the Denomination of Christians Called Baptists*, 1:96, 1:227–30; 2:418.
[986] Cotton Mather, *Magnalia Christi Americana*, book 3, chapter 12, page 100.
[987] New England and Scottish churches would use the Dunster-Lyon Psalm book until Thomas Prince of Boston's Old South Church produced a new metrical edition in 1758.

family for permission to remain a bit longer in their home.[988] As Morison notes, they received little sympathy:

> Apparently, the Overseers were more eager to get the new president installed than to make the old president comfortable; for we find Dunster again addressing the General Court on November 16. It was a moving and pathetic appeal to their humane sentiments. Winter was coming on; he and his young family had no knowledge of the place whither they were destined; their goods and cattle could be moved at that season only with great loss; Mrs. Dunster was ill and the baby too "extremely sick" for a long journey.[989]

After prolonged wrangling, the General Court of Overseers allowed the Dunster family to remain in the house until March, but the court would hound Dunster until near the end of his life with legal proceedings over his objections to infant baptism. Even after 1654, when Dunster and his family moved to Scituate (in Plymouth Colony),[990] the Cambridge Court deprived them of peace and quiet. In 1655, the court summoned Dunster back to Boston, on alleged charges of disturbing the peace when he had taught against infant baptism in the Cambridge church. The court ruled him guilty. In April 1657, the Cambridge Grand Jury summoned Dunster on charges of heresy, for failing to bring his fifth child, Elizabeth, to the "Holy Ordinance of baptism." The court found him guilty and fined him.[991] Back in

---

[988] Dunster's letters are in Harvard University Archives, in 4 folio boxes, call no. UAI 15.850. For a transcription of this letter, see Josiah Quincy, *The History of Harvard University* (Cambridge: John Owen, 1840), 1:18–20.

[989] Morison, *Harvard College in the Seventeenth Century*, 1:313.

[990] Upon leaving Cambridge, the Dunster family spent a very brief time in nearby Charlestown before moving on to Scituate that same year.

[991] On that same day and in the same place, Thomas Gould also stood before the inquisition of the Grand Jury for failing to bring one of his children into the parish church for baptism. Prior to becoming a Baptist, in 1655, Gould had served as deacon in the First Church of nearby Charlestown. After a series of unsuccessful encounters with the 1644 law, Gould, in 1665 (six years after Dunster's death), would organize Boston's First Baptist Church. See Chaplin, *Life of Henry Dunster*, 164–66.

Scituate, Dunster had succeeded his Harvard replacement, Charles Chauncy, as pastor of First Parish Church. John Lathrop, who had served as the second pastor of London's J-L-J Church, had founded Scituate church in 1634. Like Lathrop, the Scituate church would never become Baptist.[992] While there is no extant record of Dunster receiving rebaptism, his life and ministry contributed immensely to the Baptist heritage.

Dunster's Final Years

In his will, Dunster graciously left valuable books from his library to his former student, Jonathan Mitchell, of First Church, Cambridge. Five years earlier, Mitchell had described Dunster's discourses as "venom and poison." Charles Chauncy also became a beneficiary of the former president's books. In addition, Dunster left instructions for the interment of his body to be in Cambridge, near the school and the people he had served.[993] Henry Dunster died on February 27, 1658/59, and his remains lie buried in Cambridge's Old Burying Ground adjacent to First Church (now Unitarian Universalist). Harvard College would not display signs of change until the late 1600s. Following Dunster, five presidents served during the period from 1654 to 1701: Charles Chauncy,[994] Leonard Hoar,[995] Urian Oakes,[996] John Rogers,[997] and Increase Mather. Each of these

---

[992] Today, the Scituate church is the First Parish Unitarian Universalist Church of Scituate, Massachusetts. Emerging from the Scituate church during Charles Chauncey's pastorate, the nearby First Parish in Norwell, Massachusetts, is also Unitarian and Universalist.

[993] Dunster's will is in Harvard University Archives, in 4 folio boxes; call no. UAI 15.850.

[994] Charles Chauncy's scholarship was profound, even in the field of medicine. He was up at four in the morning in all seasons. All six of his sons became Harvard graduates.

[995] Leonard Hoar, a Harvard graduate, received an honorary degree from Cambridge University. Like Chauncy, he studied medicine. His presidency was only three years—1672-75.

[996] Urian Oakes served as president from 1675 to 1681. He was a Harvard graduate and noted for his proficiency in astronomy.

[997] John Rogers served as president from 1682 to 1684. He was a Harvard graduate and a descendant of John Rogers, the martyr who was burned

proved to be an example of strong character, scholarship, and spiritual depth.

The school would begin showing subtle signs of change, during Increase Mather's administration, despite Mather's strong Puritan character and preaching. Regretfully, Mather was compelled to make trips to London for renewal of the college charter. During such absences, his colleagues made a series of decisions regarding baptism and Communion that would soon fill the state churches of New England with unregenerate members and forever change the course of the college. By then, Puritanism was only a memory of the past. The seeds of its destruction had germinated within its own Reformed theology.[998] By 1805, Harvard would be a Unitarian institution. Nothing, however, can negate the fruitful labors of the courageous founders. Their God is our God, and we continue to be emboldened by the fruit of the Holy Spirit in their lives. Only eternity will reveal the true, spiritual legacy of Henry Dunster's biblical convictions and his bold preaching, supernaturally empowered in "a gentle heart" and in "a noble vein of Christian charity."[999]

John Myles (1621–83): Founder of the First Baptist Church in Wales and in Massachusetts

Swansea in Wales

Born and raised in a Welsh speaking section of Herefordshire, England, not far from the Welsh border, John Myles (Miles),[1000]

---

at Smithfield, England, during the reign of Bloody Mary.

[998] For more development, see David Beale, "Harvard College (1636–1805: Puritanism to Unitarianism," in *Historical Theology In-Depth* (Greenville, SC: Bob Jones University Press, 2013), 2:224–41.

[999] These are the words of Harvard president Josiah Quincy, *The History of Harvard University*, 21.

[1000] The best biographical information on John Myles include William H. Brackney, with Charles K. Hartman, "From Ilston to Swansea: A Historical Introduction," in *Swansea, Massachusetts*, vol. 1 of the series, Baptists in Early North America, ed. William H. Brackney (Macon, GA: Mercer University Press, 2013), xiii–cii; Henry Melville King, *Rev. John Myles and the Founding of the First Baptist Church in Massachusetts*, "an Historical

in 1636, matriculated at Brasenose College, Oxford University, at the age of fifteen. Many details of his youth lie hidden in obscurity. Upon receiving his Oxford education, he moved to South Wales and settled in the county of Glamorgan, on the Gower Peninsula. Myles resided in the village of Ilston,[1001] situated just southwest of central Swansea (now the largest city in Wales). Following the beheading of King Charles, in January 1649, Wales became a Commonwealth, governed by Oliver Cromwell's Protectorate, or Interregnum (1649-60). This was a decade of great religious freedom for Welsh Baptists. While there is no evidence to determine precisely when Myles became a Baptist, or even when he received baptism by immersion, we know that, in the spring of 1649, Myles and his colleague Thomas Proud, both of whom had already embraced Baptist views, travelled to London and acquainted themselves with the leading Particular Baptists of the English capital. Here, the two men attended the Glasshouse Church,[1002] a central meeting place for the earliest Particular Baptist gatherings, including those of John Spilsbury (ca. 1593-1668) and William Kiffin (1616-1701).[1003] The London Baptists received

---

Address Delivered at the Dedication of a Monument in Barrington, Rhode Island (Formerly Swansea, MA) June 17, 1905" (Providence: Preston and Rounds, 1905); Gary Gregor, "John Miles: Gower's 'Pilgrim Father,'" *Gower Journal of the Gower Society* 46, (1995): 48-56; John Jones, "John Myles and His Times," *Baptist Quarterly Review* 10 (1888): 30-46; D. Densil Morgan, "John Myles (1621-83) and the Future of Ilston's Past: Welsh Baptists after Three and a Half Centuries," *The Baptist Quarterly* 38, no. 4 (October 1999): 176-84; Glanmor Williams, "John Miles, Ilston, and the Baptist Denomination in Wales," *Minerva Transactions of the Royal Institution of South Wales* 7, (1999): 11-18; and Thomas W. Bicknell, "John Myles: Religious Tolerance in Massachusetts," *Magazine of New England History* 2, no. 4 (October 1892): 213-42.

[1001] See Evan Evans and Mervyn Gwent, *A Portrait of Gower* (Swansea, Wales: The Gower Society, 1952), 10-13.

[1002] At that time, William Consett and Edward Drapes were shepherding the Glasshouse Church.

[1003] *The Ilston Book: Earliest Register of Welsh Baptists*, ed. B. G. Owens (Aberystwyth: The National Library of Wales, 1996), 31-32. In 1653, the Ilston church would receive a letter of encouragement "from the church of Christ at Glasshouse, London," with William Kiffin's name topping the list of ten men who signed it. See *The Ilston Book*, 63-64.

Myles as a providential answer to their prayers for planting churches in Wales. Myles shared their conviction that believer's baptism by immersion is prerequisite for church membership and the Lord's Supper. Commissioned by London's Particular Baptists, Myles returned to Ilston, where, in October 1649, he baptized the original nucleus of the first organized Baptist church in Wales.[1004]

Surprisingly, Myles would demonstrate obliviousness toward the Baptist distinctive of separation of church and state. Considering the historical context and the short time that Myles had walked among the Baptists, perhaps his inconsistencies during this period should not shock the modern reader. Myles would not have been immune to the strong influence of the Puritan and Presbyterian presence in Wales. In behalf of Cromwell's amorphous Independent National Church of England, the Long (Rump) Parliament, in February 1650, appointed John Myles as a paid "approver," whose task was to issue a certificate upon the completion of each "examination and ejection of scandalous, malignant, and non-resident

---

Since 1618, Sir Robert Mansell, at the glasshouse, had held the sole patent for making "all sorts of glass with pit-coal." Ben Weinreb and Christopher Hibbert, eds., *The London Encyclopedia* (1983; repr., Bethesda, MD: Adler and Adler Publishers, 1986), 309; and Walter Thornbury, *Old and New London*, rev. ed. (London: Cassell, Petter, Galpin, and Co., 1881), 165. Located on Old Broad Street, the Glasshouse building later became "Pinners' Hall," when the Pinners' Company (manufacturer of pins and needles) purchased it. Supported by local merchants, this company, beginning in 1673, would allow Presbyterian, Independent, and Baptist speakers to hold weekly, Tuesday-morning lectureships in Pinners' Hall. "The Ancient Merchants' Lecture," *Congregational Historical Society Transactions* 7, no. 6 (April 1918): 300–09. The Baptist Elias Keach would lecture here in 1692.

[1004] See "The Ilston/Swansea Record Book and Its History," in Brackney, *Swansea, Massachusetts*, xv–xvin10, 32n68 (1–373); R. C. Anderson, "Swansea, Massachusetts, Baptist Church Records," *New England Historical and Genealogical Register* 139 (January 1985): 21–49; Frank Lee, "The Tercentenary of Ilston, 1649-1949," *The Baptist Quarterly* 13, no. 4 (October 1949): 147-57; and Barrington R. White, "John Miles and the Structures of the Calvinistic Baptist Mission to South Wales 1649-1660," in *Welsh Baptist Studies*, ed. Mansel John (Cardiff: The South Wales Baptist College, 1976), 35-76.

ministers and schoolmasters" from the Welsh parishes. The examiners consisted of a Commission for the Propagation of the Gospel in Wales.[1005] When the Commission expired, after three years, it ejected 278 Anglican royalists, including William Houghton, rector of St. Illtyd Parish Church of Ilston.[1006] Myles replaced Houghton at the tax-supported pastorate of the St. Illtyd Church. With a shortage of qualified replacements, many parishes throughout the county were without ministers; itinerant preachers stepped in to fill the gap.

To reach Ilston from their remote villages and hamlets all over the Gower Peninsular and beyond, many of Myles's congregation traveled countless miles over poor roads and through frequent bad weather. To remedy the hardship, the leaders agreed that the remote or outlying membership would gather only on designated Sundays. On the other Sundays and select weekdays, those living in outlying areas would divide into sub-districts, holding cottage meetings for preaching, prayer, fellowship, and Bible study. The local group in Ilston would meet every Sunday. In 1651, the Ilston congregation officially reorganized themselves into a Baptist church, by electing Myles as pastor and Morgan Jones as elder. They also ordained deacons for their church and for each of the satellite congregations.

Initially, baptism, the Lord's 'Supper, weddings, discipline, and the counseling of new members occurred only at the Ilston church, which approved and provided training sessions for the increasing numbers of new preachers and church planters.

[1005] Established by the Long Parliament and signed on February 22, 1650 (N. S.), a Commission for the Propagation of the Gospel in Wales, consisted of seventy-one members—twenty-eight in the north and forty-three in the south. John Myles was among those appointed for south Wales. C. H. Firth and R. S. Rait, eds., *Acts and Ordinances of the Interregnum 1642–1660* (London: His Majesty's Stationery Office, 1911), 2:343, 345.

[1006] Commissioners for the British House of Commons became resident protectors of non-Anglican dissenters in the Swansea area. Parliamentary Commissions in South Wales included Rowland Dawkins, Jenkin Franklen (Jenkyn Franlyn), and John Price (Ibid., 2:343). Cf. the list of names in "Insurrection in Wales, Wednesday, the 25th of June 1651," in *Journal of the House of Commons, 1648–1651* (London: His Majesty's Stationery Office, 1802), 6:591–92.

Myles gradually adjusted the program to provide for each district, according to its own changing conditions and needs.[1007] Many church plants would spring directly from the Ilston church.[1008] Of course, they would also face a host of issues, such as corporate singing of Psalms, the laying on of hands, discipline, and prerequisites to membership and the Lord's Supper. Between 1650 and 1654, six "General Meetings" gathered in various places to establish rules for organizing churches.[1009] As Gerald Priest explains, "This centralized connectionalism was obviously an expedient measure for purposes of unity and accountability, but it revealed a hierarchical relationship uncharacteristic of a Baptist polity which has traditionally viewed each local assembly as autonomous."[1010] Myles accepted an additional paid, governmental appointment as lecturer in nearby towns.[1011] In August 1654, the Lord Protector, Cromwell, activating a new "Church Ordinance on Scandalous Ministers," appointed Myles as one of twenty-four commissioners to a vast area of South Wales. Myles's work was to serve as a Trier (approver) in the ongoing investigation and ejection of Anglican ministers.[1012]

In doctrinal issues, John Myles demonstrated his mastery in the exposition of Scripture. When the Quakers persisted in their constant distribution of "slanderous" literature against the Baptists of South Wales, Myles pinned his only published work, a powerful, doctrinal treatise, titled *An Antidote against the Infection of the Times* (1656). The Scripture-packed *Antidote* consists of three messages — a compassionate gospel call to sinners, a loving assortment of admonitions to the saints, and

---

[1007] *The Ilston Book*, 11–19.
[1008] These new church plants included those at Hay-on-Wye and Llantrisant (1650), Carmarthen (1651), and Abergavenny (1652).
[1009] Barrington R. White, ed., "Association Records of the Particular Baptists of South Wales to 1656," Part 1 of *Association Records of the Particular Baptists of England, Wales, and Ireland to 1660* (Didot, Oxfordshire: Baptist Historical Society, 1971), 1–17.
[1010] Gerald Priest, "The Philadelphia Baptist Association and the Question of Authority," *Detroit Baptist Seminary Journal* 12 (2007): 58.
[1011] Thomas Richards, "John Miles in Wales, 1649–1663," *Baptist Quarterly* 5, no. 8 (October 1931): 364 (362–65).
[1012] Firth and Rait, *Acts and Ordinances of the Interregnum 1642–1660*, 2:984.

an urgent warning to backsliders. To the saints, "We thought [it] good," said Myles, "to write a few words of admonition and exhortation unto you, that (with the blessing of the Lord) may serve as Jonathan's arrows to David, to warn you against that spirit of delusion and apostasy, which is come abroad…. With the raking up of that foul dunghill of the errors of these men," our "present purpose is to … warn you against the reigning sins of these perilous times."[1013] Particular Baptist churches throughout the realm would gladly utilize the fifty-one-page masterpiece. Myles's Ilston congregation would grow from about fifty-five members in October 1650 to about 261 in August 1660.[1014] On a small country lane, the quaint, thirteenth-century Parish Church of St. Illtyd is located near the western end of the Swansea airfield. Mid-nineteenth-century renovations slightly modified the church's appearance from the days when Myles's Baptist congregation worshipped here. Sadly, their peaceful days in this place would end abruptly.

On May 21, 1660, at the Restoration of the British monarchy, Charles II initiated a reign of terror that would drive Baptists underground until the 1689 Glorious Revolution under William and Mary. Only two months after Charles II began his reign, officials ousted John Myles from Ilston's parish church and restored William Houghton. The British Parliament soon passed the Act of Uniformity (1662), which compelled every minister in the realm to declare publicly his "unfeigned assent and consent to all and everything contained and prescribed in and by the *Book of Common Prayer*," for all

---

[1013] John Myles, *An Antidote against the Infection of the Times: Or a Faithful Watchword from Mt. Sion to Prevent the Ruin of Souls*, "whereby some special considerations are presented to sinners, admonitions to saints, and invitation to backsliders, and published for the good of all by the appointment of the elders and messengers of the several churches of Ilston, Abergavenny, Tredinog, Carmarthen, Hereford, Bredwardin, Cledock and Llangors, meeting at Brecknock upon the 29th and 30th days of the fifth month" (London: Printed for T. Brewster, at the three Bibles at the west end of Pauls, 1656), 18–19. This copy is in the British Library. I have modernized a few words and punctuation.

[1014] *The Ilston Book*, 3–10.

corporate worship.[1015] Myles was among the first of nearly two thousand non-conformists and dissenters ejected from their pulpits. Strong tradition says that Myles and a portion of his congregation worshipped secretly in a secluded building, now in ruins, located down a path, a half mile from the Church of St. Illtyd. (See the Tour Guide in Appendix C).

When John Myles, Nicholas Tanner (one of his members), and possibly more fled to New England, in 1663, to plant a twin Swansea Baptist Church in Massachusetts,[1016] the Ilston Church-book of Records was stored inside Myles's luggage. From this ancient book, we can sense something of the heartbeat of John Myles and his congregation as they reminisce those amazing dozen years in Ilston:

> We cannot choose but admire at the unsearchable wisdom, power, and love of God, in bringing about his own designs, far above and beyond the capacity and understanding of the wisest of men. Thus, to the glory of his own great name, hath He dealt with us, for when there had been no companies or society of people holding forth and practicing the doctrine, worship, order, and discipline of the gospel according to primitive institution that ever we heard of in all Wales since the apostasy, it pleased the Lord to choose this dark corner to place His name here, and to honor us, undeserving creatures, with the happiness of being the first in all these parts among whom was practiced the glorious ordinance of baptism, and to gather here the first church of baptized believers.[1017]

[1015] Andrew Browning, ed., "Early Modern 1660–1714," in *English Historical Documents, 1660–1714*, ed. David C. Douglas (1966; repr., London: Routledge, 1996), 375–82.

[1016] See J. J. Thatcher, *Historical Sketch of the First Baptist Church, Swansea, MA: From Its Organization in 1663 to 1863* (Fall River, MA: First Baptist Church, Swansea, 1863).

[1017] See *The Ilston Book*, ed. B. G. Owens, 31; and "The Ilston/Swansea Record Book and Its History," in Brackney, *Swansea, Massachusetts*, 46. I modernized some spelling and punctuation. The original Swansea Record Book is on loan at Brown University's John Hay Library, in Providence, Rhode Island.

The small remnant remaining at the Ilston (Swansea) Baptist Church did persevere. Jonathan Davis recorded that these Baptists "had to meet in different places, in the most secret manner," including "different private houses in the town of Swansea." In 1698, they rented a Presbyterian meetinghouse. In 1710, ten members, including Hugh Davis, an ordained minister, immigrated to Colonial Pennsylvania.[1018] In 1758, the church in Wales erected its own meetinghouse. The rest of its history lies in obscurity.

Swansea in Massachusetts

In 1663, Myles and his small group settled at Rehoboth, in old Plymouth Colony,[1019] where, with seven charter members, not counting the women, gathered in the home of John Butterworth.[1020] Here, John Myles drew up a covenant and organized the earliest Baptist church in Massachusetts.[1021] To pacify anti-Baptist complaints, emerging from Boston magistrates and from the nearby Puritan pastor, Samuel Newman, the Plymouth Colony officials felt compelled to act. In 1667, they fined the Baptist leaders for unauthorized public worship, halted their worship services, and advised the little group to move on to some place where their presence would not "prejudice any

---

[1018] Jonathan Davis, *History of the Welsh Baptists* (Pittsburgh: D. M. Hogan, 1835), 89-90. This work is largely that of the Welsh Particular Baptist, Joshua Thomas (1719-1797), in his *Hane y Bedyddwyr* (1777).

[1019] George H. Tilton, "Early Settlers and Annals," in *A History of Rehoboth, Massachusetts: Its History for 275 Years 1643-1918* (Boston: Printed by Louis E. Crosscup, 1918), 5-61; and Eugene A. Stratton, *Plymouth Colony: Its History & People 1620-1691* (Salt Lake City, UT: Ancestry Publishing, 1986), 77-78. Plymouth Colony would merge into Massachusetts Bay Colony in 1691.

[1020] The charter members were John Myles (pastor), James Brown, Nicholas Turner, Joseph Carpenter, John Butterworth, Eldad Kingsley, and Benjamin Alby. They excluded the women's names.

[1021] The oldest copy of the original Covenant of Swansea Baptist (1663) is in the John Hay Library, Brown University. For a transcription, see Thomas Williams Bicknell, *A History of Barrington, Rhode Island* (Providence: Snow and Farnham, 1898), 126-27.

other church."[1022] More tolerant than Massachusetts toward religious freedom, the Plymouth Court soon granted to the Myles congregation a sizable block of land a few miles to the south, where they erected a meetinghouse at New Meadow Neck (later called Nockum Hill) and established the town of Swansea, Massachusetts.[1023] Closely associated with Myles, Captain Thomas Willett (1605–74), as co-founder of Swansea, had succeeded Captain Miles Standish as military commander of the *Mayflower* Pilgrims' Plymouth Colony.[1024]

Oblivious to the Baptist principle of individual freedom of conscience, John Myles wrote a town statute denying citizenship to Unitarians, Quakers, Roman Catholics, Anglicans, Lutherans, and Sabbatarians.[1025] There is no extant record of the town ever carrying out such restrictions. Ironically, though, Swansea Baptist Church functioned as the town's tax-supported, established church, consisting of pedobaptists and anti-pedobaptists; at the time, this was the only church in town. Myles quickly discarded his former practice of closed Communion and became an advocate of open Communion to all professing believers. He now practiced infant baptism and received pedobaptists into membership and Communion.[1026] Government land grants and public funds paid Myles's salary,

---

[1022] King, *Rev. John Myles and the Founding of the First Baptist Church in Massachusetts*, 30–31. Plymouth Colony, in 1642, had purchased from Massasoit the land that became the township of Rehoboth, incorporated in 1645.

[1023] The size of Swansea grew smaller in 1717, with the separate incorporation of the township of Barrington. In 1746, in a border settlement between Massachusetts and Rhode Island, a section of Swansea became Warren, Rhode Island. Other towns that fell to Rhode Island at that time were Barrington, Little Compton, Tiverton, and Bristol. For years, the dividing line between Massachusetts and Rhode Island had been an issue of dispute.

[1024] Captain Willett was not a member of Myles's church. Willett would soon become the first English mayor of New York, when the Dutch surrendered control, and his daughter, Sarah, married John Eliot, the Apostle to the Indians.

[1025] Otis Olney Wright, *History of Swansea Massachusetts 1667–1917* (Swansea, MA: Town of Swansea, 1917), 47–48.

[1026] Ibid., 48.

and, in 1673, town officials appointed him to the office of schoolmaster for life. Myles's Oxford training had prepared him to teach the required English, Latin, Greek, and Hebrew, along with rhetoric and mathematics. Reminiscent of his twelve years in Ilston, however, Myles's first dozen years in New England (since 1663) ended with a sudden disruption.

On Sunday morning, June 20, 1675, King Philip's War broke out at Swansea when most of the population was in church. The Myles home suddenly became a garrison, where John stood watch over his family and over all who could crowd into the small building. For the next four days, the Wampanoag Indians burned and destroyed most of the town. Nine of its inhabitants died and seven suffered wounds before help arrived from neighboring towns. By then, most of Swansea's inhabitants, including its church members, had scattered into the forests seeking refuge in other towns and villages. Myles promptly moved his family to Boston, where he served as interim pastor at First Baptist Church, when its founding pastor, Thomas Gould, died on October 27, 1675. There is no record of Swansea Baptist church during the first three post-war years, but, in 1678, Myles accepted an invitation to return and resume his pastorate. Two years later, the Swansea Baptist congregation erected a new building at Tyler's Point, where Myles served until his death, on February 3, 1683, at the age of sixty-two. The precise location of his grave is unknown.

John Myles's strength of character, love for souls, and willingness to suffer for the cause of Christ drew respect from friend and foe. Myles married twice. He married his first wife in Wales, but her identity is unknown. He married Ann (née Humphrey, 1625–95) in New England. Among the Myles children, there were at least two daughters and two sons: John Jr. served as Swansea's first town clerk. Samuel Myles (1665–1728) received a BA degree from Harvard, in 1684, and later traveled to England, where he earned an MA from Oxford and converted to Anglicanism. Returning to Boston, Samuel served thirty-nine years (1689–1728) as the second minister of King's Chapel, established in 1689 as the earliest Anglican Church in New England.[1027] Under its fifth minister, James Freeman, King's Chapel, in 1784, would become the first Unitarian church in the New World.

John Myles's immediate successor, Samuel Luther, served the Swansea pastorate during the years 1685–1717. During this time, under the Massachusetts Charter of 1691, Plymouth Colony merged into Massachusetts Bay Colony and became subject to its laws. Contrary to such laws, Luther came to the conviction that he must begin enforcing the Baptistic prerequisite of believer's baptism by immersion for membership and the Lord's Supper. With most of the church already Baptist, his aim was to make the Swansea Church a truly autonomous Baptist church. To accomplish this, in 1700, he led the church to re-locate from Tyler's Point to a new building in North Swansea, where most of the Baptist members resided. After a decade of wrangling, the Congregational pedobaptists separated from Swansea Baptist, in 1710, and organized their own church in the town's southwest side, where most of them resided. The Congregationalists, in 1717, finally convinced the legislature to separate the west-southwest side from the township of Swansea and to incorporate it into the township of Barrington, which, in a 1746 border settlement between Massachusetts and Rhode Island, would become Barrington, Rhode Island.[1028] Meanwhile, in due process, Swansea Baptist finally disentangled itself from government lands and monies. Upon Samuel Luther's death, his associate Ephraim Wheaton succeeded him to the pastorate, and, throughout his ministry, Swansea Baptist enjoyed spiritual refreshing. A revival that began in 1718 resulted in Wheaton's baptizing fifty new converts over the next five years. During the twentieth century, the church would affiliate with the American Baptist Churches USA. First Baptist Church of Swansea, Massachusetts, is at 21 Baptist Street. Their present building dates to 1848; its adjacent cemetery dates to 1731.

[1027] Henry Wilder Foote, *Annals of King's Chapel* (Boston: Little, Brown, and Co., 1900), 1:97–374.

[1028] Bicknell, *History of Barrington, Rhode Island*, 102–52, 184–202; and William G. McLoughlin, "Barrington Congregationalists vs. Swansea Baptists, 1711," *Rhode Island History* 32, no. 1 (February 1973): 19–21.

Thomas Gould, Founder of First Baptist Church, Boston

The Early Years

In 1640, Thomas Gould (Goold, Gold, ca. 1619–75) and his first wife Hannah joined the Puritan Church in Charlestown, Massachusetts. Thomas was a respectable farmer and wagon maker. The couple already had three babies baptized, by 1655, when Thomas came to reject the baptism of infants.[1029] That year, he refused to present their fourth newborn to the church for baptism. Two months later, the pastor summoned Gould to a meeting at the church, to explain such "negligence." At the meeting, Gould used Scripture to combat the Pedobaptist position. For over a year, the church and civil magistrates attempted unsuccessfully to change his mind. Not only was Thomas Gould one of the leading freemen and property owners of Charlestown, his reputation was as "a man of grave and serious spirit and of sober conversation." Now, he would face charges of violating the colony's anti-Baptist law of 1644. In December 1656, the grand jury of Middlesex County presented Gould to the County Court, for withholding from his infant the "efficacious" water of baptism. They warned Gould of the repercussions of non-conformity and instructed him to appear before the next County Court at Cambridge.[1030] In April 1657, the grand jury interrogated Thomas Gould and Henry Dunster

---

[1029] The two major sources for Thomas Gould and the history of Boston's First Baptist Church are Isaac Backus, "An Account of the Constitution of the First Baptist Church in Boston, in 1665, and of Their Sufferings down to 1675," in *A History of New England: with Particular Reference to the Denomination of Christians Called Baptists*, 1:287-328; and Nathan E. Wood, *The History of the First Baptist Church of Boston* (Philadelphia: American Baptist Publication Society, 1899). Other valuable sources include Henry Melville King, "The Baptists in Boston during the Last Hundred Years," in *The Memorial History of Boston, including Suffolk County, Massachusetts 1630–1880*, ed. Justin Winsor (Boston: James R. Osgood, 1881), 3:421–32; Andrew Leonard Sweet, "The Development of Local Religious Tolerance in Massachusetts Bay Colony" (MA thesis, University of Massachusetts Amherst, 1991), 47ff.; and James Pike, ed., *History of the Churches of Boston* (Boston: Ecclesia Publishing Co., 1883).
[1030] Wood, *History*, 32ff.

for their ongoing refusal to have their infants baptized.[1031] The Court ordered a twenty-pound bond to secure Gould's appearance before the next Court of Assistants.

The Birth, Persecution, and Exile of the First Baptist Church in Boston

During this time, several Baptists had been arriving from England, including Richard Goodall and his wife—recent members of William Kiffin's church in London. In 1663, the newcomers persuaded Gould to start holding private Sunday services for prayer and Bible study in his home. Mary Newell, another Baptist who had recently arrived from England, attended the meetings, along with William Turner and Robert Lambert, who had belonged to the Baptist church in Dartmouth, England. Turner would become a militia captain in 1676, during King Philip's War. Attendees from the local area included Thomas Osborne (a freeman) and his wife Sarah, who were property owners and members with Gould in the Charlestown parish church. Also attending Gould's meetings were Edward Drinker, a potter by trade, and John George, a chimney cleaner, both of whom resided in Charlestown but had no church membership. Like Turner, Drinker would become a militia captain during the Indian attacks. When the parish church became aware of the private meetings, they rebuked Gould and Osborne for failing to attend the parish churches and for spreading the "heresy of anti-pedobaptism." Such rebukes went unheeded.

Finally, in Charlestown, on May 28, 1665, nine charter members,[1032] including Thomas Gould, received baptism by immersion, and signed a covenant, thus constituting the First Baptist Church of Boston. While the records fail to reveal who administered the initial baptisms, the group consisted of seven men and two women. They chose Gould as pastor, and he probably

---

[1031] Ibid., 33ff. Cf. Chaplin, *Life of Henry Dunster*, 161–69.
[1032] The nine charter members were Thomas Gould, Thomas Osborne, Edward Drinker, John George, Richard Goodall, Mary Goodall, William Turner, Robert Lambert, and Mary Newell.

wrote their confession of faith. The first entry in their "Record Book" declares that this church, "commonly (though falsely) called Anabaptist," is "gathered together and entered into fellowship & communion" (1665).[1033] In July, the Puritan church excommunicated Thomas Gould, his second wife, Mary,[1034] and Thomas Osborne. In October, the General Court convicted and disfranchised Gould, Osborne, Drinker, Turner, and George for refusing to cease their "schismatical rending from the communion of the churches here, and setting up a public meeting in opposition to the ordinances of Christ." The Court warned them of immediate imprisonment if they gathered for any further worship.[1035]

During the following months, the courts sentenced fifteen other members of the Baptist congregation with admonitions, fines, and imprisonments. The Baptists argued that the laws of God justified the existence of a Baptist church.[1036] In April 1666, the Middlesex County Court fined Gould, Osborn, and George four pounds each for refusing to disband and return to the Puritan fold. The court ordered that each man post a twenty-pound bond, to secure his appearance at the next Court of Assistants to answer the charge of contempt. When the four Baptists refused to pay the fines or to post the bonds, officials imprisoned them.[1037] For their safety, the remainder of the congregation took exile on Noddle's Island, in the harbor of East Boston.[1038] A year later, the courts fined Gould, Osborne, and

---

[1033] Wood, *History*, 56–57. For Gould's confession of faith, see 64–66.
[1034] See Mary Gould's testimony and defense of her husband in Backus, 1:305–6.
[1035] Nathaniel B. Shurtleff, ed., *Records of the Governor and Company of Massachusetts Bay in New England* (Boston: William White, 1854), part 2, vol. 4, pages 290–91. I modernized some of the spelling. In other volumes of this set, the title has the word *Colony* rather than *Company*.
[1036] John Russell, *A Brief Narrative of Some Considerable Passages Concerning the First Gathering, and Further Progress of a Church of Christ, in Gospel-Order, in Boston, in New-England, commonly (though falsely) Called by the Name of Anabaptists, for Clearing Their Innocency from the Scandalous Things Laid to Their Charge* (London: Printed for J. D., 1680). This copy is in the library of the Massachusetts Historical Society.
[1037] Backus, *History*, 1:299.
[1038] In 1940, during World War II, engineers filled the strait dividing Noddle's

Mrs. Newell for failing to attend the Puritan church and to submit to its ordinances. Upon Gould's refusal to pay his fine, the Court ordered a levy on his property. The Baptists could see no end to the fines, imprisonments, and confiscations. Among the citizenry, though, there were now growing signs of sympathy toward peaceful Baptists who desired only the soul liberty to worship God in submission to His Word and His Spirit.

The Great Debate of 1668

In March 1668, the Governor and Council ordered "a full and free debate,"[1039] hoping to drive the Baptists "from the error of their way."[1040] The Baptists welcomed the debate. It would take place on April 14–15, 1668, at First Church, Boston, where John Davenport was the preaching elder. The debaters would be the prisoners, Thomas Gould "and company," against the colony's six leading ministers appointed by the Court. At the opening session, the Governor was present and the meetinghouse was packed. When Gould inquired if the Baptists would be legally responsible for what they said during the debate, an appointed official replied, "You come not on equal terms, but as a delinquent, to answer for what you have done."[1041] Thus, the promised "debate" turned out to be a court hearing, and the Baptists were the defendants. The Puritan clergy addressed the General Court, declaring the Baptist group to be "an enemy in this habitation of the Lord; an anti-New England in New England."[1042] Upon the clergy's advice, the magistrates sent Gould and his colleagues

---

Island from Boston's mainland to expand Logan airport. Thus, Noddle's "Island" is no longer an island.

[1039] See Martha Whiting Davidson's transcription of the debate, in William G. McLoughlin, *Soul Liberty: The Baptists' Struggle in New England, 1630–1833* (Hanover, NH: University Press of New England, 1991), 53–92; cf. Sweet, "The Development of Local Religious Tolerance in Massachusetts Bay Colony," 47–62.

[1040] Backus, *History*, 1:300.

[1041] William G. McLoughlin, *New England Dissent 1630–1833: The Baptists and the Separation of Church and State* (Cambridge, MA: Harvard University Press, 1971), 1:60–62.

[1042] Joseph B. Felt, *The Ecclesiastical History of New England* (Boston: Congregational Board of Publication, 1862), 2:426 (2:424ff.).

back to prison, and the General Court pronounced the sentence of banishment, by July 20, upon Thomas Gould and two of his members—William Turner and John Farnam (Farnum) Sr.

Just before July 20, the magistrates released the three prisoners for their preparation for exile. When they refused to leave town, the magistrates imprisoned them for life, or until they repented and submitted to voluntary exile, or until the officials forcibly banished them. Meanwhile, Gould's congregation remained on Noddle's Island, where, with the help of Obadiah Holmes and others, they continued their prayer meetings and worship services. When Boston officials published an order, in October, for the forcible banishment of the three prisoners, the town magistrates suddenly faced a petition, signed by sixty-six Boston citizens, including many outstanding individuals, requesting freedom and toleration for the prisoners. Immediately, the Court fined the petition's instigators and forced prominent signees to retract their names.[1043] This episode signifies an important shift in public opinion toward religious freedom. Meanwhile, one of the prisoners, John Farnam Sr., separated from the Baptists and returned to Boston's Second Church where Increase Mather ministered.[1044] Thomas Gould and William Turner, who was deathly ill, remained in prison for another six months. In the spring of 1669, during a three-day release for the prisoners to attend to personal business, a constable found Gould leading a Sunday service in his home, with thirteen adults and five children in attendance. Gould and Turner quickly managed to escape by boat to Noddle's Island, where Gould held services every Sunday for the next five years.

The Battle for a Baptist Meetinghouse

Apparently considering Noddle's Island a place of semi-exile, Boston officials never pursued the Baptists while they resided there. However, one day in 1670, William Turner

---

[1043] Ibid. 2:432.

[1044] The Baptist church would excommunicate John Farnam Sr. in 1683 for recanting. In 1695, Mather's church officially re-admitted Farnam, and, in 1709, Farnam embraced Quakerism, whom he considered "ye only people of god now in ye world" (Wood, *History*, 188–89).

ventured into Boston where officials captured and imprisoned him. There is no record of the date of his release, but, six years later, Captain William Turner would die in action, while fighting for his colony in King Philip's War. Meanwhile, Baptists had begun gathering private congregations in nearby towns, including Concord, Cambridge, and Newbury. Moreover, John Leverett, who had succeeded Richard Bellingham, as governor of Massachusetts Bay Colony, in 1673, displayed a more tolerant attitude toward Baptists. In the following year, Thomas Gould and his congregation unpretentiously returned from Noddle's Island and began worshipping in a private home in Boston, where Gould died on October 27, 1675. After a short pastoral interim by John Myles of Swansea, John Russell Jr. became Gould's successor in 1676.

In the spring of 1679, town authorities discovered that the Baptist congregation had erected a wooden meetinghouse on the corner of Salem and Stillman Streets, in the north end of Boston. The General Court immediately created a law, making church buildings illegal without a license. Obediently, the Baptists withdrew from their meetinghouse and quietly returned to their homes. In December, a letter from King Charles II reached Boston's officials expressing the monarch's desire "that freedom and liberty of conscience be given to such persons as desire to serve God in the way of the Church of England ... or any other his Majesty's subjects (not being papists) who do not agree in the Congregational Way."[1045] The primary purpose of the King's letter was to provide freedom for Anglican worship. Aware, however, that the term *Congregational Way* referred to the Puritan establishment, the Baptists saw in the letter a legal argument for their own freedom. To the Baptists, the royal letter called for a test. In early March 1680, the Baptists of Boston resumed the use of their building. On March 8, Boston officials boarded up the meetinghouse door and nailed to it this warning:

[1045] Thomas Hutchinson, *The History of the Colony of Massachusetts Bay*, "from the first settlement ... in 1628, until its incorporation with the Colony of Plymouth, Province of Maine ... by the Charter of King William and Queen Mary in 1691," 2nd ed. (London: Printed for M. Richardson, 1765), 326.

> All persons are to take notice, that by order of the court, the doors of this house are shut up, and that they are inhibited to hold any meeting therein, or to open the doors thereof, without license from authority, till the court take further order, as they will answer the contrary at their peril. Edward Rawson, Secretary.[1046]

Unflinchingly, on that same day, the congregation held their regular services outside their building in freezing temperatures. In the King's name, they petitioned the Court for the use of their place of worship.[1047] Two weeks later, the congregation, finding the boards removed, gladly entered to resume their worship. In May, the Court again ordered them to evacuate, but the Baptists ignored the order. Finally, in February 1681, the General Court acknowledged the Baptists' petition and granted them official permission to occupy their building. Never again would the courts harass them over the matter. In fact, in March 1682, the General Court sent a letter to its London agents to assure the King of England, "As for the Anabaptists, they are now subject to no other penal statutes than those of the Congregational way."[1048] The dawn of the eighteenth century would bring renewed persecution from incriminating, false charges of "Anabaptism," but the Baptists would face it with revitalized perseverance.

[1046] Rollin Heber Neale, *An Address Delivered on the Two Hundredth Anniversary of the Organization of the First Baptist Church, Boston, June 7, 1865* (Boston: Gould and Lincoln, 1865), 15.

[1047] Cephas B. Crane, *Bi-Centenary Commemoration of the Reopening of the First Baptist Meeting-House in Boston, after Its Doors Had Been "Nailed Up" by Order of the Governor and Council of the Colony of Massachusetts, March 8th, 1680,* "historical discourse by the pastor, Cephas B. Crane, D. D., First Baptist Church, Boston, March 21, 1880" (Boston: Tolman and White, 1880).

[1048] Shurtleff, ed., *Records of the Governor and Colony of Massachusetts Bay in New England,* 5:347. In the early 1700s, the congregation of First Baptist Church replaced the original building with a larger, wooden one on the same site. In 1882, the Church purchased its sixth (present) building from the Brattle Square Unitarian Society, situated at 110 Commonwealth Avenue. With a modern, ecumenical agenda and mission, the church now belongs to the American Baptist Churches USA.

David Beale

Select Bibliography for Further Reading

Brackney, William H., with Charles K. Hartman. "From Ilston to Swansea: A Historical Introduction." In *Swansea, Massachusetts*. Vol. 1 of the series, Baptists in Early North America, edited by William H. Brackney, xiii–cii. Macon, GA: Mercer University Press, 2013.

The Ilston Book: Earliest Register of Welsh Baptists. Transcribed and edited by B. G. Owens. Aberystwyth: The National Library of Wales, 1996.

"The Ilston/Swansea Record Book and Its History." In *Swansea, Massachusetts*. Vol. 1 of the series, Baptists in Early North America, edited by William H. Brackney, 1-373. Macon, GA: Mercer University Press, 2013.

King, Henry Melville. *Rev. John Myles and the Founding of the First Baptist Church in Massachusetts*. An Historical Address Delivered at the Dedication of a Monument in Barrington, Rhode Island (Formerly Swansea, MA) June 17, 1905. Providence: Preston and Rounds, 1905.

Lee, Frank. "The Tercentenary of Ilston, 1649-1949." *The Baptist Quarterly* 13, no. 4 (October 1949): 147-57.

McLoughlin, William G. "Barrington Congregationalists vs. Swansea Baptists, 1711." *Rhode Island History* 32, no. 1 (February 1973): 19-21.

_____. *New England Dissent 1630-1833: The Baptists and the Separation of Church and State*. 2 vols. Cambridge, MA: Harvard University Press, 1971.

_____. *Soul Liberty: The Baptists' Struggle in New England, 1630-1833*. Hanover, NH: University Press of New England, 1991.

Melnick, Arseny James. *America's Oldest Corporation and First CEO: Harvard and Henry Dunster*. West Conshohocken, PA: Infinity Publishing, 2008.

Morgan, D. Densil. "John Myles (1621-83) and the Future of Ilston's Past: Welsh Baptists after Three and a Half Centuries." *The Baptist Quarterly* 38, no. 4 (October 1999): 176-84.

Morison, Samuel Eliot. "Henry Dunster, President of Harvard." In *Builders of the Bay Colony*, 183-216. Boston: Houghton Mifflin, 1930.

Richards, Thomas. *A History of the Puritan Movement in Wales: From the Institution of the Church at Llanfaches in 1639 to the Expiry of the Propagation Act in 1653*. London: The National Eisteddfod Association, 1920.

_____. "John Miles in Wales, 1649-1663." *Baptist Quarterly* 5, no. 8 (October 1931): 362-65.

Sweet, Andrew Leonard. "The Development of Local Religious Tolerance in Massachusetts Bay Colony." MA thesis, University of Massachusetts, 1991.

Vital Records of Swansea, Massachusetts to 1850. Transcribed by H. L. Peter Rounds and edited by Jane Fletcher Fiske and Margaret F. Costello. Boston: New England Historic Genealogical Society, 1992.

Williams, Glanmor. "John Miles, Ilston, and the Baptist Denomination in Wales." *Minerva Transactions of the Royal Institution of South Wales* 7, (1999): 11-18.

Wolever, Terry, ed. *A Noble Company: Biographical Essays on Notable*

Particular-Regular Baptists in America. Vols. 1–9. Springfield, MO: Particular Baptist Press, 2006–16.

Wood, Nathan E. *The History of the First Baptist Church of Boston.* Philadelphia: American Baptist Publication Society, 1899.

Chapter 14

Church Planting, Expansion, and Higher Education: William Screven, Elias Keach, and Morgan Edwards

---

Baptist Outreach from Boston to Maine and South Carolina
William Screven (1629–1713)

Born in Somerton (Somersetshire), England, William Screven arrived in Massachusetts around 1668.[1049] He had been active among General Baptists in England for many years.[1050] He purchased land at Kittery, Maine, in 1673, and, the

---

[1049] The best sources include Robert A. Backer, *The First Southern Baptists* (Nashville: Broadman, 1966); Robert A. Backer, Paul J. Craven Jr., and R. Marshall Blalock, *History of the First Baptist Church of Charleston, South Carolina 1682–2007* (1982; repr., Springfield, MO: Particular Baptist Press, 2007); Henry S. Burrage, *History of the Baptists in Maine* (Portland, ME: Marks Printing House, 1904); H. A. Tupper, ed., *Two Centuries of the First Baptist Church of South Carolina, 1683–1883* (Baltimore: R. H. Woodward, 1889); Leah Townsend, *South Carolina Baptists, 1670–1805* (Florence, SC: Florence Printing Company, 1935); and Isaac Backus, *A History of New England: with Particular Reference to the Denomination of Christians Called Baptists*, 2nd ed. with notes by David Weston (Newton, MA: Backus Historical Society, 1871), 1:400ff., 2:479ff.

[1050] Thomas White, Jason G. Duesing, and Malcolm B. Yarnell III, eds., "The Political Theology of William Screven," in *First Freedom: The Baptist Perspective on Religious Liberty* (Nashville: B&H Publishing Group, 2007), 71–78; cf. Joshua Millet, *A History of the Baptists in Maine* (Portland: Charles Day, 1845), 24ff.

following year, he married Bridget Cutt (Cutts), daughter of a prominent shipbuilder of Kittery. The couple would have eleven children. To William Screven, Maine was his mission field. From the time of his arrival, he preached and held private meetings for Sunday worship. In 1675, a grand jury presented him to the County Court near Kittery, "for not frequenting the public meeting according to law." From the 1640s to the end of the Colonial Era, large regions of the Province of Maine remained chiefly under the governance of Massachusetts Bay Colony. In 1679–80, due to suppression of religious liberty, by Massachusetts officials, Screven joined many other residents in an unsuccessful appeal to the British Crown to take direct rule over Maine.

Since the nearest organized Baptist congregation was in Boston, William and Bridget joined Boston's First Baptist Church by baptism, on July 21, 1681. To William, this may have been a re-baptism, marking a fresh beginning as a Particular Baptist. The following year (1682), the Boston church licensed Screven to preach. He had already gathered a congregation at Kittery. In March 1682, the Provincial Court at nearby York, Maine, ordered a bond of one hundred British pounds for assurance of Screven's appearance at the Court of Pleas, for holding private, religious meetings. Refusing to pay the unreasonable bond, he suffered imprisonment. In June, the General Assembly drew a promise from Screven that he would be willing to leave the Province of Maine. No recorded date was set. On September 25, 1682, First Baptist of Boston assisted in the organization of the first Baptist church in Maine—Kittery Baptist Church, whose ten men and seven women covenanted together and adopted the Second London Confession. As in England, New England Baptists frequently re-ordained ministers who were beginning new pastorates. Thus, William Screven received ordination. After 1684, there are no records of further proceedings against Screven, who was soon accepting leadership positions in the town of Kittery. Indian uprisings, however, were becoming frequent and furious in Maine.

Just seven miles from Kittery, at the break of dawn, on January 25, 1692, Chief Madockawando and his Abnaki warriors left their snowshoes on a boulder, silently crept into the town of York, and murdered or captured three hundred sleeping inhabitants[1051] — men, women, and children — and reduced most of the town to ashes. Amid increasing threats, in the winter of 1696, sixty-seven-year-old William Screven, accompanied by his family and his congregation, set out on a voyage of over nine hundred nautical miles from Kittery to Charleston, South Carolina. Landing near Charleston, Screven settled along the Cooper River and named the place after his old English home — *Somerton* Plantation. Here, his flock of some thirty members comprised the first Baptist church in the South. Welcomed by unorganized Baptists already in the region, the church grew despite opposition from Congregationalists and Presbyterians. By 1698, Screven and his flock moved into Charleston as the town's First Baptist Church. Originally organized in Kittery, Charleston's First Baptist Church rightly uses 1682 as the year of its founding. After meeting in a home and in a temporary building for some two years, the congregation erected their first meetinghouse. Still located on Church Street, the present sanctuary dates to 1822. Screven served intermittently as pastor until his death. In 1707, he declined an invitation to the pastorate of First Baptist in Boston. By the following year, the Charleston membership had grown to ninety.[1052]

William Screven would suffer severe illness until his death in his eighty-fourth year, on October 10, 1713. His remains rest in the Screven family cemetery in Georgetown, South Carolina.[1053] William Screven wrote one work, titled *An Ornament for Church Members*. While there are no surviving copies, Morgan Edwards (1722–95), America's earliest Baptist historian, quotes a paragraph from it to conclude his section

---

[1051] A historical plaque on the boulder in York, Maine, describes the scene. The exact number of victims slightly differs among various sources.

[1052] Screven, "Letter to Mr. Callender of the Boston Church," in Tupper, ed., *Two Centuries of the First Baptist Church of South Carolina*, 58; cf. Townsend, *South Carolina Baptists*, 5ff.

[1053] Also in Georgetown, South Carolina, the remains of the notable Edmund Botsford (1745–1819), early pastor of Antipedo Baptist (later First Baptist) Church, lie buried in the Old Baptist Cemetery. See Roy Talbert Jr. and Meggan A. Farish, *The Antipedo Baptists of Georgetown County, South Carolina 1710–2010* (Columbia: University of South Carolina Press, 2015), 45–67; and Charles D. Mallary, ed., *Memoirs of Elder Edmund Botsford* (1832; repr., Springfield, MO: Particular Baptist Press, 2004).

on William Screven. In the quotation, Screven humbly lists the chief qualifications of a minister and expresses a final request to his congregation:

> And now ... all my dear brethren and sisters, whom God hath made me, poor and unworthy ... an instrument of gathering and settling in the faith and order of the Gospel, my request is that you, as speedily as possible, supply yourselves with an able and faithful minister. Be sure you take care that the person be orthodox in the faith and of blameless life, and does own the confession put forth by our brethren in London in 1689.[1054]

Baptist Roots in the Philadelphia Area and Beyond

Elias Keach (ca. 1666–99)

"By the good Providence of God,"[1055] circa 1683, five members of a Baptist Church in Radnorshire County, Wales, responded to William Penn's appeal for colonists. They arrived in the township of Lower Dublin and settled near Pennypack Creek, in present-day northeast Philadelphia. The five Baptists were John Eatton (Eaton), George Eatton (with his wife, Jane), Sarah Eatton, and Samuel Jones. John Baker, a member of a

---

[1054] Morgan Edwards, *Materials towards a History of the Baptists in the Province of South Carolina*, vol. 5 of the handwritten 6-vol. *Materials towards a History of the Baptists in the Provinces of Maryland, Virginia, North Carolina, South Carolina, and Georgia* (1772), 5:168–69. Hosted by Clemson University, the South Carolina Digital Library scanned this item from a photo-reproduction of Duke University Library's 1952 microfilm of Morgan Edwards's original manuscript. http://contentdm2.clemson.edu/cdm/compoundobject/collection/jbt/id/241. In digital format, the six volumes appear in consecutive pagination. Edwards's original manuscript has no consistent pagination.

[1055] Those are from the opening lines of the first minute book of the Pennepack Baptist Church. The American Baptist Historical Society, in Atlanta, Georgia, houses the original volume of the first minute book, 1687–1894, of Pennepack Baptist Church. The collection of the Pennepack Baptist Historical Foundation (est. 2010), at Pennepack Baptist Church, includes a copy of the first minute book and the original volume of the second minute book, 1894–1956.

Baptist Church in Kilkenny, Ireland, soon joined them. In 1687, Samuel Vaus, a Baptist, came "out of England" and united with the group. When those seven began looking for someone to organize them into a church, their prayers were answered in an unexpected manner, when Elias Keach arrived from London.

Elias was the only son of Benjamin Keach—predecessor of John Gill, at London's Horsleydown church. Elias was born in the year of London's great fire. He was two years old when his father became pastor in Southwark. Just before Elias turned five, his mother and two of his four sisters died. Within two years, his father remarried, and Elias would eventually have five more sisters. Through it all, the young man received loving familial care and regularly heard the greatest preaching of his day. Yet the shackles of sin had continued to enslave him throughout his teenage years. Elias Keach arrived in Philadelphia, in 1686-87, as an unconverted young man. Morgan Edwards reported that Elias, at nineteen or twenty years of age, came, "dressed in black" and wearing a ministerial band, "in order to pass for a minister." Meanwhile, some locals had undoubtedly recognized the name *Keach*. Upon his acceptance of their invitation to preach, many "resorted to hear the young London divine." He "performed well" until "he had advanced pretty far in the sermon." Stopping abruptly, Keach "looked like a man astonished." The "audience concluded he had been seized with a sudden disorder," but, "on asking what the matter was," they "received from him a confession of the imposture with tears in his eyes and much trembling. Great was his distress, though it ended happily." It was "from this time" that Elias Keach "dated his conversion." As the historical monument at Pennepack Baptist Church expresses it, "The deceiver had become the first convert of his own preaching." Informed that there was a Baptist pastor near Cold Spring, in Bucks County, Keach set out "to seek counsel and comfort; and by him was he baptized and ordained."[1056] The Baptist minister was Thomas Dungan (ca. 1634-88), a former member of First

---

[1056] Cf. Morgan Edwards, *Materials towards a History of the Baptists in Pennsylvania both British and German* (Philadelphia: Joseph Crukshank and Isaac Collins, 1770), 1:5-11.

Baptist at Newport, Rhode Island. In 1684, he had planted the Cold Spring church, near the Delaware River. This was the earliest Baptist church in Pennsylvania.

Keach at once surrendered to preaching the gospel, and God richly blessed his ministry. With a regenerate heart, the indwelling Holy Spirit, and God's call, Elias Keach began rightly discerning his familial training. While preaching in the Lower Dublin area, Keach began to see fruit for his labors. He was preparing now to baptize four new converts—Joseph Ashton (with his wife Jane), William Fisher, and John Watts. Just south of the Pennepack Baptist church, a stone bridge crosses over Pennypack Creek.[1057] Here at the bridge, a flat rock, affectionately called "Baptismal Rock,"[1058] still slopes down into the serene pool, in which Elias Keach administered immersion to those earliest converts. The site became the baptismal pool of the Pennepack Baptists. In January 1688, the four new baptizees joined with the earlier group of seven, along with Keach, to become the twelve charter members of Pennepack Baptist Church. Their next step was a worshipful organization service.

According to their minute book, "a day was set apart to seek God by fasting and prayer, in order to form ourselves into a church state. Whereupon Elias Keach was accepted and received for our pastor and we sat down in Communion at the Lord's Table." The record adds that, "at the same time, Samuel Vaus was chosen, and, by Elias Keach, with laying on of hands, [he was] ordained to be a deacon."[1059] In December 1690, John Watts accepted the Pennepack pastorate; Keach was already establishing mission stations in nearby settlements and towns, including Philadelphia, Chester, Burlington, Cohansey, Trenton, and Middletown.[1060] After Thomas Dungan's decease,

---

[1057] Spelling for the park and creek is *Pennypack*, an Indian word meaning "without a current."

[1058] Samuel Hazard, ed., "The Oldest Baptist Church in Pennsylvania," *The Register of Pennsylvania* 4, no. 14 (October 3, 1829): 214–15. The city severely damaged the Baptismal Rock when using dynamite nearby to make way for a storm-water pipe.

[1059] I slightly modernized some word cases and punctuation from the opening paragraphs of the handwritten minute book.

[1060] Standing today, beautifully restored, Ye Olde Yellow Meeting House, at

in 1688, Keach and Watts preached at the Cold Spring church as frequently as possible, until 1702, when the church disbanded. Much of its remnant, including Widow Dungan, had already joined the Pennepack church.[1061] Known also as Lower Dublin Baptist Church,[1062] Pennepack is the oldest surviving Baptist church in the Middle Colonies.

Reminiscent of John Myles' system of branch congregations from the Ilston Church in Wales, all the Baptists of Pennsylvania and New Jersey, during their earliest years, were members of the Pennepack Church. For the sake of distant members, Keach provided quarterly meetings in strategic towns for the administration of baptism and the Lord's Supper. Meanwhile, Keach was training more preachers. As qualified preachers became available, they assisted in organizing new churches. As the churches multiplied, they began holding General Meetings for prayer, preaching, instruction, and fellowship. These gatherings soon developed into an Annual Meeting, which became the forerunner of the regional associations.[1063] Vedder reports, "Mr. Keach toiled with unsurpassed energy and effectiveness, and we are told that 'he was considered the chief apostle of the Baptists in these parts of America.'"[1064] In 1692, Keach returned to London with his wife, Mary (née Moore), who would bear their only child, Hannah.

Upon arrival in London, Keach presented morning lectureships in Pinners' Hall, where as many as 1500 persons frequently attended.[1065] The following year, he gathered a Baptist

---

Imlaystown, New Jersey, originated about 1737 as a branch of Middletown Baptist. Abel Morgan Jr. ministered here. See the Tour Guide in Appendix C.

[1061] David Spencer, *The Early Baptists of Philadelphia* (Philadelphia: William Syckelmoore, 1877), 28–29, 42.

[1062] In the nineteenth century, the Township of Lower Dublin incorporated into the city of Philadelphia.

[1063] Horatio Gates Jones, *Historical Sketch of the Lower Dublin (or Pennepek) Baptist Church* (Morrisania [South Bronx], NY: Henry B. Dawson, 1869); idem, "The Baptists in Pennsylvania," *The Historical Magazine* 4, no. 1 (July 1868): 76–87.

[1064] Henry C. Vedder, *A History of the Baptists in the Middle States* (Philadelphia: American Baptist Publication Society, 1898), 61.

[1065] See Elias Keach, *A Plain and Familiar Discourse on Justification*, "being the

church at Wapping, Middlesex, in London's east end, where Hercules Collins, pastor of the nearby Spilsbury church, re-ordained him before "a great congregation." In a letter to Pastor John Watts, at the Pennepack church, Elias reported that in nine months he had baptized 130 believers.[1066] Among rare glimpses, we find Elias serving the pastorate of a congregation meeting in Curriers' Hall and later moving the group into Tallow Chandlers' Hall. On another occasion, he is erecting a large meetinghouse in Goodman's Fields, on Alyes Street.[1067] As in America, Elias Keach never lost his driving passion to plant sound Baptist churches and to equip the saints to do the work of the ministry. Elias Keach died on October 27, 1699, at the age of thirty-three. Nathanael Wyles, a Baptist pastor from Shadwell, West Yorkshire, preached the funeral sermon, *All Men Must Die*.[1068]

Meanwhile, back in Pennsylvania, three key topics of discord had developed among Baptist congregations. First, a temporary debate had emerged over Elias Keach's promotion of congregational singing of Psalms, hymns, and spiritual songs.[1069] This is not surprising since Benjamin Keach had become the "father of Baptist hymnody." Secondly, there arose a controversy over Elias Keach's practice of administering the

---

substance of four sermons, preached at the Morning-Lecture, at Pinners-Hall, in Broad Street, the third, tenth, seventeenth, and twenty-fourth days of September 1693" (London: Printed for John Harris, 1694). This copy is in the Cambridge University Library.

[1066] Morgan Edwards, *Materials towards a History of the Baptists in Pennsylvania both British and German*, 1:109–15 (Appendix V). Elias dated his letter "the 12th month, 20th day, 1693–94."

[1067] E.g., see Joseph Ivimey, *A History of the English Baptists: Comprising the Principal Events of the History of Protestant Dissenters, from the Revolution in 1668 Till 1760, and of the London Baptist Churches during that Period*, vol. 3 of *A History of the English Baptists* (London: B. J. Holdsworth, 1823), 3:407–8, 3:508, 3:533–41.

[1068] Nathanael Wyles, *All Men Must Die: Or the Saint's Deliverance by Death from the Evil to Come* (London: K. Astwood, 1699). This copy is in Union Theological Seminary Library, New York, NY.

[1069] Elias Keach, *A Banqueting-House Full of Spiritual Delights: Or, Hymns and Spiritual Songs on Several Occasions* (London: Printed by Benjamin Harris, 1696). For the word *banqueting*, the publisher uses the old spelling *banquetting*. This copy is in the British Library, London.

laying on of hands to every recipient of baptism, as a prerequisite to membership and the Lord's Supper. Like his father, Elias insisted that the laying on of hands enables the baptized believer to "meet with more of Christ and His Spirit."[1070] Nevertheless, he adds, "This Ordinance is not for the extraordinary Gifts of the Spirit, but for a further Reception of the Holy Spirit of Promise, or for the Addition of the Graces of the Spirit, and the Influences thereof; to confirm, strengthen, and comfort them in Christ Jesus."[1071] Elias and his father had revised the Second London Confession (1689) for their own churches, by adding two articles verbatim from Benjamin Keach's Confession:[1072] The "Singing of Psalms in Public Worship" and the "Laying on of Hands." In 1742, the Philadelphia Baptist Association would formally adopt the Keach version, known in America as the "Philadelphia Confession."[1073] Endorsing this confession, the Regular Baptists would practice both hymn singing and the laying on of hands. For the latter, Welsh Baptists would be the most persevering advocates.

[1070] Benjamin Keach, *Laying on of Hands upon Baptized Believers, as Such, Proved an Ordinance of Christ*, 2nd ed. (London: To be sold by Benjamin Harris, 1698), 78. This is in the British Library, London.

[1071] Idem, *The Articles of the Faith of the Church of Christ, or Congregation Meeting at Horsley-down*, by "Benjamin Keach, Pastor, as asserted this 10th of the 6th Month, 1697" (London: n.p., 1697), 23. This copy is in the library of Union Theological Seminary, NYC.

[1072] Ibid., 23, 27 (Articles 23 and 27).

[1073] The published title of the Philadelphia Confession is *A Confession of Faith*, "put forth by the elders and brethren of many congregations of Christians (baptized upon profession of their faith) in London and the Country, adopted by the Baptist Association met at Philadelphia, Sept. 25, 1742, 6th ed., to which are added, two articles: Of Imposition of Hands, and Singing of Psalm in Publick Worship; also, A Short Treatise of Church Discipline" (Philadelphia: Printed by B. Franklin, 1743). This copy is in the British Library. See page 83 for "Singing of Psalms, &c" (Art. 23) and page 102 for "Laying on of Hands" (Art. 31). Appended, with separate pagination (sixty-two-pages), is a copy of Benjamin Griffith, *The Short Treatise of Church Discipline* (Philadelphia: Printed by B. Franklin, 1743). Griffith sets forth three officers for the local church: minister (pastor), ruling elders, and deacons. He does not require the ruling elder to possess the gifts of teaching and preaching (10–18). Griffith uses a discipline by Elias Keach for a model.

Thirdly, there emerged a disagreement over Keach's preference of having three church officers — pastor, elders, and deacons.[1074] His father, Benjamin, had found the terms *elder* and *pastor* interchangeable in Scripture and had prescribed only two offices — an elder (or elders) and a deacon (or deacons).[1075] Except for Strict and Primitive Baptists, the ultimate standard for most Baptists would be two offices — pastor and deacons. The policy of having one *pastor*, often accompanied by one or more assistants or associates, would uproot the designations *teaching elders* and *ruling elders*. Despite challenges, Pennsylvania Baptists would now bear spiritual fruit and multiply.

The Middle Colonies, rather than New England, quickly became the center of Baptist activity, especially the Philadelphia area, due in large part to the Quaker policy of religious toleration. Quaker pacifist, William Penn Jr. (1644-1718), had established the Colony of Pennsylvania, in 1681, when King Charles II granted a large proprietorship of land. Even before the area's population fully entered its eighteenth-century surge, Pennepack Baptist, by 1700, had forty-six members meeting in homes.[1076] In 1707, the congregation of eighty-eight members constructed their first meetinghouse, on Krewstown Road, at the rim of what is now Pennypack Park. The strong pastorate of Abel Morgan Sr., during 1711-22,[1077] further buttressed

---

[1074] See Elias Keach, *The Glory and Ornament of a True Gospel-constituted Church*, "being a brief display of the discipline of the Church of Christ, formerly meeting at Curriers Hall near Cripplegate, and now meeting at Tallow Chandlers' Hall upon Dowgate-Hill" (London: n.p., 1697), 7-8. See pages 71-74 for Keach's Solemn Covenant of the Church of Christ, "meeting in White Street, at its Constitution, June 5, 1696." This copy is in the British Library, London.

[1075] Benjamin Keach, *The Articles of the Faith of the Church of Christ or Congregation Meeting at Horsley-down*, 25-26; idem, *The Glory of a True Church, and Its Discipline Display'd* (London: n.p., 1697), 15-16. This is in the British Library, London.

[1076] Following the death of its second pastor, John Watts, in 1702, the next seven of the Pennepack church's pastors, in succession, were Evan Morgan, Samuel Jones, Joseph Wood, Abel Morgan Sr., Jenkin Jones, Peter Peterson, and Samuel Jones D. D. whose pastorate ended in 1814.

[1077] See Gerald Priest, "Abel Morgan Sr. 1673-1722," in *A Noble Company: Biographical Essays on Notable Particular-Regular Baptists in America*, ed.

the church's doctrinal foundation. During the First Great Awakening (ca. 1720–60), when Jenkin Jones (ca. 1686–1760)[1078] was serving the Pennepack pastorate (1726–46), Evangelist George Whitefield recorded in his journal, on Friday, May 9, 1740, that at Pennepack he preached to an outdoor crowd of about two thousand.[1079] In 1805, at the peak of America's Second Great Awakening (ca. 1775-1840), during the ministry of the Pennepack Church's ninth pastor, Samuel Jones (1735–1814),[1080] the congregation erected its present (third) building.[1081]

In 1698, Pennepack Baptist gathered and established the original congregation of Philadelphia's First Baptist Church, which remained a satellite congregation of the Pennepack Church, until 1746, when it organized under its own constitution. At that time, Jenkin Jones transferred from Pennepack to the Philadelphia pastorate, which he held until his death, in 1760, at age seventy-four.[1082] In 1707, representatives from five churches of the region convened in the Baptist meetinghouse in Philadelphia, to form the Philadelphia Baptist Association (PBA), the first Baptist association in the New World. Following the general paradigm of their brethren in England, the five pioneering churches were those at Pennepek (Pennsylvania) and Welsh Tract (Delaware), along with three in New Jersey—Middletown,[1083]

Terry Wolever (Springfield, MO: Particular Baptist Press, 2006), 1:283–93; Horatio Gates Jones, "The Rev. Abel Morgan, Pastor of the United Baptist Churches of Pennepek and Philadelphia," *Pennsylvania Magazine of History and Biography* 6 (1882): 300–10; and Gerald Priest, "The Abel Morgans's Contribution to Baptist Ecclesiology in Colonial America," *Detroit Baptist Seminary Journal* 8 (Fall 2003): 49–68.

[1078] Thomas Ray, "Jenkin Jones c. 1686–1760," in *A Noble Company*, ed. Terry Wolever, 2:179–212.

[1079] George Whitefield, *A Continuation of Mr. George Whitefield's Journal* (London: Printed by W. Strahan, 1741), 37.

[1080] See Hywel M. Davies, "Samuel Jones 1735–1814," in *A Noble Company*, ed. Terry Wolever, 3:359–98.

[1081] This replaced their second (1770) building at 8732 Krewstown Road, in Philadelphia.

[1082] First Baptist of Philadelphia dates its origin as 1698, the year of its original gathering.

[1083] Obadiah Holmes Sr. was one of the patentees of Monmouth County, New Jersey, and, in 1688, Baptists from the Middletown, Rhode Island, area established New Jersey's earliest Baptist church—the First Baptist

Piscataway,[1084] and Cohansey.[1085] The PBA set the pattern for subsequent American associations, such as those at Charleston,

---

Church of Middletown Township. A preacher and church planter in this region, Obadiah Holmes Jr. (baptized at Salem, Massachusetts, on June 9, 1644), had his membership in this church. Local tradition often claims 1668 for the church's origin, but there are no records prior to 1688. The church originated with two congregations—one in Middletown and the other in Baptist Town (Holmdel), undoubtedly named for the Holmes influence. For many years, both congregations (situated only seven miles apart) shared the same pastors, one of the most notable being Abel Morgan Jr. (1713–85), who served from 1738 until his death. Nineteenth-century buildings have replaced the original meetinghouses. In 1967, the Middletown Baptist congregation joined the United Church of Christ (UCC) and changed their name to "Old First Church in Middletown." They belong also to the American Baptist Churches USA. Meanwhile, in 1935, the Baptist Town (Holmdel) congregation left the Baptists, merged with a Dutch Reformed Church, and took the name Holmdel Church. In the 1950s, a local Community Church joined with this merger, and, in 1968, the congregation joined the UCC, becoming the Holmdel Community Church of the UCC. See the chart in Daniel Reid, et al., eds., *Dictionary of Christianity in America* (Downers Grove, IL: Intervarsity Press, 1990), 1200; J. T. Holmes, *The American Family of Rev. Obadiah Holmes* (Columbus, OH: n.p., 1915); Thomas A. Griffiths, "Middletown and Holmdel, Churches 1667–8," in *A History of Baptists in New Jersey* (Hightstown, NJ: Barr Press, 1904), 15ff.; Gerald Priest, "Abel Morgan Jr. 1713–1785," in *A Noble Company*, ed. Wolever, 2:403–14; and Wheelock H. Parmly, "Historical Sketch of the First Baptist Church of Middletown, New Jersey," in the *1688–1888 Celebration of the Two Hundredth Anniversary of the First Baptist Church, Middletown, New Jersey* (Trenton: MacCrellish and Quigley, 1888), 9–20.

[1084] Piscataway later became absorbed into the towns of Raritan and Edison. Thus, the Piscataway Baptist Church is now Stelton Baptist Church, in Edison, New Jersey. See Charles W. Jorgensen Jr., *History of the Stelton Baptist Church (Formerly the First Baptist Church of Piscataway)* (Stelton, NJ: Stelton Baptist Church, 1964). The church is a member of the American Baptist Churches USA.

[1085] The Cohansey Church originated with Baptist migrants from Tipperary County, Ireland who settled along the Cohansey Creek. In 1690, Thomas Killingsworth, who had assisted in the organization of Baptist churches in Middletown and Piscataway, helped organize the Cohansey church. They erected their original, log meetinghouse on the south side of the Cohansey Creek. Located in Bridgeton, New Jersey, the church is a member of the American Baptist Churches USA. The inscription in marble above the door reads, "This building erected MDCCCI" [1801].

South Carolina (1751), Sandy Creek, North Carolina (1758), Ketocton, Virginia (1766), Warren, Rhode Island (1767), and Kehukee, North Carolina (1769). The PBA model would pose a challenge to one of the most vital Baptist distinctives—local church autonomy. As the denominational court of appeal, the Association reserved the authority to censure any local church that refused to follow its counsel.[1086] As one of "the harbingers of a new period" of compromise, says Robert T. Handy, "by 1806, the Association agreed that an orthodox Baptist church could receive a person baptized by a 'Tunker Universalist' without rebaptism."[1087]

Morgan Edwards (1722–95)

His ministerial preparation and experience in Wales, England, and Ireland. Born in Trevethin Parish (Monmouthshire), Wales, Morgan Edwards received infant baptism into the local Anglican parish.[1088] By the age of sixteen, he had experienced conversion, embraced Baptist principles, and surrendered to a call to the ministry. At nearby Penygarn, he studied Welsh, English, Latin, Greek, and Hebrew at Trosnant Academy. During 1742–43, he continued his studies at England's Bristol Baptist Academy (later college), where he submitted a paper defending a position perhaps best described as a "proto-pretribulational" Rapture of the Church. While Edwards depicts the

---

[1086] Robert T. Handy, "The Philadelphia Tradition," in *Baptist Concepts of the Church*, ed. Winthrop S. Hudson (Philadelphia: Judson Press, 1959), 30–52; and Gerald Priest, "The Philadelphia Baptist Association and the Question of Authority," *Detroit Baptist Seminary Journal* 12 (2007): 68, passim (51–80).

[1087] Handy, "The Philadelphia Tradition," 52.

[1088] The best sources for Morgan Edwards include Thomas R. McKibbens Jr. and Kenneth L. Smith, *The Life and Works of Morgan Edwards* (New York: Arno, 1980); David Spencer, *The Early Baptists of Philadelphia* (Philadelphia: William Syckelmoore, 1877); Howard R. Stewart, *A Dazzling Enigma: The Story of Morgan Edwards* (Lanham, MD: University Press of America, 1995); and John Rippon, ed., "Rev. Morgan Edwards, A. M. Pennsylvania," in *The Baptist Annual Register for 1794–1797* (London: Sold by Dilly, Button, and Thomas, 1797), 308–14.

entire length of the Tribulation Period as the three and a half years prior to Christ's Second Advent, the standard pretribulational view requires the full seven-year period, depicted in Daniel 9:24–27. Edwards must have consistently retained his views, since he published the fifty-six-page paper late in life.[1089] In 1744–45, Edwards began ministering to a small Baptist church in Boston, England, where he served until 1751, when he began a nine-year ministry in a church at Cork, Ireland, where he married and received his ordination. After a short pastorate in Rye, England, Edwards, in 1761, immigrated to Colonial Pennsylvania.

His initial contributions to Colonial-American Baptist history. Morgan Edwards succeeded Jenkin Jones to the pastorate of First Baptist in Philadelphia. The notable John Gill (1697–1771) of London had recommended him to the church, and the Philadelphia Association appointed him as their moderator. Edwards would join with James Manning and Hezekiah Smith, in the mid-1760s, to establish the earliest Baptist institution of higher learning in America—Rhode Island College (later Brown University). Edwards procured the school's charter. In 1762, the College of Philadelphia (later University of Pennsylvania) awarded Edwards an MA degree, and, in 1769, Rhode Island College, at its first commencement, awarded him the *ad eundem* degree. His book, *The Customs of Primitive Churches* (1768), was the first major handbook of its kind on Baptist polity.[1090] Edwards traveled in America, England, and Ireland, appealing for funds, books, and students for Rhode Island College, where he served as a board member until he voluntarily resigned in 1789. His multi-volume *Materials towards a History of the Baptists* (1770–72) made Morgan Edwards America's premier Baptist historian. He recorded valuable accounts of Colonial Baptists, during his travels as far north as New England and as far south

---

[1089] Morgan Edwards, *Two Academical Exercises on Subjects Bearing the Following Titles: Millennium; Last-Novelties* (Philadelphia: Printed by Dobson and Lang, 1788), 7, 21, 24–25; a Library of Congress copy.

[1090] William Lloyd Allen, "The Peculiar Welsh Piety of *The Customs of Primitive Churches*," in *Distinctively Baptist Essays on Baptist History: A Festschrift in Honor of Walter B. Shurden*, ed. Marc A. Jolley and John D. Pierce (Macon, GA: Mercer University Press, 2005), 171–92.

as the Carolinas.

His major plights and accomplishments to the end of his life. By 1770, Morgan Edwards was facing major crises. With America's increasing grievances against England, over taxation without representation, Edwards found himself the only prominent, Colonial Baptist of pro-British persuasion. After the Boston Massacre, in March 1770, rumors were spreading of an impending War of Independence. Philadelphia had become an unsafe place for a Tory. While Edwards's personal conviction never developed into any type of activism, he feared for his life. Based upon a premonition of impending death, Edwards inaccurately announced in a sermon the date that he believed his death would occur. Public humiliation followed. In 1771, First Baptist accepted Edwards's voluntary resignation and requested his assistance in acquiring his replacement. Edwards then moved to Delaware, where he purchased property at Newark. He would never serve another pastorate, but, in early 1772, he accepted an appointment by the Philadelphia Association to serve as their evangelist at large. He resigned from that position in October 1773, two months prior to the Boston Tea Party. In 1774, Edwards accepted an appointment as representative of the Philadelphia Association to join with James Manning and Isaac Backus in petitioning the Massachusetts delegates to the Continental Congress to oppose governmental abuse against local churches. Edwards's fellow delegates included Samuel Jones and John Gano. Edwards preached in the Delaware area until the war began, then sequestered within his home. On August 7, 1775, he publicly recanted his loyalty to the British Crown.[1091] In great grief, he outlived three wives and all but two of his many children. During these darkest years of his life—with the death of his third wife, the disappearance of his oldest son, and a debilitating illness that persisted for months—Edwards resorted to excessive wine. He soon found restoration, and the church received him back into fellowship and Communion. Thereafter, he lived an exemplary

---

[1091] The document is in William W. Keen, ed., *The Bi-Centennial Celebration of the Founding of the First Baptist Church of the City of Philadelphia 1698–1898* (Philadelphia: American Baptist Publication Society, 1899), 51–52.

life. Morgan Edwards died in the seventy-third year of his life, on January 28, 1795, and Philadelphia's First Baptist interred his body beneath an aisle of their church.[1092]

Elhanan Winchester (1751–97)

Elhanan Winchester,[1093] during his pastorate at Philadelphia's First Baptist Church,[1094] became attracted to the heresy of Universalism. He was popular among many in the congregation and among many Baptist ministers along the Atlantic seaboard. After some time, one of his church members gave to Winchester a copy of the book, *The Everlasting Gospel*, by German author Paul Siegvolck,[1095] and asked the pastor to explain its contents. Siegvolck's book teaches that God restores each of the wicked to eternal life after a limited punishment according to sins committed. By means of this book, Elhanan Winchester became a crusading Restoration Universalist. When the church dismissed him, he split the congregation. Amid this doctrinal turmoil, Samuel Jones, D. D. (1735-1814), ninth pastor of the Pennepack Church (1763-1814),[1096] came

---

[1092] When it relocated in 1860, First Baptist Church transferred Morgan Edwards's remains to Mount Moriah Cemetery, 6201 Kingsessing Avenue, Philadelphia. The church still displays Edwards's original gravestone.

[1093] See Joseph R. Sweeny, "Elhanan Winchester and the Universal Baptists" (PhD diss., University of Pennsylvania, 1969), 18–62.

[1094] In 2015, the members of First Baptist Church, Philadelphia, "in order to sustain their continued presence and ministry, found it necessary to sell their building," located at 17th and Sansom Streets. The new owner is the Liberti Church, a member of the Reformed Church in America (RCA). First Baptist Church, a member of the American Baptist Churches USA, is now leasing from Liberti Church a small chapel of the building, which will undergo renovation. http://www.firstbaptistphiladelphia.org/pages/news.html. Originating from Colonial America's Dutch Reformed heritage, the RCA became charter members of the Federal Council of Churches (1908), the World Council of Churches (1948), and the National Council of the Churches of Christ in the USA (1950).

[1095] Paul Siegvolck, *The Everlasting Gospel*, trans. from the German (Stonington Point, CT: Printed and sold by Samuel Trumbull, 1801).

[1096] Samuel Jones, *Circular Letter to the Elders and Messengers of the Several*

to the forefront and wrote two Circular Letters (1781, 1790) to the Philadelphia Baptist Association, exposing "the leprosy of Universalism" and warning against its spread among Baptists. The Association sent Jones's letters to every PBA church and to all regional associations. Subsequent warnings from Baptist pulpits held the heresy at bay until the twentieth-century.

Joseph H. Gilmore (1834–1918), Author of the Hymn, "He Leadeth Me"

In the spring of 1862, during a mid-week service at First Baptist, Philadelphia, Joseph Gilmore,[1097] supplying the pulpit, was presenting his exposition of the Twenty-Third Psalm when suddenly the words, "He Leadeth Me," gripped him as it never had. He later recalled, "At the close of the service we adjourned to Deacon Watson's pleasant home, where we were being entertained. During our conversation the blessedness of God's leading so grew upon me that I took a pencil, wrote the text just as it stands today, handed it to my wife, and thought no more of it." Without his knowledge, Mrs. Gilmore sent the four-stanza hymn to a Boston magazine, *The Watchman and Reflector*, whose editors published it without the author's knowledge. William B. Bradbury (1816–68) found the composition in the magazine, wrote two additional lines to its refrain,

---

Churches Met in Association at Philadelphia, October 23, 1781, in A. D. Gillette, ed., *Minutes of the Philadelphia Baptist Association, from A.D. 1707 to A.D. 1807* (Philadelphia: American Baptist Publication Society, 1851), 175–78; idem, *Circular Letter to the Elders and Messengers of the Several Churches Met in Association, in the City of New York, October 5, 1790*, in *Minutes of the Philadelphia Baptist Association, from A.D. 1707 to A.D. 1807*, 257–60.

[1097] Gilmore graduated from Phillips Academy, Brown University, and, finally, in 1861, Newton Theological Institution. During his final year at Newton, he was an instructor in Hebrew. In 1862, he accepted the pastorate of First Baptist, Fisherville (Penacook), New Hampshire. In 1863–64, while his father was governor of New Hampshire, he was his father's private secretary and editor of the *Concord Daily Monitor*. In 1865, Gilmore accepted the pastorate of Second Baptist in Rochester, New York. In 1867, he served as acting professor of Hebrew in Rochester Theological Seminary, and, the following year, he became professor of logic, rhetoric, and English literature in the University of Rochester.

and set the hymn to music. Three years later, Joseph Gilmore was visiting Second Baptist Church, in Rochester, New York, as a candidate for the pastorate. "Upon entering the chapel," Gilmore recalls, "I took up a hymnal, thinking, 'I wonder what they sing here.' To my amazement the book opened up at 'He Leadeth Me,' and that was the first time I knew that my hurriedly written lines had found a place among the songs of the church."[1098] The first stanza:

> He leadeth me: Oh blessed thought!
> O, words with heavenly comfort fraught!
> Whate'er I do, where'er I be,
> Still 'tis God's hand that leadeth me.
> Refrain
> He leadeth me, He leadeth me,
> By His own hand He leadeth me;
> His faithful follower I would be,
> For by His hand He leadeth me.

Select Bibliography for Further Reading

Backus, Isaac. *A History of New England: with Particular Reference to the Denomination of Christians Called Baptists*. 2nd ed. With notes by David Weston. 2 vols. Newton, MA: Backus Historical Society, 1871.

Baker, Robert A., *The First Southern Baptists*. Nashville: Broadman, 1966. This is a biography of William Screven and the beginnings of First Baptist Church, Charleston.

_____, Paul J. Craven Jr., and R. Marshall Blalock. *History of the First Baptist Church of Charleston, South Carolina 1682–2007*. 1982. Reprint, Springfield, MO: Particular Baptist Press, 2007.

Clark, James L. "Some Influences of the Philadelphia Baptist Association upon Baptists of America." ThD diss., New Orleans Baptist Theological Seminary, 1948.

Edwards, Morgan. *Materials towards a History of the Baptists*, in Delaware, Maryland, Virginia, North Carolina, South Carolina, and Georgia. Vol. 2. Edited by Eve B. Weeks and Mary B. Warren. Danielsville, GA: Heritage Papers, 1984.

[1098] Henry S. Burrage, *Baptist Hymn Writers and Their Hymns* (Portland, ME: Brown Thurston and Co., 1888), 471ff.; E. E. Ryden, *The Story of Christian Hymnody* (Philadelphia: Fortress Press, 1959), 546–47; and Kenneth W. Osbeck, *Amazing Grace: 366 Inspiring Hymn Stories for Daily Devotions* (Grand Rapids: Kregel, 1990), 22.

_____. *Materials towards a History of the Baptists in Pennsylvania both British and German*. Vol. 1. Philadelphia: Joseph Crukshank and Isaac Collins, 1770.

_____. *Materials towards a History of the Baptists in the Provinces of Maryland, Virginia, North Carolina, South Carolina, and Georgia*. 6 vols. 1772. Hosted by Clemson University, the South Carolina Digital Library scanned this item from a photo-reproduction of Duke University Library's 1952 microfilm of Morgan Edwards's original manuscript. http://contentdm2.clemson.edu/cdm/compoundobject/collection/jbt/id/241.

Gillette, A. D., ed. *Minutes of the Philadelphia Baptist Association, from A.D. 1707 to A.D. 1807: Being the First One Hundred Years of Its Existence*. Philadelphia: American Baptist Publication Society, 1851. There is also a high-quality reprint under the slightly redesigned title, *Minutes of the Philadelphia Baptist Association: 1707–1807 being the First One Hundred Years of Its Existence*. Springfield, MO: Particular Baptist Press, 2007. This "Tri-centennial Edition 1707 to 2007" features expanded indexes and references.

Goen, Clarence C. *Revivalism and Separatism in New England, 1740–1800: Strict Congregationalists and Separate Baptists in the Great Awakening*. New Haven: Yale University Press, 1962.

Guild, Reuben A. *Early History of Brown University, Including the Life, Times, and Correspondence of President Manning: 1756–1791*. Providence, RI: Snow & Farnham, 1896.

King, Joe M. *A History of South Carolina Baptists*. Columbia, SC: The General Board of the South Carolina Baptist Convention, 1964.

McKibbens, Thomas R. Jr., and Kenneth L. Smith. *The Life and Works of Morgan Edwards*. New York: Arno, 1980.

Owens, Loulie Latimer. *Saints of Clay: The Shaping of South Carolina Baptists*. Columbia, SC: The South Carolina Baptist Convention, 1971.

Stewart, Howard R. *A Dazzling Enigma: The Story of Morgan Edwards*. Lanham, MD: University Press of America, 1995.

Talbert, Roy Jr., and Meggan A. Farish. *The Antipedo Baptists of Georgetown County, South Carolina 1710–2010*. Columbia: University of South Carolina Press, 2015.

Townsend, Leah. *South Carolina Baptists, 1670–1805*. Florence, SC: The Florence Printing Company, 1935.

Vedder, Henry C. *A History of the Baptists in the Middle States*. Philadelphia: American Baptist Publication Society, 1898.

Chapter 15

The Separate Baptists: Struggle for Religious Freedom in North Carolina, Georgia, and Virginia

---❋---

Introduction

Amid America's First Great Awakening (ca. 1720–60), there emerged in New England, circa 1735, a Separate/Congregationalist movement, consisting of more than a hundred churches that were breaking away from the "Standing Order" of Old Congregationalism. The "Separates" were the *New Lights* (pro-revival), while the tax-supported majority constituted the *Old Lights* (anti-revival). In opposition to the Old Light, state churches, that offered Communion as a "converting ordinance," the Separate/Congregationalists established independent churches that preached instantaneous conversion and practiced closed Communion.

The Separate/Congregationalist movement would begin to disappear after the 1750s,[1099] as many of them were becoming New Light *Separate* Baptists. Inevitably, during the First Great Awakening, the pro-revival, Separate Baptist movement produced both growth and purification among Baptist

---

[1099] Weary of the separatist stigma, some Congregationalists returned to their old churches, while others moved to the western frontier and established independent, non-Baptist ministries.

churches. In the fall of 1740, when George Whitefield, during his second trip to America, was preaching in the open-air of Boston Common, the increasing numbers of Baptist converts prompted the British evangelist to lament, "My chickens are becoming ducks." Out of this New England landscape, Shubal Stearns and Daniel Marshall would emerge and spread the Great Awakening revivals and the Separate Baptist movement to the South.

Shubal Stearns and Daniel Marshall: Pioneer Separate Baptists
The Early Years in New England, New York,
and Pennsylvania

Born in Boston, Shubal Stearns (1706-71),[1100] early in life, moved with his family to Tolland, Connecticut, where they joined the established, tax-supported, Congregational church. In 1727, he married Sarah Johnston. During English evangelist George Whitefield's third trip to America, he preached for several months in New England. Upon hearing him, in 1745, Shubal Stearns experienced conversion, became a Separate, and embraced revival preaching. In 1751, after a careful study of the Scriptures, Stearns became a Separate Baptist and received immersion from Wait Palmer, who had established a Separate Baptist Church at North Stonington, Connecticut. Later that year, Stearns reorganized the Tolland congregation into a Separate Baptist church and received ordination under the direction of Palmer and Joshua Morse (Moss), pastor of the Separate Baptist Church in New London, Connecticut. Baptized by Stearns, Noah Alden (1725-97) would soon succeed Stearns

---

[1100] Valuable sources on Stearns include William L. Lumpkin, *Baptist Foundations in the South: Tracing through the Separates the Influence of the Great Awakening, 1754-1787* (Nashville: Broadman, 1961); George W. Purefoy, *A History of the Sandy Creek Baptist Association from Its Organization in A. D. 1758, to A. D. 1858* (New York: Sheldon and Co., 1859); John Sparks, *The Roots of Appalachian Christianity: The Life and Legacy of Elder Shubal Stearns* (Lexington: The University Press of Kentucky, 2001); and Earl Waggoner, "Shubal Stearns 1706-1771," in *A Noble Company: Biographical Essays on Notable Particular-Regular Baptists in America*, ed. Terry Wolever (Springfield, MO: Particular Baptist Press, 2013), 2:1-21.

to the pastorate of the Tolland church.[1101] Stearns was now preparing for missionary work.

Stearns's future co-laborer Daniel Marshall (1706-84) was born in Windsor, Connecticut, to a respectable and prosperous farming family. Following his conversion at the age of twenty, Marshall had served for nearly twenty years as deacon in the local, Standing Order Congregational church. In 1742, he had married Hannah Drake, who died soon after the birth of Abraham, their only child. Listening to George Whitefield's preaching during 1744-45, Daniel received the Englishman's "seraphic fire" (as his son Abraham later described it) for reaching souls for Christ. In 1747, Daniel married Shubal Stearns's sister, Martha, who would bear him ten children. Still a Separate Congregationalist, Daniel, with his family, left all worldly luxuries in the early 1750s to preach and minister among the Mohawk Indians along the Susquehanna River in New York and Pennsylvania.

Journey from Pennsylvania to Sandy Creek, North Carolina

As conditions leading to the impending French and Indian War (1754-63) were making the region increasingly dangerous, the Marshall family resided briefly in Pennsylvania's Chambersburg area, and from there they moved to Opekon (Opeckon, now Opequon), near Winchester, Virginia. Here at Opequon, the Philadelphia Baptist Association, during 1743-46, had established the Mill Creek Baptist Church, the first Baptist church ever planted west of the Blue Ridge Mountains. Becoming a Baptist, Daniel Marshall received immersion and soon a preaching license from Samuel Heaton, pastor of the Mill Creek church. In 1754, Shubal and Sarah Stearns, with five other couples from Tolland, Connecticut, joined the Marshalls at Opequon. Under Stearns's influence, the Marshalls became Separate Baptists. Facing Indian uprisings, the Mill Creek

---

[1101] Tolland Baptist Church would disband after ten years. Alden would then accept the Baptist pastorate at Bellingham, Massachusetts, where he baptized the notable John Leland. Alden was the great grandson of John and Priscilla Alden of the *Mayflower* Pilgrims.

congregation moved twenty-five miles northeast, to a village later named Gerrardstown, (now West Virginia).[1102] Meanwhile, receiving urgent requests for gospel preaching in the Piedmont region of North Carolina, Shubal Stearns, in 1755, led his group of sixteen, including the Marshalls, on a rugged, three-hundred-mile trek down the Shenandoah Valley, across the Blue Ridge, and into Orange (now Randolph) County,[1103] North Carolina. Here, they settled on the banks of Sandy Creek, near what is now the town of Liberty. The group of sixteen (not counting children) immediately built a meetinghouse, organized the Sandy Creek Baptist church, on November 22, 1755, and chose Shubal Stearns as their pastor, with Daniel Marshall and Joseph Breed as his assistants—all from New England.[1104]

Establishing and Defining the Separate Baptist Movement in the South

Without the advantage of formal training, Stearns and Marshall initiated a movement of farmer-preachers of immovable faith and courage, who studied their English Bibles and preached with a power that the South had never witnessed. For years, Separate preachers would imitate Stearns's impromptu preaching—with his "musical and strong" voice of rhythm,

---

[1102] Pastor Samuel Heaton (Eaton) removed to Pennsylvania in 1754. Near the end of the French and Indian War, in 1761, John Gerrard (Garrard, ca. 1720-87) returned to the ruins of Mill Creek church, reorganized it, and became pastor of its 159 members. The village where Mill Creek Baptist was situated took the name Gerrardstown, in 1787, in honor of John Gerrard, who had just passed away. See J. Houston Harrison, *Settlers by the Long Grey Trail* (1935; repr., Baltimore: Genealogical Publishing Co., 2007), 176. See also the historical marker at Gerrardstown, West Virginia: http://www.waymarking.com/waymarks/WMGNT8_Gerrardstown. See also: http://bradleyrymph.com/genealogy_gerrard-john.pdf.

[1103] Upon its origin in 1755, Sandy Creek Baptist Church was in Orange County, which became Guilford County in 1770 and Randolph County in 1779.

[1104] The eight constituent members of Sandy Creek Church were Shubal Stearns, Shubal Stearns Jr., Peter Stearns, Ebenezer Stearns, Daniel Marshall, Joseph Breed, Enos Stimpson, and Jonathan Polk. They were all married.

his timely gestures harmonizing with emotional persuasion and bold conviction tempered by meekness and heartfelt compassion for each one in his audience. According to contemporary accounts, Daniel Marshall, unlike Stearns, never became an eloquent speaker. His ministry, however, was extraordinarily effective and fruitful. As the founding pastor of Abbott's Creek Baptist Church (1757), near High Point, North Carolina, Marshall received his ordination as a church-planting evangelist.[1105] Later, in 1757, Marshall planted Grassy Creek Baptist Church, at Bullock, North Carolina,[1106] and James Reed (Read, 1727–98) would shepherd here while maintaining an itinerant ministry. Robert Devin, in his *History of Grassy Creek Baptist Church*, provides a typical Separate Baptist church service during the First Great Awakening: "At the close of the sermon, the minister would come down from the pulpit and while singing a suitable hymn would go around among the brethren shaking hands. The hymn being sung, he would then extend an invitation to such persons as felt themselves poor guilty sinners, and were anxiously inquiring the way of salvation, to come forward and kneel near the stand."[1107] Steve O'Kelly concluded, "This may be the earliest known record of an invitation of this type being given in American church history."[1108] McBeth wrote, "The Separates thus devised a method of encouraging on-the-spot religious decisions, to the singing of a hymn, well before the revivals of Charles G. Finney (1792–1875), who is often credited with inventing the invitation."[1109] One must add, however, that

---

[1105] Abraham Marshall received his ordination from Shubal Stearns and Henry Ledbetter, pastor of the Baptist church on Lynch's Creek, Craven County, South Carolina.

[1106] Marshall led James Reed to Christ. Today, Bullock is a rural community in Granville County, North Carolina. Near the Virginia state line, Bullock lies about thirteen miles north of Oxford, North Carolina. Grassy Creek Baptist Church has continued to this day.

[1107] Robert I. Devin, *A History of Grassy Creek Baptist Church from Its Foundation to 1880: with Biographical Sketches of Its Pastors and Ministers* (Raleigh: Edwards, Broughton and Company, 1880), 69.

[1108] Steve O'Kelly, "The Influence of Separate Baptists on Revivalistic Evangelism and Worship" (PhD diss., Southwestern Baptist Theological Seminary, Fort Worth, 1978), 130.

[1109] H. Leon McBeth, *The Baptist Heritage* (Nashville: Broadman, 1987), 231.

Stearns, Marshall, and other Separate Baptists used a simple invitation and preached sound doctrine, while Finney would use a multifaceted invitation system and preach heretical doctrines such as Pelagianism and Perfectionism.[1110] While Baptists who listened to Stearns always found him sound in doctrine, Stearns left it to the discretion of each church as to subscribing to all of his practices. Historian Morgan Edwards reported that Sandy Creek Baptist led the way in observing "nine rites: baptism, Lord's Supper, love-feast, laying-on-of-hands, washing-feet, anointing the sick, right hand of fellowship, the kiss of charity,[1111] and devoting [dedicating] children." Stearns also allowed for the use of "ruling elders," "eldresses," and "deaconesses." While Separate Baptists sometimes allowed the extreme emotionalism, Morgan Edwards, an eye-witness, explains, "These things are not true of all the Separate Baptists; there are exceptions. Neither do all regard the nine Christian rites, but only baptism, the Lord's Supper, and imposition of hands."[1112]

The Rapid and Widespread Expansion of the Separate Baptist Movement

In 1772, during a visit to Sandy Creek, Morgan Edwards reported, "The place of worship is 30 feet by 26, built in 1762." The church "began with 16 souls, and in a short time increased

---

[1110] For more discussion, see David Beale, "Charles G. Finney and Oberlin Theology," in *Historical Theology In-Depth* (Greenville, SC: Bob Jones University Press, 2013), 2:312–16.

[1111] Customarily, the "kiss of charity" was just a quick cheek-kiss.

[1112] Morgan Edwards, *Materials towards a History of the Baptists in the Province of North Carolina*, vol. 4 of the handwritten 6-vol. *Materials towards a History of the Baptists in the Provinces of Maryland, Virginia, North Carolina, South Carolina, and Georgia* (1772), 4:130–31. Hosted by Clemson University, the South Carolina Digital Library scanned this item from a photo-reproduction of Duke University Library's 1952 microfilm of Morgan Edwards's original manuscript. http://contentdm2.clemson.edu/cdm/compoundobject/collection/jbt/id/241. All future references to Edwards's *Materials* on these five provinces will be from the above collection, with all six volumes paginated consecutively. Edwards's manuscript has no consistent pagination.

to 606, spreading its branches to Deep River,"[1113] Abbotts Creek, and far beyond. The three principal founders of the Separate Baptist movement in the South were Shubal Stearns, Daniel Marshall, and the notable Samuel Harris (1724-99). Prior to his conversion, Harris had been an Anglican vestryman, Justice of the Peace, Sheriff, and Burgess in multiple counties of Virginia. In 1758, two Separate Baptist brothers, Joseph and William Murphy, were holding a preaching service in Pittsylvania County, Virginia. As the people were arriving, an unconverted Samuel Harris—Captain of Fort Mayo and Colonel of the Virginia Militia—rode up, "splendidly attired in his military habit." When he asked the reason for the meeting, the people replied, "Preaching, Colonel." He responded, "Who is to preach?" They answered, "The Murphy boys, Sir."[1114] Having recently heard Baptist preaching, and already under conviction, Harris was eager to hear more. Dismounting his horse and entering the meetinghouse, he sat respectfully in a back corner, and, by the end of the service, Colonel Samuel Harris had found peace in his soul, as a new creation in Christ. In a shout of joy, he exclaimed, "Glory, glory, glory!" Harris separated his life "unto the gospel of God" (Romans 1:1). Upon his return to Fort Mayo with provisions for the garrison, he preached so fervently to two officers that they thought he must be drunk. As they continued listening, they realized that Colonel Harris was completely sober. One of the officers became a Christian. Harris resigned all his public offices. He had been in the process of building a large home, but now decided to turn it into a meetinghouse. Daniel Marshall baptized Harris and guided

---

[1113] No one knows precisely where Deep River Baptist was located. Soon after its founding, Pastor Philip Mulkey led the members to close the church and move into South Carolina. Leah Townsend, *South Carolina Baptists, 1670-1805* (Florence, SC: The Florence Printing Company, 1935), 125-26. Mulkey would leave the Baptists, become a Tory, and join the Disciples of Christ (Campbellites) in Kentucky.

[1114] Maud Carter Clement, "The Baptists," in *The History of Pittsylvania County Virginia* (1929; repr., Santa Maria, CA: Janaway, 2011), 125-31, passim. For persecution upon Samuel Harris, see Lewis P. Little, *Imprisoned Preachers and Religious Liberty in Virginia* (Lynchburg, VA: J. P. Bell Co., 1938), 45-52.

him into the ministry. When Dutton Lane, in 1760, became founding pastor of the nearby Dan River Baptist Church—Virginia's first Separate Baptist church,[1115] Colonel Harris became a constituent member. Harris quickly became preeminent among those who carried the gospel across Virginia. The southern course of Baptist expansion and revival during this era includes a long list of preachers and church-planting evangelists. In those days, members gladly traveled forty miles each way to attend their churches. They hungered for the preaching of the Word.

In 1758, Shubal Stearns and Daniel Marshall led in the formation of the Sandy Creek Association, originally consisting of three North Carolina churches—Sandy Creek, Deep River, and Abbotts Creek—with a combined membership of nine hundred. At the annual meeting of the Sandy Creek Association, in October 1770, Stearns led in a unanimous decision to divide the association into three distinct parts—one each for Virginia, North Carolina, and South Carolina. While traveling and spreading the gospel into North Carolina and Georgia, Shubal Stearns would maintain his local pastorate, with "no salary, except presents," for sixteen years until his death on November 20, 1771, at the age of sixty-five. His remains lie buried in the Sandy Creek churchyard.[1116] In its first seventeen years, Sandy Creek had planted forty-two churches and had sent out 125 preachers of the gospel. A plaque at the church captures the essence of Morgan Edwards's description of the Sandy Creek church:

[1115] The Dan River Baptist Church, formed in Pittsylvania (then Halifax) County, Virginia, eventually went out of existence, and no one knows precisely where it had been located. Under Dutton Lane's ministry, however, at Dan River, he established five branch churches with five assistant preachers. See Edwards, *Materials towards a History of the Baptists in the Province of Virginia*, 3:41ff.

[1116] Edwards, *Materials towards a History of the Baptists in the Province of North Carolina*, 4:131–32.

> It is a mother church, nay a grandmother and a great grandmother. All the Separate Baptists sprang hence, not only eastward towards the sea, but westward towards the great river Mississippi, [and] northward to Virginia and southward to South Carolina and Georgia. The Word went forth from this Zion, and great was the company of them who published it, in so much that her converts were as drops of morning dew.[1117]

The Battle of Alamance and Its Consequences

Only six months prior to Shubal Stearns's death, and only twenty miles from the Sandy Creek Church, the Battle of Alamance, arguably the first battle of the American Revolution, raged at Great Alamance Creek, near Burlington, on May 16, 1771. British abuse of power was the essential cause of the conflict. For instance, the Royal Governor of North Carolina, Lord William Tryon, had built a luxurious palace at New Bern, with tax funds appropriated for public schools. The immediate spark that ignited the devastating battle was a disruption of the Royal Court, in nearby Hillsborough, by a band of tax opponents called *Regulators*. After destroying the Regulators in battle, Tryon unleashed tyrannical retribution against all survivors. The longstanding policy at Sandy Creek was to excommunicate any member who joined a faction or uprising against the government.[1118] Regarding all Baptists as enemies of the Church of England, Tryon went on a rampage, ordering his militia into the Sandy Creek area, confiscating livestock, and torching homes and barns at random. When the dust had settled, more than fifteen hundred families (most of the area's population) had permanently fled into South Carolina and Tennessee. Sandy Creek Baptist membership suddenly dropped from 606 to 14. As Lumpkin has observed, however, "The dispersion of the Separates south of Sandy Creek spread

---

[1117] Cf. Ibid., 4:133–34.
[1118] Devin, *A History of Grassy Creek Baptist Church from Its Foundation to 1880*, 18–19.

them abundantly along the South Carolina frontier, while the dispersion of those north of Sandy Creek sent the earliest pioneers to Tennessee.... Tryon succeeded only in spreading the virile seed all along the southern frontier."[1119]

A Birdseye View of the Regular and Separate Baptists

Originating in the Philadelphia area, the Regular Baptists, after 1752, had spread rapidly through Virginia and eastern North Carolina, where the name *Regular* distinguished them from the revivalistic *Separate* Baptists. While most Regular Baptists settled near the coastal areas, such as Savannah, Charleston, and Richmond, the Separates formed most of their churches along the expanding frontier. While both groups were largely Calvinistic and missionary-minded, the Separates displayed more fire and fervor in their preaching and witnessed the most memorable revivals of the Great Awakening. Unlike the Separates, the Regulars often took civil oaths of obedience and applied for government licenses to build their meetinghouses and to preach. In accordance with the Philadelphia Confession, the Regulars were more systematic in their Calvinism and practiced the laying of the hands. Fearing that churches might place creeds above Scripture, the Separatists typically avoided extrabiblical confessions.

Gradually, the great battle for religious liberty would become the most powerful stimulus for Separates and Regulars to coalesce. Increasing numbers of Separates would adopt the Philadelphia Confession.[1120] In Virginia, Separate and Regular churches would officially merge in 1787, quickly dropping the names *Separates* and *Regulars* and becoming the United Baptist Churches of Christ in Virginia. In North Carolina, the two groups would merge in 1788, prompting South Carolina, Georgia, and Kentucky to follow suit over the next fifteen years up to 1803.

[1119] Lumpkin, *Baptist Foundations in the South*, 85–86.
[1120] In North Carolina, the Sandy Creek Association waited until 1816 to adopt its one-page confession, known as the Principles of Faith. It was probably written in part by Luther Rice, who was present in the 1816 meeting. Purefoy, *A History of the Sandy Creek Baptist Association*, 104–5.

The Missionary versus Anti-Missionary Controversy

Erected in 1802, near the peak of the Second Great Awakening (ca. 1775–1840), the third meetinghouse still stands on the Sandy Creek properties. One of the finest examples of the few antebellum meetinghouses left in North Carolina, this log building features some original, wooden benches and even the original pulpit, or "Bible Rail," pinned together with wooden pegs. The old building witnessed powerful revivals. In May 1814, delegates from eleven states and the District of Columbia met in Philadelphia to organize the General Missionary Convention of the Baptist Denomination in the United States of America for Foreign Missions. It became known as the Triennial Convention, since it met once every three years. Its primary purpose was to promote missionaries, beginning with Adoniram Judson. Its first president was Richard Furman, pastor of First Baptist Church, Charleston, South Carolina.

In protest to the progressive missionary advance, the Primitive, Old School movement, in 1827, presented a hyper-Calvinist Resolution to the Kehukee Association of North Carolina. The delegates collectively "agreed that we discard all Missionary Societies, Bible Societies, and Theological Seminaries, and the practices heretofore resorted to for their support, in begging money from the public."[1121] With the vast loss of its missionary churches, the Kehukee Baptist Association became the "Kehukee Primitive Baptist Association." The Missionary versus Anti-Missionary controversy intensified, in 1830, with the formation of the North Carolina State Convention and its aggressive missions program.

With Sandy Creek Baptist increasingly aligning with the Primitive Baptist movement, the pro-missionary members relocated a short distance away, near a school called Shady Grove. They continued using the name *Sandy Creek Baptist Church*. The

---

[1121] Joseph Biggs, ed., *A Concise History of the Kehukee Baptist Association: From Its Original Rise to the Present Time* (Tarboro, NC: Tarboro Free Press, 1834), 241; and Byron Cecil Lambert, "The Rise of the Anti-Mission Baptists: Sources and Leaders, 1800–1840" (PhD diss., University of Chicago, 1957). A valuable source for research is the Primitive Baptist Library at Elon College, Elon, North Carolina.

Primitive Baptist congregation continued holding services in the 1802 log meetinghouse until the turn of the twentieth century, when their last few members locked the doors and ceased all services. For years, one of its last members, Mrs. Vandalia Jones (d. 1909), came to the building alone each "Meeting Day" and sat on the stone doorstep singing hymns and praying for the services to be restored. The deed to the meetinghouse, with about an acre of land, remained with one of the families. In the 1920s, a remnant returned to the log building and reorganized into a functioning church, still described by the sign out front as "Sandy Creek Primitive Baptist Church." As customary among Primitive Baptists, its members meet only on the second Sunday of each month.

Meanwhile, in 1905, members of the missionary Sandy Creek Baptist Church likewise returned to their original location,[1122] where Stearns's tombstone stands in the graveyard. Here, they erected a new meetinghouse, situated between the cemetery and the Primitive Baptists' 1802 log building. The year 2005 marked the 250th anniversary celebration of Shubal Stearns's 1755 organization of Sandy Creek Baptist Church. In 2015, the missionary Sandy Creek Baptist erected a new, picturesque church, next door to the Primitive meetinghouse. Those two buildings are the only ones left at the site.[1123]

Daniel Marshall and Kiokee Baptist Church in Georgia

The revivals had continued through the work of Stearns's fellow evangelist, Daniel Marshall (1706–84),[1124] who, in 1760,

---

[1122] Those who remained at Shady Grove changed the name of their church to Shady Grove Baptist Church, located in the town of Staley, North Carolina.

[1123] A short distance from the church, a historical marker at the intersection of Ramseur Julian Rd. and Old Liberty Rd. rightly describes Sandy Creek as the "Mother of Separate Baptist churches across the South." See also Travis Brock, *Sandy Creek Baptist Church: Celebrating 250 Years of His Story* (Liberty, NC: Sandy Creek Baptist Church, 2005). The church's address is 4765 Sandy Creek Church Rd. Liberty, NC 27298.

[1124] Valuable sources for Daniel Marshall and his family include James B. (Barnett) Taylor, "Daniel Marshall," in *Lives of Virginia Baptist Ministers*, 2nd ed. rev. (Richmond: Yale and Wyatt, 1838), 14–21; Thomas Ray, *Daniel*

moved into South Carolina and established eight churches, including Beaver Creek Baptist Church (1760), in Fairfield County, and Stephen's Creek Baptist Church (1766)—now Big Stevens Baptist Church at North Augusta.[1125] By 1770, Marshall was crossing the Savannah River and preaching in Georgia's open fields. With the established Church of England holding sway, it was illegal for Baptists to preach in Georgia. In the spring of 1772, sixty-six-year-old Marshall established the Kiokee Baptist Church, in St. Paul's Parish (now Columbia County).

A short time earlier, during one of his initial, outdoor meetings in Georgia, Marshall was on his knees offering the opening prayer, when the local constable, Samuel Cartledge, suddenly placed his hand upon his shoulder and exclaimed, "You are my prisoner!" A friend secured bail, and Marshall preached his message. In the Augusta Courtroom, on the following Monday, Marshall, facing the charge of illegal preaching, defended himself before two Church of England representatives—Colonel Edward Barnard and clergyman Edward Ellington. As the two attempted to provoke and abuse Marshall, he and his wife, Martha, quoted verse after verse of Scripture for the whole courtroom to hear. When Barnard and Ellington ordered him never again to preach in Georgia, Marshall calmly replied, "Whether it be right to obey God rather than men, judge ye."[1126] Moved by what he had seen and heard, the arresting officer, Samuel Cartledge, soon professed Christ as his Savior, and

---

and Abraham Marshall: Pioneer Baptist Evangelists to the South (Springfield, MO: Particular Baptist Press, 2006); Waldo P. Harris III, *Georgia's First Continuing Baptist Church* (Appling, GA: Kiokee Baptist Church, 1997); James Donovan Mosteller, *A History of the Kiokee Baptist Church in Georgia*, ed. and rev. Waldo P. Harris III, in *Georgia's First Continuing Baptist Church* (Appling, GA: Kiokee Baptist Church, 1997), 13–252; Gregory L. Hunt, "Daniel Marshall: Energetic Evangelist for the Separate Baptist Cause," *Baptist History and Heritage* 21 (April 1986): 5–18; and Samuel Boykin, *History of the Baptist Denomination in Georgia: With Biographical Compendium and Portrait Gallery of Baptist Ministers and Other Georgia Baptists* (Atlanta: James P. Harrison and Co., 1881).

[1125] The Beaver Creek congregation soon joined with Daniel Marshall at Stephen's Creek.

[1126] J. H. Campbell, *Georgia Baptists: Historical and Biographical* (Macon, GA: J. W. Burke and Co., 1874), 176.

Marshall had the joy of baptizing him into the membership of Kiokee Baptist.[1127] During the American War of Independence (1775-83), Daniel Marshall, Patriarch of Georgia Baptists, was the only pastor remaining in the Colony. While he served as chaplain for nearby troops, the British arrested him, jailed him, and confiscated his horses. Marshall died in 1784.

Abraham Marshall and David Barrow

Succeeding his father to the Kiokee pastorate, Abraham Marshall (1748-1819), an eloquent and dynamic speaker, preached to thousands during his evangelistic tours, and untold numbers turned to Christ. In 1786, Abraham preached a minimum of 197 times, on a six-month tour of approximately three thousand miles through eleven states, extending as far north as Massachusetts and Connecticut.[1128] While many of his audiences numbered over a thousand and at times over two thousand, Marshall never refused to preach to small groups, such as the Black Creek Baptist congregation, in Southampton County, Virginia. Riding for miles in hard rain, Marshall reached Black Creek, on Saturday May 27, in time to constitute the church with seventy members, and to induct David Barrow as pastor.[1129] Marshall committed the meeting to the Lord, with the words, "Oh, that it may produce a 'hundred, sixty, or thirty-fold.'"[1130] The church continues to this day.

Prior to his Black Creek pastorate, David Barrow (1753-1819) had experienced harsh persecution. In 1778,

---

[1127] Cartledge became one of the first deacons at Kiokee, and later became a church planter in South Carolina.

[1128] Ray, *Daniel and Abraham Marshall*, 43.

[1129] David Barrow was a soldier in the American War of Independence and served several pastorates in Virginia. At Black Creek, he served from 1786 until 1797-98, when he accepted two pastorates in Kentucky. John Bowers succeeded Barrow to the Black Creek pulpit. Other early laborers at Black Creek Baptist included James Dupee and John McGlamre. See Robert B. Semple, *A History of the Rise and Progress of the Baptists in Virginia*, rev. and extended by G. W. Beale (Richmond: Pitt and Dickinson, 1894), 442, 462; Taylor, *Lives of Virginia Baptist Ministers*, 2nd ed. rev., 1838, 232-33; and Ray, *Daniel and Abraham Marshall*, 91n68.

[1130] Jabez P. Marshall, *Memoirs of the Late Rev. Abraham Marshall*, 20-21.

twenty-five-year-old Barrow had accepted an invitation to preach to a large audience at a home on the banks of the Nansemond River. Addressing "a large concourse of people," Barrow, standing on a raised platform, opened the meeting by reading a line of a hymn for the congregation to sing. Just then, a company of some twenty "genteelly dressed men" rushed up to the platform. One of them said, "Let us sing to the praise and glory of God." They then sang an obscene song before a shocked audience. When Barrow reproved them, they mockingly replied, "We are a parcel of … bad fellows, and are come to get you to baptize us." When Barrow refused, they swore that they would baptize him. As the congregation followed at a distance, the thugs violently took Barrow and his preaching companion, Edward Mintz, nearly a half mile, to a place where a small creek empties into the James River. The men in the audience stood helplessly, and women and children shrieked in horror, as twenty large assailants gathered around Barrow and ducked him into the water twice, pressing his face into the mud bottom and holding it until he nearly drowned. They mockingly asked if he "believed." Barrow, replied, "I believe that Jesus Christ is the Son of God; and I am not ashamed of him." They again plunged him, along with Edward Mintz, and drove them away. Within weeks, several of the thugs died "in a very distracted manner, and it was said, that one of them, a while before his death, wished he had been in hell before he had joined to treat those preachers in the manner they were."[1131]

Abraham Marshall's Family, Ministry, and Legacy

When Abraham Marshall arrived back in Kiokee from his 1786 tour, he was suffering from exhaustion; he remained ill for many days. In 1792, as forty-three-year-old Abraham was preparing to repeat his preaching excursion, he was longing for a suitable wife. In his diary, he records two supplications to

---

[1131] Carter Tarrant, *A History of the Baptized Ministers and Churches in Kentucky* (Frankfort: William Hunter, 1808), 20–23. In the title, I changed the spelling *Baptised* to *Baptized*. See also Lewis Peyton Little, *Imprisoned Preachers*, 461–64, 516.

the Lord. First, "having heard it said, that women would first view a man, and then his horse," Abraham asked the Lord to provide him with a fine horse. Secondly, he prayed that, once he received the horse, the Lord might so prosper his journey that "he might meet a helpmate, a wife, 'to divide the sorrows and double the joys of life.'" In North Carolina, he met John Dinkins, a wealthy, Christian landowner, who gave him one of his finest horses. Marshall "mounted his heaven-sent horse, and went on his way rejoicing, full in the belief that as Heaven had favored him with his first request, the others would be succedaneous." As it turned out, after passing "through several stormy days and high waters," someone pointed him to the home of John Waller, a Baptist evangelist and pastor in Spotsylvania County, Virginia, where Abraham met Nancy Ann Waller, better known as *Ann*. As their eyes met, Abraham said to himself, "You are mine if I can get you." With Ann entertaining similar thoughts, they became engaged to marry. Twenty-seven-year-old Ann was the oldest of nine children born to John and Elizabeth Ann (née Curtis) Waller. Upon Abraham's return, he and Ann renewed their engagement, her parents expressed their blessings, and, after a six-day courtship, the couple "concluded they had the consent of the 'Father of worlds,' and resolved with unshaken minds to proceed." On April 3, 1792, "at seven o'clock in the evening, the nuptial rites were solemnized in the presence of a small, genteel, and well-behaved assembly." Following their affectionate and prolonged farewells to the family, the newlyweds finally set out in the rain toward their Georgia home on Big Kiokee Creek.[1132] Stopping at Fort Mill, South Carolina, for Abraham to constitute the Sugar Creek Baptist Church, he introduced Ann to John Dinkins (1731–1811), who had provided his horse. Dinkins was a charter deacon at Sugar Creek Baptist.[1133]

[1132] Jabez P. Marshall, *Memoirs of the Late Rev. Abraham Marshall*, 67ff.

[1133] Revolutionary War veteran, John Rooker (1755–1840), became the first pastor at the Sugar Creek (now Flint Hill) Baptist Church, where he established an effective missionary outreach to the Catawba Indians while serving the pastorate for nearly fifty years. See John Marvin Crowe, *The Biography of a Thriving Church: A History of First Baptist Church, Charlotte, North Carolina, 1832–1952* (Charlotte: First Baptist Church,

During Abraham Marshall's pastorate at Kiokee Baptist, he led the congregation, in 1808, to erect the Flemish bond, brick meetinghouse that still stands three miles from the Appling community.[1134] Ann Marshall would bear her husband four children. She died in 1815 at the age of fifty-three. Just short of four years later, after a fifty-year ministry, Abraham passed into eternity at the age of seventy-one. One man who had observed Abraham Marshall's ministry for many years said of his preaching, "He would portray the glories of Heaven with such matchless force and beauty, that his hearers could scarcely remain upon their seats; and then he would depict the miseries of the lost in such terrible, burning language, as almost to make the hair stand erect upon your head." The man then added, "Dr. Gill and Dr. Doddridge were, I suppose, his favorite theological authors; for he quoted from them more frequently than from any others."[1135] Abraham's son, Jabez, estimated that his father had "baptized, married, and buried ... about six thousand of his fellow creatures," with "two thousand" in each category.[1136] Jabez succeeded his father to the pastorate and served until his death in 1832. Thus, the father, son, and grandson served Kiokee Baptist for its first sixty years.

John Waller (1741–1802): His Life, Ministry, and Legacy

John Waller was born on December 23 into a modest Anglican home in Spotsylvania County, Virginia. With his uncle's financial assistance, he received substantial training in law, but the

---

1953), 4ff.; Joe M. King, *A History of South Carolina Baptists* (Columbia: General Board of the South Carolina Baptist Convention, 1964), 65–66; and Ray, *Daniel and Abraham Marshall*, 151n324.

[1134] The SBC congregation still uses the 1808 building for special services. Their regular worship is in a more modern building in Appling. Other significant, nearby sites include the Marshall home-site and the Marshall cemetery. See Waldo P. Harris III, "Locations Associated with Daniel Marshall and the Kiokee Church," in *Georgia's First Continuing Baptist Church*, 268ff.

[1135] "From the Rev. Juriah Harriss," in *Annals of the American Baptist Pulpit*, by William B. Sprague (New York: Robert Carter & Brothers, 1860), 6:170–71.

[1136] Jabez P. Marshall, *Memoirs of the Late Rev. Abraham Marshall* (1824), in *Georgia's First Continuing Baptist Church*, 159 (73–225).

uncle's death prevented John's obtaining a degree.[1137] For a time, Waller served as deputy clerk of the county court. By the age of eighteen, he had turned to a life of gambling and viewed Baptist preachers as his worst enemies. In 1766–67, Waller was a member of the grand jury that indicted Baptist evangelist, Lewis Craig (1741–1824), for illegal preaching. Craig had experienced the new birth through the preaching of Samuel Harris. Now charged for preaching the gospel without a license, Craig gave his sworn testimony, followed by these words to the jury: "I thank you, gentlemen of the grand jury, for the honor you have done me. While I was wicked and injurious, you took no notice of me, but since I have altered my course of life, and endeavored to reform my neighbors, you concern yourselves much about me. I shall take the spoiling of my goods joyfully." Astonished at the man's meek spirit, Waller became "convinced that Craig was possessed of something that he had never seen in man before. He thought, within himself, that he should be happy, if he could be of the same religion with Mr. Craig."[1138] Waller began attending Baptist meetings, and, after nearly eight months of struggling for peace, he experienced the free grace and saving work of the Holy Spirit. Waller writes:

> I had long felt the greatest abhorrence of myself, and began almost to despair of the mercy of God. However, I determined never to rest, until it pleased God to show mercy, or cut me off. Under these impressions, I was at a certain place, sitting under preaching. On a sudden, a man exclaimed that he had found mercy, and began to praise God. No mortal can describe the horror with which I was seized at that instant. I began to conclude my damnation was certain. Leaving the meeting, I hastened into a neighboring wood, and dropped on my knees before God, to beg for mercy. In an instant, I felt my heart melt,

---

[1137] Sprague, *Annals*, 6:113ff; and Edwards, *Materials towards a History of the Baptists in the Province of Virginia*, 3:62ff.

[1138] Taylor, *Lives of Virginia Baptist Ministers*, 2nd ed. rev., 1838, 77. Later known as Craig's Baptist Meeting House, Lewis Craig's church in Spotsylvania County was the first Baptist church constituted north of the James River.

and a sweet application of the Redeemer's love, to my poor soul. The calm was great, but short.[1139]

After a brief time of struggle for assurance, Waller found permanent comfort from Scripture, such as 1 John 3:14*b*, "We know that we have passed from death unto life, because we love the brethren." Upon his profession of faith, Waller went up to Orange County and received baptism at the hands of Evangelist James Reed (Read). Having gathered a sizable congregation in his own neighborhood, Waller received ordination, in 1770, and constituted the Lower Spotsylvania Baptist Church, situated at Partlow, Virginia. In later years, it affectionately became "Waller's Meetinghouse."

The Church of England was the only legal church in Virginia. On the terms of England's 1689 Act of Toleration, most Regular Baptists followed the Presbyterian practices of taking oaths of obedience and applying for licenses to preach and to build meetinghouses. Nevertheless, while England's Toleration Act was a victory, it was not a complete victory. The Toleration Act still required all dissenters to pay tithes and parochial taxes for the maintenance of the parish churches of the Church of England. To Virginia's Separate Baptists, such condescending toleration could never achieve soul liberty. They steadfastly refused to acknowledge any "right" of civil government to regulate the preaching of the gospel or the building of meetinghouses.[1140]

The Separate Baptist movement became the greatest Virginia Baptist influence for freedom of conscience. Thus, the most severe persecution came upon Separates. Unpredictably, the era of the most intense persecution (1768–77) was also an era of intense revival and remarkable church growth. In 1770, Virginia had eighteen or nineteen Baptist churches with a combined membership of about 850. By the fall of 1774, Virginia Baptists would have at least seventy-two churches with a

---

[1139] Ibid., 78; cf. Robert B. Semple, *A History of the Rise and Progress of the Baptists in Virginia* (Richmond: Printed by John O'Lynch, 1810), 403–11.

[1140] Charles F. James, *Documentary History of the Struggle for Religious Liberty in Virginia* (Lynchburg: J. P. Bell, 1900), 26; and the valuable discussion in William Fristoe, *A Concise History of the Ketocton Baptist Association* (1808; repr., Harrisonburg, VA: Sprinkle Publications, 2002), 67–70.

combined membership of over five thousand.[1141]

Persecution against Virginia Baptists had begun on June 4, 1768, when a Spotsylvania County sheriff seized five Baptist preachers—John Waller, Lewis Craig, James Chiles, James Reed (Read), and William Mash (Marsh)—in a meetinghouse yard. Charged with disturbing the peace and with ramming a text of Scripture down the throat of every man they met upon the road,[1142] they faced imprisonment in Fredericksburg. As the preachers walked along the streets from the courthouse to the prison, they sang Watts' hymn, "The Narrow Way," whose first line reads, "Broad is the Road that leads to death."[1143] After Waller's strong, legal defense, the justices offered him freedom if he would stop preaching. *Waller refused.* Brilliant attorney, Patrick Henry (1736-99), future governor of Virginia, also defended the Baptists. As Henry's grandson, William Wirt Henry, reports, "It is quite certain that Henry appeared there in their defense, but the speech attributed to him on the occasion was made up in after years from doubtful traditions."[1144]

Patrick Henry, like his father, would remain a lifelong member of the Anglican Church. From the age of twelve,

---

[1141] William Taylor Thom, "The Struggle for Religious Freedom in Virginia: The Baptists," *Johns Hopkins University Studies in Historical and Political Science* 18, nos. 10-12 (October–December 1900): 506 (479–581).

[1142] Robert B. Semple, *A History of the Rise and Progress of the Baptists in Virginia* (Richmond: Printed by John O'Lynch, 1810), 15.

[1143] Hymn 189 in *The Baptist Standard Hymnal with Responsive Readings*, ed. Willa A. Townsend (Nashville: Sunday School Publishing Board of the National Baptist Convention, USA, 1924); see also Oscar H. Darter, *The History of Fredericksburg Baptist Church* (Richmond: Garrett and Massie, 1959), 4–25; Reuben E. Alley, *A History of Baptists in Virginia* (Richmond: Virginia Baptist General Board, 1973), 44–45; and Edwards, *Materials towards a History of the Baptists in the Province of Virginia*, 3:62–64, 68, 72–74.

[1144] William Wirt Henry, *Patrick Henry: Life, Correspondence, and Speeches* (New York: Charles Scribner's Sons, 1891), 1:119; and Lewis P. Little, "Patrick Henry's Supposed Speech in Defense of Waller and His Companions," in *Imprisoned Preachers*, 106–27; see also 93–106. Lewis P. Little traces the fabricated letter to John Mason Peck's "Speech of Patrick Henry," *The Baptist Memorial and Monthly Record* 4, no. 5 (May 1845): 129–32. Faced with criticism, Peck later reported that he had come to doubt the authenticity of his account, which he had heard from Thomas Hinde of Illinois, who heard it from others.

however, Patrick had also accompanied his Presbyterian mother to the preaching of revivalist Samuel Davies,[1145] who succeeded Jonathan Edwards as Princeton's fourth president. It is no wonder that, as a Christian leader, Patrick Henry supported the revivals. He "read the Bible daily, paid for the printing and distribution of two attacks on Deism," and "distributed religious tracts while riding circuit as a lawyer."[1146] A neighbor once visited Henry and found him reading his Bible. Holding it up, Henry said, "This book is worth all the books that ever were printed." Henry's family recalled that it was his "habit to seat himself in his dining-room every morning directly after rising, and read his Bible." Moreover, "he was accustomed to read every Sunday evening to his family, after which they all joined in sacred music, while he accompanied them on the violin."[1147] As a man of strong convictions, Patrick Henry would resist the Anglican establishment and defend the Baptist cause.

In the wake of the five initial incarcerations at Fredericksburg, in 1768, the world, the state, and the church ushered in a "reign of terror" against the Separate Baptists.[1148] Uniting in the cause for religion freedom, in May 1771, the Virginia Separates organized into the General Association of the Separate Baptists of Virginia. That same spring, John Waller was conducting a preaching service in Caroline County, when the parish minister, the parish clerk, and the county sheriff suddenly interrupted him in a vicious manner. As Waller was praying, the Anglican minister approached the platform on his horse and ran the handle of his horsewhip into Waller's mouth. The parish clerk jerked Waller from the platform, repeatedly beat his head against the ground, and dragged him over to the sheriff, who horsewhipped him "with not much less than twenty lashes." Baptist elder, John Williams, described the scene: "The Lord stood by him [Waller] of a truth & poured his love into his soul without measure, & the brethren & sisters about him singing

---

[1145] William Wirt Henry, *Patrick Henry*, 1:15.
[1146] David Holmes, *The Faiths of the Founding Fathers* (Oxford: Oxford University Press, 2006), 141.
[1147] William Wirt Henry, *Patrick Henry*, 2:519.
[1148] Little, *Imprisoned Preachers*, 106, 93–98.

praises to Jehovah, so that he could scarcely feel the stripes for the love of God."[1149] Covered with blood, Waller remounted the platform, says Morgan Edwards, and "preached a most extraordinary sermon, thereby showing that beaten oil is best for the sanctuary."[1150] Edwards was referring to Exodus 27:20, "And thou shalt command the children of Israel that they bring thee pure olive oil beaten for the light, to cause the lamp to burn always." Waller's light would burn until his beaten body lay in the grave.

Sentenced for illegally preaching the gospel, in August 1771, John Waller, William Webber, James Greenwood, and Robert Ware suffered incarceration for forty-six days in a Middlesex County jail that was swarming with fleas. In October 1772, we find Waller back in the same area organizing the Glebe Landing Baptist Church, one of earliest Baptist churches in the Tidewater region. The church has continued to the present day.[1151] In 1774, at Tappahannock (Essex County), magistrates sentenced John Waller, John Shackelford, and Robert Ware with fines and imprisonments for "preaching and expounding the scriptures contrary to law."[1152] The more their enemies persecuted the Baptists the more readily the common folks embraced Baptist preaching. John Waller suffered imprisonment in at least four county jails for 113 days—Spotsylvania (43 days), Caroline (10 days), Middlesex (46 days), and Essex (14 days).[1153] Nothing could stop this man from preaching Christ. An environment of constant persecution made extemporaneous preaching the norm. While in jail, Waller preached through the iron window grates to the crowds who gathered.

[1149] John S. Moore, "John Williams' Journal: Edited with Comments," *Virginia Baptist Register* 17 (1978): 805-6, 804, 778 (795-813).

[1150] Edwards, *Materials towards a History of the Baptists in the Province of Virginia*, 3:62-66.

[1151] See Little, *Imprisoned Preachers*, 269-302. (John Waller's letter is on pages 285-86.). For an earlier Waller letter written from this prison, see Robert Lynch Montague, *Sketch of the History of Glebe Landing Baptist Church*, "address at its 150th anniversary Sunday, October 1, 1922" (Richmond: Richmond Press, 1927), 5-6. The church is now in its third location: Laneview (King William County).

[1152] Little, *Imprisoned Preachers*, 405-8.

[1153] See Little, 405, 510, and 520.

Baptist History in England and America

In 1787, he conducted one of the most widespread revivals of his era. In Virginia alone, he baptized more than two thousand converts, assisted in ordaining twenty-seven ministers, and in establishing eighteen churches.[1154] In June of that year, he led in John Leland's ordination by the laying on of hands. Hailing from Massachusetts, the well-known Leland (1754–1841) was now conducting revival meetings in Virginia.[1155] In August, Virginia's Regular and Separate Baptists consummated their permanent union.

In 1793, the year after his daughter Ann's marriage to Abraham Marshall, fifty-two-year-old John Waller left his Virginia congregation of fifteen hundred members in the capable hands of his nephew, Absalom Waller. With a large contingent of family and friends,[1156] John and Elizabeth Waller moved to the vicinity of Greenwood, South Carolina,[1157] where, in 1794, he led in establishing the Bethabara Baptist Church, in Cross Hill.[1158] Waller served its pastorate until 1799, when he became founding pastor of Siloam Baptist Church, near the town of Ninety Six, South Carolina.[1159] Waller would preach his final sermon in Siloam Baptist. The recent death of a young man in the community had prompted Waller to take his text from

---

[1154] See Taylor, *Lives of Virginia Baptist Ministers*, 2nd ed. rev., 1838, 77ff.

[1155] A local church in Culpeper, Virginia, had ordained Leland in 1777 without the customary presbytery. The re-ordination established his fellowship among both the Separates and the Regular Baptists. John Leland, *The Writings of the Late Elder John Leland: Including Some Events in His Life; Written by Himself, with Additional Sketches, & c.*, ed. L. F. Greene (New York: G. W. Wood, 1845), 26.

[1156] John and Elizabeth Waller had six daughters and three sons: Nancy Ann, John Nicodemus, Benjamin, Mary Magdalene, Thomas Baxter, Dorothy Virginia, Frances Jane, Phoebe, and Elizabeth.

[1157] Margaret Watson, *Greenwood County Sketches: Old Roads and Early Families*, revised (Greenwood, SC: The Attic Press, 1970), 404–7.

[1158] This is an SBC church at 635 Bethabara Church Road, Cross Hill, SC. In the church cemetery, there is a monument with detailed script honoring John Waller. Cf. Townsend, *South Carolina Baptists, 1670–1805*, 223–24, and 228–29.

[1159] This is an SBC church at 2409 Siloam Church Road, Greenwood, SC. There is a historical marker at the church. John Broadus and Basil Manley, founders of the Southern Baptist Theological Seminary, would later serve the Siloam pastorate.

the Zechariah 2:4a, "Run, speak to this young man." Waller preached on the urgency of reaching young people before it is eternally too late. Many recalled that, when he finished his message, there was not a dry eye in the audience. Waller was so exhausted that the men had to lift him up and carry him home. A short time later, John Waller died in the presence of his family. His grave is in a wooded area, just off a Greenwood country road. (See the Tour Guide in Appendix C.).

James Ireland and John Pickett

Born in Edinburgh, Scotland, to a Presbyterian family, James Ireland (ca. 1745-1806) received a classical education, but his tempestuous spirit prompted the youth to take to the high seas for adventure.[1160] At the age of eighteen, he began teaching school in Shenandoah County, Virginia, where he experienced the new birth and, under the influence of the Separate Baptist preacher, John Pickett (1744-1803), he became a Baptist. After visiting Sandy Creek, North Carolina, in 1769, Ireland concluded that the Separates, rather than the Regulars, "had the warmest preachers and the most fire."[1161] Aligning himself with the Separates, Ireland received his baptism and ordination under the guiding hand of Samuel Harris, at Fall Creek Baptist Meeting House, Pittsylvania County, Virginia. Ireland then joined with Harris in establishing the earliest Separate Baptist church in Fauquier County—Carter's Run Baptist Church. Within three years, its congregation grew to 240 members. In 1770, a mob broke into the meetinghouse when it was unoccupied and destroyed the pulpit and Communion table. Later, as John Pickett was preaching, the mob broke in and transported him to jail. Sentencing Pickett for preaching

---

[1160] Near the end of his life, Ireland dictated his autobiography, *The Life of the Rev. James Ireland*, "for many years, pastor of the Baptist church in Buck Marsh, Waterlick and Happy Creek, in Frederick and Shenandoah counties, Virginia" (1819; repr., Harrisonburg, VA: Sprinkle Publications, 2002).

[1161] Ibid., 116; Taylor, *Lives of Virginia Baptist Ministers*, 2nd ed. rev., 1838, 118; and Keith Harper and C. Martin Jacumin, eds., *Esteemed Reproach: The Lives of Rev. James Ireland and Rev. Joseph Craig* (Macon, GA: Mercer University Press, 2005), 105.

without a license, corrupt county justices incarcerated him for three months. Upon his release, Pickett vastly extended his ministry and served the Carter's Run pastorate from 1772 until his death in 1803.

During 1769, magistrates cast fourteen Baptists, including James Ireland, into a Culpeper jail for preaching Christ in their town.[1162] Ireland remained in jail until April 1770. During those five months, crowds gathered outside the "little iron grate" to hear him preach.[1163] As Ireland preached through the grate, oppressors rode their horses at a gallop over attendees, treading them under the horses' feet. Opponents of the gospel stripped and flogged black people found in the audience. Ireland testifies that, at times, when he preached through the grate, mockers "got a table, bench, or something else, stood upon it, and made their water right in my face."[1164] "My prison," said Ireland, was nevertheless, "a place in which I enjoyed much of the divine presence; a day seldom passed without some signal token and manifestation of the divine goodness towards me."[1165] The warden charged each of Ireland's visitors four shillings and eight pence for each visit to his cell. Providentially, a conspiracy, contrived by the jailor and a medical doctor, to poison Ireland came to naught. Mockers quickly attempted to suffocate Ireland by filling pods of Indian pepper with brimstone and setting them on fire for the smoke and fumes to fill the one-room jailhouse. Ireland managed to breath by pressing his mouth and nose to a crack in the floor. Mobs surrounded the jail, cursing and throwing rocks through the grate. Haters of the gospel exploded a keg of gunpowder underneath Ireland's cell. The explosion pushed up a plank, but left Ireland without a scratch. Shortly thereafter, the man who had supplied the gunpowder joined two other young men on a hunting excursion in the back woods. Late one night, as the three slept, a rabid wolf bit the nose of Ireland's persecutor, who died in

---

[1162] Ireland, *Life*, 143.
[1163] Ibid., 141.
[1164] Little, *Imprisoned Preachers*, 163–64.
[1165] Ireland, *Life*, 144. Pick up a free walking-tour map at Museum of Culpeper History.

excruciating pain.[1166]

James Ireland endured every affliction, but the suffering left his health badly damaged. Nevertheless, upon his release from prison, he traveled widely, planting churches.[1167] For many years in Frederick and Shenandoah counties, Ireland served as pastor of the Buckmarsh, the Waterlick, and the Happy Creek Baptist churches.[1168] Buckmarsh Baptist later became Berryville Baptist, in Berryville (Frederick County), Virginia, where an impressive monument with a bronze plaque honors the memory of James Ireland, who served the pastorate here from 1786 until his death in 1806. On the monument's base, another plaque honors his service as an American Revolutionary Patriot. Upon Ireland's death, the *Winchester Virginia Gazette* reported, "He was always distinguished as an able minister of the New Testament, rightly dividing the Word of Truth, giving to saint and sinner their portion in due season."[1169]

Virginia Baptist Preachers Imprisoned in Chesterfield Jail 1770–74

Magistrates in Chesterfield, Virginia, sentenced seven Baptist preachers to jail for preaching Christ without state-church approval. On the exact spot where the jail once stood is the Religious Freedom Monument, a granite memorial with a bronze tablet inscribed to the memory of these Baptist preachers:

[1166] Ibid., 140–44, 150–51.
[1167] See Fristoe, *A Concise History of the Ketocton Baptist Association*, 20–21.
[1168] The Waterlick Church in Shenandoah County and the Happy Creek Church in Front Royal (Frederick County) became Primitive Baptist churches in the nineteenth century. The Happy Creek church still exists. See also Semple, "Ketocton Association," in *A History of the Rise and Progress of the Baptists in Virginia*, rev. extended G. W. Beale, 412–15 (386–420).
[1169] *Winchester Virginia Gazette*, Tuesday June 17, 1806, in Harper and Jacumin, eds., *Esteemed Reproach*, 160.

> On this spot were imprisoned 1770–1774
> John Tanner   David Tinsley
> William Webber   Joseph Anthony
> Augustine Eastin Jeremiah Walker
> John Weatherford

Of those seven men, the Baptists would be obliged to excommunicate two—Augustine Eastin and Jeremiah Walker. While both began well, Eastin fell into Unitarianism,[1170] and Walker fell into immorality.[1171] Every Baptist, however, should honor and perpetuate the names of the five old warriors who kept the faith. Here is an overview.

Converted under Separate Baptist preaching, William Webber (1747–1808) and Joseph Anthony, of Goochland County, received baptism by John Waller and joined the Waller church in Spotsylvania County, where they later received ordination as church-planting evangelists. At the invitation of Chesterfield residents, in 1770, the two men came and preached Christ. Local magistrates promptly imprisoned them "for misbehavior by itinerant preaching." In January 1771, the court ruled that they could go free if they would provide bond and security that they would cease preaching in Chesterfield County. *The*

[1170] Baptists broke from Augustine Eastin when he went into Kentucky, embraced Arianism, and promoted it in his pamphlet titled *Letters on the Divine Unity* (Lexington, Kentucky: D. Bradford, 1804); idem, "Letter from the Rev. Mr. Eastin of Kentucky, to a Friend," *The Unitarian Miscellany and Christian Monitor* 1, no. 7 (July 1821): 289–92; J. L. Burrows, "Recollections of the First General Association in Kentucky," in *Memorial Volume Containing the Papers and Addresses That Were Delivered at the Jubilee of the General Association of Baptists in Kentucky* (Louisville: John P. Morton and Company, 1888), 78 (75–95); and Semple, *A History of the Rise and Progress of the Baptists in Virginia*, rev. extended G. W. Beale, 139.

[1171] David Benedict, *A General History of the Baptist Denomination in America, and Other Parts of the World* (Boston: Printed by Manning and Loring, 1813), 2:388–92; Semple, *History of the Rise and Progress of the Baptists in Virginia* (Richmond: Printed by John O'Lynch, 1810), 385–90, 81–83; cf. Jeremiah Walker, *The Fourfold Foundation of Calvinism Examined and Shaken* (Richmond: Printed by John Dixon, 1791).

men steadfastly refused. Upon magisterial order, the jailor left their cell door unlocked, in hopes that news could spread abroad that the Baptists had fled. The prisoners had a different idea. Webber and Anthony declared, "They have taken us openly, un-condemned, and have cast us into prison; and now, do they cast us out privily? Nay, verily; but let them come themselves and fetch us out."[1172] They preached through the window grates until their release, three months later. By then, many had professed Christ under their preaching.

In May 1773, John Tanner, of North Carolina, suffered imprisonment for proclaiming the gospel in Chesterfield County. Being from another colony, Tanner paid his bond and gained release. Later, in Windsor, North Carolina, a Mrs. Dawson experienced the new birth and requested baptism from the local Baptist church. Her husband threatened to shoot any Baptist who tried to baptize her. John Tanner, at that moment, was traveling on a Roanoke River ferry to reach the Windsor church in time to preach and to baptize recent converts. Moments after Tanner stepped off the ferry, Dawson, lying in wait, began firing at him at close range with a fourteen-and-a-half-inch-long flintlock, horse pistol that fired .69-caliber rounds. Dawson's seventeenth shot entered Tanner's leg and left a severe wound. Suddenly afraid that Tanner might bleed to death, Dawson sent for a doctor to remove the embedded slug. Apparently, Tanner submitted the whole episode to the Lord and never filed charges.[1173]

In May 1773, authorities imprisoned John Weatherford (1740–1833), of Hanover County. Just for preaching Christ, he remained in the Chesterfield jail for five months. James B. Taylor reports of Weatherford,

> The love of Christ constrained Him. He preached at the door of the prison as long as allowed the privilege; when refused that, he preached through the grates of the window. But such determined opposition did

---

[1172] This is a paraphrase of Acts 16:37, where the apostle Paul was in prison at Philippi. Taylor, *Lives of Virginia Baptist Ministers*, 2nd ed. rev., 1838, 44–46, 146–50; and Little, *Imprisoned Preachers*, 209ff., 269ff., 293ff., 516.

[1173] Little, *Imprisoned Preachers*, 334–38. There appears to be no other record of the Dawson couple.

he meet, that an effort was made by his enemies to put a stop to that also. For this purpose, they built an outer wall ... above the grate; but Weatherford devised means to overcome the obstacle. A handkerchief, by the congregation, was to be raised on a pole, above the wall, as a signal that the people were ready to hear. His voice being very strong, he could throw it beyond these impediments, and convey the words of life and salvation to the listening crowd.[1174]

Knife-wielding gangs slashed Weatherford's hands through the grates as he preached. He would carry the scars to his grave. Many years later, Weatherford would become a neighbor of the retired, five-term Virginia Governor Patrick Henry. In one of their conversations, the Governor casually revealed that he had anonymously paid Weatherford's prison fees and secured his liberation from the Chesterfield jail. Again, as a conservative Christian, Henry had shown kindness to the Baptists, and they honored him as an avid defender of soul liberty.[1175] John Weatherford, during his final years, would serve the pulpit of Shockoe Baptist, at Chatham, Virginia. (See Appendix C.).

The fifth of the steadfast Chesterfield prisoners was David Tinsley (1749-1801), a pastor-evangelist, ordained by Samuel Harris. The court convicted Tinsley, on February 4, 1774, "of having assembled & preached to the people at sundry times & places in the County as a Baptist preacher." Tinsley preached through the grates to large crowds, "some weeping and others rejoicing, as they received the word of truth." To stop Tinsley's preaching, the jailor confined him, for four and a half months,

---

[1174] Taylor, *Lives of Virginia Baptist Ministers* (2nd ed., 1838), 49 (46–52); and Little, *Imprisoned Preachers*, 338–60.

[1175] William Wirt Henry, *Patrick Henry*, 1:117–19; see also David L. Holmes, *The Faiths of the Founding Fathers* (Oxford: Oxford University Press, 2006), 141. With tension increasing between Virginia and England during the 1770s, the 1775 Second Virginia Convention assembled in St. John's Church in Richmond, rather than in the capital building in Williamsburg. Attendees at St. John's included such notables as George Washington, Thomas Jefferson, and Richard Henry Lee. Here, they heard the stirring words of Patrick Henry's clarion call for war, "Give me liberty or give me death."

in a dungeon, and mockers tried to suffocate him by burning tobacco and red pepper at his door.[1176] When Baptist churches set apart the second and third Saturdays in June as fast days, "in behalf of our poor blind persecutors and for the releasement of our brethren," the court released David Tinsley on the second fast day.[1177]

Elijah Baker

A Virginian by birth, Elijah Baker (1742–98)[1178] would be the first Baptist preacher to visit the Eastern Shore, and the last Baptist preacher in Virginia to suffer imprisonment for preaching the gospel. Saved and baptized, in 1769, by Samuel Harris, Elijah became a church-planting evangelist, establishing churches in Henrico, Charles City, James City, York, and Gloucester Counties. In 1776, he sailed across the Chesapeake Bay and began preaching along Virginia's Eastern Shore. Instigated by Anglican clergy, an Eastern Shore gang attempted to silence the preacher, by forcing him aboard a ship going abroad. The vessel was to "land him on any coast out of America." Driven by Baker's incessant praying, preaching, and singing, the ship's owner transferred him to another vessel, whose crew feared that Baker's presence was causing contrary winds. They placed him on a third vessel, whose captain promptly "put him ashore" not far from the Accomac area. As an obedient Jonah, Elijah Baker would obey his commission to the Eastern Shore. For the next two decades, he planted Baptist churches along the Virginia, Maryland, and Delaware shores.[1179]

[1176] Garnett Ryland, *The Baptists of Virginia* (Richmond VA: The Virginia Baptist Board of Missions and Education, 1955), 82; and James B. Taylor, *Virginia Baptist Ministers* (Philadelphia: J. B. Lippincott, 1859), 2:100–2.

[1177] Semple, *History of the Rise and Progress of the Baptists in Virginia*, rev. extended G. W. Beale, 78, 476; and Little, *Imprisoned Preachers*, 441–49.

[1178] "Genealogical Notes: Elijah Baker (1742–1798)," *Virginia Baptist Register* 6 (1967): 286–88.

[1179] Morgan Edwards, *Materials towards a History of the Baptists in Delaware*, in *The Pennsylvania Magazine of History and Biography* (Philadelphia: Historical Society of Pennsylvania, 1885), 60. See also Little, *Imprisoned Preachers*, 469–80. Semple's abbreviated account omits many details. For example, his account has only one ship; Semple, *A History of the Rise and*

By 1778, Baker had established, near Cape Charles, the Lower Northampton Baptist Church—the first of his six churches in Virginia. With Anglican clergy charging Elijah Baker with "vagrancy," authorities imprisoned him for fifty-six days in the town of Accomac.[1180] Baker preached through the grates to those who gathered. In addition to the Lower Northampton Church, three other Virginia churches founded by Elijah Baker still exist.[1181] Baker moved on to Maryland, where he organized two churches in Salisbury and fourteen more in surrounding counties. Traveling on to Delaware, he continued his church-planting ministry. Baker died in Salisbury, Maryland, but the location of his grave is unknown.[1182] At Cape Charles's Lower Northampton Baptist Church and at Accomac's Drummondtown Baptist Church, identical bronze tablets commemorate, in the following words, the sacrificial life and ministry of Elijah Baker:

Elijah Baker
Pioneer Baptist of the Eastern Shore of Virginia
who landed at Hunt's Point,
Old Plantation Creek, on Easter Sunday 1776
and the same day preached the
first Baptist sermon, "at the end of a horsing tree."
Opposition of the
Established Church caused him to be deported;
but kind Providence brought him back. He was later imprisoned
56 days in the Old Debtors' Jail at Accomac for

Progress of the Baptists in Virginia (1810), 395. Especially valuable is the work by Robert Williamson, *A Brief History of the Origin and Progress of the Baptists on the Eastern Shore of Virginia*, "embracing an account of the Accomack Association and Sketches of the Churches" (Baltimore: J. F. Weishampel Jr., 1878).

[1180] The 1783 Debtors' Prison in Accomac replaced the jail that had once confined Elijah Baker.

[1181] The other three existing Virginia churches are the Red Bank Baptist Church (est. 1783), in Marionville; the Chincoteague Baptist Church (est. 1786), in New Church; and the Pungoteague Meeting House (est. 1790, now Hollies Baptist Church), in Keller.

[1182] There is a picture of Elijah Baker in Little, *Imprisoned Preachers*, 476.

> the crime of preaching the gospel. (Acts IV; 19, 20)
> In gratitude of the rich heritage that is ours
> because of his suffering and
> imprisonment, this memorial is erected by the
> churches of the Accomac Baptist
> Association, April 4, 1926.

Conclusion

Between 1768 and 1778, at least forty-four Baptist ministers had suffered imprisonment in Virginia jails. These were warriors in the battle for soul liberty. Baptist preachers sacrificed everything, that future generations might enjoy religious liberty. Lewis Peyton Little wrote, "Body imprisonment is bad enough, but soul imprisonment is much more to be dreaded."[1183] William C. Rives, in his *History of the Life and Times of James Madison*, urges, "There is no form of tyranny so revolting to the feelings of human nature as that which is exercised over the mind of man; and no species of mental tyranny so odious as that which seeks to enslave the conscience in matters of religion."[1184] In the next chapter, we will trace the continuation of all citizens paying for the maintenance of state churches. Full freedom would become a reality, but only through the sacrificial ministries of such noble men as Isaac Backus and John Leland.

[1183] Ibid., 506.
[1184] William C. Rives, *History of the Life and Times of James Madison* (Boston: Little, Brown and Co., 1859), 1:45.

Select Bibliography for Further Reading

Clement, Maud Carter. "The Baptists." In *The History of Pittsylvania County Virginia*, 125-31. 1929. Reprint, Santa Maria, CA: Janaway, 2011.

Harper, Keith, and C. Martin Jacumin, eds. *Esteemed Reproach: The Lives of Rev. James Ireland and Rev. Joseph Craig*. Macon, GA: Mercer University Press, 2005.

Harris, Waldo P. III, "A History of the Kiokee Baptist Church 1937-1997." In *Georgia's First Continuing Baptist Church*, 303-524. Appling, GA: Kiokee Baptist Church, 1997.

_____. "Locations Associated with Daniel Marshall and the Kiokee Church." *Viewpoints: Georgia Baptist History* 6 (1978): 25-46, publication of Georgia Baptist Historical Society.

Howell, Robert Boyte C. *The Early Baptists of Virginia*. Philadelphia: The Bible and Publication Society, 1857.

Hunt, Gregory L. "Daniel Marshall: Energetic Evangelist for the Separate Baptist Cause." *Baptist History and Heritage* 21 (April 1986): 5-18.

Ireland, James. *The Life of the Rev. James Ireland*. "For many years, pastor of the Baptist church in Buck Marsh, Waterlick and Happy Creek, in Frederick and Shenandoah counties, Virginia." 1819. Reprint, Harrisonburg, VA: Sprinkle Publications, 2002.

King, Joe M. *A History of South Carolina Baptists*. Columbia, SC: The General Board of the South Carolina Baptist Convention, 1964.

Little, Lewis Peyton. *Imprisoned Preachers and Religious Liberty in Virginia*. "A narrative drawn largely from the official records of Virginia counties, unpublished manuscripts, letters, and other original sources." Lynchburg, VA: J. P. Bell Co., 1938.

Lumpkin, William L. *Baptist Foundations in the South: Tracing through the Separates the Influence of the Great Awakening, 1754-1787*. Nashville: Broadman, 1961.

Marshall, Jabez P. *Memoirs of the Late Rev. Abraham Marshall*. Mount Zion, Hancock County, GA: Printed for the author, 1824.

Mosteller, James Donovan. *A History of the Kiokee Baptist Church in Georgia*. 3rd printing revised and updated by Waldo P. Harris III, in *Georgia's First Continuing Baptist Church*, 13-252. Appling, GA: Kiokee Baptist Church, 1997.

Purefoy, George W. *A History of the Sandy Creek Baptist Association from Its Organization in A. D. 1758, to A. D. 1858*. New York: Sheldon and Co., 1859.

Ray, Thomas. *Daniel and Abraham Marshall: Pioneer Baptist Evangelists to the South*. Springfield, MO: Particular Baptist Press, 2006.

Rennie, Sandra. "The Role of the Preacher: Index to the Consolidation of the Baptist Movement in Virginia from 1760 to 1790." *The Virginia Magazine of History and Biography* 88, no. 4 (October 1980): 430-41.

Ryland, Garnett. *The Baptists of Virginia*. Richmond VA: The Virginia Baptist

Board of Missions and Education, 1955.

Semple, Robert B. (Baylor). *A History of the Rise and Progress of the Baptists in Virginia*. Revised and extended by G. W. Beale. Richmond: Pitt and Dickinson, 1894.

Sparks, John. *The Roots of Appalachian Christianity: The Life and Legacy of Elder Shubal Stearns*. Lexington: The University Press of Kentucky, 2001.

Taylor, George Braxton. *Virginia Baptist Ministers*. Series 3–5 in 3 vols. Lynchburg: J. P. Bell Co., 1912–15. This author was the grandson of James Barnett Taylor (below).

Taylor, James B. (Barnett). *Lives of Virginia Baptist Ministers*. 2nd ed. Revised. Richmond: Yale and Wyatt, 1838.

_____. *Virginia Baptist Ministers*. Series 1–2 in 2 vols. Philadelphia: J. B. Lippincott, 1859.

Thom, William Taylor. "The Struggle for Religious Freedom in Virginia: The Baptists." *Johns Hopkins University Studies in Historical and Political Science* 18, nos. 10–12 (October–December 1900): 479–581.

Townsend, Leah. *South Carolina Baptists, 1670–1805*. Florence, SC: The Florence Printing Company, 1935.

Chapter 16

Isaac Backus, John Leland, and Their Associates: Final Steps toward Religious Liberty

---❋---

Introduction

There were perhaps two dozen organized Baptist churches scattered among the colonies in 1700. By 1791, that number had grown to nearly 65,000 Baptist churches in America.[1185] Most pastors were compelled to supplement their needs, by farming or part-time work, but this gradually changed with the increasing, multifaceted demands of eighteenth-century churches. Typical of this century, Baptist congregations built their meetinghouses of wood, often with high pulpits with elevated steps. Since most meetinghouses were without heating and lighting, churches generally held one service each Sunday during the winter season and two in the summer. Few congregations used musical instruments. As Sunday Schools began their debut in the late 1700s, conversions increased and churches began installing indoor immersion tanks. Empowered by spiritual awakenings, persecuted Baptists would complete their struggle for liberty of conscience and help to unite the colonies into a nation with a Constitution and a Bill of Rights. This chapter introduces the key Baptist leaders.

[1185] Albert W. Wardin Jr., *Baptist Atlas* (Nashville: Broadman, 1980), 10.

Isaac Backus (1724–1806)

His Early Life

Born at the beginning of the first Great Awakening (ca. 1720–60) and converted under the influence of itinerant evangelists and local revivals, Isaac Backus would live to see the epitome of the Second Great Awakening (ca. 1775–1840). He would not only know true revival firsthand, as a pastor-evangelist, he would play a key role in the great struggle for religious liberty. Backus was born in Norwich, Connecticut on January 9, 1724,[1186] the second son and fourth child of Samuel and Elizabeth Backus, who baptized their children in the established (Standing Order) Congregational parish and educated them with Bible training. Elizabeth (née Tracy) Backus was a direct descendant of Edward Winslow (1595–1655), three-term governor of the *Mayflower* Pilgrims' Plymouth Colony. The Backus family were yeoman farmers who owned and managed a gristmill, sawmill, and the Backus Iron Works. In 1740, when Isaac was sixteen, his father died of measles, leaving a deeply depressed Elizabeth with several children—the youngest only six weeks old. In 1741, the local parish minister, Benjamin Lord, invited to his pulpit itinerant evangelists such as Eleazar Wheelock. Isaac Backus's mother experienced conversion to

---

[1186] The best sources include Backus, *The Diary of Isaac Backus*, ed. William G. McLoughlin, 3 vols. (Providence, RI: Brown University Press, 1979); idem, *A History of New England: with Particular Reference to the Denomination of Christians Called Baptists*, 2nd ed. with notes by David Weston, 2 vols. (Newton, MA: Backus Historical Society, 1871); idem, *Isaac Backus on Church, State, and Calvinism: Pamphlets, 1754–1789*, ed. William G. McLoughlin (Cambridge, MA: Harvard University Press, 1968); Alvah Hovey, *A Memoir of the Life and Times of the Rev. Isaac Backus, A. M.* (Boston: Gould and Lincoln, 1859); William G. McLoughlin, *Isaac Backus and the American Pietistic Tradition*, ed. Oscar Handlin (Boston: Little, Brown and Co., 1967); idem, "Isaac Backus and Separation of Church and State," *American Historical Review* 73, no. 5 (June 1968): 1392–1413; idem, *New England Dissent 1630–1833: The Baptists and the Separation of Church and State*, 2 vols. (Cambridge, MA: Harvard University Press, 1971); idem, *Soul Liberty: The Baptists' Struggle in New England, 1630–1833* (Hanover, NH: University Press of New England, 1991).

Christ during these meetings,[1187] and such preaching began to sow the Word in Isaac's heart. He recalls the very day when he was "alone in the field," August 24, 1741, when "all my past life was opened plainly before me, and I saw clearly that it had been filled up with sin.... I was enabled by divine light to see the perfect righteousness of Christ and the freeness and riches of His grace, with such clearness, that my soul was drawn forth to trust in Him for salvation." Backus adds, "My heavy burden was gone, tormenting fears were fled, and my joy was unspeakable."[1188]

His Journey into New Light, Separate Congregationalism

In July 1742, Backus, with much misgiving, joined the established church. Having adopted the creed known as the Saybrook Platform (1708), the Standing Order had stripped Connecticut's local churches of their historical, congregational governance, making them semi-Presbyterian. Due to Benjamin Lord's commitment to the New England Puritans' Half-Way Covenant (1662), his church membership now consisted of many outwardly moral, baptized, unregenerate members, and he was readily baptizing their infants. Baptized, but prohibited from the Lord's Supper, these unregenerate families were "half-way" toward full membership. "Progressing" into Stoddardism, the teachings of Solomon Stoddard (1643–1729), Congregational clergymen, across New England, began eliminating the half-way status by inviting the baptized unconverted to the Communion Table and into full membership. As infant baptism had already become the passively *regenerating* ordinance, Communion now became the *converting* ordinance. "The Lord brought me to see," recalls Isaac, "that though they had a form of godliness yet they did deny the power thereof and therefore I was commanded to turn away from them."[1189]

[1187] Elizabeth Backus had made a profession of faith around 1721. Backus, *History of New England: with Particular Reference to the Denomination of Christians Called Baptists*, 1:496n1.

[1188] Hovey, *Memoir of the Life and Times of the Rev. Isaac Backus*, 39; cf. Backus, *History of New England*, 2:107.

[1189] Backus, *Diary*, 1:3.

The legislature of Connecticut passed a law, in 1742, making it a penal offense for any person to teach or preach in any parish without an invitation from the parish minister. Even so, Isaac Backus, along with his mother[1190] and about a dozen others, left the old church in 1745 and began holding home Bible studies. In July 1746, they organized a Separate Congregational church in Norwich. Mockery and imprisonment followed. On September 27, 1746, while praying in the woods, Isaac surrendered to the call to preach. The next day, he preached at the Separate church in Norwich, and the congregation encouraged him toward the ministry. In view of the numerous, unconverted clergymen filling New England's pulpits, Backus's first published work was *A Discourse Showing the Nature and Necessity of an Internal Call to Preach the Everlasting Gospel* (1754).

After preaching in Connecticut, Rhode Island, and Massachusetts, during the next fourteen months, Backus thankfully found a group of New Light, Congregational Separates in the Titicut parish area of Massachusetts. They were seeking help in forming a local church.[1191] Titicut parish comprised part of Middleboro on the south side of the Taunton River, and part of Bridgewater on the north side. In February 1748, Backus prepared for this group a statement of faith and a covenant, signed by sixteen Separates, thus organizing the "Third Congregational Church," now named North Congregational Church, in North Middleboro.[1192] Their membership was up to thirty-four in April, when they ordained Isaac Backus as their first pastor.[1193] In November 1749, Isaac married Susanna Mason of Rehoboth, Massachusetts. The Lord would bless their home with nine children. Keeping abreast of the persecutions against the Baptists in Massachusetts, Backus reported that,

---

[1190] Backus, *History of New England*, 1:496n1.

[1191] *Titicut*, the Indian name for the Taunton River, had been home to a group of John Eliot's Praying Indians. This scenic site is a popular part of Bridgewater.

[1192] North Congregational Church is now a member of the liberal United Church of Christ (UCC).

[1193] S. Hopkins Emery, *The History of the Congregational Church of North Middleborough, Massachusetts* (Middleborough: Harlow and Thatcher, 1876).

in January 1750, the state legislature taxed the local Baptist churches in the Sturbridge area for the upkeep of the established Congregational churches. In the months that followed, authorities imprisoned five Baptists, heavily fined many others, and seized Baptists' properties, including their oxen and cattle. Although the local Baptists had consistently repudiated Anabaptism, the courts required that their churches sign certificates "that they were Anabaptists," which, Backus explains, "was a name of reproach cast upon them by their persecutors."[1194] In the wake of these events, Isaac Backus would become a Baptist.

His Baptist Stance Developed out of Scripture and Conviction

After almost two years of torturous doubt, regarding the proper subjects and mode of baptism, Backus resorted to serious and focused Bible study. Finally, in July 1751, Backus confidently announced to his Titicut church his conviction that believer's baptism by immersion is the only scriptural manner. The following month, Pastor Benjamin Pierce of Warwick, Rhode Island, baptized Isaac and Susanna Backus, and five others by immersion. Most of Titicut's Third Congregational Church remained unconvinced. After nearly five years, a New Light council of ministers persuaded the majority of Third Congregational and all other Congregational churches to reject the Baptists. Widespread persecution followed. With his small flock now driven to private worship, Isaac Backus records at least eleven Baptists who were seized and jailed in Norwich, during an eight-month span. Isaac's brother, Samuel, suffered imprisonment for twenty days. A short time later, in the Backus home, Isaac's mother, Elizabeth, "sick, and, thickly wrapped in clothes to produce perspiration, sat near the fire by her stand, reading the family Bible," when state-church, collection agents

---

[1194] Backus, *History of New England*, 2:94–96. Even Zinzendorf, founder of the Moravians, reported now that, while "the Baptist Church has not proved its origin," Baptists "have sufficiently shown that they have nothing in common with the Anabaptists." Jacob John Sessler, *Communal Pietism among Early American Moravians* (New York: Henry Holt, 1933), 56.

entered the house "about nine o'clock, in a dark rainy night," and "took her away to prison." Mrs. Backus spent the next thirteen days in prison.[1195]

Finally, in January 1756, Isaac Backus and his group organized in his home the First Baptist Church of North Middleboro,[1196] where he received ordination, in June of the same year.[1197] He would maintain this pastorate for the remaining half century of his life. Having witnessed the perils of open Communion, Backus organized First Baptist as a closed Communion church. During the next eleven years, he traveled beyond the area of his own church 14,691 miles, preached 2,412 sermons, and baptized 62 persons.[1198] Backus's local church would benefit greatly from the diverseness and widespread scope of his ministry. For thirty-four years, he served on the first Board of Trustees of Rhode Island College (later Brown University). An astute apologist and diplomat for religious liberty, Backus was also a prolific historian, producing a three-volume *History of New England: with Particular Reference to the Denomination of Christians Called Baptists* (1777, 1784, and 1796). Backus's greatest achievements came from three driving forces: (1) his deep commitment to glorify God in his whole life and ministry, (2) his uncompromising determination to safeguard the independence and autonomy of the local church, and (3) his relentless battle for the freedom of the local church from governmental intrusion. No one since Roger Williams stood so preeminently in the public arena as a champion of soul liberty as Isaac Backus. Both men penned their convictions for future generations. Unlike Williams, however, who labored totally

---

[1195] Backus, "A Fish Caught in His Own Net," in *Isaac Backus on Church, State, and Calvinism*, 188. Backus is using the word *fish* as a pun on the name *Joseph Fish*, a Connecticut clergyman of the Standing Order. See also Backus, *History of New England*, 2:98–99n3–4.

[1196] Once known as "Backus Memorial Baptist Church," it is now First Baptist Church of North Middleboro (unaffiliated). The church is in its third building since its 1756 founding. It is located at the intersection of Plymouth and Bedford Streets. Just down Plymouth Street from First Baptist stands North Congregational Church (UCC).

[1197] Backus, *History of New England*, 2:117.

[1198] Hovey, *Memoir of the Life and Times of the Rev. Isaac Backus*, 130.

outside the local church, Backus for a half century served one of the most prominent pastorates of his generation.

His Contributions toward Freedom of Religion

During the 1770s, Isaac Backus adamantly confronted the so-called "certificate system," developed by the Massachusetts legislature for handling the collection of taxes, for the support of the established Congregational Church. According to the system, the parish collectors would exempt from the tax requirement any individual—Anglican, Baptist, or Quaker—who would file an annual certificate, signed by his minister and a committee of law-abiding lay members of his church, attesting to the fact that he was a conscionable member of the church. The certificate system created immense difficulties for Baptists. Many of the parish tax collectors, fearing that their own churches might receive insufficient funds, utilized every imaginable means of invalidating the certificates. For example, collectors could automatically invalidate all certificates from any church that was temporarily without a pastor, even if their pastor had only recently died. For Baptists, the certificate system was a deadly enemy of religious freedom. After all, the use of a certificate was essentially a concession that the government had the right to control matters of conscience. In addition, "certificate families" always suffered from social prejudice as second-class citizens.

While many Baptists—both clergy and lay members—disobeyed the tax and certificate laws, scores of pastors enjoined their people to "submit to every ordinance of man for the Lord's sake" (1 Pet. 2:13a). "Let every soul be subject unto the higher powers. For there is no power but of God: the powers that be are ordained of God" (Rom. 13:1). These Baptists could not approve of doing what some might perceive as "evil that good may come" (Romans 3:8). Doing so might suggest that the end justifies the means. Thus, they practiced "obedience under protest." However, many other Baptists concluded that the issues at hand demanded a different, equally biblical, and perhaps more effective solution. They explained it this way. While God commands Christians to obey human laws, He also instructs Christians that their supreme duty is to obey God. Therefore, when a human law conflicts with the clear teaching of Scripture, "we must obey God rather than men" (Acts 5:29*b*). We will now see how this dilemma played out in eighteenth-century Baptist history.

The Warren (RI) Baptist Association (est. 1767) appointed Isaac Backus as "Agent for the Baptists in New England." His task on the Association's Grievance Committee was to collect complaints of persecution against Baptists and to seek biblical solutions. Upon his completion of the project, Backus proposed massive civil disobedience, regarding the payment of religious taxes and the use of certificates. Upon the vote of the Committee, on May 5, 1773, Backus sent out a circular letter, asking all Baptist churches of Massachusetts to consider his proposal of non-compliance and to instruct their delegates to vote for its adoption at the Association meeting in Medfield. However, when the delegates assembled in the Medfield meetinghouse, Samuel Stillman—pastor of First Baptist, Boston, and principal opponent of civil disobedience—persuaded the delegates to use an anonymous ballot and to make the outcome non-binding on those who voted against civil disobedience. The delegates voted to send the issue back to the local churches, thus leaving each local church free to decide for itself on the matter of civil disobedience.

Meanwhile, the delegates, the large majority of whom supported Backus, raised funds to publish his tract in defense of civil disobedience against the oppression. Backus's defense was *An Appeal to the Public for Religious Liberty* (1773),[1199] often called the "Baptist Declaration of Independence" against religious taxation without representation. While Backus's *Appeal* did not result in the support that most expected, the tract itself is of great significance for its brilliant appeal to church history and Scripture, and for its detailed analysis of the religious tax and the certificate system. Although rumors floated in high places of a Baptist threat to inform England's monarchy of the

---

[1199] Isaac Backus, *An Appeal to the Public for Religious Liberty, against the Oppressions of the Present Day* (Boston: John Boyle, 1773); cf. *Isaac Backus on Church, State, and Calvinism*, 303ff.

religious persecutions, Baptists never carried out the threat. During 1774, though, each member of the First Continental Congress received a copy of Backus's *Appeal*. As McLoughlin concludes, this *Appeal* "still stands as the most forceful exposition of the pietistic theory of separation of church and state written during the colonial era."[1200] The *Appeal* did produce a measure of success. "The record shows," says McBeth, that by the "policy of civil disobedience, Baptists made more progress toward religious liberty in a year than they had made in the previous decade."[1201]

Most importantly, amid the widespread preaching and evangelism that ignited the Second Great Awakening, Baptists voiced anti-establishment protests in a proliferation of petitions, public debates, articles, and private letters, calling for a repeal of unjust legislation. In October 1774, the Warren Association appointed Backus to lead a delegation to Philadelphia, to present a religious freedom petition to a committee of the First Continental Congress.[1202] Thus, in December 1774, a year after the celebrated Boston Tea Party, Isaac Backus, in behalf of the Baptist Grievance Committee at Boston, presented to the Massachusetts Congress a powerful plea for soul liberty. He closed with these words: "All America are alarmed at the tea tax; though, if they please, they can avoid it by not buying the tea; but we have no such liberty.... We cannot give in the certificates you require." To do so, Backus explained, would "implicitly" surrender "to men that authority which we believe in our consciences belongs only to God." In this, "therefore, we claim charter rights, liberty of conscience. And if any still deny it to us, they must answer ... to Him who has said, 'With what measure ye mete, it shall be measured to you again [Matt. 7:2b].'" Backus assures, "We remain hearty friends to our country, and ready to do all in our power for its general welfare."[1203]

[1200] McLoughlin, "Massive Civil Disobedience as a Baptist Tactic in 1773," 725.

[1201] H. Leon McBeth, *The Baptist Heritage* (Nashville: Broadman, 1987), 263.

[1202] Backus, *Diary*, 2:916–19.

[1203] Hovey, *Memoir of the Life and Times of the Rev. Isaac Backus*, 220–21; and Edwin S. Gaustad, ed., *A Documentary History of Religion in America: To the Civil War*, 2nd ed. (Grand Rapids: Eerdmans, 1993), 255–56.

As Massachusetts began focusing its attention on the War of Independence (1775–83), authorities would soon find little time to enforce the certificate laws. Indeed, Backus would live to see the virtual termination of imprisonments for failure to pay parish taxes. Nevertheless, while the War freed Americans from British taxes, it did not free Baptists from religious taxes. The Massachusetts Constitution (1780), whose principal author was John Adams, empowered the state to require every citizen to pay religious taxes for the support of teachers of Protestant churches. Such taxes, paid by Baptists and other dissenters, would go toward supporting of their own churches — *if they filed certificates*.[1204] Unwilling to accept the gilded shackle, Backus, until his death, in 1806, would publicly oppose all religious taxes and certificates. Backus did agree with the requirement in the Massachusetts Constitution that any person chosen to become "Governor, Lieutenant-Governor, Counselor, Senator, or Representative," swear, "I believe the Christian religion, and have a firm persuasion of its truth."[1205] Isaac Backus was "convinced that America was not only a Christian nation but a Protestant one."[1206] While graciously tolerating the well-meaning politicians who used Enlightenment terminology, such as "natural rights," Backus stood without apology for his conviction that liberty of conscience is a *supernatural* right — not a *natural* right. Sadly, Backus would not live to see the final victory, when disestablishment became a reality in Connecticut in 1818 and in Massachusetts in 1833.

When the Warren Association, in 1788, sent Backus to preach in Virginia, he witnessed great revivals. Returning to New England, the following year, he yearned for revival in

---

[1204] The Massachusetts Constitution (1780), Part 1, article 3, in Oscar Handlin and Mary Handlin, eds., *The Popular Sources of Political Authority: Documents on the Massachusetts Constitution of 1780* (Cambridge, MA: The Belknap Press, 1966), 442–43 (441–72). The contention prompted Backus's pamphlet, *An Appeal to the People* (1780), in *Isaac Backus on Church, State, and Calvinism*, 385–96.

[1205] Massachusetts Constitution (1780), Part 2, chapter 6, article 1, in Handlin, *Documents on the Massachusetts Constitution of 1780*, 467ff. Cf. *Backus on Church, State, and Calvinism*, 436.

[1206] McLoughlin, *Soul Liberty*, 259.

his own state. During the next seven years, beginning in 1790, Isaac Backus covered more than 1,100 miles a year on horseback, preaching all over New England. In 1795, Backus and the Baptist, Stephen Gano, together with twenty-one others, issued a "Circular Letter," calling for a "Concert of Prayer" for genuine revival. Backus's records reveal that, from 1748 to 1802, he made 918 trips on horseback, aggregating more than 68,600 miles.[1207] On November 20, 1806, at the peak of the Second Great Awakening, Isaac Backus finished his earthly course. In Titicut Parish Cemetery, at 41 Plymouth Street, Middleboro, Backus's granite tomb is pulpit-shaped and holds an open Bible. Underneath the Bible is a bronze memorial plaque.

John Leland (1754–1841)

Background

John Leland was born into a Congregationalist family in Grafton, Massachusetts.[1208] Upon his profession of faith, at the age of twenty, he became a Baptist and received immersion at Northbridge, Massachusetts, by Noah Alden (1725-97) of Bellingham.[1209] Two years later, John married Sallie Devine, a young woman of devout Baptist upbringing from Hopkinton, Massachusetts. The Bellingham church issued a preaching license to John, and the couple traveled to Virginia, in 1776, where they joined the Mount Pony Baptist Church, in Culpeper. Here, Leland received ordination and served the Mount Pony pastorate for a short time, before moving to a new pastorate in Orange County. Since his ordination had been without the laying on of hands by a presbytery (the normal way among Virginia's Regular Baptists), some Regulars refused to acknowledge his

---

[1207] In those days, traveling on the postal routes provided for the most accurate registering of mileage. Backus limited his mileage charts to those journeys exceeding ten miles in length from his home.

[1208] See John Leland, *The Writings of the Late Elder John Leland: Including Some Events in His Life; Written by Himself, with Additional Sketches, & c.*, ed. L. F. Greene (New York: G. W. Wood, 1845).

[1209] Baptized by Shubal Stearns, Noah Alden had succeeded Stearns to the Baptist pastorate at Tolland, Connecticut. Noah Alden was the great grandson of John and Priscilla Alden of the *Mayflower*.

ordination. From his base in Orange, however, Leland entered evangelistic work, traveling all over the colony and preaching as many as a dozen sermons a week. With the Second Great Awakening underway, his revival ministry proved to be enormously effective. Moreover, in 1787, when the Regular and Separate Baptists in Virginia united, Leland accepted a second ordination by the imposition of the hands of a presbytery, which bonded his fraternal relationship with the United Baptists.[1210] Meanwhile, John Leland would contribute immensely toward the final victory in the Baptist struggle for soul liberty.

The Virginia Declaration of Rights (1776)

Just a few months prior to Leland's arrival in the Old Dominion, and little more than two weeks prior to the adoption of the Declaration of Independence, the Virginia Convention, in June 1776, adopted the sixteen-article Virginia Declaration of Rights, whose "free exercise of religion" would ultimately make its way into the First Amendment of America's Constitution. Article 16 of the Declaration of Rights declares:

> That religion, or the duty which we owe to our Creator and the manner of discharging it, can be directed by reason and conviction, not by force or violence; and therefore, *all men are equally entitled to the free exercise of religion, according to the dictates of conscience;* and that it is the mutual duty of all to practice Christian forbearance, love, and charity towards each other.[1211]

The Virginia Bill for Establishing Religious Freedom (1786)

The reign of terror against Virginia Baptists had emerged in Fredericksburg, in 1768, with the imprisonment of five Christ-honoring preachers (discussed above). The end of that

---

[1210] William Sprague, "John Leland," in *Annals of the American Baptist Pulpit* (New York: Robert Carter & Brothers, 1860), 6:175.
[1211] Italics mine. See Robert S. Alley, ed., *James Madison on Religious Liberty* (Buffalo, NY: Prometheus Books, 1985), 51–52.

era emerged in the same town, in 1777, with a committee of five freedom-loving patriots, including Thomas Jefferson.[1212] Their goal was to end the state-church status of the Anglican Church in Virginia. In this meeting, Thomas Jefferson (1743–1826), future third president of the United States (1801–9), drafted the Virginia Statute for Establishing Religious Freedom. On January 16, 1786, after nine years of debate, the Virginia General Assembly enacted the Statute into law. Jefferson would regard this as one of three accomplishments for which he desired future generations to remember him.[1213] The Virginia Statute for Religious Freedom promises that "no man shall ... suffer on account of his religious opinions or belief."[1214] In late 1791, this Statute became the basis for the religion clause in the First Amendment and for part of Article six of the American Constitution. See "Fredericksburg" in the Tour Guide (Appendix C).

While Baptists deeply appreciated Jefferson's contributions toward religious freedom, they quietly simmered over his Enlightenment-Era approach to the Scriptures. Late in life, Jefferson decided to extract the "diamonds" of true Christianity from what he regarded as the "dunghills" of the "corrupt" text of the four Gospels. Utilizing a King James Bible, Jefferson took his penknife and cut out all "acceptable" passages. He pasted these onto eighty-seven blank pages, to produce the *Jefferson Bible*, subtitled *The Life and Morals of Jesus of Nazareth* (1820).[1215] The following letter, written by Jefferson in his later years, furnishes a résumé of his hatred toward Trinitarian Christianity. With the hope that every young man in America would grow up a Unitarian, Jefferson described two of the most notable Trinitarians—Athanasius of Alexandria, Egypt (ca. 298–373) and John Calvin of Geneva, Switzerland

---

[1212] The other four at the meeting were George Mason, Edmund Pendleton, George Wythe, and Thomas Ludwell Lee.
[1213] Jefferson considered the Declaration of American Independence and the founding of the University of Virginia as his other two key accomplishments.
[1214] Alley, *James Madison on Religious Liberty*, 60–61.
[1215] *The Jefferson Bible: The Life and Morals of Jesus of Nazareth* (1820; facsimile reprint, Washington, DC: Smithsonian Books, 2011).

(1509–64) — as "impious dogmatists":

> Verily I say these [Athanasius and Calvin] are the false shepherds foretold as to enter not by the door into the sheepfold, but to climb up some other way. They are mere usurpers of the Christian name, teaching a counter religion made up of the *deliria* of crazy imaginations, as foreign from Christianity as is that of Mahomet. Their blasphemies have driven thinking men into infidelity, who have too hastily rejected the supposed Author himself, with the horrors so falsely imputed to Him. Had the doctrines of Jesus been preached always as pure as they came from his lips, the whole civilized world would now have been Christian. I rejoice that in this blessed country of free inquiry and belief, which has surrendered its creed and conscience to neither kings nor priests, the genuine doctrine of one only God is reviving, and I trust that there is not a young man now living in the United States who will not die a Unitarian.[1216]

Final Battles toward the First Amendment to the United States Constitution (1789)

Meanwhile, the struggle for a Bill of Rights in behalf of freedom of religion still faced two challenges. The first challenge emerged in November 1784, when the Virginia Legislature produced an Assessment Bill, authorizing a state-wide taxation for the support of all "teachers of the Christian religion." Supported by petitions from the Tidewater counties, along with "a torrent of eloquence" from Patrick Henry, the bill gained enormous support, even though it required the state to subsidize religion.[1217] As a conservative Christian who fought long and hard for the disestablishment of the Church

---

[1216] Thomas Jefferson, *The Writings of Thomas Jefferson*, memorial edition, ed. Albert E. Bergh, 20 vols. (Washington, DC: Washington Jefferson Memorial Association, 1903–4), 15:383–85; cf. 15:322–24.

[1217] Ralph Ketcham, *James Madison: A Biography* (Charlottesville: University Press of Virginia, 2000), 162–67.

of England in Virginia, Henry saw the bill as an emergency solution to the widespread unpreparedness of Christian clergy against rapid inroads of French Deism.[1218] In opposition to the bill, James Madison Jr. (1751–1836), who was destined to become the two-term, fourth president of the United States (1809–17), argued heroically in a speech before the 1784 Assembly that the "obnoxious" bill would violate individual liberty of conscience, and that it would entangle the state in matters of defining the true Christian religion. As it became apparent that Patrick Henry's eloquence was winning over the majority in the House of Delegates, Madison maneuvered to have the vote on the Assessment Bill postponed until the following spring. This would allow time for Madison and others to canvass for the bill's defeat.

During the next few months, Madison cleverly supported Patrick Henry's successful campaign to return to Virginia's governorship—thus guaranteeing the loss of Henry's seat in the next House of Delegates. In April 1785, many other supporters of the Assessment Bill lost their House seats. In a further effort to ensure the defeat of the Assessment Bill, the Religious Society of Baptists in Virginia persuaded Madison to draft *A Memorial and Remonstrance against Religious Assessments* (1785).[1219] The fifteen-point *Memorial*, supported by Baptists such as Leland and Backus, served as a powerful petition that led the legislature, in their October 1785 meeting, to let the Assessment Bill die forever—a major victory for Baptists. Remarkably, in his works, James Madison never reveals his personal relationship with God. Receiving infant baptism and growing up in a respectable Anglican family, Madison graduated from the College of New Jersey (later Princeton), in 1771, and studied Hebrew and ethics under John Witherspoon, a

---

[1218] William Wirt Henry, *Patrick Henry: Life, Correspondence, and Speeches* (New York: Charles Scribner's Sons, 1891), 2:205ff., 2:575–76; and James M. Wells, "A Historical Survey of the Influence of Christianity upon the Political Career of Patrick Henry" (MA thesis, Sam Houston State Teachers College, 1960), now known as Sam Houston State University.

[1219] James Madison, *A Memorial and Remonstrance on the Religious Rights of Man*, "written in 1784–5, at the request of the Religious Society of Baptists in Virginia" (Washington City [DC]: S. C. Ustick, 1828).

strong advocate of Scottish Common Sense philosophy and the only clergyman to sign the Declaration of Independence. While Madison did have a deep interest in religion, a careful study by David Holmes concludes, "The pattern of Madison's religious associations and the comments of contemporaries clearly categorize" him as "a moderate Deist."[1220]

The second challenge in the struggle for religious freedom was the Ratification Controversy. After signing the national Constitution, on September 17, 1787, in Philadelphia, Congress sent copies to the state legislatures for ratification. Later hailed as the "Father of the Constitution," James Madison had drafted the proposed Constitution, at Montpelier, his country estate near Orange, Virginia. The document touches on religion, but only in Article 6: "No religious test shall ever be required as a qualification to any office or public trust under the United States." To the Baptists, this was essential but insufficient. John Leland, whose homestead was near Montpelier, wrote his *Objections to the Federal Constitution* (1788), and a copy soon reached James Madison, who was campaigning for a seat among the Virginia delegates who would be voting at the Ratification Convention. Many Virginians believed that, if the plainspoken Leland would campaign for the delegate seat, he could defeat Madison.

The first of Leland's objections warns, "There is no Bill of Rights" for freedom of religion and protection from the potential powers of the federal government. Another key concern for Leland was that, without more safeguards, future leaders could prohibit by law or regulation the free exercise of conscience and worship.[1221] At the advice of supporters,[1222] Madison vis-

---

[1220] David L. Holmes, "The Religious Views of James Madison," in *The Faiths of the Founding Fathers* (Oxford: Oxford University Press, 2006), 92–98.

[1221] John Leland, "My Objections to the Federal Constitution" (original), from *James Madison Papers*, digital copy, courtesy, Library of Congress, Washington DC.

[1222] E.g., "Joseph Spencer [letter] to Col. James Madison Jr., Fredericksburg, [from] Orange County, February 28, 1788" (original), from *James Madison Papers*, digital copy, courtesy, Library of Congress, Washington DC. Madison would be passing Leland's farm on his way home from Fredericksburg to Orange. Spencer advises Madison to stop at the farm and spend a few hours with Leland. Enclosed with Spencer's letter is a copy of Leland's ten "Objections."

ited with Leland to discuss Baptist concerns.[1223] Their meeting took place in an oak grove, where Leland often resorted to pray. Here, at Leland-Madison Memorial Park, a plaque mounted on a boulder memorializes this important meeting. After hours of deliberation, Madison pledged that, if Leland would support his campaign, he in turn would champion a Bill of Rights to amend the Constitution. With Leland's full support, Madison won his seat to the Ratification Convention and, later, to the First Federal Congress. The Constitution became "operational" in the summer of 1788, but, without a Bill of Rights, opposition from the State of Virginia alone could still render it ineffective. As author of the first edition, Madison acquired the title "Father of the Bill of Rights." In 1789, when Congress submitted the Bill to the states, for ratification, it still needed the approval of nine states. On December 15, 1791, the Bill of Rights—the first ten amendments—went into effect.

The Purpose and Essence of the First Amendment

The First Amendment opens with the words, "Congress shall make no Law respecting an Establishment of religion, or prohibiting the free exercise thereof."[1224] Due to archaic expressions, many today are oblivious to the fact that the word *respecting* meant *regarding*, and, as used in the First Amendment, the word *respecting* refers to "the whole subsequent clause or sentence."[1225] The phrase "Establishment of religion" meant *state church*. To the founders, the expression "an Establishment of religion" meant "any state church." The Constitution prohibits Congress from establishing and from prohibiting any state religion.[1226] Moreover, the First Amendment relegates the

---

[1223] Ketcham, *James Madison*, 251; idem, "James Madison and Religion," in *James Madison on Religious Liberty*, ed. Robert S. Alley, 185; and Sprague, *Annals of the American Baptist Pulpit*, 6:174–86.

[1224] The First Amendment also includes freedom of speech, freedom of the press, the right of the people peaceably to assemble, and the right to petition the government for a redress of grievances.

[1225] This is verbatim from Noah Webster's 1806 *Compendious Dictionary of the English Language* and his 1828 *American Dictionary of the English Language*.

[1226] See also John Harmon McElroy, "Understanding the First Amendment's

matter to the states. At the time of the ratification of the Bill of Rights, in 1791, there were fourteen states, and state churches still existed in nearly half of them. The final disestablishment would occur in Massachusetts in 1833.

It is noteworthy that the expression *separation of church and state* is not in the Constitution. Indeed, that expression has led to unconstitutional court rulings on the First Amendment's *establishment* clause. For example, rather than protecting Christian symbols and seasonal displays on public properties, court rulings have disallowed them as "establishments of religion."[1227] In effect, court rulings have dismissed God from *public* venues, by relegating freedom of religion to *non-public* venues. Due to archaic words and expressions, the restoration of the religious freedom that our founders originally intended would require a new version of the First Amendment.[1228]

The Big Cheshire Cheese

On Friday January 1, 1802, President Thomas Jefferson received a colossal, 1235-pound cheese, delivered in a wagon drawn by six horses. It was a gift from John Leland and the Baptists of Cheshire, Massachusetts. Made by the dairy women of the town, the gift became a national sensation. Two days later, on January 3, Leland volunteered to preach in the House of Representatives. Jefferson attended, and he would frequent such services regularly, until the end of his two terms. Speakers for these services would come from various denominations. At the corner of Church and School Streets, in Cheshire, a concrete replica of the cider press that made the cheese has this plaque:

Religion Clauses," *The Intercollegiate Review* 46, no. 1 (Spring 2011): 33–40.

[1227] E.g., *Engel v. Vitale* (1962) and *Wallace v. Jaffree* (1985); for more detail, see Thomas White, Jason G. Duesing, and Malcolm B. Yarnell III, eds., *First Freedom: The Baptist Perspective on Religious Liberty* (Nashville: B&H Publishing Group, 2007).

[1228] Cf. McElroy, "Understanding the First Amendment's Religion Clauses," 40.

Elder John Leland
Eloquent Preacher, Beloved Pastor, Influential Patriot, Father of Religious Liberty, with James Madison Carried Virginia in the Adoption of the Constitution of the United States and the First Amendment, Despite Opposition of Every Other Pulpit in Massachusetts, Carried Every Vote in Cheshire for the Election of President Thomas Jefferson and Presented to Him on Jan. 1, 1802, in the East Room of the White House in the Presence of Foreign Diplomats, Supreme Court Judges
and the Congress,
The Big Cheshire Cheese
Weighing 1235 Lbs.
Dedicated by the Sons of the American Revolution 1940

Origin and Meaning of Separation of Church and State in America

The expression *separation of church and state*, as we know it, first entered our vocabulary through a letter that Thomas Jefferson wrote to the Baptist Association of Danbury, Connecticut. These Baptists, congratulating the President for his love of religious freedom, had sent him a letter, dated October 7, 1801, reminding him that Connecticut's Congregationalist state church was still relegating Baptists to second-class citizenry.[1229] The letter suggests a desire for the President to work toward disestablishment in their state. On that same busy day on which he received the gift from John Leland and the Cheshire Baptists, Jefferson replied to the Danbury Baptists. In a carefully nuanced letter, dated January 1, 1802, Jefferson employs the metaphorical expression *"wall of separation* between church and state." Aware that the First Amendment relegates the Baptists' issue to the states, and that the solution to their dilemma could not become a matter of

---

[1229] Letter from "Danbury, Connecticut, Baptist Association to Thomas Jefferson, October 7, 1801" (original), from *Thomas Jefferson Papers*, digital copy, courtesy, Library of Congress, Washington, DC, Manuscript Division, Series 1: General Correspondence 1651–1827, from microfilm reel: 024.

executive order, the President shares their concern for "rights of conscience." With the Baptists, he asserts, "Religion is a matter which lies solely between man and his God."[1230] In Jefferson's libertarian worldview, the wall exists to protect church and state from one another.

The Fourteenth Amendment later extended to the states certain restrictions already placed upon Congress. For instance, "No State shall make or enforce any law which shall abridge the privileges or immunities of citizens of the United States; nor shall any State deprive any person of life, liberty, or property, without due process of law; nor deny to any person within its jurisdiction the equal protection of the laws." Thus, the Constitution protects its citizens against threats to life, liberty, and property. In addition, the Constitution grants to each citizen the freedom to choose his own religion, and the freedom to choose no religion. The Constitution neither establishes a "Christian nation" nor separates government from God and the Bible. The founders advocated a government tempered by biblical morals.

Baptists view the term *separation of church and state* as a preventive against government intrusion into the spiritual teaching and governance of the local church. Baptists base this conviction upon two principles: (1) freedom of conscience and (2) the autonomy of the local church. Baptists believe that Christians must be loyal citizens who obey the laws of civil government. They must obey the injunction of Christ to "render ... to Caesar the things that are Caesar's, and to God the things that are God's" (Mark 12:17). When civil laws clearly require disobedience to the Scriptures, Christians "ought to obey God rather than men" (Acts 5:29*b*).

Leland's Return to New England: Contributions and Controversies

In 1791, John, Sallie, and their eight children boarded a boat in Fredericksburg and returned to New England. After preaching

---

[1230] Letter from "Thomas Jefferson to Danbury, Connecticut, Baptist Association, January 1, 1802" (original), from *Thomas Jefferson Papers*, digital copy, courtesy, Library of Congress, Washington, DC, Manuscript Division, Series 1: General Correspondence. 1651-1827, from microfilm reel: 025. Italics mine.

as an itinerant for several months, Leland became pastor of the Baptist church at Cheshire, Massachusetts, where he began to reset his ministry, first, by repealing the Lord's Supper: "For more than thirty years," Leland testifies, "I have had no evidence that the bread and wine ever assisted my faith to discern the Lord's body."[1231] Thus, "for the next twenty years or more he refused to perform the ordinance."[1232] Some regarded Leland's stance as dangerously close to the Quaker practice of nullifying church ordinances on the authority of feelings. Though he strongly defended believer's baptism by immersion, Leland refused to acknowledge that baptism is exclusively a local church ordinance. Conversely, Isaac Backus, regarded baptism and the Lord's Supper as vital and exclusive components of every Baptist church.[1233] Leland warned that creeds and confessions could impede the study of Scripture and become as tyrannical as dead traditions. While Leland never opposed education, missions, or interchurch endeavors, his fear of a "clerical hierarchy" drove him to oppose seminaries, mission boards, and church associations.[1234] Having seen the tyranny of England's state-church system, he never ceased fighting, in Jeffersonian fashion, for the autonomy of the individual conscience. Isaac Backus fought for the same, but he surpassed Leland in the pastoral outworking of biblical ecclesiology.

John Leland drew both criticism and approval, when he echoed James Madison's libertarian views on three sensitive issues.[1235] First, in agreement with Madison's *laissez faire* prin-

---

[1231] Leland, *The Writings of the Late Elder John Leland*, 60 (57–61); and J. Bradley Creed, "John Leland, American Prophet of Religious Individualism" (PhD diss., Southwestern Baptist Theological Seminary, 1986), 161ff.

[1232] McLoughlin, "John Leland and the Era of 'Modern Liberality' in Connecticut, 1776–1800," in *New England Dissent 1630–1833*, 2:930.

[1233] Edwin S. Gaustad, "The Backus-Leland Tradition," in *Baptist Concepts of the Church*, ed. Winthrop S. Hudson (Philadelphia: Judson Press, 1959), 118–19.

[1234] Leland, *The Writings of the Late Elder John Leland*, 408–12, 523–24, 600–2; Creed, "John Leland, American Prophet of Religious Individualism," 197ff. Cf. Nathan O. Hatch, *The Democratization of American Christianity* (New Haven: Yale University Press, 1989), 93–101, 236–39.

[1235] See McLoughlin, "Isaac Backus and Separation of Church and State," 1392–1413; and Martha Eleam Boland, "Render unto Caesar: Sources of the Political Thought of John Leland" (PhD diss., New Orleans Baptist

ciples, Leland urged the civil government to cease legislating blue laws, and proclaiming "holy days," such as days of worship, prayer, and fasting. To Leland, such is not the role of government, and such legislation neglects groups such as Jews and Seventh Day Adventists. For Christians, the Word of God alone, not civil legislation, should determine the days of worship.[1236] Second, Leland and Madison questioned the propriety of supporting congressional and military chaplains out of the public treasury. Leland urged that the local churches should support the chaplains. Third, Leland urged that government exempt no one from military service for being an ordained minister. The law should protect ministers as citizens, but never treat them as a special class.[1237]

John Leland's populist style spoke to the common people, while Isaac Backus could adjust his appeals to all levels of society. The two differed on many issues. In a day of developing convictions, concerning church-state relations, Backus and Leland were occasionally inconsistent with their secondary, published opinions. Both men enjoyed fruitful ministries, and their unique contributions are immeasurable. Leland became seriously ill on the night of January 8, 1841, after preaching in North Adams, Massachusetts. His text was I John 2:20, 27. Six days later, he passed away in his sleep, at the age of eighty-seven. His life ended at the close of the Second Great Awakening. Together, John Leland and Isaac Backus had witnessed America's longest era of spiritual awakening—an era that included the War of Independence and the founding of the Nation they loved.

Highlights of Other Key Baptists during the

Theological Seminary, 1997).

[1236] Leland, *The Writings of the Late Elder John Leland*, 440–46, 535–40, 561–66. President Jefferson agreed with Leland on this issue and refused to proclaim any national, religious days.

[1237] See Scarberry, "John Leland and James Madison," 738–39n17.

Second Great Awakening

James Manning (1738–91)

Born in Piscataway, New Jersey,[1238] to a wealthy and upright farming family, James Manning became one of the first students to enroll at New Jersey's Hopewell Academy, a Latin, grammar school, founded in 1756 by Isaac Eaton (ca. 1725 –72),[1239] pastor of Hopewell Baptist Church.[1240] Manning experienced the new birth under Eaton's influence. Baptized by Benjamin Miller, of Scotch Plains Baptist Church, in New Jersey,[1241] twenty-year-old James Manning enrolled at the College of New Jersey (later Princeton). After four years, he received his BA degree, graduating second in his class of twenty-one. He received the MA in 1765, and, later that year, he became founding president of the first Baptist institution of higher learning in America — Rhode Island College, in Warren, Rhode Island. Its name would change, in 1804, to Brown University.[1242] The college moved to Providence in 1770, where Manning served the pastorate of First Baptist Church.

Named by Isaac Backus as one of the three best-educated

[1238] Reuben Aldridge Guild, *Early History of Brown University, Including the Life, Times, and Correspondence of President Manning: 1756–1791* (Providence, RI: Snow and Farnham, 1897); and William H. Brackney, "James Manning 1738–1791," in *A Noble Company: Biographical Essays on Notable Particular-Regular Baptists in America*, ed. Terry Wolever (Springfield, MO: Particular Baptist Press, 2013), 3:511–39.

[1239] Walter E. Johnson, "Isaac Eaton 1725–1772," in *A Noble Company*, ed. Wolever, 3:217–33.

[1240] The Hopewell Church was an offshoot of the Middletown Church. John Gano, a member of the Hopewell Church, received his ordination here in 1755. The gravestone of John Hart, signer of the Declaration of Independence, stands beside the meetinghouse. Hart was not a member of the church, but he donated the land on which the building stands. The graves of many Revolutionary War veterans are in the church's cemetery. In 1822, the congregation rebuilt the church on the foundation of the original building. The appearance of the building has not changed since 1822.

[1241] Benjamin Miller had experienced conversion under the preaching of the Presbyterian Gilbert Tennent during the First Great Awakening.

[1242] The Rhode Island College changed its name to Brown University in recognition of a five-thousand-dollar gift from Nicholas Brown, a prominent Providence executive and alumnus.

Baptists of New England,[1243] James Manning was a careful expositor of Scripture, and he depended upon the Holy Spirit to use every sermon for the glory of God. Under his ministry, as our nation stood on the brink of war, the first glimmer of the Second Great Awakening (ca. 1775–1840) emerged here in Providence Baptist. The Church Record Book relates that, in late 1774, "the sudden death of one Biggelo [Biggalo], a young man who was accidentally shot by his intimate companion playing with a gun, made a very uncommon impression upon the minds of many." First, "it pleased the Lord to make his power known to the hearts of Tamar Clemmons & Venus Arnold, two black women, who were soon added to the church by baptism, and have since maintained the dignity of their profession." As church attendance began to soar, "the sacred flame of the gospel began to spread, and in the course of fifteen months, 104 persons confessed the power of Christ in the conversion of their souls, and entered the gate of Zion with Joy."[1244] During 1774–75, an overcrowded meetinghouse compelled Manning's congregation to erect the beautiful building that still stands on North Main Street, Providence. In its tall steeple, a bell, weighing 2,515 pounds, displays these words:

> For Freedom of Conscience this town was first planted,
> Persuasion, not force, was used by the people;
> This church is the oldest, & has not recanted,
> Enjoying & granting bell temple & Steeple.[1245]

[1243] Backus named Samuel Stillman and Hezekiah Smith as the other two best-educated Baptists in New England. Guild, *Early History of Brown University*, 64.

[1244] J. Stanley Lemons, ed., "Church Records," in *First Baptist, Providence*, vol. 2 of the series, Baptists in Early North America, ed. William H. Brackney (Macon, GA: Mercer University Press, 2013), 40ff. The Rhode Island Historical Records office holds the entire First Baptist Church collection (except for recent years), including minutes of the church from 1755 forward, committee minutes, scrapbooks, photographs, publications by pastors, and hymnals. The office is located at 337 Westminster Street.

[1245] Ibid., 41.

Those words, "persuasion, not force," reflect the heartbeat of Roger Williams and the Baptist heritage. Appropriately, in the final stages of the founding of our nation, the General Assembly, by a unanimous vote, appointed James Manning as one of the delegates to the 1786 Continental Congress.

John Gano (1727–1804)

John Gano was born in Hopewell, New Jersey.[1246] His paternal, great-grandfather was a Protestant French Huguenot, who had fled from the terrors of Louis IV.[1247] When John was eighteen years of age, he experienced the new birth. About two years later (1747), he received baptism by immersion and joined the Baptist Church at Hopewell, where Isaac Eaton, in 1748, assumed the pastorate. Gano studied in the homes of several ministers, including Isaac Eaton, whose academy would become a reality in 1756. Meanwhile, Gano received the call to preach, and the Hopewell Church licensed him to fill the pulpit at the newly-established, First Baptist Church, in Morristown, New Jersey. In 1754, the Hopewell church ordained Gano, with Isaac Eaton preaching the charge. Four months later, the Philadelphia Association commissioned Gano for a missionary trip to the South. Lasting some nine months, the trip included a visit to the "Jersey Settlement," on the north bank of the Yadkin River, in Davidson County, North Carolina.[1248] From there, Gano visited Charleston, South Carolina, where Oliver Hart, at First Baptist, scheduled him to preach. Hart spread the news for miles around that John Gano would be preaching.

[1246] See Terry Wolever, *The Life and Ministry of John Gano, 1727–1804* (Springfield, MO: Particular Baptist Press, 1998); idem, *The Life of John Gano 1727–1804: Pastor-Evangelist of the Philadelphia Association* (Springfield, MO: Particular Baptist Press, 2012); idem, "John Gano 1727–1804," in *A Noble Company*, ed. Wolever, 3:235–73.

[1247] Many of John's descendants pronounce the name *Gano* with a long *a*.

[1248] This area became the "Jersey Settlement" because its original settlers came here from the Hopewell area of New Jersey to escape corrupt political leaders. Henry Sheets, "Jersey Baptist Church," *The Dispatch* 22, no. 42 (Wednesday March 2, 1904): page 2, full-page article in the local paper of Lexington, North Carolina. The article includes Gano's visit as well as a picture of the old Jersey Meetinghouse, established in 1755.

Arriving on horseback in soiled, ragged clothes, Gano had no time prior to the service to clean up and change his garments. Adding to that humiliation, he discovered that the English evangelist George Whitefield (1714–70) was sitting in the audience. Gano describes his dismay. "I went with my tattered garb on; and when I arose to speak, the sight of so numerous and brilliant an audience (among whom were twelve ministers, one of whom was Mr. Whitefield) for a moment brought the fear of man on me; but, blessed be the Lord, I was soon relieved from this embarrassment: the thought passed my mind, I had none to fear, and obey, but the Lord."[1249] Ten years later, Isaac Backus would report of Gano, "His preaching seems to be as much admired as Mr. Whitefield's."[1250]

Returning to Morristown, New Jersey, in 1755, John Gano married Sarah Stites and recommenced his pulpit ministry at the church. In 1757, the couple moved to North Carolina, where John ministered to Jersey Baptist Church, until 1760, when hostile, Cherokee Indian excursions made it necessary to leave. Another ministry would soon open, however, at the newly-established, First Baptist Church, in New York City. The roots of this church go back to 1745, when Jeremiah Dodge, a Baptist entrepreneur, initiated cottage prayer meetings. Encouraged by Benjamin Miller (1715–81), of the Scotch Plains Baptist Church, in New Jersey, the group began temporarily meeting in a rigging loft at Cart and Horse Alley (now William Street), New York. In 1753, when the group had increased to thirteen, they became a branch ministry of the Scotch Plains church, with Miller administering baptism when needed. In 1760, the group erected their own meetinghouse on Gold Street and began holding regular services. Two years later, with twenty-seven charter members, Miller assisted in constituting the group into the "First Baptist Church in the City of New York," with John Gano as their first full-time

---

[1249] This occasion was at the end of Whitefield's fifth trip to America. Whitefield would embark for England within a few days. See also John Gano, "My Own Life," in *Biographical Memoirs of the Late Rev. John Gano, of Frankfort, (Kentucky) formerly of the City of New York*, ed. his sons, Stephen Gano and Daniel Gano (New York: Southwick and Hardcastle, 1806), 67.

[1250] *Diary of Isaac Backus*, 1:583.

pastor. Their doctrinal statement was the London Confession of 1688. Gano would serve this pastorate for the next quarter of a century (1762–88), except for the years he served as chaplain for George Washington in the War of Independence.[1251] Increased membership soon compelled the congregation to enlarge its building.

As a brother-in-law of James Manning, Gano preached one of the sermons for Manning's ordination, became one of the founders of Rhode Island College, and served as a trustee and fundraiser for the college. For seven years during the Revolutionary War, the British laid siege on New York City and turned the Baptist meetinghouse into a prison, an infirmary, and even a horse stable. Gano served during the entire war as a chaplain. Untold numbers of the city's inhabitants joined the Continental Army, as families fled the city for safety. At the war's end, Gano could find only thirty-seven of his two hundred members. "Some were dead, and others scattered into almost every part of the Union."[1252] The remnant set to work repairing their meetinghouse, and, upon completion, Gano gathered his flock and rededicated their building with a timely sermon from Haggai 2:3*a*, "Who is left among you that saw this house in her first glory? and how do you see it now?" In a wave of revival, their membership "was greatly increased; and, to crown all, the word preached was accompanied with 'the power of the Holy Ghost sent down from heaven.'" During his New York pastorate, Gano baptized 297 converts and admitted twenty-three others by letter.[1253] As folklore follows great men, a Gano tradition is that John baptized George Washington. Legend, however, must never distract from the true and multifarious greatness of this bold, yet humble, servant of God.[1254]

[1251] J. T. Headley, "John Gano," in *The Chaplains and Clergy of the Revolution* (New York: Charles Scribner, 1864), 250–72.

[1252] Gano, "My Own Life," in *Biographical Memoirs*, 116–17.

[1253] William Parkinson, *A Jubilee Sermon: Containing a History of the Origin of the First Baptist Church in the City of New-York, and Its Progress during the First Fifty Years since Its Constitution*, "delivered in the meetinghouse of said church, January 1, 1813" (1813; repr., New York: John Gray, 1846), 25–28.

[1254] A full probe into this tradition is in Wolever, *The Life of John Gano 1727–1804* (2012), 451–86.

In 1788, the Gano family moved to Kentucky,[1255] where John shepherded the Town Fork Baptist Church, near Lexington, during 1788-98. John Gano died at Frankfort, Kentucky, in 1804, at the age of seventy-seven. His gravestone stands near that of Daniel Boone, in the Frankfort cemetery. John had outlived his first wife, Sarah, and remarried, but Sarah had borne all his children, one of whom was Dr. Stephen Gano—trained in medicine and ministry—who served the pastorate of First Baptist, Providence, Rhode Island, for thirty-five years (1792-1828). Stephen Gano would see great revivals at Providence, during the Second Great Awakening. The revival of 1820 produced so many converts that Stephen dismissed twenty-three of his members, to establish Third Church of Providence.[1256]

Meanwhile, First Baptist of New York City would outgrow several more buildings, and, in 1891, during the fifty-year pastorate of Isaac M. Haldeman (1845-1933), they erected their present building at 265 West 79th Street at Broadway. With the guidance of architect George M. Kaiser, Haldeman utilized biblical symbolism throughout the grand structure—made of Indiana limestone on a base of Milford granite. Over the main entrance into the auditorium, a high tower represents Christ as head of the church, and a lower tower, which appears incomplete, to symbolize the church's incompleteness prior to the Rapture. Two smaller towers represent the Old and New Testaments. High above the pulpit appears the Hebrew text for "In the beginning God" (Genesis 1:1*a*), along with the Greek text for "In the beginning was the Word" (John 1:1*a*). Above the baptistery, eight pillars represent eight fundamental doctrines "once delivered unto the saints" (Jude 3*b*):

(1) The sovereignty of our triune God (Father, Son, and Holy Spirit)
(2) The inspiration and inerrancy of Scripture

[1255] The government was offering free land on the Kentucky frontier to war veterans.

[1256] William Gammell and Samuel Lunt Caldwell, *History of the First Baptist Church in Providence 1639-1877* (Providence: J. A. & R. A. Reid, 1877), 15-16; and *A List of Members with the Covenant and Sketch of History of the Third Baptist Church of Providence, R.I.* (Providence: H. H. Brown, 1855), 5-7.

(3) The Virgin Birth and Incarnation of Christ
(4) The sinlessness and impeccability of Christ
(5) Christ's vicarious atonement at Calvary
(6) The bodily resurrection and ascension of Christ
(7) The pretribulational rapture of the church
(8) The premillennial return and reign of Christ

Besides its "Gano Chapel," the church possesses the large dispensational chart that I. M. Haldeman used in his popular Sunday school classes. In 1945, the renowned Harry A. Ironside (1876–1951) preached at First Baptist in celebration of its 200th anniversary.

Oliver Hart (1723–95)

Born in Warminster Township (Bucks County),[1257] Pennsylvania, Oliver Hart became a Christian at age seventeen, and Jenkin Jones (ca. 1686–1760), of the nearby Baptist Church at Southampton, baptized him. Five years later, Oliver

---

[1257] The best sources for John Hart include his diary, *A Memorandum Containing Some of the Most Remarkable Occurrences in Providence, Relative to Or Noticed by an Unworthy Traveler towards the New Jerusalem, who Desire[s] Ever to Esteem Himself a Stranger and Sojourner in this Dreary Wilderness*, transcribed from the original and privately printed in 1949 by Loulie L. Owens. This thirty-six-page copy is in the library at Furman University, Greenville, South Carolina. Quotes from the diary first appeared in H. A. Tupper, ed., *Two Centuries of the First Baptist Church of South Carolina, 1683–1883* (Baltimore: R. H. Woodward, 1889), 28–36. Other best sources include Joe M. King, *A History of South Carolina Baptists* (Columbia: General Board of the South Carolina Baptist Convention, 1964), 17–19, 37, 42, 5l, 62, 64–66, 76, 81–82, 89, 91–92, 136, 138, 142–143, 156–59, 212, 340, and passim; John Rippon, ed., *The Baptist Annual Register for 1794–1797* (London: Sold by Dilly, Button, and Thomas, 1797), 7–14; Leah Townsend, *South Carolina Baptists, 1670–1805* (Florence, SC: The Florence Printing Co., 1935); and Thomas Nettles, "Oliver Hart 1723–1795," in *A Noble Company*, ed. Wolever, 3:161–91. See also Robert A. Baker, Paul J. Craven Jr., and R. Marshall Blalock, *History of the First Baptist Church of Charleston, South Carolina 1682–2007* (1982; repr., Springfield, MO: Particular Baptist Press, 2007); and Wood Furman, *A History of the Charleston Association of Baptist Churches in the State of South Carolina* (Charleston: J. Hoff, 1811).

surrendered to preach. In February 1747/48, he married Sarah Brees. With South Carolina in dire need of preachers, Hart received ordination at Southampton Baptist, in October 1749, and, the next month, the couple boarded a ship for Charleston. Providentially, they arrived on December 2, the same day that Charleston Baptists were holding the funeral service for one of the last two Baptist preachers left in the colony. In February 1750, Hart began his thirty-year pastorate at First Baptist. The next year, he founded the Charleston Baptist Association, the second such association in the country, and the first in the South. In 1769, Rhode Island College awarded Hart an honorary MA degree. Sarah died in 1772 and, two years later, Oliver married Anne Seeley Grimball.[1258]

In the American War of Independence, the British siege of Charleston (1780–82) forced the Harts to return to Warminster, Pennsylvania. Richard Furman would accept the Charleston pulpit,[1259] as Hart committed to the Hopewell Baptist pastorate, in New Jersey, where he remained for the rest of his life.[1260] Hart was in constant demand as a speaker. Baptists regarded his sermon, *A Gospel Church Portrayed* (1791), delivered at the Philadelphia Association, as a model portrayal of Baptist ecclesiology. Oliver Hart passed away on December 31, 1795, with his family by his bedside. His remains lie buried at the Southampton Meeting House, Pennsylvania, where he had preached his first sermon.

Hezekiah Smith (1737–1805)

Born at Hempstead, Long Island, New York,[1261] Hezekiah

[1258] Townsend, *South Carolina Baptists, 1670–1805*, 20–25, 282.

[1259] Richard Furman would become a legend in the South. See James A. Rogers, *Richard Furman: Life and Legacy* (Macon, GA: Mercer University Press, 1985), 51ff.

[1260] Hopewell Baptist stands on West Broad Street in Hopewell, New Jersey.

[1261] The best sources for Hezekiah Smith include Reuben Aldridge Guild, *Chaplain Smith and the Baptists: Or, Life, Journals, Letters, and Addresses of the Rev. Hezekiah Smith, D. D., of Haverhill, Massachusetts, 1737–1805* (Philadelphia: American Baptist Publication Society, 1885); and John David Broome, *The Life, Ministry, and Journals of Hezekiah Smith: Pastor*

Smith grew up in Morristown, New Jersey, where, in 1756, John Gano, pastor of the local Baptist church, influenced his becoming a Christian and received the joy of baptizing him. After completing his pre-college training, under Isaac Eaton at Hopewell Baptist Academy, Smith enrolled at the College of New Jersey, where he and James Manning, his classmate, became lifetime friends. Following his graduation, in 1762, Smith traveled to the South, received his ordination under Oliver Hart, at Charleston, and became an itinerant evangelist—known as "the Baptist Whitefield." Smith accompanied Manning to Rhode Island, in 1764, and became a trustee and fellow of Rhode Island College.

Hezekiah Smith worked tirelessly for the remainder of his life, raising funds for the college, watching over its affairs, and preaching in chapel. Following a long preaching tour through New England, in 1765-66, Smith became founding pastor of First Baptist Church at Haverhill, Massachusetts, where he served for almost forty years until his death. Meanwhile, he planted some thirteen additional churches. He assisted in the organization of the Warren Baptist Association, in 1767, and joined Isaac Backus on the Association's Grievance Committee, in the struggle for religious freedom. In the War of Independence, Smith served as chaplain in the Continental Army, under George Washington. Hezekiah Smith died at Haverhill in 1805.

Summary

This chapter has covered the era of our Baptist ancestors, Isaac Backus, John Leland, James Manning, John Gano, Oliver Hart, and Hezekiah Smith, who came to the kingdom for such a time as the American Revolution and the development of the American Constitution. Such pioneers of religious freedom paved the way for the great era of Baptist missions unfolding in the following chapter.

---

of the First Baptist Church of Haverhill, Massachusetts 1765 to 1805 and Chaplain in the American Revolution 1775 to 1780 (Springfield, MO: Particular Baptist Press, 2004).

Select Bibliography for Further Reading

Alley, Reuben Edward. *A History of Baptists in Virginia*. Richmond: Virginia Baptist General Board, 1973.

Backus, Isaac. *The Diary of Isaac Backus*. Edited by William G. McLoughlin. 3 vols. Providence, RI: Brown University Press, 1979.

Boland, Martha Eleam. "Render unto Caesar: Sources of the Political Thought of John Leland." PhD diss., New Orleans Baptist Theological Seminary, 1997.

Broome, John David. *The Life, Ministry, and Journals of Hezekiah Smith: Pastor of the First Baptist Church of Haverhill, Massachusetts 1765 to 1805 and Chaplain in the American Revolution 1775 to 1780*. Springfield, MO: Particular Baptist Press, 2004.

Creed, J. Bradley, "John Leland, American Prophet of Religious Individualism." PhD diss., Southwestern Baptist Theological Seminary, 1986.

Dreisbach, Daniel L. "The President, a Monmouth Cheese, and the Wall of Separation." In *Thomas Jefferson and the Wall of Separation between Church and State*, 9–24. New York: New York University Press, 2002.

Gano, John. "My Own Life." In *Biographical Memoirs of the Late Rev. John Gano, of Frankfort, (Kentucky) formerly of the City of New York*, edited by his sons, Stephen Gano and Daniel Gano, 9–130. New York: Southwick and Hardcastle, 1806. The account of John Gano's death, pages 131–37, derives from documents belonging to Daniel Gano.

Gaustad, Edwin Scott. "A Disestablished Society: Origins of the First Amendment." *The Journal of Church and State* 11, no. 3 (Autumn 1969): 409–25.

Guild, Reuben Aldridge. *Chaplain Smith and the Baptists: Or, Life, Journals, Letters, and Addresses of the Rev. Hezekiah Smith, D. D., of Haverhill, Massachusetts, 1737–1805*. Philadelphia: American Baptist Publication Society, 1885.

Hovey, Alvah. *A Memoir of the Life and Times of the Rev. Isaac Backus, A. M.* Boston: Gould and Lincoln, 1859.

Leland, John. *The Writings of the Late Elder John Leland: Including Some Events in His Life; Written by Himself, with Additional Sketches, & c.* Edited by L. F. Greene. New York: G. W. Wood, 1845.

McLoughlin, William Gerald. *Isaac Backus and the American Pietistic Tradition*. Edited by Oscar Handlin. Boston: Little, Brown and Co., 1967.

———, ed. *Isaac Backus on Church, State, and Calvinism: Pamphlets, 1754–1789*. Cambridge, MA: Harvard University Press, 1968.

Scarberry, Mark S. "John Leland and James Madison: Religious Influence on the Ratification of the Constitution and on the Proposal of the Bill of Rights." *Penn State Law Review* 113, no. 3 (February 11, 2009): 733–800.

Sprague, William. "John Leland." In *Annals of the American Baptist Pulpit*, 6:174–86. New York: Robert Carter & Brothers, 1860.

Wolever, Terry. *The Life of John Gano 1727–1804: Pastor-Evangelist of the Philadelphia Association*. Springfield, MO: Particular Baptist Press, 2012.

Chapter 17

Pioneer Missionaries: Adoniram Judson, Luther Rice, and John Mason Peck

------------ ❈ ------------

The Haystack Prayer Meeting at Williams College (1806)

*I*n the spring of 1805, at the peak of the Second Great Awakening, a longing for revival was emerging among a few students at Williams College (Congregational, est. 1793), in Williamstown, Massachusetts. By spring and summer of 1806, several students were meeting regularly for prayer. On Wednesdays, they gathered under the willow trees, south of the West College building, and, on Saturdays, they met in the thick grove of maple trees, in Sloan's Meadow, now a part of the campus. On a sweltering Saturday in August, five students arrived at the grove just as dark clouds were appearing in the western sky. Suddenly, amid torrential rain, bolts of lightning, and rolling thunder, the students ran for shelter under the overhang of thatch protecting a nearby haystack from rain and mildew. As the young men waited for the storm to pass by, their conversation quickly turned to foreign missions. Familiar with William Carey's work in India, their prayer leader, Samuel J. Mills Jr. (1783–1818),[1262] from

---

[1262] See Gardiner Spring, *Memoirs of the Rev. Samuel J. Mills: Late Missionary*

Torringford, Connecticut, challenged the little prayer band to join him in taking the gospel to the heathen. There was no mission board in America to encourage such an endeavor. The young men prayed until the storm passed and bright skies began breaking through the darkness. During the following months, Mills organized the prayer group under the name "Brethren," and under the motto, "We can do it if we will." While they tried to avoid attention, their meetings increased in attendance. During the next twenty-six years, Williams College would experience eight revivals.

In 1867, sixty-one years after the Haystack Prayer Meeting, a group of missionary-minded Christians erected a twelve-foot-high, marble monument where the haystack had once stood. Byram Green, one of the five participants in the famous prayer meeting, returned to the campus and confirmed the location. The grove of maple trees was still standing. Surmounting the memorial monument is a globe, three feet in diameter. Below the globe are inscribed the words, "The Field is the World." Below the inscription is a sculptured haystack, encircled with the words, "The Birthplace of American Foreign Missions 1806." Underneath those words are the names of the five young men — Samuel J. Mills, James Richards, Francis L. Robbins, Harvey Loomis,[1263] and Byram Green. The inscription on a nearby plaque reads:

---

to the South Western Section of the United States and Agent of the American Colonization Society, Deputed to Explore the Coast of Africa (New York: New York Evangelical Society, 1820); Thomas C. Richards, *Samuel J. Mills: Missionary Pathfinder, Pioneer and Promoter* (Boston: The Pilgrim Press, 1906); idem, *The Haystack Prayer Meeting: An Account of Its Origin and Spirit* (Williamstown, MA: The Haystack Centennial, 1906); and *The One Hundredth Anniversary of the Haystack Prayer Meeting* (Boston: American Board of Commissioners for Foreign Missions, 1907).

[1263] Of the five, Harvey Loomis, a devout Christian brother, was the only one who stood convinced that it was not the time to advance foreign missions. Promoting home missions, Loomis established a solid church in Bangor, Maine. His death came one Sunday in January 1825, when he entered the pulpit, fell unconscious, and died within a half hour. Loomis's intended sermon for the occasion was still in his pocket. His text was from Jeremiah 28:16b, "This year thou shalt die." See Richards, "The Men of the Haystack," in *Samuel J. Mills*, 259–60.

> Haystack Monument
> On this site in the shelter of a haystack during a summer storm in 1806, five Williams College students dedicated their lives to the service of the Church around the globe. Out of their decision grew the American Foreign Mission Movement.

The Missionary Rock at Andover Theological Seminary

In late 1806, another Williams College student, Gordon Hall (1784-1826),[1264] from Tolland, Massachusetts, became a Christian and united with the praying Brethren. The next year, Luther Rice (1783-1836), from Northborough, Massachusetts, would join them. Rice had earlier come to Christ and joined the Northborough Congregational church. In 1807, after three years of training at Leicester Academy, he enrolled as a sophomore at Williams College. After their graduation, most of the Brethren enrolled at Andover Theological Seminary (Congregational, est. 1807), where they bonded with Adoniram Judson Jr. in the cause of missions.[1265] Judson's father was a Congregational minister who served several Massachusetts pastorates—the final being the Church of the Pilgrimage (1802), at Plymouth.

[1264] Horatio Bardwell, *Memoir of Rev. Gordon Hall, A. M.: One of the First Missionaries of the American Board of Commissioners for Foreign Missions at Bombay* (Andover, MA: Flagg, Gould & Newman, 1834), 16.

[1265] The best sources for Adoniram Judson include Courtney Anderson, *To the Golden Shore: The Life of Adoniram Judson* (Boston: Little, Brown and Co., 1956); Rosalie Hall Hunt, *Bless God and Take Courage: The Judson History and Legacy* (Valley Forge: Judson Press, 2005); Arabella W. Stuart, *The Lives of Mrs. Ann H. Judson and Mrs. Sarah B. Judson, with a Biographical Sketch of Mrs. Emily C. Judson, Missionaries to Burma* (Auburn, NY: Derby and Miller, 1852); Jason G. Duesing, ed., *Adoniram Judson: A Bicentennial Appreciation of the Pioneer American Missionary* (Nashville: B&H Publishing Group, 2012); Francis Wayland, *A Memoir of the Life and Labors of the Rev. Adoniram Judson, D. D.*, 2 vols. (Boston: Phillips, Sampson, and Co., 1853); and William C. Richards, *The Apostle of Burma: A Missionary Epic in Commemoration of the Centennial of the Birth of Adoniram Judson* (Boston: Lee and Shepard Publishers, 1889).

After graduating valedictorian of his class at Brown University, Judson Jr. had enrolled at Andover Seminary in 1808.

Although it originated as a reaction to the Unitarian takeover at Harvard College, Andover Seminary would become the premier institution for New Divinity theology.[1266] The Seminary resided for a century on the campus of Phillips Academy (est. 1778). In the back of Phillips Academy, one can still walk down "Judson Road" and visit the secluded area by the "Rabbit Pond," where Adoniram Judson and his Brethren dedicated their lives to God and earnestly prayed for missions. Their prayer petition for support in taking the gospel to regions beyond resulted, in 1810, in the formation of the American Board of Commissioners for Foreign Missions—the first Congregational foreign mission board in America. In this sequestered area, by the Rabbit Pond, citizens of Andover, in 1910, affixed a commemorative plaque to a boulder (affectionately called "Missionary Rock"), in celebration of the formation of the Board: Its inscription:

In the missionary woods once extending to this spot, the first missionary students of Andover Seminary walked and talked one hundred years ago, and on this secluded knoll met to pray.
In memory of these men
Adoniram Judson   Samuel Nott   Samuel J. Mills
Samuel Newell   Gordon Hall   James Richards
Luther Rice
whose consecrated purpose to carry the Gospel to the heathen, world led to the formation of the first American Society for Foreign Missions.
In recognition of the two hundred and forty-eight missionaries trained in Andover Seminary, and in gratitude to almighty God, this stone is set up in the centennial year of the American Board.
1910

[1266] See the section above on the "Influence of New Divinity Theology," in chapter 11, titled "The Rise of Evangelical Calvinism: Life of Andrew Fuller to the Prayer Call of 1784."

Judson and Rice Become Baptists by Conviction

On February 5, 1812, Adoniram Judson (1788–1850) married Ann Hasseltine of Bradford, Massachusetts. The next day, Judson, Luther Rice, Samuel Newell, Samuel Nott, and Gordon Hall received ordination in Salem, Massachusetts.[1267] On February 19, Adoniram and Ann Judson set sail from Salem, on the brig *Caravan*, for Calcutta, India. During the voyage, the Judson couple did in-depth studies through the Scriptures and church history on the topic of baptism. Soon after arriving in Calcutta, on June 17, they became Baptists by conviction. Immediately, they sent their resignation to the Congregational mission board, and, on September 6, 1812, in the Lal Bazaar Baptist chapel, in Calcutta, they received believer's baptism by immersion, at the hands of William Carey's coworker, William Ward. Upon Carey's invitation, a few days later, in the same chapel, Judson preached on *Christian Baptism*. Deeply impressed by the message, Carey urged its immediate publication.[1268] Upon reading this book, Adoniram Judson Sr., in 1817, resigned his Congregational pastorate in Plymouth, Massachusetts, and moved his membership to Second Baptist Church, in Boston. In 1819, he received Baptist ordination into the Damariscotta Baptist pastorate in Maine.[1269]

[1267] Leonard Woods, *A Sermon Delivered at the Tabernacle in Salem, Feb. 6, 1812*, on "occasion of the ordination of the Rev. Messrs. Samuel Newell, A. M. Adoniram Judson, A. M. Samuel Nott, A. M. Gordon Hall, A. M. and Luther Rice, A. B. Missionaries to the Heathen in Asia under the direction of the Board of Commissioners for Foreign Missions" (Boston: Samuel T. Armstrong, 1812).

[1268] Adoniram Judson, *Christian Baptism*, "a sermon preached in the Lal Bazar Chapel, Calcutta, on the Lord's Day, September 27, 1812" (Boston: Lincoln and Edmonds, 1812). The standard edition is the 5th American edition: *Christian Baptism* (Boston: Gould, Kendall and Lincoln, 1846).

[1269] Due to his age, Judson Sr. retired from the pastorate in 1821. During the next two years, he preached for First Baptist in Plymouth, whose congregation was then erecting its first building. He died at Scituate, Massachusetts, in 1826, at the age of seventy-six. Henry S. Burrage, *History of the Baptists in Maine* (Portland, ME: Marks Printing House, 1904), 393n1; William T. Davis, *History of the Town of Plymouth: With a Sketch of the Origin and Growth of Separatism* (Philadelphia: J. W. Lewis and Co., 1885), 125; and "A Brief Historical Sketch: The First Baptist

Meanwhile, onboard the ship *Harmony*, Luther Rice (1783-1836)[1270] had embarked from Philadelphia for Calcutta, in February 1812. He arrived about six weeks after the arrival of Ann and Adoniram Judson. Rice's earliest scruples about infant baptism had occurred while he was a student at Williams College. During the voyage, he had searched the Scriptures for the truth. In Calcutta's Lal Bazaar Baptist chapel, he had listened with keen interest to Judson's September sermon on Christian baptism. By October, Luther Rice was convinced that believer's baptism by immersion in the name of the Holy Trinity is the only proper administration of the ordinance. On November 1, Rice received believer's baptism, and, the next day, he wrote to his parents saying, "I was baptized by the Rev. Mr. Ward, and enjoyed the privilege of uniting with the Baptist church in Calcutta, in celebrating the sacred ordinance of the Lord's Supper. It was a comfortable day to my soul!"[1271] In his letter to the Congregational board, Rice explained, "I am now satisfactorily convinced, that those only who give credible evidence of piety, are proper subjects, and that immersion is the proper mode of baptism."[1272] In a letter to his brother, Rice added, "I dared not resist the light any longer, for I feared the Lord would not bless my labors, if I refused obedience to what was to my mind so perfectly clear in the Bible."[1273]

Church of Plymouth, Massachusetts," http://fbcplymouth.com/about/history/.

[1270] Helpful sources on Luther Rice include James B. (Barnett) Taylor, *Memoir of Rev. Luther Rice: One of the First American Missionaries to the East* (Nashville: Broadman, 1840); Evelyn Wingo Thompson, *Luther Rice: Believer in Tomorrow* (Nashville: Broadman, 1967); Edward B. Pollard, *Luther Rice: Pioneer in Missions and Education*, ed. Daniel Gurden (Philadelphia: Judson Press, 1928). Lynn E. May Jr., "Foundations Laid by Luther Rice: A Bicentennial Tribute," *Baptist History and Heritage* 18, no. 2 (April 1983): 2-4; Rufus W. Weaver, "Luther Rice," *Baptist Quarterly* 8, no. 3 (July 1936): 153-59; Ronald F. Deering, "Newly Discovered Love Letter from Luther Rice," *Baptist History and Heritage* 18, no. 2 (April 1983): 5-9; and John Mark Terry, "Luther Rice 1783-1836," in *A Noble Company*, ed. Wolever, 8:186-218.

[1271] Taylor, *Memoir of Rev. Luther Rice*, 104.

[1272] Ibid., 99-100.

[1273] Ibid., 111.

Later in November, the British colonial governor in Calcutta notified Rice and Judson that they could not remain in India, and that he would be deporting them to England on the next ship. With urgent prayer and William Carey's advice, Adoniram and Ann Judson immediately became missionaries to the neighboring nation of Burma (Myanmar), and Luther Rice returned to America to promote foreign missions among the Baptists. Ann and Adoniram arrived in Burma in July 1813, and Luther Rice arrived in America the following September. Judson and Rice would never see one other again in this life. Despite fragile health, throughout his life, Rice would never cease promoting the cause of Christ. Rice's extensive travels and passionate preaching would spark a deep and fruitful burden among American Baptists for the cause of foreign missions.[1274]

The Judson Family and Their Contributions to the Cause of Missions

During their voyage to Burma, Ann Judson had given birth to a stillborn son. Their second son, Roger Williams Judson, died in 1816, before reaching his first birthday. In 1819, Adoniram baptized Maung Nau, their first Burmese convert. Suspected of spying, during the First Anglo-Burmese War (1824–26), Adoniram Judson suffered incarceration, heavily bound in fetters, for over twenty months. At nighttime, the guards placed a bamboo pole between Judson's legs and drew up the chains with pulleys, so that only his head and shoulders touched the ground. His body suffered permanent damage. The crowded, one-room prison, with both men and women, had no toilets, no method of cleaning, and no food. Ann Judson managed

---

[1274] The Luther Rice collection of correspondence, financial ledgers, and logbooks, covering the twenty-year period 1812–32, is in The Gelman Library Special Collections of the George Washington University Archives. See Research Center Collection Number MS0260. The Luther Rice papers include promissory notes, financial documents, college-building appeals, and other Baptist documents, notebooks, and diaries. See also William H. Brackney, ed., *Dispensations of Providence: The Journal and Selected Letters of Luther Rice* (Rochester, NY: The American Baptist Historical Society, 1984).

to bring enough food each day to keep Adoniram and a few others alive. Besides ministering to her husband during this time, Ann gave birth to Maria Elizabeth Butterworth Judson. As hardship took its heavy toll on Ann's health, she contracted smallpox, spotted fever, and cerebral meningitis. She went into eternity in 1826, and, six months later, their baby Maria died of smallpox at the age of two.[1275] After this, Adoniram Judson spent months in depression and despair. God never left nor forsook His faithful servant.

In 1834, after twenty-four years of labor, Judson completed his Burmese translation of the whole Bible. That same year, he married Sarah Hall Boardman, widow of missionary George D. Boardman. Sarah would bear eight children—Abigail Ann (the firstborn) plus seven sons—one of whom was stillborn and two of whom would die before reaching the age of two.[1276] In 1845, eleven years after their marriage, Sarah became seriously ill and doctors recommended a family trip to America for her restoration. She died on the voyage, and her remains lie buried on St. Helena Island, off the west coast of Africa. Weeks later, Adoniram and the children finally arrived in Boston. The nine-month visit would be Judson's only furlough during his ministry of almost forty years. Having forgotten much of his native tongue, Judson used the help of a translator while in America. During his speaking tours, Adoniram met Miss Emily Chubbuck, an American poet who had often written under the penname, Fanny Forrester. Adoniram asked that Emily assist him in writing memoirs of his late wife Sarah. A romance developed, and Adoniram and Emily united in marriage. A month later, the Judson family embarked from Boston for Burma. Emily would bear a daughter (Emily Frances) and a stillborn (Charlie). Judson's health was now beginning to decline.

Adoniram Judson died during the early days of an ocean voyage, which doctors had prescribed as the only cure for his chronic illness. His remains received a sea burial on April 12,

---

[1275] See James D. Knowles, ed., *Memoir of Mrs. Ann H. Judson* (Boston: Lincoln and Edmans, 1830).

[1276] Sarah gave birth to the seven boys in this order: Adoniram Brown; Elnathan; Henry (died an infant); Luther (stillborn); Henry Hall; Charles (died an infant); and Edward.

1850, in the Bay of Bengal. After collecting materials for Francis Wayland's biography of Adoniram Judson, Emily died of tuberculosis in 1854. Her remains rest in Madison Avenue Cemetery, Hamilton, New York. Filled with trial and toil — sacrifice and suffering — the lives and labors of Adoniram Judson and his three wives, Ann, Sarah, and Emily, have provided enduring inspiration and perseverance to the thousands of missionaries who have followed their example and their passion for souls. At the time of Adoniram Judson's death, numerous Burmese pastors had received training, more than sixty Baptist congregations had emerged, and some seven thousand converts had received public baptism. Judson's Burmese Bible, Burmese grammar, and Burmese-English dictionary continue in use today. Judson had completed a full revision of his Burmese Bible in 1840. While eternity alone holds the precious crown, there is an earthly memorial to Adoniram Judson on Burial Hill, in Plymouth, Massachusetts.

Final Years of Luther Rice

Rice became the founder of Columbian College (1821), in Washington, D. C. but, five years later, the lack of finances forced the Baptists to withdraw their ties with the school. In 1904, Columbian became the present-day George Washington University. Meanwhile, Francis Wayland (1796–1865), fourth president of Brown University (1827–55), was converted and called into the ministry under Luther Rice's preaching. After delivering his final sermon, in 1836, at Pine Pleasant Baptist Church, near Saluda, South Carolina, Rice passed into eternity. His remains rest here in the churchyard. (See the Tour Guide in Appendix C.).

In May 1814, delegates from eleven states and the District of Columbia had met in Philadelphia and organized the General Missionary Convention of the Baptist Denomination in the United States of America for Foreign Missions. Meeting once every three years, it became the Triennial Convention. Its first president was Richard Furman, of First Baptist in Charleston, South Carolina. The Convention's primary purpose was to promote and support missionary work, beginning with Adoniram

Judson. Through Rice's influence, the Triennial Convention, in 1817, had begun to expand its outreach by appointing home missionaries, John Mason Peck, to establish mission stations along Missouri's western frontier, and Isaac McCoy, to minister among the Indians in Illinois.

John Mason Peck (1789-1858)

Born and raised on a farm at Litchfield, Connecticut,[1277] Peck became a Christian at the age of eighteen during a revival in the Litchfield Congregation Church. In 1809, he married Sally Paine, who had recently experienced conversion, and the couple joined the local Congregational church. Before the arrival of their first child, however, both had come to reject infant baptism. Early in 1811, they moved to Windham, New York, the region of Sally's childhood home. Here, they received baptism by immersion and joined the New Durham Baptist Church. During the next two years, Peck shepherded two small churches in upstate New York, received ordination, established a school to help support his family, and responded to the call to missions.

In early 1816, Luther Rice encouraged Peck to apply to the Triennial Convention as a missionary to the American West. At the board's suggestion, Peck moved to Philadelphia to study theology, ancient languages, liberal arts, and medicine under William Staughton.[1278] Here, Peck met James E. Welch, and, in

---

[1277] See John Mason Peck, *Memoir of John Mason Peck D. D.*, ed. Rufus Babcock (Philadelphia: American Baptist Publication Society, 1864); Matthew Lawrence, "John Mason Peck: A Biographical Sketch" (MA thesis, University of Illinois, 1914); Austen Kennedy De Blois and Lemuel Call Barnes, *John Mason Peck and One Hundred Years of Home Missions 1817-1917* (New York: American Baptist Home Mission Society, 1917); Coe Hayne, *Vanguard of the Caravans: A Life-Story of John Mason Peck* (Philadelphia: Judson Press, 1931); W. S. Stewart, "John Mason Peck," in *Early Baptist Missionaries and Pioneers*, 1:229-55; and Myron D. Dillow, "John Mason Peck 1789-1858 [and] Sarah Paine Peck 1789-1856," in *A Noble Company: Biographical Essays on Notable Particular-Regular Baptists in America*, ed. Terry Wolever (Springfield, MO: Particular Baptist Press, 2017), 9:42-119.

[1278] In 1852, Harvard University would confer an honorary degree on John

May 1817, the board appointed them both as missionaries to the Missouri Territory. Later that year, they moved with their families to the river town of St. Louis, which became their base.

Due to anti-missionary opposition and shortage of funds, in 1820, the Triennial Convention discontinued its home mission efforts and suggested that Peck join with missionary, Isaac McCoy (1784-1846), among the Indians around Ft. Wayne, Indiana — over 350 miles to the northeast.[1279] Convinced that God would have him in Missouri and Illinois, Peck remained in St. Louis without support, until 1822, when the Massachusetts Baptist Missionary Society began sporadically sending him five dollars a week. That year, the Peck family moved to a farm at Rock Spring, Illinois, and this served as their mission headquarters for the remainder of his life. Peck immediately began organizing Bible and Sunday school societies, and, for the next thirty-five years, he would saturate Missouri and Illinois — evangelizing, organizing, educating, and establishing the Baptist movement in the West.

In 1831, Peck escorted Jonathan Going (1786-1844), of Massachusetts, on a three-month excursion through the Mississippi Valley — including large portions of Illinois, Missouri, Indiana, and Kentucky. Traveling by buggy, the men witnessed countless families without Bibles, struggling churches without shepherds, and a lost frontier without missionaries. Consequently, Peck initiated the formation of the American Baptist Home Mission Society, in 1832-37, with Going as its first correspondence secretary. Peck died at Rock Spring, and the family buried his remains at Bellefontaine Cemetery in St. Louis,

---

Mason Peck.

[1279] The "Isaac McCoy Papers," in 38 volumes, are at the Kansas Historical Society, Topeka, Kansas. See also W. S. Stewart, "Isaac McCoy," in *Early Baptist Missionaries and Pioneers* (Philadelphia: Judson Press, 1925), 1:199-228; and Jeannie Watson, *Reverend Isaac McCoy and the Carey Mission* (Berrien County, Michigan: online profiles preserving local history with people, events, and places, 2013), http://berrien.migenweb.net/profiles.htm. Visit Particular Baptist Press for reprints and new editions of the best books on and by Isaac McCoy, http://www.pbpress.org/. Of special value are Gary W. Long, "Isaac McCoy 1784-1846," in *A Noble Company*, ed. Wolever, 8:286-319; and Isaac McCoy, *History of Baptist Indian Missions* (New York: H. and S. Raynor, 1840).

Missouri. In 1827, Peck had founded Rock Spring Seminary, which, four years later, moved to Upper Alton, Illinois, where, in 1836, the seminary became Shurtleff College, which is now Southern Illinois University Dental School, where a memorial plaque highlights the life and legacy of John Mason Peck.

Resultant Beginnings of Baptist Outreach Overseas

In 1835, the Triennial Convention began supporting Johann G. Oncken (1800–84),[1280] often hailed as the "Baptist Apostle to Germany" and "Father of Continental Baptists." In the previous year, Oncken had established, in Hamburg, the first German Baptist church. His church-planting ministry would reach into Denmark, Finland, Poland, Holland, Switzerland, Russia, Hungary, and Bulgaria. To keep American Baptists abreast of missionary work, at home and abroad, Luther Rice, in 1817, had led the Triennial Convention to establish the periodical *The Latter Day Luminary* (1818–25),[1281] calling for dead churches to repent and return to the Lord.

[1280] David Saxon, "'Every Baptist a Missionary': Johann G. Oncken and Disciple-making in Europe," *Maranatha Baptist Theological Journal* 5, no. 1 (Spring 2015): 1–25; John H. Cooke, *Johann Gerhard Oncken: His Life and Work* (London: S. W. Partridge, 1908); J. H. Rushbrooke, *The Baptist Movement in the Continent of Europe* (London: The Carey Press, 1923), 17ff.; W. S. Stewart, "Johann Gerhard Oncken," in *Early Baptist Missionaries and Pioneers* (Philadelphia: Judson Press, 1926), 2:1–27; Günter Balders, "Oncken, Johann Gerhard (1800–84)," in *A Dictionary of European Baptist Life and Thought* (Eugene, OR: Wipf & Stock, 2009), 364–65.

[1281] With volumes five and six combined, all six volumes of *The Latter Day Luminary* are available at https://catalog.hathitrust.org/Record/012242282.

Select Bibliography for Further Reading

Anderson, Courtney. *To the Golden Shore: The Life of Adoniram Judson*. Boston: Little, Brown and Co., 1956.

Brackney, William H., ed. *Dispensations of Providence: The Journal and Selected Letters of Luther Rice*. Rochester, NY: The American Baptist Historical Society, 1984.

Duesing, Jason G., ed. *Adoniram Judson: A Bicentennial Appreciation of the Pioneer American Missionary*. Nashville: B&H Publishing Group, 2012.

Hayne, Coe. *Vanguard of the Caravans: A Life-Story of John Mason Peck*. Philadelphia: Judson Press, 1931.

Hill, James L. *The Immortal Seven: Judson and His Associates*. Philadelphia: American Baptist Publication Society, 1913. The book covers Dr. and Mrs. Adoniram Judson, Samuel Newell, Harriet Newell, Gordon Hall, Samuel Nott, and Luther Rice.

Hunt, Rosalie Hall. *Bless God and Take Courage: The Judson History and Legacy*. Valley Forge: Judson Press, 2005.

Lawrence, Matthew. "John Mason Peck: A Biographical Sketch." MA thesis, University of Illinois, 1914.

Peck, John Mason. *Memoir of John Mason Peck D. D.* Edited by Rufus Babcock. Philadelphia: American Baptist Publication Society, 1864.

Stuart, Arabella W. *The Lives of Mrs. Ann H. Judson and Mrs. Sarah B. Judson, with a Biographical Sketch of Mrs. Emily C. Judson, Missionaries to Burma*. Auburn, NY: Derby and Miller, 1852.

Taylor, James B. (Barnett). *Memoir of Rev. Luther Rice: One of the First American Missionaries to the East*. Nashville: Broadman, 1840.

Thompson, Evelyn Wingo. *Luther Rice: Believer in Tomorrow*. Nashville: Broadman, 1967.

Wolever, Terry, ed. *A Noble Company: Biographical Essays on Notable Particular-Regular Baptists in America*. Vols. 1–9. Springfield, MO: Particular Baptist Press, 2006–16.

Chapter 18

Northern Baptist Seminaries and the Rise of Theological Liberalism

※

Introduction

*A*t the beginning of the nineteenth century, notable distinctions were apparent between Baptists in the South and their brethren in the North. While the southerners gravitated toward denominational centralization, the northerners preferred a denomination with a loose structure of autonomous societies. Functioning independently of each other, and often duplicating each other's work, two societies operated home missions, while the Triennial Convention operated as the foreign mission board. In 1845, when tensions over a variety of issues led to the formation of the Southern Baptist Convention, the Triennial Convention changed its name to the American Baptist Missionary Union (ABMU). Upon the formation of the Northern Baptist Convention (NBC) in 1907, the ABMU became its American Baptist Foreign Mission Society. In 1913, the NBC established its Ministers and Missionaries Benefit Board, as a source for insurance and pension needs. In 1950, the NBC became the American Baptist Convention, which, in 1972, became the American Baptist Churches USA (ABC/USA), with about 5,800 congregations and one and a half million members.

From its inception, in 1907, the NBC was an inclusive organization, with liberals and conservatives serving in places of leadership. The NBC has never adopted a doctrinal statement of faith. Before the turn of the twentieth century, five Baptist seminaries in the North were teaching liberal theology; these issues would become a battleground during the 1920s. At a preconvention meeting in Buffalo, New York, in 1920, conservatives would organize into the Fundamentalist Fellowship (Foundations Baptist Fellowship International, since 2017) as a voice of alarm. Fundamentalist efforts to salvage the seminaries would not cease before the 1940s. Proper appreciation for the drama that would unfold on the convention floors, during the 1920s, demands some awareness of attitudes and actions that had been developing for many years.

Andover Newton Theological School

Newton Theological Institution, in Newton Centre, Massachusetts, originated in 1825 as a Baptist seminary. A representative spectrum of its professors begins with a variety of men, such as Irah Chase, Alvah Hovey, and Nels F. S. Ferré. Irah Chase (1793–1864), professor of Biblical Theology, was Newton's first faculty member, having previously taught theology at Columbian College, Washington, D. C.[1282] Chase was a sound conservative, whose writings include *The Design of Baptism* (1851); *Infant Baptism an Invention of Men* (1863); and *The Life of Bunyan, Author of The Pilgrim's Progress* (1847).

Alvah Hovey (1820–1903),[1283] who spent most of his career at Newton, taught Hebrew, Interpretation, Theology, Apologetics, and Biblical Literature. He served Newton's presidency for thirty years (1868–98). Hovey expressed agreement with all the fundamentals of the faith, but his written works are consistently

---

[1282] Alvah Hovey, *A Tribute of Affection to the Memory of Professor Irah Chase* (Boston: George C. Rand and Avery Printers, 1865), including Chase's funeral service and a list of thirty-six of Chase's books, including *Infant Baptism an Invention of Men* (Philadelphia: American Baptist Publication Society, 1863); idem, *Historical Address Delivered at the Fiftieth Anniversary of the Newton Theological Institution, June 8, 1875* (Boston: Wright and Potter, 1875), 13ff.

[1283] Margaret Lamberts Bendroth, *A School of the Church: Andover Newton across Two Centuries* (Grand Rapids: Eerdmans, 2008), 35ff.

imprecise on the inerrancy of Scripture.[1284] Despite Hovey's critical review of Edmond Stapfer's *The Death and Resurrection of Jesus Christ*,[1285] which adamantly denies the literal, bodily resurrection of Christ, Hovey insists that Stapfer "gives evidence of being an earnest Christian" who "recognizes the lordship of Jesus Christ, and expresses the deepest interest in his kingdom and confidence in its triumphant progress."[1286] Many conservatives regarded Hovey's glowing description of Stapfer as a denigration of Christ, whose literal, bodily resurrection is the most vital part of the gospel. As his own son observed, Alvah Hovey, "as so often occurred," was a "harmonizing influence between a progressive thinker and the conservatives."[1287]

The Harvard-trained, Swedish immigrant, Nels F. S. Ferré (1908–71), taught theology at Newton from 1937 to 1950 and from 1957 to 1965. As "the leading theologian" on the campus,[1288] Ferré insisted, "We have no way of knowing that Jesus was sinless."[1289] To Ferré, "Marxism may be God's means to

---

[1284] Hovey, *Manual of Christian Theology*, 2nd ed. (Chicago: Silver, Burdett and Co., 1900), 42–106. In Henry C. King's review of this book for the University of Chicago, he describes it as a "scholarly theological treatise," in which "there is general acceptance of the theory of evolution, but no thoroughgoing application of it.… The author's doctrine of Scripture … is not extremely conservative," in *The American Journal of Theology* 5, no. 2 (April 1901): 398–99.

[1285] Edmond Stapfer, *The Death and Resurrection of Jesus Christ*, trans. Louise Seymour Houghton (New York: Charles Scribner's Sons, 1898). Stapfer taught Protestant theology in the University of Paris.

[1286] Alvah Hovey, "Stapfer on the Resurrection of Jesus Christ," *American Journal of Theology*, vol. 4 (July 1900): 550 (536–54). The journal was produced by the divinity faculty of the University of Chicago.

[1287] George Rice Hovey, *Alvah Hovey: His Life and Letters* (Philadelphia: Judson Press, 1928), 169, passim. Alvah Hovey maintained lifelong ties with notorious liberals such as William Newton Clarke (discussed below). For key examples, see Jeffrey Paul Straub, "The Making of a Battle Royal: The Rise of Religious Liberalism in Northern Baptist Life, 1870–1920" (PhD diss., Southern Baptist Theological Seminary, 2004), 55n23, 86–87n121, 95–105, passim.

[1288] Bendroth, *A School of the Church*, 156.

[1289] Nels F. S. Ferré, *The Christian Understanding of God* (New York: Harper & Brothers, 1951), 186. On page 191, the author speculates that Jesus might even have been the illegitimate son of Mary and a German soldier. See

Christian fulfillment in history."[1290] Ferré attacked all the historic fundamentals.

In 1931, the Congregationalist, Andover Theological Seminary (est. 1807) moved from Cambridge, Massachusetts, to Newton Theological Institution to form the Andover Newton Theological School.[1291] In 1965, the two schools officially merged.

Colgate Theological Seminary

Colgate Theological Seminary originated in 1817 as the Hamilton Theological and Literary Institute, in Hamilton, New York, with "thirteen men, thirteen prayers, and thirteen dollars,"[1292] as the first Baptist seminary in America. In 1890, a liberal, William Newton Clarke (1841-1912), began teaching at Colgate, where he remained until shortly before his death. Clarke's book *An Outline of Christian Theology* (1894) was the first systematic theology of American liberalism. It promptly became popular, and, by 1914, the book was in its twentieth printing. Near the end of his life, Clarke traced his own path from pious upbringing to apostasy and published it in his autobiography *Sixty Years with the Bible* (1909) — a tragic account in view of the thousands he influenced.[1293] In 1928, Colgate

---

also Ferré, *The Sun and the Umbrella* (New York: Harper & Brothers, 1953), 39, 112, 117, 122, and passim; and Gary Dorrien, *The Making of American Theology: Crisis, Irony, and Postmodernity* (Louisville: Westminster John Knox Press, 2006), 39-57.

[1290] Nels F. S. Ferré, *Christianity and Society* (New York: Harper & Brothers, 1950), 239. See also Alan P. F. Sell, *Content and Method in Christian Theology: A Case Study of the Thought of Nels Ferré* (Cambridge, United Kingdom: James Clarke and Co., 2014).

[1291] In 1907, Andover Theological Seminary had moved from Andover, Massachusetts to Cambridge, where it affiliated with Harvard University and Harvard Divinity School.

[1292] William H. Allison, "Colgate," in *The New Schaff-Herzog Encyclopedia of Religious Knowledge* (New York: Funk and Wagnalls, Company, 1911), 11:345; and Howard D. Williams, *A History of Colgate University 1819-1969* (New York: Van Nostrand Reinhold Co., 1969), 1ff.

[1293] See Straub, "The Making of a Battle Royal," 115-49; Claude L. Howe Jr., *The Theology of William Newton Clarke* (New York: Arno, 1980); idem, "William Newton Clarke: Systematic Theologian of Theological Liberalism," *Foundations* 6, no. 2 (April 1963): 123-135. For discussions

Theological Seminary and Rochester Theological Seminary merged to become Colgate Rochester Divinity School.

Rochester Theological Seminary

Rochester Theological Seminary emerged, in 1850, as part of the University of Rochester, in New York.[1294] In 1872, Augustus H. Strong (1836-1921) became president of the Seminary,[1295] after professing Christ under Charles Finney's influence, studying theology under Nathaniel Taylor at Yale Divinity School, and serving two Baptist pastorates.[1296] Three years into his presidency, Strong brought in the well-known conservative, Howard Osgood,[1297] to teach Hebrew language

---

on other early Colgate liberals, see Norman H. Maring, "Baptists and Changing Views of the Bible, 1865-1918," *Foundations* 1 (July 1958): 53-75 and (October 1958): 45 (32-61).

[1294] See Sally Dodgson, "Rochester Theological Seminary: 1850-1928," *American Baptist Quarterly* 20, no. 2 (June 2001): 115-29.

[1295] See Grant Wacker, *Augustus H. Strong and the Dilemma of Historical Consciousness* (Macon, GA: Mercer University Press, 1985), 43-57, 111-23; Leroy Moore Jr., "The Rise of American Religious Liberalism at the Rochester Theological Seminary, 1872-1928" (PhD diss., Claremont Graduate School, 1966); idem, "Academic Freedom: A Chapter in the History of the Colgate Rochester Divinity School," *Foundations* 10, no. 1 (January-March 1967): 64-79.

[1296] Augustus H. Strong, *Autobiography of Augustus Hopkins Strong*, ed. Crerar Douglas (Valley Forge: Judson Press, 1981), 86ff.

[1297] See "The Late Professor Howard Osgood," *The Biblical World* (February 1, 1912): 137-39. Born and raised an Episcopalian, Osgood (1831-1911) completed his pre-college studies at the Episcopal Institute, Flushing, New York. In 1856, he became a Baptist and received immersion at Oliver Street Baptist, New York City. During 1856-58, he served the pastorate of the Baptist church in Flushing, Long Island. In 1858, Osgood completed his AB degree at Harvard. During 1860-65, he served the pastorate of the North Church, New York City. He was honored with the DD degree from Brown University in 1868. He taught Hebrew Literature at Crozer Theological Seminary (1868-74) and at Rochester Seminary (1875-1900). Osgood addressed the conference on inspiration in Philadelphia in 1887 and the Seaside Bible Conference at Asbury Park, New Jersey, in 1893. For the 1893 Seaside Conference sermons, see *Anti-Higher Criticism: Or Testimony to the Infallibility of the Bible*, ed. Leander W. Munhall (New York: Hunt and Eaton: 1894). Princeton awarded Osgood an LLD degree in 1894.

and literature. Osgood would remain steadfast in his defense of the Scriptures.[1298]

With A. H. Strong defending cardinal doctrines and promoting missions, many considered him also as a conservative. In his final years, however, Strong insisted, "I have always held that there is a theistic evolution."[1299] To him, "Neither evolution nor the higher criticism has any terrors to one who regards them as parts of Christ's creating and educating process."[1300] Strong wrote, "I grant the composite documentary view of the Pentateuch and of its age-long days of creation, while I still hold to its substantially Mosaic authorship." Asserting that there is "more than one Isaiah," Strong adds, "Any honest Christian ... has the right to interpret Jonah and Daniel as allegories, rather than as histories."[1301] Strong's "dynamical" view of inspiration stands in opposition to plenary inspiration and the inerrant autographa of Scripture.[1302]

On the American committee for the revision of the Old Testament, Osgood helped translate the American Standard Version (1901). Osgood's works include *The Bible and Higher Criticism*, "read at the summer school of the American Institute of Christian Philosophy, July 6, 1893" (New York: W. B. Ketcham, 1893); *Christ and the Old Testament*, "a paper read April 14, 1902, at the request of the Presbyterian ministers of Rochester" (Rochester, NY: Genesee Press, 1902); and *Topics in the Psalms* (1900, unpublished copy at Princeton Seminary).

[1298] LeRoy Moore Jr., "Academic Freedom: A Chapter in the History of Colgate Rochester Divinity School," *Foundations* 10, no. 1 (January-March 1967): 68–69 (64–79).

[1299] See the newspaper accounts and full discussion in Gilbert L. Guffin, ed., *What God Hath Wrought: Eastern's First Thirty-Five Years* (Philadelphia: Judson Press, 1960), 28–29.

[1300] Augustus H. Strong, *Outlines of Systematic Theology* (Philadelphia: The Griffith and Rowland Press, 1908), ix.

[1301] Idem, *A Tour of the Missions: Observations and Conclusions* (Philadelphia: The Griffith and Rowland Press, 1918), 186.

[1302] Idem, *Outlines of Systematic Theology*, 55–60. One can trace Strong's developing liberal views by comparing the various editions of his *Systematic Theology*, which first appeared in 1886. His changes are most noticeable in the fifth edition (1896) to the eighth (final) edition of 1907. For Strong's latest word on inspiration, see his *Systematic Theology* (Philadelphia: American Baptist Publication Society, 1907), 1:211–12. See Myron James Houghton, "An Examination and Evaluation of A. H. Strong's Doctrine of Holy Scripture" (ThD diss., Concordia Seminary,

Strong's doctrine of "Ethical Monism,"[1303] that "God is in all and that all things are in God,"[1304] drew the charge of pantheism. Archibald T. Robertson concluded, "According to Strong the end of my little finger is a piece of God!"[1305] Indeed, "God *is* all," declared Strong, and "he is also in all; so, making the universe a graded and progressive manifestation of himself, both in his love for righteousness and his opposition to moral evil."[1306]

In 1897, Strong brought Walter Rauschenbusch (1861-1918), father of the Social Gospel, to Rochester's faculty.[1307] Rauschenbusch soon released his *Christianity and the Social Crisis* (1906) and *Theology of the Social Gospel* (1917). A popular speaker in Northern Baptist gatherings, Rauschenbusch continued at Rochester Seminary until his death. Augustus Strong remained there until 1912, and his successor George Cross (1862-1929) greatly increased Rochester's demise into liberalism and ecumenism.[1308]

1986); L. Russ Bush and Tom J. Nettles, *Baptists and the Bible* (Chicago: Moody, 1980), 260-73; and Maring, "Baptists," *Foundations* 1 (October 1958): 39-40.

[1303] See John Andrew Aloisi, "Augustus Hopkins Strong and Ethical Monism As a Means of Reconciling Christian Theology and Modern Thought" (PhD diss., Southern Baptist Theological Seminary, 2012); and Brandon Wilkins, "Augustus Hopkins Strong and His Journey toward Ethical Monism," *Reformed Baptist Theological Review* 4, no. 2 (July 2007): 127-42.

[1304] Strong, *Outlines of Systematic Theology*, 31; cf. idem, *Christ in Creation and Ethical Monism* (Philadelphia: Griffith and Roland, 1899); and idem, *What Shall I Believe?* (New York: Revell, 1922).

[1305] James Oliver Buswell includes this helpful discussion in his *Systematic Theology of the Christian Religion* (Grand Rapids: Zondervan, 1963), 1:97-100.

[1306] Strong, *Outlines of Systematic Theology*, 32; idem, *Systematic Theology*, 8th ed. (Valley Forge: Judson Press, 1907), 714-16, 736, 747, 750; and idem, *Christ in Creation*, passim.

[1307] A. H. Strong wrote to Rauschenbusch in 1912 that his *Christianizing the Social Order* was "a great book." In 1917, however, when Rauschenbusch dedicated his *Theology for the Social Gospel* to Strong, the latter expressed his disagreement with some of its themes. For a valuable discussion, see Grant A. Wacker Jr., "Augustus H. Strong: A Conservative Confrontation with History" (PhD diss., Harvard University, 1978), 230.

[1308] See George Cross, *Christian Salvation, a Modern Interpretation* (Chicago: University of Chicago Press, 1925).

Crozer Theological Seminary

Baptists established Crozer Theological Seminary in Upland, Pennsylvania, in 1867, as a conservative institution. It later moved to Chester, Pennsylvania. The Seminary's first president, Henry G. Weston (1820-1909), an ardent Fundamentalist,[1309] served as a consulting editor of the Scofield Reference Bible. Fundamentalist James M. Stifler (1839-1902),[1310] after serving several pastorates, taught as professor of New Testament at Crozer, from 1882 until the year of his death. Described by Ernest R. Sandeen as one of the most active millenarians of whom we have any record, Stifler participated in numerous Fundamentalist conferences, including the historic Niagara Conference.[1311] Crozer professor, George D. B. Pepper, in his *Outlines of Systematic Theology* (1873), likewise defended the doctrine of biblical inerrancy.[1312] Eventually, however, liberal theology would find its way into Crozer.

With the equivalent of a Bachelor of Divinity degree, from Rochester Theological Seminary, and then an MA from the University of Rochester, Henry C. Vedder (1853-1935) taught at Crozer Seminary, from 1894 to 1926. After completing his final edition of *A Short History of the Baptists* (1907), Vedder began vigorously attacking Christ's substitutionary atonement. He considered "the idea of sacrificial expiation, made by the innocent for the guilty," as "especially repugnant to our best ethics." He called the Old Testament sacrificial system "too revolting, too stupidly absurd, to be worthy of serious refutation."[1313] Alvah Sabin Hobart (1847-1930), who taught at

---

[1309] See Henry G. Weston, *Matthew, the Genesis of the New Testament: Its Purpose, Character, and Method* (Rochester, New York: American Baptist, n.d.); idem, *Constitution and Polity of the New Testament Church* (Philadelphia: American Baptist Publication Society, 1895).

[1310] See James Madison Stifler, *The Epistle to the Romans: A Commentary, Logical and Historical* (Chicago: Moody, 1960).

[1311] Ernest R. Sandeen, *The Roots of Fundamentalism: British and American Millenarianism, 1800-1930* (Grand Rapids: Baker, 1970), 164-65.

[1312] See Straub, "The Making of a Battle Royal," 55n24; cf. Maring, "Baptists," *Foundations* 1 (July 1958): 52-75 and (October 1958): 30-61.

[1313] *Chester Times*, April 10, 1920, in W. B. Riley, "Modernism in Baptist Schools," in *Baptist Fundamentals*, "being addresses delivered at the

Crozer during 1900–20, expressed similar views.[1314] There was no turning back. Liberal professors, such as Eric C. Rust[1315] and Morton Scott Enslin were warmly welcomed at Crozer Theological Seminary,[1316] which, in 1970, affiliated with Colgate Rochester Divinity School to form Colgate Rochester Crozer Divinity School.

The University of Chicago Divinity School

In 1891, John D. Rockefeller Sr. (1839–1937) funded the establishment of the University of Chicago. As a predecessor of the University, the Divinity School originated with the old Morgan Park Seminary chartered, in 1865, by the Baptist Theological Union.[1317] By the turn of the twentieth century, the school's teachings had created a furor among Northern Baptist conservatives. Having a Yale PhD in Semitic languages, William Rainey Harper (1856–1906) was one of the founders and the first president of the University of Chicago. As professor of

---

pre-convention conference at Buffalo June 21 and 22, 1920 (Philadelphia, Judson Press, 1920), 183–85; Henry C. Vedder, *Fundamentals of Christianity: A Study of the Teaching of Jesus and Paul* (New York: Macmillan, 1922), x–xix, 4–9, 100–3, 110–13, 190–93, 235, passim; Robert B. Hanley, "Henry Clay Vedder: Conservative Evangelical to Evangelical Liberal," *Foundations* 5 (April 1962): 135–57; G. Keith Parker, "Henry Clay Vedder: Church Historian," *The Quarterly Review* 31, no. 1 (October–December 1970): 65–86; and Dwight A, Honeycutt, "A Study of the Life and Thought of Henry Clay Vedder" (ThD diss., New Orleans Baptist Theological Seminary, 1984), 140–41, passim.

[1314] Alvah Hobart, *Transplanted Truths from Romans* (Philadelphia: Griffith and Rowland, 1916), 29.

[1315] Eric C. Rust, *Nature and Man in Biblical Thought* (London: Lutterworth Press, 1953), 20; cf. 2, 5, 17, and 195.

[1316] Morton Scott Enslin, *Christian Beginnings* (New York: Harper, 1938), see especially page 358; idem, *Prophet from Nazareth* (New York: McGraw-Hill, 1961); idem, *Reapproaching Paul* (Philadelphia: Westminster Press, 1972).

[1317] The best histories of the University of Chicago Divinity School include Arthur Cushman McGiffert Jr., *No Ivory Tower: The Story of the Chicago Theological Seminary* (Chicago: Chicago Theological Seminary, 1965); and Thomas Wakefield Goodspeed, *A History of the University of Chicago Founded by John D. Rockefeller: The First Quarter-Century* (Chicago: University of Chicago Press, 1916).

Hebrew and Old Testament, Harper established the institution as the leading, liberal Baptist seminary in America.[1318] Shailer Mathews (1863-1941),[1319] professor of New Testament and systematic theology, vigorously promoted liberalism.[1320] Other liberals representing the Chicago Divinity School included: George Burman Foster (1858-1918);[1321] Gerald Birney Smith (1868-1929);[1322] Shirley Jackson Case (1872-1947);[1323] Henry N. Wieman (1884-1975);[1324] Ernest DeWitt Burton (1856-1925);[1325] and Martin E. Marty (b. 1928).[1326] From its origins, the University of Chicago Divinity School was an official Northern Baptist institution, but, in the late 1970s, in an attempt to attract more students to its ecumenical base, the school declared itself an "unofficial" institution of the American Baptist Churches in the USA. The institution would continue its "historical and

---

[1318] Milton Mayer, *Young Man in a Hurry: The Story of William Rainey Harper, First President of the University of Chicago* (Chicago: University of Chicago Alumni Association, 1957); and James P. Wind, *The Bible and the University* (Atlanta: Scholars Press, 1987).

[1319] Shailer Matthews, *New Faith for Old: An Autobiography* (New York: Macmillan, 1936).

[1320] Idem, *The Faith of Modernism* (New York: Macmillan, 1925).

[1321] George Burman Foster, *The Finality of the Christian Religion* (Chicago: University of Chicago Press, 1906); idem, *The Function of Religion in Man's Struggle for Existence* (Chicago: University of Chicago Press, 1909).

[1322] A cross-section of the theology of the University of Chicago Divinity School appears in Gerald Birney Smith, ed., *A Guide to the Study of the Christian Religion* (Chicago: University of Chicago Press, 1916); see especially pages 27, 33-34, 42-43, 48, 55, 76, 105, 110, 130-36, 180, 190-97. This book was a major target of Fundamentalist protests when the Fundamentalist Fellowship organized in 1920.

[1323] William J. Hynes, *Shirley Jackson Case and the Chicago School: The Socio-Historical Method* (Chico, CA: Scholars Press, 1981).

[1324] E.g., Henry N. Wieman, *The Source of Human Good* (Chicago: University of Chicago Press, 1946).

[1325] http://president.uchicago.edu/directory/ernest-dewitt-burton.

[1326] Martin E. Marty and R. Scott Appleby, eds., *The Fundamentalism Project*, 5 vols. (Chicago: University of Chicago Press, 1991-95), volume 1: *Fundamentalisms Observed*; volume 2: *Fundamentalisms and Society: Reclaiming the Sciences, the Family, and Education*; volume 3: *Fundamentalisms and the State: Remaking Polities, Economies, and Militance*; volume 4: *Accounting for Fundamentalisms: The Dynamic Character of Movements*; and volume 5: *Fundamentalisms Comprehended*.

friendly" relationship with the ABCUSA.[1327] Conservatives, meanwhile, saw the Divinity School as one of the most theologically radical seminaries on the continent.

Two Conservative Reactions to the Modernism in the Seminaries

As a reaction to modernism at the University of Chicago Divinity School, conservatives under John Marvin Dean's leadership, in 1913, established Northern Baptist Theological Seminary. Dean's Second Baptist Church, in Chicago, provided the seminary's facilities during its first seven years. In 1919, Northern Seminary affiliated with the NBC and dropped Fundamentalists, W. B. Riley and J. R. Straton, from its advisory board. Northern Seminary swiftly sought to dialogue with the "Chicago Cluster of Theological Schools." After serving on the Northern faculty from 1940 to 1947, Carl Henry, dean of the "New Evangelicalism," helped establish Fuller Theological Seminary, in Pasadena, California. He propelled Northern to remain an Evangelical institution.[1328] During the 1960s, Northern moved to Lombard, Illinois.[1329]

As a reaction to modernism at Crozer Theological Seminary, evangelicals established Eastern Baptist Theological Seminary, in 1925, in Philadelphia, Pennsylvania.[1330] The seminary continued operating within the framework of the NBC. Still affiliated with the ecumenical, American Baptist Churches USA, and located in St. Davids, Pennsylvania, the school has

---

[1327] Elinor Johnson, telephone interview; Johnson was administrative secretary in the executive offices of the American Baptist Churches USA. See also *The University of Chicago Divinity School Announcements 2015–2016*.

[1328] See Carl F. H. Henry, "Cloistered Years at Northern," in *Confessions of a Theologian: An Autobiography* (Waco, TX: Word Books, 1986), 89–113.

[1329] Warren Cameron Young, *Commit What You Have Heard: A History of Northern Baptist Theological Seminary, 1913–1988* (Wheaton: Harold Shaw Publishers, 1988). Presently, Northern Seminary is moving to Chicago's Lisle area.

[1330] The earliest history of Eastern Baptist Theological Seminary is Gilbert L. Guffin, ed., *What God Hath Wrought: Eastern's First Thirty-five Years* (Philadelphia: Judson, 1960).

changed its name to Eastern University, whose seminary is Palmer Theological Seminary. In the next chapter, we will overview the Fundamentalist Baptist movement and its reactions to modernism.

Select Bibliography for Further Reading

Aloisi, John Andrew. "Augustus Hopkins Strong and Ethical Monism As a Means of Reconciling Christian Theology and Modern Thought." PhD diss., Southern Baptist Theological Seminary, 2012.

Bendroth, Margaret Lamberts. *A School of the Church: Andover Newton across Two Centuries*. Grand Rapids: Eerdmans, 2008.

Dodgson, Sally. "Rochester Theological Seminary: 1850-1928." *American Baptist Quarterly* 20, no. 2 (June 2001): 115-29.

Hanley, Robert B. "Henry Clay Vedder: Conservative Evangelical to Evangelical Liberal." *Foundations* 5 (April 1962): 135-57.

Houghton, Myron James. "An Examination and Evaluation of A. H. Strong's Doctrine of Holy Scripture." ThD diss., Concordia Seminary, 1986.

Hovey, Alvah. *Manual of Christian Theology*. 2nd edition. Chicago: Silver, Burdett and Co., 1900.

Hovey, George Rice. *Alvah Hovey: His Life and Letters*. Philadelphia: Judson Press, 1928.

Howe, Claude L. Jr. *The Theology of William Newton Clarke*. New York: Arno, 1980.

Maring, Norman H. "Baptists and Changing Views of the Bible, 1865-1918." *Foundations* 1 (July 1958): 53-75 and (October 1958): 45 (32-61).

Moore. Leroy Jr. "The Rise of American Religious Liberalism at the Rochester Theological Seminary, 1872-1928." PhD diss., Claremont Graduate School, 1966.

Riley, W. B. "Modernism in Baptist Schools." In *Baptist Fundamentals: Being Addresses Delivered at the Pre-Convention Conference at Buffalo June 21 and 22, 1920*, 183-85. Philadelphia, Judson Press, 1920.

Sell, Alan P. F. *Content and Method in Christian Theology: A Case Study of the Thought of Nels Ferré*. Cambridge, United Kingdom: James Clarke and Co., 2014.

Straub, Jeffrey Paul. "The Making of a Battle Royal: The Rise of Religious Liberalism in Northern Baptist Life, 1870-1920." PhD diss., The Southern Baptist Theological Seminary, 2004.

Strong, Augustus Hopkins. *Autobiography of Augustus Hopkins Strong*. Edited by Crerar Douglas. Valley Forge: Judson Press, 1981.

Wacker, Grant. *Augustus H. Strong and the Dilemma of Historical Consciousness*. Macon, GA: Mercer University Press, 1985.

Williams, Howard D. *A History of Colgate University 1819-1969*. New York: Van Nostrand Reinhold Co., 1969.

Chapter 19

The Rise and Development of Baptist Fundamentalism

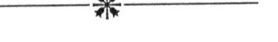

※

Introduction

As a movement, Baptist Fundamentalism emerged and developed through two primary stages. While pre-1930 Fundamentalism was *non-conformist* in practice, post-1930 Fundamentalism took a "come-out" *separatist* stance. Whether by attempting to separate liberals from institutions, or by separating from liberal institutions, each stage included some degree of separation. Like the English, non-conformist Puritans, the first group made first-degree attempts, from within, to purge their denominations of liberal doctrines and practices. Like the English Separatists, the second group eventually took the second-degree position of withdrawing from religious entities that harbored liberals, and from Evangelicals who remained within such entities. Not until the 1950s and 60s were there distinct and definitive lines of demarcation emerging between first-degree and second-degree separatism.

Many Fundamentalist Baptist churches prefer the label *unaffiliated*, rather than *independent*, since their churches do depend upon fellowship with churches of like faith and worship. Because many take the unaffiliated stance, it would be difficult if not impossible to measure the numerical strength of the movement. Ordinarily, their churches do not include the word *Fundamentalist* on their letterheads and signboards.

On the other hand, its use of the word *Fundamentalist* does not necessarily mean that a church or group still maintains a definitive, separatist stance in doctrine and worship.

The Rise of Educational Institutions among Conservative Baptists

In 1889, Adoniram Judson (A. J.) Gordon of Boston's Clarendon Street Baptist Church, founded the interdenominational, Boston Missionary Training School (now Gordon College at Wenham, MA). Its first faculty included A. J. Gordon, F. L. Chapell, James M. Gray, J. M. Stifler, and Robert Cameron. In 1902, William Bell (W. B.) Riley of First Baptist, Minneapolis, established the interdenominational, Northwestern Bible and Missionary Training School (now University of Northwestern – St. Paul). The original purpose of these conservative schools was to provide Bible training, for equipping men and women for Christian service, with an emphasis on missions.

Faith Baptist Bible College and Theological Seminary in Ankeny, Iowa

Originally challenged by Evangelist Dwight L. Moody, during the 1893 World's Fair, in Chicago, William H. Jordan, a Presbyterian pastor in Omaha, Nebraska, later founded Omaha Bible Institute (OBI), in 1921, and served its presidency until 1942. Jordan's successor, Paul Sawtell, served the office from 1943 to 1947, when the Board of Trustees considered closing the institute. A faculty member, John L. Patten, pastor of Omaha's Grace Baptist Church, promptly volunteered to lead the school into the future. During Patten's presidency (1947–65), the school was renamed Omaha Baptist Bible Institute (OBBI). In 1960, OBBI expanded into a four-year college and became Omaha Baptist Bible College (OBBC). With the OBBC outgrowing its facilities, Fundamentalist, David Nettleton (1918-1993), who served the presidency during 1965-80, tirelessly raised funds for a new campus. Finally, in 1967, OBBC relocated in Ankeny, Iowa, with its new name, Faith Baptist Bible College (FBBC). In 1986, Denver Baptist Bible College and Theological Seminary merged with FBBC on the Ankeny campus, to form Faith Baptist Bible College and Theological Seminary (FBBC&TS),[1331] which acquired regional and national accreditation. The Seminary building (Shipp Hall) was named in honor of Gordon Shipp (1930–87), the Faith president during 1980–87.[1332]

Foundations Baptist Fellowship International (FBFI)

Just as Northern Baptists were arriving in Buffalo, New York, in 1920, to convene their annual convention (June 23–29), a group of NBC conservatives (non-conformists), who had arrived two days earlier, were now adjourning a preconvention conference (June 21–22), which had begun in Delaware Avenue Baptist Church. The conservatives' theme was "The Fundamentals of Our Baptist Faith." Such a massive crowd had converged on the church that, on the second evening, they held their sessions in the Civic Auditorium, where an estimated three thousand attended. After the meeting, they attended the NBC gathering. The 1920 preconvention, whose purpose was to rescue the NBC from its drift into modernism, had launched the National Federation of Fundamentalists of the Northern Baptists,[1333] whose name changes are:
- The Fundamentalist Fellowship (FF 1920)
- The Conservative Baptist Fellowship (CBF 1946)
- The Fundamental Baptist Fellowship (FBF 1967)
- The Fundamental Baptist Fellowship International (FBFI 2001)
- The Foundations Baptist Fellowship International (FBFI, operational name 2017).

Thirteen of the sermons preached at the initial preconvention

---

[1331] Sam Bradford, pastor of Beth Eden Baptist Church, in Denver, Colorado, had founded Denver Baptist Bible College in 1952 and added the seminary in 1972. See John L. Patten, *"For the Truth's Sake": A History of Faith Baptist Bible College* (Ankeny, Iowa: Faith Baptist Bible College, 1979); and https://www.faith.edu/about-faith/history-of-faith/.

[1332] The current FBBC&TS president, Jim Tillotson, accepted the office in 2017.

[1333] *The Baptist* 1 (1920): 800, an NBC publication.

appeared under the title *Baptist Fundamentals* (1920).[1334] Jasper C. Massee (1871-1965), the Fundamentalist Fellowship's first president, concluded his "Opening Address" with an appeal for "loyalty, affection, and fraternity" toward the NBC: "We will not go [into the Convention] with swords sharpened to conflict, but with spirits prayerfully called to unity."[1335] Ironically, Curtis Lee Laws, editor of the *Watchman-Examiner* magazine, helped standardize the label *Fundamentalist*, following that first preconvention (1920): "We suggest," says Laws, "that those who still cling to the great fundamentals and who mean to do battle royal for the fundamentals shall be called 'Fundamentalists.'"[1336]

From the outset, the Fundamentalist Fellowship stated that their aims were to oppose evolution and modernism within NBC seminaries, and to secure the adoption of a confession of faith for the Convention. The FF's characteristic lack of militancy, however, provoked, in 1923, the founding of the Baptist Bible Union (BBU), in Kansas City, Missouri.[1337] The BBU elected Thomas Todhunter (T. T.) Shields (1873-1955),[1338]

[1334] *Baptist Fundamentals*, "being addresses delivered at the pre-convention conference at Buffalo June 21 and 22, 1920" (Philadelphia: Judson Press, 1920); cf. *Baptist Doctrines*, "addresses delivered at the North American pre-convention conference, Des Moines, Iowa, June 21, 1921" (N.p.: J. C. Massee, 1921).

[1335] *Baptist Fundamentals*, 11; see also C. Allyn Russell, "J. C. Massee: Moderate Fundamentalist," in *Voices of Fundamentalism: Seven Biographical Studies* (Philadelphia: The Westminster Press, 1976), 107-34; cf. Bob Dalton, "J. C. Massee: A Portrait in Spiritual Treason," *Frontline Magazine* (May-June 1998): 13-14.

[1336] Curtis Lee Laws, "Convention Side Lights," *Watchman-Examiner* (July 1, 1920): 834.

[1337] The definitive study of the BBU is Robert George Delnay, "A History of the Baptist Bible Union" (ThD diss., Dallas Theological Seminary, 1963); see also David Beale, *In Pursuit of Purity: American Fundamentalism since 1850* (Greenville: BJU Press, 1986), 209-42, 273-301; 2nd edition is forthcoming.

[1338] Valuable sources on Shields include Leslie K. Tarr, *Shields of Canada* (Grand Rapids: Baker, 1967); Gerald L. Priest, "T. T. Shields the Fundamentalist: Man of Controversy," *Detroit Baptist Seminary Journal* 10 (2005): 69-101; and Doug Adams, "The Call to Arms: The Reverend Thomas Todhunter Shields, World War One, and the Shaping of a Militant Fundamentalist,"

pastor of the Jarvis Street Baptist Church, in Toronto, Ontario, as its president. For vice presidents (North and South), the BBU elected pastors W. B. Riley (1861–1947)[1339] of First Baptist Church, Minneapolis, Minnesota, and J. Frank Norris (1877–1952),[1340] of First Baptist Church, Fort Worth, Texas. The BBU originated with the conviction that the Fundamentalist Fellowship was soft on the very evils against which it protested. Consequently, the BBU became a militant rival, drawing large crowds, while the FF declined. The BBU and the FF did resemble one another in four ways. First, each was a preacher's organization. Second, each avoided making any specific millennial view binding on its constituency. Third, each refused to operate under a come-out, separatist position. Fourth, each group would ultimately transform into a separatist organization. As we will discuss below, in 1932, the BBU executive committee dissolved their organization and reorganized into the General Association of Regular Baptist Churches (GARBC), which, by 1938, would be a separatist association, in policy and

---

in *Baptists and War: Essays on Baptists and Military Conflict, 1640s–1990s*, ed. Gordon L. Heath and Michael A. G. Haykin (Eugene, OR: Wipf and Stock, 2015), 115–49.

[1339] Valuable sources on Riley include Marie Acomb Riley, *The Dynamic of a Dream: The Life Story of Dr. William B. Riley* (Grand Rapids: Eerdmans, 1938); Lloyd B. Hull, "A Rhetorical Study of the Preaching of William Bell Riley" (PhD dissertation, Wayne State University, 1960); William Vance Trollinger Jr., *God's Empire: William Bell Riley and Midwestern Fundamentalism* (Madison, WI: The University of Wisconsin Press, 1990); Ferenc M. Szasz, "Three Fundamentalist Leaders: The Roles of William Bell Riley, John Roach Straton, and William Jennings Bryan in the Fundamentalist-Modernist Controversy" (PhD dissertation, University of Rochester, 1969); C. Allyn Russell, "William Bell Riley: Organizational Fundamentalist," in *Voices of American Fundamentalism* (Philadelphia: Westminster Press, 1976), 79–106.

[1340] Valuable sources on Norris include Barry Hankins, *God's Rascal: J. Frank Norris and the Beginnings of Southern Fundamentalism* (Lexington, KY: The University Press of Kentucky, 1996); Ray E. Tatum, *Conquest or Failure? A Biography of J. Frank Norris* (Dallas: Baptist Historical Foundation, 1966); Samuel K. Tullock, "The Transformation of American Fundamentalism: The Life and Career of John Franklyn Norris" (PhD diss., The University of Texas at Dallas, 1997); and C. Allyn Russell, "J. Frank Norris: Violent Fundamentalist," in *Voices*, 20–46.

practice. We will first trace the path of the FF, which, by 1955, would take the same separatist stance.

The FF established its foreign mission board in 1943. With an office in Chicago, the FF, in 1946, renamed itself the Conservative Baptist Fellowship (CBF) and named its mission board the Conservative Baptist Foreign Mission Society (CBFMS). Due to the NBC's prompt rejection of a competing mission board, the CBF, in 1947, sponsored the establishment of the Conservative Baptist Association of America (CBA of A), operating outside the NBC. The Conservative Baptist Home Mission Society (CBHMS) emerged during 1948-50. Meanwhile, the CBA of A's Constitution and early promotional literature were sending mixed messages regarding its position on ecclesiastical separation. The Constitution's Preamble condemned the notion of an "inclusive missionary policy" and warned that God would withhold His blessings from any "Baptist support of an affiliation with apostate ecumenical organizations."[1341] Likewise, in its pamphlet *The CBA – Its Mission*, the Association tried to assure everyone that its purpose was to build "upon a thoroughly biblical basis, un-mixed with liberals and liberalism and those who are content to walk in fellowship with unbelief and inclusivism."[1342] On the other hand, Article IV of the Association's Constitution assures that its "affiliates ... shall consist of ... autonomous Baptist churches without regard to other affiliations."[1343] This allowed for dual membership, which appealed to NBC churches desiring a conservative affiliation, without losing their properties for deserting the Convention.[1344] Thus, Article IV opened the doors for non-sep-

---

[1341] *Constitution and Historical Summary of the Conservative Baptist Association of America* (CBA of A, n.d.), booklet; Fred Moritz, *Now is the Time: A History of Baptist World Mission* (North Fort Myers, FL: Faithful Life Publishers, 2011), 124; and G. Archer Weniger, "The Conservative Baptist Association—A Separatist Movement," *Central C. B. Quarterly*, Winter 1960, 25-26.

[1342] Moritz, *Now is the Time: A History of Baptist World Mission*, 124.

[1343] Bruce L. Shelley, *A History of Conservative Baptists*, 3rd ed. (Wheaton, IL: Conservative Baptist Press, 1981), 56, 91.

[1344] Robert Irving Johnson, "An Investigation of the Abandonment of Certain Historic Baptist Principles by the Northern Baptist Convention in Court Cases against Local Churches" (BD thesis, Central Baptist Theological

aratists to move in and mold the movement's ideologies, contradicting its stated purpose of existence.

After the organization of the CBA of A, many assumed (and some hoped) that the Conservative Baptist Fellowship would simply die. Instead, the CBF obtained a voice of vigor in its research secretary, Chester E. Tulga (1896–1976),[1345] editor of CBF *News Letter* (1945–54). Providing life-preserving, financial support to the CBF, Tulga's paperback "Case" books sold by the millions. Their topics included *The Case against Modernism in Foreign Missions* (1950) and *The Case for the Virgin Birth of Christ* (1950). Tulga wrote at least sixteen Case books and twenty additional titles, including *Studies in Romans* and *The Foreign Missions Controversy in the Northern Baptist Convention 1919–1949*. Due to his well-documented exposure of liberalism within the NBC and of compromise within the CBA of A, Tulga and the CBF drew sharp criticism from both groups. In 1955, the CBF took a consistent separatist position by breaking ties with its characteristically anti-separatist, "New Evangelical" daughter — the CBA of A.

In 1953, the CBA of A adopted its Portland Manifesto,[1346] a proposal to practice biblical separation in its appointment of board members. In practice, however, they largely ignored the Manifesto from the start. In 1962, the CBA of A officially rejected its stated purpose of providing "a fellowship of churches and individuals upon a thoroughly biblical basis, unmixed with liberals and liberalism and those who are content to walk in fellowship with unbelief and inclusivism."[1347] That same year, the controversy exploded at several of the state associational

---

Seminary, Minneapolis, 1963). For other examples of property losses, see John Ballentine and Wellie Midgley, *A Light in the Darkness: A History of the Minnesota Baptist Association 1859–1982* (Minneapolis: North Star Baptist Press, 1983), 67.

[1345] See Kenneth William Rhodes, "Ambivalent Fundamentalist: The Life and Ministry of Rev. Chester E. Tulga" (PhD diss., University of Akron, 2001); and "Chester Tulga: The Convicting Conscience of Conservative Baptists," *Frontline Magazine* (May-June 1998): 15–17.

[1346] For the text of the Portland Manifesto, see Moritz, *Now is the Time: A History of Baptist World Mission*, 33–34.

[1347] Ibid., 124.

meetings. At the annual meeting of the CBA of Colorado, the deep division between Fundamentalists and New Evangelicals was particularly apparent. Edward J. (Ed) Nelson (b. 1923), of Denver's South Sheridan Baptist Church, led his congregation out of the Conservative Baptist movement, and large numbers of other churches would take the same course. In Atlantic City, 1963, the CBA of A and its agencies formally repudiated their Portland Manifesto and openly committed themselves to the New Evangelical cause.[1348] Their schools included Denver Conservative Baptist Theological Seminary (now Denver Seminary), Western Baptist Theological Seminary (now Western Seminary) in Portland, Oregon, and Southwestern Conservative Baptist Bible College (now Arizona Christian College), in Phoenix. With declining influence, the CBA of A (now CBAmerica) has become increasingly inter-denominational. The CBFMS is now WorldVenture, and small ministries, such as Missions Door, have replaced the CBHMS. CBAmerica maintains its ties with the National Association of Evangelicals.

Prior to the 1950s, the terms *evangelical* and *conservative* were virtually synonymous with *Fundamentalism*. Such is no longer the case. While all Fundamentalists are evangelical and conservative, not all evangelicals and conservatives are Fundamentalists. One might be an apologist for sound doctrine, even for the historic "fundamentals," without being a *Fundamentalist*. A Fundamentalist is both an apologist, who can explain the truth, and a polemicist who, being "separated unto the gospel of God" (Rom. 1:1*b*), compassionately stands up and welds the spiritual sword in defense of the faith. To protect their identity, Fundamentalist entities would drop the word *Conservative* from their names. In 1961, for instance, the CBF established the separatist, World Conservative Baptist Mission, known since 1966 as Baptist World Mission.[1349] Likewise, in 1967, the CBF, under the leadership of its president, G. Archer Weniger, dropped the word *Conservative* and renamed itself the

---

[1348] Ernest Pickering, *Betrayal on the Boardwalk: An Analysis of the Annual Meeting of CBA Atlantic City, May 23–28, 1963* (Minneapolis: Central Baptist Seminary, n.d.), 1 (mimeographed).

[1349] See the history by Moritz, *Now is the Time: A History of Baptist World Mission*.

Fundamental Baptist Fellowship (FBF). Many regretted that the FBF chose the word *Fundamental* rather than its original, militant label *Fundamentalist*.

G. Archer Weniger (1915–82) had trained at the University of Minnesota (*cum laude*) and in Northwestern Theological Seminary, founded in Minneapolis, in 1935, by W. B. Riley. Weniger received his ordination at First Baptist, Minneapolis, under Riley's ministry. Besides serving a forty-year pastorate (1942–82) at Foothill Baptist, in Castro Valley, California, Weniger served as editor of the *CBF Information Bulletin* (1957–62) and president of the FF, CBF, and FBF (1964–77). As a separatist, Weniger was editor of *The Blu-Print*, a periodical that for years warned Baptists of New Evangelical compromise and apostasy. As a Fundamentalist, Weniger helped establish San Francisco Baptist Theological Seminary (SFBTS), in 1958, at Hamilton Square Baptist Church (est. 1881).[1350] His older brother, Arno Q. Weniger Sr. (1905–95), during his thirty-five-year pastorate at Hamilton Square, served as the first president of SFBTS.[1351] Since 1977, David C. Innes (b. 1940) has served the Hamilton Square pastorate. During 1983–90, Innes served also as Seminary president.[1352] During its thirty-two years of existence (1958–90), SFBTS educated scores of Christian leaders.

As a fellowship of individuals, rather than churches, the FBF, in 2001, renamed itself the Fundamental Baptist Fellowship International (FBFI). In 2017, the FBFI began operating under the name Foundations Baptist Fellowship International (FBFI). Its *FrontLine* magazine is a quality, bimonthly publication. With a conservative statement of faith (including the pretribulation

---

[1350] "G. Archer Weniger: A Separatist Baptist Bulldog," *Frontline Magazine* (May–June 1998): 18–19; and David C. Innes, *The Little Church of Hamilton Square: A Grand History of 120 Years: Hamilton Square Baptist Church, San Francisco, California*, 2nd ed. (Anaheim: Printed by Pace Publication Art, 2003).

[1351] For more on FBFI history, see Beale, *In Pursuit of Purity*, 190–208, 289–301; and Philip Dale Mitchell, "Come Out from among Them and Be Ye Separate: A History of the Fundamental Baptist Fellowship" (PhD diss., University of Colorado, 1991).

[1352] With the addition of a college during its last decade, the institution was known as The Baptist College and Graduate School of the West.

Rapture), the FBFI endeavors to perpetuate the Baptist heritage. Besides sixteen regional meetings, the FBFI hosts national and international meetings.[1353] The FBFI Commission is a Chaplaincy Endorsing Agency approved by the Department of Defense.

The General Association of Regular Baptist Churches (GARBC)

An executive member of the Baptist Bible Union (BBU) and leading separatist of Michigan, Oliver W. Van Osdel (1846-1935), of Wealthy Street Baptist Church, in Grand Rapids,[1354] initiated the formation of the GARBC. The GARBC originated at the BBU's final meeting, held during May 15-18, 1932, in Chicago's Belden Avenue Baptist Church. Emboldened by Van Osdel, host pastor Howard C. Fulton (1891-1951) chaired the meeting, and the group of about thirty-five messengers, representing some twenty-two churches from eight states, adopted its new name, the General Association of Regular Baptist Churches. Thus, the old BBU gave way to a new organization that, in 1938, would declare a complete separatist stance.[1355] The GARBC elected Harry G. Hamilton (1886-1978), pastor of First Baptist Church, Buffalo, New York, as its first president (1932-33). Hamilton soon became editor of the Association's magazine, known since 1935 as the *Baptist Bulletin*. Pastor Earle Griffith, from Erie, Pennsylvania, served as the Association's

---

[1353] For the Constitution and Articles of Faith of the Foundations Baptist Fellowship International, see http://www.fbfi.org/.

[1354] The church has been Wealthy "Park" Baptist Church since 1988, when it moved into suburban Grand Rapids. David Otis Fuller (1903-88), successor to Van Osdel, served the pastorate here for forty years. Although Fuller held a KJV Only position, the GARBC never endorsed it. In 1941, Fuller founded a school later named Grand Rapids Baptist College and Seminary — renamed Cornerstone University in 1999 as an interdenominational institution.

[1355] *The Position of the General Association of Regular Baptist Churches on Separation* (pamphlet published by the GARBC); see also Paul R. Jackson, *The Position, Attitude, and Objectives of Biblical Separation* (Chicago: General Association of Regular Baptist Churches, n.d.). This was the keynote address at the twenty-seventh annual conference of the GARBC in Columbus, Ohio, May 12-16, 1958 (pamphlet).

second president (1933–34).[1356] In 1934, Robert T. (Bob) Ketcham (1889–1978) became the third president,[1357] and the Association reelected him in 1935, 1936, and 1937. Having witnessed the dangers of a "one-man affair," such as the enterprise that had developed around J. Frank Norris,[1358] Ketcham proposed that a representative council would best serve an association of churches.[1359] Thus, in 1938, with Ketcham's carefully prepared proposal in place, the offices of president, vice president, and secretary-treasurer gave way to a Council of Fourteen.[1360] In addition, the Association embraced a full, Fundamentalist position on ecclesiastical separation.[1361]

Bob Ketcham had experienced conversion to Christ on February 16, 1910, at the age of twenty. In 1919, the year Ketcham began his pastorate at First Baptist of Butler, Pennsylvania, the NBC launched its New World Movement, with emphasis on the Social Gospel. Ketcham expressed opposition to the movement, in *A Statement of the First Baptist Church, Butler, Pennsylvania, with Reference to the New World Movement and the $100,000,000 Drive*. The booklet created a sensation. Before the end of 1920, more than two hundred thousand copies had spread over the country. This not only worked as a major factor in the

---

[1356] Histories of the GARBC include Kevin Bauder and Robert Delnay, *One in Hope and Doctrine: Origins of Baptist Fundamentalism 1870–1950* (Schaumburg, IL: Regular Baptist Press, 2014); Merle R. Hull, *What a Fellowship! The First Fifty Years of the GARBC* (Schaumburg, IL: Regular Baptist Press, 1981); Calvin Odell, *The General Association of Regular Baptists and Its Attendant Movement* (Salem, OR: Western Baptist Bible Press, 1975); Joseph M. Stowell, *Background and History of the General Association of Regular Baptist Churches* (Hayward, CA: J. F. May Press, 1949); Curtis Wayne Whiteman, "The General Association of Regular Baptist Churches, 1932–1970" (PhD diss., Saint Louis University, 1982); and Paul N. Tassell, *Quest for Faithfulness: The Account of a Unique Fellowship of Churches* (Schaumburg, IL: Regular Baptist Press, 1991). Tassell argues for a euphemistic view of separation (e.g., 355–62).

[1357] J. Murray Murdoch, *Portrait of Obedience: The Biography of Robert T. Ketcham* (Schaumburg, IL: Regular Baptist Press, 1979).

[1358] Ibid., 177; and Bauder and Delnay, *One in Hope and Doctrine*, 254.

[1359] The late Oliver W. Van Osdel had expressed the same general pattern.

[1360] The Council has increased to eighteen. See *How the General Association of Regular Baptist Churches Operates* (pamphlet published by the GARBC).

[1361] Bauder and Delnay, *One in Hope and Doctrine*, 225, 243, 247ff.

Convention's abandonment of the New World Movement, it established the young pastor as an articulate representative of Fundamentalism. Ketcham had participated in the early Fundamentalist Fellowship. In 1923, he had addressed the organizational meeting of the BBU, under the big tent in Kansas City. At the organization of the GARBC, in 1932,[1362] Ketcham was just beginning his pastorate at Central Baptist Church, Gary, Indiana.[1363] During the rest of his life, he would serve the GARBC, as author, editor of the *Baptist Bulletin*, national representative, and national consultant. In 1949, he published his widely circulated booklet, *The Answer*, an exposé of modernism in the NBC.[1364] Ketcham suffered ongoing health problems, including multiple corneal transplants in 1946, and a heart attack in 1959. Several strokes led to his death in 1978. His life had personified loyalty and consistent commitment to Christ.

Since 1973, the GARBC has operated with a Council of Eighteen. The Association keeps a church directory, but, to emphasize the autonomy of the local churches, the directory avoids the word *membership*. Each GARBC church is entitled to send six messengers to the annual meetings. The churches nominate the Council members and elect six members annually to a three-year term. Prompted by controversy over potential conflict of interest in allowing agency personnel to serve on the Council of Eighteen, the GARBC, in 2000, ended its longtime system of "approving" mission boards and academic institutions.

In 2006, the GARBC severed ties with Cedarville

[1362] *The Necessity for the Formation of the General Association of Regular Baptist Churches* (pamphlet published by the GARBC); see also *What is the General Association of Regular Baptist Churches?* (pamphlet published by the GARBC).

[1363] Ketcham's predecessor at Central Baptist in Gary, Indiana, was William Ward Ayer, who recommended Ketcham to the church. Over his lifetime, Ketcham served seven pastorates: (1) First Baptist, Roullette, PA; (2) First Baptist, Brookville, PA; (3) First Baptist, Butler, PA; (4) First Baptist, Niles, OH; (5) First Baptist, Elyria, OH; (6) Central Baptist, Gary, IN; and (7) Walnut Street Baptist, Waterloo, IA.

[1364] Cf. Ketcham, *God's Provision for Normal Christian Living*; *Old Testament Pictures of New Testament Truth*; *I Shall Not Want*; *Boxes, Bottles, and Books at the Judgment Seat of Christ*, and more.

University—the representative institution of the Southern Baptist State Convention of Baptists in Ohio.[1365] Many viewed such action as consistent with the Constitution's stipulation that the GARBC will accept into its fellowship only those churches that "are not in fellowship or cooperation with any local, state, or national convention, association, or group, which permits the presence of liberals, liberalism (modernists or apostates)."[1366] In 2017, the GARBC Annual Conference resumed all former ties with Cedarville University.

In addition to its conservative Articles of Faith, ranging from a literal account of creation to a pretribulation Rapture,[1367] the GARBC also seeks to support our Baptist heritage. Their home office is in Arlington Heights, Illinois, where its ministries include the Regular Baptist Press, Gospel Literature Services, *Baptist Bulletin*, the Baptist Builders Club, Talents for Christ, the International Partnership of Fundamental Baptist Ministries, and the Regular Baptist Chaplaincy Ministries.

The Minnesota Baptist Association (MBA)

In 1897, William B. Riley (1861–1947) became pastor of First Baptist, Minneapolis, where, five years later, with seven students, he established Northwestern Bible and Missionary Training

---

[1365] See http://www.sbc.net/colleges/; and *Baptist Bulletin* (July/August 2017): 1.

[1366] Constitution of the GARBC (Article 4), in *2015–16 GARBC Church Directory*, 15; see also George Houghton, "Are Conservative Southern Baptists Fundamentalists?" *Faith Pulpit*, January/February 2004; Myron Houghton, "Secondary Ecclesiastical Separation," *Faith Pulpit*, November 1, 2003); Myron Houghton, "Why I am a Regular Baptist," *Baptist Bulletin*, January/February 2015, 50–53 (digital edition); George Houghton, "The GARBC: A Rich History and Heritage," Parts 1 and 2, *Faith Pulpit*, March 1, 2004 and April 1, 2004, a publication of Faith Baptist Theological Seminary, Ankeny, Iowa; and Paul R. Jackson, *The Position, Attitudes, and Objectives of Biblical Separation* (Schaumburg, IL: General Association of Regular Baptist Churches, n.d.), pamphlet.

[1367] Articles of Faith, in *2015–16 GARBC Church Directory*, 19–21; see also Robert G. Delnay, *A History of the GARBC Confession of Faith*, a paper presented at Baptist Bible College and School of Theology, Tuesday evening, March 15, 1983 (Schaumburg, IL: Regular Baptist Press, 1983).

School, which soon became Northwestern College.[1368] By 1935-36, when the college had grown to well over five hundred students, Riley further enhanced its significance with the addition of Northwestern Theological Seminary. During the 1940s, the college added a liberal arts program and a conservatory of music. The institution's composite name was "Northwestern Schools." With Fundamentalist graduates of Northwestern occupying the pastorates of over half the Baptist churches of the state,[1369] in 1948 (the year after Riley's death), the Minnesota Baptist Convention (MBC) voted to leave the Northern Baptist Convention.[1370]

Riley had retired from his forty-five-year pastorate, in 1943, only four years before his death. During his ministry, the church had grown from a membership of 585 to 3,600. He had received national acclaim in numerous, successful public debates with noted evolutionists.[1371] So skillful was Riley that he had difficulty finding opponents who would debate. Clarence Darrow forfeited a debate with Riley four days before it was to take place in Denver. William Jennings Bryan once described Riley as "the greatest statesman in the American pulpit."[1372] Riley had not only fought against modernism within the NBC,[1373] he had provided dynamic leadership to the World's Christian

---

[1368] Evangelist Billy Graham served during 1948-52 as Riley's successor to the presidency of Northwestern (renamed in 2015 the University of Northwestern—St. Paul). See also Dell G. Johnson, "W. B. Riley and the Developing New Evangelicalism," *Central Bible Quarterly*, Fall 1978, 2-28; idem, "Fundamentalist Responses in Minnesota to the Developing New Evangelicalism" (ThD diss., Central Baptist Theological Seminary, Minneapolis, 1982), 215-99.

[1369] Ballentine and Midgley, *A Light in the Darkness: A History of the Minnesota Baptist Association 1859-1982*, 48. See also David Becklund, "A History of the Minnesota Baptist Convention" (BD thesis, Central Baptist Theological Seminary, Minneapolis, 1967).

[1370] Larry Dean Pettegrew, *The History of Pillsbury Baptist Bible College* (Owatonna, MN: Pillsbury Press, 1981), 87.

[1371] William B. Gatewood Jr., ed., *Controversy in the Twenties: Fundamentalism, Modernism, and Evolution* (Nashville: Vanderbilt University Press, 1969), 157-61.

[1372] Quoted in Russell, *Voices of American Fundamentalism*, 80.

[1373] William Bell Riley, *The Menace of Modernism* (New York: Christian Alliance Publishing Company, 1917); see also Bruce Shelley, "William Bell Riley: A Champion of Fundamentalism," *Conservative Baptist*, Spring 1976, 3.

Fundamentals Association, the Fundamentalist Fellowship, and the Baptist Bible Union. He had authored some sixty-five books, in addition to his forty-volume *Bible of the Expositor and the Evangelist*, plus thirty-seven serial booklets and pamphlets. For many years, Riley had edited his Northwestern *Pilot* and still found time to conduct evangelistic campaigns around the world.[1374] A guiding hand in his own Minnesota Baptist Convention, Riley grieved over the liberal drift of many Northern Baptist missionaries, but he was reluctant to give up on the convention. Replacing the word *Convention* with *Association*, by 1973, the Minnesota Baptist Convention would become the Minnesota Baptist Association. Its periodical is *North Star Baptist*.[1375] Robert Delnay suggests four reasons why W. B. Riley (1861–1947) remained in the NBC for so long:

> He regarded the convention with something like loathing, but stayed in it (1) in order not to abandon the works begun by orthodox men; (2) in order not to abandon the faithful missionaries under the American Baptist Foreign Mission Society; (3) in order not to injure pastors and churches by an abortive withdrawal movement; and (4) in order to await a great realignment, interdenominational in scope, of fundamentalists and against modernists, and he preferred to give his energies to that hope. On the other hand, late in life Riley helped dissociate the Minnesota Baptist Convention from the national convention.[1376]

In 1957, the Minnesota Baptist Convention established Pillsbury Baptist Bible College, in Owatonna, Minnesota. When Pillsbury opened its first semester, its interim president was Richard V. Clearwaters (1900–96),[1377] pastor of Fourth Baptist,

---

[1374] See William Bell Riley, *The Perennial Revival: A Plea for Evangelism* (Philadelphia: American Baptist Publication Society, 1916).
[1375] http://www.mbaoc.net/.
[1376] Robert George Delnay, *A History of the Baptist Bible Union*, 61–62.
[1377] Clearwaters' autobiography, *The Upward Road* (Minneapolis: Richard Clearwater c/o Central Seminary, 1991); and Michael H. Windsor, "Valiant for Truth: The Ministry of Richard Volley Clearwaters" (ThD diss., Central Baptist Theological Seminary of Minnesota, 1991).

Minneapolis (1940–82) and founding president of Central Baptist Theological Seminary (1956–86). Fourth Baptist owns and operates the Seminary. Pillsbury Baptist Bible College, before the end of its first semester, had elected its first resident president, Monroe Parker (1909–94), an evangelist and former administrator at Bob Jones University.[1378] Parker's successor, in 1965, was B. Myron Cedarholm (1915–97), who had just resigned as national director of the Conservative Baptist Association of America. Clearwaters took Pillsbury's reins again, in 1968,[1379] when Cedarholm left to establish Maranatha Baptist Bible College (MBBC), in Watertown, Wisconsin.[1380] After fifty-one years of steadfast service, Pillsbury ceased operation, in 2008. MBBC is now Maranatha Baptist University, with over forty accredited degrees, plus a theological seminary.

The Independent Baptist Fellowship of North America (IBFNA)

Established in 1990, as a Fundamentalist fellowship of pastors and laypersons, the Independent Baptist Fellowship of North America exists for a fivefold purpose:

A. To establish a nationwide fundamentalist, separatist association of Baptists to provide fellowship, counsel, a uniform standard of biblical faith and practice, and a vehicle for cooperation in promoting the evangelistic, church-planting and educational goals of the fellowship; and further

B. To emphasize the biblical teaching on separation from unbelievers in religious work (primary separation) and separation from believers who ignore or disobey the Bible's teaching of primary separation (secondary separation); and

C. To raise a standard for personal separation from worldliness

---

[1378] See Monroe "Monk" Parker, *Through Sunshine and Shadows: My First 77 Years* (Murfreesboro, TN: Sword of the Lord Publishers, 1987).

[1379] Stephan M. Mattsen, "B. Myron Cedarholm: Man of Character, Man of God," *Frontline Magazine* (May-June 1999): 7–8; cf. Pettegrew, *The History of Pillsbury Baptist Bible College*, 148–56; and Windsor, "Valiant for Truth," 225–32.

[1380] See Bob Whitmore, "The Cedarholm/Clearwaters Conflict," *Frontline Magazine* (May-June 1999): 11–12.

and worldly practices reflecting the truth that believers are new creatures in Christ; and

D. To provide information on current issues facing fundamental Baptists and others; and

E. To produce literature for churches and pastors who desire such materials.[1381]

The IBFNA defines its aim as being a pure witness to the glory of God:

> The IBFNA is an independent, fundamental, missionary, Bible honoring, Christ exalting, separatist fellowship of Baptists. If you know what those words connote, then they identify the things for which we stand. We are unashamedly surrendered to the purpose of raising up a witness to the reliability of God's Word, to the saving power of the Person of Jesus Christ, and to the necessity of obedience to Him as our Lord and Savior into Whose image He is ultimately conforming us. We did not become this when we formed the Independent Baptist Fellowship of North America. That's what we were from the beginning and that's the reason it was formed....[1382]

The IBFNA Articles of Faith include "Ecclesiastical Separation, whereby we preach against apostasy, and withdraw from brethren who enter into memberships, affiliations and fellowships (including evangelistic crusades, youth movements, mission agencies, and schools) which seek to unite separatist fundamentalists with those who deny Biblical doctrines, including those who do not obey the Biblical teaching on separation" (Article F).

[1381] http://www.ibfna.org/v3/index.php.

[1382] Ibid. On the origin of the IBFNA, see *What Happened to the GARBC at Niagara Falls?* by L. Duane Brown, Ralph G. Colas, Richard A. Harris, and Jack Keep. The booklet is available from the IBFNA office. See Ernest Pickering, "Implementing Separatist Convictions," in *Biblical Separation: The Struggle for a Pure Church*, 2nd ed., with Myron Houghton (Schaumburg, IL: Regular Baptist Press, 2008), 275–98.

Conclusion

As with all such movements, Fundamentalist Baptists made mistakes. Many learned from them. Rather than being suspicious of scholarship, many are promoting and providing quality academics. To safeguard against searching for hidden codes and allegory, they approach Scripture as literal, except where the text or context indicates otherwise. Many are taking seriously the Christian duty to be salt and light in the world. Rather than resting ecclesiastical separation upon "guilt" by association, they recognize the importance of "identification" by association. They insist that leaders define themselves by those they endorse. The driving force for many remnants of Fundamentalist Baptists today is that spiritual oneness can be based only upon sound doctrine and practice; therefore, it is better to be divided by truth than united in error.

Select Bibliography for Further Reading

Ballentine, John, and Wellie Midgley. *A Light in the Darkness: A History of the Minnesota Baptist Association 1859–1982.* Minneapolis: North Star Baptist Press, 1983.

Bauder, Kevin, and Robert Delnay. *One in Hope and Doctrine: Origins of Baptist Fundamentalism 1870–1950.* Schaumburg, IL: Regular Baptist, 2014.

Beale, David. *In Pursuit of Purity: American Fundamentalism Since 1850.* Greenville: BJU Press, 1986. The 2nd edition is forthcoming.

Clearwaters, Richard V. *The Great Conservative Baptist Compromise.* Minneapolis: Central Seminary Press, n.d.

_____. *The Upward Road.* Minneapolis: Richard Clearwaters c/o Central Seminary, 1991.

Delnay, Robert George. "A History of the Baptist Bible Union." ThD diss., Dallas Theological Seminary, 1963.

Hankins, Barry. *God's Rascal: J. Frank Norris and the Beginnings of Southern Fundamentalism.* Lexington, KY: The University Press of Kentucky, 1996.

Hull, Merle R. *What a Fellowship! The First Fifty Years of the GARBC.* Schaumburg, IL: Regular Baptist Press, 1981.

Mitchell, Philip Dale. "Come Out from among Them and Be Ye Separate: A History of the Fundamental Baptist Fellowship." PhD diss., University of Colorado, 1991.

Moritz, Fred. *Now is the Time: A History of Baptist World Mission.* North Fort Myers, FL: Faithful Life Publishers, 2011.

Murdoch, J. Murray. *Portrait of Obedience: The Biography of Robert T. Ketcham.*

Schaumburg, IL: Regular Baptist Press, 1979.

Parker, Monroe "Monk." *Through Sunshine and Shadows: My First 77 Years.* Murfreesboro, TN: Sword of the Lord Publishers, 1987.

Pettegrew, Larry Dean. *The History of Pillsbury Baptist Bible College.* Owatonna, MN: Pillsbury Press, 1981.

Pickering, Ernest. *Biblical Separation: The Struggle for a Pure Church.* 2nd ed. with Myron Houghton. Schaumburg, IL: Regular Baptist Press, 2008.

Priest, Gerald L. "T. T. Shields the Fundamentalist: Man of Controversy." *Detroit Baptist Seminary Journal* 10 (2005): 69–101.

Rhodes, Kenneth William. "Ambivalent Fundamentalist: The Life and Ministry of Rev. Chester E. Tulga." PhD diss., University of Akron, 2001.

Riley, Marie Acomb. *The Dynamic of a Dream: The Life Story of Dr. William B. Riley.* Grand Rapids: Eerdmans, 1938.

Russell, C. Allyn. "J. Frank Norris: Violent Fundamentalist," in *Voices of American Fundamentalism*, 20–46. Philadelphia: Westminster Press, 1976.

———. "William Bell Riley: Organizational Fundamentalist," in *Voices of American Fundamentalism*, 79–106. Philadelphia: Westminster Press, 1976.

Shelley, Bruce L. *A History of Conservative Baptists.* 3rd ed. Wheaton, IL: Conservative Baptist Press, 1981.

Wardin, Albert W. Jr. *The Twelve Baptist Tribes in the USA: A Historical and Statistical Analysis.* Nashville: Fields Publishing, for Baptist History and Heritage Society, 2007.

Windsor, Michael H. "Valiant for Truth: The Ministry of Richard Volley Clearwaters." ThD diss., Central Baptist Theological Seminary of Minnesota, 1991.

Chapter 20

The Southern Baptist Convention: Its Strong Foundation, Rise of Liberalism, and Conservative Resurgence

Background and Early History of the SBC

The Southern Baptist Convention (SBC) originated as an 1845 split from the Northern Baptists. While many factors—social, economic, political, and religious—contributed to the separation, three factors deserve special mention. First, while Baptists in the South favored more centralization in their organized work, Baptists in the North favored a loose structure of autonomous societies. Second, most Baptists in the South, with their revivalist-Separatist heritage, favored a more aggressive evangelism than those in the North. Finally, there was the issue of slavery, which served as the catalyst to the division. The immediate issue involved the question of whether Baptist mission societies would approve slaveholders as missionary candidates. As a test case, in 1844, Georgia Baptists recommended to the Home Mission Society, a slaveholder, James E. Reeves, as a missionary to the Cherokee Indians. The Board rejected Reeves by a seven-to-five vote. Alabama Baptists soon followed up by recommending a slaveholder to the Foreign Mission Society. When the Board rejected the Alabama appeal, Virginia Baptists called for a regional meeting to consult on these issues. On May 8, 1845, the southern brethren met in First Baptist Church, Augusta, Georgia, and established the Southern Baptist Convention with two mission boards—home and foreign.[1383] Today, its North American Mission Board is in Alpharetta, Georgia, and its International Mission Board is in Richmond, Virginia.

William Bullein (W. B.) Johnson (1782-1862) became the first SBC president. Converted in a revival meeting, in 1804 at Beaufort, South Carolina, and trained for the ministry at Brown University,[1384] W. B. Johnson founded numerous churches and served pastorates in key areas across South Carolina, including Edgefield, Columbia, and Greenville. In 1831, an unforgettable season of revival emerged from his ministry at Edgefield. As a pioneer of higher education for women, Johnson assisted female schools in Greenville, Edgefield, and even Savannah, Georgia. He served as chancellor (1853-58) of Johnson Female University, in Anderson, South Carolina. A close friend of Luther Rice, Johnson was the only person to attend the initial meetings of both the Triennial Convention (1814) and the SBC (1845). He was the only person to serve as president of both conventions—the Triennial (1841-44) and the SBC (1845-51). Succeeding Richard Furman to the presidency of the South Carolina State Convention, Johnson, in 1826, became one of the founders of Furman Academy and Theological Institution (later Furman University). Furman's original campus was in Edgefield. Over the next three decades, the campus would change locations three times, finally settling in Greenville in 1851. The following year, under the direction of James P. Boyce, the school established its theology department.

Southern Baptist Theological Seminary (est. 1859)

Originating in Greenville, South Carolina, with twenty-six

[1383] Jesse C. Fletcher, *The Southern Baptist Convention: A Sesquicentennial History* (Nashville: B&H Publishers, 1994); and William Wright Barnes, *The Southern Baptist Convention 1845-1953* (Nashville: Broadman, 1954).

[1384] See Hortense C. Woodson, *Giant in the Land: The Life of William B. Johnson: First President of the Southern Baptist Convention 1845-1851* (1950; expanded reprint, Springfield, MO: Particular Baptist Press, 2005).

students,[1385] Southern Baptist Theological Seminary was the Convention's flagship seminary, intricately interwoven within the fabric of the Convention's earliest history. The seminary remained in Greenville for eighteen years, before moving to Louisville, Kentucky, in 1877, with eighty-nine students. In Greenville, the original faculty—James P. Boyce, William Williams, John A. Broadus, and Basil Manly Jr.—were spiritual and scholarly giants, who provided dignity and poise to the institution's character. All four stood for the full inspiration, total inerrancy, and absolute authority of the Scriptures.

James Petigru Boyce (1827–88)

Converted and baptized, in 1846, during a revival service at First Baptist, Charleston, James P. Boyce[1386] received his education at Charleston College (1843–45), Brown University (1845–47) (under Francis Wayland), and Princeton Seminary (1849–51) under Charles Hodge. Two years after completing his theological training, Boyce accepted the pastorate of First Baptist, Columbia, South Carolina. Two years later, in 1855, he accepted the professorship of Theology at Furman University, in Greenville. In his inaugural address, titled *Three Changes in Theological Institutions* (1856),[1387] Boyce set forth strong convictions on the necessity of a doctrinal statement for combating heresy and defending the faith within theological institutions. In 1859, Furman University generously released James Boyce, its theology department, and its entire theological library, as the seed of a new entity—the Southern Baptist Theological

---

[1385] See Gregory A. Wills, *Southern Baptist Theological Seminary, 1859–2009* (New York: Oxford University Press, 2009); and John R. Sampey, *Southern Baptist Theological Seminary: The First Thirty Years 1859–1889* (Baltimore: Wharton, Barron, and Co.), 1890.

[1386] See Broadus, *Memoir of James Petigru Boyce*; and Thomas J. Nettles, *James Petigru Boyce: A Southern Baptist Statesman* (Phillipsburg, NJ: P&R Publishing, 2009).

[1387] James P. Boyce, *Three Changes in Theological Institutions*, "an inaugural address delivered before the Board of Trustees of the Furman University, the night before the Annual Commencement, July 31, 1856" (Greenville, SC: C. J. Elford's Book and Job Press, 1856).

Seminary. Boyce became a key founder. Besides teaching courses in theology, homiletics, New Testament, and church history, Boyce served as the first "chairman" of Southern Seminary's original faculty. The trustees would change the title to "president" the year of his death. Boyce also served as president of the SBC from 1872 to 1879, and again in 1888. His published sermon, *The Uses and Doctrine of the Sanctuary: Making Sacred Our Houses of Worship* (1859),[1388] portrays his practical wisdom. His *Abstract of Systematic Theology* (1887)[1389] portrays his doctrinal wisdom, as he points to Scripture as the infallible authority on every doctrine.

William Williams (1821–77)

A native of Georgia, William Williams became a Christian, in 1837, and united with a Baptist Church at Athens, Georgia. Graduating from the University of Georgia, in 1840, he married Ruth Bell in 1845, earned a law degree at Harvard in 1847, and began preaching in 1851. In 1856, he succeeded John L. Dagg (1794–1884) as professor of theology at Mercer University, in Georgia. Moving to Southern Seminary in Greenville, in 1859, Williams became professor of Ecclesiastical History, Church Government, and Pastoral Duties. Due to criticism against Williams from Landmark Baptists, in 1872, Boyce transferred Williams to the chair of Systematic Theology, a position he faithfully and effectively served, until tuberculosis took his life, just before the Seminary moved to Kentucky. John Broadus observed that Williams's "legal studies and practice had disciplined his great mental acuteness," so that "he had extraordinary power in the clear and terse statements of truth, and when kindled in preaching or lecturing he spoke with such intensity

---

[1388] Idem, *The Uses and Doctrine of the Sanctuary: Making Sacred Our Houses of Worship*, "a sermon preached September 25th, 1859 at the dedication of the new house of worship of the Baptist church at Columbia, S. C." (Columbia, SC: Steam-Press of Robert M. Stokes, 1859). Among those who participated was W. B. Johnson, founding pastor of this church 1809 11. They had erected their first building in 1811.

[1389] Idem, *Abstract of Systematic Theology* (Philadelphia: American Baptist Publication Society, 1887), 48, 137.

as is rarely equaled." Broadus adds that Williams, "was also a man of great purity of character, certain to command the profoundest respect."[1390]

John Albert Broadus (1827–95)

John Broadus was born into a distinguished family in Culpeper County, Virginia. He became a Christian at about the age of sixteen. In 1850, he received his MA at the University of Virginia and married Maria Harrison, who would bear him three children. She died in 1857. Broadus taught Latin and Greek at the University of Virginia, where he served as pastor of the Charlottesville Baptist Church. Forsaking a promising future in the Old Dominion, Broadus moved to Greenville, South Carolina, in 1859, to help pioneer the founding of Southern Seminary. Here he served as professor of New Testament and Homiletics, from 1859 until his death in 1895, and as president from 1889 to 1895. Southern Seminary held its first commencement, in 1861, just as the Civil War broke out at Fort Sumter. The school immediately closed, and Broadus served as chaplain in Robert E. Lee's army.

After the war, in 1865, the original four professors met to confer over the ominous end of the Seminary's existence. Broadus extinguished all doubts, with these words: "Suppose we quietly agree that the seminary may die, but we'll die first."[1391] The school reopened on November 1, 1865, with seven students. In his Homiletics class, Broadus had only one student, and the student was blind. The carefully-prepared lectures for that blind brother became the basis of Broadus's classic work, *On the Preparation and Delivery of Sermons* (1870).

[1390] John A. Broadus, *Memoir of James Petigru Boyce, D. D., L. L. D.* (Nashville: Sunday-School Board of the Southern Baptist Convention, 1927), 203; see also Wills, *Southern Baptist Theological Seminary*, 46ff. and passim; Sampey, *Southern Baptist Theological Seminary*, 34–36; and *Encyclopedia of Southern Baptists* (Nashville: Broadman, 1958), 2:1503.

[1391] Archibald Thomas Robertson, *Life and Letters of John Albert Broadus*, 6th ed. (Philadelphia: Judson Press, 1938), 214. See also David S. Dockery and Roger D. Duke, eds., *John A. Broadus: A Living Legacy* (Nashville: B&H Publishing Group, 2008).

Many know of Broadus for his well-known *Commentary on the Gospel of Matthew* (1886). He amplifies his defense of Bible inerrancy in his *Three Questions as to the Bible* (1883) and *Paramount and Permanent Authority of the Bible* (1887). Broadus's second wife, Charlotte, bore him five children, including Ella, who would marry her father's successor, as professor of New Testament Interpretation — Archibald Thomas (A. T.) Robertson (1863–1934).

Basil Manly Jr. (1825–92)

Born in Edgefield County, South Carolina, Basil Manly Jr. spent most of his childhood in Charleston, where his father served the pastorate at First Baptist. The boy was twelve years old when the family moved to Tuscaloosa, where his father accepted the presidency of the University of Alabama. Two years later, young Basil enrolled in the University. During his first year there, he became a Christian after reading Jonathan Edwards's autobiography, known as his *Personal Narrative*.[1392] Basil immediately received baptism by immersion and united with the local Baptist church. Four years later, in 1844, he graduated at the top of his class, received a preaching license, and began his theological training at Newton Theological Institution, in Massachusetts. With the North-South division among the Baptists (1845), Manly transferred to the more-serene Princeton Seminary, where he studied under Charles Hodge and, in 1847, received a degree in theological studies.

Prior to his becoming a founder of Southern Seminary, Manly had served several pastorates, including First Baptist, Richmond, Virginia. He had also held the office of president of the Richmond Female Institute. In 1859, Manly became professor of Old Testament Interpretation at Southern. In 1871, he accepted the presidency of Georgetown College, in Kentucky. When Southern Seminary moved to Louisville, in 1877, Manly returned to his old post as professor of Old Testament. He

---

[1392] See William Edward Smallwood, "'The Most Versatile Man': The Life, Ministry, and Piety of Basil Manly Jr." (PhD diss., Southern Baptist Theological Seminary, 2015).

remained at Southern for the remainder of his life. His book, *The Bible Doctrine of Inspiration: Explained and Vindicated* (1888),[1393] is a defense of the infallibility of the original manuscripts of Scripture. Each faculty member, at his inauguration, was required to sign the Seminary's Charter, along with its twenty-article, doctrinal statement—the Abstract of Principles (1858). Basil Manly wrote its first draft, and all four faculty members contributed to the final draft. The first article affirms that "the Scriptures of the Old and New Testaments were given by inspiration of God, and are the only sufficient, certain and authoritative rule of all saving knowledge, faith and obedience." The Charter adds that the trustees will consider any departure from those principles as grounds for resignation or removal. Author of over twenty hymns, Basil Manly compiled the *Baptist Psalmody* (1850), *Baptist Chorals* (1860), and *Manly's Choice* (1891).

Crawford H. Toy (1836–1919)

Upon enrolling in the first class at Southern Seminary, Crawford Toy had already made a profession of faith and received baptism and ordination, under the ministry of John Broadus, at Charlottesville Baptist. Graduating from the University of Virginia with an MA degree, Toy had accepted a teaching position at Albemarle Female Academy, where Broadus chaired the board of trustees. At Southern, Toy excelled in Hebrew, as he sat under the tutelage of Manly and Broadus. During 1866–68, Toy studied at the University of Berlin. In 1869, he returned to Southern Seminary as professor of Old Testament Interpretation and Oriental Languages. Eventually, however, it became obvious to most that Crawford Toy had become "a pronounced evolutionist and Darwinian."[1394] He was now applying higher criticism to Old Testament interpretation. Warned by Boyce and Broadus that he had departed from Southern's Abstract of Principles, Toy submitted his

---

[1393] Basil Manly, *The Bible Doctrine of Inspiration: Explained and Vindicated* (New York: A. C. Armstrong and Son, 1888), 37.
[1394] Broadus, *Memoir of James Petigru Boyce*, 305.

resignation in 1879. The Seminary had now been in Louisville for two years. As Toy stood in the waiting room of the Louisville railway station, Boyce could not withhold his grief. Broadus recalls the scene: "Throwing his left arm around Toy's neck, Dr. Boyce lifted the right arm before him, and said, in a passion of grief, 'Oh, Toy, I would freely give that arm to be cut off if you could be where you were five years ago, and stay there.'"[1395] Crawford Toy soon became professor of Hebrew at Harvard, where he joined the nearby Unitarian church. The Unitarian Sunday School Board published his *History of the Religion of Israel* (1894).

Lottie Moon (1840–1912)

It is difficult to imagine that Crawford Toy had once considered going to Japan as a missionary. Moreover, Crawford and Charlotte (Lottie) Moon, legendary Southern Baptist missionary to China, had once considered marriage. John Broadus had baptized Lottie, during the Revival of 1859, when she was a student in Albemarle Female Institute. Rejecting Crawford's marriage proposal, during the year of his resignation from Southern, Lottie regarded Toy's new theology as untenable. She had carefully read the liberal books that he had recommended to her.

Lottie Moon spent the next forty years in China, and, in 1888, she wrote a desperate appeal for more missionaries, which resulted in the Lottie Moon Christmas Offering for International Missions. A relative asked her, in her later years, if she had ever been in love. Lottie answered, "Yes, but God had first claim on my life, and since the two conflicted, there could be no question about the result."[1396] During one of her deepest trials, Lottie wrote, "I pray that no missionary will

---

[1395] Ibid., 309. Cf. Gregory A. Wills, "Modernism's First Martyr: Crawford H. Toy and the Inspiration Controversy," in *Southern Baptist Theological Seminary, 1859–2009*, 108–49.

[1396] Irwin T. Hyatt Jr., *Our Ordered Lives: Three Nineteenth-Century American Missionaries in East Shantung* (Cambridge: Harvard University Press, 1976), 99.

ever be as lonely as I have been."[1397] When the Chinese suffered famine, she starved along with them until she weighed less than fifty pounds. Returning to America, on Christmas Eve, 1912, seventy-two-year-old Lottie Moon collapsed and died on board the ship, while it was briefly anchored at Kobe, Japan. Her ashes lie buried in Crewe Cemetery, in Crewe, Virginia.

Edgar Y. Mullins (1860-1928)

E. Y. Mullins served as president of Southern Seminary (1899-1928), the Southern Baptist Convention (1921-24), and the Baptist World Alliance (1928). He served Southern Baptist pastorates in Kentucky, Maryland, and Massachusetts. Although Mullins affirmed his belief in Christ's deity, Virgin Birth, miracles, bodily resurrection, and vicarious atonement,[1398] he was conspicuously silent on the inerrancy of the original autographa of Scripture. While claiming a neutral stance on such vital issues as creation versus evolution and of a young versus old earth, Mullins endorsed pro-evolution publications without reservation.[1399]

In 1925, Mullins served on the committee that led the SBC to adopt a modified version of the 1833 New Hampshire Confession, as its first statement of faith, known as "The Baptist Faith and Message" (BFM). It is noteworthy that, while its 2000 revision adds a strong statement embracing inerrancy, none of the three editions of the BFM has included an article on creation or on the general age of the earth. Mullins, though, had been influenced by the pragmatism of the psychologist-philosopher, William James (1842-1910), and by the personalism of

---

[1397] Catherine B. Allen, *The New Lottie Moon Story* (Nashville: Broadman Press, 1980), 275.

[1398] Mullins, "The Testimony of Christian Experience," in *The Fundamentals: A Testimony to the Truth*, 4 vols. ed. R. A. Torrey, A. C. Dixon, et al (1917; repr., Grand Rapids: Baker, 1980-88), 4:314-23.

[1399] William E. Ellis, "The Triumph of Fundamentalism," in *"A Man of Books and a Man of the People": E. Y. Mullins and the Crisis of Moderate Southern Baptist Leadership* (Macon, GA: Mercer University Press, 1985), 185-208; see also Isla May Mullins, *Edgar Young Mullins: An Intimate Biography* (Nashville: Sunday School Board of the Southern Baptist Convention, 1929).

the philosopher, Borden Parker Bowne (1847–1910). Mullins allowed their misguided pragmatism and autonomous personalism to dominate his teachings.[1400] Applied to the Bible, pragmatism is the mindset that the essential significance of the Bible's proclamations emerges from their practical effects within the human experience.

For his systematic theology course, Mullins replaced Boyce's *Abstract of Systematic Theology* (1887) with his own text, *The Christian Religion in Its Doctrinal Expression* (1917), which places heavy emphasis upon experiential theology. Rather than beginning every theological pursuit with a deductive approach, through the precepts of Scripture, Mullins began with an inductive approach, through the lens of experience.[1401] In his method of approaching Scripture, Mullins was liberal, and Southern Seminary utilized his text for over thirty years.[1402] Many who followed Mullins's pragmatic method became theological liberals.

An improper pragmatism inevitably led to a relativism that prompted liberals arbitrarily to equate the liberty of conscience with the priesthood of the believer. The terms *priesthood* and *conscience* are not synonymous. *Priesthood*, made possible by Christ's atoning blood, is the free access that belongs to all believers, by the power of the Holy Spirit, to enter directly into the presence of God in prayer and without the assistance of human, angelic, or iconic mediators (Eph. 2:18–19; Heb. 10:19–25; 1 Peter 2:5). *Conscience*, on the other hand, is the God-given, inward faculty that gages the moral quality of one's willful thoughts and deeds. The violation of one's conscience results in feelings of guilt and remorse. There is universal evidence of a sense of guilt over horrid sins such as murder. Depraved in Adam's fall, however, the conscience can become an incompetent guide if the mind is not biblically informed. For instance,

---

[1400] E. Y. Mullins, "Pragmatism, Humanism, and Personalism—The New Philosophic Movement," *Review and Expositor* 5 (1908): 501–15.

[1401] Mullins, *The Christian Religion in Its Doctrinal Expression* (Philadelphia: Roger Williams Press, 1917), 49–81.

[1402] R. Albert Mohler, "Introduction," to Mullins, *The Axioms of Religion*, ed. R. Albert Mohler, Timothy George, and Denise George (Nashville: B&H Publishers, 1997), 7.

devout Roman Catholics can feel conscience stricken over missing a Mass.

Resting upon E. Y. Mullins's arbitrary merger of freedom of conscience with individual priesthood, liberals appealed to the notion of autonomous individualism. Such individualism places the church member above the authority of pastoral leadership and of doctrinal standards. Such a merger strips local-church leadership of its biblical authority, by ignoring the scriptural command to submit one to another. Rather than providing a license for doctrinal laxity, true liberty provides the local church with freedom to teach the whole counsel of God and to discipline members who fall into heresy or immorality. As Malcom Yarnell observes, "The early Baptists were Christocentric churchmen; Mullins and his disciples are anthropocentric individualists." Between the two, there lies "a world of difference."[1403] Any member who remains in disagreement with his church's doctrinal statement, after conferring with church leaders, has an obligation to withdraw his membership. If he refuses, the church has an obligation, in due process, to remove that person from their rolls. The same principle applies to educational institutions. We will take a birds-eye view of the usage of the term *priesthood* since the New Testament.

In the New Testament, there is no church office of "priest." The word *priest*, corresponding to the Latin *sacerdos*, refers to one who offers sacrifices. Christ abolished the old sacrificial system, all Christians have direct access to God, and Christ alone is our Great High Priest. The New Testament packages the terms *pastor, elder, bishop, shepherd,* and *presbyter* all into a single office.[1404] In three steps, the church Fathers misapplied

---

[1403] Malcolm B. Yarnell III, "Changing Baptist Concepts of Royal Priesthood: John Smyth and Edgar Young Mullins," in Deryck W. Lovegrove, ed., *The Rise of the Laity in Evangelical Protestantism* (London: Routledge, 2002), 249 (236–52); and Gregory A. Wills, "E. Y. Mullins, Southern Seminary, and Progressive Theology," in *Southern Baptist Theological Seminary, 1859–2009*, 230–72.

[1404] For example, in 20:28, he describes them as "bishops" (Gk. overseers), who shepherd the flock: "Take heed therefore unto yourselves, and to all the flock, over [Gk. in] which the Holy Ghost hath made you overseers [Gk. bishops], to feed [Gk. shepherd or pastor] the church of God,

the doctrine of *priesthood*. First, they arbitrarily established a distinct office of "presbyter." Second, they changed the title *presbyter* to *priest*. Third, they required that each ministerial candidate accept ordination as a "priest," before rising to the higher status of "bishop." Each bishop retained the power of the priesthood for the remainder of the life. Such power only increased, as his priesthood duties extended to mediating between God and the people. Bishop Cyprian of Carthage (ca. 200–58) played the major role in setting such a hierarchy in motion.[1405]

The emergence of priestly bishops obliterated the biblical teaching of the priesthood of all believers. By the time of Augustine (354–430), bishops were hearing confessions and forgiving sins. Except for the Church of England, the sixteenth-century Reformation restored the doctrine of the priesthood of all believers. During the next two centuries, Baptists sacrificially recovered the doctrine of soul liberty (freedom of individual conscience) to its biblical essence and application.[1406] In summation, during the modern era, Edgar Y. Mullins and his followers corrupted the doctrines of personal *priesthood* and freedom of *conscience* by equating the two terms, thus creating a priestly, autonomous individualism that covers for heresy and undercuts the true role of the pastor and the local church. Hebrews 13:17 instructs us, "Obey them that have the rule over you, and submit yourselves: for they watch for your souls, as they that must give account, that they may do it with joy, and not with grief: for that is unprofitable for you." Autonomous individualism prompted liberal seminary professors to

---

which he hath purchased with his own blood." Likewise, when Paul left Titus in Crete to "ordain elders in every city" (Titus 1:5), his qualifications for these "elders" (Gk. presbyters) begin with the words, "A bishop [Gk. overseer] must be blameless" (vv. 6–9).

[1405] See David Beale, "The School of Carthage: Cyprian and Sacerdotalism," in *Historical Theology In-Depth* (Greenville, SC: Bob Jones University Press, 2013), 1:183–99; and Colin Bulley, *The Priesthood of Some Believers: Developments from the General to the Special Priesthood in the Christian Literature of the First Three Centuries* (Carlisle, England: Paternoster, 2000).

[1406] Cf. John Quincy Adams, *Baptists the Only Thorough Religious Reformers*, rev. ed. (New York: Sheldon and Co., 1876).

demand "academic freedom," under the guise of a supposed "priestly privilege," whereby they could sign a doctrinal statement in silent reservation concerning any part of it.[1407]

Ellis A. Fuller (1891–1950)

Ellis Fuller, Southern Seminary president (1942–50), brought in George A. Buttrick, in 1943, to present the E. Y. Mullins Lectures. Buttrick was the widely-known, liberal pastor of Madison Avenue Presbyterian Church, in New York City. When Buttrick became general editor of the twelve-volume *Interpreter's Bible*, Ellis Fuller served as consulting editor, then endorsed and promoted the set among Southern Baptists. The first volume establishes the tone for the entire set, by claiming, "The evidence is clear" that the books of the Bible "contain inaccuracies, inconsistencies, interpolations, omissions, over-statements, and so forth."[1408] The authors depict the God of Genesis as a local deity that the Hebrews picked up in Hebron. Most of Genesis is mere legend.[1409] In its "explanation" of the Day of Atonement, in Exodus 12, the *Interpreter's Bible* depicts the Hebrews as cruel, vile savages who received pleasure from cutting the throats of struggling little lambs and watching hot blood spurt.[1410] The authors of the *Interpreter's Bible* reject Jesus' miracles, including His feeding the five thousand and walking on water.[1411] Even the Gospel accounts of Jesus' resurrection are said to "contain legendary details."[1412]

Ellis Fuller had served several Southern Baptist pastorates. Known among the local churches as a warm, soul-winning evangelist, Fuller remained in popular demand for revival meetings. A collection of his sermons would appear posthumously, under the title *Evangelistic Messages* (Broadman 1953).

[1407] See Jerry Sutton, "The Priesthood of the Believer and Its Corollaries," in *The Baptist Reformation: The Conservative Resurgence in the Southern Baptist Convention* (Nashville: B&H Publishers, 2000), 425–38.

[1408] George A. Buttrick, ed., *The Interpreter's Bible*, 12 vols. (Nashville: Abingdon Press, 1951–57), 1:16.

[1409] Ibid., 1:442ff.

[1410] Ibid., 1:917–18.

[1411] Ibid., 7:127–28.

[1412] Ibid., 7:144.

Nevertheless, in his role as seminary president, Fuller embraced theological liberals. He invited John Mackay, liberal president of Princeton Seminary, to lecture at Southern in 1947. That same year, Fuller chose Nels F. S. Ferré, professor of Christian Theology, at Andover Newton Theological School (NBC),[1413] to deliver Southern Seminary's Julius B. Gay Lectures. These lectures, published under the title *Pillars of Faith* (1948), attack the inspiration and inerrancy of the Bible.[1414] In his book, *The Christian Faith* (1942), Ferré had clearly denied that Jesus is "a supernatural Savior with an eternally pre-existing personality." Ferré had insisted that the Virgin Birth never occurred.[1415] In his book, *Return to Christianity* (1943), Ferré had not only castigated the historic Christian faith; he had embraced Marxism.[1416] Throughout his book, *Faith and Reason* (1946) — a book that would soon become a text at Southern Seminary — Ferré had embraced and promoted Kierkegaardian Existentialism, which denies the reality of biblical absolutes.

Duke K. McCall (1914–2013)

Duke McCall, Southern Seminary president (1951–82),[1417] had Eric C. Rust (1910–91) teaching philosophy courses during the 1950s. While professor of Biblical Theology, at Crozer

---

[1413] Alan P. F. Sell, *Content and Method in Christian Theology: A Case Study of the Thought of Nels Ferré* (Cambridge, United Kingdom: James Clarke and Co., 2014), passim.

[1414] Nels Ferré, *Pillars of Faith* (New York: Harper, 1948), 48, 95, passim.

[1415] Idem, *The Christian Faith: An Inquiry into Its Adequacy as Man's Ultimate Religion* (New York: Harper & Brothers, 1942), 34, 102–3, 110; Idem, *The Christian Understanding of God* (New York: Harper. 1951), where Ferré claims, "We have no way of knowing that Jesus was sinless" (186). On page 191, the author speculates that Jesus might have been the illegitimate son of Mary and a German soldier.

[1416] Idem, *Return to Christianity* (New York: Harper & Brothers, 1943), 66, passim.

[1417] A Furman University graduate, McCall had been president of New Orleans Baptist Theological Seminary (SBC) from 1943 to 1946 and Executive Secretary of the SBC Executive Committee 1946 to 1951. See *Duke McCall: An Oral History*, ed. A. Ronald Tonks (Brentwood, TN: Baptist History and Heritage Society, 2001).

Theological Seminary (NBC), Rust had expressed liberal views in his book, *Nature and Man in Biblical Thought* (1953). Of the Genesis account of creation, Rust had asserted, "The Old Testament begins with two myths of creation, both of which reflect elements from pagan mythology of surrounding peoples."[1418] Throughout Duke McCall's presidency, he brought in radical speakers. The two speakers for Southern Seminary's 1955 Mullins Lectures included Robert J. McCracken, successor to the modernist, Harry Emerson Fosdick, of Riverside Church, New York City, and Harry Henry Rowley (1890-1969), professor of Old Testament, at England's University of Manchester. Rowley's lectures at Southern Seminary soon appeared in print under the title, *The Unity of the Bible*, which attempts to persuade the reader that "none of the main documents on which the Pentateuch rests can have been compiled until long after the time of Moses.... There is little which we can with confidence ascribe to Moses."[1419] During the McCall administration, faculty members who attacked the inerrancy of the biblical autographa included William E. Hull (1930-2013),[1420] E. Glenn Hinson (b. 1931),[1421] and Frank Stagg (1911-2001).[1422] The successor to Duke McCall, Roy L. Honeycutt Jr. (1926-2004),

---

[1418] Eric Rust, *Nature and Man in Biblical Thought* (London: Lutterworth Press, 1953), 20; cf. 2, 5, 17, and 195. See also *Southern Baptist Journal*, October 1980, 9.

[1419] H. H. Rowley, *The Unity of the Bible* (Philadelphia: The Westminster Press, 1955), 21. For evidences of the Mosaic authorship of the Pentateuch, see Gleason L. Archer Jr., *A Survey of Old Testament Introduction*, new ed. (Chicago: Moody Press, 2007), 117ff.

[1420] E.g., William E. Hull, "Relevance of the New Testament," *Review & Expositor* 62 (Spring 1965): 190-95 (187-200); Harold Lindsell, *The Battle for the Bible* (Grand Rapids: Zondervan, 1976), 93-95; idem, *The Bible in the Balance* (Grand Rapids: Zondervan, 1979), 158-62.

[1421] E.g., E. Glenn Hinson, *Jesus Christ* (Wilmington, NC: McGrath Publishing Co., 1977), 66, 78. Hinson insists that later writers embellished the four Gospels and that Jesus never considered Himself as divine (53-112). Hinson denies Jesus' bodily resurrection (109-11).

[1422] E.g., Frank Stagg, *New Testament Theology* (Nashville: Broadman, 1962), 39-44, 59, 131, passim, where the author rejects the doctrine of the Trinity as expressed in the ancient and orthodox creeds. Stagg also goes to great length to obliterate the propitiating work of Christ's atonement (140-45). See also Lindsell, *The Bible in the Balance*, 154-57.

president during 1982–93, rejected inerrancy[1423] and declared a "holy war" against the conservative movement.[1424] In the midst of the conservative resurgence, Richard Albert Mohler Jr. (b. 1959) would succeed Honeycutt and become the Seminary's ninth president.

Southwestern Baptist Theological Seminary (est. 1908)

Beginnings

Southwestern Seminary came into existence, in 1905, during a day of prayer and meditation in the life of Benajah Harvey Carroll (1843–1914), as he was traveling onboard a train. He had begun his adult life as a skeptic. After near-death experiences while serving in the Civil War, twenty-two-year-old B. H. Carroll accepted Christ after hearing the final sermon of a neighborhood brush-arbor revival. So rapid was his spiritual progress that, only twelve years later, the SBC invited Carroll to deliver the annual Convention sermon. For twenty-nine years, Carroll served as pastor of First Baptist, in Waco, Texas, and, for thirty-two years, he was professor of Bible and Theology at Baylor University. Following the call he received, in 1905, while traveling on a westbound train across the Texas Panhandle, Carroll reorganized Baylor's theology department into Baylor Theological Seminary. In 1907, the Texas Baptist Convention authorized a friendly separation of Baylor Theological Seminary from Baylor University, and gave it a new name—Southwestern Baptist Theological Seminary. The seminary received its charter, in 1908, and moved from Waco to Fort Worth, in 1910, with B. H. Carroll serving its presidency until his death in 1914. In his final words to his

---

[1423] E.g., Roy L. Honeycutt, "Biblical Authority: A Treasured Heritage," *Review and Expositor* 83 (Fall 1986): 605–22.

[1424] For more detail, see Gregory A. Wills, "Duke McCall and the Struggle for the Seminary's Direction," in *Southern Baptist Theological Seminary, 1859–2009*, 351–404. Cf. N. W. Hollyfield Jr., "A Sociological Analysis of the Degrees of Christian Orthodoxy among Selected Students in the Southern Baptist Theological Seminary" (MDiv Thesis, Southern Baptist Theological Seminary, 1976).

successor, L. R. Scarborough, professor of Evangelism, Carroll wrote, "My deep concern is about the seminary. Keep it on a hot trail after the lost. That is why I started the Chair of Evangelism and chose you as its professor. Never let it get away from the compassion of Calvary. Keep it missionary and true to the truth. Give it the best of your life."[1425]

Carroll held staunchly to the verbal, plenary inspiration, inerrancy, and supreme authority of the Scriptures, and he expressed these convictions in thirty-three published volumes, including his multi-volume, *An Interpretation of the English Bible* (1913). J. B. Cranfill collected Carroll's lectures on inspiration, and Fleming H. Revell published them under the title, *The Inspiration of the Bible* (1930).[1426] Two other early conservatives at Southwestern were Baptist historian Albert H. Newman (1852-1933) and Harvey E. Dana (1888-1945), professor of New Testament. Newman's works include *A History of the Baptist Churches in the United States* (1894), and Dana is noted for his book, *The Authenticity of the Holy Scriptures: A Brief Story of the Problems of Biblical Criticism* (1923).

Transition

During the 1940s, Southwestern began using liberal speakers, such as Edwin Dahlberg, chairperson of the Executive Committee of the Federal Council of Churches (later named the National Council of the Churches of Christ in the USA). During the 1950s, Charles A. Trentham, a Southwestern graduate, served there as professor of Systematic Theology. In 1963, the *Religious Herald*, official organ of the Virginia Baptist Convention, quoted Trentham as saying, "This is our heresy; we have made claims for the Bible which it does not make for itself.... The part of the truth which is being overemphasized today is that the Bible itself is the Word of God and as such is

---

[1425] "Celebrating 100 Years Est. 1908 Southwestern Baptist Theological Seminary," *Southwestern News* 66, no. 2 (2008 Special Centennial Edition): 22.

[1426] B. H. Carroll, *The Inspiration of the Bible* (New York: Revell, 1930), 20, 25-54.

the infallible authority in religion."[1427] In Neo-Orthodox vocabulary, in 1970, W. Boyd Hunt, professor of Theology, claimed, "No matter how much we stress that the Bible is the Word of God, only the Holy Spirit today can make it the Word of God for us."[1428]

John P. Newport Spreads the Influence of Paul Tillich

During the presidency of Russell H. Dilday, John P. Newport, director of the North American Paul Tillich Society, became Vice President for Academic Affairs and Provost, at Southwestern Seminary. Existentialist, Neo-Orthodox theologian Paul Tillich (1886–1965), a German Lutheran, had arrived in America in 1933. He had taught in the nation's most liberal institutions, including Harvard, the University of Chicago, and Union Seminary in New York City. Tillich's three-volume *Systematic Theology* displays shocking ignorance regarding the most cardinal Christian doctrines, such as the Trinity, and Christ's deity, incarnation, atonement, and bodily resurrection.[1429] Eight years after his death, Paul Tillich's widow, Hannah, authored a shocking autobiography titled *From Time to Time*,[1430] and Paul Tillich's longtime friend, Rollo May, wrote *Paulus* (Latin for *Paul*),[1431] an equally startling biography of Tillich. Revealing the man behind the public view, the two books, written by those who best knew and admired Tillich, expose him as a whoremonger, an adulterer, a pornographer, and a religious infidel.

A decade after the publishing of those two books, Southwestern Seminary's John P. Newport authored a glowing biography titled *Paul Tillich*. Depicting Tillich as an "apologist

---

[1427] *Religious Herald*, November 1963; and *Maranatha Gospel Messenger*, July 1968.

[1428] W. Boyd Hunt, "What is Inspiration?" in *Is the Bible a Human Book?* ed. Wayne E. Ward and Joseph F. Green (Nashville: Broadman, 1970), 125 (120-29).

[1429] Paul Tillich, *Systematic Theology*, 3 vol. (Chicago: University of Chicago, 1951-63).

[1430] Hannah Tillich, *From Time to Time* (New York: Stein and Day, 1973).

[1431] Rollo May, *Paulus: Reminiscences of a Friendship* (New York: Harper & Row, 1973).

to intellectuals," Newport assesses Tillich's theology as "surely one of the most significant contributions to Christian thought in this century."[1432] In his book's preface, Newport announces, "I am indebted to Russell Dilday of Southwestern Seminary for the constancy of his friendship and encouragement." In 1994, during the conservative resurgence, the trustees fired Dilday from the presidency and replaced him with Kenneth S. Hemphill, a conservative Virginia pastor. A leader of the conservative resurgence, Paige Patterson, after serving two terms as SBC president (1998-2000), became president at Southwestern in 2003.

New Orleans Baptist Theological Seminary (est. 1917)

New Orleans Baptist Theological Seminary originated in Louisiana, in 1917, as "Baptist Bible Institute." Prior to its transition into a seminary, in 1946, liberal views had found toleration under the presidency of Duke K. McCall (1943-46). Frank Stagg (discussed above) had served as professor and chair of the New Testament department, at New Orleans (1945-64), prior to beginning his thirteen years, as professor of New Testament at Southern Seminary (1964-77).[1433]

Theodore R. Clark

After studying under Stagg and receiving his doctorate at New Orleans Seminary, Theodore Clark taught there for more than a decade. During that time, Clark denied the inerrancy and infallibility of the Bible. In 1959, Macmillan published Clark's *Saved by His Life*, an attack against the necessity of Jesus' crucifixion. To Clark, those who sing and believe the old hymns are guilty of "Jesusolatry," a kind of "Jesus cult." Such hymns, according to Clark, include "How Firm a Foundation," "Pass Me Not," "Safe in the Arms of Jesus," "Living for Jesus," "We would See Jesus,"

[1432] John P. Newport, *Paul Tillich* (Waco, Texas: Word Books, 1984), 62-65, 220.
[1433] See Frank Stagg, *New Testament Theology* (Nashville: Broadman, 1962), 39-44, 59, 131, and passim, where the author rejects the doctrine of the Trinity as expressed in the ancient and orthodox creeds. Stagg also goes to great length to obliterate the propitiating work of Christ's atonement (140-45). See the discussion in Lindsell, *The Bible in the Balance*, 154-57.

and "Jesus Saves." Clark considers the hymn "Nothing but the Blood of Jesus" as "a most serious distortion of the Christian faith," and the hymn "Are you washed in the blood?" as "crude and even repulsive."[1434] After much conservative protest, in 1960, New Orleans Seminary President, Leo Eddleman, fired Clark. Offering vague reasons for dismissing him, the trustees agreed to pay Clark's salary for another year after his dismissal. They offered to review him for rehiring within five years.

Fisher H. Humphreys

A graduate of the institution, Fisher Humphreys, in 1970, became professor of Theology at New Orleans Seminary and remained there until the conservative resurgence of the 1980s. In 1978, Broadman Press had published Humphreys' book, *The Death of Christ*, which displays massive confusion over the doctrine of salvation. "I do not know of anyone today," says Humphreys, "who naturally assumes, as the writer of Hebrews did, that sins can be washed away only by the blood of sacrifices."[1435] Quite the contrary, however, the writer of Hebrews asserts that the blood of bulls and goats can *never* take away sins (9:12; 10:4), and that only the blood of Christ on the cross can remove sin. Humphreys, moreover, believed it "unwise to seek for a 'necessity' for the cross. It is quite possible to affirm and clarify the importance of the cross without speaking of it as necessary."[1436] Contrariwise, the book of Hebrews clearly warns, "Without shedding of blood is no remission" (9:22b). Any insistence that Jesus died for sinners is repulsive to Humphreys, who asserts, "No illustration can be given, so far as I can tell, which makes vicarious punishment morally credible to men today." Calling the doctrine of Christ's vicarious atonement "reprehensible" and "despicable," Humphreys thinks it "morally outrageous that any judge would require a substitute."[1437]

[1434] Theodore R. Clark, *Saved by His Life: A Study of the New Testament Doctrine of Reconciliation and Salvation* (New York: Macmillan, 1959), 11n1, 22-38, 59-69, 121-41, passim.
[1435] Fisher H. Humphreys, *The Death of Christ* (Nashville: Broadman, 1978), 38.
[1436] Ibid., 55.
[1437] Ibid., 61-62.

In 1990, during the conservative resurgence, Fisher Humphreys relocated to the new Beeson Divinity School, established in 1988, at Samford University, an institution affiliated with the Alabama Southern Baptist Convention. Humphreys became professor of Divinity (later Emeritus) at Beeson. In 2003, Beeson's dean and historian, Timothy F. George, honored Humphreys with the "Teaching Award." Meanwhile, in 1996, conservative Charles S. Kelley had become president at New Orleans Seminary.

Gateway Seminary of the Southern Baptist Convention (est. 1944)

Golden Gate Baptist Theological Seminary began at Golden Gate Baptist Church, in Oakland, California, and, in 1959, it relocated to Mill Valley, California. The school eventually added four regional campuses. In 2016, Golden Gate sold its Mill Valley properties, relocated four hundred miles south to Ontario, California, and changed its name to Gateway Seminary of the Southern Baptist Convention. The school's paper the *Span* reported in April 1963 that the "California Bishop of the Episcopal Church, James A. Pike, was the recent speaker in chapel services on the seminary campus." Later, Pike's mysterious death seemed to confirm his long-known involvement in the occult. Merrill F. Unger's book, *The Mystery of Bishop Pike* (Tyndale House 1971), recorded the complete story of this controversial bishop. In a 1965 article, Fred L. Fisher, professor of New Testament at Gateway, asserted, "The Bible is not a revelation of God; it is a record of that revelation." Fisher added that, in the Bible, "scientific and historical statements reflect the knowledge that men had of the world in that day; such statements may be in error." In Neo-Orthodox fashion, Fisher concludes that while "the Bible expresses God's authority … it is authoritative only when God actually speaks to us through it."[1438] During the SBC resurgence, in 2004, conserva-

---

[1438] Fred L. Fisher, "Revelation and the Bible," *California Southern Baptist* 24, no. 3 (January 21, 1965): 14–15, published by the Southern Baptist General Convention of California, http://cdm16061.contentdm.oclc.org/cdm/compoundobject/collection/p16061coll23/id/9807/rec/2. In 1970, Fisher still insisted, "We must remember that the Bible does not

tive, Jeff P. Iorg,[1439] accepted Gateway's presidency.

Southeastern Baptist Theological Seminary (est. 1951)

Situated in Wake Forest, North Carolina, Southeastern Seminary, from its early decades, displayed a tolerance toward liberal teachings. For example, John I. Durham, professor of Hebrew and Old Testament, utilized the higher-critical method for denying the Mosaic authorship of the Pentateuch. Agreeing with "current Pentateuchal studies," Durham advocated "the presence within the Pentateuch of three strata of sources: oral sources, written sources, and redactional or editorial sources."[1440] Southeastern again offended conservatives when it added Robert G. Bratcher to its summer school faculty. When Bratcher, translator of *Good News for Modern Man*, addressed the Southern Baptist Christian Life Commission, in 1981, the Baptist Press release quoted him as saying, "Only willful ignorance or intellectual dishonesty can account for the claim that the Bible is inerrant and infallible.... To invest the Bible with the qualities of inerrancy and infallibility is to idolatrize it, to transform it into a false god.... Even words spoken by Jesus in Aramaic in the thirties of the first century and preserved in Greek, thirty-five to fifty years later, do not necessarily wield compelling or authentic authority over us today."[1441] During the conservative resurgence, in 1988, Southeastern trustees replaced the controversial president, W. Randall Lolley,[1442] with a conservative,

---

speak directly to our situation in life. It was written to men of another age and time." Fisher, "How You Can Understand the Bible," in *Is the Bible a Human Book?* ed. Ward and Green, 91 (83–92). Cf. *The Southern Baptist Journal* 9, no. 2 (February 1981): 1ff. See also *The Southern Baptist Journal* 9, no. 4 (April/May 1981): 10; and *The Southern Baptist Journal* 9, no. 5 (July/August 1981): 1ff.

[1439] When the name *Iorg* is pronounced, the letter I is silent, making the name rhyme with *Gorge*.

[1440] John I. Durham, "Contemporary Approaches in Old Testament Study," *Broadman Bible Commentary*, ed. Clifton J. Allen, et al (Nashville: Broadman, 1969), 1:90.

[1441] *The Baptist Courier*, April 2, 1981, page 6. This paper is a publication of the South Carolina Baptist Convention.

[1442] As pastor of First Baptist, Winston-Salem, and as president of

Lewis A. Drummond, who was succeeded by conservatives Paige Patterson and Daniel L. Akin.

Midwestern Baptist Theological Seminary (est. 1957)

Located in Kansas City, Missouri, Midwestern Seminary hosted liberal guest speakers in the early years of its history. For example, in 1967, President Millard J. Berquist brought in Methodist Bishop Gerald Kennedy to deliver the H. I. Hester Lectures. Even after years of openly questioning Christ's Virgin Birth, deity, and blood atonement, Kennedy had recently served as chairman of Billy Graham's 1963 Los Angeles campaign. Sharply distinguishing between the words *deity* and *divinity*, Kennedy asserted, "I believe [that] the testimony of the New Testament taken as a whole is against the doctrine of the deity of Jesus, although I think it bears overwhelming witness to the divinity of Jesus."[1443]

G. Temp Sparkman

During the 1970s and 80s, G. Temp Sparkman, professor of Religious Education and Church Administration, at Midwestern, wrote books that drew criticism from conservatives.[1444] Abandoning the doctrine of original (birth) sin, Sparkman bemoans, "Man has ... been berated as a sinner and then told the good news that he can change." To Sparkman, "The order is reversed. He is already good."[1445] Thus, "It often appears," adds Sparkman, "that God himself is fickle, punishing man and

---

Southeastern Seminary, Lolley, on May 8, 1970, had offered up the public prayer at the formal, dedication ceremony of the Schlitz Brewing Company's new plant near Winston-Salem. For the text of the prayer, along with Lolley's explanation, see William A. Powell, *SBC Issue & Question* (Buchanan, GA: Baptist Missionary Service, 1977), 132ff. For just the text, see *Baptist Challenge*, July 1983, 18.

[1443] Gerald Kennedy, *God's Good News* (New York: Harper and Brothers, 1955), 125.

[1444] See the full discussion in Sutton, *The Baptist Reformation*, 24–25, and 383–90.

[1445] G. Temp Sparkman, *Being a Disciple* (Nashville: Broadman, 1972), 17.

then changing His mind."[1446] Following the teachings of Horace Bushnell (1802–76),[1447] Sparkman contends that parents must nurture children into the realization that they have been God's children from birth.[1448] Such is the essence of Sparkman's gospel. He would receive additional criticism for teaching universalism,[1449] socialism,[1450] and situation ethics.[1451]

Ralph H. Elliott

Ralph Elliott received his Bachelor of Divinity and Doctor of Theology at Southern Seminary. In 1958, he accepted the chair of Old Testament and Hebrew at Midwestern Seminary. Elliott's book, *The Message of Genesis*, published by Broadman in 1961, resulted in a major controversy that caught the attention of religious media nationwide. Taking the higher-critical approach, Elliott wrote that Genesis is not historically accurate and that Moses was not its author.[1452] To Elliott, such "stories" as creation and Adam and Eve are not real history.[1453] One must not regard the Garden of Eden as "an actual place but rather … a setting of the message to be conveyed."[1454] Moreover, to Elliott, Abraham only "thought he heard" a call from God to sacrifice his son.[1455] While Midwestern Seminary's Board of Trustees and

---

[1446] Ibid., 20.
[1447] Idem, *Salvation and Nurture of the Child of God: The Story of Emma* (Valley Forge: Judson Press, 1983), 191, where Sparkman views Bushnell's ideas "as a fresh spring rain over the Connecticut valley nurturing a budding view of humanity which the winters of stern Calvinism had stunted." For a summary of Bushnell's teachings, see David Beale, *Historical Theology In-Depth* (Greenville, SC: Bob Jones University Press, 2013), 2:308–10.
[1448] *Salvation and Nurture of the Child of God*, 16, 25, 29–31, 33, 65–66, 193–94, passim.
[1449] *Being a Disciple*, 17–18, 21–23, 32, 34, 57, 59–61, 63, 65–66, 91–92, passim; and *Salvation and Nurture of the Child of God*, 41, 43–46, 72, passim.
[1450] *Being a Disciple*, 72.
[1451] Ibid., 31–32.
[1452] Ralph H. Elliott, *The Message of Genesis* (Nashville: Broadman, 1961), 1–16.
[1453] Ibid., 19–40.
[1454] Ibid., 43.
[1455] Ibid., 145.

the Baptist Sunday School Board supported the book, conservatives demanded its withdrawal and succeeded in securing conservative appointments to Midwestern Seminary's Board of Trustees. Upon Elliott's refusal, in 1962, to promise not to republish the book, the new Board dismissed him. Elliott then moved into the American Baptist Churches USA, accepted the pastorate of First Baptist, Rochester, New York, and became Vice President for Academic Life and Dean of the Faculty at Colgate Rochester Crozer Divinity School.

Roy L. Honeycutt Jr.

Roy L. Honeycutt Jr. (1926-2004), while occupying the chair of Old Testament at Midwestern, wrote the commentary on *Exodus* (1969), in the twelve-volume *Broadman Bible Commentary*. Heavily committed to the higher critical, hypothesis of interpretation, Honeycutt asserts, "The narrators have overlaid this historical nucleus with additional material."[1456] Honeycutt portrays the burning bush of Exodus 3:1-6 as nothing more than a "visionary experience."[1457] Commenting on Exodus 12, he disagrees with verse 29, where God smote the firstborn among the Egyptians. Honeycutt prefers the reader to believe that "a fatal pestilence struck the Egyptian children," and that, over time the whole story became an exaggerated tale: "Through years of transmission within Israel the memory of the event was so shaped that ... only the firstborn were involved, and that every firstborn of both man and beast was involved."[1458] In 1975, Honeycutt moved to Southern Seminary, where, up to the time of the conservative resurgence, he served as dean of the school of theology, professor of Old Testament, provost, and president. The resurgence would emerge at Midwestern Seminary under the leadership of its Presidents Mark Coppenger and Jason K. Allen.

[1456] Roy L. Honeycutt Jr., *Exodus*, in *Broadman Bible Commentary*, 1:333; see 1:307ff.
[1457] Ibid., 1:328.
[1458] Ibid., 1:363.

The Conservative Evangelical Resurgence

Background: The Overall Structure of Southern Baptist Work

To understand how the evangelical resurgence ever became possible, we must first understand how Southern Baptist work operates at four levels, with the *local church* as the basic unit. Then the *district associations* represent churches located within city or county boundaries. Representing the third level, there are presently forty-two *state conventions*.[1459] Southern Baptist colleges and universities fall under the jurisdiction of the state conventions. The fourth level is the *national SBC*. Entities that fall under the jurisdiction of the national SBC include the seminaries, the mission boards, the Ethics and Religious Liberty Commission, and the Historical Library and Archives. Since, theoretically, Southern Baptist churches are autonomous and do not delegate their authority, representatives at the state and national conventions go as "messengers" rather than as delegates. The national SBC meets once a year. Each "cooperating" church is *de facto* qualified to send two messengers to the national convention. Based upon its yearly contributions to SBC causes, each church is qualified to send up to ten additional messengers.[1460] Such was the background of the conservative resurgence.

[1459] New England shares one convention, and the Northwest states share one convention. The following couples also share one convention: Kansas/Nebraska; Maryland/Delaware; Minnesota/Wisconsin; Pennsylvania/South Jersey; and Puerto Rico/US Virgin Islands.

[1460] There are two ways for each cooperating church to qualify for up to ten additional messengers to the national convention: (1) one additional messenger for each full percent of the church's undesignated receipts contributed to SBC causes during the preceding fiscal year through the Cooperative Program or through the SBC Executive Committee. (2) One additional messenger for each $6,000 that the church contributed to SBC causes during the preceding fiscal year through the Cooperative Program or through the SBC Executive Committee. For the full statement, see the *Annual of the 2015 Southern Baptist Convention*, page 7. See also pages 134–36.

The Origin of the Resurgence

In the 1970s, William (Bill) Powell (1925-2000), editor of the *Southern Baptist Journal* of the conservative Baptist Faith and Message Fellowship (est. 1973), observed a simple way within the structure of the SBC to turn the tide of liberalism.[1461] The key to ousting the liberals lay embedded within the Constitution and Bylaws at the national level: SBC presidents are empowered to appoint the Convention's Committee on Committees, which in turn nominates the Committee on Nominations, which nominates the trustees of the SBC agencies and institutions, including the two mission boards and the six seminaries. As general overseers of the institutions, the elected trustees hire presidents, faculties, and staffs. They also determine the missionaries who go out under the two boards, as well as the literature that emerges from the denomination's press. Generally, a trustee serves a four-or-five-year term and is eligible for two terms. Ultimately, therefore, SBC presidents can play a pivotal role in the theological makeup of the seminaries and mission boards. Powell stood confident that a ten-year succession of conservative presidents would "replace all 900 trustees at Southern Baptist institutions and give the denomination a solidly conservative cast."[1462] The structure of checks and balances was indeed in place to awaken the sleeping giant.

The Work of the Resurgence

While Bill Powell would not live long enough to see the resurgence completed, he shared his findings with Appeals Court Judge Paul Pressler,[1463] deacon at Second Baptist in Houston, Texas. Paige Patterson, associate pastor under W. A. Criswell (1909-2002) at First Baptist in Dallas, Texas, joined with Pressler, as large numbers of conservative pastors began supporting the

---

[1461] Sutton, *The Baptist Reformation: The Conservative Resurgence in the Southern Baptist Convention*, 65, 92; (see 62ff.). See also the William Powell Collection (23 boxes) in the Archives and Special Collections Department at Southwestern Baptist Theological Seminary.
[1462] "News," *Christianity Today,* July 17, 1981, 80.
[1463] Pressler, *A Hill on Which to Die,* 77-84.

plan. Emerging from conservative grassroots, local church messengers attended the annual conventions and cast their votes for conservative presidents and trustees.[1464] In 1985, 45,000 messengers attended the Convention in Dallas. Euphemistically known as "moderates," the liberals appealed to E. Y. Mullins's doctrine of autonomous individualism and accused conservatives of "power grabbing."[1465] On the evening prior to the annual SBC meeting in San Antonio, Texas, in 1988, W. A. Criswell delivered to the conservative Pastors' Conference a message titled "The Curse of Liberalism." To a cheering audience, this patriarch of the conservative resurgence opened his message with his opinion of the current usage of the word *moderate*: "Because of the opprobrious epithet 'liberal,' today they call themselves

---

[1464] Conservative accounts include Sutton, *The Baptist Reformation*; Wills, *Southern Baptist Theological Seminary, 1859–2009*; Pressler, *A Hill on Which to Die*; James C. Hefley, *The Truth in Crisis*, 5 vols. (Hannibal, MO: Hannibal Books, 1986–90); idem, *The Conservative Resurgence in the Southern Baptist Convention* (Hannibal, MO: Hannibal Books, 1991); Paige Patterson, *Anatomy of a Reformation: The Southern Baptist Convention, 1978–2004* (Fort Worth: Southwestern Baptist Theological Seminary, 2004); David S. Dockery, *Southern Baptist Consensus and Renewal: A Biblical, Historical, and Theological Proposal* (Nashville: B&H Publishing Group, 2008); and Jason K. Allen, ed., *The SBC and the 21st Century* (Nashville: B&H Publishing Group, 2016).

[1465] Moderate (liberal) accounts include Joe E. Barnhart, *The Southern Baptist Holy War* (Austin, TX: Texas Monthly Press, 1986); Nancy Tatum Ammerman, *Baptist Battles: Social Change and Religious Conflict in the Southern Baptist Convention* (New Brunswick: Rutgers University Press, 1990); Grady C. Cothen, *What Happened to the Southern Baptist Convention? A Memoir of the Controversy*, corrected ed. (Macon, GA: Smyth and Helwys Publishing, 1993); David T. Morgan, *The New Crusades, the New Holy Land: Conflict in the Southern Baptist Convention, 1969–1991* (Tuscaloosa, AL: University of Alabama Press, 1996); Walter B. Shurden, ed., *The Struggle for the Soul of the SBC: Moderate Responses to the Fundamentalist Movement* (Macon, GA: Mercer University Press, 1993); *Baptists Today* (a liberal periodical formerly called *SBC Today*), discussed in Walker L. Knight, "The History of *Baptists Today*," in *The Struggle for the Soul of the SBC*, ed. Shurden, 151–68; and the Associated Baptist Press, discussed in Stan Hastey, "The History of the Associated Baptist Press," in *The Struggle for the Soul of the SBC*, 169–85. In addition, a network called Mainstream Baptists (est. 2000) tries to unite liberal organizations.

'moderates.' A skunk by any other name still stinks!"[1466] Over the next few years, SBC executives would replace the leadership in the Home and Foreign Mission Boards and in the Baptist Press (SBC news service) with conservatives. The six seminaries gradually received conservative trustees and presidents. In 1991, Broadman and Holman began releasing its multivolume *New American Commentary*, covering the whole Bible and written by authors who held to biblical inerrancy. In 2004, the SBC withdrew from the ecumenical Baptist World Alliance. Meanwhile, in the year 2000, the Convention revised its article on "the Scriptures" in the Baptist Faith and Message statement. The first sentence of the 1963 edition had described the Bible as "the record of God's revelation of Himself to man." The 2000 edition describes the Bible as "God's revelation of Himself to man" — not merely "the record" of God's revelation. In addition, the final sentence of the same article of the 1963 edition said, "The criterion by which the Bible is to be interpreted is Jesus Christ." Any Neo-Orthodox professor could have agreed. The conservative revision (2000) replaces that sentence with, "All Scripture is a testimony to Christ, who is Himself the focus of divine revelation."[1467]

Liberal Reactions to the Conservative Resurgence

Reacting to the conservative resurgence and its strong stance on biblical inerrancy, two leftwing, liberal groups formed outside the SBC — the Alliance of Baptists (1987)[1468] and the Cooperative Baptist Fellowship (1991).[1469] Many SBC churches —

[1466] Criswell, "The Curse of Liberalism" (Dallas, TX: W. A. Criswell Foundation, 2015), 1.

[1467] Douglas K. Blount and Joseph D. Wooddell, eds., *The Baptist Faith and Message 2000: Critical Issues in America's Largest Protestant Denomination* (Lanham, MD: Rowman & Littlefield Publishers, 2007), 1–11.

[1468] The Alliance ordained women, accepted homosexuals, and joined the National Council of the Churches of Christ in the USA. See Alan Neely, "The History of the Alliance of Baptists," in *The Struggle for the Soul of the SBC*, ed. Shurden, 101–28; and *Baptists Today*, November 12, 1992, page 11, and September 2002, page 9.

[1469] Pamela R. Durso, *A Short History of the Cooperative Baptist Fellowship Movement* (Brentwood, TN: Baptist History and Heritage Society, 2006); and Walter B. Shurden, "The Cooperative Baptist Fellowship," in *The*

especially in Virginia, North Carolina, South Carolina, Georgia, Kentucky, and Texas—maintain dual affiliations with the Cooperative Baptist Fellowship and with Southern Baptist state conventions. With liberals dominating the Virginia state convention, that is, the Baptist General Association of Virginia (est. 1823), conservatives, in 1993, organized a new convention, called the Southern Baptist Conservatives of Virginia. Again, the churches have ways to maintain dual affiliations with both conventions.[1470] Likewise, in Texas, with liberals dominating the state convention, that is, the Baptist General Convention of Texas (est. 1886), conservatives, in 1998, organized a new state convention, called the Southern Baptists of Texas Convention. These churches can also maintain dual affiliations.

Divinity schools quickly emerged to accommodate displaced liberals who lost their seminary positions during the conservative resurgence. Under the large Southern Baptist umbrella, "the perspective is wide," adds William H. Brackney, who observes that the conservative resurgence has "spawned a series of new theological seminaries or programs independent of Southern Baptist controls, and this has produced a broadening definition of the overall Southern Baptist educational culture."[1471] For example, in 1991, the Alliance of Baptists founded the Baptist Theological Seminary at Richmond, Virginia,[1472] where liberals including E. Glenn Hinson, formerly at Southern Seminary, took refuge. In 1994, the board of self-perpetuating trustees at Mercer University, in Atlanta, voted to establish the McAfee School of Theology. This in part led the Georgia Baptist Convention, in 2006, to sever ties with

---

Baptist River, ed. W. Glenn Jonas Jr. (Macon, GA: Mercer University, 2006), 243–68.

[1470] See Jeffrey R. Pinder, "Forged by Conviction: An Historical Overview of the Southern Baptist Conservatives of Virginia" (DMin thesis, Liberty Baptist Theological Seminary, 2010), 85, 93, 112, 123, 142, 296, 317, 433.

[1471] William H. Brackney, "Baptists Turn toward Education: 1764," in *Turning Points in Baptist History: A Festschrift in Honor of Harry Leon McBeth*, ed. Michael E. Williams Sr. and Walter B. Shurden (Macon, GA: Mercer University Press, 2008), 138.

[1472] Thomas H. Graves, "The History of the Baptist Theological Seminary at Richmond," in *The Struggle for the Soul of the SBC*, ed. Shurden, 187–200.

Mercer over liberal teaching.[1473] Mercer presently affiliates with the Cooperative Baptist Fellowship. Other universities that formed their own divinity schools (as "moderate" alternatives to the six SBC seminaries) include Hardin-Simmons,[1474] Samford,[1475] Gardner-Webb,[1476] Baylor,[1477] Campbell,[1478] and Wake Forest.[1479] Institutions that in effect declared independence from their respective state conventions (their purported owners) include Wake Forest University and Meredith College (NC), Furman University (SC), and Stetson University (FL).

SBC Today

With about 46,500 churches and 15,500,000 members, the Southern Baptist Convention is the largest Baptist group in the world, the largest Protestant group in America, and, among

---

[1473] David Morgan recalls that *Playboy* magazine in 1987 named Mercer as America's ninth best "party school," in *The New Crusades, the New Holy Land*, 143.

[1474] Presently affiliated with the more liberal Baptist General Convention of Texas, Hardin-Simmons University, centered at Abilene, established in 1983 the Logsdon School of Theology (of which Logsdon Seminary is a part). They continue to expand their programs.

[1475] Samford University, in Birmingham, Alabama, established Beeson Divinity School in 1988. Liberal church historian Bill J. Leonard left Southern Seminary to chair the religion department at Samford. As noted above, liberal professor Fisher H. Humphreys found refuge in the divinity school at Samford when he left New Orleans Seminary.

[1476] Affiliated with the Southern Baptist State Convention of North Carolina, Gardner-Webb University, at Boiling Springs, established its Divinity School in 1993.

[1477] Affiliated with the more liberal Baptist General Convention of Texas, Baylor University (at Waco), founded the George W. Truett Theological Seminary in 1994.

[1478] Presently affiliated with the Southern Baptist State Convention of North Carolina, Campbell University, based at Buies Creek, established its Divinity School in 1996.

[1479] Wake Forest University, in Winston-Salem, North Carolina, established its School of Divinity in 1999. Liberal Bill J. Leonard, formerly at SBTS and Beeson Divinity School, became professor of Church History and founding dean of Wake's School of Divinity. See Bill J. Leonard, *God's Last and Only Hope: The Fragmentation of the Southern Baptist Convention* (Grand Rapids: Eerdmans, 1990).

American denominations, its membership ranks second only to the Roman Catholic Church. Despite its enormous size, the SBC has relatively few major divisions. Among its foremost issues, two are ongoing and noteworthy. The first concerns the doctrine of unconditional election, whose spokesmen have included President Albert Mohler of Southern Seminary, versus conditional election, whose spokesmen have included President Paige Patterson of Southwestern.[1480]

The second ongoing division is between *moderates* and *conservatives*. Southern Baptist historian, David S. Dockery, places SBC *moderates* into various categories that include pragmatists, centrists, ecumenists, doctrinal liberals, culture enthusiasts, and women in the ministry.[1481] Dockery places SBC *conservatives* into various categories that include Evangelicals of the Billy Graham type; revivalists of the old-fashioned style; Emergent/missional ministries of various types; Willow Creek Church (Heather Larson and Steve Carter, successors of Bill Hybels); Saddleback Church (Rick Warren); and Reformed ministries, such as Sovereign Grace Churches.[1482] Other Reformed SBC ministries include Founders (*Founders Journal*) and Nine Marks (Mark Dever). Prominent SBC leaders observe that the New Evangelical emphasis on cultural engagement was a key attraction that brought SBC conservatives into the Evangelical

---

[1480] "Seminary Presidents Mohler and Patterson Debate Calvinism," *Religious Herald*, June 21, 2006. Recently, a committee was appointed to try to bring both sides to agree to disagree on the matter.

[1481] Cf. Pamela R. Durso, "Baptists and the Turn toward Baptist Women in Ministry," in *Turning Points in Baptist History*, ed. Williams and Shurden, 275–87; and Libby Bellinger, "The History of Southern Baptist Women in Ministry," in *The Struggle for the Soul of the SBC*, ed. Shurden, 129–50.

[1482] Dockery, *Southern Baptist Consensus and Renewal*, 10–11. Sovereign Grace Churches are also known as *New Calvinists* and *Neo-Charismatic*. See Collin Hansen, *Young, Restless, Reformed: A Journalist's Journey with the New Calvinists* (Wheaton, IL: Crossway, 2008); Jeremy Walker, *The New Calvinism Considered* (Darlington, England: Evangelical Press, 2013); and E. S. Williams, *The New Calvinists: Changing the Gospel* (London: Wakeman Trust and Belmont House, 2014). Williams includes chapters on Tim Keller and John Piper, who are popular among many Reformed Southern Baptists.

movement.[1483] Rick Warren, with his *Purpose Driven Church* (1995), is a chief source of Southern Baptist vitality.[1484] The SBC conservative resurgence is providing new and prominent leadership to the broad Evangelical movement.

Select Bibliography for Further Reading

Barnes, William Wright. *The Southern Baptist Convention, 1845–1953.* Nashville: Broadman, 1954.
Blount, Douglas K., and Joseph D. Wooddell, eds. *The Baptist Faith and Message 2000: Critical Issues in America's Largest Protestant Denomination.* Lanham, MD: Rowman & Littlefield Publishers, 2007.
Broadus, John A. *Memoir of James Petigru Boyce, D. D., L. L. D.* Nashville: Sunday-School Board of the Southern Baptist Convention, 1927.
"Celebrating 100 Years Est. 1908 Southwestern Baptist Theological Seminary." *Southwestern News* 66, no. 2 (Special Centennial Edition 2008).
Dockery, David S. *Southern Baptist Consensus and Renewal: A Biblical, Historical, and Theological Proposal.* Nashville: B&H Publishing Group, 2008.
_____, and Roger D. Duke, eds. *John A. Broadus: A Living Legacy.* Nashville: B&H Publishing Group, 2008.
Fletcher, Jesse C. *The Southern Baptist Convention: A Sesquicentennial History.* Nashville: B&H Publishers, 1994.
Hankins, Barry. *Uneasy in Babylon: Southern Baptist Conservatives and American Culture.* Tuscaloosa: University of Alabama Press, 2002.
Lefever, Alan J. *Fighting the Good Fight: The Life and Work of Benajah Harvey Carroll.* Austin, TX: Eakin Press, 1994.
Morgan, David T. *The New Crusades, the New Holy Land: Conflict in the Southern Baptist Convention, 1969–1991.* Tuscaloosa, AL: University of Alabama Press, 1996.
Nettles, Thomas J. *James Petigru Boyce: A Southern Baptist Statesman.* Phillipsburg, NJ: P&R Publishing, 2009.
Robertson, Archibald Thomas. *Life and Letters of John Albert Broadus.* Philadelphia: American Baptist Publication Society, 1910.
Shurden, Walter B., ed. *The Struggle for the Soul of the SBC: Moderate Responses to the Fundamentalist Movement.* Macon, GA: Mercer University Press, 1993.
Smallwood, William Edward. "'The Most Versatile Man': The Life, Ministry, and Piety of Basil Manly Jr." PhD diss., Southern Baptist Theological Seminary, 2015.
Sutton, Jerry. *The Baptist Reformation: The Conservative Resurgence in the Southern Baptist Convention.* Nashville: B&H Publishers, 2000.
Wills, Gregory A. *Southern Baptist Theological Seminary, 1859–2009.* New

---

[1483] Barry Hankins, *Uneasy in Babylon: Southern Baptist Conservatives and American Culture* (Tuscaloosa: University of Alabama Press, 2002), 39.
[1484] Sutton, *The Baptist Reformation*, 482.

York: Oxford University Press, 2009.
Woodson, Hortense C. *Giant in the Land: The Life of William B. Johnson, First President of the Southern Baptist Convention (1845–1851)*. Expanded ed. Springfield, MO: Particular Baptist Press, 2005. The first edition appeared in 1950.

Part V

Sources for Baptist Ecclesiology

Chapter 21

Additional Tools and Resources

❋

The History of the New Hampshire Confession of Faith (1833)

*T*he American Baptist Publication Society (est. 1824) published the New Hampshire Confession, in 1833, along with an accompanying Church Covenant. The Confession had sixteen articles. While there are no known copies of the original, W. J. McGlothlin regards the copy in William Crowell's *The Church Member's Hand-Book* (1850) as substantially the same as the original.[1485] Twenty years after the original publication, J. Newton Brown, editorial secretary of the American Baptist Publication Society, revised the Confession and the Covenant and published them in his *Baptist Church Manual* (1853). Brown added two new articles—one on "Repentance and Faith" and one on "Sanctification."[1486] His 1853 edition of the Confession

---

[1485] W. J. McGlothlin, *Baptist Confessions of Faith* (Philadelphia: American Baptist Publication Society, 1911), 301; and William Crowell, *The Church Member's Hand-Book: A Guide to the Doctrines and Practice of Baptist Churches* (Boston: Gould, Kendall and Lincoln, 1850), 19–28. The 1833 Covenant is in Charles W. Deweese, *Baptist Church Covenants* (Nashville: Broadman, 1990), 157–58.

[1486] For Brown's 1853 revision of the New Hampshire Confession, see J. Newton Brown, *A Baptist Church Manual: Containing the Declaration of Faith, Covenant, Rules of Order and Brief Forms of Church Letters* (1853; repr., Valley Forge: Judson Press, 2014), 5–30; and McGlothlin, *Baptist Confessions of Faith*, 299–307.

and the Covenant became the standard for later versions. Many Landmark Baptists would use the New Hampshire Confession because it contains no mention of the Universal Church. To the 1853 Covenant (below) many welcomed Brown's addition of the church members' resolve "to abstain from the sale and use of intoxicating drinks as a beverage":[1487]

J. Newton Brown's 1853 Revision of the New Hampshire Covenant

Having been led, as we believe, by the Spirit of God, to receive the Lord Jesus Christ as our Savior; and, on the profession of our faith, having been baptized in the name of the Father, and of the Son, and of the Holy Spirit, we do now, in the presence of God, angels, and this assembly, most solemnly and joyfully enter into covenant with one another as one body in Christ.

We engage, therefore, by the aid of the Holy Spirit, to walk together in Christian love; to strive for the advancement of this church, in knowledge, holiness, and comfort; to promote its prosperity and spirituality; to sustain its worship, ordinances, discipline, and doctrines; to contribute cheerfully and regularly to the support of the ministry, the expenses of the church; the relief of the poor, and the spread of the gospel through all nations.

We also engage to maintain family and secret devotion[s]; to religiously educate our children; to seek the salvation of our kindred and acquaintances; to walk circumspectly in the world; to be just in our dealings, faithful in our engagements, and exemplary in our deportment; to avoid all tattling, backbiting, and excessive anger; to abstain from the sale and use of intoxicating drink as a beverage; and to be zealous in our efforts to advance the kingdom of our Savior.

[1487] For Brown's 1853 revision of the New Hampshire Covenant, see J. Newton Brown, *A Baptist Church Manual*, 31–32.

We further engage to watch over one another in brotherly love; to remember each other in prayer; to aid each other in sickness and distress; to cultivate Christian sympathy in feeling and courtesy in speech; to be slow to take offense, but always ready for reconciliation, and mindful of the rules of our Savior, to secure it without delay. We moreover engage that when we remove from this place, we will as soon as possible unite with some other church, where we can carry out the spirit of this covenant and the principles of God's Word.

Baptist Manuals

Nineteenth-century Baptists used church manuals extensively to provide guidance for the organizational life of their churches. The wide circulation of such manuals reflects their need for resources on the organizational structure of local churches. Offering a basic and systematic approach to ecclesiastical order, these manuals included William Crowell's *Church Member's Hand-Book* (1850); J. Newton Brown's *Baptist Church Manual* (1853); J. L. Dagg's *Treatise on Church Order* (1858); Edward T. Hiscox's *Baptist Church Directory* (1859); J. M. Pendleton's *Church Manual* (1867); and Hiscox's *New Directory for Baptist Churches* (1894). By 1946, Pendleton's manual had sold at least 150,000 copies. Hiscox's works, including his *Principles and Practices for Baptist Churches*, have continued in print to the present day.

Providing basic introductions in Baptist history, doctrine, and practice, Hiscox's *New Directory* includes local-church covenants and specific instructions toward a basic orthopraxy for Baptists. Hiscox delineated three methods in which individuals could unite with Baptist churches: (1) admission by baptism upon profession of faith; (2) admission by letter; and (3) admission by solid testimony of true conversion, baptism, and Christian life. The first method applied to new converts. The second method required a letter from the church where the individual last held membership. Such a letter "certifies to his good Christian character and regular standing, and commends him to the confidence of, and membership in, the other church." Once the church had adequately observed the individual's loyalty and commitment, a "vote of the Church" established formal admission into its membership. The third method, admission by testimony, or experience, applied to candidates who have received immersion, but for legitimate reasons no longer hold membership in a church.[1488]

Hiscox explains that Baptist churches generally observed Communion quarterly, bimonthly, or monthly. Many congregations offered the "hand of fellowship" to new members, on Communion Sunday. Interestingly, Hiscox observes that some Baptists objected to "individual communion cups" and "the practice of holding the bread till all are served." They feared that such formalities might "exalt the form over the spirit and make the service ritual rather than spiritual."[1489] While some churches would continue their old tradition of using wine in Communion, most shared the concerns of the temperance movement and turned to unfermented grape juice.[1490]

Select Bibliography for Baptist Ecclesiology

Bancroft, Emery H. "Ecclesiology: The Doctrine of the Church." In *Christian Theology*, 2nd ed. revised by Ronald B. Mayors, 281–306. Grand Rapids: Zondervan, 1976.

Barackman, Floyd H. "Ecclesiology: The Doctrine of the Christian Church." In *Practical Christian Theology: Examining the Great Doctrines of the Faith*, 4th ed., 413–36. Grand Rapids: Kregel, 2012.

Bauder, Kevin. *Baptist Distinctives and New Testament Church Order*. Schaumburg, IL: Regular Baptist Press, 2012.

Benedict, Willard R. *Burial or Cremation: Which Do You Choose?* North Fort Myers, FL: Faithful Life Publishers, 2014.

Brown, Jeff. *Corporate Decision-Making in the Church of the New Testament*. Eugene, OR: Wipf and Stock, 2013.

Brown, J. Newton. *A Baptist Church Manual: Containing the Declaration of Faith, Covenant, Rules of Order and Brief Forms of Church Letters*. 1853. Reprint, Valley Forge: Judson Press, 2014.

Brown, L. Duane, and Daniel R. Brown. *Biblical Basis for Baptists: A Bible Study on Baptist Distinctives*. Revised and Expanded. North Fort Myers,

---

[1488] Hiscox, *The New Directory for Baptist Churches* (Philadelphia: Judson Press, 1894), 73–79.

[1489] Ibid. 141.

[1490] H. Leon McBeth, *The Baptist Heritage* (Nashville: Broadman, 1987), 250.

FL: Faithful Life Publishers, 2009.

Brown, Laurence D. *The Call, Content, and Concern of the Gospel Ministry.* North Conway, NH: Solid Rock Publications, 2006.

_____. *Sense and Nonsense about Baptist Church Organization and Offices.* North Conway, NH: Solid Rock Publications, 2003.

Buhler, F. M. *Baptism: Three Aspects: Archaeological–Historical–Biblical.* Translated from the French by W. P. Bauman. Ontario, Canada: Joshua Press, 2004.

Conant, Thomas Jefferson. *The Meaning and Use of Baptizein.* Grand Rapids: Kregel, 1977.

Couch, Mal. *A Biblical Theology of the Church.* Grand Rapids: Kregel, 1999.

Dagg, J. L. *A Treatise on Church Order.* Charleston, SC: The Southern Baptist Publication Society, 1858.

Delnay, Robert G. *Fire in Your Pulpit.* Schaumburg, IL: Regular Baptist Press, 1990.

Deweese, Charles W. *Baptist Church Covenants.* Nashville: Broadman, 1990.

Ferguson, Everett. *Baptism in the Early Church: History, Theology, and Liturgy in the First Five Centuries.* Grand Rapids: Eerdmans, 2009.

Good, Kenneth H. *The Doctrine of the Church.* Elyria, OH: The Fellowship of Baptists for Home Missions, 1966.

Hammett, John S. *Biblical Foundations for Baptist Churches: A Contemporary Ecclesiology.* Grand Rapids: Kregel, 2005.

Hiscox, Edward T. *The Baptist Church Directory: A Guide to the Doctrines and Practices of Baptist Churches.* Revised. New York: Sheldon and Co., 1888.

_____. *The New Directory for Baptist Churches: An Indispensable Guide to the Conduct and Operation of Baptist Churches.* 1894. Reprint, Grand Rapids: Kregel, 1970.

Hudson, Winthrop Still, ed. *Baptist Concepts of the Church: A Survey of the Historical and Theological Issues Which Have Produced Changes in Church Order.* Philadelphia: Judson Press, 1956.

Jackson, Paul R. *The Doctrine and Administration of the Church.* Revised. Schaumburg, IL: Regular Baptist Press, 2010.

Jenkens, Charles A., ed. *Baptist Doctrines: Being an Exposition, in a Series of Essays by Representative Baptist Ministers, of the Distinctive Points of Baptist Faith and Practice.* St. Louis: Chancy R. Barns, 1880.

Jeter, Jeremiah B. (Bell), et al. *Baptist Principles Reset: Consisting of a Series of Articles on Distinctive Baptist Principles.* Richmond: The Religious Herald, 1901.

Judson, Adoniram. *Christian Baptism.* 5th American ed. Boston: Gould, Kendall & Lincoln, 1846.

Lehman, Victor D. *The Pastor's Guide to Weddings and Funerals.* Valley Forge: Judson Press, 2001.

Lynch, Ken. *The Evangelist: His Life and Ministry to the Church and World.* Revised and expanded edition. Kearney, NE: Morris Publishing, 2004.

Maoz, Baruch, et al. *Local Church Practice.* Haywards Heath, County Sussex,

England: Carey Publications, 1978.

Morris, Wally. *A Time to Die: A Biblical Look at End of Life Issues.* Greenville, SC: Ambassador International, 2014.

Norman, R. Stanton. *The Baptist Way: Distinctives of a Baptist Church.* Nashville: B&H Publishing Group, 2005.

Patterson, W. Morgan. "The Lord's Supper in Baptist History." *Review and Expositor* 66, no. 1 (Winter 1969): 25–34.

Pendleton, James Madison. *Church Manual: Designed for the Use of Baptist Churches.* Philadelphia: American Baptist Publication Society, n.d.

Reese, J. Irving. *A Guide for Organizing and Conducting a Baptist Church.* Cleveland, OH: Baptist Mid-Missions, n.d.

———. *A Service Manual for Ministers.* Des Plaines, IL: Regular Baptist Press, 1966.

Stander, H. F., and J. P. Louw. *Baptism in the Early Church.* Rev. ed. Leeds, England: Reformation Today Trust, 2004.

Taylor, James B. (Barnett). *Restricted Communion: Or, Baptism an Essential Prerequisite to the Lord's Supper.* Charleston: Southern Baptist Publication Society, 1856.

Tetreau, Joel. *The Pyramid and the Box: The Decision-Making Process in a Local New Testament Church.* Eugene, OR: Wipf and Stock, 2013.

Wallace, O. C. S. *What Baptists Believe: The New Hampshire Confession: An Exposition.* Nashville: Sunday-School Board of the Southern Baptist Convention, 1913.

Weston, Henry G. *Constitution and Polity of the New Testament Church.* Philadelphia: American Baptist Publication Society, 1895.

Appendix A

Reconciling Old Style–New Style Calendar Dates

---✳---

$\mathcal{U}$ntil 1752, England and her colonies used the Julian calendar (begun under Julius Caesar in 46 B.C.), which started the New Year on March 25 and was based on a miscalculation of the length of a year by eleven minutes and fourteen seconds (making a difference of one day every 128 years). In 1582, during the time of Pope Gregory XIII, when the Julian calendar had gotten ten days behind the solar year, astronomers and mathematicians created a New Style (N. S.), known as the Gregorian calendar, which adjusted the astronomical errors of the old Julian calendar. This was made possible by advancing the 1582 calendar ten days (omitting October 5 through 14), in conformity with the solar year, and starting the New Year at January 1.

England refused to use "the Pope's calendar" for the period from 1582 to 1752. This explains why historical markers and books often use double dates within the period falling between January 1 and March 24. For example, since the Julian New Year did not begin until March 25, we might find a reference using a format such as March 5, 1621/22 (O.S.). This means it was March 5, 1621 (Old Style), but March 15, 1622 (New Style). When a reference has an O.S. date, you must add ten days to get the modern (N.S.) equivalent. I often translate the O.S.

dates into N.S. dates, so that they can relate more readily to our own calendars. To make their transition to the N.S. Gregorian calendar, the British simply advanced their 1752 calendar eleven days (omitting September 3 through 13), in conformity with the solar year, and started their New Year at January 1. Some complained that the Pope had now robbed their lives of eleven days.

Appendix B

Overview of Free Will Baptists in America

---※---

$\mathcal{F}$ree Will Baptists trace their origins to two eighteenth-century Arminian groups—one in the south and the other in the north.[1491] The southern group began in 1727, when Paul Palmer (fl. 1720-40)—father of the General Baptists in North Carolina—began organizing churches. By 1750, they had sixteen churches, the earliest being in Chowan. By 1756, Palmer had deceased, and most of his churches had transformed into Regular Baptists. Palmer's small remnant, however, would become the nucleus of the Free Will Baptist movement in North Carolina.[1492] In 1921, the Free Will Baptist Churches in the south organized into a General Conference.

The Northern group began in 1780, when Benjamin Randall (1749-1808), in New Durham, New Hampshire, established

---

[1491] Helpful references include G. A. Burgess and J. T. Ward, *Free Will Baptist Cyclopaedia: Historical and Biographical* (Boston: Free Baptist Cyclopaedia Co., 1886-89); and William F. Davidson, *The Free Will Baptists in America, 1727-1984* (Nashville: Randall House, 1985).

[1492] G. W. Paschal, "Morgan Edwards' Materials towards a History of the Baptists in the Province of North Carolina," *The North Carolina Historical Review* 7, no. 3 (July 1930): 369, 369n2, 370n8, 393n107 (365-99); cf. McBeth, *The Baptist Heritage*, 222-23. See also Robert E. Picirilli, *History of Free Will Baptist State Associations* (Nashville: Randall House Publications, 1976).

the mother church of Northern Free Will Baptists.[1493] Having been converted under the influence of Evangelist George Whitefield, Randall received his ordination here at the New Durham church. Since 1982, this has been a Fundamental, Free Will Baptist church.[1494] In 1911, a merger of the northern group with the Northern Baptist Convention took a large majority of the eleven hundred Free Will Baptist churches, along with their properties and several colleges. In 1916–17, most of the churches that had rejected the merger reorganized into the Co-operative General Association of Free Will Baptists.

In 1935, the northern Co-operative General Association, descending from the Randall movement, merged with the southern General Conference, descending from the Palmer movement, to establish the National Association of Free Will Baptists (NAFWB). The NAFWB adopted a *Treatise*, setting forth their basic doctrines and practices.[1495] The NAFWB office is in Antioch, Tennessee, and its official paper is titled *ONE Magazine*. Representative NAFWB institutions include Welch College in Gallatin, Tennessee, and Randall University in Moore, Oklahoma.

[1493] See Frederick L. Wiley, *Life and Influence of the Rev. Benjamin Randall Founder of the Free Baptist Denomination* (Philadelphia: American Baptist Publication Society, 1915); John Buzzell, *The Life of Elder Benjamin Randall* (Limerick, ME: Hobbs, Woodman and Co., 1827); and Scott E. Bryant, "The Awakening of the Freewill Baptists: Benjamin Randall and the Founding of an American Religious Tradition" (PhD diss., Baylor University, 2007).

[1494] The Free Will Baptist meetinghouse, on Ridge Road, New Durham, dates to 1819 and is on the National Register of Historic Places. The church had five members, in 1982, when Jim Nason, his wife Pat, and their four sons, arrived to begin a new ministry, in accord with the Great Commission of Matthew 28:18-20. The building that the congregation regularly uses is at 20 Depot Road, New Durham, NH. They use the old meetinghouse on special occasions.

[1495] *A Treatise of the Faith and Practices of the National Association of Free Will Baptists, Inc.*, "adopted by the National Association, November 7, 1935, at Nashville, Tennessee," latest revision (Antioch, TN: Executive Office of the National Association of Free Will Baptists, 2013); cf. *A Treatise on the Faith of the Free-Will Baptists*, "with an appendix containing a summary of their usages in church government" 6th ed. (Dover, NH: Free-Will Baptist Printing Establishment, 1854).

In 1961, the North Carolina State Convention of Original Free Will Baptists (OFWB), headquartered in Mount Olive, withdrew from the NAFWB over various worship and polity issues. The OFWB sponsors the University of Mount Olive, which houses a large collection of Free Will Baptist history.[1496] Some Free Will Baptist churches and institutions, such as Southeastern Free Will Baptist College, in Wendell, North Carolina, operate as independent.

[1496] Michael R. Pelt, *A History of Original Free Will Baptists* (Mount Olive, NC: Mount Olive College, 1996); Floyd B. Cherry, *An Introduction to Original Free Will Baptists* (Ayden, NC: Free Will Baptist Press, n.d.); and *Convention of Original Free Will Baptists* (Ayden, NC: Palmer Printing Solutions, 2017).

Appendix C

A Travel Guide to Historical Baptist Sites in England, Wales, and America

---❋---

(Italics indicate key points at each site. The book's index can lead to further information.)

England and Wales
London

In the back of Amen Court, in the shadow of St. Paul's Cathedral, stands the *only surviving wall of Newgate Prison*, where many Baptists suffered and died.

Inside the *Church of St. Sepulchre without Newgate*, at Holborn Viaduct, a hand bell known as the Execution Bell, resides in a glass case, situated near the entrance of a blocked-up tunnel that once connected the church with Newgate Prison. At midnight prior to execution days, the church's bellman would walk through the tunnel and into the prison. Standing outside the cells of condemned prisoners, he would ring twelve double tolls of the bell and chant their condemnation. The church is also rich in its own history. John Rogers, once a vicar of this church, had been the first Protestant burned at the stake, during the reign of Mary Tudor. The remains of Captain John Smith, early leader at Jamestown, Virginia, lie buried in the church's cemetery. Inside the church is a brass plaque dedicated to this famous explorer.

On London's Clink Street, the *Clink Museum* stands at the ruins of this infamous prison,[1497] where John Greenwood, Henry Barrow, and Francis Johnson (of the "Ancient Church"), along with Henry Jacob, and John Lathrop (forerunners of Particular Baptists), all suffered incarceration, during 1587–1634.

Inside the nearby *Southwark Cathedral* is the tomb of Bishop Lancelot Andrewes, a translator of the King James Bible. Be sure to see the John Harvard Chapel.

Near Southwark Cathedral is a full-sized reconstruction of the warship, *Golden Hinde*, used by Sir Francis Drake when he circumnavigated the world in 1577–80.

Metropolitan Tabernacle, where Charles Spurgeon once served, is at the junction of Elephant and Castle Streets (Southwark).

Bunhill Fields, at 38 City Road, was the Burying Ground for Dissenters. Here stand the tombs of key players in Baptist history: John Rippon, Joseph Ivimey, John Gill, and John Bunyan. Important Baptists whose tombstones here have been destroyed over time include Henry Jessey, Hanserd Knollys, William Kiffin, and Vavasor Powell. See also the tombstones of notable non-Baptists, such as Daniel Defoe, author of *Robinson Crusoe*, Isaac Watts, "Father of English Hymnody," and Susanna Wesley, mother of nineteen children, of whom the most eminent were John and Charles. Just across the road from Bunhill Fields is the Wesley House.

Plymouth

Visit the *Mayflower Memorial* at the Barbican, from where the Pilgrims, in 1620, departed for the New World. Visit the Mayflower Museum just down the street.

Oxford

In 1810, the London Baptist Education Society (est. 1752) led in the founding of Stepney Academy, in East London. Moving to

---

[1497] See E. J. Burford, *A Short History of the Clink Prison* (London: published by the author, 1989).

the center of Regent's Park, London, in 1855, Stepney Academy became Regent's Park College, a constituent College of the University of London. In 1927, Regent's Park College moved to Oxford, and, since 1957, it has been a Permanent Private Hall of the University of Oxford. *The Angus Library and Archive at Regent's Park College* holds priceless treasures of Baptist history. Henry Jacob, founder of the J-L-J Church, received his BA and MA degrees from Oxford's St. Mary Hall College. Jacob also served as music director at Oxford's Corpus Christi College.

See the *Martyrs Memorial*, a stone monument, near Balliol College, at the intersection of St. Giles, Magdalen, and Beaumont Streets. The Memorial commemorates Oxford's Reformer-martyrs, Thomas Cranmer, Nicholas Ridley, and Hugh Latimer. The earliest Baptists were products of the Reformation.

Experience one of the bus tours of Oxford University. These can be booked at the *Visitor Information Centre* at 15–16 Broad Street.

University of Cambridge

At the University of Cambridge, Christ's College graduates included Francis Johnson of the Ancient Church and John Smyth of Gainsborough. John Lathrop, second pastor of London's J-L-J Church, was a Queens' College graduate. Lathrop's successor, Henry Jessey, earned his BA and MA degrees at St. John's College. London Baptist, Hanserd Knollys, received his training at St. Catherine's Hall. Roger Williams, founder of America's First Baptist Church, was a Pembroke College graduate. Henry Dunster, first president of Harvard, earned his BA and MA in Magdalene College. An excellent place to begin is the *Cambridge Visitor Information Centre*, at The Guildhall, Peas Hill CB2 3AD.

Bedford

Situated on Mill Street, *the Bunyan Meeting House* and its *Bunyan Museum* preserve priceless memorabilia of John Bunyan's life and times. The present Bunyan Meeting was built in 1849–50. A bronze statue of Bunyan stands at the north end of High Street.

Paulerspury

In the porch of *St. James Church* (Anglican), a plaque commemorates William Carey, missionary to India and father of Baptist foreign missions. A few feet away, just to the right of the porch, the grave of William's father, Edmund Carey, carries this inscription: "Reader, time is short, prepare to meet thy God." The Carey cottage, William Carey's birthplace, stood on what is now Carey Road, at Pury End, a hamlet, half a mile outside Paulerspury. In 1965, the cottage suffered demolition, to make room for modern homes. A memorial cairn, built from the original stones, is all that remains of the Carey cottage.

Piddington

The *Church of St. John the Baptist* (Anglican), in Piddington, is where William Carey and Dorothy ("Dolly") Plackett were married in 1781. (See Chapter 10.).

Hackleton

In one of the rooms of *Carey Baptist Church*, in Hackleton, one can see the pulpit from which William Carey once preached in a thatched cottage. In 1809, when the thatched cottage could no longer accommodate the growing congregation, the church moved to a nearby site and erected a "24 feet by 36 feet" chapel. (The thatched cottage eventually suffered demolition.). In 1813, they had seventy-six members. There were 129 members, in 1862, when they added a Sunday-School room and a vestry. The present edifice of Carey Baptist Church dates to 1888–89.

Olney

In 1775, John Sutcliff (1752–1814) commenced his pastorate at *Olney Baptist Church*, which continues to the present day. In 1785, young William Carey placed himself under the tutelage of Sutcliff and under the watch-care of the Olney church where he held membership. After Carey preached his first sermon to the Olney congregation, the unanimous conclusion was that the young man needed more time before they could ordain him. They promised to hear him again. Operating a little theological academy in his home, Sutcliff prepared Carey for the ministry. In 1786, Sutcliff led in Cary's ordination, and the Olney church commissioned him to preach.

Sutcliff's neighbors in Olney included the local minister of the Church of England, John Newton (1725-1807), author of "Amazing Grace." Hymn writer and poet, William Cowper (1731-1800), was a member of Newton's parish, and, at the time of Sutcliff's arrival, Newton and Cowper were composing their popular "Olney Hymns." Visit *John Newton's church and tombstone*, and the *Cowper and Newton Museum and Gardens*.

Moulton

In 1787, William Carey received ordination into his first pastorate, the Moulton Baptist congregation, later named *Carey Baptist Church*. At Carey's ordination, John Ryland Jr. asked the questions, John Sutcliff preached the charge, from 2 Timothy 4:5, and Andrew Fuller preached a challenge to the members. The congregation was soon compelled to reconstruct and enlarge their small brick building to thirty feet square. In 1870, the church enlarged the structure to its present size. In 1958, they added the William Carey Memorial Hall, whose renovation in the 1990s included a multi-panel mural, depicting the story of Carey's life and work. Church rooms underwent renovation in 2002, and the year 2009 witnessed major refurbishment of the auditorium.

Next to Carey Baptist Church is the *Carey Cottage*, where the trough he had used to soak his shoe leather is still set in the wall. Part of the cottage is a museum that includes Carey's pulpit. On the exterior wall, a tablet inscription reveals that Carey lived here from 1785 to 1789. It pays tribute to Carey as "shoemaker, schoolmaster, preacher, scholar, and missionary pioneer."

Kettering

As faithful members of Andrew Fuller's church, Beeby and Martha Wallis used their home as an inn for traveling evangelists. Many still call it the "Gospel Inn." Situated on Lower Street, in the heart of Kettering town center, the historic Wallis House is now the *"Carey Mission House,"* the featured attraction of "Martha Wallis Court," a residential facility for the elderly. The room in which fourteen men met, on October 2, 1792, to form the Baptist Missionary Society, still contains the table and chairs they used. The meeting concluded with a missionary offering. Fuller Baptist Church has Andrew Fuller's silver snuffbox he passed around the table for the offering. Near the street is a bronze memorial plaque. Across the street is the *Chesham House*, home of Thomas Gotch, the merchant for whom Carey made shoes while at Moulton.

From 1782 to the end of his life, Andrew Fuller (1754–1815) served the pastorate of the Baptist Church in Kettering. By 1786, the congregation was compelled to enlarge their chapel. With increasing growth, by 1804–5, they enlarged it again—this time to seat nine hundred persons. They replaced that building with the present Lombardian style edifice, during 1860–61, when the church's name changed from Kettering Baptist to *"Fuller Baptist Church."* It can accommodate about a thousand people. Its Heritage Room displays Andrew Fuller's pulpit, communion table, desk, and sermon notes, along with Widow Wallis's teapot. Tombstones in the small graveyard at the rear of the premises include those of Andrew Fuller and Beeby and Martha Wallis.

Thrapston

The *Baptist church at Thrapston*, Northamptonshire, was once shepherded by Reynold Hogg (1752–1843), one of the founders of the Baptist Missionary Society (1792). With the construction of the present building, in 1787, a small, Congregationalist-Separatist group opened its doors for worship. In 1790, Reynold Hogg became their preacher. In 1797, they organized into a Baptist church and ordained Hogg as pastor. He served here for seventeen years. The remains of Reynold and his wife, Ann, lie entombed underneath the church. Inside the auditorium is a Commemorative Tablet. The congregation still uses this two-storied, brick building. Town records indicate some mid-nineteenth-century renovation.

Leicester

In 1789, William Carey and his family moved into a cottage across the street from Leicester's Harvey Lane Baptist Church, which he shepherded to the time of their departure to India in 1793. The Harvey Lane building no longer exists. When Harvey Lane Baptist outgrew its building, in 1845, the congregation moved to Belvoir Street and changed its name to Belvoir Street Baptist. In 1940, Belvoir Street Baptist and Charles Street Baptist (planted by Harvey Lane in 1831) merged to form the United Baptist Church, at the Charles Street facilities. In 1983, the United Baptist Church and the Victoria Road Church merged to form the present *Central Baptist Church*, still at the Charles Street address. Meanwhile, in 1915-16, the William Carey Cottage, on Harvey Lane, became the Carey Museum, or "House of Memories." Due to street additions in the 1960s, the Carey Museum suffered demolition. A Holiday Inn now occupies the site. Across from the hotel's main entrance is a commemorative plaque to Carey. Today, the William Carey Museum, in Central Baptist Church, displays the artifacts once housed in the Carey Museum at Harvey Lane. At the top of De Montfort Square, just off New Walk, there is a statue of Baptist preacher, Robert Hall Jr. (1764-1831), who served the Harvey Lane pastorate during 1807-26. (See Chapter 10.).

Northampton

On October 5, 1783, William Carey walked five miles from Piddington to Northampton, for John Ryland Jr. (1753-1825) to immerse him in the River Nene at 6:00 AM. He was baptized on the spot where the modern railway station is now located. The construction of the station necessitated the rerouting of the River Nene. Carey's baptism took place where the station's "platform one" ends. In 2011, for the 250th anniversary of Carey's birth, a *William Carey plaque* was unveiled here at the railway station.

John Collett Ryland Sr. (1723-92) and John Ryland Jr. served the pastorate of Northampton's College Lane Baptist Church (built in 1697). The church became *College Street Baptist Church*, in 1863, when the congregation erected a new building on the same site. The church would later close, but, on College Street, one can admire this magnificent building's classical façade of Corinthian pillars. College Street Baptist records reside at the Northamptonshire Record Office.

At Doddridge Street (NN1 2RN) is *Castle Hill United Reformed Church*, once known as Castle Hill Church, where the independent Congregationalist, Phillip Doddridge (1702-51), served as pastor. While Doddridge's compromising endorsements led many young men toward erroneous doctrines, his songs, such as "O Happy Day," and his classic book, *The Rise and Progress of Religion in the Soul* (1745), are still in use. William Wilberforce's reading of *Rise and Progress* became one of the instruments, in 1784, leading to his conversion. More than two hundred students passed through *Doddridge's Academy for Dissenters*, during its twelve years of existence (1740-52). The building that housed the Academy still stands on Sheep Street, a ten-minute walk from the church.

Scrooby

Visit *St. Wilfred's Church* (Anglican) from which the Pilgrims separated. See the only remaining section of *Scrooby Manor House* where postmaster William Brewster lived, and where the Separatists organized their church in 1606. This is the church that the future Baptist, Thomas Helwys, sacrificially assisted in their escape to Holland. In 1620, many of these Pilgrims would come to the New World on the *Mayflower* ship.

Gainsborough

Visit historic *Gainsborough Old Hall* (Lincolnshire), where John Smyth held his Separatist meetings. From here, in early 1608, Smyth and most of his congregation escaped to Holland. Rich in Separatist history, the Gainsborough Old Hall is well worth a two-hour visit. It has a Gift Shop and Tea Shop.

Ilston and Swansea, Wales

John Myles organized the earliest Baptist church in Wales, in 1651. During Oliver Cromwell's rule, Myles's church occupied the thirteenth-century *Church of St. Illtyd*, located on a small country lane, at Ilston, near the west end of the Swansea airfield. At the Restoration of the British monarchy, in 1660, officials of Charles II ousted John Myles and his congregation from St. Illtyd Church. Baptists fled the area, but strong tradition testifies that Myles and a remnant of his people worshipped secretly in a secluded building, now in ruins, a half mile from the Church of St. Illtyd. For the shortest walk to the site, begin at Gower Inn, in nearby Parkmill. Near the west end of the Inn's parking lot is a wide iron gate, to the left of which is this bronze inscription:

The path beyond this gate leads to the Ilston Memorial erected in 1928. On the ruins of the meeting place of the Baptist church founded by John Myles in 1649, the Memorial is built from the original stones.

The *"Ilston Memorial"* is a stone pulpit, standing among the ancient ruins of the Baptist chapel, formerly a Roman Catholic chapel. To reach the site, follow the path for a delightful quarter-mile walk into the Ilston Valley. At certain points along the way, you will see the stream, known by locals as the "Killy Willy," running along near the path. Twisting and winding across the valley floor, the Killy Willy cuts across the path in several places, where small, wooden, foot bridges allow you to continue to the medieval chapel called *"Trinity Well."* Underneath the chapel's stone foundation is a spring to which superstitious Catholics once flocked for its promised healing powers. There is no record of when the chapel fell into disuse. The Memorial pulpit holds a carved, open Bible. Underneath the Bible is a plaque with this inscription:

> To commemorate the foundation in this valley of the first Baptist Church in Wales 1649–60 and to honor the memory of its founder John Myles. This ruin is the site of the pre-Reformation chapel of Trinity Well and is claimed by tradition as a meeting place of the above Cromwellian Church. This memorial has been erected with the permission of Admiral A.W. Heneage Vivian, C.R.M.V.O. and was unveiled by the Rt. Hon. D. Lloyd George, M.P.O.M., 13th, June 1928.

Key Baptist Sites in America

Barnstable, Massachusetts

John Lathrop, the second pastor of London's J-L-J Church, immigrated to Barnstable, where his house, built in 1644, still stands as part of the *Sturgis Library*, at 3090 Main Street. Here, one can stand in the room that once served as Lathrop's meetinghouse. On display is Lathrop's copy of the Scriptures—a 1605 Bishops' Bible. See the section, "John Lathrop (1584–1653)," in chapter five.

Organized in London, in 1616, and now situated in a seaside village, in the northwest part of Barnstable, Lathrop's church is the *West Barnstable Parish Church*, at 2049 Meetinghouse Way. It is the only existing remnant of the J-L-J Church—from whom the earliest Particular Baptists in England departed, during 1633–38, to gather their own churches. Erected in 1717 and remodeled in 1852, West Barnstable Parish Church underwent restoration, in 1953–58, including its high pulpit and sounding board. On the church tower is a half-ton bell cast by Paul Revere and Son in 1806.

Andover, Massachusetts

On the back campus of *Phillips Academy*, one can walk down "Judson Road" and visit the secluded area by the "Rabbit Pond," where Adoniram Judson, Luther Rice, and other believers kneeled each morning by a huge boulder, prayed for missions, and dedicated their lives to God. On that boulder (affectionately called *"Missionary Rock"*), citizens of Andover, in 1910, affixed a memorial plaque, honoring the faithful prayer band of Andover students. See the section, "Missionary Rock at Andover Theological Seminary," in Chapter 17.

Plymouth, Massachusetts

Upon reading his son's *Christian Baptism*, in 1817, Adoniram Judson Sr., of the *Church of the Pilgrimage*, on the north side of Town Square, became a Baptist and resigned the Congregational pastorate. After serving for most of his life in Burma, Judson Jr. died at sea. There is a cenotaph to his honor on *Burial Hill*.

Cambridge, Massachusetts

The *grave of Henry Dunster*, first president of Harvard College, is in the Old Burying Ground (adjacent to First Church, Unitarian) on Church Street. Harvard forced Dunster out of the presidency for his defense of believer's baptism by immersion. Harvard never had a greater president. (See Chapter 13.).

Boston, Massachusetts

First Baptist Church was founded by Thomas Gould, in 1665. In 1872, Brattle Square Unitarian Church erected a brick building, at 110 Commonwealth Avenue. By 1876, the church was extinct, and First Baptist purchased the building. (See Chapter 13.).

Swansea, Massachusetts

Founded by John Myles from Wales, the *First Baptist Church* of Swansea, at 21 Baptist Street, was the first Baptist church in Massachusetts. Its present building dates to 1848, and its adjacent cemetery dates to 1731. (See Chapter 13.).

Cheshire, Massachusetts

On the corner of Church and School Streets stands a concrete *replica of the cider press* that produced the gigantic cheese that

John Leland gave to President Thomas Jefferson. In Cheshire Cemetery, *Leland's obelisk grave-marker* displays a commemorative plaque. See "The Big Cheshire Cheese," in Chapter 16.

Williamstown, Massachusetts

At Williams College (Congregational), a twelve-foot-high marble, monument, called the *Haystack Prayer Meeting Memorial*, commemorates "The Birthplace of American Foreign Missions 1806," out of which came Baptists Adoniram Judson and Luther Rice. See the section, "Haystack Prayer Meeting at Williams College (1806)," in Chapter 17.

Middleboro, Massachusetts

Once known as "Backus Memorial Baptist Church," *First Baptist Church of North Middleboro*, Massachusetts, is now in its third building since Isaac Backus founded it in 1756. It stands at the intersection of Plymouth and Bedford Streets. In Titicut Parish Cemetery, at 41 Plymouth Street, *Backus's granite tomb* is pulpit-shaped and holds an open Bible. Under the Bible is a bronze memorial plaque.

Providence, Rhode Island

First Baptist Church, founded by Roger Williams in 1638, was the earliest Baptist Church in America. Erected in 1775, its present building is at 75 North Main Street. Its twelfth pastor, James Manning, was founder and president of nearby *Brown University*.

Underneath *the Roger Williams Statue*, at Prospect Terrace, lie Williams's ashes. With John Clarke, he was the co-founder of Rhode Island. (See Chapter 12.).

Newport, Rhode Island

United Baptist Church, John Clarke Memorial, at 30 Spring Street, was founded in 1644 by John Clarke. It was America's second Baptist church. Clarke was co-founder of Rhode Island

and an early defender of liberty of conscience. *John Clarke's tombstone* stands in the John Clarke Family Cemetery, on the west side of Dr. Marcus Wheatland Boulevard. The key to the cemetery's padlock is available at the United Baptist Church office. Adjoining the cemetery, a small park has two *Memorials to John Clarke*: A plaque on a small rock, and a monument, erected by the Baptist History Preservation Society.

Newport Historical Society (NHS) houses the first Seventh-Day Baptist church in America. In 1671, Stephen Mumford led a small group out of First Baptist to establish this church. In 1884, the NHS bought the Seventh-Day Baptists' 1730 wooden chapel. In 1915, the NHS moved the elegant chapel from Barney Street to the rear of their headquarters, at 82 Touro Street. Here, the NHS encased the chapel in brick and incorporated it into their facility. More restoration took place in 2009. (See Chapter 12.).

Middletown, Rhode Island

In the *Holmes family cemetery*, on the west side of Vaucluse Avenue, just north of Green End Avenue, Route 138, a memorial tombstone honors the notable Obadiah Holmes, who suffered a public beating in Boston for preaching the gospel in a private home. He became successor to Pastor John Clarke in Newport. See Chapter 12.

Imlaystown, New Jersey

Ye Olde Yellow Meeting House, located on Yellow Meetinghouse Road, off Route 526, dates to about 1737. Its earliest records, beginning in 1766, are in a 165-page, handwritten "Church Book: Giving an Account of ye First Settlement & Progress of the Baptists at Crosswicks, or Upper Freehold." In 1766, its forty-seven members organized into Crosswicks Baptist Church. In 1773, its name changed to Upper Freehold Baptist Church, located in Imlaystown since 1855. Since the 1991 restoration of Ye Olde Yellow Meeting House, including its yellow paint, it has accommodated special occasions for the congregation. The word *Ye* in its title should be pronounced *the*. Early movable type used the letter *Y* like the first two letters of the Anglo-Saxon character known as the *thorn*. Common abbreviations include yᵉ ("the"), yᵗ ("that"), and yⁿ ("then").

Hopewell, New Jersey

Hopewell Academy (est. 1756), a Latin grammar school, founded by Isaac Eaton, pastor at Hopewell Baptist, was the earliest Baptist academy in America. The building is now a private home, but a historical plaque stands near the street. The academy's alumni included James Manning, founder of Brown University. Other alumni included the "Baptist Whitefield," Hezekiah Smith, who was a classmate with Manning at Princeton and founding pastor of First Baptist at Haverhill, Massachusetts.

Hopewell Baptist Church is on West Broad Street. One of its most notable pastors was Oliver Hart (1723–95). Gravestones in the church cemetery include those of Isaac Eaton and John Hart, signer of the Declaration of Independence. Hart was not a member here, but he donated the land on which the building stands. Revolutionary War veterans lie buried here. The appearance of the Hopewell Baptist meetinghouse has not changed since 1822, when the congregation rebuilt it on its original foundation.

New York City

John Gano (1727–1804) was the first full-time pastor of *First Baptist in the City of New York* (est. 1762). During the War of Independence, Gano served as chaplain to George Washington. In 1891, during the ministry of I. M. Haldeman (1845–1933), the church erected its present building at 265 West 79th Street at Broadway. (See Chapter 16.).

Newark, Delaware

The *Welsh Tract Baptist Church*, on Welsh Tract Road, originated in 1701, when sixteen people formed the original congregation in Wales. In 1703, they settled on a forty-thousand-acre tract of land, granted by William Penn and since known as the Welsh Tract. As the first Baptist church in Delaware and situated a couple of miles south of Newark, they built a log meetinghouse in 1706. In 1746, they constructed their present brick building. In the Battle at Cooch's Bridge, on September 3, 1777, a British cannon ball passed through the auditorium. Brickwork patches on both sides of the building still mark the event. The historical marker at the nearby battle site reports that this was the "only battle of the American Revolution on Delaware soil and claimed to have been the first in which the stars and stripes were carried." A plaque at the church reads, "Old Welsh Tract Church - Oldest Primitive Baptist Church in America." With the 1814 establishment of the Triennial Convention, the Welsh Tract Church, having become hyper-Calvinist, voiced strong opposition to the Convention's missionary emphasis. In 1824, the Baptist General Tract Society made its debut. At the establishment of the American Baptist Home Mission Society, in 1832, Welsh Tract reacted by becoming a "mother church" of independent, Primitive (Old School) Baptist churches. The church broke away from mainstream Baptists at every level. Often called "Hard Shell Baptists," Primitive Baptists opposed missionary societies, Bible societies, theological seminaries, and even Sunday schools. They mockingly compared evangelistic appeals with Jehu's invitation, "Come with me, and see my zeal for the Lord" (2 Kings 10:16). Primitive Baptist ministers had little or no formal training, and seldom received a salary. Their congregations have generally used no musical instruments, but they often sing a cappella, in four-part harmony, known as Sacred Harp, a style of eighteen-century folk music. There is often a sort of music in their sermons, as preachers deliver rhythmic, extemporaneous messages in a distinctive singsong voice. Some practice foot washing as an ordinance.[1498]

[1498] See Morgan Edwards, *Materials towards a History of the Baptists in Delaware*, in *The Pennsylvania Magazine of History and Biography* (Philadelphia: Historical Society of Pennsylvania, 1885), 45–61, 197–213; *Records of the Welsh Tract Baptist Meeting: Pencader Hundred, New Castle County, Delaware, 1701–1828*, vol. 42 of *Papers of the Historical Society of Delaware* (Wilmington, DE: Historical Society of Delaware, 1904); and Richard B. Cook, *The Early and Later Delaware Baptists* (Philadelphia: American

Philadelphia, Pennsylvania

Pennepack Baptist Church, founded by Elias Keach, in 1688, is the oldest surviving Baptist church in the Middle Colonies. In 1805, at the peak of the Second Great Awakening, during the ministry of Samuel Jones, the congregation erected its present (third) building, constructed from fieldstone collected from the surrounding meadows. Straight-backed box pews occupy the main floor. An elegant, high pulpit enables ministers to look out on level with the balconies on three sides. Attached to the front of the high pulpit, a bronze plaque lists the names of the twelve charter members. In 1885, the church began using a new building, a mile away, but, in 2006, they returned to the 1805 building, at 87 Krewstown Road, where they still meet. (See Chapter 14.).

Berryville, Virginia

Berryville (formerly Buckmarsh) Baptist Church is at 114 Academy Street. John Gerrard (Garrard, ca. 1720–87), in 1772, constituted the Buckmarsh church. James Ireland (ca. 1745–1806) served the Buckmarsh pastorate from 1786 until his death. Ireland's remains lie in an unknown grave in the Buckmarsh cemetery. A historical plaque marks the site where Buckmarsh Baptist once stood. The plaque is only a few yards north of the VA 7 overpass on US 340 (southbound lane), just north of Berryville. In the 1840s, the Buckmarsh congregation moved into Berryville and changed their name to Berryville Baptist. Note: The marker on US 340 gives 1778 as the year Ireland began his pastorate at Buckmarsh, but a James Ireland memorial cenotaph, at *Berryville Baptist Church*, has a bronze plaque, giving 1786 as the date. The year 1786 is accurate, since Gerrard was pastor until near the time of his death in 1787.[1499]

Baptist Publication Society, 1880), 91 (74–96).

[1499] See chapter 15, "The Separate Baptists: Struggle for Religious Freedom in North Carolina, Georgia, and Virginia."

Fredericksburg, Virginia

On Washington Avenue, stands the *Thomas Jefferson Religious Freedom Monument*, made from stones sent from churches across the country. It commemorates Jefferson's Virginia Religious Freedom Statute, promising that "no man shall ... suffer on account of his religious opinions or belief." The Statute became the basis for the religion clause of the First Amendment.

Marked by a tall obelisk, at 1500 Washington Avenue, is the grave of George Washington's mother. Near the obelisk, an inscription on *Meditation Rock* says of her, "Here Mary Ball Washington prayed for the safety of her son and country during the dark days of the Revolution." Mary's home is at 1200 Charles Street.

Orange, Montpelier Station, and Charlottesville, Virginia

The Leland-Madison Memorial Park, six miles east of Orange, at the intersection of US 20/Constitution Highway and SR 658/Clifton Road, is the place where James Madison met in an oak grove with Baptist-Evangelist John Leland, to discuss the issue of religious freedom of conscience. This meeting led to the Bill of Rights.

Nearby is *Montpelier*, home of the two-term, fourth President, James Madison—Father of the Constitution and Architect of the Bill of Rights. It was here that Dolley Madison earned the epithet "America's first, 'First Lady'." Montpelier is at 11350 Constitution Highway, Montpelier Station.

A short drive southwest of Orange is *Monticello*, at 931 Thomas Jefferson Parkway, Charlottesville, the home of President, Thomas Jefferson—principal author of the Declaration of Independence. His tombstone inscription says:

> Here was buried Thomas Jefferson, author of
> the Declaration of American Independence, of
> the Statute of Virginia for Religious Freedom,
> and father of the University of Virginia.

Tappahannock, Virginia

In 1774, Baptists in Tappahannock established the earliest Baptist church in Essex County—Piscataway (now Mt. Zion) Baptist, on Dunbrooke Road.[1500] On that same day, inside the local Essex County Courthouse, which is now the oldest courthouse building in Virginia, officials sentenced fines and imprisonments to the three men who preached the church's opening service—John Waller, John Shackelford, and Robert Ware.[1501] Their crime was "preaching and expounding the scriptures contrary to law." Shackelford and Ware spent eight days in the local jail. Waller spent fourteen. This *1728 Essex County Courthouse*, with its thick walls of Flemish bond brick, still stands on the corner of US 360 and US 17. In a turn of irony, from 1878 to 2007, this same courthouse would serve as a church. In 1875, Frank Brown Beale had founded Tappahannock's Centennial Baptist Church, named for the forthcoming, one-hundredth anniversary of America's founding. In 1878, the church purchased the courthouse and added a bell tower to the front. Near the location of Beale's pulpit, magistrates had condemned Waller, Shackelford, and Ware for preaching Christ. These same dense walls, which had resounded condemnation against preaching, would reverberate the gospel for 130 years. When Frank Beale died in 1908, the church changed its name to Beale Memorial Baptist.[1502] During 2004–7, the church moved into new facilities on Tidewater Trail, just north of town, and sold the 1728 courthouse building back to Essex County.

Chesterfield, Virginia

The Chesterfield County Museum, at 6813 Mimms Loop, is a replica of the 1749 courthouse where magistrates, during

---

[1500] The present brick building of Mt. Zion Baptist dates to 1884–86.
[1501] Tappahannock Court Records, Order Book number 29, pages 195–96. Ivison Lewis was also apprehended, but released, since there was no proof that he preached.
[1502] Lewis Peyton Little, *Imprisoned Preachers and Religious Liberty in Virginia* (Lynchburg, VA: J. P. Bell Co., 1938), 406.

1770–74, sentenced seven Baptist preachers to jail for preaching Christ without state-church approval.[1503] Where the jail once stood, there now stands the *Religious Freedom Monument*, a granite memorial with a bronze tablet inscribed to the memory of those Baptist preachers. See the section, "Virginia Baptist Preachers Imprisoned in Chesterfield Jail 1770–74," in Chapter 15.

Brookneal, Virginia

The *grave of Virginia Governor Patrick Henry*, a friend of persecuted Baptists, is at Patrick Henry National Memorial, 1497 Red Hill Road, Brookneal, VA 24528. This beautiful plantation is called *Red Hill*.

Chatham, Virginia

The grave of the notable Baptist, John Weatherford, lies in a wooded area near *Shockoe Baptist Church*, at 16 Spring Garden Road. His tomb inscription reads:

Elder
John Weatherford
Aa devoted Baptist Minister
Born in 1740, began to preach
in 1764. [He] lay in Chesterfield
jail in 1773 5 months for
preaching.
He moved to Halifax in 1813
and died Jan. 23, 1833.

In the cemetery behind Shockoe Baptist, a *memorial cenotaph* inscription reads:

[1503] Next to the County Museum is an 1892 jail. The present courthouse dates to 1917.

Elder John Weatherford
A Devoted Baptist Minister
Born in Charlotte Co. 1740
Lay in Jail in Chesterfield Co. in 1773 five months for preaching.
Moved to Halifax in 1813, to Pittsylvania 1823
Died Jan. 23, 1833
A sufferer for conscience sake
An earnest and faithful minister of the Gospel

Liberty, North Carolina

Founded by Shubal Stearns, in 1755, *Sandy Creek Baptist Church* is located at 4765 Sandy Creek Church Road, Liberty. Stearns's obelisk tombstone stands in the church cemetery. Historical monuments on the grounds provide fascinating glimpses into the Sandy Creek heritage. The year 2005 marked the 250th anniversary of Stearns's organization of the church. In 2015, Sandy Creek Baptist erected a new, picturesque church, situated next door to an *1802 log meetinghouse* (owned and used for many years by Primitive Baptists). A short distance from the site, a historical marker, at the intersection of Ramseur Julian Road and Old Liberty Road, describes Sandy Creek as the "Mother of Separate Baptist churches across the South." (See Chapter 15.).

Cross Hill, South Carolina

In the church cemetery at *Bethabara Baptist Church*, at 635 Bethabara Church Road, there stands a memorial monument, with detailed script honoring its founder, the celebrated church planter and evangelist, John Waller, who suffered persecution for preaching the gospel without state approval.

Greenwood, South Carolina

Siloam Baptist Church, 2409 Siloam Church Road, was founded by John Waller. The historical marker at the church offers valuable information. There is also a *John Waller Highway Marker* on East Scotch Cross Road. Traveling south, if you pass Pembroke Road on the left, you just missed this marker on the right:

John Waller 1741–1802
One half mile south of the marker is the grave of John Waller, early minister of the Baptist faith in Virginia, where he is credited with founding eighteen churches. He was persecuted and imprisoned by the established church and civil authorities. In 1793, he moved to South Carolina, where he founded Bethabara and Siloam Churches.

John Waller's white marble tombstone, erected in the 1870s, replaced the original, which had been made of limestone. The inscription reads:

Eld. Jno. Waller
Died July 4 of 1802
Age 60 Yrs.

The Waller home was likely near the gravesite, which is on private property. Permission is required to visit this gravesite.

Charleston, South Carolina

First Baptist Church finds its roots in 1696, when William Screven and his twenty-eight-member church (est. 1682) moved from Kittery, Maine, and settled near Charleston, as the earliest Baptist church in the south. In 1698, they moved into Charleston, as First Baptist Church, still located on Church Street. Other early Baptist pastors here include Oliver Hart and Richard Furman.

Georgetown, South Carolina

Founded in 1729 by William Screven's son Elisha, Georgetown lies sixty miles north of Charleston. *The Screven family cemetery* is on Prince Street, near the intersection of Prince and Screven Streets. In the 700 block of Church Street, the remains of Edmund Botsford (1745-1819), early pastor of Antipedo Baptist (later First Baptist) Church, lie buried in the *Old Baptist Cemetery*. A marker was placed at Botsford's grave in 2004.

Saluda, South Carolina

Luther Rice preached his final sermon at *Pine Pleasant Baptist Church* (est. 1831). His remains were laid to rest here in the *churchyard*, at 457 Pine Pleasant Road. Under a distinctive canopy, his tomb has a marble slab with a biographical inscription.

Appling, Georgia

Old Kiokee Baptist Church, founded by Daniel Marshall, is the earliest continuing Baptist Church in Georgia. They erected their third (present) meetinghouse, in 1808, with its the quaint auditorium, gallery, and hand-hewn pews. The congregation uses this building, at 2520 Ray Owens Road, for special services. For access, contact the church (706-541-1086). Inquire about the Marshall home-site and cemetery. In the median of US 221, near the Appling courthouse, the people of Georgia, in 1903, erected a monument to Daniel Marshall and his "devotion and consecration ... to the cause of Christ." (See Chapter 15.).

Upper Alton, Illinois

Pioneer missionary, John Mason Peck (1789-1858), saturated Missouri and Illinois with the gospel, evangelizing, organizing churches, and establishing the Baptist movement in the West. At Southern Illinois University Dental School, this memorial plaque highlights his life and legacy:

John Mason Peck

On this site in 1831, John Mason Peck (1789-1858), pioneer Baptist preacher, author, and educator, established the school which became Shurtleff College. In 1817, Peck had left his home in New

England with a vision "to bring the lamp of learning and the light of the Gospel" into the undeveloped West. He, his wife Sally, and three children endured an arduous four-month trip in a small one-horse wagon, settling in Rock Spring, near O'Fallon, Illinois.

There, in 1827, Peck founded Rock Spring Seminary, the first institution of its kind in the State of Illinois. In 1831, the Seminary was moved to the growing city of Alton, where, in 1836, the name was changed to Shurtleff College, recognizing the gift of $10,000 from Dr. Benjamin Shurtleff of Boston.

John Mason Peck is well described as a missionary and a teacher, an author, and an editor, a geographer and a cartographer, and a promoter of churches, schools, and western settlement. For thirty years, he was undoubtedly one of the strongest advocates of education and righteousness in the entire Mississippi Valley. He traveled hundreds of miles by horseback or wagon, often under most difficult circumstances, while his wife and children bore his long absences with fortitude.

Peck was one of the foremost ministerial opponents of slavery in Illinois and provided great support to Governor Edward Coles' successful anti-slavery effort in 1824. In 1851, he was honored with a Doctor of Divinity degree from Harvard University. He died on March 16, 1858 and is buried in Bellefontaine Cemetery in St. Louis.

Index

A
Act of Uniformity, 26–27, 159, 407
Ainsworth, Henry, 31–34, 42, 76n152, 100, 202
Akin, Daniel L., 573
Alden, Noah, 442, 485
Allen, Jason K., 575, 578n1464
Alliance of Baptists, 579–80
American Baptist Churches USA, 520–31
Andover Newton Theological School, 521–23, 564
Angus Library and Archive, 271, 600

B
Backus, Isaac, 475–85, 495–96, 609
Baker, Elijah, 470–72
Baptist Bible Union, 535, 541
Baptist General Association of Virginia, 580
Baptist General Convention of Texas, 9, 580, 581n1474, 581n1477
Baptist Theological Seminary at Richmond, 580n1472
Barber, Edward, 66–69
Barebone, Praisegod, 102, 119–24
Barrow, David, 454–55
Barrow, Henry, 30–31
Baylor University, George W. Truett Theological Seminary, 581n1477
Beddome, Benjamin, 304–5
Bellamy, Joseph, 258–62
Black Creek Baptist Church (VA), 454
Blacklock, Samuel, 135–38
Blunt, Richard, 133–38
Booth, Abraham, 140, 268–71, 302
Boyce, James P., 552–54, 557–60
Brine, John, 165n371, 245–48
Bristol Baptist College, 173, 229, 256–57, 294, 298, 326, 329, 434
Broadus, John A., 553–58
Brown, J. Newton, 587–89
Brown, L. Duane, 4
Brown College (University), 316, 326, 435, 480, 497, 510, 515, 552, 611
Browne, Robert, 91–94
Bunyan, John, 116, 124–25n271, 173, 190–96, 251, 599, 600
Busher, Leonard, 75, 132, 383

C

Caffyn, Matthew, 80–82
Campbell University Divinity School, 581
Carey, William, 288–321
Carroll, Benajah Harvey (B. H.), 13n22, 566–67
Carroll, James Milton (J. M.), 13
Cedarholm, B. Myron, 547
Central Baptist Church (Leicester), 303n771, 604
Central Baptist Theological Seminary, 547
Chase, Irah, 521
Chesterfield Jail, 466–70
Chiles, James, 460
Church of St. Sepulchre without Newgate, 18, 598
Clarendon Code, 159–60, 162–63, 179
Clark, Theodore R., 569–70
Clarke, John, 138, 373–87, 609–10
Clarke, William Newton, 523
Clearwaters, Richard V., 546–47
Clifford, John, 86–87, 335–39
Colgate Theological Seminary, 523–24
Collegiants, 134–35
Collier, Thomas, 209–13
Collins, Hercules, 18, 21, 68n142, 137, 140, 189, 220n537, 226
Conservative Baptist Association of America (CBA of A), 537–39, 547
Conservative Baptist Fellowship (CBF), 534, 537–40
Conventicle Act, 159–60, 192
Cooperative Baptist Fellowship, 579–81
Coppenger, Mark, 575
Corporation Act, 159

Cox, Samuel, 86, 334
Coxe, Nehemiah, 211–12
Craig, Lewis, 458, 460
Crisp, Tobias, 154n344, 237–45
Criswell, W. A., 577–79
Crosby, Thomas, 7n9, 180, 188n450
Crozer Theological Seminary, 527–28

D

Dayton, Amos C., 8–9
Dean, John Marvin, 530
Delaune, Thomas, 18, 184n433
Devonshire Square Baptist Church, 168n383, 177
Doddridge, Phillip, 605
Dodge, Jeremiah, 500
Down Grade Controversy, 87, 331, 335–42
Drummond, Lewis L., 224n552, 573
Dungan, Thomas, 426–27
Dunster, Henry, 103, 363, 391–402, 413, 600, 608

E

Eastern Baptist Theological Seminary, 530–31
Eaton, Isaac, 497, 499, 505, 616
Eaton, Samuel, 18, 131
Edwards, Jonathan, 253, 258–60, 273, 277, 282, 295, 556
Edwards, Jonathan Jr., 263
Edwards, Morgan, 434–37
Elliott, Ralph H., 574–75
Emmons, Nathaniel, 261, 263
Etherington, John, 3n1, 140

F

Faith Baptist Bible College & Theological Seminary, 533–34

Fawcett, John Sr., 255–57, 313
Featley, Daniel, 139, 169, 201n474, 204–7
Ferré, Nels F. S., 521–23, 564
Fifth-Monarchist Movement, 71, 116–22, 125, 154, 157, 160, 169, 180, 375n926, 376
First Great Awakening, 386, 432, 441, 445, 476, 497n1241
Five-Mile Act, 160
Ford, Charles, 86–87, 335
Fosdick, Harry Emerson, 565
Foundations Baptist Fellowship International, 228, 521, 534–41
Fox, George (see Quaker Movement)
Free Will Baptists, 79, 227, 595–97
Fuller, Andrew, 250–87, 292–302 passim, 602–3
Fuller, Ellis A., 563–64
Fundamentalist Baptists, 341, 521, 527, 530, 532–50
Furman, Richard, 451, 504, 515, 552, 618

G
Gano, John, 436, 497n1240, 499–503, 611
Gano, Stephen, 485, 500–2
Gardner-Webb University Divinity School, 581
Gateway Seminary of the SBC, 571–72
General Association of Regular Baptist Churches, 227, 536–37, 541–44
Gerrard, John, (Gerrardstown), 444n1102, 613
Gill, John, 13n24, 231–49, 256, 325–26, 341n849, 435, 599
Gilmore, Joseph, 438–39

Goadby, Thomas, 86, 334
Going, Jonathan, 517
Gordon, Adoniram Judson (A. J.), 371–72, 533
Gould, Thomas, 400n991, 411, 413–18, 608
Grantham, Thomas, 69–73
Graves, James R., 7–15
Greenwood, James, 462
Greenwood, John, 30–31, 599
Griffith, John, 18, 113

H
Haldeman, Isaac M., 502–3, 611
Hall, Robert, 253–55, 258, 265, 276–77, 291
Hall, Robert Jr., 254n632, 604
Hamilton Square Baptist Church, 540
Hardin-Simmons Divinity School, 581
Harper, William Raincy, 528–29
Harris, Samuel, 447, 458, 464, 469–70
Hart, Oliver, 499, 503–5, 611, 618
Harvey Lane Baptist Church (Leicester) (see Central Baptist Church)
Haystack Prayer Meeting, 507–9, 609
Helwys, Edmund (Edward), 40, 61–63
Helwys, Gervase, 42, 60–61
Helwys, Thomas, 18, 21–22, 32, 39–43, 54–63, 605
Hemphill, Kenneth S., 569
Hewling, Benjamin and William, 18, 175–77
Henry, Patrick, 460–61, 469, 488–89, 616
Hiscox, Edward T., 589–90
Hogg, Reynold, 298, 304, 603

Holliman, Ezekiel, 358n875, 359
Holmes, Obadiah, 139n310, 369, 378–86, 396, 417, 432n1083, 610
Hopewell Baptist Church and Academy, 497–99, 504–5, 611
Hopkins, Samuel, 258–61
Horsleydown Baptist Church, 182–89, 233, 325, 426
Hovey, Alvah, 521–22
Hussey, Joseph, 244–45
Hutchinson, Anne, 147–51

I
Independent Baptist Fellowship of North America, 4, 227, 547–48
Innes, David C., 540
Iorg, Jeff P., 572
Ireland, James, 464–66, 613
Ivimey, Joseph, 7, 136n299, 163, 240, 270n680, 332, 599

J
Jacob, Henry, 94–102, 129–30, 202, 599–600
Jefferson, Thomas, 469n1175, 487–88, 492–93n1229, 494n1230, 495–96n1236, 609, 614
Jessey, Henry, 94, 105, 122–29, 131–36n299, 153, 168n380, 599–600
Johnson, Francis, 30–34, 95, 599–600
Johnson, William Bullein (W. B.), 552
Jones, Jenkin, 431n1076, 432, 435, 503
Jones, Samuel, 425, 431n1076, 432, 437, 613
Judson, Adoniram, 511, 608
Judson, Adoniram Jr., Ann, Sarah, and Emily, 271, 319, 507–16, 607–9

K
Keach, Benjamin, 68n141, 82, 114, 164, 178–90, 197–98, 208, 225, 233, 325
Keach, Elias, 425–31
Kelley, Charles S., 571
Ketcham, Robert T. (Bob), 542–43
Kiffin, William, 112, 121, 125, 128–30, 139, 153, 164–78, 194, 197, 202, 208–9, 211, 269n677, 403
Kilcop, Thomas, 109, 135–37
Kinghorn, Joseph, 270
Kiokee Baptist Church, 452–57 passim
Knollys, Hanserd, 109, 124–29, 137n301, 144–66, 171, 177, 183, 196–97, 208, 599–600

L
Lamb (Lambe), Thomas, 3n1, 18, 66–67, 76–78, 120–21, 202
Lane, Dutton, 448
Lathrop, John, 94, 97, 101–5, 129, 131, 401, 599–600, 607
Leland, John, 462, 483–96, 609, 614
Leveller Movement, 78, 115–16, 137
Lucar, Mark, 138, 378–80

M
Maclaren, Alexander, 339
McAfee School of Theology, 580
McCall, Duke K., 564–66n1424, 569
McCoy, Isaac, 516–17
Madison, James, 488n1217, 489–91, 495–96, 614

Manly, Basil Jr., 553, 556–57
Manning, James, 326, 366, 435–36, 497–99, 501, 505, 609, 611
Maranatha Baptist University, 547
Marshall, Abraham, 443, 445n1105, 454–57, 463
Marshall, Daniel, 442–48, 452–54
Marshman, Joshua and Hannah, 271, 313–17
Massee, Jasper C., 535
Masters, Peter, 341n849, 342
Mathews, Shailer, 529
Maurice, Matthias, 247
Mercer University, 580–81
Midwestern Baptist Theological Seminary, 573–75
Miller, Benjamin, 497, 500
Mills, Samuel J. Jr., 507–10
Milton, John, 109, 356, 375
Minnesota Baptist Association (Minnesota Baptist Convention), 544–46
Mohler, Richard Albert Jr., 566, 582
Moon, Charlotte (Lottie), 558–59
Morgan, Abel, 431n1076, 431–32n1077
Morgan, Abel Jr., 427n1060, 432n1083
Morris, John Webster, 282–83n724
Mullins, Edgar Y., 559–633, 565, 578
Mumford, Stephen, 379n936, 385, 610
Murphy, Joseph and William, 447
Murton (Morton), John, 18, 63–66

Myles, John, 113, 402–12, 418, 428, 606–8

N

New Connection General Baptists 84–87, 331–40
New Orleans Baptist Theological Seminary, 569–71
Norcott, John, 140, 159, 183, 363–64
Norris, J. Frank, 536, 542
Northern Baptist Convention (see American Baptist Churches USA)
Northern Baptist Theological Seminary, 530

O

Old Connection General Baptists, 85, 332
Olney, Thomas, 365
Oncken, Johann G., 518
Osgood, Howard, 524–25

P

Palmer, Paul, 595–96
Palmer, Wait, 386, 442
Parker, Monroe, 547
Patterson, Paige, 569, 573, 577, 582
Pearce, Samuel, 294, 298, 301, 313
Peck, John Mason, 460n1144, 516–18, 619–20
Pendleton, James M., 7–8, 11–12, 589
Penn, William Jr., 114–15, 425, 431, 612
Pennepack (Pennepek) Baptist Church, 189, 425–32, 437, 613
Pepper, George D. B., 527
Philadelphia Baptist

Association, 430, 432–34, 438, 443
Pickett, John, 464–65
Pierson, Arthur Tappan (A. T.), 341
Pillsbury Baptist Bible College, 546–47
Pinners' Hall, 189, 403–4n1003, 428
Powel, Vavasor, 171, 599
Powell, William (Bill), 577
Pressler, Paul, 577

Q
Quaker Movement, 109–15, 209, 406–7, 410, 431

R
Randall, Benjamin, 595–96
Ranter Movement, 115–16
Rauschenbusch, Walter, 526
Reed (Read), James, 445, 459–60
Religious Freedom Monument (Chesterfield, VA), 466, 616
Religious Freedom Monument (Fredericksburg, VA), 614
Rice, Luther, 509–13, 515–16, 518, 552, 607, 609, 619
Rijnsburgers (see Collegiants)
Riley, William Bell (W. B.), 530, 533, 536, 540, 544–46
Rippon, John, 183n430, 234, 256–57, 306, 319, 325–27, 332, 341n849, 599
Ritor, Andrew, 67, 141
Robertson, Archibald Thomas (A. T.), 526, 556
Rochester Theological Seminary, 524–26
Rust, Eric C., 528, 564
Ryland, John Collett Sr., 282–84, 302, 326, 604

Ryland, John Jr., 255, 258, 265, 267, 277, 279–81, 284n725, 291–98, 309, 316, 602, 604

S
Salters' Hall, 82–83
Samford University, Beeson Divinity School, 571, 581
Sandemanianism, 267–68
Scarborough, L. R., 567
Screven, William, 422–25, 618
Second Great Awakening, 366, 432, 451, 476, 482, 483–86, 496–98, 502, 507, 613
Seeker Movement, 109, 137, 362
Shackelford, John, 462, 615
Shepard, Thomas, 138
Shields, Thomas Todhunter (T. T.), 535
Singelkerk, 51–52
Skepp, John, 165n371, 244–46
Smith, Hezekiah, 435, 498n1243, 504–5, 611
Smyth, John, 32, 34–40, 42–52, 54–59, 63, 66, 71, 600, 605
Southeastern Baptist Theological Seminary, 572–73
Southern Baptist Conservative Evangelical Resurgence, 576–83
Southern Baptist Theological Seminary, 552–66
Southern Baptists of Texas Convention, 580
Southwestern Baptist Theological Seminary, 566–69
Sparkman, G. Temp, 573–74
Spilsbury, John, 102, 109, 112, 121, 123, 125, 130–31, 136n299, 138–42, 168, 202, 269
Spurgeon, Charles, 87, 183–84, 224, 234, 243, 267, 322–43, 599
Stagg, Frank, 565, 569

Staughton, William, 282, 297–99, 315n790, 516
Stearns, Shubal, 386, 442–49, 452, 617
Stifler, James M., 527, 533
Stillman, Samuel, 482, 498n1243
Stinton, Benjamin, 128n280, 128n281, 129n282, 181n420, 188n450, 233n568, 325, 341n849
Stinton, Thomas, 188n450
Strong, Augustus H., 524–26
Sutcliff, John, 255–58, 267, 279–82, 292–95, 298, 301, 601–2

T
Taylor, Abraham, 247–48, 253
Taylor, Dan, 84–87, 331–32, 339
Terrill, Edward (see Bristol Baptist College)
Thomas, John, 301–15 passim
Toleration Act, 163, 177, 209, 228, 459
Toy, Crawford H., 557–58
Triennial Convention, 299, 451, 515–18, 520, 552, 612
Tulga, Chester E., 538

U
Underwood, William, 334
University of Chicago Divinity School, 528–30

V
Van Osdel, Oliver W., 541
Vedder, Henry C., 7, 17, 527n1313
Virginia Declaration of Rights, 486
Virginia Statute for Establishing Religious Freedom, 486–87

W
Wake Forest University Divinity School, 581
Walker, Jeremiah, 467
Waller, John, 456–64, 467, 615, 617–18
Ward, William, 271, 306, 313, 316–17, 511
Ware, Robert, 462, 615
Waterlander Mennonites, 47–57n114 passim
Wayland, Francis, 515, 553
Weatherford, John, 467–69, 616–17
Welch, James E., 516
Weniger, Arno Q. Sr., 540
Weniger, G. Archer, 539–40
West, Stephen, 261–62
Weston, Henry G., 527
Wheelwright, John, 146–52
Whitsitt, William H., 132
Wightman, Valentine, 386
Wilberforce, William, 266, 290, 305–6, 605
Williams, Roger, 65, 114, 148, 347–72, 374–90 passim, 480, 499, 600, 609
Williams, William, 553–54
Winchester, Elhanan, 437–38